A SACRIFICE
OF PRAISE

A SACRIFICE OF PRAISE

*An Anthology of Christian Poetry in English
from Caedmon to the Twentieth Century*

Selected and Arranged with Notes on the Poets,
Periods, and Genres

Ed., James H. Trott

"What is it then? I will pray with the spirit, and I will
pray with the understanding also: I will sing with the spirit,
and I will sing with the understanding also."
I Corinthians 14:15

CUMBERLAND HOUSE PUBLISHING
NASHVILLE, TENNESSEE

Published by Cumberland House Publishing, Inc., 431 Harding Industrial Drive, Nashville, Tennessee 37211.

Jacket design by Karen Phillips.
Text design by Julie Pitkin.

Library of Congress Cataloging-in-Publication Data

A sacrifice of praise : an anthology of Christian poetry in English from
    Caedmon to the mid-twentieth century / selected and arranged with notes
    on the poets, periods, and genres, ed., James H. Trott.
        p. cm.
    Includes bibliographical references (p.   ) and indexes.
    ISBN: 1-58182-044-5 (alk. paper)
    I. Christian poetry, English.   I. Trott, James H., 1949–
PR1191.S194   1999
821.008'03823—dc21   99-33977
                                                                     CIP

Printed in the United States of America
1 2 3 4 5 6 7 8 , 03 02 01 00 99

Satire III
by John Donne

Kinde pitty chokes my spleene; brave scorn forbids
Those teares to issue which swell my eye-lids;
I must not laugh, nor weepe sinnes, and be wise,
Can railing then cure these worne maladies?
Is not our Mistresse faire Religion,
As worthy of all our Soules devotion,
As vertue was to the first blinded age?
Are not heavens joys as valiant to asswage
Lusts, as earths honour was to them? Alas,
As wee do them in meanes, shall they surpasse
Us in the end, and shall thy fathers spirit
Meete blinde Philosophers in heaven, whose merit
Of strict life may be imputed faith, and heare
Thee, whom hee taught so easie wayes and neare
To follow, damn'd? O if thou dar'st, feare this;
This feare great courage, and high valour is.
Dar'st thou ayd mutinous Dutch, and dar'st thou lay
Thee in ships wooden Sepulchers, a prey
To leaders rage, to stormes, to shot, to dearth?
Dar'st thou dive seas, and dungeons of the earth?
Hast thou couragious fire to thaw the ice
Of frozen North discoveries? and thrise
Colder than Salamanders, like divine
Children in th'oven, fires of Spaine, and the line,
Whose countries limbecks to our bodies bee,
Canst thou for gaine beare? and must every hee
Which cryes not, Goddesse, to thy Mistresse, draw,
Or eat thy poisonous words? courage of straw !
O desperate coward, wilt thou seeme bold, and
To thy foes and his (who made thee to stand
Sentinell in his worlds garrison) thus yeeld,
And for the forbidden warres, leave th'appointed field?
Know thy foes: The foule Devill (whom thou
Strivest to please,) for hate, not love, would allow
Thee faine, his whole Realme to be quit; and as
The worlds all parts wither away and passe,

Kinde pitty chokes my spleene - 'natural sympathy inhibits my emotions'; asswage -
assuage; thrise - thrice; Salamanders - mythologically thought to be fire-proof; lim-
becks - retorts or ovens; draw - draw his sword; faine - to be happy or to be glad to

So the worlds selfe, thy other lov'd foe, is
In her decrepit wayne, and thou loving this,
Dost love a withered and worne strumpet; last,
Flesh (it selfes death) and joyes which flesh can taste,
Thou lovest; and thy faire goodly soule, which doth
Give this flesh power to taste joy, thou dost loath.
Seeke true religion. O where? Mirreus
Thinking her unhous'd here, and fled from us,
Seekes her at Rome; there, because hee doth know
That shee was there a thousand yeares agoe,
He loves her ragges so, as wee here obey
The statecloth where the Prince sate yesterday,
Crantz to such brave Loves will not be inthrall'd,
But loves her onely, who at Geneva is call'd
Religion, plaine, simple, sullen, yong,
Contemptuous, yet unhansome; As among
Lecherous humours, there is one that judges
No wenches wholsome, but course country drudges.
Graius stayes still at home here, and because
Some Preachers, vile ambitious bauds, and lawes
Still new like fashions, bid him thinke that shee
Which dwels with us, is onely perfect, hee
Imbraceth her, whom his Godfathers will
Tender to him, being tender, as Wards still
Take such wives as their Guardians offer, or
Pay valewes. Carlesse Phrygius doth abhorre
All, because all cannot be good, as one
Knowing some women whores, dares marry none.
Graccus loves all as one, and thinkes that so
As women do in divers countries goe
In divers habits, yet are still one kinde,
So doth, so is Religion; and this blind-
nesse too much light breeds; but unmoved thou
Of force must one, and forc'd but one allow;
And the right; aske thy father which is shee,
Let him aske his; though truth and falshood bee
Neare twins, yet truth a little elder is;
Be busie to seeke her, beleeve mee this,
Hee's not of none, nor worst, that seekes the best.
To adore, or scorne an image, or protest,

wayne - wane (as in the waning of the moon); inthrall'd - enslaved; valewes - penalties

May all be bad; doubt wisely; in strange way
To stand inquiring right, is not to stray;
To sleepe, or runne wrong, is. On a huge hill,
Cragged, and steep, Truth stands, and hee that will
Reach her, about must, and about must goe;
And what the hills suddennes resists, winne so;
Yet strive so, that before age, deaths twilight,
Thy Soule rest, for none can worke in that night.
To will, implyes delay, therefore now doe:
Hard deeds, the bodies paines; hard knowledge too
The mindes indeavours reach, and mysteries
Are like the Sunne, dazling, yet plaine to all eyes.
Keepe the truth which thou hast found; men do not stand
In so ill case here, that God hath with his hand
Sign'd Kings blanck-charters to kill whom they hate.
Nor are they Vicars, but hangmen to Fate.
Foole and wretch, wilt thou let thy Soule be tyed
To mans lawes, by which she shall not be tryed
At the last day? Oh, will it then boot thee
To say a Philip, or a Gregory,
A Harry, or a Martin taught thee this?
Is not this excuse for mere contraries,
Equally strong? cannot both sides say so?
That thou mayest rightly obey power, her bounds know;
Those past, her nature, and name is chang'd; to be
Then humble to her idolatrie.
As streames are, Power is: those blest flowers that dwell
At the rough streames calme head, thrive and do well,
But having left their roots, and themselves given
To the streames tyrannous rage, alas are driven
Through mills, and rockes, and woods, and at last, almost
Consum'd in going, in the sea are lost:
So perish Soules, which more chuse mens unjust
Power from God claym'd, than God himselfe to trust.

suddennes - steepness; in so ill case - in such bad condition; blanck-charters - free
licenses; Philip - Philip II, King of Spain; Gregory - Pope Gregory; Harry - Henry
VIII, King of England; Martin - Martin Luther; bounds - limits

TABLE OF CONTENTS

FOREWORD

Poetry was my pursuit in high school. Then in 1960 I attended the University of Illinois, with 35,000 students in residence, in Urbana, plus a small number meeting on a pier in Lake Michigan. The Urbana population formed a community, mostly cohesive, and it was here that my faint faith faded and went underground for a decade.

Agnosticism and atheism and a welter of other isms, including a new one, existentialism, were in the air along with whiffs, near the end of my tenure, of a blue-gray smoke that smelled like burning leaves. Professors and grad assistants held forth at the front of classrooms from oak lecterns, set on desks, that looked like the sawed-off upper half of pulpits. It was a new religion they preached.

A professor of mine, an impeccable scholar widely published, with a sweet and engaging sense of humor, a true gentleman, referred to people who brought up their beliefs as "Christers," as in "That Christer!"—dissing them, as we say now. It first hurt me to hear this from a dear man otherwise so tolerant and kind, and then I fell into his way. Or anyway imagined the label amused me.

There was nobody to tell me you need faith to write poetry—a larger view to pull your arrangement of words free from their mere verbal advance, no matter how technically pyrotechnic, into a realm where they sing in unrestrained song. I enrolled in an advanced course in the metaphysical poets—Donne and Herbert and Marvell—because one of the draws was the instructor. He glowed with intelligence and was lively and witty, able to make students hardened by years of trying learn to laugh. I preferred the precise and subtly dodging movements of his mind, revealed in his lectures, to my generally flat-footed way of getting at things, but I grew disenchanted with the class. I couldn't imagine why; I even troubled myself about it. For a while I found it difficult to attend, and sometimes didn't.

Now I suspect it was because he never said that the poets we studied were applying their Christian faith or singing in ecstasy out of its holy strictures. I was drawn to the poets, pulled into the world of each on my own, but I don't recall any explanation of what they were involved in or what the force was behind their writing, or its source—other than they followed the form of metaphysical conceit or strained extended metaphor to the breaking, and so forth.

Let me confess that I did well enough in science but wasn't the sophisticated or discriminating student fit for literary dissection. What I probably needed to hear was "This is faith, baby!" And one of the lows in my academic life came in that class when I submitted a paper on Marvell I had worked over in my dogged way and got it back with a grade of C and the explanation: "Sensitive as far as it goes but needs detail"—words along those lines. After class I asked what detail was required, since I thought I had a bit, and the instructor said, "You can't possibly know if you haven't attended all my lectures."

I hope this doesn't seem a disaffected student taking a poke at a professor who gave him a C—I've been a professor and know about that; I admired the man as much as my other professor; but it helps define from another angle the atmosphere in the early sixties at Urbana. In retrospect, I sense I was given a glimpse of the "Me Generation" soon to implode over the U.S. and then the world. That would become the animating religion behind most of the new poetry.

What I needed was a collection like the one you hold, *A Sacrifice of Praise*, with its gentle and discerning guide, James Trott. Here you will encounter what I was able only to suspect in some small area sovereignly preserved in me: that the tradition in western literature is Christian.

Arbiters of consensus, let's call them, who are largely drawn from the academic community, are working to erode the central fact of history—anyway for those in the Christian community. They would like to remove the slightest suggestion that God, as Jesus Christ, appeared incarnate on the same earth the poets included here celebrate, so they are now busy changing the designation AD (the Latin *Anno Domini* meaning "in the year of our Lord") to CE, *Common Era*.

No matter how you fuddle with naming or centuries of acknowledgment of historical fact, however, or even artfully sift the entries in the pantheon of poets of the past, you always come up against that unassailable truth: *the tradition in western literature is Christian.*

You see glimmers of this even in Beowulf, then the metier arrives full-blown in Chaucer, with subject matter unclouded by Victorianism, which is not Christian, and which dampens the appreciation of poetry by present-day Christians. The subject and object of the body, for example, is holy to God, is indeed what we are to offer as a sacrifice to Him, in the way Christian painters have through the centuries, yet I have heard Christian writers criticized in their community for using a word like *naked*, one the Bible leans on. If that is your view, watch out for Chaucer, watch out for Donne, watch out for Ann Bradstreet, watch out for Eliot, watch for those doubling metaphors in Emily Dickinson, and watch out for most here.

But, dear reader, I expect better from you, and propose you take the hand of your guide, Brother Trott, and let him lead you through the magnificence of what follows in these pages—centuries of poetry with Christ at its center. It is a commendable work Brother Trott has performed for the church, under the view not of a befogging cloud but a cloud of clear-eyed witnesses, an uncountable number already gathered in the general assembly of the true Parnassus, Heaven. You will find Samsons and Jobs and Jepthahs and Jepthah's daughters present, all engaged in a spiritual stretch and hope that the highest reach of their arranged words will touch the hem of The Word.

A few years ago I was working on a novel and hit one of those stretches, as one does, where the words ran effortlessly for a dozen pages. It was always my habit before to write in pencil, for first drafts, anyway, but on this afternoon I was at a computer, due to time constraints and a variety of reasons, gliding through a section of action that had me so engaged I couldn't pause to hit the "save" button. Then a lightning bolt hit close.

Out went the computer and the twelve pages sank into a sinking dot in the screen. This had happened before and I knew that even with all the well-intentioned effort I might summon I could never recreate the pages as they arrived. It doesn't do any good to turn on God or shake your fist at the electric company. By a sovereign act, the pages were gone, and perhaps a distillation of them would be better—as I was beginning to be enabled to think. There was no indication that the electricity was going to come on soon, because we were in the midst of a thunderous downpour of the sort the arid plains can receive on a sweltering summer day.

We live in the country, a dozen miles from the closest town, and are dependent on the fallible intricacies of rural electricity. So I did what my children were doing, put on rubber boots and a slicker to go out and enjoy the visitation on our parched land. I've seldom been in a rain so heavy; I felt we were standing in a cataract, the weight of the water over our gear giving a heightened gravity to every movement. Runnels and rivulets were flowing where I'd never seen water, bending grass over. Our lane was puddling and slick, and ditches in every direction were running muddy brown. The rain kept up, even seemed to increase, and a narrow creek at the bottom of our pasture, often all but dry at this time of year, was spreading so wide it had started to climb the incline of the pasture.

According to a later report we had something near six inches of rain in an hour. A gravel road runs between our pasture and our neighbors', at the base of our lane, and a mile and a half into his fields a rambling hogback butte rises over a hundred feet for the length of a mile. Now I heard runoff from the butte hit the already pouring water in the pasture across the road and I moved my children to higher ground, and then it came, a rumbling sea wave, as if watery vaults of the earth were opened wide, and started boiling and rising toward the level of the road, banked high here for the spanning bridge across our creek.

The pressure sent water shooting in a fifty-foot column under the bridge, raising the level in our pasture as fast as you could watch, and I understood the bridge was not going to be able to handle the onslaught for much longer and, sure enough, soon the water rose to the level of the road and began to slither in sheets across it, then was pouring over the stretch that held our bridge in a thundering waterfall. My children were young enough to cheer and that took enough of the pressure from me that I was weighing my lost pages against this. All the interconnected technology that I and others depended on so fully every day seemed insignificant, a ripple across the many inventions of the centuries, compared to this. And I realized that no matter what provision I might have made to preserve what I had, and no matter how much effort the many people over the years put into the local landscape to direct and contain the aftermath of rains and melts, nothing could contain a force like this that was up to do what it wanted.

And nothing can contain the outpouring of poetry that carries us on a current that is our true source of power, ordained by hands other than ours from before the beginning of time, and that onrushing stream is the tradition pouring through the chapters of this book; it is pouring out of centuries past and will keep pouring in thunderous collusion to His glory into centuries to come.

Larry Woiwode

PREFACE

It comes as a shock to those of us who have undergone secular educations to discover the vast majority of poets writing and being published in English have been Christians. The English-speaking church has sung hymns of praise, faith, and wrestling with God from the beginning. The English-speaking church has long labored to communicate the gospel of its great Savior in winsome words. There have been many whose faith in Jesus Christ replaced a former reliance on Apollo or Nature—many who found the Holy Spirit a truer inspirer than the Muses or the Oversoul. The church ought to affirm its unity in time as well as in space—with those of the past as well as with those of other lands and tongues.

This collection of much of the best Christian poetry in one volume is also an offer of evidence for that unity of the church in Christ. The Prefatory Poem, John Donne's "Satire III," is an exhortation to faith despite the dilemmas forced on the believer by warring factions. In our times, such a faith and such a sense of unity are important.

The collection is in one sense very broad. I have drawn poetry from the ancient church, the medieval church, from Anglican, Roman Catholic, Reformed and Evangelical poets. It is in another sense narrow, in that I have resisted the urge to "baptize" poets who would likely have resisted the effort. I have not knowingly dragged anyone "kicking and screaming into the kingdom" (to use C. S. Lewis's description of his own conversion). Neither have I deliberately included poems which are exclusive to one branch of the church or another. For instance, on the one hand, I have left out Protestant poems which are fulminations against the Roman Catholic church and, on the other, I have included no poems which are solely given to the adoration of the Mother of Christ. I have tried to represent a fairly broad range of nations and dialects. For this reason, the anthology might serve as an introduction to the history of the English language and as a secondary text for teaching literature. (Anglo-Saxon poems are for the most part given in translation, but the Middle English poems are in the original, with footnotes to aid the reader.)

The task of selection, even within these guidelines, has been at times arduous. The more specific factors which went into selection were 1) poetic unity: the integration of theme and stylistic elements which produces all great poetry, 2) length: few long poems are included, and therefore some "famous" poems are left out or in some cases excerpts taken from them, 3) distinctiveness: I have tried to maintain a breadth of subject and theme, as well as a range of styles and genres of poetry, 4) diversity: an attempt has been made to include poems of every period and every genre, as well as as many poets as possible, in order to help the reader perceive the progress of Christian poetry through the ages, and finally, 5) my personal tastes. This last factor is undeniable. Why Anne Ridler is my favorite living poet would take hours to explain. Furthermore, it is no doubt a dysfunction beyond most Christian counselors that causes me to like John Donne so well and barely tolerate Milton—especially his longer works. I would like to think the former is simply a better poet than the latter. That is certainly not the whole story, however. Since I am yet a sinner with particular weaknesses and strengths, I am sure my particular sins and tastes have affected my selection.

The original impetus toward making this collection was my own bewilderment as a Christian writing poetry. The Bible is a tremendous model of the highest possible use of words. It contains words from the Word and words to the Word. The Bible shows us man, the creature—in God's image interpreting for the whole creation which is, without words, declaring the glory of God, and it shows us the Word among us speaking words, sometimes plain and sometimes difficult. But we also see the Spirit of Christ leading Him to speak gently, wisely, winsomely on the most important subjects to particular people and peoples, in order that they understand him (or in some cases so that they couldn't understand him—yet!) The Bible also shows us the church following the Lord's return to heaven: men and women called to speak clearly and winsomely, but also to be "all things to all men" and "so far as it is possible for you, to live at peace with all men." It was a desire to know how the Christian poet should write and speak to his own "tribe" in his own "tongue" that led me to begin this collection.

Sometimes the Christian writer has felt very lonely. William Cowper once wrote:

> Pity, religion has so seldom found
> A skillful guide into poetic ground!
> The flowers would spring where'er she deigned to stray,
> And every muse attend her on her way.

But the Christian poet is not at all alone—nor are skillful guides "seldom found." We who speak English have thirteen centuries of Christian poetry behind us. Christian poetry in English is a deep and broad stream of praise, frequently poured out by men and women who died for the faith in a context of persecution. (To our confusion and, let us pray, to our instruction, all too often these died in a context of warfare among those who named Christ.) This stream or tradition of Christian poetry includes every genre, form and style from private meditations and psalms to great public works of literature on epic scales. The glory of God may have been diminished by sectarian motives at various times and in various hearts, but the "channel" of the stream was always faith— and a good deep channel it remained, even in the worst of times. There was an unbroken succession of men and women praising God—to which we belong. How encouraging to study the record of what they have done, and how they have done it—to be inspired by their praises and intreaties to further praises of our own. A collection like this may serve to direct and instruct those who write poetry, but beyond that it is a hymnbook for all God's people.

I offer this anthology as a mere starting point. By God's grace the reader will find particular poetry and poets attractive. By all means pursue those attractions. Libraries abound in little used collections of poetry. Every twenty or thirty years another significant anthology of Christian poetry has been published. Oxford University Press and many other publishers have produced anthologies from your favorite period of English literature, and *somewhere* there is a collection of poems by your favorite poet, no matter how obscure he or she may be.

Poetry is a vehicle of praise, exhortation, meditation and understanding. Let us read it, recite it, study it, memorize it, and where the Spirit leads, write it to Christ's glory.

James H. Trott
Philadelphia, 1999

Chapter One

ANGLO-SAXON POETRY

As the roots of the English language are in Anglo-Saxon, so the beginnings of English poetry are in Anglo-Saxon poetry. From early on, Anglo-Saxon poetry became intimately connected with the Christian gospel. There are few Anglo-Saxon poems extant which do not show Christian influence—in most cases, strong Christian influence. The best known of all Anglo-Saxon poems, *Beowulf*, although showing clear evidence of pagan origins, is so much a Christian poem that one of its better-known students, Fr. Klaeber, says "The Christian elements are almost without exception so deeply ingrained in the very fabric of the poem that they cannot be explained away as the work of a reviser or later interpolator." (Introduction to *Beowulf and The Fight at Finnsburg*)

The message of Christ the Savior reached Britain during the Roman occupation. There were Bishops from London, York, and Lincoln present at the Council of Arles in 314, and representatives of the British church at the Council of Rimini in 359. St. Augustine (of Hippo's) famous heretical adversary, Pelagius, was of British origin. The church was weakened by the withdrawal of Roman forces and various Germanic invasions until in 597 another Augustine arrived in Kent with his band of missionaries. It was from the center of Canterbury that the English church began to be steadily strengthened. In 627, Edwin, King of Northumbria and ruler over all other kingdoms but Kent, began the spread of the gospel in northern England. A pagan reaction after his death was gradually overcome and Northumbria became the center for Christian learning in Britain.

Much of our record of the early English church is told by Bede, a scholar at Yarrow, in *The Ecclesiastical History of the English People*. We owe him the account of the first recorded poet, Caedmon. The second poet, Cynewulf, is known for little more than his name. He wrote four poems which include his name in runes—not to get credit for them, but rather as part of a request that his readers pray for him. Most of the other Anglo-Saxon poets remain anonymous, although many poems have been attributed to Caedmon, Cynewulf, or their followers.

Anglo-Saxon poetry was preserved in the monastic libraries of Canterbury, Yarrow, and York which became centers for preserving Greek and Latin classical works, as well. Four extensive manuscripts remain, to which we owe almost everything we have of Anglo-Saxon poetry. In the ninth century, with the beginning and intensification of Danish raids on the Northumbrian countryside and on the monasteries, Anglo-Saxon poetry dwindled. With the victories of the

West Saxons over the Danes in the latter part of that century, the chief influence on letters shifted from the ecclesiastical schools of the north to the Court at Winchester. Prose became the leading form of literary expression under the influence of Alfred's court.

In 1066, as a natural result of their conquest, the Norman's brought their language and literary traditions which led to the Middle English language and a different sort of English poetry.

Anglo-Saxon poetry is all the more remarkable in light of the fact that there is almost no poetry extant from continental Christendom before 1000 A.D. The zeal of the British church is affirmed by records of missionaries sent from the British Isles all over the known world. Their poetry came out of this same zeal. "The vitality of this religious verse grows from the fact that the Old English poets sang of what they believed, and of its supreme importance." (Charles W. Kennedy, Introduction in *Early English Christian Poetry*)

A Brief Chronology of The Anglo-Saxon Period

314	Council of Arles, Bishops from London, York, and Lincoln present
359	Council of Rimini, representatives of British Church present
450	Approximate time of Anglo-Saxon conquest after Roman withdrawal
597	Augustine (*not* of Hippo) and missionary band arrive at Kent and begin post-Roman evangelization of Britain from Canterbury
627	Conversion of Edwin, King of Northumbria
664	Synod of Whitby in which differences in practice between Celtic church (centered in Northumbria) and Roman church (centered in Canterbury) were resolved
658–700	Probable period of Caedmon's writing
750–783	Probable period of Cynewulf's writing
781	Alcuin, scholar and contributor to York library, leaves England to serve Charlemagne.
700–850	Rise and development of vernacular poetry in England, probable time of writing of *Beowulf, Seafarer,* and *Dream of the Rood.*
800–878	Increasing Danish raids hit Northumbria in particular and slow the stream of Anglo-Saxon poetry.
878	West Saxon victory and terms of Wedmore mark movement of literary center from Northumbria to Court at Winchester
1066	Norman Conquest marks end of Anglo-Saxon era

CAEDMON (fl. 658–680) is the first Anglo-Saxon or Old English poet of whom we have record. Bede's *Ecclesiastical History of the English People* records his story. He was an untaught herdsman who slipped away from a circle of revellers because each was supposed to perform a story or song and Caedmon knew he could not. That night he had a vision in which he found himself declaiming verses in praise of God. When he told this vision to a bailiff with whom he worked, the bailiff took him to the monastery at Streaneshalch where the Abbess Hilda accepted Caedmon's newfound poetic ability as divinely inspired. He took up residence in the monastery and turned the Scriptures which were taught him into vernacular verse. "Caedmon's Hymn," the song he is said to have been given in the vision, is the only poem which can be attributed to him with certainty. Tradition for many years assigned other extant works to him, the most likely being those in the group known as Christ and Satan, including a lament of the fallen angels, the harrowing of hell and Christ's temptations. Bede recorded "Caedmon's Hymn" in Latin. Two centuries later, in Alfred's court, it was translated back into Anglo-Saxon, in which several versions are extant. Bede's Latin is included here, an Anglo-Saxon and a modern version.

Nunc laudare debemus Auctorem regni caelestis, potentiam Creatoris, et consilium illius, facta Patris gloriae. Quomodo ille, cum sit eternus Deus, omnium miraculorum auctor exstitit, qui primo filiis hominum cælum pro culmine tecti, dehinc terram Custos humani generis omnipotens creavit.

Nu sculon herigean   heofonrices weard,
meotodes meahte   and his modgeþanc,   [þ = th]
weorc wuldorfader   swa he wundra gehwæs,
ece drihten,   or onstealde.
He ærest sceop   eorþan bearnum
heofon to hrofe,   halig scyppend;
þa middangeard   moncynnes weard,
ece drihten,   æfter teode
firum foldan,   frea aelmihtig.

It is meet that we worship   the Warden of heaven,
The might of the Maker,   His purpose of mind,
The Glory-Father's work   when of all His wonders
Eternal God   made a beginning.
He earliest stablished   for earth's children
Heaven for a roof,   the Holy Shaper;
Then mankind's Warden   created the world,
Eternal Monarch,   making for men
Land to live on,   Almighty Lord!

CYNEWULF (works preserved in late 10th century mss.), is the author of four Old English poems, the epilogues of which request prayer for the author and include his name in runic characters. His work shows the effect of Latin rhetoric on the native Anglo-Saxon. The narrative is orderly, while the imagery is native and the style in keeping with Anglo-Saxon epic tradition. His known works include *Juliana, Elene, Christ II (The Ascension)*, and *Fates of the Apostles.* The last is a versified martyrology describing the ministry and death of each of the twelve apostles. We know next to nothing about Cynewulf, himself. It seems likely he was a cleric.

Lines from The Ascension
from The Redeemer
Translated by Charles W. Kennedy
(lines 743–866)

As here on earth's soil   God's Son Eternal
Mounted by leaps   above the high hills,
Bold on the mountains,   so we mortal men
In our hearts' musings   must mount by leaps
From strength to strength,   and strive for glory,
That we may ascend   by holy works
To the highest heavens,   where are joy and hope,
A goodly band of thanes.   Great is our need
In our secret souls   that we seek salvation,
If we have in our hearts   a fervent faith
That the Healing Son,   the Living Saviour,
With our own body   ascended from earth.
    Wherefore we should ever   despise idle lusts,
The wounds of sin,   finding bliss in the better.
We have for our comfort   our Father on high,
Almighty God.   From heaven the Holy One
Sends His angels   hither to earth,
Who shield us from spoilers   and their deadly darts
Lest the fiends work wounds   when the Author of evil
Against God's people   shoots bitter shafts
From his bended bow.   Therefore fast and firm
We must warily watch   against the sudden shot
Lest poisoned arrow   or pitiless dart,
Or the Foe's swift cunning,   should pierce our frame.
Grievous that hurt,   most ghastly of wounds!
    Let us guard against it   while we dwell on earth.
Let us pray the Father   that He grant us peace,

The Son of God,   and the blithe Spirit,
That He who shaped us   with life and limbs,
With body and soul,   may shield us well
From the wiles of the wicked,   the weapons of foes.
To Him be praise   and glory in heaven
For ever and ever,   world without end.

    Nor need any man   of the race of men
Fear darts of devils   or spear-flights of fiends
If the Lord God of   hosts is his defence.
The Judgment is near;   we shall know reward
According as we have won it   by our works
During days of life   dwelling on earth.
The Scriptures tell us   how the Treasure of might,
God's Glorious Son,   in the beginning
Stooped to the world,   to the womb of the Virgin,
Holy from heaven.   Verily I await,
And also dread,   a sterner doom
When the King of angels   shall come again—
I who obeyed not well   what my Saviour bade me
In the Books.   I shall surely see
The terror of vengeance of sin,   as I count it true,
Where many shall be summoned   to the Assembly
Before the face   of the Eternal Judge.

C   Then even the *bold*   shall tremble in terror
Hearing the King,   the Ruler of heaven,
Speak wrathful words   to those in the world
YN   Who obeyed Him feebly   when *affliction* and *need*
Most easily may find comfort.   There many a one
In that place shall wearily   await with fear
What dreadful punishment   God shall ordain
W   According to man's works.   *Winsomeness* of earth's treasures
U   Shall be departed.   *Our* portion of life's joy
LF   Was long washed with *floods,*   all *wealth* on earth.
In that day earth's treasures   shall burn in the blast;
Fiercely shall ravage   the swift, red flame.
It shall rush in rage   over the wide world;
Plains shall perish,   castles shall crumble;
The fire shall be fleet;   most greedy of spirits
It shall eat up all   the ancient treasure
Men gained of old   when was glory on earth.
    Therefore I urge   each of my beloved

That he never slight   the need of his soul,
Nor engulf it in pride   while God may will
That here in the world   he has his dwelling
While soul fares in body,   that friendly inn.
Let each of men earnestly   in his days on earth
Muse in his heart   how the Lord of might
First came with pity   by the angel's promise.
But He shall be grim   when He comes again,
Just and stern.   Then the heavens shall be shaken,
And the mighty limits   of earth shall be moved.
He shall give their reward   to those who through wickedness
Lived upon earth   soiled with their sin.
Soul-weary and sad   they shall long receive,
In the bath of fire   begirt with flame,
In return for their sin   a terrible requital.
    Then the King of might   shall come to that meeting
With the greatest of hosts;   loud shall be heard
The terror of men   'mid the tumult of heaven,
The wailing of them that weep.   The lost shall lament
Before the face   of the Eternal Judge,
Those who rely but little   on their works.
To many shall be manifest   more of terror
Than ever was known   from the world's creation.
To every sinner   in that sudden hour
It shall be dearer far   than all this fleeting world
That he may have shelter   in that happy band
When the Lord of hosts,   the Prince of princes,
Shall judge unto all,   the loved and the loathed,
Unto every one   a just reward.
Dire is our need   ere that day of terror
That we think of the soul's beauty   in this barren time.
    Now is it most like   as if on ocean
Across cold water   we sail in our keels,
Over the wide sea   in our ocean-steeds,
Faring on in our flood-wood.   Fearful the stream,
The tumult of waters,   whereon we toss
In this feeble world.   Fierce are the surges
On the ocean lanes.   Hard was our life
Before we made harbour   o'er the foaming seas.
Then help was vouchsafed us   when God's Spirit-Son
Guided us to the harbour of salvation   and granted us grace
That we may understand   over the ship's side

Where to moor our sea-steeds,   our ocean-stallions,
Fast at anchor.   Let us fix our hope
Upon that haven   which the Lord of heaven,
In holiness on high,   has opened by His Ascension.

BEDE (aka: BAEDA or BEDA), "Venerable Bede" (c. 673–735), historian, theologian, and scientist was possibly the most learned Western European of his day. He was probably born near Yarrow, and was educated at Saint Peter's, near Wearmouth, and at Saint Paul's, at Yarrow. At 19 he became a deacon and at 20 a priest. His *Ecclesiastical History of the English People*, written in Latin, is the most valuable record we have, especially of the century and a half just prior to his writing it (731). Although historical scholars discount some parts of this work as legendary, even these sections are highly valued by students of literature. The most famous passages are the record of Caedmon's dream (see above) and *The Conversion of Edmund*, in which man's life is likened to the flight of a small bird out of the cold and dark into a warm and lighted hall, and back out again. Wordsworth used this theme in a sonnet. Bede also wrote a history of the abbots of Wearmouth and Yarrow, and a scientific treatise, *De natura rerum (Of the Nature of Things)* based largely on Pliny and Isidore of Seville. He wrote a work on medieval finger symbolism and one on arithmetic and chronology, *De temporum ratione*. From this work it is apparent that Bede used personal observation in his studies and usually cited his sources when observations were not his own. His collected works were published in Paris in 1544–5 and were reprinted in 1554. There have been a number of English translations since then.

A Hymn
Translated by Elizabeth Charles

A hymn of glory let us sing;
New songs throughout the world shall ring;
By a new way none ever trod
Christ mounteth to the throne of God.

The apostles on the mountain stand,
The mystic mount, in Holy Land;
They with the virgin mother, see
Jesus ascend in majesty.

The angels say to the eleven:
"Why stand ye gazing into heaven?
This is the Savior, this is He!
Jesus hath triumphed gloriously!"

They said the Lord should come again,
As these beheld him rising then,
Calm soaring through the radiant sky,
Mounting its dazzling summits high.

May our affections thither tend,
And thither constantly ascend,
Where, seated on the Father's throne,
Thee reigning in the heavens we own!

Be thou our present joy, Oh Lord!
Who wilt be ever our reward;
And, as the countless ages flee,
May all our glory be in Thee!

The Seafarer
Anonymous
Translated by Margaret Williams

Full little he thinks   who has life's joy
and dwells in cities   and has few disasters,
proud and wine-flushed,   how I, weary often,
must bide my time   on the brimming stream.
Night-shades darken,   it snows from the north,
frost binds the ground,   hail falls on the earth,
the coldest corn.   For this my heart-thoughts
are knocking now,   for I must set out
on the high streams,   the rolling salt-waves.
Hour by hour   my heart's lust urges
my spirit to go forth,   that far from here
I may seek a land   of strange people.
There is no one so proud   among earth's men,
nor so gifted with goods   nor so bold in youth,
nor so brave in deeds,   with a lord dear to him,
that he has not sorrow   in his sea-faring—
too little the Lord   will do for him
He thinks not of the harp   nor of ring-giving
nor of the joy of a woman,   nor of the world's hope,
nor of ought else save the   roll of the waves;
But ever he feels longing,   who goes on the waters.
The woods have bright blossoms,   the burghs are fair,
plains gleam with loveliness,   the world full of life;

all these urge on   the eager heart
to go journeying,   for the man who thinks
to go afar   on the flood-ways.
And the cuckoo warns   with wailing voice;
summer's guardian sings,   telling the sorrow
bitter in its breast-hoard.   The man who is well off
knows but little   of what they endure
who go in exile   the farthest away.
So my thought wanders   over my heart treasures,
my inner spirit goes   over the sea-flood,
over the whale's home,   wanders away
on the earth's face.   It comes back to me
hungry and greedy;   the lone flier cries,
urges unceasing   the heart to roam
on the whale-way   of the wide waters,
the broad streams.   Thus the joys of the Lord
are hotter within me   than this dead life
passing over the land.   I do not believe
that the wealth of the earth   will stand forever.

Early Greek and Latin Hymns

Although all the following are nineteenth century translations, the original hymns were possibly sung by the early British Christians in Latin. It seems strange to modern Americans that a converted people should worship God in a language other than their own. The English-speaking branches of the Roman Catholic tradition have used some Latin up to the present, however. The rest of us might draw a parallel with our experience learning Bible verses in the sometimes "foreign" words and grammar of King James English.

Latin not only influenced the medieval English church, but it was the official language thereof, so that singing Latin hymns (and carols as we shall see later) was a common part of Christian worship. The earliest missionaries obviously had to translate the gospel into the language of the people in order to communicate it, however. And by the time of Caedmon, at least, Christians were composing and translating poetry in the vernacular (the native language). But Latin was so much a part of Christian life that the least educated Christian eventually learned much of the Latin church service by heart, and anyone mildly educated used it frequently in his daily speech.

The Latin service, the Vulgate (the Latin translation of the Bible) and Latin hymns, then, were an important part of early English literature—much more than the classical (pagan Greek and Roman) texts which were later held up as models for English composition.

Some of the Latin (and a few Greek) hymns we have in translation go back as far as the fourth century after Christ. Various accounts are given of how hymns arose as part of the church's literature. They may have been sung in the catacombs for mutual encouragement. Later hymn-singing came into vogue in some parts of the church as a defensive tactic against heretics, some of whom (such as the Arians) were active hymn-singers.

Gradually hymns came to have a particular orientation toward the "offices" of the church. Albert Edward Bailey (*The Gospel in Hymns*) comments:

> . . . In the parish churches a man was thought to be doing his full duty if he attended "Lauds" in the morning and "Vespers" in the evening; . . . These Church Offices were not as simple as at first appears. Not only were there eight canonical Hours but the Office was changed to fit the great festivals of the Church year and the saint's days. Thus practically there was a different set of offices for every day of the year. The immense literature that grew up to provide material for these Offices was gathered into books, which had become so voluminous that before the days of Henry VIII the Church had standardized them and cut them down to two: (1) the *Breviary*, detailing the various offices for the use of the clergy; (2) the *Missal*, which gives the ritual of the Mass.

In contrast to what went on in the Protestant Reformation of Europe, English hymn-singing came to a halt with the break from the Roman church:

> . . .[In] the new ritual that had to be made for the national Church, Cranmer omitted all hymns. There were practical reasons behind this act. Ordinary citizens could not read Latin—or English, for that matter; and without choirs of monks who knew the intricacies of plainsong tunes, singing by the congregation was impossible. (Bailey)

The real return of English hymn-writing and a concurrent burst of translating Greek and Latin hymns did not come until the Restoration, Romantic, and Victorian eras. Hymns, not only from the western (Latin) church, but also from the eastern (Greek) church were translated and continue to be important parts of our worship today.

The Latin and Greek hymns themselves influenced the early English church, however, and that is why we give a number of them here.

O Splendour of God's Glory Bright (Splendor paternae gloriae)
St. Ambrose, 340–97.   Translated by R. Bridges.

O splendour of God's glory bright,
O thou that bringest light from light,
O Light of light, light's living spring,
O Day, all days illumining,

O thou true Sun, on us thy glance
Let fall in royal radiance,
The Spirit's sanctifying beam
Upon our earthly senses stream.

The Father, too, our prayers implore,
Father of glory evermore;
The Father of all grace and might,
To banish sin from our delight:

To guide whate'er we nobly do,
With love all envy to subdue,
To make ill-fortune turn to fair,
And give us grace our wrongs to bear.

Of The Father's Love Begotten
Aurelius Clemens Prudentius, 348–413
Translated by John Mason Neale, 1818–1866

Of the Father's love begotten Ere the worlds began to be,
He is Alpha and Omega, He the source, the ending he,
Of the things that are, that have been, And that future years shall see.

This is he whom heav'n-taught singers Sang of old with one accord,
Whom the Scriptures of the prophets Promised in their faithful word;
Now he shines, the long-expected; Let creation praise its Lord.

O ye heights of heav'n, adore him Angel hosts, his praises sing;
All dominions, bow before him, And extol our God and King;
Let no tongue on earth be silent, Every voice in concert ring.

Thee let age and thee let manhood, Thee let boys in chorus sing;
Matrons, virgins, little maidens, With glad voices answering;
Let their guileless songs re-echo, And their heart Its music bring.

Christ, to thee, with God the Father, And, O Holy Ghost, to thee,
Hymn, and chant, and high thanksgiving, And unwearied praises be,
Honor, glory, and dominion, And eternal victory.

Ye Clouds And Darkness, Hosts Of Night (Nox Et Tenebrae Et Nubila)
Aurelius Clemens Prudentius, 348–413
Translated by R. M. Pope

Ye clouds and darkness, hosts of night,
That breed confusion and affright,
Begone! o'erhead the dawn shines clear
The light breaks in, and Christ is here.

Earth's gloom flees broken and dispersed,
By the sun's piercing shafts coerced:
The day-star's eyes rain influence bright,
And colours glimmer back to sight.

Thee, Christ, alone we know; to thee
We bend in pure simplicity;
Our songs with tears to thee arise;
Prove thou our hearts with thy clear eyes.

Though we be stained with blots within,
Thy quickening rays shall purge our sins;
Light of the Morning Star, thy grace
Shed on us from thy cloudless face.

Let All Mortal Flesh Keep Silence
From the Greek Liturgy of St. James, circa 5th century
Translated by Gerard Moultrie, 1864

Let all mortal flesh keep silence, And with fear and trembling stand;
Pondering nothing earthly-minded, For with blessing in His hand,
Christ our God to earth descendeth, Our full homage to demand.

King of kings, yet born of Mary, As of old on earth He stood,
Lord of lords, in human vesture—In the body and the blood—
He will give to all the faithful His own self for heavenly food.

Rank on rank the host of heaven Spreads its vanguard on the way,
As the Light of light descendeth From the realms of endless day,
That the powers of hell may vanish As the darkness clears away.

At His feet the six-winged seraph; Cherubim, with sleepless eye,
Veil their faces to the presence, As with ceaseless voice they cry,
Alleluia,   Alleluia,   Alleluia, Lord Most High!

Fierce Was The Wild Billow
Ascribed to Anatolius, 7th century   Translated by John Mason Neale, 1862

Fierce was the wild billow, Dark was the night;
Oars labored heavily, Foam glimmered white;
Trembled the mariners, Peril was nigh:
Then said the God of God, "Peace! it is I."

Ridge of the mountain wave, Lower thy crest!
Wall of Euroclydon, Be thou at rest!
Sorrow can never be, Darkness must fly,
Where saith the Light of light, "Peace! it is I."

Jesus, Deliverer, Come thou to me;
Soothe my voyaging Over life's sea:
Thou, when the storm of death Roars, sweeping by,
Whisper, O Truth of Truth, "Peace! it is I."

O Christ, Our Hope, Our Heart's Desire
Latin hymn, 7th or 8th century, Translated by John Chandler, 1837

O Christ, our hope, our heart's desire, Redemption's only spring!
Creator of the world thou art, Its Saviour and its King.

How vast the mercy and the love Which laid our sins on thee,
And led thee to a cruel death, To set thy people free.

But now the bands of death are burst, The ransom has been paid;
And thou art on thy Father's throne, In glorious robes arrayed.

O Christ, be thou our lasting joy, Our ever great reward!
Our only glory may it be To glory in the Lord.

Jesus The Very Thought Of Thee
Anonymous, Latin, 11th century, Translated by Edward Caswell, 1849

Jesus, the very thought of thee   With sweetness fills my breast;
But sweeter far thy face to see,   And in thy presence rest.

Nor voice can sing, nor heart can frame,   Nor can the mem'ry find
A sweeter sound than thy blest Name   O Saviour of mankind.

O Hope of ev'ry contrite heart,   O Joy of all the meek,
To those who fall, how kind thou art!   How good to those who seek!

But what to those who find? Ah, this   Nor tongue nor pen can show:
The love of Jesus, what it is   None but his loved ones know.

Jesus, our only Joy be thou,   As thou our Prize wilt be;
Jesus, be thou our Glory now,   And through eternity.

O Sacred Head Now Wounded
Ascribed to Bernard of Clairvaux, 1091–1153
Translated by Paul Gerhardt, 1656
Translated by James Waddell Alexander, 1830

O sacred Head, now wounded,   With grief and shame weighed down;
Now scornfully surrounded,   With thorns thine only crown;
O sacred Head, what glory,   What bliss till now was thine!
Yet, though despised and gory,   I joy to call thee mine.

What thou, my Lord, has suffered   Was all for sinners' gain:
Mine, mine was the transgression,   But thine the deadly pain.
Lo, here I fall, my Saviour!   'Tis I deserve thy place;
Look on me with they favor,   Vouchsafe to me thy grace.

What language shall I borrow   To thank thee, dearest Friend,
For this thy dying sorrow,   Thy pity without end?
O make me thine for ever;   And should I fainting be,
Lord, let me never, never   Outlive my love to thee.

Be near when I am dying,   O show thy cross to me;
And for my succour flying,   Come, Lord, to set me free:
These eyes, new faith receiving,   From Jesus shall not move;
For he who dies believing,   Dies safely, through thy love.

Jesus, Thou Joy Of Loving Hearts
Attributed to Bernard of Clairvaux, circa 1150
Translated by Ray Palmer,1859

Jesus, thou Joy of loving hearts,
Thou Font of life, thou Light of men,

From the best bliss that earth imparts
We turned unfilled to thee again.

Thy truth unchanged hath ever stood;
Thou savest those that on thee call;
To them that seek thee thou art good,
To them that find thee All in all.

We taste thee, O thou living Bread,
And long to feast upon thee still;
We drink of thee, the Fountainhead,
And thirst our souls from thee to fill.

Our restless spirits yearn for thee,
Where e'er our changeful lot is cast;
Glad when thy gracious smile we see,
Blest when our faith can hold thee fast.

O Jesus, ever with us stay,
Make all our moments calm and bright;
Chase the dark night of sin away,
Shed o'er the world thy holy light.

O Come, O Come, Emmanuel
Latin antiphons, 12th century. Latin hymn 1710
Translated by John Mason Neale, 1851

O come, O come, Emmanuel,
And ransom captive Israel,
That mourns in lonely exile here
Until the Son of God appear.

   Rejoice! Rejoice! Emmanuel
   Shall come to thee, O Israel.

O come, O come, thou Lord of might,
Who to thy tribes on Sinai's height,
In ancient times didst give the law
In cloud and majesty and awe.

O come, thou Rod of Jesse, free
Thine own from Satan's tyranny;
From depths of hell thy people save,
And give them vict'ry o'er the grave.

O come, thou Dayspring from on high
And cheer us by thy drawing nigh;
Disperse the gloomy clouds of night,
And earth's dark shadows put to flight.

O come, thou Key of David, come
And open wide our heav'nly home;
Make safe the way that leads on high,
And close the path to misery.

Veni, Creator Spiritus
Translated by John Dryden (1631–1700)

Creator Spirit, by whose aid
The world's foundations first were laid,
Come visit every pious mind,
Come pour thy joys on human-kind;
From sin and sorrow set us free,
And make thy temples worthy thee.

O source of uncreated light,
The Father's promised Paraclete!
Thrice holy fount, thrice holy fire,
Our hearts with heavenly love inspire;
Come, and thy sacred unction bring,
To sanctify us while we sing.

Plenteous of grace, descend from high,
Rich in thy seven-fold energy!
Thou strength of His Almighty hand,
Whose power does heaven and earth command!
Proceeding Spirit, our defense,
Who dost the gifts of tongues dispense,
And crown'st thy gift with eloquence!

Refine and purge our earthly parts;
But, O, inflame and fire our hearts!
Our frailties help, our vice control,
Submit the senses to the soul;
And when rebellious they are grown,
Then lay thy hand and hold them down.

Chase from our minds the infernal foe,

And peace, the fruit of love, bestow;
And, lest our feet should step astray,
Protect and guide us in the way.
Make us eternal truths receive,
And practice all that we believe;
Give us thyself, that we may see
The Father, and the Son, by thee.

Immortal honour, endless fame,
Attend the Almighty Father's name;
The Saviour Son be glorified,
Who for lost man's redemption died;
And equal adoration be,
Eternal Paraclete, to thee.

The Advent of Our God (Instantis adventum Dei)
C. Coffin, 1676–1749   Pr. S. P.

The advent of our God   With eager hearts we greet,
And singing, haste upon the road   His coming Reign to meet.

For, lo, God's Word and Son   Came down to make us free,
And he a servant's form put on,   To bring us liberty.

Daughter of Sion, rise   To meet thy lowly King;
Let not thy heart in haste despise   The peace he comes to bring.

For judgment doth befall   The stubborn who refuse.
But God doth give his light to all   Who cherish his Good News.

Then evil flee away   Before the rising dawn!
Let this old Adam day by day   God's image still put on.

Thou Liberator true,   All glory be to thee,
To whom in God our praise is due   For all eternity.

Thee We Adore (Adoro te devote)
Thomas Aquinas, 1227–74
Translated by Bp. F. R. Woodford

Thee we adore, O hidden Saviour, thee,
Who in thy Supper with us deign'st to be;
Both flesh and spirit in thy presence fail,
Yet here thy presence we devoutly hail.

O blest memorial of our dying Lord,
Who living bread to men doth here afford!
O may our souls for ever feed on thee,
And thou, O Christ, for ever precious be.

Fountain of goodness, Jesus, Lord and God,
Cleanse us, unclean in thy most cleansing flood;
Increase our faith and love, that we may know
The hope and peace which from thy presence flow.

O Christ, whom now beneath a veil we see,
May what we thirst for soon our portion be,
To gaze on thee unveiled, and see thy face,
The vision of thy glory and thy grace.

Chapter Two

MIDDLE ENGLISH PERIOD

1066–Norman Conquest   1485–Caxton publishes *Le Morte D'Arthur*

The conquest of England by the Normans (descendants of Norsemen who invaded France and adapted themselves to its culture and language), specifically by Duke William at the Battle of Hastings in 1066, seems to have brought English poetry to a halt until the beginning of the thirteenth century. Anglo-Norman (mostly French) became the official court language under the new rulers, but Middle English developed slowly and naturally out of a combination of Anglo-Saxon and French.

The literature of the twelfth century seems to have been chiefly "modern" translations of Anglo-Saxon and Latin ecclesiastical writings such as King Alfred's translation of Boethius' *Consolations of Philosophy*. Moral and homiletic writings continued to be favored (as in several of Chaucer's *Canterbury Tales*) up to the fifteenth century.

Middle English poetry began to cover a broader range of experience with a broader tone than Anglo-Saxon poetry, however. A modern sense of humor seems to have made its way in, either with the Normans, or out of the vicissitudes of being a conquered people. Everyday affairs and people become subjects of literature, down to the "barnyard" matters of Chaucer's bawdier tales.

The Latin of the church, the universal language of Europe, which had been a strong influence on Anglo-Saxon writers, was an even greater influence on Middle English writers, whose language and literature under the Normans was further conformed to that continental (Romance) language and literature.

In approximately 1205, a Middle English poem using Anglo-Saxon alliterative style, *Brut*, was written by a man named Layamon. It is a mythological history of England, taking its name from Brutus (a supposed descendant of Trojan Aeneas and forefather of the British). It is the first English work to deal with the Arthurian legend. The writer took some of his material from the Latin of Gregory of Monmouth, and apparently imagined the rest.

Alliterative poetry included two ancient elements of style: alliteration within each line rather than rhymed endings, and Anglo-Saxon four-part lines divided in the middle by a pause or caesura. It continued to be used in the Middle English period—by William Langland in *Piers Plowman* and by the "Gawain poet" in *Gawain and the Green Knight* (both approximately 1375).

Rhymed couplets were borrowed from French as early as the twelfth century, and this "modern" style of poetic rhyme and rhythm with its many variations comes to dominate in the works of Chaucer and continues to the present.

During the Middle English period, the romance came to replace the Anglo-Saxon epic style of poetry. The romance, best exemplified in *Gawain and the Green Knight*, was an account of the doings of kings and knights and courtly ladies—more elaborate than the more stoic Anglo-Saxon narratives. Many of the English romances are largely translations and composites taken from French romances. But the romantic or chivalric tradition had an effect on religious poetry as well. While Christ was portrayed somewhat in the tradition of Germanic epic heroes in the Anglo-Saxon *Dream of the Rood*, he is portrayed in chivalric or knightly terms in many Middle English poems.

Poets seem to have been sponsored both by ecclesiastical bodies and by the Norman court. John Gower, Chaucer's contemporary, illustrates the breadth of the Middle English poet—writing three major works, one in Latin, one in Norman French and one in English.

The effect of Latin on Middle English poetry comes out clearly in fourteenth and fifteenth century carols, which frequently utilized Latin refrains, "burdens" (the section sung first, then used as a chorus between verses) or even "macaronic" combinations of Latin and English in the verse lines themselves. While clerics may have written many of these, it appears Latin was familiar enough to many Englishmen to make such bilingual poetry natural to them. We continue to sing some of these Christmas carols today. Whether carols were sung principally by "carolers" or as aristocratic entertainments is not clear, but most of them are sincere expressions of heartfelt faith.

Many of the Middle English Christian poems are neither carols nor moral lessons, but personal cries to the Lord. While Anglo-Saxon poetry has a certain conventional formality to it, even at its most passionate, Middle English poems may be almost embarrassingly informal and personal. To our ears they have a greater ring of sincerity.

Fifteenth century Middle English poetry uses language closer to our own than that of the twelfth century, but the subjects, themes, and styles of the Middle English period changed little. In Scotland several poets, including William Dunbar, carried on the Chaucerian manner.[1] Many fifteenth century poems and carols are only polished versions or variations on earlier works. The greatest addition to English literature of that century seems to have been the morality play, of which *Everyman*, at the end of the century is the best example.

Middle English poetry appears at first sight to be almost as foreign as Anglo-Saxon, but on looking closer one quickly realizes it is largely decipherable. There are many variations in spelling, even within one author's works, and

---

[1]C.S.Lewis and others point out it is an error to call these poets "Scottish Chaucerians," because they were not literary descendants of Chaucer, but rather of a parallel tradition. (See Sixteenth Century Introduction.)

plenty of extra final "e's" (most of which are supposed to be pronounced in reading), but only the more difficult words are translated here in footnotes. Simple guides to pronunciation may be found in collections such as Volume I of the *Norton Anthology of English Literature.*

By the time Caxton published Malory's *Le Morte D'Arthur*, in 1485, the English language was very close to what it is today.

A Brief Chronology of the Middle English Period

1066	Norman Conquest. Duke William defeats King Harold at the Battle of Hastings. Norman French becomes court language of England
1066–1216	William and his six successors are generally absentee rulers, reigning much of the time from Normandy and Europe
1205	Approximate year Layamon's *Brut* was composed
1216–1272	Henry III, first of the line to be principally an English king
1309	Richard Rolle drops out of Oxford to become a hermit
c.1333	William Herebert, Franciscan theologian and poet dies
c.1370	William Langland completes *Piers Plowman* Geoffrey Chaucer writes *The Book of the Duchess*
c.1375-1400	*Gawain and the Green Knight* written, probably by unknown author of the three long Christian poems, "Patience," "Purity," and "Pearl"
1377–1400	Approximate period of Chaucer's service as "court poet" to John of Gaunt, Richard II, and Henry IV
1385	Chaucer begins *Troilus and Criseyde;* Approximate date of *The Second Shepherd's Play*, a medieval "mystery play" centering on Christ's birth and his redemption of mankind as experienced by a group of shepherds
1386-1390	Period of John Gower's composing *Confessio Amantis*, octosyllabic couplets in English
1386-1400	Chaucer writes *Canterbury Tales*
1390-1410	Both Chaucer and John Walton complete verse translations of Boethius' *Consolation of Philosophy*
c.1470–1500	*Everyman*, a morality play about a spiritual pilgrimage, is written (several editions printed after 1500)
1485	Caxton publishes Malory's *Morte D'Arthur*, one of the first books printed in English

Carols

Carols are songs of praise and of great joy, associated originally with dancing and dance tunes. The term "carol" itself may derive from "chorus" or from "corolla," a garland or circle as in a ring dance.

To what degree dancing was part of early Christian carol-singing is difficult to determine, but the third council of Toledo forbade dance in the church on saints' days, so some dancing must have been going on. The council of Auxerre in 599 and the council of Avignon in 1209 forbade secular dance and song in the churches. The crèche or "crib" was central in the Christmas celebrations of many churches of Europe and apparently dances around it were part of the rejoicing.

Part of the English carol tradition originated in pagan Yuletide festivals with customs like bringing in a boar's head and decorating with holly and ivy. There is an Anglo-Norman carol or "noel" from about 1200, which concludes with the old Saxon toasts "Wesseyl" and "Drinc-heyl."

The term "carole" for a sacred song, usually of Christmas, began to be used in England in the fourteenth century. The French called such "noels" (from Latin *natalem* - birthday). About 1429, John Audelay wrote in his manuscript containing carols and other works, "I pray you, sirs, both more and less,/ Sing these carols in Christmas." The earliest sacred carols are closely modeled on Latin hymns. Many are in fact "macaronic" (combinations), with both Latin and English phrases. In time, Latin faded from the carol, receding to a refrain, or disappearing altogether.

Fifteenth century carols are of a wide variety, covering many holidays of the Christian year as well as other gospel subjects. There are a few extant which are thoroughly secular—drinking songs and pretexts for alms-begging. Most are of a folk-song flavor, and a few preserve medieval legends such as the "Cherry-tree Carol," "When Joseph Was An Old Man," and "I Saw Three Ships." An indication some carols were either composed by "the folk" or long popular among them is the existence of many variant versions. Words tend to change when transmitted solely by oral tradition.

Many fifteenth and most sixteenth century carols appear to be less folk-songs than studied compositions. Some are re-writings of folk carols, and others are likely original compositions of the authors who signed them. In 1521 Wynkyn de Worde published *New Christmas Carols.* Between 1546 and 1552 Richard Kele issued *Christmas Carols, Newly Imprinted.* The Wedderburns put out several issues of *Compendious Book of Godly Songs* and *Ballads,* the first as far back as 1567.

The Reformation affected English carols by bringing about the exclusion of many sorts: those addressed to saints, adoring Mary, and focusing on church festivals. Christmas, the Saviour's Advent, and Easter, his Resurrection, became the only accepted subjects of carols. The Shepherd's part in the Christmas story continued to be a favorite theme.

(In the late eighteenth and nineteenth centuries there was a resurgence of carol writing. Charles Wesley was among the best writers of carols as well as of other hymns, his "Hark the Herald Angels Sing" being one of the most popular.)

The Christmas carol is a genre that continues to find writers up to the present, but many of today's favorites, like "In Excelsis Deo" are part of an ancient tradition going far back to early Latin hymns.

Mirabile Misterium
Anonymous

Mirabile misterium! The Son of God is man become

A marvelous thing I have mused in my mind,
How that Veritas sprang right of the ground,
And Justicia, for all mankind,
From heaven to earth he came adown.
Mirabile misterium!
The Son of God is man become.

Then Mary, that merciful may,
Seeing man damned for his trespass
Hath sent down Sapientia, the sooth to say;
Man is redeemed and brought to grace.
Mirabile misterium!
The Son of God is man become.

Celestial citizens, for us that you pray
To Him that is both Alpha and O,
That we may be saved on Doomsday,
And brought to that bliss He bought us to!
Mirabile misterium!
The Son of God is man become.

Veritas - *Lat.*, truth; Justicia - *Lat.*, justice; Sapientia - *Lat.*, wisdom; sooth - truth

Hand by Hand We Shall us Take *c. 1350*
Anonymous

Honnd by honnd we schulle ous take,
And joye and blisse schulle we make,
For the deuel of ele man haght forsake,
And Godes Sone ys maked oure make.

A child is boren amonges man,
And in that child was no wam;
That child ys God, that child is man,
And in that child oure life bygan.

Senful man, be blithe and glad:
For your mariage thy peys ys grad
Wan Crist was boren;
Com to Crist; thy peys ys grad;
For the was hys blod ysched
That were forloren.

Senful man, be blithe and bold,
For euene ys bothe boght and sold,
Euereche fote.
Com to Crist; thy peys ys told,
For the he yahf a hondrefold
Hys lif to bote.

deuel - devil; ele - hell; haght - hath; make - mate; wam - blemish; peys - peace; grad -
granted; the - thee; ysched - shed; euene - heaven; euereche fote - every foot; yahf - gave;
to bote - for a ransom or gift

Man Be Merie As Bryd On Berie
Anonymous

Man be merie as bryd on berie,
And al thi care let away.

This tyme is born a chyld ful good,
He that us bowt vpon the rod;
He bond the deuyl, that is so wod,
Til the drydful domysday.

Quat the chyld of meche myght
Wold be born of Mary bryght,
A tokene he sente to kyng and knyght,
A sterre that schon both nyght and day.

The sterre scon as bryght as fer
Ouer all the world bothe fer and ner,
In tokene he was withoutyn per,
And pereles he xal lastyn ay.

The eighth day he was circumsise
For to fulfylle the profecyes;
The profetes with wordes wyse
Hym present with ryche aray.

The twelfth day come kynges thre
Out of the est with herte fre;
To worchepyn him thei knelyd on kne
With gold and myr and francincens.

bryd bird; wod - insane; quat - what; meche - meek; fer - fire; xal - shall

There blows a colde wynd todaye
Anonymous

There blows a colde wynd todaye, todaye,
The wynd blows cold todaye;
Cryst sufferyd his passyon for manys saluacyon,
To kype the cold wynd awaye.

Thys wynde be reson ys callyd tentacyon;
Yt rauyghth both nyghth and daye.
Remember, man, how the Sauyor was slayne
To kype the colde wynde awaye.

Pride and presumcyon and fals extorcyon,
That meny man dothe betraye—
Man, cum to contrycyon and axe confessyon
To kype the colde wynd awaye.

O Mary myld, for love of the chyld
That dyed on Good Frydaye,
Be owr saluacyon frome mortall damnacyon,
To kype the cold wynd awaye.

He was naylyd, his blode was halyd,
Owre remyssyon for to by,
And for owr synnys all he dronke both eysell and gall,
To kype the cold wynd awaye.

rauyghth - ravishe; halyd - hallowed; eysell - wine dregs

Slowthe, enuy, couytis, and lechere
Blewe the cold wynd, as Y dare saye;
Agene suche pusyn he sufferryd his paysscyon
To kype the cold wynd awaye.

O man, remember the Lord so tender
Whyche dyed withowte denaye;
Hys hondes so smert laye next to his hart
To kype the cold wynd awaye.

Now pray we all to the Kyng selestyall,
That borne he was off mayde,
That we maye loue so with other mo,
To kype the cold wynd awaye.

At the day of dome when we schall cum
Owr synns not for to denaye,
Mary, praye to the Sone that syghthy yn hys trone
To kype the cold wynd awaye.

At the last ynde, man, thou schalt send
And kype bothe nyghth and daye;
The most goodlyst tresyor ys Cryst the Sauyor
To kype the cold wynd awaye.

Here let vs ynde, and Cryst vs defend
All be the nyghth and be daye,
And bryng vs to hys place where ys myrthe and solas
To kype the cold wynd awaye.

paysscyon - passion; other mo - others

A Lyke-Wake Dirge
Anonymous

This ae night, this ae night,
Every night and alle,
Fire and sleet and candle-lighte,
And Christ receive thy saule,

When thou from hence away art past,
Every night and alle,
To Whinny-muir thou com'st at last;
And Christ receive thy saule.

Whinny-muir - thorny moor (a mythical place of passage for the dead)

If ever thou gavest hosen and shoon.
Every night and alle,
Sit thee down and put them on;
And Christ receive thy saule.

If hosen and shoon thou ne'er gav'st none
Every night and alle,
The whins shall prick thee to the bare bone;
And Christ receive thy saule.

From Whinny-muir when thou may'st pass,
Every night and alle,
To Bridge o' Dread thou com'st at last;
And Christ receive thy saule.

From Bridge o' Dread when thou may'st pass,
Every night and alle,
To Purgatory fire thou com'st at last;
And Christ receive thy saule.

If ever thou gavest meat or drink,
Every night and alle,
The fire shall never make thee shrink;
And Christ receive thy saule.

If meat or drink thou ne'er gav'st none,
Every night and alle,
The fire will burn thee to the bare bone;
And Christ receive thy saule.

This ae night, this ae night,
Every night and alle,
Fire and sleet and candle-light,
And Christ receive thy saule.

whin - thorn

Mervell nothyng, Joseph, that Mary be with chyld
Anonymous

'Mervell nothyng, Joseph, that Mary be with chyld;
She hath conceyved vere God and man and yet she undefiled.'

'Conceyved man, how may that be by reason broght abowte?'
'By gode reason above all reasons, hit may be withouten dowte;

For God made man aboue all reasons of slyme erthe most wyld;
Wherfore, Joseph, marvell not though Mary be with chyld.

'Mary was bothe wyf and mother, and she a verrey mayde,
And conceyved God, our brother, as prophettes before hade saide.
Sithe God made reason, why may not reason of his werkes be begyld?
Wherfore, Joseph, mervell not though Mary be with chyld.

'The erthe, ayer, sonne, and mone, fyre, water, and every sterr
Is gode reason that above all reasons shuld passe our reasons ferr.
To reason with hym that made reason our reasons are but wyld,
Wherfore, Joseph, mervell not though Mary be with chyld.'

The hye and holy sacrament in verrey forme of bred
Is God and man, flesshe and blode, he that was quyck and ded.
Did reason this dede? Nay, nay; reason is ferr begylde;
His is gode reason above all reasons, Mary to be with chyld.

God, angell, soole, and devyll lett all clerks determyne;
By reason the be, but what the be reason cannot defyne.
Then serve the fyrst, and save the thrydde; the forte let be resyled,
And mervell no more, but fast beleve Mary was maide with chyld.

slyme erthe - mud; begyld - bewildered; resyled - resisted

Com home agayne
Anonymous

Com home agayne,
Com home agayne,
Min owine swet hart, com home agayne;
Ye are gone astray
Owt of youer way;
Therefore com home agayne.

Mankend I cale, wich lyith in frale;
For loue I mad the fre;
To pay the det the prise was gret,
From hell that I ranssomed the.

Mi blod so red for the was shed;
The prise it ys not smale;
Remembre welle what I the tell,
And com whan I the kale.

frale - weakness or slavery

Mi prophetes all, they ded the cale;
For loue I mad the free;

. . .

And I miselfe and mi postels twelfe,
To prech was all mi thouth
Mi Faders kyngedom both hole and sound,
Which that I so derly bouth.

Therefore refreyne, and torne agayne,
And leve thyne owene intent,
The which it is contrare, iwos,
Onto mi commaundment.

Thow standest in dout and sekest about
Where that thow mayst me se;
Idoules be set, mony for to gyt,
Wich ys made of stone and tre.

I am no stoke, nor no payncted bloke,
Nor mad by no mannes hand,
Bot I am he that shall los the
From Satan the phinnes bonde.

postels - apostles; thouth - thought; bouth - bought; iwos - certainly; Idoules - idols;
stoke - stump; payncted bloke - painted block; los - loose; phinnes - fiend's

Amendith me, and pair me noght
Anonymous

I pray yow all with on thoght,
Amendith me, and pair me nogh[t].

Holy Wret seth—nothing ys sother—
That no man schuld apeir other:
Seth in God I am thi brother,
Amendyth me, and payr me noght.

The lore in the gospell ilk man may se:
Yf thi brother trespas to the,
Betwen vs two snyb thou me;
Amendyth me, and peyr me noght.

Yf thou se I do amysse,
And no man wot bot thou of this,

amendith - correct; pair/peir - judge or defame; snyb - rebuke

Mak it noght so il as it ys;
Amend me, and peyr me noght.

God byddes thou schalt no man defame,
Nor apeyr no mans name,
Bot, euen as thou wold han the same,
Amend me, and peyr me noght.

Apeyr thou no man with thi word,
Nother in ernest ne in bowrd;
Lat thi tong, that is thi sword,
Amend ever and peyr noght.

Now to amend God gyf vs grace,
Of repentaunce and verre space,
In heuen ther to se hys face,
Qwer we schall mend and peyr noght.

wot - knows; bowrd - jest; qwer - where

Timor mortis conturbat me
Anonymous

In what estate so ever I be,
Timor mortis conturbat me.

As I went in a mery mornyng,
I hard a byrd bothe wep and syng;
Thys was the tenowr of her talkyng:
'Timor mortis conturbat me.'

I asked that byrd what sche ment.
'I am a musket bothe fayer and gent;
For dred of deth I am al schent;
Timor mortis conturbat me.

'Whan I schal dey, I know no day;
What countre or place I cannot sey;
Wherfor this song syng I may:
"Timor mortis conturbat me."

'Jhesu Cryst, whane he schuld dey,
To hys Fader he gan sey;

Timor mortis. . . "The fear of death disturbs me"; tenowr - tenor, gist; musket - male
sparrow hawk; schent - devastated

"Fader," he seyd, "in Trinyte,
Timor mortis conturbat me."

'Al Crysten pepull, behold and se:
This world is but a vanyte
And replet with necessyte;
Timor mortis conturbat me.

'Wak I or sclep, ete or drynke,
Whan I on my last end do thynk,
For grete fer my sowle do shrynke;
Timor mortis conturbat me.'

God graunte us grace hym for to serve,
And be at owr end whan we sterve,
And frome the fynd he us preserve;
Timor mortis conturbat me.

replet - full; fynd - fiend

My Hope is in God
Anonymous

Spes mea in Deo est;
Spes mea in Deo est.

When lordechype ys loste and lusti lekyng withall,
When felichepe fayleth, and frendechepe dothe falle,
Then can Y no comfort but cry and call,
'Spes mea in Deo est.'

When maystery ne mayntenaunce, manhode ne myght,
When reson ne rechesse may rewell me aryght,
Then Y, wit sorwe and care within my herte plyght:
'Spes mea in Deo est.'

When age dothe growe, then grucche Y and grone;
When febelnesse fallith, then fawte Y sone;
Then can Y non other but cry and call anone,
'Spes mea in Deo est.'

lordechype - authority; ne - nor; lusti leyking - happy thriving; maystery - rule, the rule
of ones own will; mayntenaunce - demeanor; rechesse - reckoning,duty or discipline;
plyght - plight, condition; grucche - grouch, complain; sone - soon

In Slumber Late
Anonymous

In a slumbir late as I was,
I harde a voice lowde call and crye,
'Amende the, man, of thi trespace,
And aske forgeveness or evyr thou dye.'
In a slumbir late as I was,
I harde a voice lowde call and crye,
'Amende the, man, of thi trespace,
And aske forgeveness or evyr thou dye.

'Beholde,' he saide, 'my creature,
Whome I did make so lyke unto me,
What payns I sofferd, I the ensure,
Where thou were thrall, to make the free.
Upon the cross with naylis thre
Fast I was naylyd for thyne offence;
Therfore remembir the or thou go hence.'

the - thee; thi - thy; thrall - slave

God and Man Set as One
Anonymous

By reason of two and poore of one
This tyme God and man was set at one.

God against nature thre wonders haith wrought:
First of the vile earthe mad man without man,
Then woman without woman of man maid of nought,
And so man without man in woman than.
Thus, lo, God and man together begane,
As two for to joine together in one,
As at this good tyme to be sett at one;
Thus God begane
This world for to forme and to encrease man.

Angell in heaven for offence was damned,
And man also for beinge variable;
Whether shuld be saved was examyned,
Man or yet angell; then God was greable
To answer for man, for man was not able,
And said man had mocyon and angell had none,

Wherefore God and man shuld be seit at one.
Thank we him than
That thus did leaue angell and saved man.

The devill clamed man by bargan as this:
For an appell, he said, man was bought and solde;
God aunswered and said the bargan was his:
'Withe myne to be thyne how durst thoue be so bolde?
Man myne, syne thyne; wherfore thoue art now told
Thoue bought nought; then taike nought; thi bargan is don;
Wherfore God and man shal be set att one.'
Nowe blessed be he,
For we that are bownde, loe, nowe are maid free.

Betwene God and man ther was great distaunce,
For man said that God shuld haue kept him upryght,
And God said man maid all the variaunce,
For th'apple to sett his commaundement so light;
Wherfore, of his mercye sparinge the ryght,
He thought God and man shuld be set at one.
Seing that God and man was set at one,
What kindnes was this
To agree with man and the fault not his!

Withe man and woman ther was great traverse:
Man said to the woman, 'Woe myght thou be!'
'Nay,' quod the woman, 'Why dost thoue reverse?
For womans entisinge woe be to the!
For God made man the heade and ruler of me.'
Thus God sawe man and woman were not at one;
He thought in a woman to sett theime at one
To our solace;
His mercye he graunted for our trespace.

Of womanhede, lo, thre degres there be:
Widowehede, wedlocke, and virginnitie.
Widowehede clamed heauen; her title is this:
By oppressions that mekelie suffrethe she,
And wedlocke by generacion heauen hires shuld be,
And virgins clame by chastite alone.
Then God thought a woman shoulde set them at one
And cease ther strife,
For Marie was maden, widowe, and wife.

mocyon - motion, feeling or desire; mekelie - meekly

The ritche and the pore ther title did reherse:
The pore clamed heauen throughe his pacient havour;
He saide, ' Beati pauperes,' and further the verse;
The riche man by ritches thought hym in favour,
For who was so ritche as was our Saviour?
And againe who so pure as he was one
In hey when he ley to set us at one?
Who graunt us peace
And at the last ende the great joyes endles.

Beati pauperes - Lat. "Blessed are the poor"

I Pray You Be Merry

I pray you, be mery and synge with me
In worship of Cristys nativite.

Into this world this day dide com
Jhesu Criste, bothe God and man,
Lorde and servant in on person,
Born of the blessid virgin Mary.

He that was riche withowt any nede
Appered in this world in right pore wede
To mak us that were pore indede
Riche withowt any nede trewly.

A stabill was his chambre; a crach was his bed;
He had not a pylow to lay under his hed;
With maydyns mylk that babe was fedde;
In pore clothis was lappid the Lord Almyghty.

A noble lesson here is us tawght:
To set all wordly riches at nawght,
But pray we that we may be theder browght
Wher riches ys everlastyngly.

RICHARD OF CHICHESTER, SIR, (c.1197–1253)

Day by Day

Day by Day,
Dear Lord, of thee three things I pray:
To see thee more clearly,

Love thee more dearly,
Follow thee more nearly,
Day by day.

HEREBERT, WILLIAM (d. 1333?), a Franciscan theologian, is thought to have entered the Minorite order at Hereford and been sent from there to Oxford. He was in Paris, at least for a while in 1290. He returned to Oxford where he was known as a preacher and philosopher. He became the forty-third reader in Divinity to the University. A sermon of his on "They have no wine" is preserved with other of his writings. He returned to Hereford where he was buried in the old Minorite convent where he had been taught. He is supposed to have written theological works and commentaries on *Deuteronomy* and *Revelations*. Most of his verses are translations or paraphrases of Latin hymns.

Steddefast Cross

Steddefast cross, inmong alle other
Thou art a tree mikel of prise;
In braunche and flowre swilk another
I ne wot non in wode no rise.
Swete be the nailes, and swete be the tree,
And sweter be the birden that hanges upon thee.

inmon - among; mikel of prise - of great price; swilk - such; no rise - nor thicket

My Folk, What Have I Done Thee?

My folk, what habbe I do thee,
Other in what thing teened thee?
Gin nouthe and answere thou me.

For from Egypte ich ladde thee
Thou me ledest to roode-tree
My folk, what habbe I do thee? *etc.*

Through wildernesse ich ladde thee,
And fourty yeer bihedde thee,
And angeles bred ich yaf to thee,
And into reste ich broughte thee.
My folk, what habbe I do thee? *etc.*

habbe - have; Other - or; teened - vexed; Gin nouthe -begin now; For - because; ich ladde - I led; bihedde - looked after; yaf - gave;

What more shulde ich haven y-don
That thou ne havest nought underfon?
My folk, what habbe I do thee? *etc.*

Ich thee fedde and shrudde thee,
And thou with eisil drinkst to me,
And with spere stingest me.
My folk, what habbe I do thee? *etc.*

Ich Egypte beet for thee,
And here teem I slow for thee,
My folk, what habbe I do thee? *etc.*

Ich delede the see for thee,
And dreinte Pharaon for thee,
And thou to princes sellest me.
My folk, what habbe I do thee? *etc.*

In beem of cloude ich ladde thee,
And to Pilat thou ledest me.
My folk, what habbe I do thee? *etc.*

With angeles mete ich fedde thee,
And thou bufetest and scourgest me.
My folk, what habbe I do thee? *etc.*

Of the stone ich drank to thee,
And thou with galle drincst to me.
My folk, what habbe I do thee? *etc.*

Kinges of Canaan ich for thee beet,
And thou betest myn heved with reed.
My folk, what habbe I do thee? *etc.*

Ich yaf thee crowne of kinedom,
And thou me yifst a crowne of thorn.
My folk, what habbe I do thee? *etc.*

Ich muchel worship dide to thee,
And thou me hangest on roode-tree.
My folk, what habbe I do thee? *etc.*

underfon - received; shrudde - clothed; with eisil drinkst to me - give me vinegar to
drink; teem - offspring; slow - slew; delede - divided; dreinte - drowned; beem - pillar;
ich drank to thee - I gave you drink; heved - head; kinedom - kingship; worship -honour

Veni creator spiritus.

Com, shuppere holy gost, of-sech oure *þouhtes;
Vul wyth grace of hevene heortes þat þu wrouhtest,
þou þat art cleped vor-spekere and gyft vrom god y-send,
Welle of lyf, vur, charite and gostlych oynement.
þou gyfst þe sevene gyftes, þou vinger of godes honde,
þou makest tonge of vlesge speke leodene of uche londe.
Tend lyht in oure wyttes, in our heortes love,
þer oure body is leoþe-wok gyf strengþe vrom above.
Shyld ous from þe veonde and gyf ous gryth anon,
þat woe wyten ous vrom sunne þorou þe lodes-mon.
Of þe vader and þe sone þou gyf ous knoulechinge,
To leve þat uul of boþe þou ever boe lovinge.
Woele to þe vader and to þe sone þat vrom deth aros,
And also to þe holy gost ay boe worshipe and los.

[*NOTE: Angl-Saxon þ or "thorn" was used well into the fourteenth century. It is pronounced as the "th"; note also; "v" is at times equivalent to modern "f"]

shuppere - creator; of-sech - seek out; wrouhtst - made; cleped - called; for-spekere - intercessor; gyft - gift; vur - fire; oynement - ointment; sevene - seven; vlesge - flesh; leodene - languages; uche - each; Tend lyht in oure wyttes - "nurture light in our wits"; leoþe-wok - life-weak; gryth - sanctuary; þat woe wyten ous vrom sunne þorou þe lodes-mon - "that we know us (ourselves to be) from the son through the pilot"; uul - will, pleasure; woele - power or glory; ay - always; boe - be; los - praise

Who is This that Cometh from Edom?

'What is he, this lordling, that cometh from the fight
With blood-rede wede so grisliche y-dight,
So faire y-cointised, so seemlich in sight,
So stifliche gangeth, so doughty a knight?'

'Ich it am, ich it am, that ne speke bute right,
Champioun to helen mankinde in fight.'

'Why thenne is thy shroud red, with blood al y-meind,
Ase troddares in wringe with must al bespreind?'

'The wring ich habbe y-trodded al myself one,
And of al mankinde ne was none other wone.

grisliche. . . - terribly arrayed; y-cointised: apparelled; seemlich. . . - fair to see; So. . . gadgeth - who goes so bravely; Ich it am - It is I; helen - save; shroud - clothing; meind - mingled; line 8 - like treaders in the wine-press all spattered with must; habbe - have; one - alone; of - for; wone - hope;

Ich hem habbe y-trodded in wrathe and in grame,
And al my wede is bespreind with here blood y-same,
And al my robe y-fouled to here grete shame.
The day of th'ilke wreche liveth in my thought;
The yeer of medes yelding ne foryet ich nought.
Ich looked al aboute some helping mon;
Ich soughte al the route, but help n'as ther non.
It was myn owne strengthe that this bote wroughte,
Myn owe doughtinesse that help ther me broughte.'

'On Godes milsfulnesse ich wil bethenche me,
And herien Him in alle thing that He yeldeth me.'

'Ich habbe y-trodded the folk in wrathe and in grame,
Adreint al with shennesse, y-drawe down with shame.'

hem - them; grame - anger; line 12, here. . . - their blood together; y-fouled - defiled; here - their; wreche - vengeance; medes yelding - reward-giving; foryet -forget; line 16, some. . . - for some man who would help; soughte - searched; route - crowd; bote - salvation; owe - own; milsfulnesse - mercifulness; bethenche - bethink; herien - praise; yeldeth - grants; Adreint - drowned; shennesse - shame

Christ's Coming

I sagh Him with flesh al bi-spred: He cam from Est.
I sagh Him with blood al bi-shed: He cam from West.
I sagh that manye He with Him broughte: He cam from South.
I sagh that the world of Him ne roughte: He came from North.

'I come from the wedlok as a swete spouse that habbe my wif with me y-nume.
I come from fight as staleworthe knight that mine fo habbe overcume.
I come from the cheping as a riche chapman that mankinde habbe y-bought.
I come from an uncouthe lande as a sely pilgrim that ferr habbe y-sought.'

I. . . bi-spred - I saw Him with body all spread out; bi-shed - drenched; roughte of - career about; habbe y-nume - have taken; staleworthe - stalwart; cheping - market; chapman - merchant; uncouthe - unknown; sely -innocent; ferr habbe y-sought - have travelled far

ROLLE, RICHARD, of Hampole (c.1290-1349), dropped out of Oxford at the age of nineteen to become a hermit. He began his hermit's life near his home, but his family opposed it, for which reason he became a wanderer until a college friend recognized him after he preached a powerful sermon near Rotherham. John de Dalton provided him thereafter with a fitting hermit's cell and necessities, and Rolle began to devote himself to contemplation and devotional writing. He apparently had many ecstatic experiences, describing his steps toward divine rapture in his *Incendium Amoris*. He read and wrote a great deal in Latin, but also wrote much in English, including translations of Psalms, Canticles (Song of Solomon), The Lord's Prayer, and parts of Job, and Jeremiah. He was at odds with the scholastics, although himself a learned man. He strongly advocated asceticism. "The Pricke of Conscience," his major poem, is in rhymed couplets with four-accent lines. In it he deals with man's life, the unstable world, earth, purgatory, judgement day, heaven, and hell. He apparently loved song and used musical terminology frequently in his devotional expressions. He eventually established himself in Hampole near a Cistercian nunnery. He is thought to have died in the great outbreak of plague in 1349. After his death his grave was long visited and venerated.

Love Is Life

Love is life that lasteth ay, ther it in Crist is fest,
When wele ne wo it chaunge may, as written hath men wisest;
The night is turned into day, the travail into rest.
If thou wil love as I thee say, thou may be with the best.

Love is thought with gret desire of a fair loving;
Love is likened to a fire that quenchen may no thing;
Love us clenseth of our sin, love our bot shal bring;
Love the King's hert may win, love of joy may sing.

The sete of love is set ful hegh, for into heven it ran;
Me think that it in erth is slegh, that maketh man pale and wan;
The bed of blisse it goth ful negh—I tel thee as I can;
Though us think the way be dregh, love coupleth God and man.

Love is hotter than the cole; love may non beswike;
The flaume of love who might it thole if it were ever y-like?
Love us covereth and maketh in quert and lifteth to hevenrike;
Love ravisheth Crist into our hert—I wot no lust it like.

Ler to love, if thou wil live when thou shal hethen fare.
Al thy thought to Him thou yive that may it kepe fro care.
Loke thy hert fro Him not twin, though thou in wandring ware;
So thou may Him weld with win, and love Him evermare.

ay - always; fest - fastened; wele ne - blessing nor; bot - comfort; slegh - sly; negh - near; dregh - tediously; beswike - betray; thole -suffer; y-like - like that; maketh in quert - makes well; hevenrike - heaven kingdom; wot - know; hethen - hence; twin - part; weld - weld, join

Jesu, that me lif hath lent, into thy love me bring;
Tak to thee al myn entent, that thou be my desiring.
Wo fro me away wer went and comen my coveiting,
If that my soul had herd and hent the song of thy praising.

Thy love is ever-lastand fro that we may it fele;
Therin me make brenand that no thing may me kele.
My thought take in thy hand and stabil it every dele,
That I be not heldand to love this worldes wele.

If I love an erthly thing that payeth to my will,
And set my joy and my liking when it may cum me till;
I may me drede of deperting, that wil be hote and ill;
For al my welth is but weping when pine my soul shal spill.

The joy that men hath sene is likened to the hay,
That now is fair and grene and now witing away.
Such is this world, I wene, and shal be to domes day
In travail and in tene, for flee no man it may.

If thou love in al thy thought, and hate the filth of sin,
And gif thy hert Him that it bought, that He it weld with win,
As thy soul Crist hath sought and therof wold not blin,
So thou shal to blisse be brought and heven won within.

The kind of love this es, ther it is trusty and trew:
To stand in stableness and chaunge for no new.
The lif that love might find, or ever in hert it knew—
Fro care turneth that kind, and led in mirth and glew.

For-thy love thou, I rede, Crist, as I thee telle.
With aungels take thy stede; that joy looke thou not selle.
In erthe thou hate no quede but that thy love might felle;
For love is stalwarth as dede, love is hard as helle.

Love is a light birthine, love gladdeth yonge and olde;
Love is withouten pine, as lovers han me tolde;
Love is a gostly wine that maketh bigge and bolde;
Of love no thing shal tine that it in hert wil holde.

win - joy; coveiting - desiring; hent - seized; fro that we may it fele - "from the time we feel it"; brenand - burning; every dele - completely; heidand - constrained; wele - success; payeth - satisfies; pine -sorrow; witing - wilting; domesday - judgment day; tene - grief; blin - cease; lines 43-44 - "In order that love might find life and know it always—that kind of love turns from care and is led into joy and rejoicing; forthy - therefore; rede - counsel; stede - place; looke - be careful; hate no quede - dread no harm; felle - overcome; dede - death; birthine - burden; tine - be afflicted;

Love is the swetest thing that man in erth hath tone;
Love is Goddes derling, love bindeth blood and bone.
In love be our living—I wot no better wone;
For me and my loving love maketh both be one.

But fleshly love shal fare as doth the flowr in May,
And lasting be no mare than it wer but a day;
And soroweth sethen ful sare her proudehede and her play,
When they been casten in care til pine that lasteth ay.

When erth and air shal bren, then may they quake and drede,
And up shal rise al men to answer for her dede.
If they been seen in sin, as now her lif they lede,
They shal sit hell within, and derkness have to mede.

Rich men her hand shal wring and wicked werkes bye;
In flaume of fire knight and king with sorow and shame shal lye.
If thou wil love, then may thou sing to Crist in melodye;
The love of Him overcometh al thing, in love we live and dye.

tone - bitten, tasted (?); wone - abode; sethen - boil, afflict; proudehede - pridefulness;
casten in care - thrown into suffering; bren - burn; her. . . - "fleshly love's. . ."; to mede
- for a reward

A Song of the Passion

My trewest tresowre sa trayturly was taken,
Sa bytterly bondyn wyth bytand bandes,
How sone of thi seruandes was thou forsaken,
And lathly for my lufe hurld with thair handes.

My well of my wele sa wrangwysly wryed,
Sa pulled owt of preson to pilate at prime;
Thaire dulles and thaire dyntes ful drerely thou dreed
Whan thai schot in thi syght bath slauer and slyme.

My hope of my hele sa hyed to be hanged,
Sa charged with thi crosce and corond with thorne,
Ful sare to thi hert thi steppes thai stanged—
Me thynk thi bak burd breke; it bendes for-borne.

bytand - biting; lathly - hatefully; hurld - shoved; of my wele - source of my joy; wrang-
wysly wryed - unjustly twisted; dulles- wounds; drerely thou dreed- grievously thou suf-
fered; hele - salvation; hyed - hurried, pushed on; tha stanged - they goaded; burd- must;
for-borne - overloaded

My salue of my sare sa saryful in syght,
Sa naked and nayled thi ryg on the rode,
Ful hydusly hyngand, thai heued the on hyght,
Thai lete the stab in the stane all stekked that thar stode.

My dere-worthly derlyng, sa dolefully dyght,
Sa straytly vpryght streyned on the rode;
For thi mykel mekenes, thi mercy, thi myght,
Thow bete al my bales with bote of thi blode.

My fender of my fose, sa fonden in the felde,
Sa lufly lyghtand at the euensang tyde;
Thi moder and hir menghe vnlaced thi scheld—
All weped that thar were, thi woundes was sa wyde.

My pereles prynce als pure I the pray,
The mynde of this myrour thou lat me noght mysse;
Bot wynd vp my wylle to won wyth the ay,
That thou be beryd in my brest and bryng me to blysse.
Amen.

ryg - back; lete the stab in the stane - caused you (the cross) to be thrust into the stone
(socket); stekked - fixed; bete all my bales - didst assuage all my sorrows; bote - remedy;
fonden - tested; lufly lyghtand - lovely descending; menghe - companions; the mynde of
this myrour - the purpose of this example; won - dwell.

Cantus Amoris II

Hail Ihesu, my creator, of the sorrowing, medicine!
Hail Ihesu, my saviour, that for me suffered pine!
Hail Ihesu, help and succour, my love be ay thine!
Hail Ihesu, the blessed flower of thy mother, virgin!

Hail Ihesu, leader to light, in sawl thou art full sweet!
Thy love shines day and night, that strongs me in this street;
Lene me langing for thy sight and give me grace til greet,
For thou, Ihesu, has that might that all my bale may bete.

Ihesu, thy grace my heart inspire, that me til bliss may bring;
On thee I set all my desire, thou art my love langing,
Thy love is burning, as the fire that ever on high will spring;
Far fro me put pride and ire, for them I love na thing.

strongs me in this street - 'strengthens me in this way' (or life); give me grace to greet -
'give me grace to groan' (or pray)

Hail Ihesu, price of my prayer, Lord of majesty!
Thou art joy that lastes ay, all delight thou art to see,
Give me grace, as thou well may, thy lover for to be.
My langing wends never away til that I come til thee.

Ihesu to love ay be me lief, that is my ghostly good.
Allas, my God is, as a thief, nailed til the rood!
His tender veins begin to brest, running with his blood,
Hands and feet with nails are fest; that changes my mood.

Ihesu my king is me full dear, that with his blood me bought;
With spitting spread, is all that chere, to death with beating brought.
For me he tholed these pains sere, for me, wretched, he wrought;
Forthy they sit my heart full near, that I forget them nought.

Ihesu, by fortune of ilk a sight thou grant me grace to speed,
That I may love thee aright, and have thee to my meed.
Thy love is fast in ilk fanding, and ever at all our need;
Thou through thy grace art my yearning, in til thy light me lead.

my langing wends never away - 'my longing never turns away' (or departs); ay - always;
lief - delight (desire, choice); spread - covered; chere - face; sere - severe; ilk - such; meed
- reward; fast - fixed; fanding - finding; in til - into

Prayer to Jesus I

Jhesu, since thou me made and bought,
Thou be my love and all my thought,
And help that I may to Thee be brought;
Withouten thee I may do nought.

Jhesu, since thou must do thy will,
And naething is that thee may let;
With thy grace my heart fulfill,
My love and my liking in thee set.

Jhesu, at thy will
I pray that I might be;
All my heart fulfill
With perfect love to thee.

That I have done ill,
Jhesu, forgive thou me;
And suffer me never to spill,
Jhesu, for pity!   Amen.

The Seven Sins
Anonymous

With a garland of thornes kene
My hed was crowned, and that was sene;
The stremes of blood ran by my cheke: SUPERBIA
Thou proude man, lerne to be meke.

When thou art wroth and wolde take wreche
Kepe wel the lore that I thee teche.
Through my right hand the nail it goth: IRA
Forgive therfore and be not wroth.

With a spere sharp and grill
My hert was wounded, with my will,
For love of man that was me dere: INVIDIA
Envious man, of love thou lere.

Rise up, unlust, out of thy bedde!
Think on my feet that are for-bledde   ACCIDIA
And harde nailed upon a tree:
Think theron, man; this was for thee.

Through my left hand the nail was drive:
Think theron if thou wilt live,
And worship God with almes-dede,   AVARICIA
If thou in hevene wilt have thy mede.

In alle my paines I sufferd on roode
Man gave me drinke no thing goode,
Eisell and galle for to drinke: GULA
Gloton, theron ever thou thinke.

Of a maiden I was born
To save the folk that were forlorn;
All my body was beten for sin: LUXURIA
Lecher, therfor I rede thee blin.

I was beten for thy sake:
Sin thou leve and shrift thou take;
Forsake thy sin and love me;   JESUS
Amend thee, and I forgive thee.

wreche - revenge; kepe - observe; grill - cruel; with my will - by my choice; of love thou
lere - learn about loving; un-lust - sloth; for-bledde - covered in blood; drinke - to drink;
Eisell - vinegar; forlorn - doomed; rede thee blin - advise you to cease

Candet Nudatum Pectus (White Was His Naked Breast)
Anonymous (Two versions)

Wyth was hys nakede brest and red of blod hys syde.
Bleyc was his fair handled, his wnde dop ant wide,
And hys armes ystreith hey up-hon þe rode;
On fif studes on his body þe stremes ran o blode.

wnde - wound; ystreith - stretched; studes - places

Wit was his nakede brest and red of blod his side,
Blod was his faire neb, his wnden depe an uide,
Starke waren his armes hi-spred op-on þe rode;
In fif steden an his bodi stremes hurne of blode.

neb - mouth; uide - wide; steden - places

Prayer For the Journey
Anonymous

Here I am and forth I must,
And in Jesus Criste is all my trust.
No wicked thing do me no dere,
Nother here nor elleswhere.
The Father with me, the Sone with me,
The Holy Gost, and the Trinité,
Be betwixt my gostly enemé and me.
In the name of the Father and the Son
And the Holy Gost, Amen.

must - must (go); do me no dere - [let no wicked thing] do me any harm; Nother - neither; gostly - spiritual

All Other Love is Like the Moon
Anonymous

All other love is like the moone
That wexth and waneth as flowr in plain,
As flowr that faireth and falweth soone,
As day that clereth and endth in rain.

All other love biginth by blisse,
In wop and wo makth his ending;

wop - weeping

No love ther n'is that evre habbe lisse
But what areste in Hevene-King,
Whos love is fresh and evre greene
And evre full without wanying;
His love sweeteth withoute teene,
His love is endless and a-ring.

All other love I flee for thee;
Tell me, tell me where thou list.
'In Marie mild and free
I shall be found, ac more in Crist.'

no. . . n'is - intensive "no"; habbe - has; lisse - comfort; areste - rests; wanying - waning;
teene - sorrow; a-ring - resounding; list - desire; ac - but

Make Me Loathe Earthly Likings
Anonymous

Good god, make me for þi love & þi desyre
ley doune þe birden of fleshly myre
And erthly lykingis to lothe:
My wille of þe flesh haue ladiship,
Reson of my wille haue lordship,
& þi grace be lorde vppon them boþe;
And so throw me withinne & withowte
to be soget ondir þi wille alle abowte
to alle þat is reson Right & soþe.

myre - mire; lykingis - likings, lusts; of þe flesh - over the flesh; throw - through; soget
- subject; soþe - sooth, truth

For Thy Sake Let the World Call Me Fool
Anonymous

O Ihu, lett me neuer forgett thy byttur passion,
That thou suffred for my transgression,
ffor in thy blessyd wondes is the verey scole
That must teche me with the worlde to be called a fole.
O Ihu, ihu, ihu, grauntt that I may loue the soo,
þat the wysdom of the worlde be cleene fro me A-goo,
And brennyngly to desyre to come to see thy face,
In whom is all my comford, my joy and my solace.
　　　　Amen - Ihesus - maria - Iohannes.

Ihu - Jehu, Jesus; scole - school; A-goo - gone; brennyngly - burningly

Christ Triumphant
Anonymous

I have labored sore and suffered deth,
And now I rest and draw my breth;
But I shall come and call right sone
Heven and erth and hell to dome;
And then shall know both devil and man
What I was and what I am.

dome - judgment

I Would be Clad in Christis Skin
Anonymous

Gold and all this werdis win
Is nought but Cristes rode.
I wolde ben clad in Cristes skin
That ran so longe on blode,
And gon t'is herte and taken myn in—
There is a fulsum fode.
Then yef I littel of kith or kin,
For there is alle gode.

werdis win - world's joy and wealth; Is nought but - 'Is nothing without; rode - rood, cross; t'is - to his; fulsum fode - plentiful or rich food; Then yef I little of - 'Then I would care little about.'; kith and kin - friends and family

Christ's Love
Anonymous
From a manuscript in the National Library of Scotland

Love me brought
And love me wrought,
Man, to be thy fere;
Love me fed,
And love me led,
And love me letteth here.

Love me slew,
And love me drew
And love me laid on bier;
Love is my peace,

For love I chese
Man to buyen dear.

Ne dread thee nought,
I have thee sought
Both by day and night,
To haven thee;
Well is to me,
I have thee won in fight.

fere - companion, friend; letteth - keeps, retains; chese - chose.

Jesu Christ, my Leman Swete
Anonymous

Jesu Crist, myn leman swete,
That for me diedes on roode-tree,
With al myn herte I thee biseke
For thy woundes two and three,
That al so faste into myn herte
Thy love rooted mote be
As was the spere into thy side,
When thou suffredes ded for me.

Leman - lover; biseke - beseech; al so - just as; into - in; mote - may; ded - death

Christ pleads with His Sweet Leman
Anonymous

Lo! lemman swete, now may þou se
þat I haue lost my lyf for þe.
What myght I do þe mare?
For-þi I pray þe speciali
þat þou forsake ill company
þat woundes me so sare;

And take myne armes pryuely
& do þam in þi tresory,
In what stede sa þou dwelles,
And, swete lemman, forget þow noght

do þe mare - more for you; for-þi - therefore; sare - sorely; take myne armes - take up
my weapons and/or armor; pryuely - privately, personally; do þam - place them; treso-
ry - treasury; stede - place

þat I þi lufe sa dere haue boght,
And I aske þe noght elles.

þi - thy; noght elles - nothing else.

Mercy
Anonymous

Mercy is hendest where sinne is mest,
Mercy is lattere there sinne is lest;
Mercy abideth and loketh al day
When man fro sinne wille turnen away;
Mercy saveth that lawe wolde spille:
Mercy asketh but Godes wille.

hendest - readiest; mest - greatest; lattere - slower; there - where; loketh - watches; that - him whom; spille - destroy; asketh but - only seeks

All Is Phantom
Anonymous

Al it is fantam þat we mid fare,
Naked and poure henne we shul fare,
Al shal ben oþer mannes þat we fore care,
But þat we don for godes loue haue we no mare.

we mid fare - we sojourn with; henne - hence; ben oþer mannes - belong to other men; fore care - care for; But þat - Except for that; mare - more

Christ's Prayer in Gethsemane
Anonymous

A Sory beuerech it is & sore it is a-bouth
Nou in þis sarpe time þis brewing hat me brouth
fader, if it mowe ben don als i haue be-south,
Do awey þis beuerich, þat i ne drink et nouth.

& if it mowe no betre ben, for alle mannis gilth,
þat it ne muste nede þat my blod be spilth,
Suete fader, i am þi sone, þi wil be ful-filt!
I am her þin owen child, I wil don as þu wilt.

beuerech - beverage; a-bouth - bought; hat - hath; brouth - brought; mowe - might; be-south - sought; ne. . . nouth - not; gilth - guilt; suete -sweet

RYMAN, JAMES (fl. 1342), is known almost soley by his works, particularly his songs and lullabies. All we have of his works is contained in a single manuscript in the University Library of Cambridge. Other than this we have only a note in Tanner's *Bibliotheca Britannica* that reads: Jacobus Ryman, frater ordinis Minorum, poeta Anglicanus, floruit A.D. 1342. "James Ryman, brother of the order of Minorites (Franciscans), English poet, flourished in 1342." (Given in *Spiritual Songs - from English MSS. of Fourteenth to Sixteenth Centuries*, Ed. Frances M. M. Comper)

Ther is a chielde, a heuenly childe

Ther is a chielde, a heuenly childe,
Iborne this nyght of Marie myelde.

This chielde is, was, and ay shall be
One in Godhede, in persones thre.
There is a childe, a heuenly childe. . .

This chielde is named Criste Jhesus
That nowe is borne for loue of vs.
There is a child, a heuenly childe. . .

Mortall nature this chielde hath take
Of oure thraldome vs free to make.
There is a child, a heuenly childe. . .

This chielde is God and man also,
Now borne to bringe vs out of wo.
There is a child, a heuenly childe. . .

His Fader is God of Heven Blis,
And virgyne Mary his moder is.
There is a child, a heuenly childe. . .

Fro heven to erthe this chielde come is
To suffre dethe for mannys mys.
There is a child, a heuenly childe. . .

On Good Friday vppon the roode
To save mankyende he shed his bloode.
There is a child, a heuenly childe. . .

This chielde was dede and in graue laye
And rose ayene on the thirde daye.
There is a child, a heuenly childe. . .

thraldome - slavery; mys - sins

By his grete myght to blis he stide
And sittith on his Faders right side.
There is a chield, a heuenly childe...

Whenne he shalle come and jugement make,
To blis with hym this chielde vs take.
There is a chield, a heuenly childe...

Nunc Puer Nobis Natus Est ("Now unto us a son is born")

Now in this fest, this holy fest,
Nunc puer nobis natus est,
Nunc puer nobis natus est,
Et puer nobis datus est.

Thus it is seide in prophecye
(I take witnesse of Ysay):
'A mayde shall bere a chielde, truly,
Whose name shall be called Messy.'
Now in this fest, this holy fest...

'He is oure Lorde,' seith Jheremy,
'And none like hym is ferre ne nye;
In erthe he is seyn, verily,
Conuersaunt with people playnly.'
Now in this fest, this holy fest...

This is the stone cut of the hille,
Crist borne of Mary vs vntille,
Without synne in dede, thought, and wille,
The wille of God for to fulfille.
Now in this fest, this holy fest...

'Alle kinges vnto hym shall pray,
And alle people hym shall obay
And serue hym bothe by nyght and day.'
Thus seith Dauid, as ye rede may.
Now in this fest, this holy fest...

'O Sonne of God,' Abacuc sayde,
'By whome al thing is wrought, now layde
In an oxe stalle, borne of a mayde,

Et puer.... - "And unto us a son is given"; ferre ne nye - neither far nor near; syn - seen;
us untille - unto us;

And man become for mannys ayde.'
Now in this fest, this holy fest. . .

Nowe preyse we alle this Prince of Peas
Now borne oure bondes to release
And alle oure care and woo to cease,
Oure joy and myrth for to increase.
Now in this fest, this holy fest. . .

ayde - aid

A Song of the Eucharist

Eat ye this bread, eat ye this bread,
Eat it so ye be not dead.

This bread giveth eternal life
Both unto man, to child and wife;
It yieldeth grace and bateth strife.
     Eat ye it so ye be not dead.

It seemeth white, yet it is red,
And it is quick, yet seemeth dead,
For it is God in form of bread.
     Eat ye it so ye be not dead.

This blessed bread is angel's food,
Mannis also, perfect and good;
Therefore eat it with mild mood.
     Eat ye it so ye be not dead.

This bread from heaven did descend
Us fro all ill for to defend,
And to give us life without end.
     Eat ye it so ye be not dead.

In Virgin Mary this bread was bake,
When Crist of her manhood did take,
Free of all sin mankind to make.
     Eat ye it so ye be not dead.

Eat ye this bread withouten sin,
Eternal bliss then shall ye win.
God grant us grace to dwell therein!
     Eat ye it so ye be not dead.

with mild mood - with gentleness

LANGLAND, WILLIAM (c.1330-c.1400), is thought to be author of *Piers Plowman*, one of the greatest Middle English poems. Little is known about him. It is thought he was born in Worcestershire and may have been educated at the Benedictine school in Great Malvern. He may have been a cleric and lived in London. He knew medieval theology and had a particular interest in the asceticism of Bernard of Clairvaux. *Piers Plowman* is much more centrally concerned with Christian life and doctrine than the major works of Langland's contemporaries, Chaucer and Gower. It is a tale of a spiritual pilgrimage, in the genre of Dante's *Divine Comedy* and a forerunner of Bunyan's *Pilgrim's Progress*.

The Trinity from Piers Plowman

For to a torche or to a taper the Trinite is likened,
As wax and a wike were twined togederes,
And thenne flauming fyr forth of hem bothe;
And as wax and wike and warm fyr togederes
Fostren forth a flaume and a fair leye,
That serveth these swinkeres to see by a-nightes,
So doth the Sire and the Sone and Saint Spirit togederes
Fostren forth amonges folke fyn love and beleve,
That alle kinne cristene clenseth of sinne.
And as thou seest some time sodeinliche of a torche
The blase be y-blowen out, yet brenneth the wike,
Withouten leye and lighte lith fyr in the mache,
So is the Holy Gost God and grace withouten mercy
To alle unkinde creatures that coveiten to destruye
Leel licame and lyf that oure Lord shupte.
And as glowing gledes gladeth not these werkmen
That worchen and waken in winteres nightes
As doth a kix or a candle that caught hath fyr and blaseth,
No more doth Sire ne the Sone ne Saint Spirit togederes
Graunten any grace ne forgivenesse of sinnes
Til that the Holy Gost ginne to glowe and blase:
So that the Holy Gost gloweth but as a glede
Til that love and beleve leliche to him blowe;
And thenne flaumeth he as fyr on Fader and on Filius,

As - as if; togederes - together; forth of hem - forth from them; fostren forth - engender; fair leye - fine flame; alle kinne cristene - all kinds of Christians; sodeinlich - suddenly; brenneth - burns; lith - lies; mache - wick; unkinde - wicked; coveiten to destruye - desire to destroy; Leel licame and lyf - faithful body and life; shupte - created; gledes - live coals; worchen - work; waken - keep awake; kix - dry stalk; ginne - begins; beleve - faith; leliche - steadfastly; Isekeles in evesinges - icicles in the eaves; swinkeres - workers; a-nightes - at night; Saint - Holy; fyn - pure

And melteth mighte into mercy, as we may see a winter
Isekeles in evesinges thorgh hete of the sunne
Melteth in a mint-while to mist and to water;
So grace of the Holy Gost the grete mighte of the Trinite
Melteth al to mercy to merciable and to non othere.
And as wax withouten more upon a warm glede
Wil brennen and blasen, be they togederes,
And solacen that mowen not see sitting in derknesse,
So wil the Fader foryive folke of milde hertes
That reufulliche repenten and restitucion make
In as muche as they mowen amenden and payen;
And if it sufficeth not for asseth that in such a will deyeth,
Mercy, for his mekenesse, wil maky good the remenaunt.
And as the wike and warm fyr wil make a faire flaume:
For to murthe men with that in merke sitten,
So wil Crist of His curtesye, and men crien Him mercy,
Bothe foryive and foryete, and yet bidde for us
To the Fader of hevene foryivenesse to have.
Ac hewe fyr at a flint foure hundred winter,
Bute thou have tasch to take it with, tender and broches,
Al thy labor is loste and al thy longe travaile.

mint-while - space of a minute; lines 28-29: so the grace of the Holy Ghost complete-
ly melts the great might of the Trinity to mercy for the merciful and for no others; more
- anything else; be they - if they are; that mowen not: those who cannotmilde - humble;
mowen - can; line 36: and if anyone has not enough to make full reparation and dies
intending it; for - because of; murthe (with) - gladden; merke - darkness; and - if; bidde.
. . To - intercede with; Ac hewe at - but strike from; Bute - unless; tasch to take it with
- touchwood to kindle it; tender and broches - tinder and sticks

Et Incarnatus Est

Love is the plant of peace and most precious of virtues;
For heaven hold it ne might so heavy it seemed,
Till it had on earth yoten himself.
Was never leaf upon linden lighter thereafter,
As when it had of the fold flesh and blood taken;
Then was it portative and piercing as the point of a needle.
May no armour it let, neither high walls.
For-thy is love leader of our Lord's folk of heaven.

yoten - gotten; fold - earth; portative - portable; let - keep out; for-thy - therefore

CHAUCER, GEOFFREY (c.1343-1400), is the most noted English man of letters before Shakespeare. His best known work, *Canterbury Tales*, is the centermost composition in Middle English, although it was not completed. He was born of a prosperous middle class family and after serving as a page to a noble family of Ulster, he was involved in military service, where he was taken prisoner and ransomed. He became a court official and frequently traveled as a diplomat, but also wrote extensively, producing a variety of long poems, and a translation of Boethius' *Consolation of Philosophy*. *Troilus and Criseyde* is considered his second-best work. After more military service, he became a custom-controller in London, and rose in royal favor, obtaining various other valuable appointments. He was in favour at court in the 1390s, having a close relationship with the Earl of Derby, who later was crowned Henry IV. Chaucer was living near Westminster when he died, and his remains buried in Westminster Abbey. Other of his works extant include *The Book of the Duchess*, *The Complaint to His Purse*, *The Astrolabe*, *The House of Fame*, *The Legend of Good Women*, and *the Parliament of Fowls* (incomplete). He may also be the author of *The Romaunt of the Rose*. *Canterbury Tales* is thought to have been written over a period of time as long as twenty-five years.

Truth

> Flee fro the prees and dwell with soothfastnesse;
> Suffice unto thy thing, though it be smal;
> For hord hath hate, and climbing tikelnesse,
> Prees hath envye, and wele blent overal;
> Savour no more than thee behove shal.
> Wirche wel thyself, that other folk canst rede;
> And trouthe shal delivere, it is no drede.
>
> Tempest thee not al croked to redresse,
> In trust of hir that turneth as a bal—
> For grete rest stant in litel bisinesse;
> And eek be ware to sporne ayenst an al;
> Strive not as doth the crokke with the wal.
> Daunte thyself, that dauntest otheres dede;
> And trouthe shal delivere, it is no drede.

prees - throng; soothfastnesse - truth; Suffice unto thy thing - be satisfied with what you have; hord hath hate - hoarding brings hatred; tikelnesse - insecurity; wele blent overal - prosperity blinds entirely; Savour - desire; thee behove shal - you shall need; Wirche wel -Act well; that other folke canst rede - so that you who know how to advise other people; trouthe shal delivere - and truth shall set (you) free; it is no drede - there is no doubt; Tempest thee not - Do not distress yourself; al croked - all that is awry; grete -great; stant - stands; eek - also; sporne - kick; al - awl; crokke - crock; Daunte - Govern

That thee is sent, receive in buxumnesse;
The wrestling for this worlde asketh a fal:
Here n'is none home, here n'is but wildernesse:
Forth, pilgrim, forth! Forth, beest, out of thy stal!
Know thy countree, look up, thank God of al.
Hold the high way and let thy gost thee lede;
And trouthe shal delivere, it is no drede.

buxumnesse - submissiveness; asketh - asks for; of al - for all; gost - spirit

The Parson and the Plowman Described
from The General Prologue to *The Canterbury Tales*

And was a povre Persoun of a Toun,
But riche he was of hooly thoght and werk.
He was also a lerned man, a clerk,
That Cristes gospel trewely wolde preche;
His parisshens devoutly wolde he teche.
Benygne he was, and wonder diligent,
And in adversitee ful pacient,
And swich he was ypreved ofte sithes.
Ful looth were hym to cursen for his tithes,
But rather wolde he yeven, out of doute,
Unto his povre parisshens aboute
Of his offryng and eek of his substaunce.
He koude in Yitel thyng have suffisaunce.
Wyd was his parisshe, and houses fer asonder,
But he ne lefte nat, for reyn ne thonder,
In siknesse nor in meschief to visite
The ferreste in his parisshe, muche and lite,
Upon his feet, and in his hand a staf.
This noble ensample to his sheep he yaf,
That first he wroghte, and afterward he taughte.
Out of the gospel he tho wordes caughte,
And this figure; he added eek therto,
That if gold ruste, what shal iren do?
For if a preest be foul, on whom we truste,
No wonder is a lewed man to ruste;

povre - poor; persoun - parson; werk - work; parisshens - parishioners; benygne - gracious; wonder - wondrously; swich - such; ypreved - proved; sithes - since; looth - loathe, unwilling; cursen - excommunicate; yeven - give; eek - also; ne lefte nat - did not neglect; ferreste - farthest; muche and lite - big and little (most and leastinfluential)

And shame it is, if a prest take keep,
A shiten shepherde and a clene sheep.
Wel oghte a preest ensample for to yive,
By his clennesse, how that his sheep sholde lyve.
He sette nat his benefice to hyre
And leet his sheep encombred in the myre
And ran to Londoun unto Seinte Poules
To seken hym a chaunterie for soules,
Or with a bretherhed to been withholde;
But dwelte at hoom, and kepte wel his folde,
So that the wolf ne made it nat myscarie;
He was a shepherde and noght a mercenarie.
And though he hooly were and vertuous,
He was to synful men nat despitous,
Ne of his speche daungerous ne digne,
But in his techyng discreet and benygne.
To drawen folk to hevene by fairnesse,
By good ensample, this was his bisynesse.
But it were any persone obstinat,
What so he were, of heigh or lough estat,
Hym wolde he snybben sharply for the nonys.
A bettre preest I trowe that nowher noon ys.
He waited after no pompe and reverence,
Ne maked him a spiced conscience,
But Cristes loore and his apostles twelve
He taughte, but first he folwed it hymselve.
With hym ther was a Plowman, was his brother,
That hadde ylad of dong ful many a fother;
A trewe swynkere and a good was he,
Lyvynge in pees and parfit charitee.
God loved he best with al his hoole herte
At alle tymes, thogh him gamed or smerte,
And thanne his neighebor right as hymselve.
He wolde thresshe, and therto dyke and delve,
For Cristes sake, for every povre wight,

ensample - example; gaf - gave; wroghte - worked, did; tho - those; lewed - unlearned, coarse; shiten - befouled; sette nat his benefice - does not hire out his office; leet - allow; encombred in the myre - to be stuck in the mud; And ran - while running; seken - seek; chaunterie -endowment to provide for masses being said; bretherhed - monastery; hoom - home; ne made it nat - did not make it; despitous - spiteful; daungerous ne digne - grudging nor scornful; snybben - snub, rebuke; for the nonys - impulsively; trowe - trow, swear; spiced - too fastidious; ylad - loaded; dong - dung; a fother - a load; swinkere - laborer; parfit - perfect; gamed or smerte - was pleased or in pain; dyke and delve - make ditches and dig

Withouten hire, if it lay in his myght.
His tithes payde he ful faire and wel,
Bothe of his propre swynk and his catel.
In a tabard he rood upon a mere.

withouten hire - without pay; swynk and his catel - of his earnings and chattels; tabard
- laborer's loose coat; mere - mare

Conclusion to "The Canon's Yeoman's Tale"
from *The Canterbury Tales*

Also ther was a disciple of Plato,
That on a tyme seyde his maister to,
As his book Senior wol bere witnesse,
And this was his demande in soothfastnesse:
"Telle me the name of the privee stoon?"

And Plato answerde unto hym anoon,
"Take the stoon that Titanos men name."
"Which is that?" quod he. "Magnasia is the same,"
Seyde Plato. "Ye, sire, and is it thus?
This is ignotum per ignocius.
What is Magnasia, good sire, I yow preye?"
"It is a water that is maad, I seye,
Of elementes foure," quod Plato.

"Telle me the roote, good sire," quod he tho,
"Of that water, if it be youre wil."
"Nay, nay," quod Plato, "as certein, that I nyl.
The philosophres sworn were everychoon
That they sholden discovere it unto noon,
Ne in no book it write in no manere.
For unto Crist it is so lief and deere
That he wol nat that it discovered bee,
But where it liketh to his deitee
Men for t'enspire, and eek for to deffende
Whom that hym liketh; lo, this is the ende."

Thanne conclude I thus, sith that God of hevene
Ne wil nat that the philosophres nevene
How that a man shal come unto this stoon,

soothfastnesse - truthfulness; privee stone - 'philosophers stone'; ignotum per ignocius -
Lat. " the unknown through the more unknown"; preye - ask nyl - will not; lief - beloved;
eek - also; sith - since; nevene - mention

I rede, as for the beste, lete it goon
For whoso maketh God his adversarie,
As for to werken any thyng in contrarie
Of his wil, certes, never shal he thryve,
Thogh that he multiplie terme of his lyve.
And there a poynt; for ended is my tale.
God sende every trewe man boote of his bale!

rede - counsel; certes - surely; boote - comfort; of his bale - for his sorrow

Conclusion to *Troilus and Criseyde*

Swich fyn hath, lo, this Troilus for love!
Swich fyn hath al his grete worthynesse!
Swich fyn hath his estat real above,
Swich fyn his lust, swich fyn hath his noblesse!
Swych fyn hath false worldes brotelnesse!
And thus bigan his lovyng of Criseyde,
As I have told, and in this wise he deyde.

O yonge, fresshe folkes, he or she,
In which that love up groweth with youre age,
Repeyreth hom fro worldly vanyte,
And of youre herte up casteth the visage
To thilke God that after his ymage
Yow made, and thynketh al nys but a faire
This world, that passeth soone as floures faire.

And loveth hym, the which that right for love
Upon a crois, oure soules for to beye,
First starf, and roos, and sit in hevene above;
For he nyl falsen no wight, dar I seye,
That wol his herte al holly on hym leye.
And syn he best to love is, and most meke,
What nedeth feynede loves for to seke?

Lo here, of payens corsed olde rites,
Lo here, what alle hire goddes may availle;
Lo here, thise wrecched worldes appetites;
Lo here, the fyn and guerdoun of travaille

swich fyn - such an end; brotelnesse - fickleness; repeyreth - return; up casteth - turn up;
visage - face; thilke - the same; nys - is not; nyl falsen - will not treat falsely; syn - since;
feynede - fained; payens - pagans; corsed - cursed; hire - their; guerdoun - reward

Of Jove, Appollo, of Mars, of swich rascaille!
Lo here, the forme of olde clerkis speche
In poetrie, if ye hire bokes seche.

O moral Gower, this book I directe
To the and to the, philosophical Strode,
To vouchen sauf, ther nede is, to correcte,
Of youre benignites and zeles goode.
And to that sothefast Crist, that starf on rode,
With al myn herte of mercy evere I preye,
And to the Lord right thus I speke and seye.

Thow oon, and two, and thre, eterne on lyve,
That regnest ay in thre, and two, and oon,
Uncircumscript, and al maist circumscrive,
Us from visible and invisible foon
Defende, and to thy mercy, everichon,
So make us, Jesus, for thi mercy digne,
For love of mayde and moder thyn benigne. Amen.

vouchen sauf - vouchsafe; benignities - kindnesses; zeles - zeal; sothefast - faithful; foon - foes; everichon - every one; digne - worthy

English Hymns

As the earliest piece of English poetry we have is the Anglo-Saxon "Caedmon's Hymn," so hymns, that is songs addressed to God or celebrating His nature and works before men, have made up a significant part of English poetry since. While there are hymns extant which were addressed to the Chinese, Greek, and Egyptian gods, the Psalms are the typical "hymn lyrics" of Judaeo-Christian poetry, and have been the chief models of English hymns along with such scripture passages, as the songs of Moses, Miriam, Mary, and Elizabeth.

The Psalms have a wide-range of "moods," subjects, and themes. A typical Psalm may begin with a cry for help or with an affirmation that God is almighty and merciful. It may go on to speak of the depth of the singer's need or the many mighty acts of God. It may become prophetic and declare God's blessing on the righteous and his curse upon the wicked. It may declare the singer's sinfulness and acknowledge his need for cleansing. But invariably it involves an affirmation of faith in the God who lives, moves, and acts on behalf of his people. English hymns have conformed to different psalm-models at different times, usually under the influence of the contemporary poetic schools.

Some of the earliest records of Christian hymns come from the Eastern

Church. Antiphonal singing (singing in which one group of singers alternates with another, "answering" them as it were) was practiced in the churches of Bithynia, and Antioch by the beginning of the second century. From the Latin "antiphons"comes the Old English word "antefne." This is the word which has become our "anthem." Some of the Greek hymns written from the middle of the third up to the seventh century are sung in our churches today. One of the best collections of translations is *Songs and Hymns of Earliest Greek Christian Poets* (1876) by Allen Chatfield. A few more of our English hymns derive from the Eastern church of the eighth century and after.

Latin hymns did not arise as early. Apparently it was the example of the Eastern church and a need to meet the Arian hymn-singers on their own ground that brought hymn-singing to the Western church. Hilary of Poitiers and Ambrose of Milan are credited with the introduction of hymns. Augustine records that Ambrose encouraged hymn-singing among those keeping vigil in the church premises to prevent the Arians from staging a coup, as it were. Benedict, in constituting his religious order (about 530) fixed Ambrose's hymns in an order to be sung at certain hours. Later, different hymns were deemed proper for different seasons and different holy days and these were fixed into "breviaries" which continued in use for several centuries with little change.

Gregory the Great (sixth century) wrote and encouraged the writing of new hymns. This "Gregorian" music supplanted "Ambrosian" hymns. We find hymns written by Hrabanus Maurus, archbishop of Mainz, pupil of British Alcuin (circa 800).

The tenth century saw the introduction of non-metrical "sequences," lines of praise, into the church service. These may have involved borrowing from Greek hymnody. Later a metrical form of the "sequence" began to dominate over the earlier rhythmical but unmetrical type. The distinction here is in many ways parallel, though not necessarily otherwise connected, to the difference between Old English verse and the metrical Middle English poetry.

Vernacular (in the common language rather than in Latin) "sequences" were allowed in parts of Europe. In Germany these were found as early as the twelfth century. "Caedmon's Hymn" is of course much older than that.

A Petition to Father and Son and Holy Ghost
Anonymous

> Almyghty god, fadir of heuene,
> ffor cristis loue þat dyde on rode,
> I praye þe, lorde, þou here my steuene,
> And fulfill my will in gode.

steuene - voice

Crist, thi fader for me praye,
ffor hir loue þou lighted inne,
He yeue me myght, or þat I dye,
Me to amende of all my synne.

The holy gost, þou graunte me grace,
Wiþ such werkes my lif to lede,
That I may se god in his face
On domys day wiþouten drede.

The Wounds, as Wells of Life
Anonymous

Ihesus woundes so wide
ben welles of lif to þe goode,
Namely þe stronde of hys syde,
þat ran ful breme on þe rode.

Gif þee liste to drinke,
to fle fro þe fendes of helle,
Bowe þu doun to þe brinke
& mekely taste of þe welle.

strond - shore; breme - brim; gif - if; fendes - fiends

All Ten Commandments I Have Broken
Anonymous

The ten comawndementis I haue broke
Many a tyme with wickede skylle;
To falce goddus I haue spoke
And wrowghte, a-gaynes my lordis wille.

Many tyme I haue take
Goddes name in Idylsheppe,
There-fore I tremell, drede and quake.
Mercy! god, for thi lordshepe.

Myne holidai I haue myspent,
Ther-for myne herte it is ful sore;
Ffadur and modur I haue forfende—
Now mercy, lord, I wylle no more.

forfende - resisted

Mansleer I was with all my mygt,
In thougte, in worde and eke in dede;
Befowlyd womman bothe day and nygt,
There-of toke I litil heede.

To do thefte wolde y nogt reste,
Wrougt I haue agens thy lore;
To bere fals wytnesse wold I ay preste—
Now mercy, lord, I wole no more.

Ffor to desyre my neygborus howse—
Lytil hede there-of I rowgte—
Also his wyfe that was his spouse,
And odur catelle that he owgte.

Thus haue I my lorde forsake,
And alle his comaundementis I-broke;
To thi mercy I me take,
Ffor-sothe I can no bettur grope.

mansleer - manslayer; eke - also; befowled - adulterated; nott - not; agens - against; lore
- teaching; ay prest - always ready; grope - effort, attempt

World's Bliss, Have Good Day!
Anonymous

Worlde's blisse, have good day!
Now from myn herte wend away.

Him for to loven myn hert is went
That thurgh His side spere rent;
His herte-blood shed He for me,
Nailed to the harde tree;
That swete body was y-tent,
Prened with nailes three.

Ha Jesu! thyn holy heved
With sharpe thornes was bi-weved;
Thy feire neb was al bi-spet,
With spot and blood meind al bi-wet;
Fro the crune to the to

wend - turn; went - turned; thurgh -through; rent - tore; y-tent - stretched; Prened -
pierced; heved - head; bi-weved - encircled; neb - face; bi-spet - spat upon; meind - min-
gled

Thy body was ful of pine and wo,
And wan and red.

Ha Jesu! thy smarte ded
Be my sheld and my red
From develes lore.
Ha! swete Jesu, thyn ore!
For thine pines sore,
Tech herte myn right love thee
Whos herte-blood was shed for me.

pine - pain; wan - discoloured; smarte ded - painful death; red - help; ore - mercy; right love thee - to love thee aright

GOWER, JOHN (c.1330-14), once matched Chaucer in reputation as a Middle English poet. He wrote in French, English and Latin, and produced works in the tradition of courtly love and moral allegory. To modern readers, many of his works, like those of Chaucer, appear syncretistic, combining classical tradition, courtly love, and Christian doctrine. Before we draw such a simplified conclusion, however, we need to understand the men and their times, and interpret their works accordingly.

Conclusion to **This World fares as a Fantasy**

Of fantasye is all oure fare,
Olde and yonge and alle yfere;
But make we murye and slee care,
And worshipe we God whil we ben here,
Spende oure good and littel spare,
And uch mon cherise otheres chere.
Thenk how we, comen hider all bare,
Oure way-wending is in a were.
Pray we the prince that hath no pere
Take us hool to his mercy
And kepe oure concience clere,
For this world is but fantasy.

fare - business; yfere - together; murye - merry; slee - slay; uch mon - each man; cherise - covets; chere - joy; hider - hither; were - state of doubt; pare - peer; hool - whole, wholly

'Peace'
(from the verses addressed to Henry IV)

For vein honour or for the worldes good
Thei that whilom the stronge werres made,
Wher be thei now? Bethenk wel in thi mod.
The day is goon, the nyght is derk and fade,
Her crualte, which mad hem thanne glade,
Thei sorwen now, and yit have noght the more;
The blod is schad, which no man mai restore.

The werre is modir of the wronges alle;
It sleth the prest in holi chirche at masse,
Forlith the maide and doth hire flour to falle.
The werre makth the grete citee lasse,
And doth the lawe his reules overpasse.
There is no thing wherof meschef mai growe
Which is noght caused of the werre, y trowe.

The werre bringth in poverte at hise hieles,
Wherof the comon poeple is sore grieved;
The werre hath set his cart on thilke whieles
Wher that fortune mai noght be believed.
For whan men wene best to have achieved,
Ful ofte it is al newe to beginne:
The werre hath no thing siker, thogh he winne.

Forthi, my worthi prince, in Cristes halve,
As for a part whos feith thou hast to guide,
Ley to this olde sor a newe salve,
And do the werre awei, what so betide:
Pourchace pes, and set it be thi side,
And suffre noght thi poeple be devoured,
So schal thi name evere after stonde honoured.

If eny man be now or evere was
Ayein the pes thi preve counseillour,
Let god ben of thi counseil in this cas,
And put awei the cruel werreiour.

whilom - formerly; hem - them; schad - shed; modir - mother; forlith - despises, forsakes; lasse - languish; y trowe - I believe; at hise hieles - on his heels; thilke - such; whieles - wheels; wene - suppose; siker -certain; halve - behalf; ley to - lay on; do. . .awei - end; pourchace - purchase; Ayein - against

For god, which is of man the creatour,
He wolde noght men slowe his creature
withoute cause of dedly forfeture.

slowe - slew

WALTON, JOHN (fl. 1410), much confused with later writers of the same name, appears to have been Canon of Osney in 1410 when he completed his verse translation of Boethius' *Consolation of Philosophy*. Chaucer had already completed his translation and Walton appears to make use of Chaucer's version in his. He mentions both Chaucer and Gower in his work. Ten manuscripts of his translation are extant. It was printed in 1525 and as extracts in various books thereafter.

God, the Port of Peace

Now cometh alle ye that been y-brought
In bondes full of busy bitternesse,
Of erthly lust abiding in your thought!
Here is the rest of all your bisynesse,
Here is the port of pees and restfulnesse
To them that stand in stormes and disese,
Refut overt to wreches in distresse,
And al comfort of mischief and misese.

refute - refuge; misese - discomfort

DE CAISTRE, RICHARD (died 1420), took his name from Caistor, the place near Norwich where he is supposed to have been born. He was made Vicar of St. Stephen's in Norwich in 1402. His prayer (see below) is found in sixteen manuscripts and is among the first non-liturgical prayers extant. The versions vary somewhat. De Caistre may have expanded an existing work in writing it.

Prayer Of Richard De Castre

Jesu, Lord, that madist me.
And with Thy blessed blood hast bought,
Forgive that I have greved Thee
With word, with wil, and eek with thought.

Jesu, in whom in al my trust,
That died upon the roode tree,

Withdrawe myn herte from fleshy lust,
And from al worldly vanyte!

Jesu, for Thy woundis smerte
On feet and on Thyn handis two.
Make me meeke and low of herte,
And Thee to love as I should do.

Jesu, for Thy bitter wound
That wente to Thine herte roote,
For synne that hath myn herte bounde,
Thy blessid blood mote be my boote.

And Jesu Christ, to Thee I calle.
That art God, full of might;
Keep me cleane, that I ne falle
In deadly sinne neither by day ne night.

Jesu, grante me mine asking,
Perfect pacience in my disease;
And never mote I do that thing
That should Thee in ony wise displease.

Jesu, that art our heavenly kinge,
Soothfast God, and man also,
Give me grace of good endinge,
And them that I am holden unto.

Jesu, for the deadly tearis
That Thou sheddest for my gilt,
Heare and speede my prayers.
And spare me that I be not spilt.

Jesu, for them I Thee beseche
That wrathen Thee in ony wise,
Withhold from them Thine hand of wreche
And let them live in Thy service.

Jesu, moost coumfort for to see
Of Thy saintis evereachone,
Coumfort them that careful been,
And help them that ben woo-begone.

Jesu, keep them that been goode.
Amend them that han grieved Thee,

And send them fruytis of earthly foode
As each man needeth in his degree.

Jesu, that art withouten lees,
Almighty God in Trynyte.
Ceasse these werris and send us pees
With lasting love and charitee.

Jesu, that art the ghostly stone
Of al Holy Church in middle erthe,
Bring Thy foldis and flockis in oon,
And rule them rightly with oon herde.

Jesu, for Thy blessidful blood
Bringe, if Thou wilt, the soulis to bliss
Fro whom I have had ony good,
And spare them that have done amiss. Amen.

AUDELAY (or AWDLAY), JOHN (fl. 1426), of a monastery in Shropshire,
wrote chiefly devotional verses. His life before coming there may have been con-
siderably more worldly according to the contents of some of his more peniten-
tial poems, but "Judging by his writings, he seems to have been of an unworld-
ly and devout character." (A.H.B. in *Dictionary of National Biography*) His work is
known from a solitary manuscript in the Bodleian Library of Oxford
University, which includes a number of autobiographical notes. A selection of
Audelay's work was first published in 1744. Audelay is noted for having con-
verted caroles, secular dancing songs, into devotional songs. Haghmon Abbey
where he lived belonged to the order of Augustinian Canons, but Audelay may
have been a secular priest who took refuge there after becoming blind. From his
autobiographical notes and the contents of his songs, it appears that the onset
of his physical blindness and later deafness brought him out of spiritual blind-
ness and deafness into a special kind of seeing and hearing. He wrote many
songs of celebration, often including requests that those who read them pray for
him.

The Seven Gifts of the Holy Ghost

God hath yeuen, of myghtis most,
The *vii* yiftis of the Hole Gost.

Mynd, resun, vertu, and grace,
Humelete, chast, and charete,
These *vii* yiftis God yeuen has

By the vertu of the Hole Gost to mon onle;
Ellis were we lost.

Mynd makis a mon himselue to know,
And resun him reulis in his werkis all,
And vertu makis his goodnes yknow,
And grace is grownde of hem all;
Ellis were we lost.

Humelete pride he dothe downe falle;
Chast kepis the clene in thi leuyng;
Then charete is chef of hem all;
Mon soule to blis he dothe hom breng;
Ellis were we lost.

Haue faythe, hope, and charete;
These be the grownd of thi beleue;
Ellis sauyd thou myght not be,
Thus Poule in his pistil he doth preue;
Ellis were we lost.

Thi faythe is thi beleue of Hole Cherche;
Onle in hope God hathe hordent the,
Good workis that thou schuld werche
And be rewardid in heuen on hye
Ellis were we lost.

Then charete, chef callid is he;
He cownselis vche mon that is leuyng
To do as thou woldist men did be the,
And kepe Godis est and his bidyng;
Ellis were we lost.

grownde - foundation; leuyng - living; sauyd - saved; hordent the - ordained thee; est - behest

LYDGATE, JOHN (c.1370-c.1450), was a very productive writer. Today, 145,000 lines of his verse survive (*Encyclopedia Britannica*). While a boy he became a novice in the Benedictine abbey of Bury St. Edmunds and a priest in 1397. Among his long works are *The Troy Booke*, *The Falle of Princis*, *Reason and Sensuality* (on the theme of chastity), *Complaint of the Black Knight*, *The Temple of Glass*, and *The Pilgrimage of Man*. Several of these are largely translations of medieval French works. He also wrote stories of the lives of saints, versions of Aesop's fables, and many shorter poems both lyrical and occasional. He became Court poet under royal patronage, and therefore was obliged to write poems as he was commanded. He was the first to introduce Latin words into written English. Lydgate was esteemed almost as highly as Chaucer in the sixteenth century.

Vox Ultima Crucis

Tarye no longer; toward thyn herytage
Hast on thy weye, and be of ryght good chere.
Go eche day onward on thy pylgrymage;
Thynke howe short tyme thou hast abyden here.
Thy place is bygged above the sterres clere,
Noon erthly palys wrought in so statly wyse.
Come on, my frend, my brother most entere!
For the I offered my blood in sacryfice.

bygged - built; palys - palace.

Like a Midsummer Rose

Let no man boste of cunning nor vertu,
Of tresour, richesse, nor of sapience,
Of worldly support, for al cometh of Jesu,
Counsail, confort, discrecioun, prudence,
Provisioun, forsight, and providence,
Like as the Lord of grace list dispose:
Some man hath wisdom, some man hath eloquence—
Al stant on chaunge like a midsomer rose. . .

Holsom in smelling be the swote flowres,
Ful delitable outward to the sight;
The thorn is sharp, cured with fresh coloures;
Al is not gold that outward sheweth bright.
A stokfish bone in derknesse yeveth a light,
Tween fair and foul, as God list dispose
A difference atwixen day and night—
Al stant on chaunge like a midsomer rose. . .

The golden char of Phebus in the air
Chaseth mistes blak that they dare not appeere,

cunning - learning; Provisioun - looking ahead; stant on - is founded on; swote - sweet; delitable - delightful; cured - covered; stokfish - dried fish; yeveth a light - gives a light (because rotten); Tween fair and foul - which looks fair and is foul; atwixen - between; char - chariot

At whos uprist mountains be made so fair
As they were newly gilt with his beemes cleere;
The night doth folwe, appalleth al his cheere
When western wawes his streemes over-close.
Rekne al beute, al freshness that is heere
Al stant on chaunge like a midsomer rose. . .

Constraint of colde maketh flowres dare
With winter frostes that they dare not appeere.
Al clad in russet the sod of green is bare;
Tellus and Jove be dulled of their cheere
By revolucioun and turning of the yeere.
As gery March his stoundes doth disclose—
Now rein, now storm, now Phebus bright and cleere—
Al stant on chaunge like a midsomer rose. . .

Wher is now David, the most worthy king
Of Juda and Israel, most famous and notable?
And wher is Solomon most sovereign of cunning,
Richest of bilding, of tresour incomparable?
Face of Absolon, most fair, most amiable?
Rekne up echone, of trouthe make no glose,
Rekne up Jonathas, of frenship immutable—
Al stant on chaunge like a midsomer rose. . .

Wher is Julius, proudest in his empire,
With his triumphes most imperial?
Wher is Pirrus, that was lord and sire
Of al Inde in his estat royal?
And wher is Alisaunder that conquered al,
Failed leiser his testament to dispose?
Nabugodonosor or Sardanapal?
Al stant on chaunge like a midsomer rose. . .

Wher is Tullius with his sugred tunge?
Or Crisistomus with his golden mouth?
The aureat ditees that be red and sunge
Of Omerus, in Greece both north and south?

As - as if; appalleth - dims; cheere - face; wawes - waves; streemes - beams; freshness -
brightness; dare - lie hidden; Tellus and Jove - earth and heaven; gery March - fitful
March; stoundes - varieties (lit. times); cunning - wisdom; glose - falsification; Failed
leiser - lacked the leisure; Nabugodonosor - Nebuchadnezzar; Sardanapal -
Sardanapalus; Tullius - Cicero; Crisistomus - Chrysostom; ditees - compositions;
Omerus - Homer

The tragedyes divers and uncouth
Of moral Senek, the mysteryes to unclose?
By many example this matere is ful couth—
Al stant on chaunge like a midsomer rose. . .

Wher been of Fraunce al the Dozepeers
Which in Gaule hadde the governaunce?
'Vowes of the Pecok,' with al their proude cheers?
The Worthy Nine with al their high bobbaunce?
Troian knightes, grettest of alliaunce?
The flees of gold conquered in Colchose?
Rome and Cartage, most soverein of puissaunce?
Al stant on chaunge like a midsomer rose. . .

The remembraunce of every famous knight,
Ground considered, is bilt on rightwisnesse.
Race out ech quarel that is not bilt on right;
Withoute trouth what vaileth high noblesse?
Laurer of martirs founded on holynesse—
White was made red their triumphes to disclose:
The white lillye was their chast clennesse,
Their bloody suffraunce was no somer rose.

It was the Rose of the bloody feeld,
Rose of Jericho that grew in Bedleem;
The five Roses portrayed in the sheeld,
Splayed in the baner at Jerusalem.
The sonne was clips and derk in every rem
When Crist Jesu five welles list unclose
Toward Paradis, called the rede strem,
Of whos five woundes print in your hert a rose.

uncouth - marvellous; ful couth - well known; Dozepeers - twelve peers of Charlemagne;
Vowes of the Pecok - martial vows made to a peacock in the Alexander romance Les
Voeux du Paon; proude cheers - proud bearing; bobbaunce - pride; grettest of alliance -
most united of companies; Colchose - Colchis; Ground considered - when the grounds
are examined; Race out - erase; quarel - claim; vaileth - avails; noblesse - nobility; Laurer
- laurel; clennesse - purity; Splayed - displayed; clips - eclipsed; rem - realm

Thank God For All

By a way wandering as I went,
Well sore I sorrowed, for sighing sad
Of hard haps that I had hent

Mourning me made almost mad;
Till a letter all one me lad,
That well was written on a wall,
A blissful word that on I rad,
That alway said, 'Thank God for all.'

And yet I read furthermore—
Full good intent I took there till:
Christ may well your state restore;
Nought is to strive against his will;
He may us spare and also spill:
Think right well we be his thrall.
What sorrow we suffer, loud or still,
Alway thank God for all.

Though thou be both blind and lame,
Or any sickness be on thee set,
Thou think right well it is no shame—
The grace of God it hath thee gret.
In sorrow or care though ye be knit,
And worldes weal be from thee fall,
I cannot say thou mayst do bet,
But alway thank God for all.

Though thou wield this world's good,
And royally lead thy life in rest,
Well shaped of bone and blood,
None the like by east nor west;
Think God thee sent as him lest;
Riches turneth as a ball;
In all manner it is the best
Alway to thank God for all.

If thy good beginneth to pass,
And thou wax a poor man,
Take good comfort and bear good face,
And think on him that all good wan;
Christ himself forsooth began—
He may renew both bower and hall:
No better counsel I ne kan
But alway thank God for all.

all one me lad - led me to unity; rad - read; till - to; spill - give calamity; thrall -servant;
gret - greeted; bet - better; wan - won

Think on Job that was so rich:
He waxed poor from day to day;
His beastes died in each ditch;
His cattle vanished all away;
He was put in poor array,
Neither in purple nor in pall,
But in simple weed, as clerkes say,
And alway he thanked God for all.

For Christes love so do we;
He may both give and take;
In what mischief that we in be,
He is mighty enough our sorrow to slake.
Full good amends he will us make,
And we to him cry or call:
What grief or woe that do thee thrall,
Yet alway thank God for all.

Though thou be in prison cast,
Or any distress men do thee bede,
For Christes love yet be steadfast,
And ever have mind on thy creed;
Think he faileth us never at need,
The dearworth duke that deem us shall;
When thou art sorry, thereof take heed,
And alway thank God for all.

Though thy friendes from thee fail,
And death by rene hend their life,
Why shouldest thou then weep or wail?
It is nought against God to strive:
Himself maked both man and wife—
To his bliss he bring us all:
However thou thole or thrive,
Alway thank God for all.

What diverse sonde that God thee send,
Here or in any other place,
Take it with good intent;
The sooner God will send his grace.

simple weed - plain clothes; thrall - enslave bede - offer; dearworth duke - precious lord;
by rene hend - beyond renewal seize; diverse sonde - varying message; sonde - message,
decree

Though thy body be brought full base,
Let not thy heart adown fall,
But think that God is where he was,
And alway thank God for all.

Though thy neighbour have world at will,
And thou far'st not so well as he,
Be not so mad to think him ill,
For his wealth envious to be:
The king of heaven himself can see
Who takes his sonde, great or small;
Thus each man in his degree,
I rede thanks God for all.

For Cristes love, be not so wild,
But rule thee by reason within and without;
And take in good heart and mind
The sonde that God sent all about;
Then dare I say withouten doubt,
That in heaven is made thy stall.
Rich and poor that low will lowte,
Alway thank God for all.

stall - room; lowte - bow

Chapter Three

SIXTEENTH CENTURY POETRY

1485–Caxton publishes *Morte d'Arthur*   1603–Death of Elizabeth

C.S. Lewis, in *English Literature in the Sixteenth Century*, says one of the most useful lessons of anthologies is "Periods are largely the invention of the historians. The poets themselves are not conscious of living in any period and refuse to conform to the scheme." The Sixteenth century is especially arbitrary as a literary period with all the cross-currents of ancient, medieval, and "renaissance" thought, letters, and life which run through it, having very few neat beginnings or endings.

It is common to read about the "Renaissance" greatly affecting Europe and England, but there is very little but wishful thinking to testify to this "re-birth" of culture. Lewis argues that many of the real influences of the "Renaissance" were in fact more a strait-jacketing of culture than a cultural renewal. The modern definition of the "Renaissance" is predicated on the concept of a "Dark Ages," that is a repressed and stultified period of several hundred years during which nobody in Europe was allowed to know or think much of anything. In this view, the Christian faith, or at least the church was the chief agent of repression and stultification. The preceding poetry has demonstrated such was not the case. Neither did the men of the sixteenth century think they were breaking out of a period of oppressive ignorance into a period of artistic and intellectual freedom.

What was new in the sixteenth century was the mixture. "Science," as we call it, was of interest to many sixteenth century writers, but in quite a different relation to faith than it is on the contemporary American scene. Science might be a hobby to a sixteenth century man, but his faith was central to his life and art. Lewis says that "scientific" interest blended into astrology and magic, which, he points out, were logically in opposition, the former at one extreme of determinism or fatalism, the latter at the other extreme of humanism and faith in human power to affect change.

Puritans, Christians who wished to abolish the Anglican office of bishop and reform or "purify" Anglican doctrine along Calvinist lines, were beginning to have, in Lewis's analogy, an effect on the period like that of Marxists in the 1930s—they were bold and outspoken, and their ideas were very popular, even stylish. Humanism or classicism was proposing to rebuild learning and culture on the "ancient classics" as distinct from the medieval junkpile (as the human-

ist saw it). Lewis says the humanists did us a great favor in translating and pre-
serving a large number of Greek, Latin, and Hebrew works, but also a large dis-
service in promulgating the idea that the best was lost in the past so that all our
struggle must be to recover it. Puritans were often (but not always or in all ways)
humanists. Sixteenth century humanism and Puritanism both looked down on
the Middle Ages—especially on chivalrous romance and scholastic philosophy.
Ancient and medieval Christian literature were not two widely separated efflu-
ences however, but pretty much one stream. This same river rolled on into the
sixteenth century. Middle English genres and styles continued. There was a lot
more poetry translated from and modeled on classical Latin works than in the
previous century, however, and this, with the desire of humanist and Puritan to
be disassociated from the Middle Ages, had a significant effect on poetry in
general.

Political and religious tides swept back and forth through the period, at least
until the reign of Elizabeth. Both Roman Catholic and Protestant became mar-
tyrs for their faiths and political allegiances. (When it came to martyrdom the
boundary between religious and political allegiances often became indistinct.)

During the sixteenth century the Bible became available in several English
versions, the earliest complete version being Coverdale's in 1535, which bor-
rowed a number of books that Tyndale had translated earlier. It became illegal
for a while for any but the upper class to have an English Bible, and then for any
private person to possess one. Under Elizabeth the English Bible was brought
back, however, and new translations were made.

Literature got a boost from an economic point of view, in the Stationer's
Company being incorporated. Through their charter, bookcopy became the
property of the bookseller, so an author could now sell his work, rather than
having to rely on a wealthy sponsor to support his writing.

Lewis divides the period's poetry into three groups which he calls the Late
Medieval, the Drab, and the Golden. He dates the period of the first roughly
to the end of the reign of Edward VI, the second beginning toward the end of
Henry VII and ending in the late '70's, and the period of the third, basically
coinciding with the reign of Elizabeth.

Late Medieval poetry was largely the work of Scottish poets, like William
Dunbar. These are sometimes called "Chaucerian" poets, although most were of
a parallel tradition rather than imitators of Chaucer. Among these Lewis
includes a few later English poets on the basis of their style. Allegorical inter-
pretation (a favorite medieval approach to scripture) continued to thrive in six-
teenth century poetry and poetry reading.

"Drab poetry" was stylistically regular, but without much life. Two collec-
tions which represent it are Tottel's *Miscellany* (1557) and *The Mirror of Magistrates*
(c.1559). Lewis feels the Drab period differed from the Golden primarily in
that the former lacked great poets.

The Golden poetry of the sixteenth century includes Sidney, Spenser, Raleigh, Davies, Greville, and Sylvester. When Elizabeth came to the throne, the return of Protestant exiles became a major factor in the life and art of England. Lewis says the Golden age's unity consisted chiefly in a common defense and theory of poetry—a defense not of prose against verse, but of fiction against fact, and a theory that is largely neoplatonic. While the neoclassical humanist might quote Plato to the effect that poetry is lies or insane ramblings, the neo-Platonist poets argued that poets created purer and saner truth with their imaginations. Unlike poets of later periods the sixteenth century poets did not argue that they were accurately depicting nature or Nature. To argue that would have seemed to them to run afoul of Plato's argument that Nature, the world of matter and seen things, is more delusive than the world of ideas and unseen things, therefore not worth depicting. In other words the Golden poets did not put any priority on portraying the "real" or "actual."

The poets of the Golden age had basic metrical and rhyme techniques which were more or less fixed and could be learned. It was during the Golden Age of sixteenth century poetry that the sonnet and the sonnet sequence came to epitomize poetry.

There are a number of poets whom Lewis calls non-Golden poets, although they wrote during the Golden Age. These include some whom he classifies as Drab, some who are Metaphysical (anticipating an important kind of seventeenth century poetry), and various mixtures. (For example, Chapman was part Golden, part Metaphysical, while Southwell was part Drab, part Metaphysical, but not Golden, in Lewis's analysis.)

Shakespeare's plays, at least from our age's perspective, seem to dominate Elizabethan literature. Lewis classifies his sonnets and a few other poems as part Golden and part Metaphysical. To debate whether Shakespeare was a Christian or not may be futile, but to discuss his writing without reference to Christianity, as some critics try to do, is ludicrous.

In many ways the sixteenth century is the beginning of "tradition" in English poetry, the beginning of a unified literary consciousness. It is also the last period in which poets were of one mind about what made good poetry—and what good poetry was for. The seventeenth century (beginning late in the sixteenth) had several minds about what poets should do and what poetry should be. Seventeenth century literature was "twice-born," in C.S. Lewis's terms, that is, building self-consciously on what had gone before. Sixteenth century literature contributed to English literary tradition without much consciousness of a prior tradition or at least without self-consciousness.

Brief Chronology of the Sixteenth Century

1485	Caxton publishes *Morte D'Arthur*
	Henry VII accedes to throne, first of Tudor kings
1509	Henry VIII accedes to throne
1513	Battle of Flodden, James IV of Scotland defeated and killed
1517	Luther's *Wittenberg Theses*, Reformation begins
1525	Tyndale's New Testament first English translation printed
1535	Henry VIII acknowledged Anglican "Supreme Head on Earth"
1537	Beginning of Calvin's "theocracy" at Geneva
1538	English Bible ordered placed in every church
1539	Coverdale's Great Bible issued in name of Henry VIII
1543	Act "For the advancement of religion" restricts Bible reading
1553	Mary accedes to throne, retains title "supreme head"
1557	Tottel's *Miscellany* published
1558	Elizabeth accedes to throne
1568	College of Douai founded in France by English Roman Catholics
1576	Theatre built, first in England
1577	Drake begins voyage around world
1579	Jesuit mission to England organized
1582	Rheims version of English New Testament issued in Rheims, France (full Roman Catholic Rheims-Douay version in 1610)
1586	Star Chamber forbids publication of books without church approval
1587	Execution of Mary
1588	Spanish Armada defeated
1603	Death of Elizabeth, James I accedes, first of Stuart kings

SKELTON, JOHN (c.1460–1529), apparently attended both Oxford and Cambridge and studied both the classics and contemporary French literature. He began at an early age to write poems, often in Latin, many of them in honor of the royal family. Skelton translated a French poem (upon which Lydgate had begun) "Of Mannes Lyfe the Peregrynacioun." He was appointed tutor to Henry VII's second son, Prince Henry, later Henry VIII. For his student he wrote "Speculum Principis," a treatise on the demeanor of a prince. Although it is not certain whether it was the same man, a John Skelton was committed to prison in 1502 by the order of the king in council. In any case Skelton was not a typical courtier and often wrote of his contempt for the insincerity of court life. He depicted the sins of the court in an early poem, "The Bowge (right to rations) of Court." He was nevertheless much honored by Henry VII, being made the king's poet laureate. In 1498 he took holy orders. About this time he seems to have adopted his distinctive style of irregular meter with short rhyming lines. He wrote a light poem, "Boke of Phylyp Sparowe," which may have been the source for the nursery rhyme, "Who Killed Cock Robin," and a satire against a worldly clergyman, "Ware the Hauke." Skelton was apparently taken to task for living with a woman, whom he claimed to have secretly married. Partly due to his bent toward practical jokes and satire, he had many enemies in court and literature, including Alexander Barclay, but he also had friends including the Countess of Surrey, mother of Surrey the poet. He sought the favor of Cardinal Wolsey in the early days of Henry VIII's reign, and dedicated to him "A Replycacioun against certayne young scolers," which was directed against criticism by some Cambridge scholars of current theology. Wolsey does not seem to have been overly fond of Skelton, who directed occasional satires against the cardinal. ("Colyn Cloute" is directed principally against the corruptions of the church, but incidentally attacks Wolsey. In "Why come ye not to court?" he more directly attacked Wolsey, as he did in "Speake Parrot.") Tradition has it that Skelton went to prison for the latter. The next time Wolsey sent officers to arrest Skelton, he took sanctuary in Westminster, where he stayed the rest of his life. Skelton's "A Balade of the Scotyshe Kynge" is one of the earliest ballads printed in English.

Woefully Arrayed

Woefully araid
My blode man for thee ran;
It may not be naid;
My body blo and wan,
Wofully araid.

Beholde me, I pray thee, with all thi hole reson,
And be not hard hartid, and for this encheson,
That I, for thi saule sake was slayne, in good seson,
Begylde and betraide by Judas fals treson;
Vnkindly intretid,
With sharp corde sore fretid,
The Iues me thretid,
They mowid, they grynned, they scornyd,
Condemned to deth, as thou maist se.
Wofully araid. . .

Thus nakyd am I maked, O man, for thy sake!
I loue thee, then loue me. Why slepist thou? awake!

naid - denied; blo - livid; encheson - cause, motive; intretid - treated; Iues - Jews; thretid - reproved

Remember my tender hart-rote for thee brake,
With paynes my veines constreyned to crake;
Thus was I defasid,
Thus was my flesh rasid,
And I to deth chasid.
Like a lambe led vnto sacrifice,
Slayne I was in most cruell wise.
Wofully araid. . .

Of sharpe thorne I haue worne a crowne on my hed,
So rubbid, so bobbid, so rufulle, so red,
Sore payned, sore strayned, and for thy loue ded,
Vnfayned, not deined, my blod for to shed,
My fete and handes sore
The sturdy nailis bore;
What myght I suffer more
Than I haue don, O man, for thee?
Cum when thou list, welcome to me.
Wofully araid. . .

Deyr brother, non other thyng of thee I desyre,
But geue me thi hert fre, to rewarde myne hire.
I am he that made thee erth, water and fire.
Sathanas, that slouen and right lothely sire,
Hym haue I ouer-caste,
In hell presoune bounde faste,
Wher ay his woo shall laste.
I haue puruaide a place full clere
For mankynde, whom I haue bought dere.

defasid - defaced; mowid - made grimaces at; bobbid - beaten

Prayer to the Father in Heaven

O Radiant Luminary of light interminable,
Celestial Father, potential God of might,
Of heaven and earth O Lord incomparable,
Of all perfections the Essential most perfite!
O Maker of mankind, that formed day and night,
Whose power imperial comprehendeth every place!
Mine heart, my mind, my thought, my whole delight
Is, after this life, to see thy glorious Face.

Whose magnificence is incomprehensible,
All arguments of reason which far doth exceed,
Whose Deity doubtless is indivisible,
From whom all goodness and virtue doth proceed,
Of thy support all creatures have need:
Assist me, good Lord, and grant me of thy grace
To live to thy pleasure in word, thought, and deed,
And, after this life, to see thy glorious Face.

DUNBAR, WILLIAM (c.1460–c.1530), a Middle Scots poet, was associated with the court of James IV. He was probably a Franciscan novice who travelled to England and France in the King's service, entering the priesthood by 1504. Most of his extant poetry is short occasional verse, ranging from earthy satire to divine praise. He wrote several longer poems, including the dream allegory, *The Golden Targe.* According to the *Encyclopedia Britannica,* "He was at ease in hymn and satire, morality and obscene comedy, panegyric and begging complaint, elegy and lampoon. His poetic vocabulary ranged through several levels and he moved freely from one to another for satiric effect. He wrote with uncommon frankness and wit, manipulating old themes and forms with imagination and originality."

All Erdly Joy Returns In Pane

Of Lentren in the first morning,
Airly as did the day up spring,
Thus sang ane bird with voce upplane:
All erdly joy returns in pane.

O man, haif mind that thou mon pas,
Remembir that thou art bot as
And sall in as revert agane:
All erdly joy returns in pane.

Haif mind that eild follows youth,
Deth follows life with gaipand mouth
Devoring fruct and flouring grane:
All erdly joy returns in pane.

Welth, wardly gloir and rich array
Are all bot thorns laid in thy way

upplane - out plane (loudly) or a-plain (plainly); erdly - earthly, worldly; returns in - changes into; mon - must; as - ashes; revert - return; eild - Age; grane - grain, seed; gloir - glory;

Owrcoverd with flours laid in ane trane:
All erdly joy returns in pane.

Corn nevir yit May so fresh and grene,
Bot Januar com als wood and kene;
Wes nevir sic drouth bot anis com rane:
All erdly joy returns in pane.

Evirmair unto this warldis joy
As nerrest heir succeidis noy;
Thairfoir, when joy ma nocht remane,
His verry heir succeidis pane.

Heir helth returnis in seikness,
And mirth returns in haviness,
Toun in desert, forest in plane:
All erdly joy returns in pane.

Fredom returns in wrechitness,
And treuth returns in doubilness
With fenyeit words to mak men fane:
All erdly joy returns in pane.

Vertew returnis in to vice,
And honour in to avarice;
With cuvatice is consciens slane:
All erdly joy returns in pane.

Sen erdly joy abidis nevir,
Wirk for the joy that lestis evir,
For uder joy is all bot vane:
All erdly joy returns in pane.

Owrcoverd - covered over; in ane trane - as a snare; als wood - as furious; line 19 - "There was never such a drought but that rain came once more."; succeidis - follows; noy - trouble; ma - may; verry - true; haviness - dreariness; plane - open country; fenyeit - feigned; fane - happy; cuvatice - covetous-ness; Sen - since

Now cumis aige quhair yewth hes bene

Now cumis aige quhair yewth hes bene.
And trew luve rysis fro the splene.

Now culit is Dame Venus brand,
Trew luvis fyre is ay kindilland,

quhair - where; culit - cooled;

And I begyn to vndirstand
In feynit luve quhat foly bene.

Quhill Venus fyre be deid and cauld,
Trew luvis fyre nevir birnis bauld;
So as the ta lufe vaxis auld,
The tothir dois incress moir kene.

No man hes curege for to wryte
Quhat plesans is in lufe perfyte
That hes in fenyeit lufe delyt
Thair kyndnes is so contrair clene.

Full weill is him that may imprent
Or onywayiss his hairt consent
To turne to trew luve his intent
And still the quarrell to sustene.

I haif experience by mysell:
In luvis court anis did I dwell;
Bot quhair I of a joy cowth tell
I culd of truble tell fyftene.

Befoir quhair that I wes in dreid
Now haif I confort for to speid;
Quhair I had maugre to my meid
I trest rewaird and thankis betuene.

Quhair lufe wes wont me to displeiss
Now find I into lufe grit eiss;
Quhair I had denger and diseiss
My breist all contort dois contene.

Quhair I wes hurt with jelosy
And wald no luver wer bot I,
Now quhair I lufe wald all wy
Als weill as I luvit, I wene.

Befoir quhair I durst nocht for schame
My lufe discure nor tell hir name,

---

feynit - feigned; quhat - what; bauld - bold; ta. . . tothir - the one. . . the other; vaxis - grows; kene - keen; curege - courage; kyndnes - natures; clene - completely; imprent - impress; onywayiss - anyway; anis - once; cowth/culd - could; speid - flourish; maugre to my meid - little for my reward; grit eiss - great ease; waid no luver wer - wished no lover existed; wald all wy - would always; wene - suppose; discure - reveal

Now think I wirschep wer and fame
To all the warld that it war sene.

Befoir no wicht I did complene,
So did hir denger me derene,
And now I sett nocht by a bene
Hir bewty nor hir twa fair ene.

I haif a luve farar of face,
Quhome in no denger may haif place,
Quhilk will me guerdoun gif and grace
And mercy ay quhen I me mene.

Vnquyt I do no thing nor sane
Nor wairis a luvis thocht in vane;
I sal be als weill luvit agane;
Thair may no jangler me prevene.

Ane lufe so fare, so gud, so sueit,
So riche, so rewthfull and discreit,
And for the kynd of man so meit
Nevirmoir sal be nor yit hes bene.

Is none sa trew a luve as he
That for trew lufe of ws did de:
He suld be luffit agane, think me,
That wald sa fane our luve obtene.

Is non but grace of God, I wiss,
That can in yewth considdir thiss:
This fals dissavand warldis bliss
So gydis man in flouris grene.

wirschep - honor; wicht - wight, being; complene - complain to; derene - injur; bene -
bean; farar - fairer; quhome - whom; quhilk - which; quhen - when; me mene - declare
myself; unquyt - unrequited; sane - say; wairis - curse; jangler - "wind-bag"; prevene -pre-
vent; rewthfull - kind; meit - right; ws - us; de - die; suld be luffit agane - should be loved,
in return; waid sa fare - so desired; dissavand - deceitful; gydis - giddies

Done is a Battle on the Dragon Black

Done is a battle on the dragon black,
Our campion Christ confoundit has his force;
The yettis of hell are broken with a crack,
The sign triumphal raisit is of the cross,

yettis - gates

The devillis trymmillis with hiddous voce,
The saulis are borrowit and to the bliss can go,
Christ with his blood our ransonis dois indoce:
Surrexit Dominus de sepulchro.

Dungen is the deidly dragon Lucifer,
The cruel serpent with the mortal stang;
The auld keen tiger, with his teeth on char,
Whilk in a wait has lyen for us so lang,
Thinking to grip us in his clawis strang;
The merciful Lord wald nocht that it were so,
He made him for to failye of that fang:
Surrexit Dominus de sepulchro.

He for our sake that sufferit to be slain,
And like a lamb in sacrifice was dicht,
Is like a lion risen up again,
And as gyane raxit him on hicht;
Sprungen is Aurora radious and bricht,
On loft is gone the glorious Apollo,
The blissful day departit fro the nicht:
Surrexit Dominus de sepulchro.

The great victour again is risen on hicht,
That for our quarrel to the death was woundit;
The sun that wox all pale now shinis bricht,
And darkness clearit, our faith is now refoundit;
The knell of mercy fra the heaven is soundit,
The Christian are deliverit of their woe,
The Jewis and their error are confoundit:
Surrexit Dominus de sepulchro.

The foe is chasit, the battle is done cease,
The prison broken, the jevellouris fleit and flemit;
The weir is gone, confermit is the peace,
The fetteris lowsit and the dungeon temit,
The ranson made, the prisoneris redeemit;
The field is won, owrecomen is the foe,
Despoilit of the treasure that he yemit.
Surrexit Dominus de sepulchro.

---

trymmillis - tremble; our ransonis - ransom; indoce - endorse; Surrexit Dominus de sepulchro - "The Lord has risen from the grave"; Dungen - struck down; stang - Sting; on char - ajar; fang - prey; dicht - prepared; gyane - giant; raxit - stretched; radious - radiant; jevellouris - jailers; fleit - put to flight; flemit - terrified; temit - emptied; yemit - guarded

O Wretch, Beware

O wretch, beware! this world will wend thee fro,
Whilk has beguilit mony great estate;
Turn to thy friend, believe nocht on thy foe,
Sen thou man go, be graithing to thy gait;
Remeid in time, and rue nocht all too late;
Provide thy place, for thou away man pass
Out of this vale of trouble and dissait:
Vanitas Vanitatum, et omnia Vanitas.

Walk furth, pilgrim, while thou has dayis licht,
Dress fro desert, draw to thy dwelling-place;
Speed home, for-why anon comis the nicht
Whilk does thee follow with ane ythand chase!
Bend up thy sail, and win thy port of grace;
For and the death owretak thee in trespass,
Then may thou say thir wordis with alas!
Vanitas Vanitatum, et omnia Vanitas.

Here nocht abidis, here standis no thing stable,
For this false world aye flittis to and fro;
Now day up bricht, now nicht as black as sable,
Now ebb, now flood, now friend, now cruel foe;
Now glad, now sad, now weel, now into woe;
Now clad in gold, dissolvit now in ass;
So dois this warld transitory go:
Vanitas Vanitatum, et omnia Vanitas.

graithing to thy gait - making ready for thy journey; dress fro - withdraw from; for-why
- because; ythand - busy; ass - ash

MORE, Sir THOMAS (1477–1535), son of a London lawyer, was to become
a central figure in the drama of Henry VIII's break with the Roman church.
When he was about twelve, he became a page in the household of the
Archbishop of Canterbury, John Morton, who was also Henry VII's Chancellor.
He went to Oxford 1492-1494, after which he pursued a legal career at the Inns
of Court. At the age of 21 he served as a member of Parliament. Apparently
under the influence of John Colet he considered a career in the church and lived
in the London Charter-house of the Carthusian Monks for about four years.
He married in 1504 and had four children. When Erasmus visited England in
1499, he and More became close friends. The title (in Latin) of Erasmus' satire
"In Praise of Folly," is a friendly pun on More's name. Erasmus' Christian

humanism seems to have encouraged More. His first literary works date from the period of their friendship and he delivered his London lectures on Augustine's *City of God* about 1501. In 1510 he became undersheriff of London,and was in favor with Henry VIII, whom he had praised in a series of Latin poems. The King sent him on his first royal mission to Europe where he met many of the humanists whose circle revolved around Erasmus. By June 1518 he was a royal counselor and resigned as undersheriff. His first book, *Utopia,* was published in 1516. In 1521 he became undertreasurer and was knighted. In 1523 he was speaker of Parliament, the next year high steward of Oxford, and the following year high steward of Cambridge. Hans Holbein stayed at his house in 1526 or 1527, and painted a famous portrait of More while there. More's official duties began to center on the campaign against Lutheran literature which was flowing into England in the 1520s. He was authorized to read Prostestant works to refute them and wrote against Martin Luther on the King's behalf. From 1529 to 1534 he wrote against William Tyndale, Simon Fish, Robert Barnes and other English Protestants. When Henry VIII began to contemplate divorcing Catherine of Aragon, More made it clear he could not support this and was allowed to resign the seals. The King turned elsewhere, but when Wolsey was unable to satisfy the king, More was made chancellor in his place (1529). He refused to attend the coronation of Anne, telling his friends that though "he might be devoured, he would never be deflowered." He was willing to accept the Act of Succession, but would not take the Oath of Supremacy, and so was put in the tower in 1534. He swore he would reveal his conscience to no one, and with his legal knowledge was a hard prisoner to interrogate. He was convicted of treason in 1535, on debatable evidence, and executed. His literary works include *Book of Hours, A Dialogue of Comfort Against Tribulation,* and *Expositio Passionis (Treatise on the Passion).* The latter two were completed during his imprisonment.

Consider Well

Consider well that both by night and day
While we most busily provide and care
For our disport, our revel, and our play,
For pleasant melody and dainty fare,
Death stealeth on full slily; unaware
He lieth at hand and shall us all surprise,
We wot not when nor where nor in what wise.

When fierce temptations threat thy soul with loss
Think on His Passion and the bitter pain,
Think on the mortal anguish of the Cross,

Think on Christ's blood let out at every vein,
Think on His precious heart all rent in twain;
For thy redemption think all this was wrought,
Nor be that lost which He so dearly bought.

Fortune

Eye-flattering fortune, look thou never so fair,
Or never so pleasantly begin to smile
As though thou wouldst my ruin all repair;
During my life thou shalt me not beguile.
Trust shall I God, to enter in a while
His haven of heaven, sure and uniform;
Ever after thy calm, look I for a storm.

WYATT, THOMAS (1503–1542) was born at Allington Castle, which had been presented to his father as reward for his hardships suffered on behalf of the Tudors under Richard III. Wyatt went to St. John's College and in 1520 married the daughter of Lord Cobham, Elizabeth, which union brought two children, before Wyatt concluded his wife was unfaithful and separated from her. He held various posts at court and in 1526 participated in a French Embassy, followed by a mission to the Pope, during which he was captured by Spanish troops, from whom he escaped. He served as Marshall of Calais, Commissioner of the Peace, and was made deputy of his father, the Chief Ewer, at Anne Boleyn's coronation. Wyatt was imprisoned for a while in 1536, partly at least, because of a quarrel with the Duke of Suffolk. In 1537 he was appointed Ambassador to Spain. Thomas Cromwell gave him both friendship and influential help. Nevertheless, Wyatt was present at Cromwell's execution in 1540—he expressed his grief in a sonnet (#173). Not long after this he retreated to his father's castle where he wrote his *Penitential Psalms*—paraphrases of seven Psalms of David with narrative sections between them. In 1541, he was arrested, apparently at the instigation of Bishop Bonner, and his goods confiscated under charges including treason and immorality. He defended himself well enough to get a full pardon, under the condition that he take back his former wife. The level of immorality among the royalty and nobility was terrible at this time, and Wyatt seems to have been caught up in a number of adulterous relationships. He was soon restored to favor, elected to Parliament, and appointed a Vice-Admiral. While escorting a Spanish envoy to London, he caught a fever and died at Sherbourne, where he is buried. Apart from his poems, we have some letters, notably two to his son, exhorting him to honesty and integrity.

The Argument

[Eight lines, possibly addressed to the Earl of Surrey, probably belong to one
of Wyatt's psalm paraphrases—pages are missing in the manuscript]

Somtyme the pryde of mye assured trothe
Contemned all helpp of god and eke of man:
But when I saw man blyndlye how he goi'the
In demyng hartes, whiche none but god there can,
And his domes hyd, wheareby mans Malyce grow'th;
Myne Earle, this doute my hart did humble than,
Ffor errour so might murder Innocence.
Then sang I thus in god my Confydence.

Introductory poem to the Penitential Psalms

Love to gyve law unto his subject hertes
Stode in the Iyes of Barsabe the bryht;
And in a look annone hymsellff convertes,
Cruelly plesant byfore kyng David syght;
First dasd his Iyes, and forder forth he stertes,
With venemd breth as sofftly as he myght
Towcht his sensis and overronnis his bonis
With creping fyre, sparplid for the nonis.

And when he saw that kendlid was the flame,
The moyst poyson in hiss hert he launcyd,
So that the sowle did tremble with the same;
And in this brawle as he stode and trauncyd,
Yelding unto the figure and the frame
That those fayre Iyes had in his presens glauncid,
The forme that love had printyd in his brest
He honorth it as thing off thinges best.

So that forgott the wisdome and fore-cast
(Wych wo to Remes when that thes kynges doth lakk)
Forgettyng eke goddes majestie as fast
Ye, and his own, forthwith he doth to mak
Urye to go into the feld in hast,
Urye, I say, that was his Idolles mak,
Under pretence off certen victorye,
For enmy's swordes a redy pray to dye.

Barsabe - Bathsheba; venom'd - poison; sparplyd - sparkled; moyst - fresh; Remes -
Realms; eke - also; Urye - Uriah

Wherby he may enjoy her owt of dowt,
Whom more then god or hymsellff he myndyth;
And after he had browght this thing abowt
And off that lust posest hym sellff, he fyndyth
That hath and doth reverse and clene torn owt
Kynges from kyndomes and cytes undermyndyth:
He blyndyd thinkes this trayne so blynd and closse
To blynd all thing that nowght may it disclosse.

But Nathan hath spyd owt this trecherye
With rufull chere, and settes afore his face
The gret offence, outrage and Injurye,
That he hath done to god as in this Case,
By murder for to clok Adulterye;
He shewth hym ek from hevyn the thretes, alas;
So sternly sore this prophet, this Nathan,
That all amasid this agid woofull man:

Lyke hym that metes with horrour and with fere,
The hete doth strayt forsake the lymms cold,
The colour eke drowpith down from his chere,
So doth he fele his fyer maynifold.
His hete, his lust and plesur all in fere
Consume and wast; and strayt his crown of gold,
His purpirll pall, his sceptre he lettes fall,
And to the ground he throwth hymsellff withall.

The pompous pryd of state and dygnite
Forthwith rabates repentant humblenes;
Thynner vyle cloth then clothyth poverte
Doth skantly hyde and clad his nakednes;
His faire, hore berd of reverent gravite
With ruffeld here knowyng his wykednes:
More lyke was he the sellff same repentance
Then statly prynce off worldly governance.

His harpe he taketh in hand to be his guyde,
Wherwith he offerth his plaintes his sowle to save,
That from his hert distilles on every syde,
Withdrawyng hym into a dark Cave
Within the grownd wherin he myght hym hyde,

---

undermyndyth - undermineth; trayne - trick or treachery; rabates - reduces ('humbleness reduces pride')

Fleing the lyght, as in pryson or grave:
In wych as sone as David enterd had,
The dark horrour did mak his fawte a drad.

But he withowt prolonging or delay
Rof that that myght his lord, his god, apese,
Fallth on his knees and with his harp, I say,
Afore his brest, frawtyd with disese
Off stormy syghes, his chere colourd lyk clay,
Dressyd upryght, seking to conterpese
His song with syghes, and towching of the strynges
With tendre hert, Lo thus to god he synges.

[In his paraphrases Wyatts' Psalm 6 follows]

fawte - fate or fault; drad - dread; Rof - Rove, meaning "to shoot randomly" - to make random efforts; frawtyd - fraught

ASKEW (ASCUE), ANNE (c.1521–1546), daughter of Sir William Askew of Lincoln, came to London where she made friends with various Protestants, including Joan Bocher, already reputed to be heterodox. Anne was examined by the Lord Mayor, then by Bishop Bonner, and finally charged as a sacramentarian (one who believes the sacraments involve a spiritual presence of Christ, but no physical or corporeal presence) at the Guildhall in 1545. These efforts failed to convict her, but she was brought before a special commission in 1546, without jury and without witnesses, where she was condemned to be burned on her own confession. She was tortured on the rack the following day, and after four more weeks in prison, was burned at Smithfield on July 16. It seems likely that the dogged judicial pursuit of this young woman was intended to intimidate other Protestants who were suspected of like beliefs. Her principle form of "heresy" seems to have been her view of the Eucharist. That both she and Thomas More should be martyred under Henry VIII indicates the intensity of religious conflict in England during this time.

Lines In Prison

Like as the armed knight,
Appointed to the field,
With this world will I fight,
And faith shall be my shield.

Faith is that weapon strong,
Which will not fail at need;

My foes therefore among
Therewith will I proceed.

As it is had in strength
And force of Christ his way,
It will prevail at length
Though all the devils say nay.

Faith in the Fathers old
Obtained righteousness,
Which maketh me so bold
To fear no world's distress.

I now rejoice in heart,
And hope bids me do so,
For Christ will take my part
And ease me of my woe.

Thou say'st, Lord, whoso knock
To them wilt thou attend;
Undo therefore the lock,
And thy strong power down send.

More enemies I have
Than hairs to crown my head,
Let them not me deprave,
But fight thou in my stead.

On thee my care I cast,
For all their cruel spite;
I set not by their haste,
For thou art my delight.

I am not she that list
My anchor to let fall
For every drizzling mist,
My ship's substantial.

Not oft use I to write
In prose, nor yet in rime;
Yet will I show one sight
That I saw in my time.

I saw a royal throne
Where justice should have sit,

But in her stead was one
Of moody cruel wit.

Absorbed was righteousness
As by a raging flood;
Satan in fierce excess
Sucked up the guiltless blood.

Then thought I—Jesu, Lord!
When thou shalt judge us all,
Hard is it to record
On these men what will fall.

Yet Lord, I thee desire,
For what they do to me
Let them not taste the hire
Of their iniquity.

GASCOIGNE, GEORGE (c.1534-1577) was the eldest son of Sir John Gascoigne. He studied at Cambridge, and afterward at Gray's Inn, but his temperament was less for the law than it was lawless. He lived a reckless life as a young man. His favorite motto was *Tam Marti quam Mercurio* (as much Mars as Mercury). He Went to Holland to take part in the struggle against Spain, and served under William of Orange with bravery and some distinction. He wrote an account of his voyage in "The Fruits of War." After he returned to England, from Holland in 1574, Gascoigne published a collection of his poems " corrected, perfected, and augmented by the author," under the title, *The Posies of George Gascoigne, Esquire.* This was followed by *The Steele Glas* and *The Complaynte of Phylomene,* which were published together in 1576. Gascoigne's reputation was growing, and he had good prospects of Court favor but his health was already failing, and he died in 1577. According to a biographer, Gascoigne "lived to amend his ways, and became a wise and good man. He died in a religious, calm, and happy frame of mind."

De Profundis

From depth of dole, wherein my soul doth dwell,
From heavy heart, which harbors in my breast,
From troubled sprite, which seldom taketh rest,
From hope of heaven, from dread of darksome hell,
O gracious God, to thee I cry and yell:
My God, my Lord, my lovely Lord, alone
To thee I call, to thee I make my moan.

And thou, good God, vouchsafe in grace to take
This woful plaint
Wherein I faint;
Oh! hear me, then, for thy great mercy's sake.

Oh! bend thine ears attentively to hear,
Oh! turn thine eyes, behold me how I wail!
Oh! hearken, Lord, give ear for mine avail,
Oh! mark in mind the burdens that I bear;
See how I sink in sorrows everywhere.
Behold and see what dolors I endure,
Give ear and mark what plaints I put in ure,
Bend willing ears; and pity therewithal
My willing voice,
Which hath no choice
But evermore upon thy name to call.

If thou, good Lord, shouldst take thy rod in hand,
If thou regard what sins are daily done,
If thou take hold where we our works begun,
If thou decree in judgment for to stand,
And be extreme to see our 'scuses scanned;
If thou take note of every thing amiss,
And write in rolls how frail our nature is,
O glorious God, O King, O Prince of power!
What mortal wight
May thus have light
To feel thy power, if thou have list to lower?

But thou art good, and hast of mercy store,
Thou not delight'st to see a sinner fall,
Thou hearkenest first, before we, come to call,
Thine ears are set wide open evermore,
Before we knock thou comest to the door;
Thou art more prest to hear a sinner cry
Than he is quick to climb to thee on high.
Thy mighty name be praised then alway,
Let faith and fear
True witness bear,
How fast they stand which on thy mercy stay.

I look for thee, my lovely Lord, therefore
For thee I wait, for thee I tarry still,

ure - use

Mine eyes do long to gaze on thee my fill,
For thee I watch, for thee I pry and pore,
My soul for thee attendeth evermore.
My soul doth thirst to take of thee a taste,
My soul desires with thee for to be placed.
And to thy words, which can no man deceive,
Mine only trust,
My love and lust,
In confidence continually shall cleave.

Before the break or dawning of the day,
Before the light be seen in lofty skies,
Before the sun appear in pleasant wise,
Before the watch, (before the watch, I say,)
Before the ward that waits therefore alway,
My soul, my sense, my secret thought, my sprite,
My will, my wish, my joy, and my delight,
Unto the Lord, that sits in heaven on high,
With hasty wing
From me doth fling,
And striveth still unto the Lord to fly.

O Israel! O household of the Lord!
O Abraham's sons! O brood of blessed seed!
O chosen sheep, that love the Lord indeed!
O hungry hearts! feed still upon his word,
And put your trust in Him with one accord.
For He hath mercy evermore at hand,
His fountains flow, his springs do never stand;
And plenteously He loveth to redeem
Such sinners all
As on Him call,
And faithfully his mercies most esteem.

He will redeem our deadly, drooping state,
He will bring home the sheep that go astray
He will help them that hope in Him alway,
He will appease our discord and debate,
He will soon save, though we repent us late.
He will be ours, if we continue his,
He will bring bale to joy and perfect bliss;
He will redeem the flock of his elect

bale - misery

From all that is
Or was amiss
Since Abraham's heirs did first his laws reject.

Excerpt from "The Steele Glas"

These knacks, my lord, I cannot call to mind;
Because they shew not in my glass of steel.
But holloa! here I see a wondrous sight,
I see a swarm of saints within my glass:
Behold, behold, I see a swarm indeed
Of holy saints which walk in comely wise,
Not decked in robes, nor garnished with gold,
But some unshod, yea some full thinly clothed,
And yet they seem so heavenly for to see
As if their eyes were all of diamonds,
Their face of rubies, sapphires, and jacinets,
Their comely beards and hair of silver wires
And to be short, they seem angelical.
What should they be, my lord, what should they be?

O gracious God, I see now what they be.
These be my priests which pray for every state,
These be my priests divorced from the world
And wedded yet to heaven and holiness,
Which are not proud, nor covet to be rich,
Which go not gay, nor feed on dainty food,
Which envy not nor know what malice means,
Which loath all lust, disdaining drunkenness,
Which cannot feign, which hate hypocrisy,
Which never saw Sir Simony's deceits,
Which preach of peace, which carp (chide) contentions,
Which loiter not but labour all the year,
Which thunder threats of God's most grievous wrath,
And yet do teach that mercy is in store.

Lo, these, my lord, be my good praying priests,
Descended from Melchisedec by line,
Cousins to Paul, to Peter, James and John,
These be my priests, the seasoning of the earth,
Which will not lease their savouriness I trow.
Not one of these, for twenty hundred groats,
Will teach the text that bids him take a wife,

And yet be cumbered with a concubine;
Not one of these will read the holy writ
Which doth forbid all greedy usury,
And yet receive a shilling for a pound;
Not one of these will preach of patience,
And yet be found as angry as a wasp;
Not one of these can be content to sit
In taverns, inns, or alehouses all day,
But spends his time devoutly at his books;
Not one of these will rail at rulers' wrongs,
And yet be bloated with extortion;
Not one of these will paint out worldly pride,
And be himself as gallant as he dare;
Not one of these rebuketh avarice,
And yet procureth proud pluralities;
Not one of these reproveth vanity,
Whiles he himself, with hawk upon his fist
And hounds at heel, doth quite forget his text;
Not one of these corrects contentions
For trifling things, and yet will sue for tithes;
Not one of these, not one of these, my lord,
Will be ashamed to do even as he teacheth.
My priests have learned to pray unto the Lord,
And yet they trust not in their lip-labour.
My priests can fast and use all abstinence
From vice and sin, and yet refuse no meats.
My priests can give in charitable wise
And love also to do good almes deeds,
Although they trust not in their own deserts.
My priests can place all penance in the heart,
Without regard of outward ceremonies.
My priests can keep their temples undefiled
And yet defy all superstition.

Lo now, my lord, what think you by my priests?
Although they were the last that shewed themselves,
I said at first their office was to pray,
And since the time is such even now-a-days
As hath great need of prayers truly prayed,
Come forth, my priests, and I will bid your beads:
I will presume, although I be no priest,
To bid you pray as Paul and Peter prayed.

Then pray, my priests, yea pray to God himself
That he vouchsafe, even for his Christes sake
To give his word free passage here on earth,
And that his church (which is now militant)
May soon be seen triumphant over all,
And that he deign to end this wicked world,
Which walloweth still in sinks of filthy sin.

BYRD, WILLIAM (c.1543-1623), chiefly noted as a musician and composer, wrote some fine lyrics as well. He was organist for Lincoln Cathedral at the age of twenty. In 1570 he was appointed a Gentleman of the Chapel. When he was twenty-nine, he joined Thomas Tallis as co-organist in the Chapel Royal of London. Byrd is credited with many influential contributions to church music, including solo songs, string fantasias, and verse anthems. His early motets include settings of hymns, responsories and antiphons based on Sarum chants (ecclesiastical musical forms in use at Salisbury from the 11th century). He published *Psalmes, sonets & songs of sadnes and pietie* in 1588. Most of his later music is written for the Roman rite, although Catholic services could only be held in strict privacy.

A Song

Let not the sluggish sleep
Close up thy waking eye,
Until with judgement deep
Thy daily deeds thou try:
He that one sin in conscience keeps
When he to quiet goes,
More venturous is than he that sleeps
With twenty mortal foes.

FLETCHER, GILES "the Elder" (c.1548-1611), was chiefly notable as a diplomat, although he was also a poet and author. He travelled to Scotland, Germany, Holland, and Russia. In 1588 he was sent to conclude an alliance with Tsar Fyodor I. He returned in 1589 and two years later published *Of Russe Common Wealth*, a comprehensive account of Russia, the land, government, church and customs. He also wrote some Latin poems and a series of love sonnets. He was the father of the poets (and playwrights) Giles and Phineas Fletcher.

Crucify Him!

Frail multitude, whose giddy law is list.
And best applause is windy flattering;
Most like the breath of which it doth consist,
No sooner blown but as soon vanishing,
As much desired as little profiting;
That makes the men that have it oft as light
As those that give it; which the proud invite,
And fear: the bad man's friend, the good man's hypocrite.

It was but now their sounding clamours sung,
'Blessed is he that comes from the Most High.'
And all the mountains with Hosanna rung;
And now, 'Away with him-away!' they cry.
And nothing can be heard but 'Crucify!'
It was but now the crown itself they gave,
And golden name of King unto him gave;
And now, no king but only Caesar they will have.
It was but now they gathered blooming may.
And of his arms disrobed the branching tree,
To strow with boughs and blossoms all thy way,
And now, the branchless trunk a cross for thee,
And may, dis-mayed, thy coronet must be.
It was but now they were so kind to throw
Their own best garments where thy feet should go,
And now, thyself they strip, and bleeding wounds they show.

VERSTEGAN, RICHARD (ROWLANDS) (c.1550-1640) son of a Dutch immigrant entered Oxford under the family Christian surname, Rowlands. He entered in 1565, but could not take a degree as a Catholic. About 1570 he became a goldsmith and engraver in London, also doing some printing and publishing a book on Campion's martyrdom in 1582. In 1583 his press was discovered and he had to flee to Paris. There he was arrested at the instigation of the English ambassador when he published an illustrated account of Catholic persecution in England. Cardinal William Allen secured his release, after which he travelled in Europe and settled in Antwerp in 1587. He became an important communication link for English Catholics, publishing and distributing many recusant books printed in Antwerp. He gradually became fully involved in Dutch life, particularly after his second marriage in 1610. He wrote, in four languages, not only many religious and political tracts, but epigrams and emblem verse as well as other forms of poetry.

Our Lady's Lullaby

Upon my lap my Sovereign sits,
And sucks upon my breast;
Meanwhile, His love sustains my life,
And gives my body rest.

> Sing lullaby, my little Boy.
> Sing lullaby, my life's joy.

When thou hast taken thy repast,
Repose, my Babe, on me;
So may thy Mother and thy Nurse
Thy cradle also be.

My Babe, my Bliss, my Child, my Choice,
My Fruit, my Flower, and Bud,
My Jesus, and my only Joy,
The Sum of all my good.

Thy fruit of death from Paradise
Made thee exiled mourn;
My fruit of life to Paradise
Makes joyful thy return.

The shepherds left their keeping sheep
For joy to see my Lamb;
How may I more rejoice to see
Myself to be the Dam.

Three kings their treasure hither brought
Of incense, myrrh and gold,
The heaven's Treasure and the King
That here they might behold.

One sort an angel did direct;
A star did guide the other;
And all the fairest Son to see
That ever had a mother.

> Sing lullaby, my little Boy.
> Sing lullaby, my life's Joy.

Times Go by Turns

The lopped tree in time may grow again;
Most naked plants renew both fruit and flower;
The sorriest wight may find release of pain,
The driest soil suck in some moistening shower;
Times go by turns and chances change by course,
From foul to fair, from better hap to worse.

The sea of Fortune doth not ever flow,
She draws her favors to the lowest ebb;
Her time hath equal times to come and go,
Her loom doth weave the fine and coarsest web;
No joy so great but runneth to an end,
No hap so hard but may in fine amend.

Not always full of leaf nor ever spring,
No endless night, yet not eternal day;
The saddest birds a season find to sing,
The roughest storm a calm may soon allay;
Thus with succeeding turns God tempereth all,
That man may hope to rise, yet fear to fall.

A chance may win that by mischance was lost;
The net that holds no great, takes little, fish;
In some things all, in all things none are crossed;
Few all they need, but none have all they wish;
Umeddled joys here to no man befall,
Who least, hath some; who most, hath never all.

SPENSER, EDMUND (1552/3–1599) is renowned as the author of *The Faerie Queen*, the long allegorical poem which is often ranked with Milton's *Paradise Lost* as nearly an English epic. It was at one time thought of as the English *Aeniad* glorifying Spenser's land and language as Virgil did his own. Spenser also wrote *The Shepheardes Calendar*, a series of ecologues, and a book of love sonnets, the *Amoretti*. He was for a time secretary to the lord deputy of Ireland, and neighbor there of Sir Walter Raleigh, who helped him in getting *The Faerie Queen* published. His remains are buried in Westminster Abbey.

Mutability

When I bethink me on that speech whilere,
Of Mutability, and well it weigh:

Me seems that though she all unworthy were
Of the Heav'ns Rule; yet very sooth to say,
In all things else she bears the greatest sway.
Which makes me loathe this state of life so tickle,
And love of things so vain to cast away;
Whose flow'ring pride, so fading and so fickle,
Short Time shall soon cut down with his consuming sickle.
Then gin I think on that which Nature said.
Of that same time when no more Change shall be,
But steadfast rest of all things firmly stayed
Upon the pillars of Eternity,
That is contrare to Mutability:
For, all that moveth, doth in Change delight:
But thence-forth all shall rest eternally
With Him that is the God of Sabbaoth hight:
O that great Sabbaoth God, grant me that Sabbaoth's sight.

Sonnet LXVIII from The Amoretti (Easter Morning)

Most glorious Lord of life, that on this day
Didst make Thy triumph over death and sin,
And having harrowed hell didst bring again
Captivity thence captive, us to win;
This joyous day, dear Lord, with joy begin,
And grant that we, for whom Thou diddest die,
Being with Thy dear blood clean washed from sin,
May live for ever in felicity;
And that Thy love we weighing worthily,
May likewise love Thee for the same again;
And for Thy sake that all like dear didst buy,
With love may one another entertain.
So let us love, dear love, like as we ought;
Love is the lesson which the Lord us taught.

Sonnet LXI from the Amoretti

The glorious image of the Maker's beauty,
My sovereign saint, the idol of my thought,
Dare not henceforth, above the bounds of duty,
T'accuse of pride, or rashly blame for ought.
For being, as she is, divinely wrought,
And of the brood of angels heavenly born,

And with the crew of blessed saints upbrought,
Each of which did her with their gifts adorn—
The bud of joy, the blossom of the morn,
The beam of light, whom mortal eyes admire;
What reason is it then but she should scorn
Base things that to her love too bold aspire!
Such heavenly forms ought rather worship be
Than dare be loved by men of mean degree.

An Hymn Of Heavenly Love

Before this world's great frame, in which all things
Are now contained, found any being place,
Ere flitting Time could wag his eyas wings
About that mighty bound which doth embrace
The rolling spheres, and parts their hours by space,
That high eternal power, which now doth move
In all these things, moved in itself by love.

It loved itself, because itself was fair,
For fair is loved; and of itself begot
Like to itself his eldest son and heir,
Eternal, pure, and void of sinful blot,
The firstling of his joy, in whom no jot
Of love's dislike or pride was to be found,
Whom he therefore with equal honour crowned.

　　　•　　•　　•　　•

Out of the bosom of eternal bliss,
In which He reigned with his glorious Sire.
He down descended, like a most demisse
And abject thrall, in flesh's frail attire,
That he for him might pay sin's deadly hire,
And him restore unto that happy state
In which he stood before his hapless fate.

　　　•　　•　　•　　•

O blessed Well of love! O Flower of grace!
O glorious Morning Star! O Lamp of light!
Most lively Image of Thy Father's face!
Eternal King of glory, Lord of might!
Meek Lamb of God, before all worlds behight!
How can we Thee requite for all this good?
Or what can prize with Thy most precious blood?

eyas - young eagle; demisse - submissive; thrall - slave; behight - promised; prize - be
equal in value

Yet nought Thou ask'st in lieu of all this love
But love of us, for guerdon of Thy pain:
Ay me! what can us less than that behove?
Had He required life for us again,
Had it been wrong to ask His own with gain?
He gave us life; He it restored lost;
Then life were least that us so little cost.

But He our life hath left unto us free,
Free that was thrall, and blessed that was banned;
Ne ought demands but that we loving be,
As He Himself hath loved us aforehand,
And bound thereto with an eternal band,
Him first to love that us so dearly bought,
And next our brethren, to His image wrought.

Him first to love great right and reason is,
Who first to us our life and being gave,
And after, when we fared had amiss,
Us wretches from the second death did save;
And last, the food of life, which now we have,
Even he himself, in his dear sacrament,
To feed our hungry souls, unto us lent.

Then next, to love our brethren that were made
Of that self mould, and that self Maker's hand,
That we, and to the same again shall fade,
Where they shall have like heritage of land,
However here on higher steps we stand;
Which also were with selfsame price redeemed,
That were, however, of us light esteemed.

And were they not, yet since that loving Lord
Commanded us to love them for his sake,
Even for his sake, and for his sacred word,
Which in his last bequest he to us spake,
We should them love, and with their needs partake;
Knowing that, whatsoever to them we give,
We give to him by whom we all do live.

Such mercy he by his most holy rede
Unto us taught, and to approve it true,
Ensampled it by his most righteous deed,
Shewing us mercy, miserable crew!

Ne ought - nor anything

That we the like should to the wretches shew,
And love our brethren; thereby to approve
How much himself that loved us we love.

Then rouse thyself, O earth! out of thy soil,
In which thou wallowest like to filthy swine,
And dost thy mind in dirty pleasures moyle,
Unmindful of that dearest Lord of thine;
Lift up to him thy heavy clouded eyne,
That thou this sovereign bounty mayst behold,
And read through love his mercies manifold.

Begin from first, where he encradled was
In simple cratch, wrapt in a wad of hay,
Between the toilful ox and humble ass;
And in what rags, and in what base array
The glory of our heavenly riches lay,
When him the silly shepherds came to see,
Whom greatest princes sought on lowest knee.

From thence read on the story of his life,
His humble carriage, his unfaulty ways,
His cankered foes, his fights, his toil, his strife,
His pains, his poverty, his sharp assays,
Through which he passed his miserable days,
Offending none, and doing good to all,
Yet being maliced both by great and small.

And look at last, how of most wretched wights
He taken was, betrayed, and false accused;
How with most scornful taunts and fell despites
He was reviled, disgraced, and foul abused;
How scourged, how crowned, how buffeted, how bruised;
And, lastly, how 'twixt robbers crucified,
With bitter wounds through hands, through feet, and side!

•   •   •   •   •

With sense whereof whilst so thy softened spirit
Is inly touched, and humbled with meek zeal
Through meditation of his endless merit,
Lift up thy mind to th' author of thy weal,
And to his sovereign mercy do appeal;
Learn him to love that loved thee so dear,
And in thy breast his blessed image bear.

assays - trials

With all thy heart, with all thy soul and mind,
Thou must him love, and his behests embrace;
All other loves with which the world doth blind
Weak fancies, and stir up affections base,
Thou must renounce and utterly displace,
And give thyself unto him full and free,
That full and freely gave himself to thee.

Thenceforth all world's desire will in thee die,
And all earth's glory, on which men do gaze,
Seem dust and dross in thy pure-sighted eye,
Compared to that celestial beauty's blaze,
Whose glorious beams all fleshly sense do daze
With admiration of their passing light,
Blinding the eyes and lumining the sprite.

Then shalt thy ravished soul inspired be
With heavenly thoughts far above human skill,
And thy bright radiant eyes shall plainly see
The Idea of his pure glory present still
Before thy face, that all thy spirits shall fill
With sweet enragement of celestial love,
Kindled through sight of those fair things above.

SIDNEY, Sir PHILIP (1554–1586), Oxford educated soldier, statesman, and poet, was knighted in 1583 after serving several years in Parliament for Kent. He was much favored by Queen Elizabeth. Although the fact that he addressed his Petrarchan love sonnets chiefly to another man's wife can hardly be commended, the influence of those sonnets did much to popularize the sonnet sequence. Shakespeare's sonnets are said to be considerably influenced by Sidney's. He also established the pastoral romance with his *Arcadia*, written in both prose and lyrical poetry. His essay *An Apologie for Poetry* is perhaps the best of Elizabethan criticism. Spenser eulogized Sidney in *Astrophel*, after Sidney was killed in battle. According to Fulke Greville, who wrote a biography of him, Sidney refused a drink of water as he was dying on the battlefield, offering it instead to a wounded soldier, saying, "Thy necessity is greater than mine."

Splendidis Longum Valedico Nugis
(A Long farewell to glittering trifles)

Leave me, O Love, which reachest but to dust;
And thou, my mind, aspire to higher things;

Grow rich in that which never taketh rust:
What ever fades, but fading pleasure brings.
Draw in thy beams, and humble all thy might
To that sweet yoke where lasting freedoms be;
Which breaks the clouds and opens forth the light
That doth both shine and give us sight to see,
O take fast hold; let that light be thy guide,
In this small course which birth draws out to death;
And think how evil becometh him to slide
Who seeketh heaven, and comes of heavenly breath.
Then farewell, world; thy uttermost I see:
Eternal Love, maintain thy life in me.

RALEGH (RALEIGH), Sir WALTER (1554-1618), an English adventurer, was a favorite of Queen Elizabeth. He was knighted in 1585 and became captain of the Queen's guard in 1587. He was the force behind the ill-fated American colony on Roanoke, the famous "Lost Colony." He also led expeditions to Guyana in South America. He was neighbor to Edmund Spenser in Ireland, and helped Spenser get *The Faerie Queen* published in London. His last royal appointment was as governor of Jersey (the Channel Islands), but he was accused of treason by Elizabeth's successor, James I, and imprisoned in the Tower of London from 1603 to 1616. He was finally beheaded, but not before he wrote some beautiful poems of faith.

The Passionate Man's Pilgrimage

Give me my scallop-shell of Quiet;
My staff of Faith to walk upon;
My scrip of Joy, immortal diet;
My bottle of Salvation;
My gown of Glory, hope's true gage;
And thus I'll take my pilgrimage.
Blood must be my body's balmer—
No other balm will there be given—
Whilst my soul like a white palmer
Travels to the land of Heaven;
Over the silver mountains,
Where spring the nectar fountains—
And there I'll kiss
The bowl of Bliss.

scallop shell: badge of a person on pilgrimage; scrip - wallet or small pack; palmer - pilgrim

And drink my everlasting fill
On every milken hill.
My soul will be a-dry before,
But after, it will ne'er thirst more;
And by the happy blissful way
More peaceful pilgrims I shall see,
That have shook off their gowns of clay
And go appareled fresh like me.
I'll bring them first
To slake their thirst,
And then to taste those nectar suckets,
At the clear wells
Where sweetness dwells,
Drawn up by saints in crystal buckets.
And when our bottles and all we
Are filled with immortality,
Then the holy paths we'll travel,
Strewed with rubies thick as gravel,
Ceilings of diamonds, sapphire floors,
High walls of coral, and pearl bowers.
From thence to heaven's bribeless hall
Where no corrupted voices brawl;
No conscience molten into gold;
Nor forged accusers bought and sold;
No cause deferred; nor vain-spent journey;
For there Christ is the King's Attorney,
Who pleads for all without degrees,
And he hath angels, but no fees.
When the grand twelve million jury
Of our sins and sinful fury,
'Gainst our souls black verdicts give,
Christ pleads his death, and then we live.
Be thou my speaker, taintless Pleader,
Unblotted Lawyer, true Proceeder,
Thou movest salvation even for alms,
Not with a bribed lawyer's palms.
And this is my eternal plea
To him that made heaven, earth, and sea,
Seeing my flesh must die so soon,
And want a head to dine next noon,—

suckets - candies; angel - word-play on angel, being also the common name for a gold
coin of the day.

Just at the stroke when my veins start and spread,
Set on my soul an everlasting head.
Then I am ready, like a palmer fit,
To tread those blest paths which before I writ.
Of death and judgment, heaven and hell
Who oft doth think, must needs die well.

Verses Found In His Bible In The Gatehouse At Westminster

Even such is time, which takes in trust
Our youth, our joys, and all we have,
And pays us nought but age and dust,
Which in the dark and silent grave,
When we have wandered all our ways,
Shuts up the story of our days;
And from which grave, and earth, and dust,
The Lord shall raise me up I trust.

The Lie

Tell them that brave it most,
They beg for more by spending,
Who, in their greatest cost,
Seek nothing but commending:
And if they make reply,
Then give them all the lie.

Tell zeal it wants devotion;
Tell love it is but lust;
Tell time it is but motion;
Tell flesh it is but dust:
And wish them not reply,
For thou must give the lie.

Tell age it daily wasteth;
Tell honour how it alters;
Tell beauty how she blasteth;
Tell favour how it falters:
And as they shall reply,
Give every one the lie.

Tell wit how much it wrangles
In tickle points of niceness;

Tell wisdom she entangles
Herself in over-wiseness:
And when they do reply,
Straight give them both the lie.

Tell physic of her boldness;
Tell skill it is pretension;
Tell charity of coldness;
Tell law it is contention:
And as they do reply,
So give them still the lie.

Tell fortune of her blindness;
Tell nature of decay;
Tell friendship of unkindness;
Tell justice of delay:
And if they will reply,
Thou give them all the lie.

Tell arts they have no soundness,
But vary by esteeming;
Tell schools they want profoundness,
And stand too much on seeming:
If arts and schools reply,
Give arts and schools the lie.

Tell faith it's fled the city;
Tell how the country erreth;
Tell manhood shakes off pity;
Tell virtue least preferreth:
And if they do reply,
Spare not to give the lie.

So when thou hath, as I
Commanded thee, done blabbing,—
Although to give the lie
Deserves no less than stabbing,—
Stab at thee he that will,
No stab the soul can kill.

Go, Soul, the body's guest,
Upon a thankless arrant:
Fear not to touch the best,
The truth shall be thy warrant:

Go, since I needs must die,
And give the world the lie.

Say to the court, it glows
And shines like rotten wood;
Say to the church, it shows
What's good, and doth no good:
If church and court reply,
Then give them both the lie.

Tell potentates, they live
Acting by others' action;
Not loved unless they give,
Not strong but by a faction:
If potentates reply,
Give potentates the lie.

Tell men of high condition,
That manage the estate,
Their purpose is ambition,
Their practice only hate:
And if they once reply,
Then give them all the lie.

GREVILLE, FULKE, First Baron Brooke (1554–1628), like most of the poets of his age was involved with the court, in his case as a favorite of the Queen and a diplomat to Europe. He became treasurer of the navy in 1598, and a Knight of the Bath after James I came to the throne, being made chancellor of the Exchequer in 1614 and a baron in 1621. Like many others in Elizabethan England, he leaned toward Calvinistic or Puritan Christianity. He wrote verse treatises and plays, including the tragedy *Mustapha*. His sonnet collection, *Caelica*, differed in tone from many contemporary cycles in its ironic realism. His poem "Humane Learning" is skeptical of the value of worldly education and he emphasizes practical knowledge as did his friend Francis Bacon. He was "a constant courtier of the ladies," but never married. He died of stab wounds received from a manservant.

Sonnet lxxxix

The Manicheans did no idols make
Without themselves, nor worship gods of wood,
Yet idols did in their Ideas take,
And figured Christ as on the cross he stood.

Thus did they when they earnestly did pray,
Till clearer Faith this idol took away.

We seem more inwardly to know the Son,
And see our own salvation in his blood.
When this is said, we think the work is done,
And with the Father hold our portion good,
As if true life within these words were laid
For him that in life never words obeyed.

If this be safe, it is a pleasant way,
The cross of Christ is very easily borne,
But six days' labour makes the sabbath day,
The flesh is dead before grace can be born,
The heart must first bear witness with the book,
The earth must burn, ere we for Christ can look.

Sonnet xcvii

Eternall Truth, almighty, infinite,
Onely exiled from man's fleshly heart,
Where ignorance and disobedience fight,
In hell and sinne, which shall have greatest part:
When thy sweet mercy opens forth the light,
Of Grace which giveth eyes unto the blind,
And with the Law even plowest up our sprite
To faith, wherein flesh may salvation finde:
Thou bidst us pray, and wee doe pray to thee,
But as to power and God without us plac'd,
Thinking a wish may weare out vanity,
Or habits be by miracles defac'd.
One thought to God wee give, the rest to sinne,
Quickely unbent is all desire of good,
True words passe out, but have no being within,
Wee pray to Christ, yet helpe to shed his blood;
For while wee say beliefe, and feele it not,
Promise amends, and yet despaire in it,
Heare Sodom judg'd, and goe not out with Lot,
Make Law and Gospell riddles of the wit:

We with the Jewes even Christ still crucifie,
As not yet come to our impiety.

Sonnet xcix

Downe in the depth of mine iniquity,
That ugly center of infernall spirits,
Where each sinne feels her owne deformity,
In these peculiar torments she inherits,
Depriv'd of human graces, and divine,
Even there appeares this saving God of mine.

Sonnet civ

O False and treacherous Probability,
Enemy of truth, and friend to wickednesse;
With whose bleare eyes opinion learnes to see,
Truth's feeble party here, and barrennesse.
When thou hast thus misled Humanity,
And lost obedience in the pride of wit,
With reason dar'st thou judge the Deity,
And in thy flesh make bold to fashion it.
Vaine thought, the word of Power a riddle is,
And till the vayles be rent, the flesh newborne,
Reveales no wonders of that inward blisse,
Which but where faith is, every where findes scorne;
Who therfore censures God with fleshly sprite,
As well in time may wrap up infinite.

sprite - spirit

Sonnet cv

Three things there be in Mans opinion deare,
Fame, many Friends, and Fortunes dignities.
False visions all, which in our sense appeare,
To sanctifie desires Idolatry.
For what is Fortune, but a wat'ry glasse?
Whose chrystall forehead wants a steely backe,
Where raine and stormes blowe all away that was,
Whose ship alike both depths and shallowes wracke.
Fame againe, which from blinding power takes light,
Both Caesar's shadow is, and Cato's friend,
The child of humour, not allyed to right,
Living by oft exchange of winged end.
And many Friends, false strength of feeble mind,

Betraying equals, as true slaves to might;
Like Ecchoes still send voyces down the wind,
But never in adversity finde right.
Then Man, though vertue of extremities
The middle be, and so hath two to one,
By Place and Nature constant enemies,
And against both these no strength but her owne,
Yet quit thou for her, Friends, Fame, Fortune's throne;
Divels there many be, and Gods but one.

Stanzas from A Treatise of Religion

What is the chain which draws us back again,
And lifts man up unto his first creation?
Nothing in him his own heart can restrain
His reason lives a captive to temptation;
Example is corrupt; precepts are mixed;
All fleshly knowledge frail, and never fixed.

It is a light, a gift, a grace inspired;
A spark of power, a goodness of the Good
Desire in him, that never is desired;
An unity, where desolation stood;
In us, not of us, a Spirit not of earth,
Fashioning the mortal to immortal birth.

    •   •   •   •

Sense of this God, by fear, the sensual have,
Distressed Nature crying unto Grace;
For sovereign reason then becomes a slave,
And yields to servile sense her sovereign place,
When more or other she affects to be
Than seat or shrine of this Eternity.

Yea, Prince of Earth let Man assume to be,
Nay more—of Man let Man himself be God,
Yet without God, a slave of slaves is he;
To others, wonder; to himself, a rod;
Restless despair, desire, and desolation;
The more secure, the more abomination.

Then by affecting power, we cannot know him.
By knowing all things else, we know him less.
Nature contains him not. Art cannot show him.

Opinions idols, and not God, express.
Without, in power, we see him everywhere;
Within, we rest not, till we find him there.

Then seek we must; that course is natural—
For owned souls to find their owner out.
Our free remorses when our natures fall—
When we do well, our hearts made free from doubt—
Prove service due to one Omnipotence,
And Nature of religion to have sense.

Questions again, which in our hearts arise—
Since loving knowledge, not humility—
Though they be curious, godless, and unwise,
Yet prove our nature feels a Deity;
For if these strifes rose out of other grounds,
Man were to God as deafness is to sounds.

    •   •   •   •

Yet in this strife, this natural remorse,
If we could bend the force of power and wit
To work upon the heart, and make divorce
There from the evil, which preventeth it,
In judgment of the truth we should not doubt
Good life would find a good religion out.

KETHE, WILLIAM (fl. 1555–93), one of the early Scots Psalm paraphrasers, was probably a Puritan. He fled the Marian Persecution in 1555, going first to Frankfurt and then to Geneva. He translated what is known as the *Geneva Bible*, the version most used by Puritans, including those who brought it to America on the *Mayflower*. He contributed twenty-five paraphrases of Psalms to the Anglo-Genevan metrical Psalter. They were reprinted in the Sternhold and Hopkins *One and Fiftie Psalmes of David in Englishe Metre* in 1562 and in the *Scottish Psalter* in 1564. The one included here has long been called "Old Hundredth" from Psalm 100. The tune, by Louis Bourgeois, had a "sprightly" rhythm originally and Albert Edward Bailey, in *The Gospel in Hymns*, says "it was tunes like these that won from Queen Elizabeth the scornful term for hymns, 'Geneva jiggs'."

Scotch Te Deum

All people that on earth do dwell,
Sing to the Lord with cheerful voice;

Him serve with mirth, His praise forth tell,
Come Ye before Him and rejoice.

The Lord ye know is God indeed.
Without our aid He did us make;
We are His folk, He doth us feed,
And for His sheep he doth us take.

O enter then His gates with praise,
Approach with joy His courts unto;
Praise, laud, and bless His name always,
For it is seemly so to do.

For why? the Lord our God is good,
His mercy is forever sure;
His truth at all times firmly stood
And shall from age to age endure.

MARCKANT, JOHN (fl. c. 1560) was a priest at Clacton Magna (1559) and Shopland (1563–8), but is otherwise known only as author of several short works: a political poem on Lord Wentworth (1558–9); a New Year's gift intitled "With speed return to God"; and "Verses to divers good purposes" (c.1580–1). He contributed four psalms to the 1562 edition of the *Old Metrical Version of the Psalms*, which originally was published by Thomas Sternhold in 1549, and went through many expanded editions thereafter.

The Lamentation
(Old Version, 1562)

O Lord, turn not away thy face
From him that lies prostrate,
Lamenting sore his sinful life
Before thy mercy-gate;

Which gate thou openest wide to those
That do lament their sin:
Shut not that gate against me, Lord,
But let me enter in.

So come I to thy mercy-gate,
Where mercy doth abound,
Requiring mercy for my sin
To heal my deadly wound.

> Mercy, good Lord, mercy I ask,
> This is the total sum;
> For mercy, Lord, is all my suit:
> Lord, let thy mercy come.

SOUTHWELL, ROBERT (c. 1561–1595), born in Norfolk, was sent by his parents to Douai in France, which drew many disenfranchised English Catholics. He was ordained a Jesuit priest in 1584 and requested that he be sent back to England, although his presence there for more than forty days was illegal and punishable by death. His request was granted, and he spent six years ministering secretly to English Catholics before he was arrested. He was imprisoned and repeatedly tortured for three years, being finally hanged at Tyburn in 1595. He wrote a number of religious tracts before, and much of his poetry after he was imprisoned. Ben Jonson is quoted as saying, "I would willingly tear up many of my works to be the author of 'The Burning Babe'."

New Prince, New Pomp

> Behold, a Silly, tender Babe,
> In freezing winter night,
> In homely manger trembling lies,
> Alas! a piteous sight.
> The inns are full, no man will yield
> This little pilgrim bed;
> But forced is He with silly beasts
> In crib to shroud His head.
> Despise Him not for lying there;
> First what He is enquire;
> As orient pearl is often found
> In depth of dirty mire.
> Weigh not His crib, His wooden dish,
> Nor beasts that by Him feed;
> Weigh not His mother's poor attire,
> Nor Joseph's simple weed.
> This stable is a Prince's court,
> The crib His chair of state;
> The beasts are parcel of His pomp,
> The wooden dish His plate.
> The persons in that poor attire
> His royal liveries wear;
> This Prince Himself, is come from heaven;

silly - innocent, helpless.

This pomp is prized there.
With joy approach, O Christian wight!
Do homage to thy King;
And highly praise this humble pomp
Which He from Heaven doth bring.

A Child My Choice

Let folly praise that fancy loves, I praise and love that child
Whose heart no thought, whose tongue no word,
        whose hand no deed defiled.
I praise him most, I love him best, all praise and love is his;
While him I love, in him I live, and cannot live amiss.
Love's sweetest mark, laud's highest theme,
        man's most desired light,
To love him life, to leave him death, to live in him delight.
He mine by gift, I his by debt, thus each to other due,
First friend he was, best friend he is, all times will try him true.
Though young, yet wise; though small, yet strong;
        though man, yet God he is;
As wise he knows, as strong he can, as God he loves to bliss.
His knowledge rules, his strength defends,
        his love doth cherish all;
His birth our joy, his life our light, his death our end of thrall.
Alas! he weeps, he sighs, he pants, yet do his angels sing;
Out of his tears, his sighs and throbs, doth bud a joyful spring.
Almighty Babe, whose tender arms can force all foes to fly,
Correct my faults, protect my life, direct me when I die!

The Burning Babe

As I in hoary winter's night stood shivering in the snow,
Surprised I was with sudden heat which made my heart to glow;
And lifting up a fearful eye to view what fire was near,
A pretty babe all burning bright did in the air appear;
Who, scorched with excessive heat, such floods of tears did shed
As though his floods should quench his flames which with his tears
    were fed.
'Alas,' quoth he, ' but newly born in fiery heats I fry,
Yet none approach to warm their hearts or feel my fire but I!
My faultless breast the furnace is, the fuel wounding thorns,
Love is the fire, and sighs the smoke, the ashes shames and scorns;

The fuel justice layeth on, and mercy blows the coals,
The metal in this furnace wrought are men's defiled souls,
For which, as now on fire I am, to work them to their good,
So will I melt into a bath to wash them in my blood!'
With this he vanished out of sight, and swiftly shrunk away,
And straight I called unto mind that it was Christmas day.

Of the Blessed Sacrament of the Aulter

The angells' eyes, whome veyles cannot deceive,
Might best disclose that best they do descerne;
Men must with sounde and silent faith receive
More then they can by sence or reason lerne;
God's poure our proofes, His workes our witt exceede,
The doer's might is reason of His deede.

A body is endew'd with ghostly rightes;
And Nature's worke from Nature's law is free;
In heavenly sunne lye hidd eternall lightes,
Lightes cleere and neere, yet them no eye can see;
Dedd formes a never-dyinge life do shroude;
A boundlesse sea lyes in a little cloude.

The God of hoastes in slender hoste doth dwell,
Yea, God and man with all to ether dewe,
That God that rules the heavens and rifled hell,
That man whose death did us to life renewe:
That God and man that is the angells' blisse,
In forme of bredd and wyne our nurture is.

Whole may His body be in smallest breadd,
Whole in the whole, yea whole in every crumme;
With which be one or be tenn thowsand fedd,
All to ech one, to all but one doth cumme;
And though ech one as much as all receive,
Not one too much, nor all too little have.

One soule in man is all in everye part;
One face at once in many mirrhors shynes
One fearefull noyse doth make a thowsand start;
One eye at once of countlesse thinges defynes;
If proofes of one in many, Nature frame,
God may in straunger sort performe the same.

God present is at once in everye place,
Yett God in every place is ever one;
So may there be by giftes of ghostly grace,
One man in many roomes, yett filling none;
Sith angells may effects of bodyes shewe,
God angells' giftes on bodyes may bestowe.

I Dye Alive

O life! what letts thee from a quicke decease?
O death! what drawes thee from a present praye?
My feast is done, my soule would be at ease,
My grace is saide; O death! come take awaye.

I live, but such a life as ever dyes;
I dye, but such a death as never endes;
My death to end my dying life denyes,
And life my living death no whitt amends.

Thus still I dye, yet still I do revive;
My living death by dying life is fedd;
Grace more then nature kepes my hart alive,
Whose idle hopes and vayne desires are deade.

Not where I breathe, but where I love, I live;
Not where I love, but where I am, I die;
The life I wish, must future glory give,
The deaths I feele in present daungers lye.

HERBERT, MARY, COUNTESS OF PEMBROKE (1561–1621), younger sister of Philip Sidney is noted as a writer and a literary patroness. Her brother wrote the first version of *Arcadia* for her. She became his executrix after his death in 1586, overseeing publication of various of his works. She completed the Psalm translations her brother had begun. He completed the first 42 in a variety of verse forms. A selection of them was published by Ruskin in 1877 as *Rock Honeycomb*. In 1592 two works which she translated were published: Du Plessis Mornay's *Discourse of Life and Death*, and R. Garnier's Senecan tragedy, *Antonius*. Later she translated Petrarch's *Trionfo della morte*. Among her literary friends were Edmund Spenser, Ben Jonson, Samuel Daniel (who was tutor to her son, William), Nicholas Breton, and Sir John Harington. She is reputed to have been acquainted with Shakespeare, and her son William (3rd earl of Pembroke) is thought possibly to be the "W. H." of Shakespeare's sonnets. William Browne wrote a famous epitaph about her: Underneath this sable hearse / Lies the subject of all verse: / Sidney's sister, Pembrokes' mother; / Death, ere thou hast slain another, Fair, / and learn'd, and good as she, / Time shall throw a dart at thee.

Verses from **Our Saviour's Passion**

He placed all rest, and had no resting place;
He healed each pain, yet lived in sore distress;
Deserved all good, yet lived in great disgrace;
Gave all hearts joy, himself in heaviness;
Suffered them live, by whom himself was slain:
Lord, who can live to see such love again?

Whose mansion heaven, yet lay within a manger;
Who gave all food, yet sucked a virgin's breast;
Who could have killed, yet fled a threatening danger;
Who sought all quiet by his own unrest;
Who died for them that highly did offend him,
And lives for them that cannot comprehend him.

Who came no further than his Father sent him,
And did fulfil but what he did command him;
Who prayed for them that proudly did torment him
For telling truly of what they did demand him;
Who did all good that humbly did intreat him,
And bare their blows, that did unkindly beat him.

Had I but seen him as his servants did,
At sea, at land, in city, or in field,
Though in himself he had his glory hid,
That in his grace the light of glory held,
Then might my sorrow somewhat be appeased,
That once my soul had in his sight been pleased.

No! I have ran the way of wickedness,
Forgetting what my faith should follow most;
I did not think upon thy holiness,
Nor by my sins what sweetness I have lost.
Oh sin! for sin hath compassed me about,
That, Lord, I know not where to find thee out.

Where he that sits on the supernal throne,
In majesty most glorious to behold,
And holds the sceptre of the world alone,

Hath not his garments of embroidered gold,
But he is clothed with truth and righteousness,
Where angels all do sing with joyfulness,

Where heavenly love is cause of holy life,
And holy life increaseth heavenly love;
Where peace established without fear or strife,
Doth prove the blessing of the soul's behove;
Where thirst nor hunger, grief nor sorrow dwelleth,
But peace in joy, and joy in peace excelleth.

behove - need

SYLVESTER, JOSUAH (1563–1618), was young when both his parents died. At age ten a relative sent him to a select school, where he was required to converse in French. He entered a trading firm after three years, and had a difficult time gaining promotion. Meanwhile he wrote poetry and dedicated it to various desirable patrons, receiving little return or attention. In 1613 he obtained a secretaryship in the Merchant Adventurers of Stade. His most notable literary work is his translations of the scriptural epics of the Gascon Huguenot, Guillaume de Saluste, seigneur du Bartas (1544–1590). Du Bartas's poetry was translated into many languages, and particularly found popularity among the Germans and the English. According to Southey, Sylvester shared the title of most popular poet with Spenser in the reign of James I. These two authors' works were the principle literary influences on the youthful Milton and impressed the young Dryden. The latter did not regard them very highly in his maturity. Sylvester's translations of Du Bartas were especially popular among Puritans. Anne Bradstreet speaks of Du Bartas as the Christian poet laureate.

The Father

Alpha and Omega, God alone:
Eloi, My God, the Holy-One;
Whose Power is Omnipotence:
Whose Wisedome is Omni-science:
Whose Beeing is All Soveraigne Blisse:
Whose Worke Perfection's Fulnesse is;
Under All things, not under-cast;
Over All things, not over-plac't;

Within All things, not there included;
Without All things, not thence excluded:
Above All, over All things raigning;

Beneath All, All things aye sustayning:
Without All, All conteyning sole:
Within All, filling-full the Whole:
Within All, no where comprehended;
Without All, no where more extended;
Under, by nothing over-topped:
Over, by nothing under-propped:

Unmov'd, Thou mov'st the World about;
Unplac't, Within it, or Without:
Unchanged, time-lesse, Time Thou changest:
Th' unstable, Thou, still stable, rangest;
No outward Force, nor inward Fate,
Can Thy dread Essence alterate:

To-day, To-morrow, yester-day,
With Thee are One, and instant aye;
Aye undivided, ended never:
To-day, with Thee, indures for-ever.

Thou, Father, mad'st this mighty Ball;
Of nothing thou created'st All,
After th' Idea of thy Minde,
Conferring Forme to every kinde.
Thou wert, Thou art, Thou wilt be ever;
And Thine Elect, rejectest never.

MARLOWE, CHRISTOPHER (baptized 1564–1593), was a significant poet and playwright in Elizabethan England. His plays introduced the inner conflicts of the main character as a central issue of drama, which continued central in the work of Shakespeare and subsequent dramatists. He also initiated the use of blank verse in drama. He apparently worked as an espionage agent for the crown while at Cambridge and continued in that capacity most of his life. *Tamburlane the Great* was the only of his plays to be published during his lifetime. Marlowe was killed in a tavern brawl. Others of his major works are *The Tragicall History of Dr. Faustus, The Famous Tragedy of the Rich Jew of Malta,* and *The Troublesome Raigne and Lamentable Death of Edward the Second, King of England.*

Excerpts from the play, **Dr. Faustus**
[Doctor Faustus speaking after he has made his bargain with Lucifer
and received Mephistophilis for his servant:]

Had I as many souls as there be stars,
I'd give them all for Mephistophilis.

By him I'll be great emperor of the world,
And make a bridge thorough the moving air,
To pass the ocean with a band of men:
I'll join the hills that bind the Afric shore,
And make that country continent to Spain,
And both contributory to my crown.
The Emperor shall not live but by my leave.
Nor any potentate of Germany.
Now that I have obtain'd what I desire,
I'll live in speculation of this art
Till Mephistophilis return again.

[Mephistophilis answering Faustus's questions about hell and
about how Mephisto can be serving Faustus outside of it:]

Why, this is hell, nor am I out of it:
Think'st thou that I, that saw the face of God,
And tasted the eternal joys of heaven,
Am not tormented with ten thousand hells,
In being deprived of everlasting bliss?. . .
Hell hath no limits, nor is circumscribed
In one self-place; but where we are is hell,
And where hell is, there must we ever be:
And to be short, when all the world dissolves,
And every creature shall be purified,
All places shall be hell that are not heaven.

[Faustus speaking, when Mephistophilis makes Helen of Troy appear:]

Was this the face that launch'd a thousand ships,
And burnt the topless towers of Ilium?
Sweet Helen, make me immortal with a kiss.
Her lips suck forth my soul: see, where it flies.
Come, Helen, come, give me my soul again.
Here will I dwell, for heaven is in these lips,
And all is dross that is not Helena. . . .
O, thou art fairer than the evening air
Clad in the beauty of a thousand stars;
Brighter art thou than flaming Jupiter
When he appear'd to hapless Semele. . .

Ilium - Troy; hapless Semele - Semele was a mortal woman whom Jupiter loved. He once
promised to grant any request she should make. Her request was that he should show
himself to her as full-dressed king of the gods as he appeared on Mount Olympus.
Jupiter resisted; but Semele was insistent. When Jupiter appeared before her in full regalia
she was consumed by his thunderbolts.

SHAKESPEARE, WILLIAM (1564–1616), son of a tradesman and town official, is thought to have gone to grammar school to study Latin and classical works. He did not attend any university, but married Anne Hathaway in 1582. They had several children, including one boy, Hamnet, who died at eleven years old. Stories abound about Shakespeare's early manhood, but the first sure reference to his involvement with the theatre is a brief sarcastic paragraph written in 1592. He is thought to have written the three plays, *Henry VI, Richard III,* and *The Comedy of Errors* before then. By 1596, he had probably written five more plays including *A Midsummer's Night's Dream* and *Romeo and Juliet.* That year his father applied for a coat of arms. By 1597, William was able to purchase a large house in his native town. Probably from 1594 he was a member of the Lord Chamberlain's players (The King's Men under James I). Their leading actor was James Burbage, their theatre, *the Globe,* and their playwright, Shakespeare. He dedicated himself to writing plays for twenty years. Two of his sonnets appeared in *The Passionate Pilgrim* in 1599, but the rest were published in 1609 for the first time. It is not known when they were actually written. His last three plays, performed for the first time in 1611-1613, are thought to be *The Tempest, Henry VIII,* and *The Two Noble Kinsmen.* He lived for a time with a Huguenot family in London. On the evidence of a court case he was a congenial and familiar border. His will is often noted for his giving his wife his "second-best bed," as an afterthought. No one is certain what was intended by this legacy. He was buried in the parish church of Stratford-on-Avon beneath a memorial, possibly of his own composition:

> Good friend, for Jesus' sake forbear
> To dig the dust enclosed here.
> Blest be the man that spares these stones,
> And curst be he that moves my bones.

While many of the themes and subjects of Shakespeare's plays and sonnets reflect the Christian influences all around him, there is little in his work from which to draw certain conclusions concerning the personal faith of the author. No English author had had more influence on our literature nor any works more influence on our language (excepting the King James Bible) than Shakespeare and his plays.

Sonnet CXLVI

> Poor soul, the centre of my sinful earth,
> Fooled by these rebel powers that thee array,
> Why dost thou pine within and suffer dearth,
> Painting thy outward walls so costly gay?
> Why so large cost, having so short a lease,

Dost thou upon thy fading mansion spend?
Shall worms, inheritors of this excess,
Eat up thy charge? Is this thy body's end?
Then, soul, live thou upon thy servant's loss,
And let that pine to aggravate thy store;
Buy terms divine in selling hours of dross;
Within be fed, without be rich no more:
So shalt thou feed on Death, that feeds on men,
And Death once dead, there's no more dying then.

NASHE (NASH), THOMAS (1567–1601), was a Cambridge graduate and one of the "University Wits," a group of young men, including Christopher Marlowe, who went from college to pursue literary careers in London. He was involved in a pamphlet war between Puritans and the Anglican hierarchy, "The Marprelate Controversy." Hired or encouraged by the Anglican authorities, he wrote several tracts in 1589 in reply to the pseudonymous "Martin Marprelate." Satire and controversy seem to have been his strong suits. He wrote *Pierce Penniless, His Supplication to the Devil* (1592) as a satire on contemporary society and attacked Gabriel Harvey in a heavy duel of literary repartee in 1593. He published a reconciliatory preface to *Christ's Tears over Jerusalem* in 1593, but in response to further attack by Harvey, counterattacked again. In 1599 the Archbishop of Canterbury ordered that all the writings produced in this controversy be burned and forbade their reprinting. Among Nashe's other works are *The Unfortunate Traveller, or the Life of Jack Wilton* (1594). It is a prose romance and a precursor to the English (picaresque) novel. One of Nashe's plays is still extant, *Summer's Last Will and Testament* (1593). He is thought to have worked with both Christopher Marlowe and Ben Jonson on dramatic works and their production.

Litany In Time of Plague

Adieu; fare-well earth's bliss,
This world uncertain is:
Fond are life's lustful joys,
Death proves them all but toys.
None from his darts can fly:
I am sick, I must die—
Lord have mercy on us!

Rich men, trust not in wealth.
Gold cannot buy you health;
Physic himself must fade;

All things to end are made;
The plague full swift goes by;
I am sick, I must die—
Lord have mercy on us!

Beauty is but a flower,
Which wrinkles will devour;
Brightness falls from the air;
Queens have died young and fair;
Dust hath closed Helen's eye;
I am sick, I must die—
Lord have mercy on us!

Strength stoops unto the grave;
Worms feed on Hector brave;
Swords may not fight with fate;
Earth still holds ope her gate.
Come, come, the bells do cry;
I am sick, I must die—
Lord have mercy on us!

Wit with his wantonness,
Tasteth death's bitterness.
Hell's executioner
Hath no ears for to hear
What vain art can reply;
I am sick, I must die—
Lord have mercy on us!

Haste therefore each degree
To welcome destiny:
Heaven is our heritage,
Earth but a player's stage.
Mount we unto the sky;
I am sick, I must die—
Lord have mercy on us!

ANONYMOUS (The following two poems are from *The Gude and Godlie Ballatis,*
1567)

Ane Sang of the Birth of Christ, with the Tune of Baw Lula Low
[A translation of Luther's hymn for Christmas Eve 'Vom himel hoch da
kom ich her'. The first six stanzas are here omitted.]

My saul and life stand up and see
Wha lyis in ane crib of tree.
What Babe is that, sa gude and fair?
It is Christ, Goddis son and heir.

Welcome now, gracious God of micht,
To sinners vile, puir, and unricht.
Thou come to save us from distress;
How can we thank thy gentleness?

God that made all creature,
How art thou now becumit sa puir,
That on the hay and stray will lie,
Amang the asses, oxen, and kye!

And war the warld ten times sa wide,
Cled owre with gold and stanes of pride,
Unworthy it war, yet to thee,
Under thy feet ane stool to be.

The silk and sandell thee to ease,
Are hay, and simple sweilling claes,
Wherein thou glories, greatest King,
As thou in heaven war in thy Ring.

Thou took sic painis temporal,
To make me rich perpetual,
For all this warldis wealth and gude
Can nathing rich thy celsitude.

O my dear heart, young Jesus sweet,
Prepare thy cradle for my spreit,
And I sall rock thee in my heart,
And never mair fra thee depart.

But I sall praise thee evermore
With sangis sweet unto thy gloir;
The knees of my heart sall I bow,
And sing this richt Balulalow.

kye - cows; sendal - rich silk; sweilling - swaddling; Ring - kingdom; sic - such; rich thy
celsitude - enrich your heavenly state; Balulalow - lullaby

Gloir be to God eternallie,
Whilk gave his only Son for me:
The angellis joyis for to hear
The gracious gift of this New Year.

Go, Heart, Unto The Lamp Of Licht

Go, heart, unto the lamp of licht,
Go, heart, do service and honour,
Go, heart, and serve him day and nicht,
Go, heart, unto thy Saviour.

Go, heart, to thy only remeid,
Descending from the heavenly tour:
Thee to deliver from pyne and deide,
Go, heart, unto thy Saviour.

Go, heart, but dissimulatioun,
To Christ, that took our vile nature,
For thee to suffer passioun,
Go, heart, unto thy Saviour.

Go, heart, richt humill and meek,
Go, heart, as leal and true servitour,
To him that heill is for all seek,
Go, heart, unto thy Saviour.

Go, heart, with true and haill intent,
To Christ thy help and haill succour,
Thee to redeem he was all rent,
Go, heart, unto thy Saviour.

To Christ, that raise from death to live,
Go, heart, unto thy latter hour,
Whais great mercy can nane discrive,
Go, heart, unto thy Saviour.

remeid - remedy; pyne and deid - pain and death; but dissimulatioun - without dissimulation; heill - health; seek - sick; live - life; discrive - describe.

CAMPION, THOMAS (1567–1620), poet and musician, is known for his lyrics for which he composed the music. He was a physician, a critic and playwright, as well as an excellent player of the lute. He published a book of Latin verses in 1595, and *A Booke of Ayres* in 1601. He published another songbook,

Two Bookes of Ayres about 1613, and a third and fourth book circa 1617. His *Observation in the Art of English Poesy* (1602) argued for the use of classical metre and was rebutted by Samuel Daniel in *Defence of Rhyme* (1602). He also wrote a book of musical theory, *New Way of Making Foure Parts in Counterpoint* (1617).

Out of my Soul's Depth

Out of my soul's depth to thee my cries have sounded:
O Let thine ears my plaints receive, on just fear grounded.
Lord, shouldst thou weigh our faults, who's not confounded?

But with grace thou censur'st thine when they have erred,
Therefore shall thy blessed name be lov'd and feared.
Ev'n to thy throne my thoughts and eyes are reared.

Thee alone my hopes attend, on thee relying;
In thy sacred word I'll trust, to thee fast flying,
Long ere the watch shall break, the morn descrying.

In the mercies of our God who live secured,
May of full redemption rest in him assured,
Their sin-sick souls by him shall be recured.

Never Weather-beaten Sail

Never weather-beaten Sail more willing bent to shore,
Never tired Pilgrim's limbs affected slumber more,
Than my wearied sprite now longs to fly out of my troubled breast.
O come quickly, sweetest Lord, and take my soul to rest.

Ever-blooming are the joys of Heav'n's high paradise,
Cold age deafs not there our ears, nor vapour dims our eyes:
Glory there the sun outshines, whose beams the blessed only see;
O come quickly, glorious Lord, and raise my sprite to thee.

Seek the Lord!

Seek the Lord, and in His ways persevere
    O faint not, but as eagles fly;
     For His steep hill is high;
Then striving gain the top, and triumph ever.

When with glory there thy brows are crowned,
    New joys so shall abound in thee,

Such sights thy soul shall see,
That worldly thoughts shall by their beams be drowned.

Farewell, World, thou mass of mere confusion,
    False light, with many shadows dimmed,
    Old Witch, with new foils trimmed,
Thou deadly sleep of soul, and charmed illusion.

I the King will seek, of kings adored;
    Spring of light, tree of grace and bliss,
    Whose fruit so sovereign is
That all who taste it are from death restored.

View Mee, Lord

View mee, Lord, a worke of thine:
Shall I then lye drown'd in night?
Might thy grace in mee but shine,
I should seeme made all of light.

But my soule still surfets so
On the poysoned baytes of sinne,
That I strange and ugly growe,
All is darke and foule within.
Clense mee, Lord, that I may kneele
At thine Altar, pure and white:
They that once thy Mercies feele,
Gaze no more on earths delight.

Worldly joyes like shadowes fade,
When the heav'nly light appeares;
But the cov'nants thou hast made,
Endlesse, know nor days, nor yeares.

In thy word, Lord, is my trust,
To thy mercies fast I flye;
Though I am but clay and dust,
Yet thy grace can lift me high.

WOTTON, Sir HENRY (1568–1639), diplomat, artist, and poet, was secretary to the Earl of Essex, served James I as ambassador to Venice and became a long-standing member of Parliament. He was made provost of Eton and took holy orders. While in Venice he became interested in architecture and painting. Sometime later he wrote *The Elements of Architecture* and *The State of Christendom*. Twelve years after his death *Reliquiae Wottonianae* was published. It contains most of his extant works. "You Meaner Beauties of the Night," addressed to Elizabeth, Queen of Bohemia, is among his best known poems.

A Hymn to my God in a night of my late Sicknesse

Oh thou great Power, in whom I move,
For whom I live, to whom I die,
Behold me through thy beams of love,
Whilst on this couch of fears I lye;
And Cleanse my sordid soul within,
By thy Christs Blood, the bath of sin.

No hallowed Oyls, no grains I need,
No rags of Saints, no purging fire,
One rosie drop from David's Seed
Was worlds of Seas, to quench thine Ire.
O precious Ransome! which once paid,
That Consummatum est was said.

And said by him, that said no more,
But seal'd it with his sacred Breath.
Thou then, that hast dispung'd my score,
And dying, wast the death of Death;
Be to me now, on thee I call,
My Life, my Strength, my Joy, my All.

A Dialogue betwixt God and the Soul
Imitatio Horatiana Odes 9. lib. 3 donec gratis eram tibi

Soul. Whilst my Souls eye beheld no light
But what stream'd from thy gracious sight,
To me the worlds greatest King,
Seem'd but some little vulgar thing.

God. Whilst thou prov'dst pure; and that in thee
I could glass all my Deity:
How glad did I from Heaven depart,
To find a lodging in thy heart!

Soul. Now Fame and Greatness bear the sway,
('Tis they that hold my prisons Key:)
For whom my soul would die, might she
Leave them her Immortalitie.

God. I, and some few pure Souls conspire,
　　And burn both in a mutual fire,
　　For whom I'ld die once more, ere they
　　Should miss of Heavens eternal day.

Soul. But Lord! what if I turn again,
　　And with an adamantine chain,
　　Lock me to thee? What if I chase
　　The world away to give thee place?

God. Then though these souls in whom I joy
　　Are Seraphins, Thou but a toy,
　　A foolish toy, yet once more I
　　Would with thee live, and for thee die.

D. O. M.*

Eternall Mover, whose diffused glory,
To show our grovelling reason what Thou art,
Unfolds itself in clouds of nature's story,
Where Man, Thy proudest creature, acts his part;
Whom yet, alas, I know not why, we call
The world's contracted sum, the little all;

For what are we but lumps of walking clay?
Why should we swell? whence should our spirits rise?
Are not brute beasts as strong, and birds as gay,—
Trees longer lived, and creeping things as wise?
Only our souls were left an inward light,
To feel our weakness, and confess Thy might.

Thou then, our strength, Father of life and death,
To whom our thanks, our vows, ourselves we owe,
From me, Thy tenant of this fading breath,
Accept those lines which from Thy goodness flow;
And Thou, that wert Thy regal Prophet's muse,
Do not Thy praise in weaker strains refuse!

Let these poor notes ascend unto Thy throne,
Where majesty doth sit with mercy crown'd,
Where my Redeemer lives, in Whom alone
The errors of my wandering life are drown'd:

---

* D.O.M. most commonly meant Deo Optimo Maximo (see other poems by that title
in this collection) - "To God, the best, the greatest," but it also sometimes meant Datur
Omnibus Mori "It is given to all to die."

Where all the choir of Heaven resound the same,
That only Thine, Thine is the saving Name!

Well, then, my soul, joy in the midst of pain;
Thy CHRIST, that conquer'd Hell, shall from above
With greater triumph yet return again,
And conquer His own justice with His love;
Commanding earth and seas to render those
Unto His bliss, for whom He paid His woes.

Now have I done; now are my thoughts at peace;
And now my joys are stronger than my grief:
I feel those comforts, that shall never cease,
Future in hope, but present in belief;
Thy words are true, Thy promises are just,
And Thou wilt find Thy dearly-bought in dust!

The Character Of A Happy Life

How happy is he born and taught,
That serveth not another's will;
Whose armour is his honest thought,
And silly truth his highest skill;

Whose passions not his masters are;
Whose soul is still prepared for death,
Untied to the world with care
Of prince's grace or vulgar breath;

Who hath his life from humours freed;
Whose conscience is his strong retreat;
Whose state can neither flatterers feed,
Nor ruin make accusers great;

Who envieth none whom chance doth raise
Or vice; who never understood
How swords give slighter wounds than praise.
Nor rules of state, but rules of good;

Who God doth late and early pray
More of his grace than gifts to lend;
And entertains the harmless day
With a well-chosen book or friend.

This man is free from servile bands
Of hope to rise, or fear to fall:
Lord of himself, though not of lands
And having nothing, yet hath all.

DAVIES, JOHN (c.1569–1626), was a poet and writing master. His poetry is in the same vein as Spenser's. He wrote *Orchestra*, about the poetry of dance and *Hymns to Astrea*, acrostic poems praising Queen Elizabeth. Among his most major works were *Microcosmos*, a theological treatise, and *Nosce Teipsum*, a philosophical poem. He mentions his contemporaries, Ben Jonson and William Shakespeare, in the epigrammatic *Scourge of Folly*. He wrote a number of other Christian treatises in verse including *Wittes Pilgrimage*, some love sonnets, and *The Writing Schoole-Master*, a popular manual of writing.

Reasons drawn from Divinity
from Nosce Teipsum

God doubtless makes her, and doth make her good.
And graffs her in the body, there to spring;
Which, though it be corrupted, flesh and blood
Can no way to the Soul corruption bring:

And yet this Soul (made good by God at first,
And not corrupted by the body's ill)
Even in the womb is sinful, and accurst,
Ere she can judge by wit or choose by will.

Yet is not God the Author of her sin,
Though Author of her being and being there,
And, if we dare to judge our judge herein,
He can condemn us and Himself can clear.

First, God from infinite eternity
Decreed what hath been, is, or shall be done;
And was resolv'd that every man should be.
And in his turn his race of life should run:

And so did purpose all the souls to make
That ever have been made or ever shall,
And that their being they should only take
In human bodies, or not be at all.

Was it then fit that such a weak event
(Weakness itself, the sin and fall of Man)

His counsel's execution should prevent,
Decreed and fixt before the World began?

Or that one penal law by Adam broke
Should make God break His own eternal Law,
The settled order of the World revoke,
And change all forms of things which He foresaw?

Could Eve's weak hand, extended to the tree,
In sunder rend that adamantine chain
Whose golden links effects and causes be,
And which to God's own chair doth fixt remain?

Oh could we see, how cause from cause doth spring,
How mutually they linkt and folded are,
And hear how oft one disagreeing string
The harmony doth rather make than mar,

And view at once how death by sin is brought,
And how from death a better life doth rise,
How this God's justice and His mercy taught,
We this decree would praise, as right and wise.

But we that measure times by first and last
The sight of things successively do take,
When God on all at once His view doth cast,
And of all times doth but one instant make.

All in Himself as in a glass He sees,
For from Him, by Him, through Him, all things be:
His sight is not discursive, by degrees,
But, seeing the whole, each single part doth see.

He looks on Adam as a root or well,
And on his heirs as branches and as streams;
He sees all men as one Man, though they dwell
In sundry cities and in sundry realms.

And as the root and branch are but one tree,
And well and stream do but one river make,
So, if the root and well corrupted be,
The stream and branch the same corruption take.

So, when the root and fountain of mankind
Did draw corruption, and God's curse, by sin,
This was a charge that all his heirs did bind,

And all his offspring grew corrupt therein.

And as when the hand doth strike, the Man offends
—For part from whole Law severs not, in this—
So Adam's sin to the whole kind extends,
For all their natures are but part of his.

Therefore this sin of kind, not personal,
But reall and hereditary was,
The guilt whereof, and punishment, to all
By course of Nature and of Law doth pass.

For as that easy Law was given to all,
To ancestor and heir, to first and last,
So was the first transgression general,
And all did pluck the fruit and all did taste.

Of this we find some footsteps in our Law,
Which doth her root from God and Nature take;
Ten thousand men she doth together draw,
And of them all one corporation make:

Yet these and their successors are but one,
And if they gain or lose their liberties
They harm or profit, not themselves alone,
But such as in succeeding times shall rise.

And so the ancestor and all his heirs,
Though they in number pass the stars of heaven,
Are still but one; his forfeitures are theirs,
And unto them are his advancements given.

His civil acts do bind and bar them all,
And as from Adam all corruption take,
So, if the father's crime be capital
In all the blood Law doth corruption make.

Is it then just with us, to disinherit
The unborn nephews for the father's fault?
And to advance again for one man's merit,
A thousand heirs that have deserved naught?

And is not God's decree as just as ours,
If He, for Adam's sin, his sons deprive
Of all those native virtues and those powers
Which He to him and to his race did give?

For what is this contagious sin of kind
But a privation of that grace within,
And of that great rich dowry of the mind
Which all had had but for the first man's sin?

If then a man on light conditions gain
A great estate, to him and his for ever,
If wilfully be forfeit it again
Who doth bemoan his heir or blame the giver?

So, though God make the Soul good, rich, and fair,
Yet when her form is to the body knit
Which makes the Man, which man is Adam's heir
Justly forthwith He takes His grace from it:

And then the Soul, being first from nothing brought,
When God's grace fails her doth to nothing fall;
And this declining proneness unto naught,
Is even that sin that we are born withal.

Yet not alone the first good qualities,
Which in the first soul were, deprived are:
But in their place the contrary do rise,
And reall spots of sin her beauty mar.

Nor is it strange that Adam's ill desart
Should be transferred unto his guilty Race,
When Christ His grace and justice doth impart
To men unjust and such as have no grace.

Lastly, the Soul were better so to be
Born slave to sin than not to be at all,
Since (if she do believe) One sets her free,
That makes her mount the higher for her fall.

Yet this the curious wits will not content;
They yet will know: sith God foresaw this ill,
Why His high Providence did not prevent
The declination of the first man's will.

If by His Word He had the current stay'd
Of Adam's will, which was by nature free,
It had been one as if His Word had said:
'I will henceforth that Man no man shall be.'

For what is Man without a moving mind
Which hath a judging wit and choosing will?
Now, if God's power should her election bind,
Her motions then would cease and stand all still.

And why did God in man this soul infuse
But that he should his Maker know and love?
Now, if love be compell'd and cannot choose,
How can it grateful or thankworthy prove?

Love must free-hearted be, and voluntary,
And not enchanted, or by Fate constrain'd;
Not like that love which did Ulysses carry
To Circe's isle, with mighty charms enchain'd.

Besides, were we unchangeable in will,
And of a wit that nothing could misdeem,
Equal to God, whose wisdom shineth still,
And never errs, we might ourselves esteem.

So that if Man would be unvariable,
He must be God, or like a rock of tree;
For even the perfect Angels were not stable,
But had a fall, more desperate than we.

Then let us praise that Power which makes us be
Men as we are, and rest contented so;
And knowing Man's fall was curiosity,
Admire God's counsels, which we cannot know.

And let us know that God the Maker is
Of all the souls in all the men that be:
Yet their corruption is no fault of His,
But the first man's that broke God's first decree.

Three Kinds of Life Answerable to the Three Powers of the Soul

For as the Soul's essential powers are three
The quickening power, the power of sense and reason—
Three kinds of life to her designed be
Which perfect these three powers in their due season.

The first life in the mother's womb is spent,
Where she her nursing power doth only use;

Where, when she finds defect of nourishment,
She expels her body, and this world she views.

This we call birth; but if the child could speak
He death would call it, and of Nature plain
That she would thrust him out naked and weak
And in his passage pinch him with such pain.

Yet, out he comes, and in this world is placed
Where all his Senses in perfection be,
Where he finds flowers to smell, and fruits to taste,
And sounds to hear and sundry forms to see.

When he hath past some time upon this stage,
His Reason then a little seems to wake,
Which, though she spring, when sense doth fade with age,
Yet can she here no perfect practice make.

Then doth the aspiring Soul the body leave:
Which we call death, but, were it known to all
What life our souls do by this death receive,
Men, would it birth or jail-delivery call.

In this third life, Reason will be so bright
As that her spark will like the sunbeams shine,
And shall of God enjoy the reall sight,
Being still increast by influence divine.

An Acclamation

Oh what is Man, great Maker of mankind,
That Thou to him so great respect dost bear,
That Thou adornst him with so bright a mind,
Mak'st him a king, and even an angel's peer!

Oh what a lively life, what heavenly power,
What spreading virtue, what a sparkling fire!
How great, how plentiful, how rich a dower
Dost Thou within this dying flesh inspire!

Thou leav'st Thy print in other works of Thine,
But Thy whole image Thou in Man hast writ;
There cannot be a creature more divine
Except, like Thee, it should be infinit.

But it exceeds man's thought to think how high
God hath rais'd Man since God a man became:
The angels do admire this mystery,
And are astonisht when they view the same.

The Intellectual Powers of the Soul

But now I have a will, yet want a wit,
To express the working of the wit and will;
Which, though their root be to the body knit,
Use not the body when they use their skill.

These powers the nature of the Soul declare,
For to man's soul these only proper be;
For on the Earth no other wights there are
That have these heavenly powers, but only we.

The Wit the pupil of the Soul's clear eye,
And in man's world the only shining star,
Looks in the mirror of the Fantasy,
Where all the gatherings of the Senses are.

From thence this power the shapes of things abstracts,
And them within her passive part receives,
Which are enlightned by that part which acts,
And so the forms of single things perceives.

But after, by discoursing to and fro,
Anticipating, and comparing things,
She doth all universal natures know,
And all effects into their causes brings.

When she rates things and moves from ground to ground,
The name of Reason she obtains by this;
But when by Reason she the truth hath found
And standeth fixt, she Understanding is.

When her assent she lightly doth incline
To either part, she is Opinion light:
But when she doth by principles define
A certain truth, she hath true Judgment's sight.

And as from Senses Reason's work doth spring,
So many reasons understanding gain;

And many understandings knowledge bring;
And by much knowledge wisdom we obtain.

So, many stairs we must ascend upright
Ere we attain to Wisdom's high degree:
So doth this Earth eclipse our Reason's light,
Which else (in instants) would like angels see.

Yet hath the Soul a dowry natural.
And sparks of light some common things to see;
Not being a blank where naught is writ at all,
But what the writer will, may written be.

For Nature in man's heart her laws doth pen.
Prescribing truth to wit, and good to will,
Which do accuse, or else excuse all men,
For every thought or practice, good or ill:

And yet these sparks grow almost infinite,
Making the World and all therein their food;
As fire so spreads, as no place holdeth it,
Being nourisht still with new supplies of wood.

And though these sparks were almost quencht with sin,
Yet they whom that just One hath justified
Have them increas'd with heavenly light within,
And like the widow's oil still multiplied.

And as this wit should goodness truly know,
We have a Will, which that true good should choose,
Though Will do oft (when wit false forms doth show)
Take ill for good, and good for ill refuse.

Will puts in practice what the Wit deviseth:
Will ever acts, and Wit contemplates still;
And as from Wit the power of wisdom riseth,
All other virtues daughters are of Will.

Will is the prince, and Wit the counsellor,
Which doth for common good in Counsel sit;
And when Wit is resolv'd, Will lends her power
To execute what is advis'd by Wit.

Wit is the mind's chief judge, which doth control
Of Fancy's court the judgments false and vain;

Will holds the royal sceptre in the soul
And on the passions of the heart doth reign.

Will is as free as any emperor;
Naught can restrain her gentle liberty;
No tyrant nor no torment hath the power
To make us will when we unwilling be.

Madrigals

Madrigals are a definite musical form. The term "madrigal" is from Greek *mandra* or "fold" (sheep-fold), thus the madrigal was originally a pastoral song. The term apparently originally meant a short lyrical song, often a love-song, to an unaccompanied contrapuntal part-song for several voices. It was used early in ecclesiastical music, but by the middle of the sixteenth century the Italian madrigal had become the highest form of secular music. Petrarch's sonnets to the Virgin in memory of Laura were composed as "spiritual madrigals," by Palestrina who also produced masses founded on madrigal themes, despite the secular origins of some of them. Madrigals were a popular literary form in England for a time and a few were composed on Christian subjects. They were a courtly "art-form" from the beginning in English. It was fashionable to set Petrarchan poetry in madrigals. Unlike carols, they were apparently never meant as dance-tunes.

O All Ye Nations
Thomas Norton

O all ye nations of the Lord,
Praise ye the Lord always;
And all ye people everywhere
Set forth His noble praise.
For great His kindness is to His,
His truth endures for aye;
Wherefore praise ye the Lord our God,
Praise ye the Lord I say.

Ye People All
John Hopkins

Ye people all in one accord
Clap hands and eke rejoice;

Be glad and sing unto the Lord
With sweet and pleasant voice.
Sing praises to our God, sing praise,
Sing praises to our King,
For God is King of all the earth,
All thankful praises sing.

Madrigal
Anonymous

If that a sinner's sighs be angels' food,
Or that repentant tears be angels' wine;
Accept, O Lord! in this most pensive mood
These hearty sighs and tears of mine:
That went with Peter forth most sinfully;
But not with Peter wept most bitterly.

If I had David's crown to me betide,
Or all his purple robes that he did wear;
I would lay then such honour all aside,
And only seek a sackcloth weed to bear:
His palace would I leave, that I might show
And mourn in cell for such offence, my woe.

There should these hands beat on my pensive breast;
And sad to death, for sorrow rend my hair:
My voice to call on Thee, should never rest;
Whose grace I seek, Whose judgment I do fear.
Upon the ground, all grovelling on my face,
I would beseech Thy favour and good grace!

But since I have not means to make the show
Of my repentant mind, and yet I see
My sin, to greater heap than Peter's grow,
Whereby the danger more it is to me:
I put my trust in His most precious blood,
Whose life was paid to purchase all our good.

Thy mercy greater is than any sin!
Thy greatness none can ever comprehend!
Wherefore, O Lord! let me Thy mercy win,
Whose glorious name, no time can ever end:
Wherefore, I say, " All praise belongs to Thee!"
Whom I beseech be merciful to me.

Chapter Four

SEVENTEENTH CENTURY POETRY

1603—Death of Elizabeth   1660—End of the Protectorate

T.S. Eliot in an essay "The Metaphysical Poets" puts forth the idea that something very significant happened in seventeenth century poetry, something which he calls "a dissociation of the sensibility." He says:

> A thought to Donne was an experience; it modified his sensibility. When a poet's mind is perfectly equipped for its work, it is constantly amalgamating disparate experience; the ordinary man's experience is chaotic, irregular, fragmentary. The latter falls in love, or reads Spinoza, and these two experiences have nothing to do with each other, or with the noise of the typewriter or the smell of cooking; in the mind of the poet these experiences are always forming new wholes.
> . . . The poets of the seventeenth century, the successors of the dramatists of the sixteenth, possessed a mechanism of sensibility which could devour any kind of experience. They are simple, artificial, difficult, or fantastic, as their predecessors were. . . In the seventeenth century a dissociation of sensibility set in, from which we have never recovered. . .

C. S. Lewis told us (see introduction to the sixteenth century) that the difference between sixteenth century poetry and what followed was the simplicity and relative un-selfconsciousness of the sixteenth. The literature of the seventeenth century indeed became more complex, for instead of one standard of poetic excellence, there came to be two or three. There began divisions in the "poetic consciousness" of England. Eliot is arguing that another kind of division began to open in the consciousness of the individual poets as well.

But Eliot says this "dissociation of sensibility" was great in Milton and Dryden, who may be associated with the following period. At least one of the "schools" of seventeenth century poetry before the Restoration (1660) maintained the sixteenth century association of sensibility and intellect. These were the "metaphysical poets" of whom John Donne is foremost. The other two "schools," the "Cavalier," led by Ben Jonson, and the "Spenserian" (including no primary "great," but men like William Browne of Tavistock and Giles and Phineas Fletcher) tended toward the "dissociation"—especially the later ones. Those who wrote early in the century were better able to "feel their thoughts," while those who came later were losing that ability. While these generalizations break down in relation to particular poets, they are useful to the student of poetry and history.

The seventeenth century saw several major changes in society which significantly affected poetry. Although the reigns of Elizabeth and James I were periods of relative peace in England, by mid-century the English Civil War was to greatly divide and shake the country. Religious controversy had been squelched at the beginning of Elizabeth's reign and she had maintained gentle but firm "tolerance" thereafter for a variety of religious allegiances (not including those of Roman Catholics). By the middle of the seventeenth century religious controversy was to become very heated again and politically significant. No one of any religious or political camp opposed monarchy in principle at the beginning of the seventeenth century, yet by mid-century a king would be executed and a protectorate (under Oliver Cromwell) established. Although it did not last very long, this had a tremendous impact on the mind of England.

Secular critics argue that the "Christian" or "medieval" worldview of the sixteenth century could not hold up to the scientific advancements being made in the seventeenth century. The argument might be paraphrased, that dissociation of sensibility from intellect was due to loss of the lovely but (to a secularist way of thinking) illusory view of the universe as integrated and ordered under its Creator:

> The king was to his subjects as Michael was to the other archangels, as the bishop was to his pastors, as the Archbishop of Canterbury was to his bishops, as the lion was to other beasts, as the eagle was to other birds, as the diamond was to other stones, as gold was to other metals. Within every category and species, there was an order of excellence; and though the noblest lion was less than the lowest man, yet he was a monarch of his species. That the king was "father of his country" was a metaphor, to be sure; but that a father was "king of his family" was also a metaphor, and both were metaphors derived from the central fact that God the Father was King of Kings. (*Norton Anthology of English Literature*, "Introduction, Seventeenth Century")

We might argue that the movement away from this "medieval" view was a loss of faith. It was indeed an age increasingly focused on reasoning. And to a certain degree that was a strength of the age. The scientific leaders of the age were Christians. Some of the power in metaphysical poetry comes from new-found knowledge about how the universe was made and how it operated. Furthermore, much of the superstitious interest in "occult" things (astrology and magic) faded before the power of reason. As the *Norton Anthology* puts it:

> Astrology gave way to astronomy, alchemy to chemistry, and the immense corpus of "curious learning," accumulated from generation

to generation, and cherished less because it was presumed true than because it was thought instructive, was subjected to the cruel test of fact.

But at the same time:

The test of truth gradually changed, under the double impulsion of scientific method and prolonged, inconclusive sectarian conflict, from conformity with a large-scale view, philosophical or religious, to conformity with experimental data, manipulative fact. (ibid.)

And another shift was underway:

The pursuit of the heavenly kingdom gave way to the pursuit of earthly prosperity; the ideal of strenuous intellectual and spiritual effort gave way to the ideal of gentlemanly good taste; the rule of the saints gave way to the rule of the well-to-do and respectable. Truth, instead of standing on a rough, high hill up which each man must find his own difficult way [See Satire III, prefatory poem to this anthology] became plain, natural, easy, and common to all (ibid.)

The three "schools" of poetry during this period did not differ so much on these weightier matters as on matters of taste and literary theory, however. There were Christian poets in all three schools—perhaps more in the metaphysical camp and fewer in the Cavalier—but representatives in all, nonetheless. The Metaphysical school (consisting chiefly of John Donne, George Herbert, Richard Crashaw, Henry Vaughan, and to some degree Andrew Marvell and Abraham Cowley) is noted for its striking imagery, and "strong conceits."

The word "conceit" derives not from the notion of egotism in the author, but from the Italian concetto; it is most closely allied to the English "concept." In this sense, it is an almost separable unit of intellectual or verbal ingenuity, which occurs in a poem but can be detached from it and appreciated separately.
. . . The metaphysical conceit is often consciously odd and far-fetched; hence it takes some getting used to. But its ultimate effect is one of highly compressed, sharply angled perspectives on an object of contemplation, glittering and intellectually provocative. (Norton Anthology)

One external influence on English poetry, especially that of the Metaphysicals, was the ambitious Christian poetry of the Gascon Huguenot, Guillaume de Salluste du Bartas (1544-1590), whose works had been translated in part by Joshua Sylvester in *Divine Weeks and Works* (1605).

The Cavalier poets (sometimes called "sons of Ben" Jonson) were dedicated to a less striking and more "classical" style. These men, including Lovelace and Herrick, Carew, Waller and Suckling were moderate in their imagery and language, avoiding both the stark and unusual images of the metaphysicals and the ornate and archaic flourishes of the Spenserians.

> . . . Ben Jonson and his followers produced verse which had the special Latin quality of being "lapidary." At its best their poetry gave the impression of being written to be carved in marble. Restrained in feeling, deliberately limited in its subject matter, intellectually thin but meticulously clear and incisive in expression. . . strong syntactically . . . as a poem by Donne is strong metaphorically. (ibid.)

Jonson became poet laureate under James I and had written largely for the court up to that time (1616). His position and influence did much to establish the "Cavalier" poets as the dominant school in their heyday.

The Spenserian school modeled its poetry on that of Edmund Spenser. Few of this school are as well-known today. They carried through a tradition which Milton was to continue, however. It was characterized by allegorical romance, being strongly moral and religious in theme, and usually ornate in style. Thomas Browne and Giles and Phineas Fletcher are among the Spenserian poets whose works are included here.

In their own time, the metaphysical poets were not very popular, except among circles of intellectual society. John Donne became a well-known preacher during his lifetime, but it has only been relatively recently that he has been recognized for the greatness of his poetry and poetic vision.

The English Civil War and the Protectorate were periods of heavy political writing during which little good poetry was written. They constituted a break in the tradition which the Restoration could not quickly repair.

Brief Chronology of the Seventeenth Century up to the Restoration

1603   Death of Elizabeth I, accession of James I
1605   Gunpowder plot, last major effort of Catholic militants
1615   John Donne ordained
1616   Ben Jonson appointed poet laureate
1620   Pilgrims emigrate to America
1625   Death of James I, accession of Charles I
1631   John Donne dies
1637   Ben Jonson dies
1642   Beginning of English Civil War
1649   Charles I executed, beginning of Cromwell's Protectorate
1651   John Milton becomes blind

1658   Milton begins *Paradise Lost*
1660   End of the Protectorate; Charles II restored to the throne

DONNE, JOHN (c.1572–1631) wrote one style of poetry from two differ-ent worldviews, first from a somewhat cynical version of the courtly love tradi-tion, and then as a Christian. He is the chief and founder of the "metaphysical school" of poetry (although the title was not used by the poets or their con-temporaries) which also includes Herbert, Crashaw, Herrick, Vaughan and Marvell. Donne's father died when he was four. His mother married a Roman Catholic, and Donne was raised in that church. He was educated at Oxford and Cambridge, but as a Catholic could receive no degree from either university. He was enrolled as a law student at Lincoln's Inn in 1592. His younger brother Henry died in prison in 1593 after being arrested for harboring a Roman Catholic priest. At some point during this period Donne renounced his Catholic affiliation. His dilemma regarding religious alliance is powerfully por-trayed in "Satire III." (Prefatory Poem of this book) In 1596, Donne served in a military capacity with the Earl of Essex, and in 1597 became secretary to Sir Thomas Egerton, the Lord Keeper of the Great Seal. He lost his position when he secretly married the Lord Keeper's niece, Ann More, for which he was impris-oned for a time, but the marriage was found valid and he was released. He came to the notice of James I after much effort to gain a government post. Advisors urged him to seek a post in the Anglican church, however, and after he was ordained in 1615, he found a "living" there. His wife died in 1617 at the age of thirty-three after giving birth to their twelfth child. In 1621 he became dean of St. Paul's Cathedral and eventually a most influential preacher. Several vol-umes of his sermons were published after his death. His "Holy Sonnets" are among the most powerful of English devotional poems. There is an integrity of theme and style in his poetry which has made it very influential in his century and in ours. Donne was out of fashion in the eighteenth century, however, and was only being "rediscovered" in the nineteenth.

Holy Sonnets

iii

O might those sighes and teares returne againe
Into my breast and eyes, which I have spent,
That I might in this holy discontent
Mourne with some fruit, as I have mourn'd in vaine;
In mine Idolatry what showres of raine
Mine eyes did waste? what griefs my heart did rent?
That sufferance was my sinne; now I repent;

'Cause I did suffer I must suffer paine.
Th'hydroptique drunkard, and night-scouting thiefe,
The itchy Lecher and self-tickling proud
Have the remembrance of past joyes, for reliefe
Of coming ills. To (poore) me is allow'd
No ease; for, long, yet vehement griefe hath beene
Th'effect and cause, the punishment and sinne.

vii

At the round earths imagin'd corners, blow
Your trumpets, Angells, and arise, arise
From death, you numberlesse infinities
Of soules, and to your scattred bodies goe,
All whom the flood did, and fire shall o'erthrow,
All whom warre, dearth, age, agues, tyrannies,
Despaire, law, chance, hath slaine, and you whose eyes,
Shall behold God, and never taste deaths woe.
But let them sleepe, Lord, and mee mourne a space,
For, if above all these, my sinnes abound,
'Tis late to aske abundance of thy grace,
When wee are there; here on this lowly ground,
Teach mee how to repent; for that's as good
As if thou 'hadst seal'd my pardon, with thy blood.

x

Death be not proud, though some have called thee
Mighty and dreadfull, for, thou art not soe,
For, those, whom thou think'st, thou dost overthrow,
Die not, poore death, nor yet canst thou kill mee.
From rest and sleepe, which but thy pictures bee,
Much pleasure, then from thee much more must flow,
And soonest our best men with thee doe goe,
Rest of their bones, and soules deliverie.
Thou art slave to Fate, Chance, kings, and desperate men,
And dost with poyson, warre, and sicknesse dwell,
And poppie, or charmes can make us sleepe as well,
And better than thy stroake; why swell'st thou then?
One short sleepe past, wee wake eternally,
And death shall be no more; death, thou shalt die.

xiv

Batter my heart, three person'd God; for, you
As yet but knocke, breathe, shine, and seeke to mend;
That I may rise, and stand, o'erthrow mee,'and bend

Your force, to breake, blowe, burn and make me new.
I, like an usurpt towne, to'another due,
Labour to'admit you, but Oh, to no end,
Reason your viceroy in mee, mee should defend,
But is captiv'd, and proves weake or untrue.
Yet dearely I love you, and would be loved faine,
But am betroth'd unto your enemie:
Divorce mee, untie, or breake that knot againe,
Take mee to you, imprison mee, for I
Except you'enthrall mee, never shall be free,
Nor ever chaste, except you ravish mee.

Goodfriday, 1613. Riding Westward

Let mans Soule be a Spheare, and then, in this,
The intelligence that moves, devotion is,
And as the other Spheares, by being growne
Subject to forraigne motions, lose their owne,
And being by others hurried every day,
Scarce in a yeare their natural forme obey:
Pleasure or businesse, so, our Soules admit
For their first mover, and are whirld by it.
Hence is't, that I am carryed towards the West
This day, when my Soules forme bends toward the East.
There I should see a Sunne, by rising set,
And by that setting endlesse day beget;
But that Christ on this Crosse did rise and fall,
Sinne had eternally benighted all.
Yet dare I almost be glad, I do not see
That spectacle of too much weight for mee.
Who sees Gods face, that is selfe life, must dye;
What a death were it then to see God dye?
It made his owne Lieutenant Nature shrinke,
It made his footstoole crack, and the Sunne winke.
Could I behold those hands which span the Poles,
And turne all spheares at once, peirc'd with those holes?
Could I behold that endlesse height which is
Zenith to us, and our Antipodes,
Humbled below us? or that blood which is
The seat of all our Soules, if not of his,
Made dirt of dust, or that flesh which was worne
By God, for his apparell, ragg'd, and torne?

If on these things I durst not looke, durst I
Upon his miserable mother cast mine eye,
Who was Gods partner here, and furnish'd thus
Halfe of that Sacrifice, which ransom'd us?
Though these things, as I ride, be from mine eye,
They'are present yet unto my memory,
For that looks towards them; and thou look'st towards mee,
O Saviour, as thou hang'st upon the tree;
I turne my backe to thee, but to receive
Corrections, till thy mercies bid thee leave.
O thinke mee worth thine anger, punish mee,
Burn off my rusts, and my deformity,
Restore thine Image, so much, by thy grace,
That thou may'st know mee, and I'll turne my face.

A Hymn to Christ, at the Authors last going into Germany

In what torne ship soever I embarke,
That ship shall be my embleme of thy Arke;
What sea soever swallow mee, that flood
Shall be to mee an embleme of thy blood;
Though thou with clouds of anger do disguise
Thy face; yet through that maske I know those eyes,
Which, though they turne away sometimes,
They never will despise.

I sacrifice this Iland unto thee,
And all whom I lov'd there, and who lov'd mee;
When I have put our seas twixt them and mee,
Put thou thy sea betwixt my sinnes and thee.
As the trees sap doth seeke the root below
In winter, in my winter now I goe,
Where none but thee, th'Eternall root
Of true Love I may know.

Nor thou nor thy religion dost controule,
The amorousnesse of an harmonious Soule,
But thou would'st have that love thy selfe: As thou
Art jealous, Lord, so I am jealous now,
Thou lov'st not, till from loving more, thou free
My soule: Who ever gives, takes libertie:
O, if thou car'st not whom I love
Alas, thou lov'st not mee.

Seale then this bill of my Divorce to All,
On whom those fainter beames of love did fall;
Marry those loves, which in youth scattered bee
On Fame, Wit, Hopes (false mistresses) to thee.
Churches are best for Prayer that have least light:
To see God only, I goe out of sight:
And to scape stormy dayes, I chuse
An Everlasting night.

A Hymn to God the Father

Wilt thou forgive that sin, where I begun,
Which is my sin, though it were done before?
Wilt thou forgive those sinns through which I runn
And doe them still, though still I doe deplore?
When thou hast done, thou hast not done,
for I have more.

Wilt thou forgive that sin, by which I'have wonne
Others to sin, and made my sin their dore?
Wilt thou forgive that sin which I did shunne
A yeare or twoe, but wallowed in a score?
When thou hast done, thou hast not done,
for I have more.

I have a sin of feare that when I have spun
My last thred, I shall perish on the shore;
Sweare by thy self that at my Death, thy Son
Shall shine as he shines nowe, and heretofore;
And having done that, thou hast done,
I have noe more.

Upon The Translation Of The Psalms By Sir Philip Sidney, And The Countess Of Pembroke, His Sister

Eternal God—for whom who ever dare
Seek new expressions, do, the circle square,
And thrust into straight corners of poor wit
Thee, who art cornerless and infinite—
I would but bless Thy name, not name Thee now
—And Thy gifts are as infinite as Thou,—
Fix we our praises therefore on this one,
That, as thy blessed Spirit fell upon

These Psalms' first author in a cloven tongue
—For 'twas a double power by which he sung
The highest matter in the noblest form—
So Thou hast cleft that Spirit, to perform
That work again, and shed it here, upon
Two, by their bloods, and by Thy Spirit one;
A brother and a sister, made by Thee
The organ, where Thou art the harmony.
Two that make one John Baptist's holy voice,
And who that Psalm, " Now let the Isles rejoice,"
Have both translated, and applied it too,
Both told us what, and taught us how to do.
They show us islanders our Joy, our King;
They tell us why, and teach us how to sing.
Make all this all three choirs, heaven, earth, and spheres;
The first, Heaven, hath a song, but no man hears;
The spheres have music, but they have no tongue,
Their harmony is rather danced than sung;
But our third choir, to which the first gives ear
—For angels learn by what the Church does here—
This choir hath all. The organist is he
Who hath tuned God, and man, the organ we;
The songs are these, which heaven's high holy Muse
Whisper'd to David, David to the Jews;
And David's successors in holy zeal,
In forms of joy and art do re-reveal
To us so sweetly and sincerely too,
That I must not rejoice as I would do,
When I behold that these Psalms are become
So well attired abroad, so ill at home,
So well in chambers, in Thy Church so ill,
As I can scarce call that reform'd until
This be reform'd; would a whole state present
A lesser gift than some one man hath sent?
And shall our Church unto our Spouse and King
More hoarse, more harsh than any other, sing?
For that we pray, we praise Thy name for this,
Which, by this Moses and this Miriam, is
Already done; and as those Psalms we call,
—Though, some have other authors—David's all,
So though some have, some may some Psalms translate,
We Thy Sidneian psalms shall celebrate,
And, till we come th' extemporal song to sing

—Learn'd the first hour that we see the King,
Who hath translated those translators—may
These their sweet learned labours, all the way,
Be as our tuning, that when hence we part,
We may fall in with them, and sing our part!

Ode

Vengeance will sit above our faults; but till
    She there do sit
We see her not, nor them. Thus blind, yet still
We lead her way; and thus, whilst we do ill,
    We suffer it.

Unhappy he whom youth makes not beware
    Of doing ill:
Enough we labor under age and care:
In number, th' errors of the last place are
    The greater still.

Yet we, that should the ill we now begin
    As soon repent,
Strange thing! perceive not; our faults are not seen,
But past us; neither felt, but only in
    The punishment.

But we know ourselves least; mere outward shows
    Our minds so store,
That our souls, no more than our eyes disclose
But form and color; only he who knows
    Himself, knows more.

JONSON, BEN (c.1573-1673), played the melody to which Donne was counterpoint in the seventeenth century. Representing the tradition which built on classical models, subjects, and themes, he was a poet and a dramatist having a lasting effect on English letters. At about the age of twenty-five, he was put in prison for manslaughter, having killed a man in a duel (1598). While in prison he converted to Roman Catholicism, remaining a member of that communion for twelve years. He was released by benefit of clergy, forfeited his property, and received a brand on his thumb. His "Every Man In His Own Humour" was in effect a comic morality play—intended to bring the audience to see their own folly. He wrote several effective tragedies, Including *Volpone* and *Bartholomew Fair.* His tragedies focus on the despicable depths to which men will go in pursuing their ends. He contributed to the importance of the court masque, composing many until the accession of Charles I. He fell from favor thereafter, and becoming an invalid, he continued to be the head of a coterie of young men, "the sons of Ben," many of whom became leading Cavalier poets late in the century. Perhaps his best known poem is "To Celia," much recited and put to music, beginning, "Drink to me only with thine eyes."

A Hymne to God the Father from The Sinner's Sacrifice

Heare mee, O God!
A broken heart,
Is my best part:
Use still thy rod,
That I may prove
Therein, thy Love.

If thou hadst not
Beene stern to mee,
But left me free,
I had forgot
My selfe and thee.

For sin's so sweet,
As minds ill bent
Rarely repent,
Untill they meet
Their punishment.

Who more can crave
Than thou hast done:
That gav'st a Sonne,
To free a slave?
First made of nought;
With All since bought.

Sinne, Death, and Hell,
His glorious Name
Quite overcame,
Yet I rebell,
And slight the same.

But, I'll come in,
Before my losse,

Me farther tosse,
As sure to win
Under his Crosse.

To The Holy Trinity from The Sinner's Sacrifice

O holy, blessed, glorious Trinity
Of persons, still one God in Unity,
The faithful man's believed mystery,
Help, help to lift
Myself up to thee, harrowed, torn, and bruised
By sin and Satan, and my flesh misused,
As my heart lies—in pieces, all confused—
O take my gift.

All-gracious God, the sinner's sacrifice,
A broken heart, thou wert not wont despise,
But, 'bove the fat of rams or bulls, to prize
An offering meet
For thy acceptance: Oh, behold me right,
And take compassion on my grievous plight!
What odour can be, than a heart contrite,
To thee more sweet?

Eternal Father, God, who didst create
This All of nothing, gav'st it form and fate,
And breath'st into it life and light, with state
To worship thee!
Eternal God the Son, who not deniedst
To take our nature, becam'st man, and diedst,
To pay our debts, upon thy cross, and criedst
All's done in me!

Eternal Spirit, God from both proceeding,
Father and Son—the Comforter, in breeding
Pure thoughts in man, with fiery zeal them feeding
For acts of grace!
Increase those acts, O glorious Trinity
Of persons, still one God in Unity,
Till I attain the longed-for mystery
Of seeing your face,

Beholding one in three, and three in one,
A Trinity, to shine in Union—

The gladdest light, dark man can think upon—
O grant it me,
Father, and Son, and Holy Ghost, you three,
All co-eternal in your majesty,
Distinct in persons, yet in unity
One God to see;

My Maker, Saviour, and my Sanctifier,
To hear, to meditate, sweeten my desire,
With grace, with love, with cherishing entire!
O then, how blest
Among thy saints elected to abide,
And with thy angels placed, side by side!
But in thy presence truly glorified,
Shall I there rest!

To Heaven

Good, and great God, can I not thinke of thee,
But it must, straight, my melancholy bee?
Is it interpreted in me disease,
That, laden with my sinnes, I seeke for ease?
O, be thou witnesse, that the reines dost know,
And hearts of all, if I be sad for show,
And judge me after: if I dare pretend
To ought but grace, or ayme at other end.
As thou art all, so be thou all to mee,
First, midst, and last, converted one, and three;
My faith, my hope, my love: and in this state,
My judge, my witnesses and my advocate.
Where have I beene this while exil'd from thee?
And whither rap'd, now thou but stoop'st to mee?
Dwell, dwell here still: O, being everywhere,
How can I doubt to finde thee ever, here?
I know my state, both full of shame, and scorne,
Conceiv'd in sinne, and unto labour borne,
Standing with feare, and must with horror fall,
And destin'd unto judgement, after all.
I feele my griefs too, and there scarce is ground,
Upon my flesh t'inflict another wound.
Yet dare I not complaine, or wish for death

reines - kidneys

With holy PAUL, lest it be thought the breath
Of discontent; or that these prayers bee
For weariness of life, not love of thee.

A Hymn On The Nativity Of My Saviour from A Sinner's Sacrifice

I sing the Birth was born to-night,
The Author both of life and light;
   The angels so did sound it,
And like the ravished shepherds said,
Who saw the light, and were afraid,
   Yet searched, and true they found it.

The Son of God, th' Eternal King,
That did us all salvation bring,
   And freed the soul from danger;
He whom the whole world could not take,
The Word, which Heaven and Earth did make,
   Was now laid in a manger.

The Father's wisdom willed it so,
The Son's obedience knew no No.
   Both wills were in one stature,
And as that wisdom had decreed,
The Word was now made Flesh indeed,
   And took on Him our nature.

What comfort by Him do we win,
Who made Himself the price of sin
   To make us heirs of glory?
To see this Babe all innocence,
A martyr born in our defence:
   Can man forget this story?

HALL, JOSEPH (1574–1656), educated at Cambridge, was bishop first at Exeter (1627) and then at Norwich (1641). During his time at Cambridge he published two volumes of satires and a play. He introduced a variety of genres to English: he was the first to publish his letters (1608–10); he was first to publish "character writing" (brief general description of a class or type of person in prose); he introduced Juvenalian satire; and he was the first Protestant to publish meditations (taken from his sermons). He was a favorite of King James and went on three embassies abroad for him. The king used him as a controversialist and Bishop Laud used him in this capacity against Smectymnuus, the anti-episcopal "author " (actually several Presbyterians). He went to prison for five months in 1641, during an attack on the episcopacy, and in 1643 he was sequestered at Norwich, while his property was seized and the cathedral desecrated. He is noted for his plain (Senecan) prose style. His complete works are in ten volumes.

Anthem For The Cathedral Of Exeter.

Lord, what am I? A worm, dust, vapour, nothing!
What is my life? A dream, a daily dying!
What is my flesh? My soul's uneasy clothing!
What is my time? A minute ever flying:
My time, my flesh, my life, and I,
What are we, Lord, but vanity?

Where am I, Lord? Down in a vale of death.
What is my trade? Sin, my dear God offending;
My sport sin too, my stay a puff of breath.
What end of sin? Hell's horror never ending:
My way, my trade, sport, stay, and place,
Help to make up my doleful case.

Lord, what art thou? Pure life, power, beauty, bliss.
Where dwell'st thou? Up above in perfect light.
What is thy time? Eternity it is.
What state? Attendance of each glorious sprite:
Thyself, thy place, thy days, thy state
Pass all the thoughts of powers create.

How shall I reach thee, Lord? Oh, soar above,
Ambitious soul. But which way should I fly?
Thou, Lord, art way and end. What wings have I?
Aspiring thoughts—of faith, of hope, of love:
Oh, let these wings, that way alone
Present me to thy blissful throne.

For Christmas Day

Immortal babe, who this dear day
Didst change thine heaven for our clay,
And didst with flesh thy Godhead veil,
Eternal Son of God, all hail!

Shine, happy star! Ye angels, sing
Glory on high to heaven's king!
Run, shepherds, leave your nightly watch!
See heaven come down to Bethlehem's cratch!

Worship, ye sages of the east,
The king of gods in meanness drest!
O blessed maid, smile, and adore
The God thy womb and arms have bore!

Star, angels, shepherds, and wise sages!
Thou virgin-glory of all ages!
Restored frame of heaven and earth!
Joy in your dear Redeemer's birth.

cratch - cretch, manger

SANDYS, GEORGE (1578–1664), a foreign service officer and writer, wrote extensively of his travels and translated numerous classical works. His *Relation of a Journey*, a journal of Mideast travels, was very popular in the seventeenth century and his verse translations of Ovid's *Metamorphoses* and Book I of Virgil's *Aeniad* were his major literary works. He was treasurer and director of industry and agriculture for the colony of Virginia from 1621 to 1626. His writings provided geographical and mythological data used by such writers as Sir Francis Bacon, Milton, and Keats. "In his compression, latinization of syntax, and balanced antithesis, he prepared the way for the heroic couplet of Dryden and Pope." (*Encyclopedia Britannica*) He also wrote numerous Biblical paraphrases and translations.

Deo Optimo Maximo

O Thou, who all things hast of nothing made,
Whose hand the radiant firmament displayed,
With such an undiscerned swiftness hurled
About the steadfast centre of the world;
Against whose rapid course the restless sun,
And wandering flames in varied motions run,
Which heat, light, life infuse; time, night, and day
Distinguish; in our human bodies sway:
That hung'st the solid earth in fleeting air
Veined with clear springs, which ambient seas repair,
In clouds the mountains wrap their hoary heads;
Luxurious valleys clothed with flowery meads;

Her trees yield fruit and shade; with liberal breasts
All creatures she, their common mother, feasts.
Then man Thy image madest; in dignity,
In knowledge, and in beauty, like to Thee,
Placed in a heaven on earth; without his toil
The ever-flourishing and fruitful soil
Unpurchased food produced; all creatures were
His subjects, serving more for love than fear.
He knew no lord but Thee; but when he fell
From his obedience, all at once rebel,
And in his ruin exercise their might;
Concurring elements against him fight;
Troops of unknown diseases, sorrow, age,
And death assail him with successive rage.
Hell let forth all her furies; none so great
As man to man:—ambition, pride, deceit,
Wrong armed with power, lust, rapine, slaughter reigned,
And flattered vice the name of virtue gained.
Then hills beneath the swelling waters stood,
And all the globe of earth was but one flood,
Yet could not cleanse their guilt. The following race
Worse than their fathers, and their sons more base;
Their god-like beauty lost; sin's wretched thrall;
No spark of their divine original
Left unextinguished; all enveloped
With darkness; in their bold transgressions dead:
When Thou didst from the East a light display,
Which rendered to the world a clearer day;
Whose precepts from Hell's jaws our steps withdraw,
And whose example was a living law;
Who purged us with His blood; the way prepared
To Heaven, and those long chained-up doors unbarred.
How infinite Thy mercy! which exceeds
The world thou madest, as well as our misdeeds;
Which greater reverence than Thy justice wins,
And still augments Thy honour by our sins.
O who hath tasted of Thy clemency
In greater measure or more oft than I!
My grateful verse Thy goodness shall display,
O Thou who went'st along in all my way,
To where the morning with perfumed wings
From the high mountains of Panchaea springs;
To that new found-out world, where sober Night

Takes from the Antipodes her silent flight;
To those dark seas where horrid Winter reigns,
And binds the stubborn floods in icy chains;
To Libyan wastes, whose thirst no showers assuage,
And where swoln Nilus cools the lion's rage,
Thy wonders in the deep have I beheld;
Yet all by those on Judah's hills excelled,
There, where the Virgin's Son His doctrine taught,
His miracles and our redemption wrought;
Where I, by Thee inspired, His praises sung,
And on His Sepulchre my offering hung.
Which way soe'er I turn my face or feet,
I see Thy glory, and Thy mercy meet;
Met on the Thracian shores, when in the strife
Of frantic Simoans Thou preservedst my life;
So, when Arabian thieves belaid us round,
And when, by all abandoned, Thee I found.
That false Sidonian wolf, whose craft put on
A sheep's soft fleece, and me, Bellerophon,
To ruin by his cruel letter sent,
Thou didst by Thy protecting hand prevent.
Thou savedst me from the bloody massacres
Of faithless Indians; from their treacherous wars;
From raging fevers; from the sultry breath
Of tainted air, which cloyed the jaws of death;
Preserved from swallowing seas, when towering waves
Mixed with the clouds, and opened their deep graves;
From barbarous pirates ransomed; by those taught,
Successfully with Salian Moors we fought;
Then brought'st me home in safety, that this earth
Might bury me, which fed me from my birth;
Blest with a healthful age, a quiet mind;
Content with little; to this work designed;
Which I at length have finished by Thy aid,
And now my vows have at Thy altar paid.

Hymn Written At The Holy Sepulchre In Jerusalem

Saviour of mankind, Man, Emmanuel!
Who sinless died for sin, who vanquished hell;
The first-fruits of the grave; whose life did give
Light to our darkness; in whose death we live:—

Oh! strengthen Thou my faith, convert my will,
That mine may Thine obey; protect me still,
So that the latter death may not devour
My soul, sealed with Thy seal.— So, in the hour
When Thou (whose body sanctified this tomb,
Unjustly judged), a glorious judge shall come
To judge the world with justice; by that sign
I may be known, and entertained for Thine.

BOLTON, EDMUND (c.1575–1633), a historian and poet, who with Raleigh, Spenser, and Jonson contributed to *England's Helicon*, a popular anthology of lyrical and pastoral poetry. He held a minor position in court, but did not obtain a public office largely due to his being a Roman Catholic. He wrote a number of books on Roman history and one on armor. He promoted a plan for a royal academy of letters and science, but despite favorable reception by James I, it was never instituted. He also planned histories of England and London which did not come to fruition. He was imprisoned for recusancy (refusal to attend Church of England services), and apparently died in poverty.

Madrigal

Sweet music, sweeter far
Than any song is sweet:
Sweet Music, heavenly rare,
Mine ears (O peeres), doth greet.
You gentle flocks, whose fleeces, pearled with dew,
Resemble heaven, whom golden drops make bright,
Listen, O listen, now, O not to you
Our pipes make sport to shorten weary night:
But voices most divine
Make blissful harmony;
Voices that seem to shine,
For what else clears the sky?
Tunes can we hear, but not the singers see,
The tunes divine, and so the singers be.

Lo, how the firmament
Within an azure fold
The flock of stars hath pent,
That we might them behold.
Yet from their beams proceedeth not this light,
Nor can their crystals such reflection give.

What then doth make the element so bright?
The heavens are come down upon earth to live.
But hearken to the song,
Glory to Glory's king,
And peace all men among,
These choristers do sing.
Angels they are, as also, Shepherds, he
Whom in our fear we do admire to see.

FLETCHER, PHINEAS (1582–1650), elder son of Giles Fletcher the elder and brother of Giles the younger, he published *The Purple Island*, a Christian and scientific poem, in 1633. It includes his "Piscatorie Eclogs and Other Poetical Miscellany" and "The Purple Island: of the Isle of Man." The "Eclogs" are pastorals set on the banks of the Cam River. "The Purple Island" is a poem in 12 cantos describing the human body and soul in allegorical terms. It is written in the manner of Spenser and some critics see it as the link between Spenser and John Bunyan.

The Divine Wooer

Me, Lord? Canst Thou misspend
One word, misplace one look on me?
Call'st me Thy love, Thy friend?
Can this poor soul the object be
Of these love-glances, those life-kindling eyes?
What? I the centre of Thy arms' embraces?
Of all Thy labour I the prize?
Love never mocks, truth never lies.
Oh, how I quake! Hope fear, fear hope displaces.
I would but cannot hope: such wondrous love amazes.

See, I am black as night,
See, I am darkness: dark as hell.
Lord, Thou more fair than light:
Heaven's sun Thy shadow. Can suns dwell
With shades? 'twixt light and darkness what commerce?
' True, thou art darkness, I thy light: My ray
Thy mists and hellish fogs shall pierce.
With Me, black soul, with Me converse.
I make the foul December flowery May:
Turn thou thy night to Me, I'll turn thy night to day. '

See, Lord, see I am dead,
Tombed in myself, myself my grave:
A drudge, so born, so bred—
Myself even to myself a slave.
Thou, Freedom, Life; can Life and Liberty
Love bondage, death? ' Thy Freedom I, I tied
To loose thy bonds: be bound to Me.
My yoke shall ease, My bonds shall free.
Dead soul, thy spring of life My dying side:
There die, with Me to live: to live in thee I died. '

An Hymne

Drop, drop, slow tears, and bathe those beauteous feet,
Which brought from heav'n the news and Prince of peace:
Cease not, wet eyes, his mercies to entreat;
To crie for vengeance sinne doth never cease:
In your deep floods drown all my faults and fears;
Nor let his eye see sinne, but through my tears.

To A Rich Man

If well thou view'st us with no squinted eyes,
No partial judgment, thou wilt quickly rate
Thy wealth no richer than my poverty;
My want no poorer than thy rich estate:
Our ends and births alike; in this, as I;
Poor thou wert born, and poor again shalt die.

My little fills my little-wishing mind;
Thou having more than much, yet seekest more:
Who seeks, still wishes what he seeks to find;
Who wishes, wants; and who so wants, is poor;
Then this must follow of necessity—
Poor are thy riches, rich my poverty.

Though still thou gett'st, yet is thy want not spent,
But as thy wealth, so grows thy wealthy itch:
But with my little I have much content;
Content hath all, and who hath all is rich:
Then this in reason thou must needs confess—
If I have little, yet that thou hast less.

Whatever man possesses, God hath lent,
And to his audit liable is ever,
To reckon, how, and where, and when he spent:
Then thus thou bragg'st, thou art a great receiver:
Little my debt, when little is my store:
The more thou hast, thy debt still grows the more.

But seeing God himself descended down
T'enrich the poor by his rich poverty;
His meat, his house, his grave, were not his own,
Yet all is his from all eternity:
Let me be like my Head, whom I adore;
Be thou great, wealthy, I still base and poor.

The Dying Husband's Farewell

My dearest consort, my more loved heart,
I leave thee now: with thee all earthly joying:
Heaven knows with thee I sadly part:
All other earthly sweets have had their cloying;
Yet never full of thy sweet loves' enjoying,
Thy constant loves, next Heaven I did refer them;
Had not much grace prevail'd, 'fore Heaven I should
    prefer them.

I leave them, now the trumpet calls away;
In vain thine eyes beg for some time's reprieving;
Yet in my children here immortal stay:
In one I die, in many ones am living:
In them, and for them, stay thy too much grieving;
Look but on them, in them thou still wilt see
Marry'd with thee again thy twice-two Antony.

And when with little hands they stroke thy face,
As in thy lap they sit (ah, careless!) playing,
And stammering ask a kiss, give them a brace;
The last from me: and then a little staying,
And in their face some part of me surveying,
In them give me a third, and with a tear
Show thy dear love to him who loved thee ever dear.

And now our falling house leans all on thee;
This little nation to thy care commend them;
In thee it lies that hence they want not me;

Themselves yet cannot, thou the more defend them;
And when green age permits, to goodness bend them;
A mother were you once, now both you are:
Thou with this double style double your love and care.

Turn their unwary steps into the way:
What first the vessel drinks, it long retaineth;
No bars will hold, when they have used to stray:
And when for me one asks, and weeping plaineth,
Point thou to heaven, and say, " He there remaineth:"
And if they live in grace, grow, and persevere,
There shall they live with me: else they shall see me never.

My God, oh! I in thy fear here let me live!
Thy wards they are, take them to thy protection;
Thou gavest them first, now back to thee I give;
Direct them now, and help her weak direction;
That re-united by thy strong election,
Thou now in them, they then may live in thee;
And seeing here thy will, may there thy glory see.

Farewell, farewell! I feel my long long rest,
And iron sleep my leaden heart oppressing:
Night after day, sleep after labour's best;
Port after storms, joy after long distressing:
So weep thy loss, as knowing 'tis my blessing;
Both as a widow and a Christian grieve:
Still live I in thy thoughts, but as in heaven I live.

The Triumph Of The Church

With that a thundering noise seemed shake the sky,
As when with iron wheels through stony plain
A thousand chariots to the battle fly;
Or when with boisterous rage the swelling main,
Puffed up by mighty winds, does hoarsely roar,
And breaking with his waves the trembling shore,
His sandy girdle seems, and breaks earth's rampart door.

And straight an angel, full of heavenly might,
(Three several crowns circled his royal head,)
From northern coast heaving his blazing light,
Through all the earth his glorious beams dispread,
And open lays the beast and Dragon's shame;

For to this end the Almighty did him frame,
And therefore from supplanting gave his ominous name.

A silver trumpet oft he loudly blew,
Frighting the guilty earth with thundering knell;
And oft proclaimed, as round the world he flew,
"Babel, great Babel, lies as low as hell.
Let every angel loud his trumpet sound,
Her heaven-exalted towers in dust are drowned;
Babel, proud Babel's fallen, and lies as low as ground!"

The broken heavens dispart with fearful noise,
And from the breach outshoots a sudden light;
Straight shrilling trumpets, with loud-sounding voice,
Give echoing summons to new bloody fight:
Well knew the Dragon that all-quelling blast,
And soon perceived that day must be his last,
Which struck his frightened heart and all his troops aghast.

Yet full of malice and of stubborn pride,
Though oft had strove, and had been foiled as oft,
Boldly his death and certain fate defied;
And, mounted on his flaggy sails aloft,
With boundless spite he longed to try again
A second loss, and new death;—glad and fain
To show his poisonous hate, though ever showed in vain.

So up he arose upon his stretched sails,
Fearless expecting his approaching death;
So up he arose, that the air starts and fails,
And overpressed, sinks his load beneath;
So up he arose, as doth a thunder-cloud,
Which, all the, earth with shadows black doth shroud;
 So up he arose, and through the weary air he rowed.

Now his Almighty foe far off he spies,
Whose sun-like arms dazzled the eclipsed day,
Confounding with their beams less glittering skies,
Firing the air with more than heavenly ray,
Like thousand suns in one:—such is their light,
A subject only for immortal sprite,
Which never can be seen but by immortal sight.

His threatening eyes shine like that dreadful flame
With which the Thunderer arms his angry hand:

Himself had fairly wrote his wondrous name,
Which neither earth nor heaven could understand:
A hundred crowns, like towers, be set around
His conquering head; well may they there abound,
When all his limbs and troops with gold are richly crowned.

His armor all was dyed in purple blood,
(In purple blood of thousand rebel kings,)
In vain their stubborn powers his aim withstood;
Their proud necks chained he now in triumph brings,
And breaks their spears and cracks their traitor-swords;
Upon whose arms and thigh in golden words
Was fairly writ, "The King of kings, and Lord of lords."

His snow-white steed was born of heavenly kind,
Begot by Boreas on the Thracian hills,
More strong and speedy than his parent wind,
And (which his foes with fear and horror fills)
Out from his mouth a two-edged sword he darts,
Whose sharpest steel the bone and marrow parts,
And with his keenest point unbreast the naked hearts.

The Dragon, wounded with his flaming brand,
They take, and in strong bonds and fetters tie:
Short was the fight, nor could he long withstand
Him whose appearance is his victory.
So now he's bound in adamantine chain:
He storms, he roars, he yells for high disdain;
His net is broke, the fowl go free, the fowler's ta'en.

Soon at this sight the knights revive again,
As fresh as when the flowers from winter's tomb,
When now the sun brings back his nearest train,
Peep out again from their fresh mother's womb:
The primrose, lighted new, her flame displays,
And frights the neighbor hedge with fiery rays!
And all the world renew their mirth and sportive plays.

The prince, who saw his long imprisonment
Now end in never-ending liberty,
To meet the victor from his castle went,
And falling down, clasping his royal knee,
Pours out deserved thanks in grateful praise:
But him the heavenly Saviour soon doth raise,
And bids him spend in joy his never-ending days.

BEAUMONT, JOHN (1583–1627), elder brother of the dramatist, Francis, studied at Oxford and succeeded to his father's estates on the death of a yet older brother. He published a mock-heroic poem in 1602, *The Metamorphosis of Tobacco*. A long work, *The Crown of Thorns*, was lost in manuscript. He was "created" a baronet in 1626, and was buried in Westminster Abbey on his death a year later. In 1629 his son, Sir John, published his collected poetry as *Bosworth Field, with a Taste of the Variety of other Poems, left by Sir John Beaumont*.

Of The Epiphany

Fair eastern star, that art ordained to run
Before the sages, to the rising sun,
Here cease thy course, and wonder that the cloud
Of this poor stable can thy Maker shroud:
Ye, heavenly bodies, glory to be bright,
And are esteemed as ye are rich in light;
But here on earth is taught a different way,
Since under this low roof the highest lay.
Jerusalem erects her stately towers,
Displays her windows, and adorns her bowers;
Yet there thou must not cast a trembling spark:
Let Herod's palace still continue dark;
Each school and synagogue thy force repels,
There Pride, enthroned in misty errors, dwells;
The temple, where the priests maintain their choir,
Shall taste no beam of thy celestial fire,
While this weak cottage all thy splendour takes:
A joyful gate of every chink it makes.
Here shines no golden roof, no ivory stair,
No king exalted in a stately chair,
Girt with attendants, or by heralds styled,
But straw and hay enwrap a speechless child;
Yet Sabae's lords before this babe unfold
Their treasures, offering incense, myrrh, and gold,
The crib becomes an altar: therefore dies
No ox nor sheep; for in their fodder lies
The Prince of Peace, who, thankful for his bed,
Destroys those rites in which their blood was shed:
The quintessence of earth he takes and fees,
And precious gums distilled from weeping trees;
Rich metals and sweet odours now declare
The glorious blessings which his laws prepare,

To clear us from the base and loathsome flood
Of sense, and make us fit for angels' food,
Who lift to God for us the holy smoke
Of fervent prayers with which we him invoke,
And try our actions in that searching fire,
By which the seraphims our lips inspire:
No muddy dross pure minerals shall infect,
We shall exhale our vapours up direct:
No storms shall cross, nor glittering lights deface
Perpetual sighs which seek a happy place.

In Desolation

O thou who sweetly bend'st my stubborn will,
Who send'st thy stripes to teach and not to kill!
Thy cheerful face from me no longer hide;
Withdraw these clouds, the scourges of my pride;
I sink to hell, if I be lower thrown
I see what man is, being left alone.
My substance, which from nothing did begin,
Is worse than nothing by the weight of sin:
I see myself in such a wretched state
As neither thoughts conceive, nor words relate.
How great a distance parts us! for in thee
Is endless good, and boundless ill in me.
All creatures prove me abject, but how low
Thou only know'st, and teachest me to know.
To paint this baseness, nature is too base;
This darkness yields not but to beams of grace.
Where shall I then this piercing splendour find?
Or found, how shall it guide me, being blind?
Grace is a taste of bliss, a glorious gift,
Which can the soul to heavenly comforts lift:
It will not shine to me, whose mind is drowned
In sorrows, and with worldly troubles bound;
It will not deign within that house to dwell,
Where dryness reigns, and proud distractions swell.
Perhaps it sought me in those lightsome days
Of my first fervour, when few winds did raise
The waves, and ere they could full strength obtain,
Some whispering gale straight charmed them down again;
When all seemed calm, and yet the Virgin's child

On my devotions in his manger smiled;
While then I simply walked, nor heed could take
Of complacence, that sly, deceitful snake;
When yet I had not dangerously refused
So many calls to virtue, nor abused
The spring of life, which I so oft enjoyed,
Nor made so many good intentions void,
Deserving thus that grace should quite depart,
And dreadful hardness should possess my heart:
Yet in that state this only good I found,
That fewer spots did then my conscience wound;
Though who can censure whether, in those times,
The want of feeling seemed the want of crimes?
If solid virtues dwell not but in pain,
I will not wish that golden age again
Because it flowed with sensible delights
Of heavenly things: God hath created nights
As well as days, to deck the varied globe;
Grace comes as oft clad in the dusky robe
Of desolation, as in white attire,
Which better fits the bright celestial choir.
Some in foul seasons perish through despair,
But more through boldness when the days are fair.
This then must be the medicine for my woes—
To yield to what my Saviour shall dispose;
To glory in my baseness; to rejoice
In mine afflictions; to obey his voice,
As well when threatenings my defects reprove
As when I cherished am with words of love;
To say to him, in every time and place,
"Withdraw thy comforts, so thou leave thy grace."

PESTEL (PESTELL), THOMAS (c.1584–c.1659), after graduating from
Cambridge, became a vicar in Leicestershire. A little later he became chaplain to
the earl of Essex. He was highly reputed as a preacher and published a few of
his sermons. He was appointed a royal chaplain after 1630 and preached before
the king, and in 1640 he preached before the council. He resigned his "living"
to his son in 1644. He complained of having been several times robbed and
plundered during the civil wars. He collected some of his verse and sermons in
Sermons and Devotions, Old and New, revewed and publisht . . . with a Discourse of Duels in
1659, not long before he died.

Psalm For Christmas Day

Behold the great Creator makes
    Himself an house of clay,
A robe of Virgin-flesh He takes
    Which He will wear for aye.

Hark, hark, the wise eternal Word
    Like a weak infant cries;
In form of servant is the Lord.
    And God in cradle lies.

This wonder struck the world amazed,
    It shook the starry frame;
Squadrons of spirits stood and gazed,
    Then down in troops they came.

Glad shepherds ran to view this sight;
    A quire of angels sings;
And eastern sages with delight
    Adore this King of kings.

Join then, all hearts that are not stone.
    And all our voices prove,
To celebrate this Holy One,
    The God of peace and love.

DRUMMOND, WILLIAM (Of Hawthornden), (1585—1649), studied at Edinburgh and went to Paris and Bourges to study law until the death of his father. He then returned and settled on his father's estate at Hawthornden, where he devoted himself to writing and mechanical experiments. He was the first major Scots poet to write exclusively in English. His friends included Ben Jonson, who stayed with him for a time, and Michael Drayton, the poet. Drummond adapted and translated poems from French, Italian, and Spanish, as well as borrowing from Sir Philip Sidney. Some of his best known poems are near-translations of Renaissance love poetry. Among his poetic works is *Flowers of Zion*. His prose work *Cypresse Grove* is a meditation of death and mutability. A staunch Royalist, he also wrote a number of political pamphlets and a history of Scotland.

Madrigal

Ah! silly soul, what wilt thou say,
When he whom earth and heavens obey,
Comes man to judge in the last day;

When he a reason asks, why grace
And goodness thou would'st not embrace,
But steps of vanity didst trace?

That day of terror, vengeance, ire,
Now to prevent thou should'st desire,
And to thy God in haste retire.

With wat'ry eyes, and sigh-swoll'n heart,
O beg, beg in his love a part,
Whilst conscience with remorse doth smart.

Sonnet vi
The Booke Of The World

Of this faire Volumne which wee World doe name,
If wee the sheetes and leaves could turne with care,
Of Him who it correctes, and did it frame,
Wee cleare might read the Art and Wisedome rare?
Finde out his Power which wildest Pow'rs doth tame,
His Providence extending everie-where,
His justice which proud Rebels doeth not spare,
In everie Page, no, Period of the same:
But sillie wee (like foolish Children) rest
Well pleas'd with colour'd Velame, Leaves of Gold,
Faire dangling Ribbones, leaving what is best,
On the great Writers sense ne'er taking hold;
Or if by chance our Mindes doe muse on ought,
It is some Picture on the Margine wrought.

Sonnet vii
The Miserable Estate Of The World Before The Incarnation Of God

The Griefe was common, common were the Cryes,
Teares, Sobbes, and Groanes of that afflicted Traine,
Which of Gods chosen did the Summe containe,
And Earth rebounded with them, pierc'd were Skies;

All good had left the World, each Vice did raigne,
In the most hideous shapes Hell could devise,
And all degrees, and each Estate did staine,
Nor further had to goe, whom to surprise:
The World beneath the Prince of Darknesse lay,
In everie Phane who had himselfe install'd,
Was sacrifiz'd unto, by Prayers call'd,
Responses gave, which (Fooles) they did obey:
When (pittying Man) God of a Virgines wombe
Was borne, and those false Deities strooke dombe.

Phane - Temple

Sonnet x
Amazement At The Incarnation Of God

To spread the azure Canopie of Heaven,
And make it twinkle with those spangs of Gold,
To stay this weightie masse of Earth so even,
That it should all, and nought should it up-hold;
To give strange motions to the Planets seven,
Or Jove to make so meeke, or Mars so bold,
To temper what is moist, drie, hote, and cold,
Of all their Jarres that sweete accords are given:
LORD, to thy Wisedome nought is, nor thy Might;
But that thou shouldst (thy Glorie laid aside)
Come meanelie in mortalitie to bide,
And die for those deserv'd eternall plight,
A wonder is so farre above our wit,
That Angels stand amaz'd to muse on it.

spangs - spangles, ornaments

Madrigall ii
Faith Above Reason

Soule, which to Hell wast thrall,
Hee, Hee for thine offence,
Did suffer Death, who could not die at all
O soveraigne Excellence,
O Life of all that lives,
Eternall Bounty which each good thing gives,
How could Death mount so hie?

No wit this hight can reach,
Faith only doth us teach,
For us Hee died, at all who could not dye.

Sonnet xvii
Mans Knowledge, Ignorance In The Misteries Of God

Beneath a sable vaile, and Shadowes deepe,
Of Unaccessible and dimming light,
In Silence ebane Clouds more blacke than Night,
The Worlds great King his secrets hidde doth keepe:
Through those Thicke Mistes when any Mortall Wight
Aspires, with halting pace, and Eyes that weepe,
To pore, and in his Misteries to creepe,
With Thunders hee and Lightnings blastes their Sight.
O Sunne invisible, that dost abide
Within thy bright abysmes, most faire, most darke,
Where with thy proper Rayes thou dost thee hide;
O ever-shining, never full seene marke,
To guide mee in Lifes Night, thy light mee show,
The more I search of thee, The lesse I know.

ebane - ebony; proper - own

Sonnet xxvi
The Blessednesse Of Faithfull Soules By Death

Let us each day enure our selves to dye,
If this (and not our Feares) be truely Death;
Above the Circles both of Hope and Faith
With faire immortall pinniones to flie?
If this be Death our best Part to untie
(By running the Jaile) from Lust and Wrath,
And every drowsie languor heere beneath,
In turning deniz'd Citizen of Skie?
To have, more knowledge than all Bookes containe,
All Pleasures even surmounting wishing Powre,
The fellowship of Gods immortall Traine,
And these that Time nor force shall er'e devoure?
If this be Death? what Joy, what golden care
Of Life, can with Deaths ouglinesse compare?

deniz'd - denizened, resident; Skie - Heaven

Madrigal—Life as a Bubble

This life, which seems so far,
Is like a bubble blown up in the air
By sporting children's breath,
Who chase it everywhere,
And strive who can most motion it bequeath.
And though it sometimes seems of its own might,
Like to an eye of gold to be fixed there,
And firm to hover in that empty height,
That only is because it is so light.
But in that pomp it doth not long appear;
For, when 'tis most admired in a thought,
Because it erst was naught, it turns to naught.

erst - at first

Closing Section of **A Hymn to the Fairest Fair**

O king, whose greatness none can comprehend,
Whose boundless goodness doth to all extend!
Light of all beauty! ocean without ground,
That standing flowest, giving dost abound!
Rich palace, and indweller ever blest,
Never not working, ever yet in rest!
What wit cannot conceive, words say of thee,
Here, where, as in a mirror, we but see
Shadows of shadows, atoms of thy might,
Still owly-eyed while staring on thy light,
Grant that, released from this earthly jail,
And freed of clouds which here our knowledge veil,
In heaven's high temples, where thy praises ring,
I may in sweeter notes hear angels sing.

AUSTIN, WILLIAM (1587–1634), a lawyer of Lincoln's Inn, did not publish his own poetry during his lifetime, despite the urging of his friend James Howell. He lived for many years in Southwark where he had a considerable local reputation from circulating his poems among friends. In 1635 *Certayne Devout, Godly, and Learned Meditations: written by the Excelently Acomplisht Gentleman, William Austin of Lincolnes Inne, Esquier* was published by his wife, Anne. It includes carols and meditations and ends with a prose sermon. In 1637, along with a second edition of his poems, *Haec Homo, wherein the Excellency of the Creation of Woman is* described by way of an *Essay* was published by Austin's friends. Another of his works, *Cato Major*, or *the Book of Old Age*. . . was published by a London stationer several decades later.

To a Musician

Many musicians are more out of order than their instruments; such as are so, may by singing this Ode become reprovers of their own untunable affections: they who are better tempered, are hereby remembered what music is most acceptable to God, and most profitable to themselves.

> What helps it those,
> > Who skill in song have found,
> Well to compose
> > Of disagreeing notes,
> By artful choice,
> > A sweetly pleasing sound,
> To fit their voice,
> > And their melodious throats?
> What helps it them
> > That they this cunning know,
> If most condemn
> > The way in which they go?
> What will he gain
> > By touching well his lute,
> Who shall disdain
> > A grave advice to hear?
> What from the sounds
> > Of organ, fife, or lute,
> To him redounds,
> > Who doth no sin forbear?
> A mean respect,
> > By tuning strings he hath,
> Who doth neglect
> > A rectified path.
> Therefore, O Lord!
> > So tuned let me be
> Unto Thy Word,
> > And Thy ten-stringed law,
> That in each part
> > I may thereto agree,
> And feel my heart
> > Inspired with loving awe;

He sings and plays
>The songs which best thou lovest,
Who does and says
>The things which Thou approvest.
Teach me the skill
>Of him whose harp assuaged
Those passions ill
>Which oft afflicted Saul;
Teach me the strain
>Which calmeth minds enraged,
And which from vain
>Affections doth recall:
So to the choir
>Where angels music make,
I may aspire
>When I this life forsake.

FLETCHER, GILES the Younger (1588–1623), like his brother Phineas was a poetical follower of Spenser. He went to Cambridge, was ordained, and held a college position. His sermons at St. Mary's were famous. He left Cambridge and received a rectory in Suffolk. His masterpiece, *Christs Victorie, and Triumph in Heaven, and Earth, over, and after death* somewhat resembles the *Devine Weeks and Workes* (translated) of Du Bartas, the French Protestant poet. (Du Bartas was apparently a significant influence on Protestant poetry of the period. Anne Bradstreet regarded him as a laureate.) Fletcher's work is not mere translation or paraphrase, however. *Christs Victorie* is a Baroque poem of strong passion and vision, especially in depicting paradise. It, in turn, is thought to have influenced Milton's *Paradise Regained.*

The Celestial City from Christ's Triumph after Death
(stanzas 30-43)

Here let my Lord hang up his conquering lance,
And bloody armour with late slaughter warme,
And looking downe on his weake Militants,
Behold his Saints, 'midst of their hot alarme,
Hang all their golden hopes upon his arme.
And in this lower field dispacing wide,
Through windie thoughts, that would their sayles misguide,
Anchor their fleshly ships fast in his wounded side.

Here may the Band, that now in tryumph shines,
And that (before they were invested thus)
In earthly bodies carried heavenly mindes,
Pitcht round about in order glorious,
Their sunny Tents, and houses luminous,
All their eternall day in songs employing,
Joying their ends, without ende of their joying,
While their almightie Prince Destruction is destroying.

Full, yet without satietie, of that
Which whets and quiets greedy Appetite,
Where never Sunne did rise, nor ever sat,
But one eternall day, and endless light
Gives time to those, whose time is infinite,
Speaking with thought, obtaining without fee,
Beholding him, whom never eye could see,
And magnifying him, that cannot greater be.

How can such joy as this want words to speake?
And yet what words can speake such joy as this?
Far from the world, that might their quiet breake,
Here the glad Soules the face of beauty kisse,
Pour'd out in pleasure, on their beds of blisse.
And drunke with nectar torrents, ever hold
Their eyes on him, whose graces manifold,
The more they doe behold, the more they would behold.

Their sight drinkes lovely fires in at their eyes,
Their braine sweete incense with fine breath accloyes,
That on Gods sweating altar burning lies,
Their hungrie cares feede on their heav'nly noyse,
That Angels sing, to tell their untold joyes;
Their understanding naked Truth, their wills
The all, and selfe-sufficient Goodnesse fills,
That nothing here is wanting, but the want of ills.

No Sorrowe now hangs clouding on their browe,
No bloodless Maladie empales their face,
No Age drops on their hairs his silver snowe,
No Nakednesse their bodies doth embase,
No Povertie themselves, and theirs disgrace,
No feare of death the joy of life devours,
No unchast sleepe their precious time deflowrs,
No losse, no griefe, no change waite on their winged hours.

But now their naked bodies scorne the cold,
And from their eyes joy lookes, and laughs at paine,
The infant wonders how he came so old,
And old man how he came so young againe;
Still resting, though from sleepe they still refraine,
Where all are rich, and yet no gold they owe,
And all are Kings, and yet no Subjects knowe,
All full, and yet no time on foode they doe bestowe.

A heav'nly feast, no hunger can consume,
A light unseene, yet shines in every place,
A sound, no time can steale, a sweet perfume,
No windes can scatter, an intire embrace,
That no satietie can e'er unlace,
Ingrac'd into so high a favour, there
The saints, with their Beau-peers, whole worlds outwear,
And things unseene doe see, and things unheard doe hear.

Ye blessed soules, growne richer by your spoile,
Whose losse, though great, is cause of greater gaines,
Here may your weary Spirits rest from toyle,
Spending your endlesse ev'ning, that remaines,
Among those white flocks, and celestiall traines,
That feed upon their Sheapheards eyes, and frame
That heav'nly musique of so wondrous fame,
Psalming aloude the holy honours of his name.

Had I a voice of steel to tune my song,
Were every verse as smoothly fil'd as glasse,
And every member turned to a tongue,
And every tongue were made of sounding brasse,
Yet all that skill, and all this strength, alas,
Should it presume to gild, were misadvis'd,
The place, where David hath new songs devis'd,
As in his burning throne he sits emparadis'd.

Mercy Replies to Justice From Christ's Victory and Triumph

He was but dust: how could he stand before him?
And being fallen, why should he fear to die?
Cannot the hand that made him first, restore him?
Depraved of sin, should he deprived lie
Of grace? Can He not find infirmity
That gave him strength? Unworthy the forsaking

He is, whoever weighs without mistaking
Or Maker of the man, or manner of his making.

Who shall thy temple incense any more,
Or at thy altar crown the sacrifice,
Or strew with idle flowers the hallowed floor?
Or what should prayer deck with herbs and spice,
Her vials breathing orisons of price?
If all must pay that which all cannot pay,
Oh! first begin with me, and Mercy slay,
And thy thrice-honored Son that now beneath doth stray.

But if or He or I may live and speak,—
And heaven can joy to see a sinner weep,—
Oh! let not Justice' iron sceptre break
A heart already broke, that low doth creep,
And with proud humbless her feet's dust doth sweep.
Must all go by desert? Is nothing free?
Ah! if but those who only worthy be,
None should Thee ever see, none should thee ever see!

What hath man done that man shall not undo
Since God to him is grown so near akin?
Did his foes slay him? He shall slay his foe:
Hath he lost all? He all again shall win:
Is sin his master? He shall master sin.
Too hardy soul, with sin the field to try:
The only way to conquer was to fly;
But thus long death hath lived, and now death's self shall die.

He is a path, if any be misled;
He is a robe, if any naked be;
If any chance to hunger, He is bread;
If any be a bondman, He is free;
If any be but weak, how strong is He!
To dead men life He is, to sick men health,
To blind men sight, and to the needy wealth;
A pleasure without loss, a treasure without stealth.

Who can forget—never to be forgot—
The time that all the world in slumber lies,
When like the stars the singing angels shot
To earth, and heaven awaked all his eyes
To see another sun at midnight rise?

On earth? was never sight of pariel fame;
For God before man like Himself did frame,
But God Himself now like a mortal man became.

A child He was, and had not learned to speak,
That with his word the world before did make;
His mother's arms Him bore, He was so weak,
That with one hand the vaults of heaven could shake.
See how small room my infant Lord doth take,
Whom all the world is not enough to hold!
Who of his years or of his age hath told?
Never such age so young, never a child so old.

And yet but newly He was infanted,
And yet already He was sought to die;
Yet scarcely born, already banished;
Not able yet to go, and forced to fly;
But scarcely fled away, when, by and by,
The tyrant's sword with blood is all defiled,
And Rachel, for her sons, with fury wild,
Cries, O thou cruel king! and, O my sweetest child!

Egypt his nurse became, where Nilus springs,
Who straight to entertain the rising sun,
The hasty harvest in his bosom brings;
But now for drought the fields were all undone,
And now with waters all is overrun:
So fast thy Cynthian mountains poured their snow,
When once they felt the sun so near them glow,
That Nilus Egypt lost, and to a sea did grow.

The angels carolled loud their song of peace;
The cursed oracles were stricken dumb;
To see their Shepherd the poor shepherds press;
To see their King, the kingly sophics come;
And then, to guide unto his master's home,
A star comes dancing up the orient,
That springs for joy over the strawy tent,
Where gold to make their prince a crown they all present.

Young John, glad child, before he could be born,
Leaped in the womb, his joy to prophesy;
Old Anna, though with age all spent and worn,

pariel - equal; sophics - wise men

Proclaims her Saviour to posterity;
And Simeon fast his dying notes doth ply.
Oh, how the blessed souls about him trace!
It is the sire of heaven thou dost embrace:
Sing, Simeon, sing—sing, Simeon, sing apace.

With that the mighty thunder dropt away
From God's unwary arm, now milder grown,
And melted into tears; as if to pray
For pardon and for pity, it had known
That should have been for sacred vengeance thrown;
There, too, the armies angelic devowed
Their former rage, and all to Mercy bowed;
Their broken weapons at her feet they gladly strowed.

Bring, bring, ye Graces, all your silver flaskets,
Painted with every choicest flower that grows,
That I may soon unflower your fragrant baskets,
To strow the fields with odors where He goes;
Let whatsoe'er He treads on be a rose.
So down she lets her eyelids fall to shine
Upon the rivers of bright Palestine,
Whose woods drop honey, and her rivers skip with wine.

To Whom Else Can We Fly?

Should any to himself for safety fly?
The way to save himself, if anywhere,
Were to fly from himself; should he rely
Upon the promise of his wife? but there
What can he see but that he most may fear,
A syren sweet to death? upon his friends?
Who, that he needs, or that he hath not, lends?
Or wanting aid himself, aid to another sends?

His strength? but dust: his pleasure? cause of pain:
His hope? false courtier: youth or beauty? brittle:
Entreaty? fond: repentance? late and vain:
Just recompense? the world were all too little:
Thy love? he hath no title to a tittle:
Hell's force, in vain her furies hell shall gather:
His servants, kinsmen, or his children rather?
His child, if good, shall judge; if bad, shall curse his father:

His life? that brings him to his end and leaves him:
His end? that leaves him to begin his wo:
His goods? what good in that, that so deceives him?
His gods of wood? their feet, alas! are slow
To go to help, that must be helped to go:
Honor? great worth? ah! little worth they be
Unto their owners: wit? that makes him see
He wanted wit, that thought he had it wanting Thee.

The sea to drink him quick? that casts his dead:
Angels to spare? they punish: night to hide?
The world shall burn in light: the heavens to spread
Their wings to save him? heaven itself shall slide
And roll away, like melting stars that glide
Along their oily threads: his mind pursues him:
His house to shroud, or hills to fall and bruise him?
As sergeants both attach and witnesses accuse him.

WITHER, GEORGE (1588–1667) dropped out of Oxford after two years in order to study law, devoted himself thereafter to literature, producing some fine lyric poetry and pointed satire. He became a noted member of the London literary establishment and counted among his acquaintances William Browne and Michael Drayton. His *Epithalamia: or Nuptiall Poems,* celebrating the marriage of Princess Elizabeth, pleased her and she became Wither's most powerful patron. Wither went to prison, however, over a book of satirical essays and poems which struck the authorities as seditious. He was released due to Elizabeth's intervention, after writing some of his better poems in prison. He and William Browne affected each other's pastoral poetry over the next few years. Wither angered the printers and booksellers (The Stationer's Company) in 1623 by gaining special patents from James I which included a compulsory order that a copy of his *Hymnes and Songs of the Church* be included in all authorized Psalm books thereafter. He also enjoyed the antipathy of Ben Jonson and his band of disciples. Wither published a popular poem called "Wither's Motto. Nec habeo, nec careo, nec curo," which John Winthrop saw as a sign of hope for 'our modern spirit of poetry.' Wither was sued for libel over this poem but won the case. He became a convinced Puritan like his contemporary Milton. He published a book of Christian poems, *Hallelujah,* in 1641 as the best of a long series of published religious works including a number of psalm translations, hymns, and moral odes. In 1642 he sold his estate to raise a troop of horse for Parliament and served briefly as a captain of Farnham Castle. He was captured by a troop of royalists and owed his life, apparently, to the intercession of Sir John Denham who pleaded that "so long as Wither lived, he [Denham] would not be accounted the worst poet in England." From 1645 on he occupied himself in writing and in "discovering" the estates of royalists including Sir John Denham, from whose lands he received an income for a number of years. He did not soften his position at the approach of Charles II's restoration, so that upon the restoration, his papers were searched and he was sent to Newgate prison from which he was released after a year on a bond for good behavior. He continued to write steadily on politically dangerous subjects as well as such subjects as the plague of 1665, and the Lord's Prayer.

The Marigold
"Whil'st I, the Sunne's bright Face may view,
I will noe meaner Light pursue"

When with a serious musing, I behold
The faithfull, and obsequious Marigold,
How duely, ev'ry morning, she displayes
Her open breast, when Titan spreads his Rayes;
How she observes him in his daily walke,
Still bending towards him, her tender stalke;
How, when he downe declines, she droopes and mournes,
Bedew'd (as 'twere) with teares, till he returnes;
And, how she vailes her Flow'rs, when he is gone,
As if she scorned to be looked on
By an inferiour Eye; or, did contemne
To wayt upon a meaner Light, than Him.
When this I meditate, me-thinkes, the Flowers
Have spirits, farre more generous, than ours;
And, give us faire Examples, to despise
The servile Fawnings, and Idolatries,
Wherewith we court these earthly things below,
Which merit not the service we bestow.
But, oh my God! though groveling I appeare
Upon the Ground, (and have a rooting here,
Which hales me downwards) yet in my desire,
To that, which is above mee, I aspire:
And, all my best Affections I professe
To Him, that is the Sunne of Righteousnesse.
Oh! keepe the Morning of his Incarnation,
The burning Noone tide of his bitter Passion,
The Night of his Descending, and the Height
Of his Ascension, ever in my sight:
That imitating him, in what I may,
I never follow an inferiour Way.

When We Cannot Sleep

What ails my heart, that in my breast
It thus unquiet lies;
And that it now of needful rest
Deprives my tired eyes?

Let not vain hopes, griefs, doubts, or fears,
Distemper so my mind;
But cast on God thy thoughtful cares,
And comfort thou shalt find.

In vain that soul attempteth ought,
And spends her thoughts in vain,
Who by or in herself hath sought
Desired peace to gain.

On thee, O Lord, on thee therefore,
My musings now I place;
Thy free remission I implore,
And thy refreshing grace.
Forgive thou me, that when my mind
Oppressed began to be,
I sought elsewhere my peace to find,
Before I came to thee.

And, gracious God, vouche to grant,
Unworthy though I am,
The needful rest which now I want,
That I may praise thy name.

Extract from **A Prisoner's Lay**

First think, my soul, if I have foes
That take a pleasure in my care,
And to procure those outward woes
Have thus enwrapt me unaware;
    Thou shouldst by much more careful be,
    Since greater foes lay wait for thee.

By my late hopes that now are crossed,
Consider those that firmer be,
And make the freedom I have lost,
A means that may remember thee.

Had Christ not thy Redeemer been,
What horrid state hadst thou been in!

Or when through me then seest a man
Condemned unto a mortal death,
How sad he looks, how pale, how wan,
Drawing, with fear, his panting breath
    Think if in that such grief thou see,
    How sad will "Go ye cursed" be!

These iron chains, these bolts of steel,
Which often poor offenders grind;
The wants and cares which they do feel
May bring some greater things to mind.
    For by their grief thou shalt do well
    To think upon the pains of Hell.

Again, when he that feared to die
(Past hope) doth see his pardon brought,
Read but the joy that's in his eye,
And then convey it to thy thought;
    Then think between thy heart and thee,
    How glad will "Come ye blessed" be!

Prayer For His Wife And Children, Written In Newgate.

Thereof be therefore heedful,
Them favor not the less,
Supply with all things needful
In this our great distress.

And when Thou me shalt gather,
Out of this Land of Life,
Be Thou my children's Father,
A Husband to my wife.

When I to them must never
Speak more with tongue or pen,
And they be barred forever
To see my face again—

Preserve them from each folly,
Which, ripening into sin,
Makes root and branch unholy,
And brings destruction in.

Let not this world bewitch them
With her besotting wine,
But let Thy grace enrich them
With faith and love divine.

And whilst we live together,
Let us upon Thee call,
Help to prepare each other,
For what may yet befall:

So just, so faithful-hearted,
So constant let us be,
That when we here are parted,
We may all meet in Thee.

HERRICK, ROBERT (1591–1674), is noted as a lyric poet. His best known poem is "To the Virgins, to Make Much of Time" which begins, "Gather ye rosebuds while ye may," which was very popular in the last half of the seventeenth century. After attending Cambridge, he took Anglican orders in 1623 and was made a vicar in Devonshire in 1629. At first he apparently regarded this as something of an exile. His poems came to express a contentment with country life, however. He was ejected from his position in 1647 by the Puritans and reinstated in 1662. In the interim he lived happily in London. Herrick was of the Cavalier school (followers of Jonson) as seen in his use of classical imagery and models. Though not a direct follower of Donne, but like Donne's, his poetry uses startling metaphor and falls into two categories: courtly love poems, and Christian poems. There is a certain forced quality in many of his Christian poems, but it disappears in the better ones.

The Argument of his Book.

I sing of Brooks, of Blossomes, Birds, and Bowers:
Of April, May, of June, and July-Flowers.
I sing of May-poles, Hock-carts, Wassails, Wakes,
Of Bride-grooms, Brides, and of their Bridall-cakes.
I write or Youth, of Love, and have Accesse
By these, to sing of cleanly-Wantonnesse.
I sing of Dewes, of Raines, and piece by piece
Of Balme, of Oyle, of Spice, and Amber-Greece.
I sing of Times trans-shifting; and I write
How Roses first came Red, and Lillies White.
I write of Groves, of Twilights, and I sing

The Court of Mab, and of the Fairie-King.
I write of Hell; I sing (and ever shall)
Of Heaven, and hope to have it after all.

His Prayer for Absolution

For those my unbaptized Rhimes,
Writ in my wild unhallowed Times;
For every sentence, clause and word,
That's not inlaid with Thee, (my Lord)
Forgive me God, and blot each Line
Out of my Book, that is not Thine.
But if, 'mongst all, thou find'st here one
Worthy thy Benediction;
That One of all the rest, shall be
The Glory of my Work, and Me.

Gods Providence

If all transgressions here should have their pay,
What need there then be of a reckning day:
If God should punish no sin, here, of men,
His Providence who would not question then?

Persecutions Purifie

God strikes His Church, but 'tis to this intent,
To make, not marre her, by this punishment:
So where He gives the bitter Pills, be sure,
'Tis not to poyson, but to make thee pure.

His Letanie to the Holy Spirit

1. In the houre of my distresse,
   When temptations me oppresse,
   And when I my sins confesse,
   Sweet spirit comfort me!

2. When I lie within my bed,
   Sick in heart, and sick in head,
   And with doubts discomforted,
   Sweet spirit comfort Me!

3. When the house doth sigh and weep,
   And the world is drown'd in sleep,
   Yet mine eyes the watch do keep;
   Sweet spirit comfort me!

4. When the artlesse Doctor sees
   No one hope but of his Fees,
   And his skill runs on the lees;
   Sweet Spirit comfort Me!

5. When his Potion and his Pill,
   Has, or none, or little skill,
   Meet for nothing, but to kill;
   Sweet Spirit comfort me!

6. When the passing-bell doth tole,
   And the Furies in a shole
   Come to fright a parting soule;
   Sweet Spirit comfort me!

7. When the tapers now burne blew,
   And the comforters are few,
   And that number more then true;
   Sweet Spirit comfort me!

8. When the Priest his last hath praid,
   And I nod to what is said,
   'Cause my speech is now decaid;
   Sweet Spirit comfort me!

9. When (God knowes) I'm tost about,
   Either with despaire, or doubt;
   Yet before the glasse be out,
   Sweet Spirit comfort me!

10. When the Tempter me pursu'th
    With the sins of all my youth,
    And halfe damns me with untruth;
    Sweet Spirit comfort me!

11. When the flames and hellish cries
    Fright mine eares, and fright mine eyes,
    And all terrors me surprize;
    Sweet Spirit comfort me!

12. When the judgment is reveal'd,
     And that open'd which was seal'd,
     When to Thee I have appeal'd;
     Sweet Spirit comfort me!

To God

If any thing delight me for to print
My Book, 'tis this; that Thou, my God, art in't.

To His Saviour

Lord, I confesse, that Thou alone art able
To purifie this my Augean stable:
Be the Seas water, and the Land all Sope,
Yet if Thy Bloud not wash me, there's no hope.

Temptation

God tempteth no one (as S. Aug'stine saith)
For any ill; but, for the proof of Faith:
Unto temptation God exposeth some;
But none, of purpose, to be overcome.

Gods Presence

God 's evident, and may be said to be
Present with just men, to the veritie:
But with the wicked if He doth comply,
'Tis (as S. Bernard saith) but seemingly.

Hell (#1)

Hell is no other, but a soundlesse pit,
Where no one beame of comfort peeps in it.

To God

God' s undivided, one in Persons Three;
And Three in Inconfused Unity:
Originall of Essence there is none
'Twixt God the Father, Holy Ghost, and Sonne:

And though the Father be the first of Three,
'Tis but by order, not by Entitie.

Sabbaths

Sabbaths are threefold (as S. Austine sayes:)
The first of Time, or Sabbath here of Dayes;
The second is a Conscience trespasse-free;
The last the Sabbath of Eternitie.

Temporall goods

These temp'rall goods God (the most Wise) commends
To th' good and bad, in common, for two ends:
First, that these goods none here may o're esteem,
Because the wicked do partake of them:
Next, that these ills none cowardly may shun;
Being, oft here, the just mans portion.

Predestination

Predestination is the Cause alone
Of many standing, but of fall to none.

Gods Keyes

God has foure keyes, which He reserves alone;
The first of Raine, the key of Hell next known:
With the third key He opes and shuts the wombe;
And with the fourth key He unlocks the tombe.

No Coming to God Without Christ

Good and great God! How sho'd I feare
To come to Thee, if Christ not there!
Co'd I but think, He would not be
Present, to plead my cause for me;
To Hell I'd rather run, then I
Wo'd see Thy Face, and He not by.

His Saviours Words, Going to the Crosse

Have, have ye no regard, all ye
Who passe this way, to pitie me,
Who am a man of miserie!

A man both bruis'd, and broke, and one
Who suffers not here for mine own,
But for my friends transgression!

Ah! Sions Daughters, do not feare
The Crosse, the Cords, the Nailes, the Speare,
The Myrrhe, the Gall, the Vineger:

For Christ, your loving Saviour, hath
Drunk up the wine of Gods fierce wrath;
Onely, there's left a little froth,

Lesse for to tast, then for to shew,
What bitter cups had been your due,
Had He not drank them up for you.

The White Island: or Place of the Blest

In this world (the Isle of Dreames)
While we sit by sorrowes streames,
Teares and terrors are our theames
Reciting:

But when once from hence we flie,
More and more approaching nigh
Unto young Eternitie
Uniting:

In that whiter Island, where
Things are evermore sincere;
Candor here, and lustre there
Delighting:

There no monstrous fancies shall
Out of hell an horrour call,
To create (or cause at all)
Affrighting.

There in calm and cooling sleep
We our eyes shall never steep;
But eternall watch shall keep,
Attending

Pleasures, such as shall pursue
Me immortaliz'd, and you;
And fresh joyes, as never too
Have ending.

To Keep A True Lent.

Is this a fast, to keep
The larder lean?
And clean
From fat of veals, and sheep?

Is it to quit the dish
Of flesh, yet still
To fill
The platter high with fish?

Is it to fast an hour,
Or ragged to go,
Or show
A downcast look, and sour?

No: 'tis a fast, to dole
Thy sheaf of wheat,
And meat,
Unto the hungry soul.

It is to fast from strife,
From old debate,
And hate;
To circumcise thy life.

To show a heart grief-rent;
To starve thy sin,
Not bin;
And that's to keep thy Lent.

QUARLES, FRANCIS (baptized 1592–1644), was educated at Cambridge
and at Lincoln's Inn. He wrote metaphysical poetry something in the manner of

George Herbert. His earlier poetry was collected and printed in *Divine Poems* in 1630. Being more or less of independent means, he seems to have preferred writing in an atmosphere of scholarly seclusion, but his major work, *Emblemes and Hieroglyphickes* became the most popular book of verse of the seventeenth century. It was an emblem book, a genre popular throughout western Europe during that century. Emblem books had their origin in the medieval emblems, such as the pelican (supposed to feed its young with its own blood), which were types of Christ or of other Biblical figures. The books collated these emblems, and mottoes or verses were printed with them. Both George Wither's emblem book and Quarles' first edition were printed In 1635. Most of the emblem illustrations used in Quarles' first edition of the book originated in two Jesuit works, although Quarles himself was a staunch Anglican. He became city chronologer for London in 1640. He wrote a book of aphorisms, *Enchiridion*, which was highly popular. His Royalist loyalties caused him some hardship at the time of the Civil war.

On the Plough-man

I heare the whistling Plough-man all day long,
Sweetning his labour with a chearful song;
His Bed's a Pad of Straw; his dyet, coarse;
In both, he fares not better than his Horse;
He seldom slakes his thirst, but from the Pump;
And yet his heart is blithe, his visage, plump;
His thoughts are ne'er acquainted with such things,
As Griefs or Fears; he only sweats and sings:
When as the landed Lord, that cannot dine
Without a Qualm, if not refresht with Wine;
That cannot judge that controverted case,
Twixt meat and mouth, without the Bribe of Sauce;
That claims the service of the purest linnen,
To pamper and to shroud his dainty skin in;
Groans out his days, in lab'ring to appease
The rage of either Business or Disease;
Alas, his silken Robes, his costly Diet,
Can lend a little pleasure, but no Quiet:
The untold sums of his descended wealth
Can give his Body plenty, but not Health:
The one, in Pains, and want, possesses all;
T'other, in Plenty, finds no peace at all;
'Tis strange! And yet the cause is easly showne;
T' one's at God's finding; t'other at his owne.

Wherefore hidest thou thy face, and holdest me for thine enemy?
(Job xiii. 24)

Why dost thou shade thy lovely face? O why
Doth that eclipsing hand so long deny
The Sun-shine of thy soul-enliv'ning eye?

Without that Light, what light remaines in me?
Thou art my Life, my Way, my Light; in thee
I live, I move, and by thy beams I see.

Thou art my Life; if thou but turn away,
My life's a thousand deaths: thou art my Way:
Without thee, Lord, I travel not, but stray.

My Light thou art; without thy glorious sight,
Mine eyes are darkned with perpetuall night.
My God, thou art my Way, my Life, my Light.

Thou art my Way; I wander, if thou fly:
Thou art my Light; If hid, how blind am I!
Thou art my Life; If thou withdraw, I die.

Mine eyes are blind and dark; I cannot see;
To whom, or whither should my darkness flee,
But to the Light? And who's that Light but thee?

My path is lost; my wandring steps do stray;
I cannot safely go, nor safely stay;
Whom should I seek but thee, my Path, my Way?

O, I am dead: to whom shall I, poor I,
Repair? to whom shall my sad ashes fly
But Life? And where is Life but in thine eye?

And yet thou turn'st away thy face, and fly'st me;
And yet I sue for grace, and thou deny'st me;
Speak, art thou angry, Lord, or only try'st me?

Unscreen those Heav'nly lamps, or tell me why
Thou shad'st thy face; perhaps thou thinkst, no eye
Can view those flames, and not drop down and die.

If that be all, shine forth, and draw thee nigher;
Let me behold and die, for my desire
Is Phoenix-like to perish in that fire.

Death-conquer'd Laz'rus was redeem'd by thee;
If I am dead, Lord, set death's prisoner free;
Am I more spent, or stink I worse than he?

If my puff'd light be out, give leave to tine
My flameless snuff at that bright Lamp of thine;
O what's thy Light the lesse for lightning mine?

If I have lost my Path, great Shepherd, say,
Shall I still wander in a doubtfull way?
Lord, shall a Lamb of Israel's sheepfold stray?

Thou art the Pilgrim's Path; the blind man's Eye;
The dead man's Life; on thee my hopes rely;
If thou remove, I erre; I grope; I die.

Disclose thy Sun beams; close thy wings, and stay;
See, see how I am blind, and dead, and stray,
O thou, that art my Light, my Life, my Way.

tine - tind, kindle

I Am My Beloved's, And His Desire Is Towards Me
(Canticles, vii. 10)

Like to the Artick needle, that doth guide
The wand'ring shade by his magnetick pow'r,
And leaves his silken Gnomon to decide
The question of the controverted houre;
First franticks up and down, from side to side,
And restlesse beats his crystall'd Iv'ry case
With vain impatience; jets from place to place,
And seeks the bosome of his frozen bride;
At length he slacks his motion, and doth rest
His trembling point at his bright Poles beloved brest.

Ev'n so, my soul, being hurried here and there,
By ev'ry object that presents delight,
Fain would be settled, but she knowes not where;
She likes at morning what she loaths at night;
She bowes to honour; then she lends an eare
To that sweet swan like voice of dying pleasure,
Then tumbles in the scatter'd heaps of treasure;
Now flatter'd with false hope; now foyl'd with fear:

Thus finding all the worlds delights to be
But empty toyes, good God, she points alone to thee.

But hath the virtued steel a power to move?
Or can the untouch'd needle point aright?
Or can my wandring thoughts forbear to rove,
Unguided by the virtue of thy spirit?
O hath my leaden soul the art t'improve
Her wasted talent, and unrais'd, aspire
In this sad moulting time of her desire?
Not first belov'd have I the pow'r to love?
I cannot stirre, but as thou please to move me,
Nor can my heart return thee love, untill thou love me.

The still Commandresse of the silent night
Borrows her beams from her bright brother's eye;
His fair aspect fines her sharp horns with light;
If he withdraw, her flames are quench'd and die:
Even so the beams of thy enlightning sp'rite
Infus'd and shot into my dark desire,
Inflame my thoughts, and fill my soul with fire,
That I am ravisht with a new delight;
But if thou shroud thy face, my glory fades,
And I remain a Nothing, all compos'd of shades.

Eternall God, O thou that onely art
The sacred Fountain of eternall light,
And blessed Loadstone of my better part;
O thou my heart's desire, my soul's delight,
Reflect upon my soul, and touch my heart,
And then my heart shall prize no good above thee;
And then my soul shall know thee; knowing, love thee;
And then my trembling thoughts shall never start
From thy commands, or swerve the least degree,
Or once presume to move, but as they move in thee.

Christ and Our Selves

Wish a greater knowledge, then t'attaine
The knowledge of my selfe: A greater Gaine
Then to augment my selfe; A greater Treasure
Then to enjoy my selfe: A greater Pleasure
Then to content my selfe; How slight, and vaine
Is all selfe-Knowledge, Pleasure, Treasure, Gaine;

Unlesse my better knowledge could retrive
My Christ; unles my better Gaine could thrive
In Christ; unles my better Wealth grow rich
In Christ; unles my better Pleasure pitch
On Christ; Or else my Knowledge will proclaime
To my owne heart how ignorant I am:
Or else my Gaine, so ill improv'd, will shame
My Trade, and shew how much declin'd I am;
Or else my Treasure will but blurre my name
With Bankrupt, and divulge how poore I am;
Or else my Pleasures, that so much inflame
My Thoughts, will blabb how full of sores I am:
Lord, keepe me from my Selfe; 'Tis best for me,
Never to owne my Selfe, if not in Thee.

Mercy Tempering Justice

Had not the milder hand of Mercy broke
The furious violence of that fatal stroke
Offended Justice struck, we had been quite
Lost in the shadows of eternal night.
Thy mercy, Lord, is like the morning sun,
Whose beams undo what sable night hath done;
Or like a stream, the current of whose course,
Restrained a while, runs with a swifter force.
Oh! let me glow beneath those sacred beams,
And after bathe me in those silver streams;
To Thee alone my sorrows shall appeal.
Hath earth a wound too hard for heaven to heal?

HERBERT, GEORGE (1593–1633), unlike most other Christian poets of his age, wrote almost nothing but explicitly Christian poetry. In 1610 he sent his mother two poems on the theme that love for God is a fitter poetic subject than love for women. He obtained a fellowship at Trinity College and became public orator of the University. He was ordained a deacon in 1625 and a priest in 1630. For the brief remainder of his life he was parish priest at Bemerton. At Bemerton he revised his earlier poems and wrote many more. He also wrote a prose treatise, *A Priest to the Temple*, dealing with the duties of a parish priest. He was a good musician and wrote accompaniments for some of his poems which became hymns a century later. None of his poetry was published during his lifetime. The year of his death he sent a manuscript volume of them to Nicholas Ferrar (founder of the Christian community at Little Gidding) for him to publish or destroy as he saw fit. Published after his death as *The Temple; Sacred Poems and Private Ejaculations,* Herbert's poetry quickly became very popular. It is said to have sold more than 20,000 copies by 1670. John Donne was a friend of the Herbert family. Herbert's poetry is similar to Donne's in its use of striking imagery from ordinary life. He used emblem and allegory, as well, however, making him somewhat more difficult to understand for the modern reader. He is also noted for his versatility in using and inventing metrical variations in his verse. (George Herbert's brother, Edward, First Baron Herbert of Cherbury, is noted for his pioneering of "natural religion," that is deism. His *De Veritate* "On Truth" puts forth his theories that there are five God given Ideas innate to all men, that reason is the supreme means to religious understanding, and that no revelation can be taken as authoritative.) George Herbert died of tuberculosis at the age of forty.

Prayer (i)

Prayer the Churches banquet, Angels age,
Gods breath in man returning to his birth,
The soul in paraphrase, heart in pilgrimage,
The Christian plummet sounding heav'n and earth;
Engine against th' Almightie, sinners towre,
Reversed thunder, Christ-side-piercing spear,
The six-daies world transposing in an houre,
A kinde of tune, which all things heare and fear;
Softnesse, and peace, and joy, and love, and blisse,
Exalted Manna, gladnesse of the best,
Heaven in ordinarie, man well drest,
The milkie way, the bird of Paradise,
Church-bels beyond the starres heard, the souls bloud,
The land of spices; something understood.

Iesu

IESU is in my heart, his sacred name
Is deeply carved there: but th'other week
A great affliction broke the little frame,
Ev'n all to pieces: which I went to seek:
And first I found the corner, where was I,
After, where E S, and next where U was graved.
When I had got these parcels, instantly
I sat me down to spell them, and perceived
That to my broken heart he was I ease you,
And to my whole is I E S U.

Time

Meeting with Time, Slack thing, said I,
Thy sithe is dull; whet it for shame.
No marvell Sir, he did replie,
If it at length deserve some blame:
But where one man would have me grinde it,
Twentie for one too sharp do finde it.

Perhaps some such of old did passe,
Who above all things lov'd this life;
To whom thy sithe a hatchet was,
Which now is but a pruning-knife.
Christs coming hath made man thy debter,
Since by thy cutting he grows better.

And in his blessing thou art blest:
For where thou onely wert before
An executioner at best;
Thou art a gard'ner now, and more,
An usher to convey our souls
Beyond the utmost starres and poles.

And this is that makes life so long,
While it detains us from our God.
Ev'n pleasures here increase the wrong,
And length of dayes lengthen the rod.
Who wants the place, where God doth dwell,
Partakes already half of hell.

Of what strange length must that needs be,
Which ev'n eternitie excludes!
Thus farre Time heard me patiently:
Then chafing said, This man deludes:
What do I here before his doore?
He doth not crave lesse time, but more.

Paradise

Blesse thee, Lord, because I GROW
Among thy trees, which in a ROW
To thee both fruit and order OW.

What open force, or hidden CHARM
Can blast my fruit, or bring me HARM,
While the enclosure is thine ARM?

Inclose me still for fear I START.
Be to me rather sharp and TART,
Then let me want thy hand & ART.

When thou dost greater judgements SPARE,
And with thy knife but prune and PARE,
Ev'n fruitfull trees more fruitfull ARE.

Such sharpnes shows the sweetest FREND:
Such cuttings rather heal then REND:
And such beginnings touch their END.

The Holdfast

I Threatned to observe the strict decree
Of my deare God with all my power & might.
But I was told by one, it could not be;
Yet I might trust in God to be my light.
Then will I trust, said I, in him alone.
Nay, ev'n to trust in him, was also his:
We must confesse that nothing is our own.
Then I confesse that he my succour is:
But to have nought is ours, not to confesse
That we have nought. I stood amaz'd at this,
Much troubled, till I heard a friend expresse,
That all things were more ours by being his.
What Adam had, and forfeited for all,
Christ keepeth now, who cannot fail or fall.

The Collar

I Struck the board, and cry'd, No more.
      I will abroad.
What? shall I ever sigh and pine?
My lines and life are free; free as the rode,
Loose as the winde, as large as store.
      Shall I be still in suit?
Have I no harvest but a thorn
To let me bloud, and not restore

What I have lost with cordiall fruit?
Sure there was wine
Before my sighs did drie it: there was corn
Before my tears did drown it.
Is the yeare onely lost to me?
Have I no bayes to crown it?
No flowers, no garlands gay? all blasted?
All wasted?
Not so, my heart: but there is fruit,
And thou hast hands.
Recover all thy sigh-blown age
On double pleasures: leave thy cold dispute
Or what is fit, and not. Forsake thy cage,
Thy rope of sands,
Which pettie thoughts have made, and made to thee
Good cable, to enforce and draw,
And be thy law,
While thou didst wink and wouldst not see.
Away; take heed:
I will abroad.
Call in thy deaths head there: tie up thy fears.
He that forbears
To suit and serve his need,
Deserves his load.
But as I rav'd and grew more fierce and wilde
At every word,
Me thought I heard one calling, Childe:
And I reply'd, My Lord.

The Call

Come, my Way, my Truth, my Life:
Such a Way, as gives us breath:
Such a Truth, as ends all strife:
Such a Life, as killeth death.

Come, my Light, my Feast, my Strength:
Such a Light, as shows a feast:
Such a Feast, as mends in length:
Such a Strength, as makes his guest.

Come, my Joy, my Love, my Heart:
Such a Joy, as none can move:

Such a Love, as none can part:
Such a Heart, as joyes in love.

Dotage

False glozing pleasures, casks of happinesse,
Foolish night-fires, womens and childrens wishes,
Chases in Arras, guilded emptinesse,
Shadows well mounted, dreams in a career,
Embroider'd lyes, nothing between two dishes;
These are the pleasures here.

True earnest sorrows, rooted miseries,
Anguish in grain, vexations ripe and blown,
Sure-footed griefs, solid calamities,
Plain demonstrations, evident and cleare,
Fetching their proofs ev'n from the very bone;
These are the sorrows here.

But oh the folly of distracted men,
Who griefs in earnest, joyes in jest pursue;
Preferring, like brute beasts, a lothsome den
Before a court, ev'n that above so cleare,
Where are no sorrows, but delights more true
Then miseries are here!

Marie Magdalene

When blessed Marie wip'd her Saviours feet,
(Whose precepts she had trampled on before)
And wore them for a jewell on her head,
Shewing his steps should be the street,
Wherein she thenceforth evermore
With pensive humblenesse would live and tread:

She being stain'd her self, why did she strive
To make him clean, who could not be defil'd?
Why kept she not her tears for her own faults,
And not his feet? Though we could dive
In tears like seas, our sinnes are pil'd
Deeper then they, in words, and works, and thoughts.

Deare soul, she knew who did vouchsafe and deigne
To bear her filth; and that her sinnes did dash

Ev'n God himself: wherefore she was not loth,
As she had brought wherewith to stain,
So to bring in wherewith to wash:
And yet in washing one, she washed both.

Jordan

When first my lines of heav'nly joyes made mention,
Such was their lustre, they did so excell,
That I sought out quaint words, and trim invention;
My thoughts began to burnish, sprout, and swell,
Curling with metaphors a plain intention,
Decking the sense, as if it were to sell.

Thousands of notions in my brain did runne,
Off'ring their service, if I were not sped:
I often blotted what I had begunne;
This was not quick enough, and that was dead.
Nothing could seem too rich to clothe the sunne,
Much lesse those joyes which trample on his head.

As flames do work and winde, when they ascend,
So did I weave my self into the sense.
But while I bustled, I might heare a friend
Whisper, How wide is all this long pretence!
There is in love a sweetnesse readie penn'd:
Copie out onely that, and save expense.

Aaron

Holinesse on the head,
Light and perfections on the breast,
Harmonious bells below, raising the dead
To leade them unto life and rest:
Thus are true Aarons drest.
Profanenesse in my head,
Defects and darknesse in my breast,
A noise of passions ringing me for dead
Unto a place where is no rest:
Poore priest thus am I drest.

Onely another head
I have, another heart and breast,

Another musick, making live not dead,
Without whom I could have no rest:
In him I am well drest.

Christ is my onely head,
My alone onely heart and breast,
My onely Musick, striking me ev'n dead;
That to the old man I may rest,
And be in him new drest.

So holy in my head,
Perfect and light in my deare breast,
My doctrine tun'd by Christ, (who is not dead,
But lives in me while I do rest)
Come people; Aaron's drest.

Easter Wings

Lord, who createdst man in wealth and store,
Though foolishly he lost the same,
Decaying more and more,
Till he became
Most poore:
With thee
O let me rise
As larks, harmoniously,
And sing this day thy victories:
Then shall the fall further the flight in me.

My tender age in sorrow did beginne:
And still with sicknesses and shame
Thou didst so punish sinne,
That I became
Most thinne.
With thee
Let me combine,
And feel this day thy victorie:
For, if I imp my wing on thine,
Affliction shall advance the flight in me.

imp - strengthen by grafting

Teach Me, My God And King

Teach me, my God and King,
In all things thee to see,
And what I do in anything,
To do it as for thee.

A man that looks on glass,
On it may stay his eye,
Or, if he pleaseth, through it pass,
And then the heav'n espy.

All may of thee partake:
Nothing can be so mean
Which with this motive, "For thy sake,"
Will not grow bright and clean.

This is the famous stone
That turneth all to gold;
For that which God doth touch and own
Cannot for less be told.

WILLIAMS, ROGER (c.1604–1683) graduated from Cambridge in 1626 and served as chaplain to a peer, refusing other preferments over a dislike of Anglican liturgy. In 1630 he left England and John Winthrop noted the arrival of "a good minister" in Massachusetts. Williams did not find the "unseparated" colonial church, in which he held a number of positions, much better than the home church. In 1635, he became chief teacher in Salem, where he taught the importance of self-government. That eventually brought him under the discipline of the general council. He objected to the council's authority under their charter, saying the land belonged not to the king but to the Indians. In 1635 he was summoned to the general court in Boston on two charges, and since he would not change his position was ordered out of the colony, although allowed to stay in Salem until spring, providing he did not teach his "different opinions." When it was decided he'd broken this condition and a ship was dispatched to deport him to England, Winthrop dropped a hint he ought to flee. After a hard fourteen weeks of winter with a few companions among the Narragansett Indians, he purchased land and began a new colony. In 1639 he was publically immersed and started the first Baptist church in Providence. Later he disputed the validity of immersion and severed his connection with the Baptists, becoming a "seeker" (one dissatisfied with existing sects). Williams went back to England in order to obtain firmer title to the colony's lands, and on the way compiled a vocabulary of the Narragansett language. He was granted a charter in 1644. While in England he published two tracts against the Massachusetts colony and its apologists, one of which "The Bloudy Tenent of Persecution, for the cause of Conscience,. . ." was ordered burned by the House of Commons a month after Williams sailed. He returned to England in 1651, to defend Rhode Island's charter and to publish more refutations of his detractors. While in England he met many Puritans who would soon be active in the civil wars, including Milton. After two and a half years in England, he returned to become governor of Rhode Island. In 1656 he issued a warrant for the arrest of William Harris who promoted doctrines claiming the unlawfulness of all earthly powers and the bloodguiltiness of all penal discipline. When Rhode Island was granted a new charter in 1663, Williams became assistant to the new governor, Benedict Arnold. During Philip's war with the Indians, he served as a captain of militia and afterwards on the committee which allotted captives as slaves among the families in Providence. Milton spoke highly of Williams. Bradford spoke highly of his zeal, but not of his judgment. Cotton Mather said he had a windmill inside his head. Southey held his memory "in veneration."

"The Observation Generall From Their Eating, Etc."

It is a strange truth, that a man shall generally finde more free entertainment and refreshing amongst these Barbarians, then amongst thousands that call themselves Christians.

More particular

Course bread and water's most their fare,
O Englands diet fine;
Thy cup runs ore with plenteous store
Of wholesome beare and wine.

Sometimes God gives them Fish or Flesh,
Yet they're content without;
And what comes in, they part to friends
and strangers round about.

Gods providence is rich to his,
Let none distrustfull be;
In wildernesses in great distresses
These Ravens have fed me.

God Makes A Path

God makes a path, provides a guide,
And feeds a wilderness;

His glorious name, while breath remains,
O that I may confess.

Lost many a time, I have had no guide,
No house but a hollow tree!
In stormy winter night no fire,
No food, no company;

In Him I found a house, a bed,
A table, company;
No cup so bitter but's made sweet,
Where God shall sweetening be.

BROWNE, Sir THOMAS (1605–1682), a physician and writer, attended Oxford and received his M.D. at Leiden in 1633. He appears to have been orthodox, latitudinarian, and mystical. While practicing medicine in Yorkshire he wrote a journal dealing with the mysteries of God, man and the creation. After circulating among some of his friends, it was published in 1642 without his permission in London. It therefore had to be acknowledged and an authorized version, *Religio Medici* ("A Doctor's Religion") was published in 1643. It quickly became popular and was translated into Latin, French and Dutch. Browne's thought is a fusion of scientific scepticism and Christian faith. He also wrote *Pseudodoxia Epidemica*, in which he tried to correct many commonly held superstitions and ignorant ideas. He also wrote *Hydriotaphia, Urne-Buriall*, and *The Garden of Cyrus*, the former reflections on death, the latter, a history of ancient gardens. He was knighted when Charles II visited Norwich In 1671.

A Colloquy with God

The night is come, like to the day;
Depart not thou, great God, away.
Let not my sins, black as the night,
Eclipse the lustre of thy light:
Keep still in my Horizon; for to me
The Sun makes not the day, but thee.
Thou, whose nature cannot sleep,
On my temples sentry keep;
Guard me 'gainst those watchful foes,
Whose eyes are open while mine close.
Let no dreams my head infest,
But such as Jacob's temples blest.
While I do rest, my Soul advance;

Make my sleep a holy trance;
That I may, my rest being wrought,
Awake into some holy thought;
And with as active vigour run
My course, as doth the nimble Sun.
Sleep is a death; O make me try,
By, sleeping, what it is to die;
And as gently lay my head
On my grave, as now my bed.
Howe'er I rest, great God, let me
Awake again at last with thee;
And thus assur'd, behold I lie
Securely, or to awake or die.
These are my drowsie days; in vain
I do now wake to sleep again:
O come that hour, when I shall never
Sleep again, but wake for ever.

Verses Of Mans Mortalitie,
With An Other Of The Hope Of His Resurrection
Anonymous

Like as the Damaske Rose you see,
Or like the blossome on the Tree,
Or like the dainty flowre of May,
Or like the morning to the day,
Or like the Sunne, or like the shade,
Or like the Gourd which Jonas had:
Even such is Man; whose thred is spun,
Drawne out, and cut, and so is done.
The Rose withers, the Blossom blasteth,
The Flower fades, the Morning hasteth:
The Sun sets, the shadow flyes;
The Gourd consumes, and Man he dyes.
Like to the grasse that 's newly sprung,
Or like a Tale that's new begun:
Or like the Bird that's here to day,
Or like the pearled dew of May;
Or like an houre, or like a span,
Or like the singing of a Swan:
Even such is Man, who lives by breath;
Is here, now there: so life, and death.

The grasse withers, the tale is ended,
The Bird is flowne, the Dew's ascended,
The Houre is short, the span not long;
The Swan's neere death: Mans life is done.
Like to the Bubble in the Brooke,
Or in a Glasse much like a looke,
Or like a shuttle in Weavers hand,
Or like a writing in the sand,
Or like a thought, or like a dreame,
Or like the gliding of the streame:
Even such is Man, who lives by breath;
Is here, now there: so life, and death.
The Bubble's cut, the look's forgot,
The Shuttle's flung, the writing's blot,
The thought is past, the dream is gone;
The water glides; Mans life is done.
Like to an Arrow from the Bow,
Or like swift course of watery flow,
Or like the time 'twixt floud and ebbe,
Or like the Spiders tender webbe,
Or like a Race, or like a Goale,
Or like the dealing of a Dole:
Even such is Man, whose brittle state
Is always subject unto Fate.
The arrow's shot, the flood soone spent,
The time no time, the web soone rent,
The Race soone run, the Goale soone won,
The Dole soone dealt, Mans life fast done.
Like to the lightning from the skie,
Or like a Post that quicke doth hie,
Or like a quaver in short song,
Or like a journey three dayes long,
Or like the snow when Summers come,
Or like the Peare, or like the Plum:
Even such is man who heapes up sorrow,
Lives but this daye, and dyes to morrow.
The lightning's past, the Post must go,
The song is short, the journey's so,
The Peare doth rot, the Plum doth fall,
The Snow dissolves, and so must all.
Like to the seed put in Earths wombe,
Or like dead Lazarus in his tombe;

Or like Tabitha being asleepe,
Or Jonas-like within the deepe;
Or like the Night, or Stars by day,
Which seeme to vanish cleane away:
Even so this Death, Mans life bereaves,
But being dead, Man death deceaves.
The Seed it springeth, Lazarus standeth,
Tabitha wakes, and Jonas landeth;
The night is past, the Stars remaine,
So man that dyes shall live againe.

The Guest
From Christ Church Manuscript: After 1620
Anonymous

Yet if his majesty, out sovereign lord,
Should of his own accord
Friendly himself invite,
And say, 'I'll be your guest to-morrow night,'
How should we stir ourselves, call and command
All hands to work! 'Let no man idle stand!

'Set me fine Spanish tables in the hall,
See they be fitted all;
Let there be room to eat,
And order taken that there want no meat.
See every sconce and candlestick made bright,
That without tapers they may give a light.

'Look to the presence: are the carpets spread,
The dazie o'er the head,
The cushions in the chairs,
And all the candles lighted on the stairs?
Perfume the chambers, and in any case
Let each man give attendance in his place.'

Thus if the King were coming would we do,
And 'twere good reason too;
For 'tis a duteous thing
To show all honour to an earthly king,
And after all our travail and our cost,
So he be pleased, to think no labour lost.

But at the coming of the king of Heaven
All's set at six and seven:
We wallow in our sin,
Christ can not find a chamber in the inn.
We entertain Him always like a stranger,
And, as at first, still lodge Him in the manger.

Hierusalem, My Happy Home
Anonymous

Hierusalem, my happy home,
When shall I come to thee?
When shall my sorrows have an end,
Thy joys when shall I see?

O happy harbour of the Saints!
O sweet and pleasant soil!
In thee no sorrow may be found,
No grief, no care, no toll.

There lust and lucre cannot dwell,
There envy bears no sway;
There is no hunger, heat, nor cold,
But pleasure every way.

Thy walls are made of precious stones,
Thy bulwarks diamonds square;
Thy gates are of right orient pearl,
Exceeding rich and rare.

Thy turrets and thy pinnacles
With carbuncles do shine;
Thy very streets are paved with gold
Surpassing clear and fine.

Ah, my sweet home, Hierusalem,
Would God I were in thee!
Would God my woes were at an end,
Thy joys that I might see!

Thy gardens and thy gallant walks
Continually are green;
There grow such sweet and pleasant flowers
As nowhere else are seen.

Quite through the streets, with silver sound,
The flood of Life doth flow;
Upon whose banks on every side
The wood of Life doth grow.

There trees for evermore bear fruit,
And evermore do spring;
There evermore the angels sit,
And evermore do sing.

Out Lady sings Magnificat
With tones surpassing sweet;
And all the virgins bear their part,
Sitting about her feet.

Hierusalem, my happy home,
Would God I were in thee!
Would God my woes were at an end,
Thy joys that I might see!

DAVENANT (D'AVENANT), Sir WILLIAM (baptized 1606–1668), was born at his father's inn in Oxford, where Shakespeare is said to have been a frequent guest. He became page to the duchess of Richmond, then entered the household of Fulke Greville, Lord Brooke. After Brooke's death he became a playwright, producing *Albovine, King of the Lombard* in 1692 and *The Wits* in 1633. He was much in favor at court and succeeded Ben Jonson as poet laureate. He remained a loyalist through the civil war, joining Henrietta Maria in France and travelling at her commission. He was knighted in 1643 after participating in the seige of Gloucester. He was captured several times by the Parliamentary party, and was finally imprisoned upon being intercepted in the Channel on his way to Virginia as head of a colonizing expedition. While in the Tower, he wrote the epic poem *Gondibert*. It is said he was released at last upon the personal intercession of Milton, for whom, in turn, he interceded after the restoration. He had been manager of the Drury Lane theatre before the Puritans closed the theatres. He was able to get around the law by giving semi-private performances in private homes, and in these performances began some of the innovations which led away from the traditions of ancient theatre. In 1658 he was permitted to open the Cockpit Theatre for historical drama. At the restoration he was licensed to set up a players company, which became known as the Duke of York's players. They performed many musical plays which began to be called operas. Davenant re-produced some earlier plays as well as freely adapting plays of Shakespeare, Jonson, Fletcher, and a few French dramas. His remains were buried in Westminster Abbey. Davenant is often grouped with the Cavalier poets.

To a Mistress Dying

Lover:

Your beauty, ripe and calm and fresh
As eastern summers are,
Must now, forsaking time and flesh,
Add light to some small star.

Philosopher:

Whilst she yet lives, were stars decayed,
Their light by hers relief might find;
But Death will lead her to a shade
Where Love is cold and Beauty blind.

Lover:

Lovers, whose priests all poets are,
Think every mistress, when she dies,
Is changed at least into a star:
And who dares doubt the poets wise?

Philosopher:

But ask not bodies doomed to die
To what abode they go;
Since Knowledge is but Sorrow's spy,
It is not safe to know.

Praise and Prayer

Praise is devotion fit for mighty minds,
The diff'ring world's agreeing sacrifice;
Where Heaven divided faiths united finds:
But Prayer in various discord upward flies.

For Prayer the ocean is where diversely
Men steer their course, each to a sev'ral coast;
Where all our interests so discordant be
That half beg winds by which the rest are lost.

By Penitence when we ourselves forsake,
'Tis but in wise design on piteous Heaven;
In Praise we nobly give what God may take,
And are, without a beggar's blush, forgiven.

WALLER, EDMUND (1606–1687) was educated at Eton and Cambridge, and entered Parliament as "an active member of the opposition." He became a royalist and was arrested in 1643 as head of a plan to seize London for Charles I. After his first wife died (1643) he courted, but was not accepted by the "Saccharisa" of his poems (Lady Dorothy Sidney), then married again in 1644.

He wrote a complimentary poem, "His Majesty's Escape at St. Andre" (about Prince Charles's shipwreck) in heroic couplets—one of the earliest examples of what became a popular form of English verse. Dryden praised him as "Father of our English numbers." His *Poems* were published in 1645, and his *Divine Poems* in 1685. The poem given here is one of his best known.

Of the Last Verses in the Book

When we for Age could neither read nor write
The subject made us able to indite.
The Soul with nobler Resolutions deckt,
The Body, stooping, does Herself erect:
No Mortal Parts are requisite to raise
Her, that Unbody'd can her Maker praise.

The Seas are quiet, when the Winds give o'er
So calm are we, when Passions are no more:
For then we know how vain it was to boast
Of fleeting Things, so certain to be lost.
Clouds of Affection from our younger Eyes
Conceal that emptiness, which Age descries.

The Soul's dark Cottage, batter'd and decay'd,
Lets in new light thro' chinks that time has made.
Stronger by weakness, wiser Men become.
As they draw near to their Eternal home:
Leaving the old, both Worlds at once they view,
That stand upon the threshold of the New.

WASHBOURNE, THOMAS (1606–1687), graduate of Oxford, became a rector in Northamptonshire and Gloucestershire until 1643, during the civil war, when he was secretly installed as "Prebend" (one who gets his living from the church revenues) in Gloucestershire Cathedral. He apparently did not lose his position during the Commonwealth, but he was honored after the Restoration, not only with a formal presentation, but with a D.D. from Oxford. He published two sermons and *Divine Poems* (London, 1654, 8 volumes), with an introductory poem addressed to Edward Phillips, Milton's nephew.

Casting All Your Care upon God, for He Careth for You

Come, heavy souls, oppressed that are
With doubts, and fears, and carking care.

Lay all your burthens down, and see
Where's One that carried once a tree
Upon His back, and, which is more,
A heavier weight, your sins, He bore.
Think then how easily He can
Your sorrows bear that's God and Man;
Think too how willing He's to take
Your care on Him, Who for your sake
Sweat bloody drops, prayed, fasted, cried,
Was bound, scourged, mocked and crucified.
He that so much for you did do,
Will do yet more, and care for you.

God's Two Dwellings

Lord thou hast told us that there be
Two dwellings which belong to thee,
And Those two, that's the wonder,
Are far asunder.

The one the highest heaven is,
The mansions of eternal bliss;
The other's the contrite
And humble sprite.

Not like the princes of the earth,
Who think it much below their birth
To come within the door
Of people poor.

No, such is thy humility,
That though thy dwelling be on high,
Thou dost thyself abase
To the lowest place.

Where'er thou seest a sinful soul
Deploring his offences foul,
To him thou wilt descend,
And be his friend.

Thou wilt come in, and with him sup,
And from a low state raise him up,
Till thou hast made him eat
Blest angel's meat.

Thus thou wilt him with honour crown
Who in himself is first cast down,
And humbled for his sins,
That thy love wins.

Though heaven be high, the gate is low,
And he that comes in there must bow:
The lofty looks shall ne'er
Have entrance there.

O God! since thou delight'st to rest
In the humble contrite breast
First make me so to be,
Then dwell with me.

MILTON, JOHN (1608–1674), frequently numbered among the greatest poets of the English language, is most famous for *Paradise Lost,* one of the few contenders for the title "English epic" since Beowulf. Milton was an able scholar at Cambridge, where he became versed in Latin and Italian. His first major work was *Comus* a dramatization of the conflict between good and evil. He wrote it and the poem "Lycidus" while engaged in private study after receiving his MA from Cambridge. He was a convinced Puritan and worked chiefly as a pamphleteer from 1641 to 1660. He became blind in 1651–2. He was arrested after the Restoration, but was soon released. *Paradise Lost* was published in 1667, both *Paradise Regained* and *Samson Agonistes* in 1671. Milton was married three times. His first marriage is frequently termed "unhappy." His daughters of that marriage do not seem to have been on very good terms with him. Milton is often portrayed as the struggling genius who failed to meet his responsibilities to his family. His other two marriages seem to have been happy, however. His longer poems seem very ponderous to our modern ears. They have always been regarded by the great stylists of English literature as among the best, however. Milton's sonnets strike a stronger chord of response in this editor.

On the Morning of Christs Nativity

This is the Month, and this the happy morn
Wherin the Son of Heav'ns eternal King,
Of wedded Maid, and Virgin Mother born,
Our great redemption from above did bring;
For so the holy sages once did sing,
That he our deadly forfeit should release,
And with his Father work us a perpetual peace.

That glorious Form, that Light unsufferable,
And that far-beaming blaze of Majesty,
Wherwith he wont at Heav'ns high Councel-Table,
To sit the midst of Trinal Unity,
He laid aside; and here with us to be,
Forsook the Courts of everlasting Day,
And chose with us a darksom House of mortal Clay.

Say Heav'nly Muse, shall not thy sacred vein
Afford a present to the Infant God?
Hast thou no verse, no hymn, or solemn strein,
To welcom him to this his new abode,
Now while the Heav'n by the Suns team untrod,
Hath took no print of the approching light,
And all the spangled host keep watch in squadrons bright?

See how from far upon the Eastern rode
The Star-led Wisards haste with odours sweet,
O run, prevent them with thy humble ode,
And lay it lowly at his blessed feet;
Have thou the honour first, thy Lord to greet,
And joyn thy voice unto the Angel Quire,
From out his secret Altar toucht with hallow'd fire.

On Time

Fly envious Time, till thou run out thy race,
Call on the lazy leaden-stepping hours,
Whose speed is but the heavy Plummets pace;
And glut thy self with what thy womb devours,
Which is no more than what is false and vain,
And meerly mortal dross;
So little is our loss,
So little is thy gain.
For when as each thing bad thou hast entomb'd,
And last of all, thy greedy self consum'd,
Then long Eternity shall greet our bliss
With an individual kiss;
And Joy shall overtake us as a flood,
When every thing that is sincerely good
And perfectly divine,
With Truth, and Peace, and Love shall ever shine.

Sonnet xvi

When I consider how my light is spent,
Ere half my days, in this dark world and wide,
And that one Talent which is death to hide,
Lod'g with me useless, though my Soul more bent
To serve therewith my Maker, and present
My true account, lest he returning chide,
Doth God exact day-labour, light deny'd,
I fondly ask, But patience to prevent
That murmur, soon replies, God doth not need
Either man's work or his own gifts, who best
Bear his milde yoak, they serve him best, his State
Is Kingly, Thousands at his bidding speed
And post o'er Land and Ocean without rest:
They also serve who only stand and waite.

Sonnet xix

Methought I saw my late espoused Saint
Brought to me like Alcestis from the grave,
Whom Joves great Son to her glad Husband gave,
Rescu'd from death by force though pale and faint.
Mine as whom washt from spot of child-bed taint,
Purification in the old Law did save,
And such, as yet once more I trust to have
Full sight of her in Heaven without restraint,
Came vested all in white, pure as her mind:
Her face was vail'd, yet to my fancied sight,
Love, sweetness, goodness, in her person shin'd
So clear, as in no face with more delight.
But O as to embrace me she enclin'd
I wak'd, she fled, and day brought back my night.

At A Solemn Music

Blest pair of sirens, pledges of heaven's joy
Sphere-born harmonious sisters, Voice and Verse,
Wed your divine sounds, and mixed power employ—
Dead things with inbreathed sense able to pierce—
And to our high-raised phantasy present
That undisturbed song of pure concent
Aye sung before the sapphire-coloured throne

To him that sits thereon,
With saintly shout, and solemn jubilee;
Where the bright seraphim, in burning row,
Their loud uplifted angel trumpets blow;
And the cherubic host in thousand choirs,
Touch their immortal harps of golden wires,
With those just spirits that wear victorious palms,
Hymns devout and holy psalms
Singing everlastingly;
That we on earth, with undiscording voice,
May rightly answer that melodious noise—
As once we did, till disproportioned
Sin jarred against Nature's chime, and with harsh din
Broke the fair music that all creatures made
To their great Lord, whose love their motion swayed
In perfect diapason, whilst they stood
In first obedience and their state of good.
O may we soon again renew that song,
And keep in tune with heaven, till God ere long
To his celestial consort us unite,
To live with him, and sing in endless morn of light!

concent - harmonious singing; diapason - (octave) harmony; consort - royal bride (also may be pun on "concert")

GODOLPHIN, SIDNEY (1610–1643), a lyrical poet killed while fighting as a royalist in the English Civil War, was a friend of Ben Jonson and the political philosopher Thomas Hobbes. Educated at Oxford, he entered Parliament for Cornwall in 1628. He was one of the last to leave the House of Commons when Charles I ordered his followers to withdraw. His poem "The Passion of Dido for Aeneas," a translation from the Aeniad, was completed by Edmund Waller and published in 1658. Other of his poems survive in manuscript collections.

Hymn

Lord, when the wise men came from far,
Led to thy cradle by a star,
Then did the shepherds too rejoice,
Instructed by thy angel's voice.
Blest were the wise men in their skill,
And shepherds in their harmless will.

Wise men, in tracing Nature's laws,
Ascend unto the highest cause;
Shepherds with humble fearfulness
Walk safely, though their light be less.
Though wise men better know the way,
It seems no honest heart can stray.

There is no merit in the wise
But love, the shepherds' sacrifice.
Wise men, all ways of knowledge passed,
To the shepherds' wonder come at last.
To know can only wonder breed,
And not to know is wonder's seed.

A wise man at the altar bows,
And offers up his studied vows,
And is received. May not the tears,
Which spring too from a shepherd's fears,
And sighs upon his frailty spent,
Though not distinct, be eloquent?

'Tis true, the object sanctifies
All passions which within us rise,
But since no creature comprehends
The cause of causes, end of ends,
He who himself vouchsafes to know
Best pleases his creator so.

When then our sorrows we apply
To our own wants and poverty,
When we look up in all distress,
And our own misery confess,
Sending both thanks and prayers above,
Then, though we do not know, we love.

BRADSTREET, ANNE (DUDLEY) (c.1612–1672), wife of the colonial governor of Massachusetts, was the first poet of note in America. Her father, Thomas Dudley was steward to the Puritan Earl of Lincoln. She married Simon Bradstreet when she was sixteen and they and her parents came with other Puritans to settle in Massachusetts. She had eight children and was under the burden not only of frontier hardships, but of being a frequent hostess and having to move frequently (to Cambridge, to Ipswich, and to Andover). Her first published poems were put out in England by her brother-in-law without her permission. They were published in 1650 as *The Tenth Muse Lately Sprung Up in America.* She wrote an introductory poem to the American edition which came out in 1678. Many of her best Christian poems, written for her family, were not published until 1867. In our century, the very personal tone and simple style of these poems has earned her genuine respect and critical acceptance.

To my Dear and Loving Husband

If ever two were one, then surely we.
If ever man were lov'd by wife, then thee.
If ever wife was happy in a man,
Compare with me, ye women, if you can.
I prize thy love more than whole Mines of gold,
Or all the riches that the East doth hold.
My love is such that Rivers cannot quench,
Nor ought but love from thee give recompence.
Thy love is such I can no way repay;
The heavens reward thee manifold I pray.
Then while we live, in love lets so persever,
That when we live no more, we may live ever.

Upon the Burning Of Our House, July 10th, 1666

In silent night when rest I took,
For sorrow near I did not look,
I waken'd was with thundring noise
And piteous shreiks of dreadfull voice.
That fearfull sound of 'Fire!' and 'Fire!'
Let no man know is my Desire.

I, starting up, the light did spye,
And to my God my heart did cry
To strengthen me in my Distress,
And not to leave me succourlesse.
Then coming out, beheld apace
The flame consume my dwelling place.

And when I could no longer look,
I blest his Name that gave and took,
That layd my goods now in the dust:
Yea so it was, and so 'twas just.
It was his own: it was not mine;
Far be it that I should repine.

He might of All justly bereft,
But yet sufficient for us left.
When by the Ruines oft I past,
My sorrowing eyes aside did cast,
And here and there the places spye
Where oft I sate, and long did lye.

Here stood that Trunk, and there that chest;
There lay that store I counted best:
My pleasant things in ashes lye,
And them behold no more shall I.
Under thy roof no guest shall sitt,
Nor at thy Table eat a bitt.

No pleasant tale shall e'er be told,
Nor things recounted done of old.
No Candle e'er shall shine in Thee,
Nor bridegroom's voice e'er heard shall bee.
In silence ever shalt thou lye;
Adieu; Adieu; All's vanity.

Then streight I 'gan my heart to chide:
And did thy wealth on earth abide?
Didst fix thy hope on mouldring dust,
The arm of flesh didst make thy trust?
Raise up thy thoughts above the skye,
That dunghill mists away may flie.

Thou hast an house on high erect,
Fram'd by that mighty Architect,
With glory richly furnished,
Stands permanent though this bee fled.
It's purchased, and paid for, too,
By Him who hath enough to doe.

A Prise so vast as is unknown,
Yet, by his Gift, is made thine own.
There's wealth enough, I need no more;
Farewell my Pelf, farewell my Store.
The world no longer let me Love,
My Hope and Treasure lyes Above.

"Before the Birth of One of Her Children"

All things within this fading world hath end,
Adversity doth still our joyes attend;
No tyes so strong, no friends so dear and sweet,
But with deaths parting blow is sure to meet.
The sentence past is most irrevocable,
A common thing, yet oh inevitable;
How soon, my Dear, death may my steps attend,
How soon't may be thy Lot to lose thy friend,
We both are ignorant, yet love bids me
These farewell lines to recommend to thee,
That when that knot's unty' d that made us one,
I may seem thine, who in effect am none.
And if I see not half my dayes that's due,
What nature would, God grant to yours and you;
The many faults that well you know I have,
Let be interr'd in my oblivions grave;
If any worth or virtue were in me,
Let that live freshly in thy memory
And when thou feel'st no grief, as I no harms,
Yet love thy dead, who long lay in thine arms:
And when thy loss shall repaid with gains
Look to my little babes my dear remains.
And if thou love thy self, or loved'st me
These O protect from step Dames injury.
And if chance to thine eyes shall bring this verse,
With some sad sighs honour my absent Herse;
And kiss this paper for thy loves dear sake,
Who with salt tears this last Farewel did take.

"As Weary Pilgrim, Now at Rest."

As weary pilgrim, now at rest,
    Hugs with delight his silent nest
His wasted limbes, now lye full soft
    That myrie steps, have troden oft
Blesses himself, to think upon
    his dangers past, and travailes done
The burning sun no more shall heat
    Nor stormy raines, on him shall beat.
The bryars and thornes no more shall scratch

nor hungry wolves at him shall catch
He erring pathes no more shall tread
    nor wild fruits eate, in stead of bread,
for waters cold he doth not long
    for thirst no more shall parch his tongue
No rugged stones his feet shall gaule
    nor stumps nor rocks cause him to fall
All cares and feares, he bids farwell
    and meanes in safity now to dwell.
A pilgrim I, on earth, perplext
    with sinns with cares and sorrows vext
By age and paines brought to decay
    and my Clay house-mouldring away
Oh how I long to be at rest
    and soare on high among the blest.
This body shall in silence sleep
    Mine eyes no more shall ever weep
No fainting fits shall me assaile
    nor grinding paines my body fraile
With cares and fears ne'r cumbred be
    Nor losses know, nor sorrowes see
What tho my flesh shall there consume
    it is the bed Christ did perfume
And when a few yeares shall be gone
    this mortall shall be cloth'd upon
A Corrupt Carcasse downe it lyes
    a glorious body it shall rise
In weaknes and dishonour sowne
    in power 'tis rais'd by Christ alone
Then soule and body shall unite
    and of their maker have the sight
Such lasting joyes shall there behold
as eare ne'r heard nor tongue e'er told
Lord make me ready for that day
    then Come deare bridgrome Come away.

TAYLOR, JEREMY (baptized 1613–1667), clergyman and writer, went to Cambridge and was ordained, in 1633. He was granted a fellowship at Cambridge by Archbishop Laud, and made a doctor of divinity by royal decree of Charles I in 1643. A royalist, he was captured in Wales in 1645 and thereafter set up a school in Carmarthenshire. He wrote his important works, *The Rule and Exercises of Holy Living*, by 1650, and *The Rule and Exercises of Holy Dying*, by 1651, to aid members of the church of England deprived of regular ministry during the Commonwealth. Both works grew to be popular, influencing John Wesley in the next century. He continued to minister to scattered groups of Anglican royalists until the Restoration, when he was made bishop of Down and Connor. He served on the Irish privy council and helped reconstitute the University of Dublin. He was noted as a preacher for his poetic imagination and use of metaphor.

A Prayer (I)

O beauteous God! uncircumscribed treasure
Of an eternal pleasure!
Thy throne is seated far
Above the highest star;
Where thou preparest a glorious place
Within the brightness of thy face,
For every spirit
To inherit,
That builds his hopes upon thy merit;
And loves thee with an holy charity.
What ravish'd heart, seraphic tongues, or eyes
Clear as the morning rise,
Can speak, or think, or see
That bright eternity,
Where the great King's transparent throne
Is of an entire jasper-stone.
There the eye
O' th' chrysolite,
And a sky
Of diamonds, rubies, chrysoprase,
And above all, thy holy face
Makes an eternal charity.
When thou dost bind thy jewels up—that day
Remember us, we pray;
That where the beryl lies,
And the crystal 'bove the skies,
There thou may'st appoint us place,
Within the brightness of thy face;
And our soul
In the scroul
Of life and blissfulness enroul,
That We may praise thee to eternity.

A Prayer (II)

My soul doth pant towards thee
My God, source of eternal life:
    Flesh fights with me,
      O! end the strife
And part us, that in peace I may
    Unclay

My wearied spirit, and take
My flight to thy eternal spring;
    Where for his sake
      Who is my king,
I may wash all my tears away
    That day.

Thou conqueror of death,
Glorious triumpher o'er the grave,
    Whose holy breath
      Was spent to save
Lost mankind; make me to be styled
    Thy child,

And take me when I die
And go unto my dust, my soul
    Above the sky
      With saints enroll,
That in thine arms for ever I
    May lie.

Hymn For Advent

Lord, come away!
Why dost Thou stay?
Thy road is ready; and Thy paths made straight
With longing expectations wait
The consecration of Thy beauteous feet.
Ride on triumphantly; behold, we lay
Our lusts and proud wills in Thy way!

Hosanna! Welcome to our hearts! Lord, here
Thou hast a temple too; and full as dear
As that of Sion, and as full of sin:
Nothing but thieves and robbers dwell therein:

Enter, and chase them forth, and cleanse the floor:
Crucify them, that they may never more
Profane That holy place
Where Thou hast chose to set Thy face!

And then if our stiff tongues shall be
Mute in the praises of Thy Deity,
The stones out of the Temple wall
Shall cry aloud and call
Hosanna! And Thy glorious footsteps greet!

A Prayer For Charity

Full of mercy, full of love,
Look upon us from above;
Thou who taught'st the blind man's night
To entertain a double light,
Thine and the day's—and that thine too:
The lame away his crutches threw;
The parched crust of leprosy
Returned unto its infancy;
The dumb amazed was to hear
His own unchain'd tongue strike his ear;
Thy powerful mercy did even chase
The devil from his usurped place,
Where thou thyself shouldst dwell, not he:
Oh let thy love our pattern be;
Let thy mercy teach one brother
To forgive and love another;
That copying thy mercy here,
Thy goodness may hereafter rear
Our souls unto thy glory, when
Our dust shall cease to be with men. Amen.

AUSTIN, JOHN (1613–1669), a native of Norfolk, attended Cambridge for several years where he embraced the Roman Catholic faith about 1640. He left Cambridge and entered as a student at Lincoln's Inn. He is thought to have distinguished himself as a lawyer, but his religious affiliation and the turbulence of the civil war period prevented him from making the law his livelihood. He served as a tutor to a family in Staffordshire during the civil war. He apparently acquired some property through the death of a relative in 1652. Under the pseudonym William Birchley, he wrote several tracts describing and defending

Roman Catholicism and arguing for religious toleration. He also wrote a book of devotions published in France in 1672, the second part of which, lessons on the four gospels, was republished by the Protestant Dr. Hickes for use by his congregation. It was, among other things, a harmony of the gospels. The devotions included psalms, hymns, and prayers, some of which are also fine poetry.

The Love Of Christ

Come, let's adore the King of Love,
And King of Sufferings too;
For Love it was that brought Him down
And set Him here in woe.

Love drew Him from His Paradise,
Where flowers that fade not grow;
And planted Him in our poor dust,
Among us weeds below.

Here for a time this heavenly Plant
Fairly grew up and thrived;
Diffused its sweetness all about,
And all in sweetness lived.

But envious frosts and furious storms
So long, so fiercely chide;
This tender Flower at last bowed down,
And hung its head and died.

O narrow thoughts, and narrower speech,
Here your defects confess;
The Life of Christ, the Death of God,
How faintly you express!

Help, O thou Blessed Virgin Root,
Whence this fair Flower did spring,
Help us to raise both heart and voice,
And with more spirit sing.

CRASHAW, RICHARD (c. 1613–1649), perhaps the most baroque of the major metaphysical poets, was born the son of a learned Puritan minister. He was educated at Cambridge and learned Latin, Greek, Hebrew, Spanish, and Italian. He published *epigrammatum Sacrorum Liber* ("Book of Sacred Epigrams") in 1634. He held a fellowship and was ordained at Cambridge, but his position there became difficult due to his high church beliefs in the midst of the first

Civil War (1642–51). He was inclining toward Roman Catholicism, and resigned his post before he was evicted. He prepared *Steps to the Temple, Sacred Poems, With other Delights of the Muses* for publication in 1646. He went to France in 1644 and entered the Roman Church. His friend Abraham Cowley found him living in poverty in Paris two years later. Queen Henrietta Maria, consort of Charles I, sent him to Rome with a strong recommendation, but he did not receive a decent position until a short time before his death. His English religious poems were republished in Paris as *Carmen Deo Nostro* ("Hymn to Our Lord") in 1652. Coleridge said Crashaw's "Flaming Heart" inspired the second part of his "Christabel." Crashaw's translation of the Italian Baroque poet, Marino, is thought to have been an influence on Milton's "On the Morning of Christ's Nativity."

Act. 8
On the baptized Aethiopian

Let it no longer be a forlorne hope
To wash an Aethiope:
He's washt, His gloomy skin a peacefull shade
For his white soule is made:
And now, I doubt not, the Eternall Dove,
A black-fac'd house will love.

Matthew. 27
And he answered them nothing.

O Mighty Nothing! unto thee,
Nothing, wee owe all things that bee.
God spake once when hee all things made,
Hee sav'd all when hee Nothing said.
The world was made of Nothing then;
'Tis made by Nothing now againe.

Luke 10.

And a certaine Priest comming that way
looked on him and passed by.

Why dost Thou wound my wounds, O Thou that passest by
Handling & turning them with an unwounded eye?
The calm that cools thine eye does shipwrack mine, for O!
Vnmov'd to see one wretched, is to make him so.

Luc. 7
**She began to wash his feet with teares and
wipe them with the haires of her head.**

Her eyes flood lickes his feets faire staine,
Her haires flame lickes up that againe.
This flame thus quench't hath brighter beames:
This flood thus stained fairer streames.

On St. Peter casting away his Nets at our Saviours call.

Thou hast the art on't Peter; and canst tell
To cast thy Nets on all occasions well.
When Christ calls, and thy Nets would have thee stay:
To cast them well's to cast them quite away.

Steps to the Temple from Sospetto d'Herode

22.

That the Great Angell-blinding light should shrinke
His blaze, to shine in a poore Shepheards eye.
That the unmeasur'd God so low should sinke,
As Pris'ner in a few poore Rags to lye.
That from his Mothers Brest hee milke should drinke
Who feeds with Nectar Heav'ns faire family.
That a vile Manger his low Bed should prove,
Who in a Throne of stars Thunders above.

23.

That hee whom the Sun serves, should faintly peepe
Through clouds of Infant flesh: that hee the old
Eternall Word should bee a Child, and weepe.
That hee who made the fire, should feare the cold;
That Heav'ns high Majesty his Court should keepe
In a clay-cottage, by each blast control'd.
That Glories selfe should serve our Griefs, & feares:
And free Eternity, submit to yeares.

24.

And further, that the Lawes eternall Giver,
Should bleed in his owne lawes obedience:
And to the circumcising Knife deliver
Himselfe, the forfeit of his slaves offence.

That the unblemisht Lambe, blessed for ever,
Should take the marke of sin, and paine of sence.
These are the knotty Riddles, whose darke doubt
Intangles his lost Thoughts, past getting out.

25.

While new Thoughts boyl'd in his enraged Brest,
His gloomy Bosomes darkest Character,
Was in his shady forehead seen exprest.
The forehead's shade in Griefes expression there,
Is what in signe of joy among the blest
The faces lightning, or a smile is here.
Those stings of care that his strong Heart opprest,
A desperate, Oh mee, drew from his deepe Brest.

First eighteen lines from:
**In Memory of the Vertuous and Learned Lady Madre de Teresa
that Sought an Early Martyrdome**

Love thou art absolute, sole Lord
Of life and death—To prove the word,
Wee need to goe to none of all
Those thy old souldiers, stout and tall
Ripe and full growne, that could reach downe,
With strong armes their triumphant crowne:
Such as could with lusty breath,
Speake lowd unto the face of death
Their great Lords glorious name, to none
Of those whose large breasts built a throne
For love their Lord, glorious and great,
Weell see him take a private seat,
And make his mansion in the milde
And milky soule of a soft childe.

Scarce had shee learnt to lisp a name
Of Martyr, yet shee thinkes it shame
Life should so long play with that breath,
Which spent can buy so brave a death.

Christ's Victory

Christ, when he died,
Deceived the cross,

And on death's side
Threw all the loss:
The captive world awaked and found
The prisoners loose, the jailor bound.

O dear and sweet dispute
'Twixt death's and love's far different fruit,
Different as far
As antidotes and poisons are:
By the first fatal tree
Both life and liberty
Were sold and slain;
By this they both look up and live again.

MORE, HENRY (1614–1687), belonged to the philosophical group known
as the Cambridge Platonists. He published *An Anti-dote against Atheism* (1653),
Divine Dialogues (1668), and *A Brief Discourse of the Real Presence* (1681). The
Cambridge Platonists were theological philosophers who opposed Hobbe's
materialism and sought to reconcile reason and religious mystery. They followed
Plato and the Neoplatonists in much of their thought and language, agreeing
in the idea of God and absolute right and wrong. The group included Ralph
Cudworth, Nathaniel Culverwel, Joseph Glanville, Benjamin Whichcote, and
John Smith. Benet *(The Reader's Encyclopedia)* observes their thought may be sum-
marized in Smith's words, "To follow reason is to follow God." More was a
staunch Royalist.

Charity And Humility

Far have I clamored in my mind
But nought so great as love I find;
Deep searching wit, mount-moving might,
Are nought compar'd to that good sprite.
Life of delight and soul of bliss!
Sure source of lasting happiness!
Higher then Heaven! lower then hell!
What is thy tent? Where maist thou dwell?
"My mansion hight humility,
Heaven's vastest capability.
The further it doth downward tend
The higher up it doth ascend;
If it go down to utmost nought,
It shall return with that it sought."

Lord, stretch thy tent in my strait breast;
Enlarge it downward, that sure rest
May then be pight; for that pure fire
Wherewith thou wontest to inspire
All self-dead souls. My life is gone,
Sad solitude's my irksome wonne.
Cut off from men and all this world,
In Lethe's lonesome ditch I'm hurl'd;
Nor might nor sight doth aught me move,
Nor do I care to be above.
O feeble rayes of mentale light!
That best be seen in this dark night,
What are you? What is any strength
If it be not laid in one length
With pride or love? I nought desire
But a new life, or quite t' expire.
Could I demolish with mine eye
Strong towers, stop the fleet stars in skie,
Bring down to earth the pale-faced Moon,
Or turn black midnight to bright Noon;
Though all things were put in my hand—
As parch'd, as dry as th' Libyan sand
Would be my life, if Charity
Were wanting. But Humility
Is more than my poor soul durst crave
That lies entomb'd in lowly grave.
But if 'twere lawful up to send
My voice to Heaven, this should it rend:
"Lord, thrust me deeper into dust,
That thou maist raise me with the just."

BAXTER, RICHARD (1615–1691), studied divinity and was ordained in 1638 in the Church of England. He soon became an ally of the Puritans in opposing the established episcopacy. Although he was ill much of his life, he had a vigorous and exemplary ministry in a parish of Worcestershire where the church building had to be enlarged to accomodate those who came to hear his preaching. He also was in great demand as a pastor and counsellor. People came to him and wrote to him from all over England. Baxter was in the midst of many of the controversies of the seventeenth century, usually as a peacemaker. He favored a limited monarchy, but served as a chaplain to the parliamentary army. Then in 1660 he helped bring about the restoration of the king. He worked for toleration of moderate dissent within the Church of England after the

Restoration. He was imprisoned in 1685 for eighteen months, but with the Revolution of 1688, and the Act of Toleration under William and Mary, Baxter saw the sort of religious freedom established for which he had long stood. He was a prolific writer, producing nearly 200 works, most of them prose, including a popular autobiography.

The Good Shepherd

Christ who knows all His sheep
Will all in safety keep;
He will not lose His blood,
Nor intercession:
Nor we the purchased good
Of His dear Passion.

I know my God is just,
To Him I wholly trust
All that I have and am,
All that I hope for.
All's sure and seen to Him,
Which I here grope for.

Lord Jesus, take my spirit:
I trust Thy love and merit:
Take home this wandering sheep,
For Thou hast sought it:
This soul in safety keep,
For Thou hast bought it.

The Resolution

It's no great matter what men deem,
Whether they count me good or bad:
In their applause and best esteem,
There's no contentment to be had.
Thy steps, Lord, in this dirt I see;
And lest my soul from God should stray,
I'll bear my cross and follow thee:
Let others choose the fairer way.
My face is meeter for the spit;
I am more suitable to shame,
And to the taunts of scornful wit:
It's no great matter for my name.

My Lord hath taught me how to want
A place wherein to put my head:
While he is mine, I'll be content
To beg or lack my daily bread.
Must I forsake the soil and air
Where first I drew my vital breath?
That way may be as near and fair:
Thence I may come to thee by death.
All countries are my Father's lands;
Thy sun, thy love, doth shine on all;
We may in all lift up pure hands,
And with acceptance on thee call.

What if in prison I must dwell?
May I not there converse with thee?
Save me from sin, thy wrath, and hell,
Call me thy child, and I am free.
No walls or bars can keep thee out;
None can confine a holy soul;
The streets of heaven it walks about;
None can its liberty control.
This flesh hath drawn my soul to sin:
If it must smart, thy will be done!
O fill me with thy joys within,
And then I'll let it grieve alone.

Frail, sinful flesh is loath to die;
Sense to the unseen world is strange;
The doubting soul dreads the Most High,
And trembleth at so great a change.
O let me not be strange at home,
Strange to the sun and life of souls,
Choosing this low and darkened room,
Familiar with worms and moles!
Am I the first that go this way?
How many saints are gone before!
How many enter every day
Into thy kingdom by this door!

Christ was once dead, and in a grave;
Yet conquered death, and rose again;
And by this method he will save
His servants that with him shall reign.

The strangeness will be quickly over,
When once the heaven-born soul is there:
One sight of God will it recover
From all this backwardness and fear.
To us, Christ's lowest parts, his feet,
Union and faith must yet suffice
To guide and comfort us: it's meet
We trust our head who hath our eyes.

Stanzas from **The Return**

Who was it that I left behind
When I went last from home,
That now I all disordered find
When to myself I come?

I left it light, but now all's dark,
And I am fain to grope:
Were it not for one little spark
I should be out of hope.

My Gospel-book I open left,
Where I the promise saw;
But now I doubt it's lost by theft:
I find none but the Law.

The stormy rain an entrance hath
Through the uncovered top:
How should I rest when showers of wrath
Upon my conscience drop?

I locked my jewel in my chest;
I'll search lest that be gone:—
If this one guest had quit my breast,
I had been quite undone.

My treacherous Flesh had played its part,
And opened Sin the door;
And they have spoiled and robbed my heart,
And left it sad and poor.

Yet have I one great trusty friend
That will procure my peace,
And all this loss and ruin mend,
And purchase my release.

The bellows I'll yet take in hand,
Till this small spark shall flame:
Love shall my heart and tongue command
To praise God's holy name.

I'll mend the roof; I'll watch the door,
And better keep the key;
I'll trust my treacherous flesh no more,
But force it to obey.

What have I said? That I'll do this
That am so false and weak,
And have so often done amiss,
And did my covenants break?

I mean, Lord—all this shall be done
If thou my heart wilt raise;
And as the work must be thine own,
So also shall the praise.

BEAUMONT, JOSEPH (1616–1699), scholar and poet, received his M.A. at Peterhouse, Cambridge in the same year as Crashaw. In 1644 he was one of the royalists ejected from Cambridge. He retired to his old home and wrote the epic poem "Psyche," which was published in 1648. The poem showed the soul led by divine grace through various temptations into eternal joy. Not much is known of him during the Commonwealth. After marrying in 1650, he lived on his wife's property in Suffolk where he wrote most of his minor poems. His wife died of fen fever in 1662, leaving him with six children, only one of whom lived to adulthood. He was appointed master of Jesus College, Cambridge, in 1662. He carried on a long controversy with Dr. Henry More, the Platonist, after 1665. In 1674 he was appointed Regius professor of divinity of the university and he gave a course of lectures on Romans and Colossians. In 1689 he was appointed to meet with the leaders of the Nonconformists as a commissioner of comprehension. He remained in good health until 1699, when he preached before the university at eighty-four years of age. He died two weeks later.

Morning Hymn

What's this morn's bright eye to me,
If I see not Thine and Thee,
Fairer Jesu; in whose face
All my heaven is spread!—Alas,

Still I grovel in dead night,
Whilst I want Thy living light;
Dreaming with wide open eyes
Fond fantastic vanities.

Shine, my only Day-Star, shine;
So mine eyes shall wake by Thine;
So the dreams I grope in now
To clear visions all shall grow;
So my day shall measured be
By Thy grace's clarity;
So shall I discern the path
Thy sweet Law prescribed hath;
For Thy ways cannot be shown
By any light but by Thine own.

COWLEY, ABRAHAM (1618–1667), son of a stationer (bookseller), graduated with Bachelor's and Master's degrees from Cambridge (1639, 1642). While still in school, he published *Poetical Blossoms* (1633), to be followed by *Love's Riddles* in 1638. Allying himself with the Royalists, he went to France with Queen Henrietta Maria in 1646. He carried messages back to England for the exiles, himself encoding messages from the queen to Charles I. In 1646 he published a pastoral play, *The Mistress.* He returned to England in 1656, publishing *Miscellanies* or *Poems* the same year. The first collected edition of his work appeared in 1668. He is counted among the metaphysical poets, and noted for his "wit" (a term which was derogatory in the mouths of Dryden, then Samuel Johnson.) As much or more than the other metaphysical poets, Cowley used "fantastic," that is unexpected and sometimes discordant metaphor. He wrote many prose essays, the simple style of which is much praised. He is also noted as the originator of the English Pindaric ode. His unfinished epic, *Davideis,* about David, is one of his well-known poems.

Reason

The Holy Book like the Eighth Sphere, does shine
With thousand lights of truth divine:
So numberless the stars, that to the eye
It makes but all one galaxy:—
Yet Reason must assist too, for in seas
So vast and dangerous as these,
Our course by stars above we cannot know,
Without the compass too below.

Though Reason cannot through Faith's mysteries see,
It sees that there and such they be;
Leads to Heaven's-door, and there does humbly keep,
And there through chinks and key-holes peep.
Though it, like Moses, by a sad command
Must not come into the Holy Land,
Yet thither it infallibly does guide,
And from afar 'tis all descried.

Eighth sphere - the sphere of the fixed stars in medieval astronomy

Christ's Passion

Enough, my muse, of earthly things,
And inspirations but of wind;
Take up thy lute, and to it bind
Loud and everlasting strings,
And on them play, and to them sing,
The happy mournful stories,
The lamentable glories
Of the great crucified King!
Mountainous heap of wonders! which dost rise
Till earth thou joinest with the skies!

Too large at bottom, and at top too high,
To be half seen by mortal eye;
How shall I grasp this boundless thing?
What shall I play? what shall I sing?
I'll sing the mighty riddle of mysterious love,
Which neither wretched man below, nor blessed spirits above,
With all their comments can explain,
How all the whole world's life to die did not disdain!

I'll sing the searchless depths of the compassion divine,
The depths unfathomed yet
By reason's plummet, and the line of wit;
Too light the plummet, and too short the line;
How the eternal Father did bestow
His own eternal Son as ransom for his foe;
I'll sing aloud that all the world may hear
The triumph of the buried Conqueror;
How hell was by its prisoner captive led,
And the great slayer, Death, slain by the dead.

Methinks I hear of murdered men the voice
Mixed with the murderers' confused noise,
Sound from the top of Calvary;
My greedy eyes fly up the hill, and see
Who 'tis hangs there, the midmost of the three;
O! how unlike the others he;
Look! how he bends his gentle head with blessings from the tree,
His gracious hands, ne'er stretched but to do good,
Are nailed to the infamous wood!
And sinful man does fondly bind
The arms which he extends to embrace all human kind.

Unhappy man! canst thou stand by and see
All this as patiently as he?
Since he thy sins doth bear,
Make thou his sufferings thine own,
And weep, and sigh, and groan,
And beat thy breast, and tear
Thy garments and thy hair,
And let thy grief, and let thy love,
Through all thy bleeding bowels move!

Dost thou not see thy Prince in purple clad all o'er,
Not purple brought from the Sidonian shore,
But made at home with richer gore?
Dost thou not see the roses which adorn
The thorny garland by him worn?
Dost thou not see the livid traces
Of the sharp scourges' rude embraces?
If yet thou feelest not the smart
Of thorns and scourges in thy heart,
If that be yet not crucified,
Look on his hands, look on his feet, look on his side!

Open, Oh! open wide the fountains of thine eyes,
And let them call
Their stock of moisture forth, where'er it lies;
For this will ask it all.
'Twould all, alas! too little be,
Though thy salt tears come from a sea.
Canst thou deny him this, when he
Has opened all his vital springs for thee?
Take heed, for by his side's mysterious flood

May well be understood
That he will still require some waters to his blood.

MARVELL, ANDREW (1621–1678), son of the Reverend Andrew Marvell, was educated at Cambridge. After the death of his parents he travelled four years in Europe (thus perhaps deliberately avoiding involvement in the civil war). After his return to London, he moved in literary circles. His poems to Richard Lovelace and on the death of Lord Hastings were published in 1649. In 1650 he wrote "An Horatian Ode upon Cromwell's Return from Ireland." He tutored Cromwell's ward, William Dutton and in 1655 wrote "The First Anniversary," which put him in place as unofficial poet to Cromwell. In 1657 he was appointed Latin secretary to the Council of State. He was elected to Parliament in 1659 (the year after Cromwell's death). At the Restoration he used his influence to get Milton released from prison. He went to Holland, possibly on a mission of espionage, and travelled as secretary to the Earl of Carlisle in Russia and Scandanavia. He wrote a satire on corruption at court, "Last Instructions to a Painter," and a treatise advocating toleration for Dissenters, *The Rehearsal Transpos'd*. He was watched by government spies who reported he was working on behalf of Holland in England under the title, "Mr. Thomas." He published many anonymous works against royal power. His *Miscellaneous Poems* were published in 1681. He was well-known as a satirist and enemy of tyranny; however he remained relatively unknown as a poet until the twentieth century when, along with the other "metaphysical" poets, he became more popular.

The Coronet

When for the thorns with which I long too long,
With many a piercing wound,
My Saviour's head have crowned,
I seek with garlands to redress that wrong,
Through every garden, every mead
I gather flowers—my fruits are only flowers—
Dismantling all the fragrant towers
That once adorned my shepherdess's head;
And now, when I have summed up all my store,
Thinking—so I myself deceive—
So rich a chaplet thence to weave
As never yet the King of glory wore;
Alas! I find the serpent old,
That, twining in his speckled breast,
About the flowers disguised does fold,

With wreaths of fame and interest.
Ah, foolish man that wouldst debase with them
And mortal glory, heaven's diadem!
But thou who only couldst the serpent tame,
Either his slippery knots at once untie,
And disentangle all his winding snare,
Or shatter too with him my curious frame,
And let these wither, that so he may die,
Though set with skill, and chosen out with care;
That they, while thou on both their spoils dost tread,
May crown thy feet that could not crown thy head.

VAUGHAN, HENRY (1622–1695), metaphysical poet native to southern Wales, is often called "The Silurist" after an ancient name of his native region. He wrote and published two books of secular verse, *Poems*, in 1646, and *Olor Iscanus*, in 1651, before beginning to write Christian poetry. He is the most respected of the followers of George Herbert. He wrote "The first that with any effective success attempted a diversion of this foul and overflowing stream was the blessed man, Mr. George Herbert, whose holy life and godly verse gained many pious converts, of whom I am the least." Herbert's influence upon his verse is significant—in a number of cases he uses themes and images direct from Herbert's work as springboards for his poems, but his poems nevertheless have a life of their own, being more than imitations. His poem beginning, "I saw Eternity the other night," is one of his best known. Madeleine L'Engle's novel, *A Ring of Pure and Endless Light* takes its title from that poem. Wordsworth was considerably influenced by his poetry, especially by his anagogical approach to the natural world.

The Search (lines 75-96)

Leave, leave, thy gadding thoughts
Who Pores
and spies
Still out of Doores
descries
Within them nought.

The skinne, and shell of things
Though faire,
are not
Thy wish, nor pray'r
but got

By meer Despair
of wings.

To rack old Elements,
or Dust
and say
Sure here he must
needs stay
Is not the way,
nor just.

Search well another world; who studies this,
Travels in Clouds, seeks Manna, where none is.

The Pursuite

Lord! what a busie, restles thing
   Hast thou made man?
Each day, and houre he is on wing,
   Rests not a span;
Then having lost the Sunne, and light
   By clouds surpriz'd
He keepes a Commerce in the night
   With aire disguis'd;
Hadst thou given to this active dust
   A state untir'd,
The lost Sonne had not left the huske
   Nor home desir'd;
That was thy secret, and it is
   Thy mercy too,
For when all failes to bring to blisse,
   Then, this must doe.
Ah! Lord! and what a Purchase will that be
To take us sick, that sound would not take thee?

The Incarnation, and Passion

Lord! when thou didst thy selfe undresse
Laying by thy robes of glory,
To make us more, thou wouldst be lesse,
And becam'st a wofull story.

To put on Clouds instead of light,
And cloath the morning-starre with dust,

Was a translation of such height
As, but in thee, was ne'r exprest;

Brave wormes, and Earth! that thus could have
A God Enclos'd within your Cell,
Your maker pent up in a grave,
Life lockt in death, heav'n in a shell;

Ah, my deare Lord! what couldst thou spye
In this impure, rebellious clay,
That made thee thus resolve to dye
For those that kill thee every day?

O what strange wonders could thee move
To slight thy precious bloud, and breath!
Sure it was Love, my Lord; for Love
Is only stronger far than death.

Rom. Chap. 8. ver. 19

*Etenim res Creatae, exerto Capite observantes
expectant revelationem Filiorum Dei.*

And do they so? have they a Sense
    Of ought but Influence?
Can they their heads lift, and expect,
    And grone too? why th' Elect
Can do no more: my volumes sed
    They were all dull, and dead,
They judg'd them senslesse, and their state
    Wholly Inanimate.
Go, go; Seal up thy looks,
    And burn thy books.

I would I were a stone, or tree,
    Or flowre by pedigree,
Or some poor high-way herb, or Spring
    To flow, or bird to sing!
Then should I (tyed to one sure state,)
    All day expect my date;
But I am sadly loose, and stray
    A giddy blast each way;
O let me not thus range!
    Thou canst not change.

Sometimes I sit with thee, and tarry
    An hour, or so, then vary.
Thy other Creatures in this Scene
    Thee only aym, and mean;
Some rise to seek thee, and with heads
    Erect peep from their beds;
Others, whose birth is in the tomb,
    And cannot quit the womb,
Sigh there, and grone for thee,
    Their liberty.

O let not me do lesse! shall they
    Watch, while I sleep, or play?
Shall I thy mercies still abuse
    With fancies, friends, or newes?
O brook it not! thy bloud is mine,
    And my soul should be thine;
O brook it not! why wilt thou stop
    After whole showres one drop?
Sure, thou wilt joy to see
    Thy sheep with thee.

Easter Hymn

Death, and darkness get you packing,
Nothing now to man is lacking,
All your triumphs now are ended,
And what Adam marr'd, is mended;
Graves are beds now for the weary,
Death a nap, to wake more merry;
Youth now, full of pious duty,
Seeks in thee for perfect beauty,
The weak, and aged tir'd, with length
Of daies, from thee look for new strength,
And Infants with thy pangs Contest
As pleasant, as if with the brest;
Then, unto him, who thus hath thrown
Even to Contempt thy kingdome down,
And by his blood did us advance
Unto his own Inheritance,
To him be glory, power, praise,
From this, unto the last of daies.

Love, and Discipline

Since in a land not barren stil
(Because thou dost thy grace distil,)
My lott is fain, Blest be thy will!

And since these biting frosts but kil
Some tares in me which choke, or spil
That seed thou sow'st, Blest be thy skil!

Blest be thy Dew, and blest thy frost,
And happy I to be so crost,
And cur'd by Crosses at thy cost.

The Dew doth Cheer what is distrest,
The frosts ill weeds nip, and molest,
In both thou work'st unto the best.

Thus while thy sev'ral mercies plot,
And work on me now cold, now hot,
The work goes on, and slacketh not,

For as thy hand the weather steers,
So thrive I best, 'twixt joyes, and tears,
And all the year have some green Ears.

The World

I saw Eternity the other night
Like a great Ring of pure and endless light,
    All calm, as it was bright,
And round beneath it, Time in hours, days, years
    Driv'n by the spheres
Like a vast shadow mov'd, In which the world
    And all her train were hurl'd;
The doting Lover in his queintest strain
    Did there Complain,
Neer him, his Lute, his fancy, and his flights,
    Wits sour delights,
With gloves, and knots the silly snares of pleasure
    Yet his dear Treasure
All scattered lay, while he his eys did pour
    Upon a flow'r.

The darksome States-man hung with weights and woe
Like a thick midnight-fog mov'd there so slow
   He did nor stay, nor go;
Condemning thoughts (like sad Ecclipses) scowl
   Upon his soul,
And Clouds of crying witnesses without
   Pursued him with one shout.
Yet dig'd the Mole, and lest his ways be found
   Workt under ground,
Where he did Clutch his prey, but one did see
   That policie,
Churches and altars fed him, Perjuries
   Were gnats and flies,
It rain'd about him bloud and tears, but he
   Drank them as free.

The fearfull miser on a heap of rust
Sate pining all his life there, did scarce trust
   His own hands with the dust,
Yet would not place one peece above, but lives
   In feare of theeves.
Thousands there were as frantick as himself
   And hug'd each one his pelf,
The down-right Epicure plac'd heav'n in sense
   And scornd pretence
While others slipt into a wide Excesse
   Said little lesse;
The weaker sort slight, triviall wares Inslave
   Who think them brave,
And poor, despised truth sate Counting by
   Their victory.

Yet some, who all this while did weep and sing,
And sing, and weep, soar'd up into the Ring,
   But most would use no wing.
O fools (said I,) thus to prefer dark night
   Before true light,
To live in grots, and caves, and hate the day
   Because it shews the way,
The way which from this dead and dark abode
   Leads up to God,
A way where you might tread the Sun, and be
   More bright than he.

But as I did their madnes so discusse
   One whisper'd thus,
This Ring the Bride-groome did for none provide
   But for his bride.

John Chap. 2. ver. 16, 17.

All that is in the world, the lust of the flesh, the lust of the Eys,
and the pride of life, is not of the father, but is of the world.
And the world passeth away, and the lusts thereof, but he that
doth the will of God abideth for ever.

The Water-fall

With what deep murmurs through times silent stealth
Doth thy transparent, cool and watry wealth
   Here flowing fall,
     And chide, and call,
As if his liquid, loose Retinue staid
Lingring, and were of this steep place afraid,
   The common pass
     Where, clear as glass,
      All must descend
       Not to an end:
But quickned by this deep and rocky grave,
Rise to a longer course more bright and brave.

     Dear stream! dear bank, where often I
     Have sate, and pleas'd my pensive eye,
     Why, since each drop of thy quick store
     Runs thither, whence it flow'd before,
     Should poor souls fear a shade or night,
     Who came (sure) from a sea of light?
     Or since those drops are all sent back
     So sure to thee, that none doth lack,
     Why should frail flesh doubt any more
     That what God takes, hee'l not restore?
     O useful Element and clear!
     My sacred wash and cleanser here,
     My first consigner unto those
     Fountains of life, where the lamb goes?
     What sublime truths, and wholesome themes,
     Lodge in thy mystical, deep streams!
     Such as dull man can never finde

Unless that Spirit lead his minde,
Which first upon thy face did move,
And, hatch'd all with his quickning love.
As this loud brooks incessant fall
In streaming rings restagnates all,
Which reach by course the bank, and then
Are no more seen, just so pass men.
O my invisible estate,
My glorious liberty, still late!
Thou art the Channel my soul seeks,
Not this with Cataracts and Creeks.

QUARLES, JOHN (1624–1665), one of the eighteen children of Francis Quarles, was another of the poets tossed about on the currents of the English civil wars. He went to Oxford, but does not seem to have finished there. He was part of a royal garrison at Oxford and was promoted to the rank of captain. He was imprisoned and banished during the Commonwealth, apparently for supporting the King. In banishment in Flanders he wrote the poems published as *Fons Lachrymarum* ("Fountain of Tears"). He was in London in 1648, but had to leave again the following year. When he returned again to London, he barely was able to support himself with his writing. *Fons Lachrymarum* was subtitled "From whence flow England's Complaint, Jeremiah's Lamentations Paraphrased," and was followed in 1655 with *Divine Meditations upon Several Subjects*, subtitled "whereunto is annexed God's Love to Man's Unworthiness, with several Divine Ejaculations." He published many other miscellaneous writings. His poetry has that note of alien longing which comes so naturally to the Christian exile.

At Home

Long did I toil and knew no earthly rest,
Far did I rove and found no certain home;
At last I sought them in His sheltering breast,
Who opes His arms and bids the weary come:
With Him I found a home, a rest divine,
And I since then am His, and He is mine.

The good I have is from His stores supplied,
The ill is only what He deems the best;
He for my friend I'm rich with nought beside,
And poor without Him, though of all possessed;
Changes may come, I take or I resign,
Content, while I am His, while He is mine.

Whate'er may change, in Him no change is seen,
A glorious Sun that wanes not nor declines,
Above the storms and clouds He walks, serene,
And on His people's inward darkness shines;
All may depart, I fret not, nor repine,
While I my Saviour's am, while He is mine.

While here, alas! I know but half His love,
But half discern Him and but half adore;
But when I meet him in the realms above
I hope to love Him better, praise Him more,
And feel, and tell, amid the choir divine,
How fully I am His and He is mine.

SPEED, SAMUEL (d. 1681), a London stationer and Fleet Street bookseller, was arrested in 1666 for publishing and dispersing seditious books. He was released on giving his bond to do so no more. He appears to have been author of *Fragmenta Carceris; or the King's Bench Scuffle, with Humours of the Common Side* (1674) and *Prison Pietie, or Meditations, Divine and Moral, digested into practical heads on mixt and various subjects.* The poetry of Quarles and Herbert influenced the latter work considerably. (Another contemporary, Samuel Speed, 1631–1682, was an exile during the Commonwealth and came back to become a vicar and chaplain at the Restoration, but seems to have died in debtor's prison.)

Peace

I sought for Peace, but could not find;
     I sought it in the city,
But they were of another mind,
     The more's the pity!

I sought for Peace of country swain,
     But yet I could not find;
So I returning home again,
     Left Peace behind.

Sweet Peace, where dost thou dwell? said I.
     Methought a voice was given:
'Peace dwelt not here, long since did fly
     To God in heaven.'

Thought I, this echo is but vain,
     To folly 'tis of kin;

Anon I heard it tell me plain,
'Twas killed by sin.'

Then I believed the former voice,
And rested well content,
Laid down and slept, rose, did rejoice,
And then to heaven went.
There I enquired for Peace, and found it true,
An heavenly plant it was, and sweetly grew.

CROSSMAN, SAMUEL (c. 1624–1684), graduated from Cambridge in 1660 and was ordained, but in 1662 was ejected from his rectory in Essex for nonconformity. He later came into conformity with the Church of England and became one of the king's chaplains. He published *The Young Mans Monitor, or a modest Offer toward the Pious and Vertuous Composure of Life from Youth to Riper Years* (1664), and *The Young Mans Meditation, or some few Sacred Poems upon Select Subjects and Scriptures* (1664), as well as various sermons.

No Story So Divine

My song is love unknown;
My Saviour's love to me;
Love to the loveless shown,
That they might lovely be.
   O who am I
   That for my sake,
   My Lord should take
   Frail flesh, and die?

He came from His blest Throne,
Salvation to bestow:
But men made strange and none
The longed-for Christ would know.
   But O my Friend!
   My Friend indeed,
   Who at my need
   His life did spend.

Sometimes they strew His way,
And His sweet praises sing;
Resounding all the day,
Hosannas to their King.
   Then: Crucify!

Is all their breath,
And for His death
They thirst and cry.

Why, what hath my Lord done,
What makes this rage and spite?
He made the lame to run,
He gave the blind their sight.
    Sweet injuries!
    Yet they at these
    Themselves displease,
    And 'gainst Him rise.

They rise and needs will have
My dear Lord made away;
A murderer they save;
The Prince of life they slay.
    Yet cheerful He
    To suffering goes,
    That He His foes
From thence might free.

In life, no house, no home
My Lord on earth might have;
In death, no friendly tomb
But what a stranger gave.
    What may I say?
    Heaven was His home;
    But mine the tomb
    Wherein He lay.

Here might I stay and sing,
No story so divine;
Never was love, dear King,
Never was grief like Thine.
    This is my Friend,
    In whose sweet praise
    I all my days
    Could gladly spend.

BUNYAN, JOHN (1628–1688), is the most enduring and popular of seventeenth century Christian authors. His *Pilgrim's Progress* has had tremendous influence on English-speaking Christians ever since it was first published in 1678. He served in the military, and according to his autobiography, *Grace Abounding To* the *Chief of Sinners* (1666), was a thoroughly hardened man, but he underwent a gradual conversion and became a Baptist preacher. He was arrested for nonconformity and imprisoned for twelve years. He did considerable writing in prison. Among his other works are *The Holy War* and *The Life and Death of Mr. Badman.* His use of allegory harkens back to Spenser, although his works are much less literary and thus have been popular among less educated as well as learned readers.

Christian Loses His Burden (from Pilgrim's Progress)

So I saw in my dream that just as Christian came up with the cross, his burden loosed from off his shoulders and fell from off his back, and began to tumble and so continued to do till it came to the mouth of the sepulchre, where it fell in, and I saw it no more. . . . Then Christian gave three leaps for joy and went on singing:

> Thus far I did come laden with my sin;
> Nor could aught ease the grief that I was in,
> Till I came hither. What a place is this!
> Must here be the beginning of my bliss?
> Must here the burden fall from off my back?
> Must here the strings that bound it to me crack?
> Blessed cross! Blessed sepulchre! Blessed rather be
> The Man that there was put to shame for me!

The Shepherd Boy sings in the Valley of Humiliation

> He that is down needs fear no fall,
> He that is low, no pride:
> He that is humble ever shall
> Have God to be his guide.
>
> I am content with what I have,
> Little be it or much:
> And, Lord, contentment still I crave.
> Because Thou savest such.
>
> Fullness to such a burden is
> That go on pilgrimage:
> Here little, and hereafter bliss,
> Is best from age to age.

Who Would True Valor See

> Who would true valor see,
> Let him come hither;

One here will constant be,
Come wind, come weather;
There's no discouragement
Shall make him once relent
His first avowed intent
To be a pilgrim.

Whoso beset him round
With dismal stories,
Do but themselves confound—
His strength the more is.
No lion can him fright;
He'll with a giant fight,
But he will have a right
To be a pilgrim.

Hobgoblin nor foul fiend
Can daunt his spirit;
He knows he at the end
Shall life inherit.
Then fancies fly away,
He'll fear not what men say;
He'll labor night and day
To be a pilgrim.

German Hymns

The Protestant Reformation, if we mark its beginning with Luther's ninety-five theses in 1517, was also the beginning of modern hymn-writing. English hymn-writing, however, did not begin in earnest for another two hundred years. The British church, in its split from Rome, put an end to public hymn-singing:

> . . . Since the new ritual that had to be made for the national Church, Cranmer *omitted all hymns.* There were practical reasons behind this act. Ordinary citizens could not read Latin—or English, for that matter; and without choirs of monks who knew the intricacies of plainsong tunes, singing by the congregation was impossible. (Albert Edward Bailey, *The Gospel in Hymns*)

Psalm-singing, alone, was allowed in the strongly puritan Anglican and Scottish churches. In the Anglican church even metrical psalms were only for private worship. In 1549 a small book was published, *Certayne Psalmes chose out of the Psalter of David and drawn into Englishe metre by Thomas Sternhold, grome to ye Kynges Majesties robes.* From that edition to the nineteenth century, approximately 325 different version of metrical psalmes were published in England.

Despite the official ban on worshipping with hymns of "human composure," poets and composers continued to produce hymns—literary as well as musical. In fact various of the best poems from the sixteenth and seventeenth centuries were entitled "Hymne. . . ."

The real return of English hymn-writing, however, started with the Restoration and reached its peak in the late Romantic and Victorian eras, with a concurrent burst of translating Greek, Latin, and German hymns. The Victorian Evangelicals led in hymn-writing, while the High Church brethren (Oxford movement) led in translation of ancient hymns.

During the two hundred years when the English were not writing or using many hymns for worship, the Germans were writing and singing tens of thousands of them. These German hymns were an influence on the revival of hymns in England. German Moravians, among whom the Wesleys found much inspiration, were great hymn-singers and writers. Translations of German hymns from the last half of the nineteenth century are among our best English hymns.

A Mighty Fortress Is Our God
Martin Luther, 1529   Translated by Frederick H. Hedge, 1853

> A mighty Fortress is our God,
>   A Bulwark never failing
> Our Helper he amid the flood
>   Of mortal ills prevailing.
> For still our ancient foe
>   Doth seek to work us woe;
> His craft and power are great;
>   And, armed with cruel hate,
> On earth is not his equal.
>
> Did we in our own strength confide,
>   Our striving would be losing;
> Were not the right Man on our side,
>   The Man of God's own choosing.
> Dost ask who that may be?
>   Christ Jesus, it is he,
> Lord Sabaoth his Name,
>   From age to age the same,
> And he must win the battle.
>
> And though this world with devils filled,
>   Should threaten to undo us,
> We will not fear, for God hath willed

His truth to triumph through us.
The prince of darkness grim,
    We tremble not for him;
His rage we can endure,
    For lo! his doom is sure;
One little word shall fell him.

That Word above all earthly powers,
    No thanks to them, abideth;
The Spirit and the gifts are ours
    Through him who with us sideth;
Let goods and kindred go,
    This mortal life also;
The body they may kill:
    God's truth abideth still;
His kingdom is forever.

Praise To The Lord The Almighty
Joachim Neander, 1680   Translated by Catherine Winkworth, 1863

Praise to the Lord, the Almighty, the King of creation
O my soul praise him for he is thy health and salvation!
All ye who hear, Now to his temple draw near,
Join me in glad adoration.

Praise to the Lord, who o'er all things so wondrously reigneth,
Shelters thee under his wings, yea, so gently sustaineth!
Hast thou not seen How thy desires ever have been
Granted in what he ordaineth?

Praise to the Lord, who doth prosper thy work and defend thee!
Surely his goodness and mercy here daily attend thee;
Ponder anew What the Almighty will do,
If with his love he befriend thee!

Praise thou the Lord, who with marvelous wisdom hath made thee,
Decked thee with health, and with loving hand guided and stayed thee.
How oft in grief Hath not he brought thee relief,
Spreading his wings to o'er-shade thee!

Praise to the Lord! O let all that is in me adore him!
All that hath life and breath, come now with praises before him!
Let the Amen Sound from his people again;
Gladly for aye we adore him.

If Thou But Suffer God To Guide Thee
Georg Neumark, 1641   Translated by Catherine Winkworth, 1855, 1863

If thou but suffer God to guide thee,
And hope in him through all thy ways,
He'll give thee strength, what-e'er betide thee,
And bear thee through the evil days:
Who trusts in God's unchanging love
Builds on the rock that naught can move.

What can these anxious cares avail thee,
These never ceasing moans and sighs?
What can it help, if thou bewail thee
O'er each dark moment as it flies?
Our cross and trials do but press
The heavier for our bitterness.

Only be still, and wait his leisure
In cheerful hope, with heart content
To take what-e'er thy Father's pleasure
And all-discerning love hath sent;
Nor doubt our inmost wants are known
To him who chose us for his own.

All are alike before the Highest;
'Tis easy to our God, we know,
To raise thee up though low thou liest,
To make the rich man poor and low;
True wonders still by him are wrought
Who setteth up and brings to naught.

Sing, pray, and keep his ways unswerving,
So do thine own part faithfully,
And trust his Word, though undeserving,
Thou yet shalt find it true for thee;
God never yet forsook at need
The soul that trusted him indeed.

Silent Night
Joseph Mohr, 1818   Translated by Jane Campbell

Silent night! Holy night! All is calm, all is bright
Round yon virgin mother and Child. Holy Infant so tender and mild,
Sleep in heavenly peace, Sleep in heavenly peace.

Silent night! Holy night! Shepherds quake at the sight!
Glories stream from heaven afar, Heav'nly hosts sing: Alleluia,
Christ, the Savior, is born! Christ, the Saviour, is born!

Silent night! Holy night! Son of God, love's pure light
Radiant beams from thy holy face, With the dawn of redeeming grace,
Jesus, Lord, at thy birth, Jesus, Lord, at they birth.

When Morning Gilds The Skies
German hymn, 1828   Translated by Edward Caswall, 1854, and others

When morning gilds the skies,
My heart awaking cries: May Jesus Christ be praised:
Alike at work and prayer
To him I would repair: May Jesus Christ be praised.

Whene'er the sweet church bell
Peals over hill and dell: May Jesus Christ be praised.
O hark to what it sings;
As joyously it rings: May Jesus Christ be praised.

When sleep her balm denies,
My silent spirit sighs: May Jesus Christ be praised.
When evil thoughts molest,
With this I shield my breast: May Jesus Christ be praised.

Does sadness fill my mind?
O solace here I find: May Jesus Christ be praised.
Or fades my earthly bliss?
My comfort all is this: May Jesus Christ be praised.

Let earth's wide circle round
In joyful notes resound: May Jesus Christ be praised.
Let air, and sea, and sky
From depth to height reply: May Jesus Christ be praised.

Be this, while life is mine,
My canticle divine: May Jesus Christ be praised.
Be this the eternal song
Through all the ages long: May Jesus Christ be praised.

Ye nations of mankind,
In this your concord find: May Jesus Christ be praised.

Let all the earth around
Ring joyous with the sound: May Jesus Christ be praised.

Be Still My Soul
Katharina von Schlegel, b.1697   Translated by Jane Borthwick, 1855

Be still, my soul: the Lord is on thy side;
Bear patiently the cross of grief or pain;
Leave to thy God to order and provide;
In ev'ry change he faithful will remain.
Be still, my soul: thy best and heav'nly Friend
Through thorny ways leads to a joyful end.

Be still, my soul: thy God doth undertake
To guide the future as he has the past.
Thy hope, thy confidence let nothing shake;
All now mysterious shall be bright at last.
Be still, my soul: the waves and wind still know
His voice who ruled them while he dwelt below.

Be still, my soul: when dearest friends depart,
And all is darkened in the vale of tears,
Then shalt thou better know his love, his heart,
Who comes to soothe thy sorrow and thy fears.
Be still, my soul: thy Jesus can repay
From his own fullness all he takes away.

Be still, my soul: the hour is hast'ning on
When we shall be for ever with the Lord,
When disappointment, grief, and fear are gone,
Sorrow forgot, love's purest joys restored.
Be still, my soul: when change and tears are past,
All safe and blessed we shall meet at last.

Now Thank We All Our God
Martin Rinkart, c. 1636   Translated by Catherine Winkworth, 1858

Now thank we all our God   With heart and hands and voices,
Who wondrous things hath done,   In whom his world rejoices;
Who from our mothers' arms,   Hath blessed us on our way
With countless gifts of love,   And still is ours today.

O may this bounteous God   Through all our life be near us,
With ever joyful hearts   And blessed peace to cheer us;

And keep us in his grace,   And guide us when perplexed,
And free us from all ills   In this world and the next.

All praise and thanks to God,   The Father, now be given,
The Son and Him who reigns   With them in highest heaven,
The One Eternal God   Whom earth and heav'n adore;
For thus it was, is now,   And shall be evermore.

O Let Him Whose Sorrow No Relief Can Find
Wem in Leidenstagen
H. S. Oswald, 1751–1834   Translated by F. E. Cox

O let him whose sorrow
No relief can find,
Trust in God, and borrow
Ease for heart and mind.

Where the mourner weeping
Sheds the secret tear,
God his watch is keeping,
Though none else be near.

God will never leave thee,
All thy wants he knows,
Feels the pains that grieve thee,
Sees thy cares and woes.

Raise thine eyes to heaven
Should thy spirits quail,
When, by tempests driven
Sight and steering fail.

All our woe and trouble
Justice will requite,
All our joys redouble
In the eternal height.

Jesus gracious Saviour,
In the realms above
Crown us with Thy favour,
Fill us with thy love.

Ah, Holy Jesus, How Hast Thou Offended
Herzliebster Jesu
F. Heermann, 1585-1647 Translated by R. Bridges

Ah, holy Jesus, how hast thou offended,
That man to judge thee hath in hate pretended?
By foes derided, by thine own rejected,
O most afflicted.

Who was the guilty? Who brought this upon thee?
Alas, my treason, Jesus, hath undone thee.
'Twas I, Lord Jesus, I it was denied thee:
I crucified thee.

Lo, the good Shepherd for the sheep is offered;
The slave hath sinned, and the Son hath suffered;
For man's atonement, while he nothing heedeth,
God intercedeth.

For me, kind Jesus, was thy incarnation,
Thy mortal sorrow, and thy life's oblation;
Thy death of anguish and thy bitter passion,
For my salvation.

Therefore, kind Jesus, since I cannot pay thee,
I do adore thee, and will ever pray thee,
Think on thy pity and thy love unswerving,
Not my deserving.

Chapter Five

RESTORATION AND EIGHTEENTH CENTURY POETRY

1660—Charles II restored to throne   1776—American Revolution

The period of English history known as "The Restoration" was not as healthy an age for Christian poetry as the preceding one. During the eighteenth century there came extensive periods of spiritual revival and renewal, but the primary poetic evidence of a resurgence of faith is found in hymn lyrics.

The English Civil War was a source of great disillusionment in England, much as the American Civil War was to be a century later in the United States. No matter how high the ideals which ignite a civil war, those who idolize them, will sooner or later find them considerably shabbied by blood. Other unsettling events came soon after Charles' restoration: the Plague of 1664–5 and the Great Fire of London in 1666. These catastrophes and a lack of real political resolution during the reigns of Charles II and James II may have contributed to the dirth of Christian poetry during that time.

Further factors, however, which continued on into the eighteenth century were the lack of court sponsorship (earlier poets had often relied upon noble "patrons" for financial support in their writing) and a general distrust among those in power of anything which looked like "enthusiasm." Although enthusiasm is no longer a negative term, its meaning was similar to that of "fanaticism" in contemporary English. The worst tendencies in a caricature of a Puritan or of a "Nonconformist" (so-called for refusal to obey the Act of Uniformity of 1662) were summarized as "enthusiasm." Literary voices as well as the political powers called for calm and reasonableness. The poetry that was produced in response to this call, although stylistically excellent, was seldom a poetry of the heart.

Many aspects of Restoration and eighteenth century poetry were defined in reaction to the English Civil War and The Puritan Protectorate. Cromwell and Milton had claimed the Bible as their official guidebook. Many of the poets of this period felt inclined to avoid that association and to look elsewhere. There was as always a deep desire for an abiding human tradition to build upon, however. The dominant poetic tradition of the period, the neoclassical, harkened back to the ancient pagan writers and particularly to those of the pre-Christian Augustan period—the period of relative peace and prosperity under Augustus Caesar which followed the Roman civil war (after the death of Julius Caesar).

A parallel was seen in the historical context as well as the literary. The two greatest poets of the English Augustan Age were Alexander Pope and John Dryden. Neither is widely noted as a Christian poet, although a number of Pope's poems are included here.

An American colonist was among the better Christian poets of the Restoration period. Edward Taylor was a great poet, although he was not to be published for more than two hundred years after his death. The kind of "enthusiasm" which many of the post-Protectorate British dreaded reached its peak in America in 1692 with the Salem witch trials. Little poetry of significance was produced in America after Taylor's death in 1729.

The novel began to rise as a major literary genre during this time. John Bunyan's *Pilgrim's Progress* is often mentioned as the first English novel. The first full-blown novels of Defoe, Richardson, and Fielding, although dealing with issues of morals and manners, were not centrally concerned with Christian faith and faithfulness.

The Eighteenth Century brought many social problems which concerned Christian reformers: slavery, child labor, factory safety, alcoholism, and education issues, which were to continue as central concerns through the Romantic and Victorian periods.

The mid-Eighteenth Century also brought "revivals" of faith and a new era of evangelism. With this came a new emphasis on the hymn lyric as a central and popular genre of Christian poetry. Hymn-writing began to flourish among a wide range of Anglicans, Calvinists, Methodists, and Independents. These were sung by all classes of people from coal miners to countesses. Their language was often high-flown, but nevertheless of the heart and centered in Christ. Many of the great hymns we sing today were written during the century. [See Eighteenth Century Hymnology toward the end of this chapter.]

Apart from hymns, Restoration and Eighteenth Century poetry tended to be more sceptical than devotional, avoiding metaphysical and religious themes as well as the styles associated with them. The poetry was often satirical or elegiac. Among "men of letters" it was largely a period of reaction against the immediate past and conformity to an ideal of the distant past.

The end of the period included some poetry which would come to be called Romantic: reflective poetry on subjects chiefly from "nature."

A Brief Chronology of The Restoration and Eighteenth Century

1660   Charles II is restored to the throne
1662   Charles charters the Royal Society of London (scientific society)
1664–65   The European Plague strikes London, killing about one-sixth of the inhabitants, and driving about two-thirds of them into the country

1666	The Great Fire of London
1667	Milton's *Paradise Lost* is published
1671	Milton's *Paradise Regained* and *Samson Agonistes* published
1675	John Bunyan writes *Pilgrim's Progress* while in prison for the second time (published-1678-9)
1688–89	"The Glorious Revolution"—James II deposed and William and Mary accede to the throne
1690	John Locke's *Essay Concerning Human Understanding* states "Our business here is not to know all things, but those which concern our con duct."
1692	Witch trials were conducted in Salem, Massachusetts
1700	John Dryden dies
1707	Act of Union forms "Great Britain" of Scotland and England
1707–09	Isaac Watts *Hymns and Spiritual Songs* published
1714	George I accedes to throne (begins rule of House of Hanover)
1719	Daniel Defoe's *Robinson Crusoe* published
1726	Jonathan Swift, Dean of St. Patrick's Cathedral, Dublin, publishes *Gulliver's Travels*
1729	Edward Taylor dies
1737	Charles Wesley "found rest for his soul," began writing hymns
1740	Samuel Richardson's *Pamela* published
1742	Henry Fielding's *Joseph Andrews* published (Tom Jones - 1749)
1744	Alexander Pope dies
1745	Jonathan Swift dies
1776	Augustus Toplady publishes hymns including "Rock of Ages"
1776	American Revolution
1779	John Newton and William Cowper publish *Olney Hymns*

WIGGLESWORTH, MICHAEL (1631–1705), was born in England where his father was persecuted for his Puritan faith. The family emigrated in 1638 and settled in New Haven. Michael graduated from Harvard in 1651. He became a tutor and Fellow of the college from 1652–54 and again from 1697–1705. Like nearly all other major universities of the world, Harvard was founded as a center of Christian education. With most of his fellow graduates, Wigglesworth became a pastor, preaching at Charlestown and then at Malden. Although his health was often poor, he remained pastor at Malden from 1656 to his death in 1705. He published various poetical works, including *The Day of Doom; or a Poetical Description of the Great and Last Judgment* (1662), and though very popular during it's day contains some embarrasingly harsh passages reflecting "Calvinism" at its worst.

A Farewel to the World

Now farewel World, in which is not my Treasure,
I have in thee enjoy'd but little Pleasure.
And now I leave thee for a better Place,
Where lasting Pleasures are before CHRIST's Face.

Farewel, ye Sons of Men, who do not favour
The things of God; who little prize his Favour.
Farewel, I say with your Fools Paradise,
Until the King of Terrors you Surprise,
And bring you trembling to CHRIST's Judgment seat,
To give Account of your Transgressions Great.

Farewel, New-England, which hast long Enjoy'd
The Day of Grace, but hast most vainly toy'd,
And trifled with the Gospels Glorious Light;
Thou mayst expect a dark Egyptian Night.

Farewel, Young Brood and Rising Generation,
Wanton and Proud, Ripe for Gods Indignation;
Which neither you, nor others can prevent,
Except in Truth you speedily Repent.

Farewel, sweet Saints of God, Christ's little Number,
Beware lest ye thro' sloth securely Slumber.
Stand to your Spiritual Arms, and keep your Watch,
Let not your Enemy you napping catch.
Take up your Cross, prepare for Tribulation,
Thro' which doth ly the way unto Salvation.
Love JESUS CHRIST, with all Sincerity:
Eschew Will-Worship and Idolatry.
Farewel again, until we all appear
Before our Lord, a Well-done there to hear.

Farewel ye faithful Servants of the Lord,
Painful dispensers of His Holy Word;
From whose Communion and Society
I once was kept thro' long Infirmity;

This of my Sorrows was an Aggravation;
But, Christ be thanked, thro' whose Mediation,
I have at length obtained Liberty
To dwell with Soul-delighting Company,

Where many of our Friends are gone before,
And you shall follow with as many more.
Mean while stand fast, the Truth of God maintain,
Suffer for Christ, and great shall be your Gain.

Farewel, my natural Friends and dear Relations,
Who have my Trials seen and great Temptations;
You have no Cause to make for me great Moan;
My Death to you is little Loss or none.
But unto me it is no little Gain;
For Death at once frees me from all my Pain.
Make Christ your greatest Friend, who never dies;
All other Friends are fading Vanities.
Make him your Light, your Life, your End, your All:
Prepare for Death, be ready for his call.

Farewel, vile Body subject to Decay,
Which art with lingering Sickness worn away,
I have by thee much Pain and Smart endur'd,
Great Grief of Mind thou hast to me Procur'd;
Great Grief of Mind, by being impotent,
And to Christ's Work an awkward Instrument.
Thou shalt not henceforth be a clog to me,
Nor shall my Soul a burthen be to thee.

Rest in thy Grave, until the Resurrection,
Then shalt thou be revived in Perfection:
Endow'd with wonderful Agility,
Cloathed with Strength, and Immortality;
With shining brightness, gloriously array'd,
Like to Christ's glorious Body, glorious made.
Thus Christ shall thee again to me restore,
Ever to live with Him, and part no more.
Mean while my Soul shall enter into Peace,
Where Fears and Tears, where Sin & Smart shall cease.

WANLEY, NATHANIEL (1634–1680), clergyman and compiler, graduated from Cambridge and after being ordained, took a rectory in Leicestershire. He published *Vox Dei, or the Great Duty of Self-reflection upon a Man's own Wayes* in 1658. When John Bryan, D.D., nonconformist vicar of Trinity Church, Coventry, resigned, Wanley was made his successor. Bryan was ministering to a nonconformist congregation, but continued to attend Wanley's services. Wanley is said to have been in touch with the prevailing puritanism of Coventry. Bryan and

Wanley became intimate friends and on the former's death in 1676, Wanley preached the funeral sermon honoring their friendship and the Lord. Wanley published *War and Peace Reconciled. . .* (1670) a translation from the Latin author Justus Lipsius. He also published *The Wonders of the Little World; or a General History of Man In Six Books* (1678).

Royal Presents

The off'rings of the Eastern kings of old
Unto our lord were incense, myrrh and gold;
Incense because a God; gold as a king;
And myrrh as to a dying man they bring.
Instead of incense (Blessed Lord) if we
Can send a sigh or fervent prayer to thee,
Instead of myrrh if we can but provide
Tears that from penitential eyes do slide,
And though we have no gold; if for our part
We can present thee with a broken heart
Thou wilt accept: and say those Eastern kings
Did not present thee with more precious things.

TRAHERNE, THOMAS (c.1636–1674), attended Oxford after which he became a rector and later chaplain to the Lord Keeper of the Seals. The only one of his works to appear before his death was *Roman Forgeries*, a controversial work about Roman Catholic documents. *Christian Ethics* was published in 1675, and in 1699 a friend published *A Serious and Pathetic Contemplation of the Mercies of God*. Traherne's poems were not published until 1903! In 1908 *Centuries of Meditations*, reflections on ethics and religion, was published. Traherne was an admirer of the neo-Platonist "Hermes Trismegistus." Stylistically he is usually referred to as a metaphysical poet.

An Hymn upon St. Bartholomew's Day

What powerful Spirit lives within!
What active Angel doth inhabit here!
What heavenly light inspires my skin,
Which doth so like a Deity appear!
A living Temple of all ages, I
Within me see
A Temple of Eternity!
All Kingdoms I descry
In me.

An inward Omnipresence here
Mysteriously like His within me stands,
Whose knowledge is a Sacred Sphere
That in itself at once includes all lands.
There is some Angel that within me can
Both talk and move,
And walk and fly and see and love,
A man on earth, a man
Above.

Dull wars of clay my Spirit leaves,
And in a foreign Kingdom doth appear,
This great Apostle it receives,
Admires His works and sees them, standing here,
Within myself from East to West I move
As if I were
At once a Cherubim and Sphere,
Or was at once above
And here.

The Soul 's a messenger whereby
Within our inward Temple we may be
Even like the very Deity
In all the parts of His Eternity.
O live within and leave unwieldy dross!
Flesh is but clay!
O fly my Soul and haste away
To Jesus' throne or Cross!
Obey!

The Salutation

These little Limbs,
These Eys & Hands which here I find,
This panting Heart wherwith my Life begins;
Where have ye been? Behind
What Curtain were ye from me hid so long!
Where was, in what Abyss, my new-made Tongue?
When silent I
So many thousand thousand Years
Beneath the Dust did in a Chaos ly.
How could I Smiles, or Tears,

Or Lips, or Hands, or Eys, or Ears perceiv?
Welcom ye Treasures which I now receiv.

I that so long
Was Nothing from Eternity,
Did little think such Joys as Ear & Tongue
To celebrat or see:
Such Sounds to hear, such Hands to feel, such Feet,
Such Eys & Objects, on the Ground to meet.

New burnisht Joys!
Which finest Gold & Peart excell!
Such sacred Treasures are the limbs of Boys
In which a Soul doth dwell:
Their organized Joints & azure Veins
More Wealth include than the dead World conteins.

From Dust I rise
And out of Nothing now awake;
These brighter Regions which salute mine Eys
A Gift from God I take:
The Earth, the Seas, the Light, the lofty Skies,
The Sun & Stars are mine; if these I prize.

A Stranger here
Strange things doth meet, strange Glory see,
Strange Treasures lodg'd in this fair World appear,
Strange all & New to me:
But that they mine should be who Nothing was,
That Strangest is of all; yet brought to pass.

The Apostacy

One Star
Is better far
Than many Precious Stones:
One Sun, which is by its own lustre seen,
Is worth ten thousand Golden Thrones:
A juicy Herb, or Spire of Grass,
In useful Virtu, native Green,
An Em'rald doth surpass;
Hath in 't more Valu, tho less seen.

No Wars,
Nor mortal Jars,
Nor bloody Feuds, nor Coin,
Nor Griefs which those occasion, saw I then;
Nor wicked Thievs which this purloin;
I had no Thoughts that were impure
Esteeming both Women & Men
God's Work, I was secure,
And reckon'd Peace my choicest Gem.

As Eve
I did believ
My self in Eden set,
Affecting neither Gold, nor Ermin'd Crowns,
Nor ought els that I need forget;
No Mud did foul my limpid Streams,
No Mist eclypst my Sun with frowns;
Set off with hev'nly Beams,
My joys were Meadows, Fields, & Towns.

Those things
Which Cherubins
Did not at first behold
Among God's Works, which Adam did not see;
As Robes, & Stones enchas'd in Gold,
Rich Cabinets, & such like fine
Inventions; could not ravish me:
I thought not Bowls of Wine
Needful for my Felicity.

All Bliss
Consists in this,
To do as Adam did;
And not to know those superficial Joys
Which were from him in Eden hid:
Those little new-invented Things,
Fine Lace & Silks, such Childish Toys
As Ribbans are & Rings,
Or worldly Pelf that Us destroys.

For God,
Both Great & Good,
The Seeds of Melancholy

Created not: but only foolish Men,
Grown mad with customary Folly
Which doth increase their Wants, so dote
As when they elder grow they then
Such Baubles chiefly note;
More Fools at Twenty Years than Ten.

But I,
I know not why,
Did learn among them too
At length; & where I once with blemisht Eys
Began their Pence & Toys to view,
Drown'd in their Customs, I became
A Stranger to the Shining Skies,
Lost as a dying Flame;
And Hobby-horses brought to prize.

The Sun
And Moon forgon,
As if unmade, appear
No more to me; to God & Heven dead
I was, as tho they never were:
Upon som useless gaudy Book,
When what I knew of God was fled,
The Child being taught to look,
His Soul was quickly murthered.

O fine!
O most divine!
O brave! they cry'd; & shew'd
Som Tinsel thing whose Glittering did amaze,
And to their Cries its beauty ow'd
Thus I on Riches, by degrees,
Of a new Stamp did learn to gaze;
While all the World for these
I lost: my joy turn'd to a Blaze.

The Review

My Child-hood is a Sphere
Wherin ten thousand hev'nly joys appear:
Those Thoughts it doth include,

And those Affections, which review'd,
Again present to me
In better sort the Things that I did see,
Imaginations Reall are,
Unto my Mind again repair:
Which makes my Life a Circle of Delights;
A hidden Sphere of obvious Benefits:
An Earnest that the Actions of the just,
Shall still revive, & flourish in the Dust.

KEN, THOMAS (1637–1711), orphaned early, was brought up in the home of Isaac Walton (his brother-in-law). He attended Oxford and after ordination, ministered in a number of clerical posts, twice taking gratuitous charge of a needy parish. After receiving a D.D., he was appointed chaplain to Mary, the king's sister, wife of William II. He went to live in the Hague where he not only rebuked Mary's husband for his treatment of her, but further angered William by persuading a man of his court to marry rather than abandon a woman he had seduced. Ken resigned his post, but William, apparently in admiration for his courage asked him to remain. In 1684 King Charles II chose Ken as bishop of Bath and Wells. He was summoned to Charles's deathbed in 1655 where he tried to awaken the king's conscience. He interceded with James II on behalf of the prisoners at Wells, reportedly saving a hundred from death and visiting others, supplying what needs he could. Ken gave a large sum of money in 1686 to the fund for Huguenot refugees. He published *Practice of Divine Love* and *Directions for Prayer* for the people of his diocese, also making considerable effort to promote the religious education of children, setting up schools and furnishing books to clergy for that purpose. He preached boldly before James in 1687, openly opposing the Roman Catholic distinctives which James was promoting. He was one of the "seven bishops" who were sent to the tower briefly and tried (but released) over a seditious pamphlet. After the revolution of 1688, he was equally bold in refusing the oaths required by William and Mary. In 1691 he was deprived of his see. Thereafter he lived in Wiltshire and Somerset, sometimes staying at Isaac Walton's rectory in Wiltshire. He disapproved of all actions which furthered the schism in the church and country, and desired to see the schism die with the death of the remaining unseed bishops, including himself. His published works include a prayer manual for Winchester scholars, several hymns, a few sermons and letters, and the two works mentioned above. His poetical works were published in four volumes in 1721. Probably we know his work best in the last stanza of his "Morning and Evening Hymns," which we sing as the Doxology ("Praise God from whom all blessings flow. . .").

Morning Hymn

Awake, my Soul, and with the Sun
Thy daily stage of Duty run,
Shake off dull sloth, and joyful rise,
To pay thy Morning sacrifice.

Thy precious Time misspent, redeem,
Each present Day thy last esteem,
Improve thy Talent with due care,
For the Great Day thyself prepare.

'Wake, and lift up thyself, my Heart,
And with the Angels bear thy part,
Who all night long unwearied sing,
High Praise to the Eternal King.

I wake, I wake, ye Heavenly Choir,
May your devotion me inspire,
That I like you my Age may spend,
Like you may on my God attend.

May I like you in God delight,
Have all day long my God in sight,
Perform like you my Maker's Will,
O may I never more do ill.

Had I your Wings, to Heaven I'd fly,
But God shall that defect supply,
And my Soul wing'd with warm desire,
Shall all day long to Heav'n aspire.

   •   •   •   •

I would not wake, nor rise again,
Ev'n Heaven itself I would disdain,
Wert not Thou there to be enjoy'd,
And I in Hymns to be employ'd.

   •   •   •

Lord, I my vows to Thee renew,
Disperse my sins as Morning dew,
Guard my first springs of Thought and Will,
And with Thyself my spirit fill.

Direct, control, suggest, this day,
All I design, or do, or say,
That all my Powers, with all their might,
In Thy sole Glory may unite.

Praise God from whom all blessings flow,
Praise him all creatures here below,
Praise him above ye heavenly host,
Praise Father, Son, and Holy Ghost.

An Evening Hymn

All Praise to Thee, my God, this night,
For all the Blessings of the Light;
Keep me, O keep me, King of Kings,
Beneath Thy own Almighty Wings.

Forgive me, Lord, for Thy dear Son,
The ill that I this day have done;
That with the World, myself and Thee,
 I, ere I sleep, at peace may be.

Teach me to live, that I may dread
The Grave as little as my Bed;
To die, that this vile Body may
Rise glorious at the Awful Day.

O! may my Soul on Thee repose,
And may sweet sleep my Eyelids close;
Sleep that may me more vigorous make,
To serve my God when I awake.

When in the night I sleepless lie,
My Soul with Heavenly Thoughts supply;
Let no ill Dreams disturb my Rest,
No powers of darkness me molest.

    •   •   •

O when shall I in endless Day,
For ever chase dark sleep away;
And Hymns with the Supernal Choir,
Incessant sing, and never tire?

O may my Guardian, while I sleep,
Close to my Bed his Vigils keep;
His Love angelical instil;
Stop all the avenues of ill.

May he Celestial joy rehearse,
And thought to thought with me converse,

Or in my stead, all the night long,
Sing to my God a grateful Song.

Praise God from whom all blessings flow,
Praise him all creatures here below,
Praise him above ye heavenly hosts,
Praise Father, Son, and Holy Ghost.

Now

The Past can be no more—
Whose misemploying I deplore:
The Future is to me
An absolute uncertainty:
The Now, which will not with me stay,
Within a second flies away.

I heard God often say,
Now, of salvation is the day,—
But turn'd from heaven my view,
I still had something else to do;
Till God a dream instructive sent,
To warn me timely to repent.

Methought Death, with his dart,
Had mortally transfix'd my heart;
And devils round about,
To seize my spirit flying out,
Cried—'Now, of which you took no care,
Is turn'd to Never and despair!'

I gave a sudden start,
And waked, with Never in my heart:
Still I that Never felt,
Never upon my spirit dwelt;—
A thousand thanks to God I paid,
That my sad Never was delay'd.

The Priest Of Christ

Give me the priest these graces shall possess;
Of an ambassador the just address,
A Father's tenderness, a Shepherd's care,

A Leader's courage, which the cross can bear,
A Ruler's arm, a Watchman's wakeful eye,
A Pilot's skill, the helm in storms to ply,
A Fisher's patience, and a Labourer's toil,
A Guide's dexterity to disembroil,
A Prophet's inspiration from above,
A Teacher's knowledge, and a Saviour's love.
Give me a priest, a light upon a hill,
Whose rays his whole circumference can fill,
In God's own Word and Sacred Learning versed,
Deep in the study of the heart immersed,
Who in such souls can the disease descry,
And wisely fair restoratives supply.

TAYLOR, EDWARD (c.1645–1729), major American colonial poet along with Anne Bradstreet, was born near Coventry, Leicestershire, and being unwilling to take an oath of conformity, emigrated to America in 1668, where he entered Harvard College. He became minister in the frontier town of Westfield, Massachusetts, in 1671, marrying twice and having thirteen children. He wrote some pamphlets attacking the liberal ideas of Solomon Stoddard, Jonathon Edward's grandfather. At the age of forty he began to compose his *Preparatory Meditations* regularly as part of his spiritual preparation for the Lord's Supper. In 1685 he wrote a long poem, "God's Determination Touching his Elect." By his express desire, his 400 page poetic manuscript was not published by his heirs. It was given to Yale University by an heir in 1883 and his poetry was finally published in 1939, two hundred and ten years after his death! His work is often classed with metaphysical poetry, because of his common diction, imagery taken from daily life, and the use he makes of these in dealing with Christian themes.

Huswifery

Make me, O Lord, thy Spining Wheele compleate.
Thy Holy Worde my Distaff make for mee.
Make mine Affections thy Swift Flyers neate
And make my Soule thy holy Spoole to bee.
My Conversation make to be thy Reele
And reele the yarn thereon spun of thy Wheele.

Make me thy Loome then, knit therein this Twine:
And make thy Holy Spirit, Lord, winde quills:
Then weave the Web thyselfe. The yarn is fine.
Thine Ordinances make my Fulling Mills.

Then dy the same in Heavenly Colours Choice,
All pinkt with Varnisht Flowers of Paradise.

Then cloath therewith mine Understanding, Will,
Affections, Judgment, Conscience, Memory,
My Words, and Actions, that their shine may fill
My wayes with glory and thee glorify.
Then mine apparell shall display before yee
That I am Cloathd in Holy robes for glory.

Upon Wedlock, and Death of Children

A Curious Knot God made in Paradise,
And drew it out inamled neatly Fresh.
It was the True-Love Knot, more sweet than spice
And set with all the flowres of Graces dress.
Its Weddens Knot, that ne're can be unti'de.
No Alexanders Sword can it divide.

The slips here planted, gay and glorious grow:
Unless an Hellish breath do sindge their Plumes.
Here Primrose, Cowslips, Roses, Lilies blow
With Violets and Pinkes that voide perfumes.
Whose beauteous leaves ore laid with Hony Dew.
And Chanting birds Cherp out sweet Musick true.

When in this Knot I planted was, my Stock
Soon knotted, and a manly flower out brake.
And after it my branch again did knot
Brought out another Flowre its sweet breathd mate.
One knot gave one tother the tothers place.
Whence Checkling smiles fought in each others face.

But oh! a glorious hand from glory came
Guarded with Angells, soon did Crop this flowre
Which almost tore the root up of the same
At that unlookt for, Dolesome, darksome houre.
In Pray're to Christ perfum'de it did ascend,
And Angells bright did it to heaven tend.

But pausing on't, this sweet perfum'd my thought,
Christ would in Glory have a Flowre, Choice, Prime,
And having Choice, chose this my branch forth brought.
Lord take't. I thanke thee, thou takst ought of mine,

It is my pledg in glory, part of mee
Is now in it, Lord, glorifi'de with thee.

But praying ore my branch, my branch did sprout
And bore another manly flower, and gay
And after that another, sweet brake out,
The which the former hand soon got away.
But oh! the tortures, Vomit, screechings, groans,
And six weeks Fever would pierce hearts like stones.

Griefe o're doth flow: and nature fault would finde
Were not thy Will, my Spell, Charm, Joy, and Gem:
That as I said, I say, take, Lord, they're thine.
I piecemeale pass to Glory bright in them.
I joy, may I sweet Flowers for Glory breed,
Whether thou getst them green, or lets them seed.

10. Meditation. Joh. 6.55. My Blood is Drinke Indeed

Stupendious Love! All Saints Astonishment!
Bright Angells are black Motes in this Suns Light.
Heav'ns Canopy the Paintice to Gods tent
Can't Cover't neither with its breadth, nor height.
Its Glory doth all Glory else out run,
Beams of bright Glory to't are motes i'th' sun.

My Soule had Caught an Ague, and like Hell
Her thirst did burn: she to each spring did fly,
But this bright blazing Love did spring a Well
Of Aqua-Vitae in the Deity,
Which on the top of Heav'ns high Hill out burst
And down came running thence t'allay my thirst.

But how it came, amazeth all Communion.
Gods onely Son doth hug Humanity,
Into his very person. By which Union
His Humane Veans its golden gutters ly.
And rather than my Soule should dy by thirst,
These Golden Pipes, to give me drink, did burst.

This Liquour brew'd, thy sparkling Art Divine
Lord, in thy Chrystall Vessells did up tun,
(Thine Ordinances,) which all Earth o're shine
Set in thy rich Wine Cellars out to run.

Lord, make thy Butlar draw, and fill with speed
My Beaker full: for this is drink indeed.

Whole Buts of this blesst Nectar shining stand
Lockt up with Saph'rine Taps, whose splendid Flame
Too bright do shine for brightest Angells hands
To touch, my Lord. Do thou untap the same.
Oh! make thy Chrystall Buts of Red Wine bleed
Into my Chrystall Glass this Drink-Indeed.

How shall I praise thee then? My blottings Jar
And wrack my Rhymes to pieces in thy praise.
Thou breath'st thy Vean still in my Pottinger
To lay my thirst, and fainting spirits raise.
Thou makest Glory's Chiefest Grape to bleed
Into my cup: And this is Drink-Indeed.

Nay, though I make no pay for this Red Wine,
And scarce do say I thank-ye-for't; strange thing!
Yet were thy silver skies my Beer bowle fine
I finde my Lord, would fill it to the brim.
Then make my life, Lord, to thy praise proceed
For thy rich blood, which is my Drink-Indeed.

40. Meditation. I. Joh. 2.2. He is a Propitiation for Our Sin

Still I complain; I am complaining still.
Oh! woe is me! Was ever Heart like mine?
A Sty of Filth, a Trough of Washing-Swill,
A Dunghill Pitt, a Puddle of mere Slime.
A Nest of Vipers, Hive of Hornets; Stings.
A Bag of Poyson, Civit-Box of Sins.

Was ever Heart like mine? So bad? black? Vile?
Is any Divell blacker? Or can Hell
Produce its match? It is the very Soile
Where Satan reads his Charms, and sets his Spell.
His Bowling Ally, where he sheeres his fleece
At Nine Pins, Nine Holes, Morrice, Fox and Geese.

His Palace Garden where his courtiers walke.
His Jewells Cabbinet. Here his Caball
Do sham it, and truss up their Privie talk
In Fardells of Consults and bundles all.

His shambles, and his Butchers stale's herein.
It is the Fuddling Schoole of every sin.

Was ever Heart like mine? Pride, Passion, fell,
Ath'ism, Blasphemy, pot, pipe it, dance
Play Barlybreaks, and at last Couple in Hell.
At Cudgells, Kit-Cat, Cards and Dice here prance.
At Noddy, Ruff-and-trumpet, Jing, Post-and-Pare,
Put, One-and-thirty, and such other ware.

Grace shuffled is away: Patience oft sticks
Too soon, or draws itselfe out, and's out Put.
Faith's over trumpt, and oft doth lose her tricks.
Repentance's Chalkt up Noddy, and out shut.
They Post, and Pare off Grace thus, and its shine.
Alas! alas! was ever Heart like mine?

Sometimes methinks the serpents head I mall:
Now all is still: my spirits do recreute.
But ere my Harpe can tune sweet praise, they fall
On me afresh, and tare me at my Root.
They bite like Badgers now nay worse, although
I tooke them toothless sculls, rot long agoe.

My Reason now's more than my sense, I feele
I have more Sight than Sense. Which seems to bee
A Rod of Sun beams t'whip mee for my steele.
My Spirits spiritless, and dull in mee
For my dead prayerless Prayers: the Spirits winde
Scarce blows my mill about. I little grinde.

Was ever Heart like mine? My Lord, declare.
I know not what to do: What shall I doe?
I wonder, split I don't upon Despare.
Its grace's wonder that I wrack not so.
I faintly shun't: although I see this Case
Would say, my sin is greater than thy grace.

Hope's Day-peep dawns hence through this chinck.
    Christs name
Propitiation is for sins. Lord, take
It so for mine. Thus quench thy burning flame
In that clear stream that from his side forth brake.
I can no Comfort take while thus I see
Hells cursed Imps thus jetting strut in mee.

Lord take thy sword: these Anakims destroy:
Then soake my soule in Zions Bucking tub
With Holy Soap, and Nitre, and rich Lye.
From all Defilement me cleanse, wash and rub.
Then wrince, and wring mee out till th'water fall
As pure as in the Well: not foule at all.

And let thy Sun, shine on my Head out cleare.
And bathe my Heart within its radient beams:
Thy Christ make my Propitiation Deare.
Thy Praise shall from my Heart breake forth in streams.
This reeching Vertue of Christs blood will quench
Thy Wrath, slay Sin and in thy Love mee bench.

66. Meditation. Joh. 15.13.
Greater Love hath no man than this
That a man lay down his Life for his Friends.

O! what a thing is Love? who can define
Or liniament it out? Its strange to tell.
A Sparke of Spirit empearld pill like and fine
In't shugard pargings, crusted, and doth dwell
Within the heart, where thron'd, without Controle
It ruleth all the Inmates of the Soule.

It makes a poother in its Secret Sell
Mongst the affections: oh! it swells, its paind,
Like kirnells soked untill it breaks its Shell
Unless its object be obtained and gain'd.
Like Caskd wines jumbled breake the Caske, this Sparke
Oft swells when crusht: untill it breakes the Heart.

O! Strange Strange Love! 'Stroy Life and't selfe thereby.
Hence lose its Object, lay down all't can moove.
For nothing rather choose indeed to dy,
And nothing be, than be without its love.
Not t'be, than be without its fanci'de bliss!
Is this Love's nature? What a thing is this?

Love thus ascending to its highest twig,
May sit and Cherp such ditties. Sing and dy.
This highest Note is but a Black-Cap's jig
Compar'd to thine my Lord, all Heavenly.

A greater love than such man ne'er mentain'd.
A greater Love than such thou yet hast gain'd.

Thy Love laid down thy Life hath for thy Sheep:
Thy friends by grace: thy foes by Nature's Crimes.
And yet thy Life more precious is and sweet
More worth than all the World ten thousand times.
And yet thy Love did give bright Wisdoms Shine
In laying down thy precious life for thine.

This Love was ne'er adulterate: e're pure.
Noe Whiffe of Fancy: But rich Wisdomes Beams,
No Huff of Hot affection men endure.
But sweetend Chimings of Celestiall gleams
Play'd and Display'd upon the golden Wyer
That doth thy Human Cymball brave, attire.

Thy Love that laid thy life all down for thine
Did not thereby destroy itselfe at all.
It was preserved in thy Selfe Divine
When it did make thy Humane Selfe down fall.
And when thy body as the Sun up rose
It did itselfe like flaming beames disclose.

Lord, let thy Love shine on my Soule! Mee bath
In this Celestiall Gleame of this pure Love.
O! gain my heart and thou my Love shalt have
Clime up thy golden Stares to thee above.
And in thy upper Chamber sit and sing
The glory of thy Love when Entred in.

SEWALL, SAMUEL (1652–1730), was a colonial merchant and a judge in the Salem witchcraft trials. He graduated from Harvard in 1671 and received a master of divinity degree in 1674. He was at different times manager of the colonial printing press, a member of Council, and chief justice of the Superior Court. He was also a commissioner for the Society for the Propagation of the Gospel in New England and an overseer of Harvard College. In 1692 he was appointed by the governor as one of the commissioners trying the Salem witchcraft cases out of which nineteen persons were condemned to death. In 1697, on a day marked for repentance concerning mistakes in those trials, Sewall alone of the judges publicly stood in Old South Church, Boston, while his confession of error and guilt was read aloud. He is noted for his *Diary* published by the Massachusetts Historical Society in 1878, and for some anti-slavery and religious tracts.

WEDNESDAY, January I. 1701. A little before Break-a-Day, at Boston of the Massachusets

Once more! Our GOD, vouchsafe to Shine:
Tame Thou the Rigour of our Clime.
Make haste with thy Impartial Light,
And terminate this long dark Night.

Let the transplanted ENGLISH Vine
Spread further still: still Call it Thine.
Prune it with Skill: for yield it can
More Fruit to Thee the Husbandman.

Give the poor INDIANS Eyes to see
The Light of Life: and set them free;
That they Religion may profess,
Denying all Ungodliness.

From hard'ned JEWS the Vail remove,
Let them their Martyr'd JESUS love;
And Homage unto Him afford,
Because He is their Rightful LORD.

So false Religions shall decay,
And Darkness fly before bright Day:
So Men shall GOD in CHRIST adore;
And worship Idols vain, no more.

So ASIA, and AFRICA,
EUROPA, with AMERICA;
All Four, in Consort join'd, shall Sing
New Songs of Praise to CHRIST our KING.

MATHER, COTTON (1663–1728), son of Increase Mather, was a minister and author of more than 400 works. He spent his whole life in Boston, going to Harvard at the age of twelve, and beginning to preach in 1680. He was ordained in 1685 and became his father's colleague. During the witchcraft trials of 1692, with his father he opposed the use of "spectre evidence" (Satan appearing in the guise of "spectres") as proof of satanic involvement. He gave himself largely to charitable activities, including leading the effort for inoculation against smallpox, despite public opposition. His scientific interests won him membership in the Royal Society of London.

Epitaph

Dummer the Shepherd Sacrific'd
By Wolves, because the Sheep he priz'd.
The Orphans Father, Churches Light,
The Love of Heav'n, of Hell the Spight.
The Countries Gapman, and the Face
That Shone, but knew it not, with Grace.
Hunted by Devils, but Reliev'd,
The Martyr'd Pelican, who Bled
Rather than leave his Charge Unfed.
A proper Bird of Paradise,
Shot, and Flown thither in a Trice.

Lord, hear the Cry of Righteous Dummer's Wounds,
Ascending still against the Salvage Hounds,
That Worry thy dear Flocks, and let the Cry
Add Force to Theirs that at thine Altar lye.

The Excellent WIGGLESWORTH, Remembred by some Good Tokens.

His Pen did once MEAT FROM THE EATER fetch;
And now he's gone beyond the Eaters reach.
His Body, once so Thin, was next to None;
From Thence, he's to Unbodied Spirits flown.
Once his rare skill did all Diseases heal;
And he does nothing now uneasy feel.
He to his Paradise is Joyful come;
And waits with Joy to see his DAY OF DOOM.

ADDISON, JOSEPH (1672–1719), often mentioned in conjunction with Richard Steele, with whom he shared many literary activities after they were educated together at the Charterhouse school. He studied the classics at Queens College, Oxford, and Magdalene. He became a fellow of Magdalene, and from 1699 to 1703 travelled in Europe and Asia. In 1705, he wrote a poem in heroic couplets, *The Campaign,* a celebration of Blenheim, the decisive battle (1704) in the war of the Spanish Succession. He became undersecretary of state and a member of parliament. He was in and out of office with the rise and fall of his party, the Whigs, but remained in parliament until his death. In 1709 he went to Ireland as secretary to Lord Wharton, the lord-lieutenant. He was an important member of the Whig "Kit-Kat Club," which included Steele, Richard Congreve, Samuel Garth, Jon Vanbrugh, and the publisher Jacob Tonson. From 1709 to 1711, Addison contributed a number of articles to Steele's *The Tatler,* a polite periodical focused on taste and manners. Addison and Steele together produced its successor, *The Spectator*, from 1711–12. His tragedy *Cato* was successful in 1713, but his comedy *The Drummer* (1715) proved less successful. He started a political newspaper, *The Freeholder* (1715–16), and married the countess of Warwick in 1716. His remains were buried in Westminster Abbey. He was extolled by Samuel Johnson as a model for prose style. Bonamy Dobrée called him "The First Victorian," largely in reference to his contribution to establishing a middle class standard of taste in literature.

Hymn—When all thy mercies, O my God

When all thy mercies, O my God,
My rising soul surveys,
Transported with the view, I'm lost
In wonder, love and praise.

Unnumbered comforts to my soul
Thy tender care bestowed,
Before my infant heart conceived
From whom those comforts flowed.

When in the slippery paths of youth
With heedless steps I ran,
Thine arm, unseen, conveyed me safe,
And led me up to man.

When worn with sickness oft hast thou
With health renewed my face;
And when in sins and sorrows sunk,
Revived my soul with grace.

Through every period of my life
Thy goodness I'll pursue,
And after death in distant worlds
The glorious theme renew.

Through all eternity to thee
A joyful song I'll raise;
For O! eternity's too short
To utter all thy praise.

WATTS, ISAAC (1674–1748), often called the father of English hymn-writing, studied at the Dissenting Academy, London, and thereafter spent two years at his home in Southampton, writing many of the *Hymns and Songs* that were eventually published in 1707–9. He spent the next six years as a tutor to the son of a leading Puritan while he studied theological and philosophical subjects. He preached his first sermon at twenty-four, being ordained in 1702 as pastor of an Independent congregation. In 1712 his health was ruined by fever. He received the degree of D. D. from Edinburgh in 1728. He published many philosophical, theological and devotional works which have had long-lasting impact such as *Logic, Divine and Moral Songs,* and *Speculations on the Human Nature of the Logos.* His hymns, however, are his most enduring works.

How Sweet And Awful Is The Place

How sweet and awful is the place
With Christ within the doors,
While everlasting love displays
The choicest of her stores.

While all our hearts and all our songs
Join to admire the feast,
Each of us cry with thankful tongues,
"Lord, why was I a guest?

"Why was I made to hear thy voice,
And enter while there's room,
When thousands make a wretched choice,
And rather starve than come?"

'Twas the same love that spread the feast
That sweetly drew us in;
Else we had still refused to taste,
And perished in our sin.

Pity the nations, O our God,
Constrain the earth to come;
Send thy victorious Word abroad,
And bring the strangers home.

We long to see thy churches full,
That all the chosen race
May with one voice and heart and soul,
Sing thy redeeming grace.

Jesus Shall Reign

Jesus shall reign wher-e'er the sun
Does his successive journeys run;
His kingdom stretch from shore to shore,
Till moons shall wax and wane no more.

For him shall endless prayer be made,
And praises throng to crown his head;
His Name, like sweet perfume, shall rise
With every morning sacrifice.

People and realms of every tongue
Dwell on his love with sweetest song;
And infant voices shall proclaim
Their early blessings on his Name.

Blessings abound wher-e'er he reigns;
The prisoner leaps to lose his chains,
The weary find eternal rest
And all the sons of want are blessed.

Let every creature rise and bring
Peculiar honors to our King,
Angels descend with songs again,
And earth repeat the loud Amen.

O God, Our Help

Our God, our help in ages past,
Our hope for years to come;
Our shelter from the stormy blast,
And our eternal home.

Under the shadow of thy throne
Thy saints have dwelt secure;
Sufficient is thine arm alone,
And our defence is sure.

Before the hills in order stood,
Or earth received her frame,
From everlasting thou art God,
To endless years the same.

Thy word commands our flesh to dust,
' Return, ye sons of men: '
All nations rose from earth at first,
And turn to earth again.

A thousand ages in thy sight
Are like an evening gone;
Short as the watch that ends the night
Before the rising sun.

The busy tribes of flesh and blood,
With all their lives and cares,
Are carried downwards by thy flood,
And lost in following years.

Time like an ever-rolling stream,
Bears all its sons away;
They fly, forgotten as a dream
Dies at the opening day.

Like flowery fields the nations stand,
Pleased with the morning light:
The flowers beneath the mower's hand
Lie withering ere 'tis night.

Our God, our help in ages past,
Our hope for years to come,
Be thou our guard while troubles last,
And our eternal home.

The Cross

When I survey the wondrous cross
On which the Prince of glory died,
My richest gain I count but loss,
And pour contempt on all my pride.

Forbid it, Lord, that I should boast,
Save in the death of Christ my God;
All the vain things that charm me most,
I sacrifice them to his blood.

See from his head, his hands, his feet,
Sorrow and love flow mingled down!

Did e'er such love and sorrow meet?
Or thorns compose so rich a crown?

His dying crimson, like a robe,
Spreads o'er his body on the tree;
Then am I dead to all the globe,
And all the globe is dead to me.

Were the whole realm of nature mine,
That were a present far too small;
Love so amazing, so divine,
Demands my soul, my life, my all.

Felicity

No 'tis in vain to seek for bliss;
For bliss can ne'er be found
'Till we arrive where Jesus is,
And tread on heav'nly ground.

There's nothing round these painted skies,
Or round this dusty clod;
Nothing, my soul, that's worth thy joys,
Or lovely as thy God.

'Tis heav'n on earth to taste his love,
To feel his quick'ning grace;
And all the Heav'n I hope above
Is but to see his face.

Joy To The World

Joy to the world! the Lord is come:
Let earth receive her King;
Let every heart prepare him room,
And heav'n and nature sing.

Joy to the earth! the Saviour reigns:
Let men their songs employ;
While fields and floods, rocks, hills, and plains
Repeat the sounding joy.

No more let sin and sorrows grow,
Nor thorns infest the ground;

He comes to make his blessings flow
Far as the curse is found.

He rules the world with truth and grace,
And makes the nations prove,
The glories of his righteousness
And wonders of his love.

Launching Into Eternity

It was a brave attempt! adventurous he,
Who in the first ship broke the unknown sea,
And leaving his dear native shores behind,
Trusted his life to the licentious wind.
I see the surging brine: the tempest raves
He on a pine plank rides across the waves,
Exulting on the edge of thousand gaping graves:
He steers the winged boat, and shifts the sails,
Conquers the flood, and manages the gales.

Such is the soul that leaves this mortal land,
Fearless when the great Master gives command.
Death is the storm: she smiles to hear it roar,
And bids the tempest waft her from the shore:
Then with a skilful helm she sweeps the seas,
And manages the raging storm with ease;
Her faith can govern death, she spreads her wings
Wide to the wind, and as she sails she sings,
And loses by degrees the sight of mortal things.
As the shores lessen, so her joys arise;
The waves roll gentler, and the tempest dies:
How vast eternity fills all her sight!
She floats on the broad deep with infinite delight,
The seas for ever calm, the skies for ever bright.

The Incomprehensible

Far in the Heavens my God retires:
My God, the mark of my desires.
      And hides His lovely face;
When He descends within my view,
He charms my reason to pursue,
But leaves it tired and fainting in th' unequal chase.

Or if I reach unusual height
   Till near His presence brought,
There floods of glory check my flight
Cramp the bold pinions of my wit,
   And all untune my thought;
Plunged in a sea of light I roll,
Where wisdom, justice, mercy, shines;
Infinite rays in crossing lines
Beat thick confusion on my sight, and overwhelm my soul.

Great God! behold my reason lies
Adoring: yet my love would rise
   On pinions not her own:
Faith shall direct her humble flight,
Through all the trackless seas of light,
To Thee, th' Eternal Fair, the Infinite Unknown.

YOUNG, EDWARD (1683–1765), clergyman, poet and dramatist, after graduating from Oxford was disappointed in his goal of practicing law. He became a rural rector in Hertfordshire in 1730. His major poem, "Complaint: or Night Thoughts on Life, Death, and Immortality" was at least partly inspired by the deaths of his stepdaughter, her husband, and Young's wife within a few years. This poem is the central work of what some call the "graveyard school" of eighteenth century poetry, is nearly 10,000 lines written in blank verse, being chiefly a poem of Christian consolation. He also wrote several tragedies including *Revenge*, another long poem, "Resignation," and some prose essays, among which "Conjectures on Original Composition" is considered a brilliant summary of much of what was later to be called Romantic thought.

Excerpt from **Night Thoughts**

"What am I? and from whence?—I nothing know
But that I am; and, since I am, conclude
Something eternal: had there e'er been nought,
Nought still had been; eternal there must be.—
But what eternal?—Why not human race?
And Adam's ancestors without an end?
That's hard to be conceived since every link
Of that long-obtain'd succession is so frail.
Can every part depend, and not the whole?
Yet grant it true; new difficulties rise;
I'm still quite out at sea, nor see the shore.

Whence earth and these bright orbs?—Eternal too?
Grant matter was eternal; still these orbs
Would want some other father;—much design
Is seen in all their motions, all their makes;
Design implies intelligence, and art;
That can't be from themselves—or man: that art
Man scarce can comprehend, could man bestow?
And nothing greater yet allow'd than man.—
Who, motion, foreign to the smallest grain,
Shot through vast masses of enormous weight?
Who bid brute matter's restive lump assume
Such various forms, and gave it wings to fly?
Has matter innate motion? then each atom,
Asserting its indisputable right
To dance, would form an universe of dust:
Has matter none? Then whence these glorious forms
And boundless flights, from shapeless, and repos'd?
Has matter more than motion? has it thought,
Judgment and genius? is it deeply learn'd
In mathematics? Has it fram'd such laws,
Which but to guess, a Newton made immortal?—
If so, how each sage atom laughs at me,
Who think a clod inferior to man!
If art, to form; and counsel, to conduct;
And that with greater far than human skill,
Resides not in each block;—a Godhead reigns.
Grant, then, invisible, eternal, Mind;
That granted, all is solv'd—But, granting that,
Draw I not o'er me a still darker cloud?
Grant I not that which I can ne'er conceive?
A being without origin, or end!—
Hail, human liberty! There is no God—
Yet why? On either scheme that knot subsists;
Subsist it must, in God, or human race:
If in the last, how many knots beside,
Indissoluble all?—Why choose it there,
Where chosen, still subsist ten thousand more?
Reject it, where, that chosen, all the rest
Dispers'd, leave reason's whole horizon clear;
This is not reason's dictate; reason says,
'Close with the side where one grain turns the scale;'
What vast preponderance is here! can reason

With louder voice exclaim—'Believe a God?'
And reason heard, is the sole mark of man.
What things impossible must man think true,
On any other system! and how strange
To disbelieve, through mere credulity!"
If, in this chain, Lorenzo finds no flaw,
Let it for ever bind him to belief.
And where the link, in which a flaw he finds?
And, if a God there is, that God how great!
How great that power, whom providential care
Through these bright orbs' dark centres darts a ray!
Of Nature universal threads the whole!
And hangs creation, like a precious gem,
Though little, on the footstool of his throne!

ERSKINE, RALPH (1685–1752), grandson of Ralph Erskine of Sheffield, and son of Rev. Henry Erskine of Cornwall and Chirnside, went to the University of Edinburgh, where he completed courses in Philosophy, Divinity, Greek, and Logic, after which he concentrated on Theology. His brother, Ebenezer, was also an active Scots Presbyterian. Ralph was licensed and ordained in the Presbytery of Dumferline in 1709 and 1711 respectively, and was called to the congregation of Dumferline, itself, in 1711, where he served as minister for forty-two years. In 1714 he married Margaret Dewar, a daughter of the Laird of Lassodie. She lived about sixteen years and had ten children. In 1732, he married Margaret Simpson, who bore four more children. During his lifetime Erskine published some of his sermons and *The Gospel Sonnets, or Spiritual Songs, in Six Parts* (1732). In 1758 he published a poetical paraphrase of the Song of Solomon. His Synod encouraged him thereafter to turn various poetical scripture passages into common metre, which were published as *Scripture Songs*. He also published several tracts, including a treatise, *Faith no Fancy: or, A Treatise of Mental Images*, which speaks to issues still significant today. He died of "nervous fever." *Gospel Sonnets* had reached its twenty-fifth edition by 1795.

The Believer's Riddle
SECT. I - The mystery of the Saints' Pedigree, and especially of their relation to Christ's wonderful person.

My life's a maze of seeming traps,
A scene of miseries and mishaps;
A heap of jarring to and froes,
A field of joys, a flood of woes.

I'm in mine own and others' eyes,
A labyrinth of mysteries,
I'm something that from nothing came,
Yet sure it is, I nothing am.

Once I was dead, and blind, and lame,
Yea, I continue still the same;
Yet what I was, I am no more,
Nor ever shall be as before .

SECT. II. - The mystery of the saint's life, state, and frame

My life's a pleasure and a pain;
A real loss, a real gain;
A glorious paradise of joys,
A grievous prison of annoys.

I daily joy, and daily mourn,
Yet daily wait the tide's return:
Then sorrow deep my spirit chears,
I'm joyful in a flood of tears.

On this condition I have all,
Yet all is unconditional.

Though freest mercy I implore,
Yet I am safe on justice' score.
Which never could the guilty free,
Yet fully clears most guilty me.

SECT. VIII. - The mystery of sanctification imperfect in this life; or, the believer doing all, and doing nothing.

Mine arms embrace my God, yet I
Had never arms to reach so high;
And though my good to him ascends,
My goodness to him ne'er extends.

I take hold of his cov'nant free.
But find it must take hold of me.
I'm bound to keep it, yet 'tis bail
And bound to keep me without fail.

The bond on my part cannot last,
Yet on both sides stands firm and fast.
I break my bands at every shock,
Yet never is the bargain broke.

Daily, alas! I disobey,
Yet yield obedience ev'ry day.
I'm an imperfect perfect man,
That can do all, yet nothing can.

I'm from beneath, and from above,
A child of wrath, a child of love.
A stranger e'en where all may know;
A pilgrim, yet I no where go,

I trade abroad, yet stay at home.
My tabernacle is my tomb.
I can be prison'd, yet abroad;
Bound hand and foot, yet walk with God.

My Father lives, my father's gone,
My vital head both lost and won.
My parents cruel are and kind,
Of one, and of a diff'rent mind.

My father, poison'd me to death,
My mother's hand will stop my breath,
Her womb, that once my substance gave;
Will very quickly be my grave.

My sisters all my flesh will eat,
My brethren tread me under feet,
My nearest friends are most unkind,
My greatest foe's my greatest friend.

He could from feud to friendship pass,
Yet never change from what he was,
He is my Father, he alone,
Who is my Father's only Son.

I am his mother's son, yet more,
A son his mother never bore,
But born of him, and yet aver
His Fathers sons my mother's were.

I am divorc'd, yet marry'd still,
With full consent against my will.
My husband present is, yet gone,
We differ much, yet still are one.

He is the first, the last, the all,
Yet number'd up with insects small.
The first of all things, yet alone,
The second of the great Three-one.

A creature never could he be,
Yet is a creature strange I see,
And own this uncreated one,
The son of man, yet no man's son.

He's omnipresent all may know;
Yet never could be wholly so.
His manhood is not here and there,
Yet he is God-man ev'ry where.

He comes and goes, none can him trace;
Yet never could he change his place.
But though he's good, and ev'ry where,
No good's in hell, yet he is there.

I by him, in him chosen was,
Of the choice he's not the cause:
For sov'reign mercy ne'er was bought,
Yet through his blood a vent is sought.

In him concenter'd at his death
His Father's love, his Father's wrath;
Ev'n he whom passion never seiz'd,
Was then most angry when most pleas'd.

Justice requir'd that he should die,
Who yet was slain unrighteously;
And died in mercy and in wrath,
A lawful and a lawless death.

With him I neither liv'd nor died,
And yet with him was crucify'd.
Law-curses stopt his breath, that he
Might stop its mouth from cursing me.

'Tis now a thousand years and more
Since heav'n receiv'd him; yet I know,
When he ascended up on high
To mount the throne, ev'n so did I.

Hence though earth's dunghill I embrace,
I sit with him in heav'nly place,
In divers distant orbs I move,
Inthrall'd below, inthron'd above.

SECT. IX. - The mystery of various names given to saints and church of Christ; or the flesh and Spirit described from inanimate things, vegetables and sensitives.

To tell the world my proper name,
Is both my glory and my shame:
For like my black, but comely face,
My name is Sin, my name is Grace.

Most fitly I'm assimilate
To various things inanimate;
A standing lake, a running flood,
A fixed star, a passing cloud.

A cake unturn'd, nor cold, nor hot;
A vessel sound, a broken pot:
A rising sun, a drooping wing;
A flinty rock, a flowing spring,

A rotten beam, a virid stem;
A menstrous cloth, a royal gem;
A garden barr'd, an open field;
A gilding stream, a fountain seal'd.

I'm with'ring grass, and growing corn;
A pleasant plant, an irksome thorn;
An empty vine, a fruitful tree;
An humble shrub, a cedar high.

A noxious brier, a harmless pine;
A sapless twig, a bleeding vine:
A stable fir, a plaint bush;
A noble oak, a naughty rush.

With sensitives I may compare,
While I their various nature share;
Their distinct names may justly suit
A strange, a reasonable brute.

The sacred page my state describes,
From volatile and reptile tribes;
From ugly vipers, beauteous birds;
From soaring hosts, and swinish herds.

I'm rank'd with beasts of different kinds,
With spiteful tygers, loving hinds;
And creatures of distinguish'd forms,
With mounting eagles, creeping worms.

A mixture of each sort I am;
A hurtful snake, a harmless lamb;
A tardy ass, a speedy roe;
A lion bold, a tim'rous doe.

A slothful owl, a busy ant;
A dove to mourn, a lark to chant:
And with less equals to compare,
An ugly toad, an angel fair.

SECT. XIV. - The mystery of the Believer's pardon and security from revenging wrath, notwithstanding his sins' desert.

I though from condemnation free,
Find such condemnables in me,
As make more heavy wrath my due
Than falls on all the damned crew.

But though my crimes deserve the pit,
I'm no more liable to it:
Remission seal'd with blood and death,
Secures me from deserved wrath.

In point of application free;
Lord, wash anew, and pardon me.

A Fourfold Exercise For The Believer in His Lodging On Earth

I. The Holy Law; or The Ten Commandments, Exod. xx. 3-17

1. No God but me thou shalt adore.
2. No image frame to bow before.
3. My holy name take not in vain.
4. My sacred Sabbath don't profane.
5. To parents render due respect.
6. All murder shun, and malice check.
7. From filth and whoredom base abstain;
8. From theft and all unlawful gain.
9. False witness flee, and slandering spite;
10. Nor covet what's thy neighbour's right.

II. The Unholy Heart the direct opposite of God's holy and righteous Law, Rom. vii. 14 or The Knowledge of Sin by the Law, Rom. iii. 20

1. My heart's to many gods a slave;
2. Of imagery an hideous cave.
3. An hoard of God-dishon'ring crimes:
4. A waster base of holy times;
5. A throne of pride and self-conceit;
6. A slaughterhouse of wrath and hate;
7. A cage of birds and thoughts unclean;
8. A den of thieves and frauds unseen;
9. A heap of calumnies unspent;
10. A gulph of greed and discontent.

III. The Glorious Gospel or Christ the end of the Law for Righteousness. Rom. x. 4.; and the absolute need of this remedy inferred from the premises.

Hence I conclude, and clearly see,
There's by the law no life for me;
Which damns each soul to endless thrall
Whose heart and life fulfil not all.
What shall I do, unless for bail
I from the law to grace appeal?
She reigns thro' Jesus' righteousness,
Which, giving Justice full redress,
On grace's door this motto grav'd,
'Let sin be damn'd, and sinners sav'd.'

O wisdom's deep mysterious way!
Lo, at this door I'll waiting stay,
Till sin and hell both pass away.
But in this bliss to shew my part,
Grant, thro' thy law grav'd in my heart,
My life may shew thy graving art.

IV. The Prayer of Faith; Which may be conceived in the following words of a certain author

Sim tuus in vita, tua sint mea funera, Christe;
Da, precor, imperii sceptra tenere tui.
Cur etenim moriens tot vulnera saeva tulisti,
Si non sum regni portio parva tui?

Cur rigido latuit tua vita inclusa sepulcho,
Si non est mea mors morte fugata tua?
Ergo mihi certam praestes, O Christe, salutem;
Meque tuo lotum sanguine, Christe, juva.

POPE, ALEXANDER (1688—1744), son of a prosperous linen draper, was educated irregularly, mostly at home. He studied so intensely as a teenager that his health was impaired. He recovered his health and was introduced to many literary figures who welcomed him as a child prodigy. He quickly became known for his wit and ability at satire. Both John Dryden and George Sandys influenced Pope's poetry, which is often seen as the epitome of the neoclassical school. His most arduous work was a translation of Homer which was said to be good poetry, but a poor translation. He also translated some of Chaucer's *The Canterbury Tales.* He became friends with Joseph Addison and published in Addison's *Spectator.* He published his best known Poem "Rape of the Lock" in 1712. It is a light-hearted mock-heroic poem. His *Windsor Forest* (1713) became, itself, the butt of various satirical pieces, and Pope returned the sallies of his literary enemies. He became estranged from Addison over this literary warfare the same year he got acquainted with Jonathon Swift. Swift started the Brother's Club, with its offshoot, the Scriblerus Club. Besides Pope and Swift, this included Arbuthnot, Congreve, and others. Pope published a version of Shakespeare as well as his *Iliad* and *Odyssey.* His *Dunciad,* another mock-heroic poem, ridiculed the "bad writers" of his day, especially those who were Whigs. (Pope, himself, was strongly connected with Tory interests.) In keeping with the politics and literature of the time, a certain amount of intrigue and hypocrisy characterized much of Pope's work. He seems a sincere Christian in his devotional poems, although his "Universal Prayer" is hardly orthodox.

Ode on Solitude

Happy the man whose wish and care
A few paternal acres bound,
Content to breathe his native air
     In his own ground.

Whose herds with milk, whose fields with bread,
Whose flocks supply him with attire;
Whose trees in summer yield him shade,
     In winter fire.

Blest, who can unconcernedly find
Hours, days, and years glide soft away
In health of body, peace of mind;
     Quiet by day,

Sound sleep by night; study and ease
Together mixed, sweet recreation,
And innocence, which most doth please,
     With meditation.

Thus let me live, unseen, unknown;
Thus unlamented let me die;
Steal from the world, and not a stone
     Tell where I lie.

The Dying Christian to His Soul

Vital spark of heavenly flame!
Quit, O quit this mortal frame!
Trembling, hoping, lingering, flying,
O the pain, the bliss of dying!
Cease, fond Nature, cease thy strife,
And let me languish into life!

Hark! they whisper; angels say,
'Sister spirit, come away!'
What is this absorbs me quite?
Steals my senses, shuts my sight,
Drowns my spirits, draws my breath?
Tell me, my soul, can this be death?

The world recedes; it disappears!
Heaven opens my eyes, my ears

With sounds seraphic ring.
Lend, lend your wings! I mount! I fly!
O Grave! where is thy victory?
O Death! where is thy sting?

Lines from an Essay on Man

Know then thyself, presume not God to scan;
The proper study of mankind is man.
Placed on this isthmus of a middle state,
A being darkly wise, and rudely great;
With too much knowledge for the sceptic side,
With too much weakness for the stoic's pride,
He hangs between; in doubt to act, or rest;
In doubt to deem himself a God, or beast;
In doubt his mind or body to prefer;
Born but to die, and reasoning but to err;
Alike in ignorance, his reason such,
Whether he thinks too little, or too much;
Chaos of thought and passion, all confused;
Still by himself abused or disabused;
Created half to rise, and half to fall;
Great lord of all things, yet a prey to all;
Sole judge of truth, in endless error hurled:
The glory, jest, and riddle of the world!

Rise, Crowned with Light
from The Messiah

Rise, crowned with light, imperial Salem, rise!
Exalt thy towering head and lift thine eyes.
See heaven its sparkling portals wide display,
And break upon thee in a flood of day.

See a long race thy spacious courts adorn,
See future sons, and daughters yet unborn,
In crowding ranks on every side arise,
Demanding life, impatient for the skies.

See barbarous nations at thy gates attend,
Walk in thy light, and in thy temple bend:
See thy bright altars thronged with prostrate kings,
While every land its joyous tribute brings.

The seas shall waste, the skies to smoke decay,
Rocks fall to dust, and mountains melt away;
But fixed His word, His saving power remains;
Thy realm shall last, thy own Messiah reigns.

Beauty

Christ, keep me from the self-survey
Of beauties all Thine own;
If there is beauty, let me pray,
And praise the Lord alone.

Pray—that I may the fiend withstand,
Where'er his serpents be;
Praise—that the Lord's almighty hand
Is manifest in me.

It is not so—my features are
Much meaner than the rest;
A glow-worm cannot be a star,
And I am plain at best.

Then come, my Love, Thy grace impart,
Great Savior of mankind;
O come and purify my heart
And beautify my mind.

Then will I Thy carnations nurse
And cherish every rose,
And empty to the poor my Purse
Till grace to glory grows.

Hymn—What Conscience Dictates

What conscience dictates to be done,
Or warns me not to do,
This, teach me ever, Lord, to shun,
That, ever to pursue.

If I am right, thy grace impart
Still in the right to stay;
If I am wrong, O teach my heart
To find that better way.

Save me alike from foolish pride
Or impious discontent
At aught thy wisdom has denied
Or aught thy goodness lent.

Teach me to feel anothers woe,
To hide the fault I see;
The mercy I to others show,
That mercy show to me.

BYROM, JOHN (1692–1763), Cambridge graduate, was best known in his own time for his system of shorthand. He began his adult life as a scholar, studied medicine abroad, and in 1721 married his cousin. Since his elder brother had inherited the family estates, Byrom decided to earn his living by teaching the system of shorthand he and a friend had devised at Cambridge. He persevered in this and became well-reputed, having a number of famous men as his students. Byrom was acquainted with John Wesley and "took a great interest in all the religious speculations of the time" *(Dictionary of National Biography)*. He was particularly drawn to mystics. With William Law, whose disciple he became, he much admired Malebranche, the French Cartesian philosopher. (Law was tutor to Gibbon's father and had gone to Cambridge with him. Byrom also followed Law in studying Jacob Boehme, the German mystic.) In 1760 Byrom's family holdings devolved on him. He published various political writings from a Jacobite point-of-view. His system of shorthand was published after his death, but was superceded by simpler systems. His *Miscellaneous Poems* were published posthumously (in 1773). His epigrams were much quoted, including:

God bless the king, God bless our faith's defender,
God bless—no harm in blessing—the Pretender;
But who pretender is, and who is king,
God bless us all! that's quite another thing.

My Spirit Longeth for Thee

My spirit longeth for thee
Within my troubled breast;
Although I be unworthy
Of so divine a Guest.

Of so divine a Guest,
Unworthy though I be;
Yet has my heart no rest,
Unless it come from thee.

Unless it come from thee,
In vain I look around;
In all that I can see,
No rest is to be found.

No rest is to be found,
But in thy blessed love;
O, let my wish be crowned,
And send it from above.

Hymn—Christians, Awake, Salute The Happy Morn

Christians, awake, salute the happy morn
Whereon the Saviour of the World was born;
Rise to adore the mystery of love,
Which hosts of angels chanted from above;
With them the joyful tidings first begun
Of God incarnate and the Virgin's Son.

Then to the watchful shepherds it was told
Who heard the angelic herald's voice, 'Behold,
I bring good tidings of a saviour's birth
To you and all the nations upon earth;
This day hath God fulfilled his promised word,
This day is born a saviour, Christ the Lord.'

He spake; and straightway the celestial choir
In hymns of joy, unknown before, conspire.
The praise of redeeming love they sang,
And heaven's whole orb with alleluyas rang:
God's highest glory was their anthem still,
Peace upon earth, and unto men good will.

To Bethlehem straight the enlightened shepherds ran,
To see the wonder God had wrought for man.
He that was born upon this joyful day
Around us all his glory shall display:
Saved by his love, incessant we shall sing
Eternal praise to heaven's almighty King.

DODDRIDGE, PHILIP (1702–1751), grandson of a minister ejected under the Commonwealth, and son of a London oilman, he attended a Nonconformist seminary. In 1723 he became a pastor at Kibworth. In 1729 he was appointed to Castle Hill Meeting in Northampton, where he ran a seminary. He trained two hundred students from England, Scotland, and Holland in a wide range of subjects and eventually received a D.D. from Aberdeen. He was a friend of Watts, Hervey, and Warburton, and welcomed Wesley and Whitfield, entertaining the latter when he visited Northampton. He was author of *Rise and Progress of Religion in the Soul,* (1745) and *The Family Expositor* (6 vols. 1739–56). He remained in Northampton until 1751 when, in the last stages of consumption (tuberculosis), he sailed for Lisbon. His hymns were published after his death in 1755 by his friend Job Orton. Some may be found in most contemporary hymnals.

Hark The Glad Sound

Hark, the glad sound! the Saviour comes,
The Saviour promised long;
Let every heart prepare a throne,
And every voice a song! . . . .

He comes, the prisoners to release,
In Satan's bondage held;
The gates of brass before him burst,
The iron fetters yield.

He comes, from thickest films of vice
To clear the mental ray,
And on the eyelids of the blind
To pour celestial day.

He comes, the broken heart to bind,
The bleeding soul to cure,
And with the treasures of his grace
To enrich the humble poor. . . .

Our glad hosannas, Prince of Peace,
Thy welcome shall proclaim,
And Heaven's eternal arches ring
With thy beloved name.

Live While You Live

'Live while you live,' the Epicure would say,
'And seize the pleasures of the present day.'
'Live while you live,' the sacred Preacher cries,

'And give to God each moment as it flies.'
Lord, in my views let both united be;
I live in pleasure, when I live to Thee.

WESLEY, JOHN (1703–1791), perhaps the most widely recognized of the Reawakening evangelists, was also a hymn writer and poet, although not generally as gifted in this area as his brother Charles. Nonetheless, inspired partly by the model of the Moravians, who were great singers of (German) hymns, he translated and wrote many hymn lyrics. He is credited with publishing the first hymnbook used in an Anglican church, *A Collection of Psalmes and Hymns*, printed in 1737 at Savannah, Georgia, during his short period of ministry there. Although a number of his hymns appear in contemporary hymnbooks, his greatest contributions to English hymnody were in supporting the writing and use of hymns generally, and the printing of his brother Charles's hymns in particular. Although he owed a great deal more to George Whitefield in this than is commonly recognized, John Wesley is regarded as founder of the Methodist churches.

Jesus, Thy Blood and Righteousness
Translated from Count Nikolaus Ludwig von Zinzendorf

Jesus, thy blood and righteousness
My beauty are, my glorious dress;
'Midst flaming worlds, in these arrayed
With joy shall I lift up my head.

Bold shall I stand in thy great day;
For who ought to my charge shall lay?
Fully absolved through these I am
From sin and fear, from guilt and shame.

When from the dust of death I rise
To claim my mansion in the skies,
Ev'n then this shall be all my plea,
Jesus hath lived, hath died for me.

Jesus, be endless praise to thee,
Whose boundless mercy hath for me—
For me a full atonement made,
An everlasting ransom paid.

O let the dead now hear thy voice;
Now bid thy banished ones rejoice;

Their beauty this, their glorious dress,
Jesus, thy blood and righteousness.

Commit thy way unto the Lord
translated from Paul Gerhardt

Commit thou all thy griefs   And ways into his hands;
To his sure truth and tender care,   Who earth and heav'n commands.

Who points the clouds their course,   Whom winds and seas obey,
He shall direct thy wand'ring feet,   He shall prepare thy way.

Give to the winds thy fears;   Hope, and be undismayed;
God hears thy sighs, and counts thy tears,   God shall lift up thy head.

What though thou rulest not?   Yet heav'n and earth and hell
Proclaim, God sitteth on the throne,   And ruleth all things well.

Leave to his sovereign sway   To choose and to command;
So shalt thou wond'ring own, his way   How wise, how strong his hand!

Ye Golden Lamps of Heaven

Ye golden lamps of Heaven, farewell,
With all your feeble light;
Farewell, thou ever-changing moon,
Pale empress of the night.

And thou, refulgent orb of day,
In brighter flames array'd;
—My soul, that springs beyond thy sphere,
No more demands thine aid.

Ye stars are but the shining dust
Of my Divine abode,
The pavement of those heavenly courts
Where I shall reign with God.

The Father of eternal light
Shall there His beams display;
Nor shall one moment's darkness mix
With that unvaried day.

No more the drops of piercing grief
Shall swell into mine eyes;

Nor the meridian sun decline
Amidst those brighter skies.

WESLEY, CHARLES (1707–1788), was, after George Whitfield and his brother John Wesley, a prominent figure in the religious movement which began at Oxford and was significant in the Great Awakening of England, Wales, and America. Charles was ordained in 1735, and travelled briefly to Georgia with his brother John. Like John he came under the influence of Count Zinzendorf and the Moravians upon his return to England. On Whitsunday (Pentecost), 1737 he "found rest for his soul." After a brief curateship where he met with opposition he went back to working as a field preacher with John, and they continued to work together for the rest of their lives. He married Miss Sarah Gwynne in 1749, and she accompanied him on his itinerations. Unlike his brother John, he never broke with the Church of England. He was and is particularly noted for his hymns. He wrote constantly and for all occasions, ecclesiastical, personal, national and local, and on a wide variety of striking scripture passages. The editor of *A Dictionary of Hymnology* suggests that he may have been the greatest hymn writer of all ages, having written no less than 6,500 hymns, many of which are among the finest in English.

Catholic Love

Weary of all this wordy strife,
These notions, forms, and modes, and names,
To Thee, the Way, the Truth, the Life,
Whose love my simple heart inflames,
Divinely taught, at last I fly,
With Thee, and Thine to live, and die.

Forth from the midst of Babel brought,
Parties and sects I cast behind;
Enlarged my heart, and free my thought,
Where'er the latent truth I find,
The latent truth with joy to own,
And bow to Jesu's name alone.

Redeem'd by Thine almighty grace,
I taste my glorious liberty,
With open arms the world embrace,
But cleave to those who cleave to Thee;
But only in Thy saints delight,
Who walk with God in purest white.

One with the little flock I rest,
The members sound who hold the Head;
The chosen few, with pardon blest,
And by the anointing Spirit led
Into the mind that was in Thee,
Into the depths of Deity.

My brethren, friends, and kinsmen these,
Who do my heavenly Father's will;
Who aim at perfect holiness,
And all Thy counsels to fulfil,
Athirst to be whate'er Thou art,
And love their God with all their heart.

For these, howe'er in flesh disjoin'd,
Where'er dispersed o'er earth abroad,
Unfeigned unbounded love I find,
And constant as the life of God,
Fountain of life, from thence it sprung,
As pure, as even, and as strong.

Joined to the hidden church unknown
In this sure bond of perfectness,
Obscurely safe, I dwell alone,
And glory in the uniting grace,
To me, to each believer given,
To all thy saints in earth and heaven.

Arise My Soul Arise

Arise, my soul, arise, Shake off thy guilty fears:
The bleeding Sacrifice In my behalf appears:
Before the Throne my Surety stands,
Before the Throne my Surety stands,
My name is written on his hands.

He ever lives above, For me to intercede,
His all-redeeming love, His precious blood to plead;
His blood atoned for ev'ry race,
His blood atoned for ev'ry race,
And sprinkles now the throne of grace.

Five bleeding wounds he bears, Received on Calvary;
They pour effectual prayers, They strongly plead for me;

Forgive him, O forgive, they cry,
Forgive him, O forgive, they cry,
Nor let that ransomed sinner die!

My God is reconciled; His pard'ning voice I hear;
He owns me for his child, I can no longer fear;
With confidence I now draw nigh,
With confidence I now draw nigh,
And "Father, Abba, Father!" cry.

Hark! The Herald Angels Sing

Hark! the herald angels sing,   "Glory to the newborn King;
Peace on earth, and mercy mild,   God and sinners reconciled!"

Joyful, all ye nations, rise,   Join the triumph of the skies;
With th'angelic host proclaim,   "Christ is born in Bethlehem!"

Christ, by highest heav'n adored,   Christ, the Everlasting Lord!
Late in time behold him come,   Offspring of the Virgin's womb.

Veiled in flesh the Godhead see;   Hail th'Incarnate Deity,
Pleased as man with men to dwell,   Jesus, our Emmanuel.

Hail, the heav'n-born Prince of Peace!   Hail, the Sun of
    Righteousness!
Light and life to all he brings,   Ris'n with healing in his wings.

Mild he lays his glory by,   Born that man no more may die,
Born to raise the sons of earth,   Born to give them second birth.

Hark the herald angels sing,   "Glory to the newborn King."

Hark, How All The Welkin Rings!
(version from Anglican Song book)

Hark, how all the welkin rings! 'Glory to the King of Kings,
Peace on earth and mercy mild, God and sinners reconciled,'

Joyful, all ye nations, rise, Join the triumph of the skies;
Universal nature say 'Christ the Lord is born to-day.'

Christ, by highest heaven adored, Christ, the everlasting Lord,
Late in time behold him come Offspring of the Virgin's womb.

Veiled in flesh, the Godhead see! Hail the incarnate Deity!
Pleased as man with men to appear, Jesus, our Emmanuel here!

Hail the heavenly Prince of Peace! Hail the Sun of Righteousness!
Light and life to all he brings, Risen with healing in his wings.

Mild he lays his glory by, Born that man no more may die,
Born to raise the sons of earth, Born to give them second birth!

Come, Desire of Nations, come, Fix in us thy humble home;
Rise, the woman's conquering seed, Bruise in us the serpent's head.

Now display thy saving power, Ruined nature now restore,
Now in mystic union join Thine to ours, and ours to thine.

Rejoice, Again I Say Rejoice

> Rejoice! The Lord is King,
> Your Lord and King adore;
> Mortals, give thanks and sing,
> And triumph evermore:
>
> Lift up your heart, lift up your voice;
> Rejoice, again I say, rejoice.
>
> Jesus, the Saviour, reigns,
> The God of truth and love;
> When he had purged our stains,
> He took his seat above:
>
> His kingdom cannot fail;
> He rules o'er earth and heaven;
> The keys of death and hell
> Are to our Jesus given:
>
> He sits at God's right hand
> Till all his foes submit,
> And bow to his command,
> And fall beneath his feet:

Love Divine, All Loves Excelling

Love Divine, all loves excelling,   Joy of heav'n to earth come down:
Fix in us thy humble dwelling,   All thy faithful mercies crown:
Jesus, thou art all compassion,   Pure, unbounded love thou art;
Visit us with thy salvation,   Enter ev'ry trembling heart.

Breathe, O breathe thy loving Spirit   Into ev'ry troubled breast;
Let us all in thee inherit,   Let us find the promised rest:
Take away the love of sinning;   Alpha and Omega be;
End of faith, as its Beginning,   Set our hearts at liberty.

Come, Almighty to deliver,   Let us all thy life receive;
Suddenly return, and never,   Never more thy temples leave.
Thee we would be always blessing,   Serve thee as thy hosts above,
Pray, and praise thee, without ceasing,   Glory in thy perfect love.

Finish, then, thy new creation;   Pure and spotless let us be:
Let us see thy great salvation   Perfectly restored in thee;
Changed from glory into glory,   Till in heav'n we take our place,
Till we cast our crowns before thee,   Lost in wonder, love, and praise.

For the Anniversary Day of One's Conversion
(Stanzas 7–12 are familiar as "O For A Thousand Tongues")

Glory to God, and praise, and love   Be ever, ever given,
By saints below and saints above,   The church in earth and heaven.

On this glad day the glorious Sun   Of Righteousness arose;
On my benighted soul He shone,   And filled it with repose.

Sudden expired the legal strife;   'Twas then I ceased to grieve;
My second, real, living life   I then began to live.

Then with my heart I first believed,   Believed with faith Divine;
Power with the Holy ghost received   To call the Saviour mine.

I felt my Lord's atoning blood   Close to my soul applied,
Me, me He loved—the Son of God   For me, for me He died!

I found, and owned His promise true,   Ascertained of my part;
My pardon passed in heaven I knew,   When written on my heart.

O for a thousand tongues to sing   My great Redeemer's praise!
The glories of my God and King,   The triumphs of His grace.

My gracious Master and my God   Assist me to proclaim,
To spread through all the earth abroad,   The honors of Thy name.

Jesus, the name that charms our fears,   That bids our sorrows cease;
'Tis music in the sinner's ears,   'Tis life, and health, and peace.

He breaks the pow'r of cancelled sin,   He sets the prisoner free;
His blood can make the foulest clean,   His blood availed for me.

He speaks; and, listening to His voice,　New life the dead receive;
The mournful, broken hearts rejoice,　The humble poor believe.

Hear Him, ye deaf; His praise, ye dumb,　Your loosened tongues
　　employ;
Ye blind, behold your Saviour come;　And leap, ye lame, for joy.

Look unto Him, ye nations; own　Your God, ye fallen race!
Look, and be saved through faith alone;　Be justified by grace!

See all your sins on Jesus laid;　The Lamb of God was slain,
His soul was once an offering made　For every soul of man.

Harlots, and publicans, and thieves　In holy triumph join;
Saved is the Sinner that believes　From crimes as great as mine.

Murderers, and all ye hellish crew,　Ye sons of lust and pride,
Believe the Saviour died for you;　For me the Saviour died.

Awake from guilty nature's sleep,　And Christ shall give you light,
Cast all your sins into the deep,　And wash the Ethiop white.

With me, your chief, you then shall know,　Shall feel your sins
　　forgiven;
Anticipate your heaven below,　And own that love is heaven.

Jesu, Lover of my Soul

> Jesu, Lover of my soul,
> Let me to Thy bosom fly,
> While the nearer waters roll,
> While the tempest still is high:
> Hide me, O my Saviour, hide
> Till the storm of life is past,
> Safe into the haven guide,
> O receive my soul at last!
>
> Other refuge have I none;
> Hangs my helpless soul on Thee;
> Leave, ah! leave me not alone,
> Still support and comfort me!
> All my trust on Thee is stay'd,
> All my help from Thee I bring:
> Cover my defenceless head
> With the shadow of Thy wing!

Wilt Thou not regard my call?
Wilt Thou not accept my prayer?
Lo! I sink, I faint, I fall—
Lo! on Thee I cast my care!
Reach me out Thy gracious hand:
While I of Thy strength receive,
Hoping against hope I stand,
Dying, and behold I live!

Plenteous grace with Thee is found,
Grace to cover all my sin;
Let the healing streams abound;
Make and keep me pure within:—
Thou of Life the Fountain art,
Freely let me take of Thee;
Spring Thou up within my heart,—
Rise to all eternity!

Free Grace (And Can It Be)

And can it be, that I should gain
An interest in the Saviour's blood?
Died he for me, who caused his pain,
For me, who him to death pursued?
Amazing Love! How can it be
That thou, my God, shouldst die for me?

'Tis Mystery all! the Immortal dies!
Who can explore his strange design?
In vain the first-born seraph tries
To sound the depths of love divine.
'Tis Mercy all! Let earth adore;
Let angel minds enquire no more.

He left his Father's throne above,
(So free, so infinite his Grace!)
Emptied himself of all but Love,
And bled for Adam's helpless race:
'Tis Mercy all, immense and free!
For, O my God, it found out me!

Long my imprisoned spirit lay,
Fast bound in sin and nature's night:

Thine eye diffused a quickening ray;
I woke; the dungeon flamed with light;
My chains fell off, my heart was free,
I rose, went forth, and followed thee.

Still the small inward voice I hear
That whispers all my sins forgiven;
Still the atoning blood is near
That quenched the wrath of hostile heaven:
I feel the life his wounds impart;
I feel my Saviour in my heart.

No condemnation now I dread,
Jesus, and all in him, is mine:
Alive in him, my living Head,
And clothed in Righteousness divine,
Bold I approach the eternal throne,
And claim the crown, through Christ, my own.

Still, O Lord, for Thee I Tarry

Still, O Lord, for Thee I tarry,
Full of sorrows, sins, and wants;
Thee, and all thy Saints I weary
With my sad but vain complaints;
Sawn asunder by temptation,
Tortur'd by distracting care,
Kill'd by doubts' severe vexation,
Sorer evil than despair.

Will the fight be never over?
Will the balance never turn?
Still 'twixt life and death I hover,
Bear what is not to be borne;
Who can bear a wounded spirit?
Whither must my spirit go?
Shall I Heaven or Hell inherit?
Let me die my doom to know.

All in vain for death I languish,
Death from his pursuer flies:
Still I feel the gnawing anguish,
Feel the worm that never dies:
Still in horrid expectation

Like the damn'd in Hell I groan,
Envy them their swift damnation,
Fearful to enhance my own.

Jesus, see thy fallen creature,
Fallen at thy feet I lie,
Act according to thy nature,
Bid the sinner live or die;
Of my pain fill up the measure,
If Thou canst no more forgive:
If Thou in my life hast pleasure,
Speak, and now my soul shall live.

The True Use of Music

Listed into the cause of sin,
Why should a good be evil?
Music, alas! too long has been
Prest to obey the devil:
Drunken, or lewd, or light the lay
Flowed to the soul's undoing,
Widened, and strewed with flowers the way
Down to eternal ruin.

Who on the part of God will rise,
Innocent sound recover,
Fly on the prey, and take the prize,
Plunder the carnal lover,
Strip him of every moving strain,
Of every melting measure,
Music in virtue's cause retain,
Rescue the holy pleasure?

Come let us try if Jesu's love
Will not as well inspire us:
This is the theme of those above,
This upon earth shall fire us.
Say, if your hearts are tuned to sing,
Is there a subject greater?
Harmony all its strains may bring,
Jesus's name is sweeter.

Jesus the soul of music is;
His is the noblest passion:

Jesus's name is joy and peace,
Happiness and salvation:
Jesus's name the dead can raise,
Shew us our sins forgiven,
Fill us with all the life of grace,
Carry us up to heaven.

Who hath a right like us to sing,
Us whom his mercy raises?
Merry our hearts, for Christ is king,
Cheerful are all our faces:
Who of his love doth once partake
He evermore rejoices;
Melody in our hearts we make,
Melody with our voices.

He that a sprinkled conscience hath,
He that in God is merry,
Let him sing psalms, the Spirit saith,
Joyful, and never weary,
Offer the sacrifice of praise,
Hearty, and never ceasing,
Spiritual songs and anthems raise,
Honour, and thanks, and blessing.

Then let us in his praises join,
Triumph in his salvation,
Glory ascribe to love divine,
Worship and adoration.
Heaven already is begun,
Opened in each believer;
Only believe, and still sing on,
Heaven is ours forever.

SMART, CHRISTOPHER (1722–1771), a Christian poet, educated at Cambridge, having achieved considerable acclaim at the university, tried to support himself in London, by means of his writing. However, bouts of "madness" seem to have burdened his life. He was for two years confined in an asylum (1756-58). It seems likely in retrospect that what was fashionable to call "madness" in the late eighteenth century might be called "depression" today; however, some of Smart's compositions of that time undeniably have the free-associative qualities commonly attributed to insanity. Among his friends were Samuel

Johnson, David Garrick, and Oliver Goldsmith. His best known poem, "A Song of David," far from being the product of a deranged mind, is beautiful and passionate praise to Christ. He published *Hymns. . . for the Fasts and Festivals* in 1765. His *Poems* were published, in two volumes, in 1771. He died in a London's debtor's prison. *Hymns for the Amusement of Children* was published in 1775 and *Rejoice in The Lamb,* (a stream-of-consciousness litany of praise) not until 1939.

From A Song To David
(Complete poem has 86 stanzas; only 1, 72–79, 84–86 given here)

Oh thou that sit'st upon a throne
With harp of high majestic tone,
To praise the King of Kings:
And voice of heaven-ascending swell
Which, while its deeper notes excel,
Clear as a clarion rings.

Sweet is the dew that falls betimes,
And drops upon the leafy limes;
Sweet Hermon's fragrant air:
Sweet is the lily's silver bell,
And sweet the wakeful tapers smell
That watch for early prayer.

Sweet the young nurse, with love intense.
Which smiles o'er sleeping innocence;
Sweet when the lost arrive:
Sweet the musician's ardour beats,
While the vague mind's in quest of sweets,
The choicest flowers to hive.

Sweeter, in all the strains of love,
The language of thy turtle-dove,
Pair'd to thy swelling chord;
Sweeter, with every grace endued,
The glory of thy gratitude,
Respired unto the Lord.

Strong is the horse upon his speed;
Strong in pursuit the rapid glede,
Which make at once his game:
Strong the tall ostrich on the ground;
Strong through the turbulent profound
Shoots Xiphias to his aim.

Strong is the lion—like a coal
His eye-ball—like a bastion's mole
His chest against his foes:
Strong the gier-eagle on his sail,
Strong against tide the enormous whale
Emerges as he goes.

But stronger still in earth and air,
And in the sea, the man of prayer,
And far beneath the tide:
And in the seat to faith assign'd,
Where ask is have, where seek is find,
Where knock is open wide.

Beauteous the fleet before the gale;
Beauteous the multitudes in mail,
Rank'd arms, and crested heads;
Beauteous the garden's umbrage mild,
Walk, water, meditated wild,
And all the bloomy beds.

Beauteous the moon full on the lawn,
And beauteous when the veil's withdrawn,
The virgin to her spouse:
Beauteous the temple, deck'd and fill'd,
When to the heaven of heavens they build
Their heart-directed vows.

Glorious the sun in mid career;
Glorious th'assembled fires appear;
Glorious the comet's train:
Glorious the trumpet and alarm
Glorious the Almighty's stretch'd-out arm,
Glorious the enraptured main:

Glorious the northern light's astream;
Glorious the song, when God's the theme;
Glorious the thunder's roar:
Glorious the hosannah from the den;
Glorious the catholic amen;
Glorious the martyr's gore;

Glorious—more glorious is the crown
Of Him that brought salvation down,
By meekness call'd thy Son;

Thou that stupendous truth believed,
And now the matchless dead's achieved,
Determined, dared, and done.

The Nativity of Our Lord and Saviour Jesus Christ

Where is this stupendous stranger?
Swains of Solyma, advise,
Lead me to my Master's manger,
Shew me where my Saviour lies.

O most Mighty! O most Holy!
Far beyond the seraph's thought,
Art thou then so mean and lowly,
As unheeded prophets taught?

O the magnitude of meekness!
Worth from worth immortal sprung;
O the strength of infant weakness,
If eternal is so young!

If so young and thus eternal,
Michael tune the shepherd's reed,
Where the scenes are ever vernal,
And the loves be love indeed!

See the God blasphemed and doubted
In the schools of Greece and Rome.
See the powers of darkness routed,
Taken at their utmost gloom.

Nature's decorations glisten
Far above their usual trim;
Birds on box and laurels listen,
As so near the cherubs hymn.

Boreas now no longer winters
On the desolated coast;
Oaks no more are riven in splinters
By the whirlwind and his host.

Spinks and ouzels sing sublimely
'We too have a Saviour born';
Whiter blossoms burst untimely
On the blest Mosaic thorn.

God all-bounteous, all creative,
Whom no ills from good dissuade,
Is incarnate and a native
Of the very world he made.

Hymn To The Supreme Being

When Israel's ruler on the royal bed
In anguish and in perturbation lay,
The down relieved not his anointed head,
And rest gave place to horror and dismay.
Fast flowed the tears, high heaved each gasping sigh,
When God's own prophet thundered—
    Monarch, thou must die.

And must I go, the illustrious mourner cried,
I who have served thee still in faith and truth,
Whose snow-white conscience no foul crime has dyed
From youth to manhood, infancy to youth,
Like David, who have still revered thy word,
The sovereign of myself and servant of the Lord!

The judge almighty heard his suppliant's moan,
Repealed his sentence, and his health restored;
The beams of mercy on his temples shone,
Shot from that heaven to which his sighs had soared;
The sun retreated at his maker's nod,
And miracles confirm the genuine work of God.

But, O immortals! what had I to plead
When death stood o'er me with his threatening lance,
When reason left me in the time of need,
And Sense was lost in terror or in trance,
My sinking soul was with my blood inflamed,
And the celestial image sunk, defaced and maimed.

I sent back memory, in heedful guise,
To search the records of preceding years;
Home, like the raven to the ark, she flies,
Croaking bad tidings to my trembling ears.
O sun! again that thy retreat was made,
And threw my follies back into the friendly shade!

But who are they, that bid affliction cease!—
Redemption and forgiveness, heavenly sounds!
Behold the dove that brings the branch of peace,
Behold the balm that heals the gaping wounds—
Vengeance divine's by penitence suppressed—
She struggles with the angel, conquers, and is blest.

Yet hold, presumption, nor too fondly climb,
And thou too hold, O horrible despair!
In man humility's alone sublime,
Who diffidently hopes he's Christ's own care—
O all-sufficient Lamb! in death's dread hour
Thy merits who shall slight, or who can doubt thy power?

But soul-rejoicing health again returns,
The blood meanders gentle in each vein,
The lamp of life renewed with vigour burns,
And exiled reason takes her seat again—
Brisk leaps the heart, the mind's at large once more,
To love, to praise, to bless, to wonder and adore.

The virtuous partner of my nuptial bands,
Appeared a widow to my frantic sight;
My little prattlers lifting up their hands,
Beckon me back to them, to life, and light;
I come, ye spotless sweets! I come again,
Nor have your tears been shed, nor have ye knelt in vain.

All glory to the Eternal, to the Immense,
All glory to the Omniscient and Good,
Whose power 's uncircumscribed, whose love 's intense;
But yet whose justice ne'er could be withstood
Except through him—through him, who stands alone,
Of worth, of weight allowed for all mankind to atone!

He raised the lame, the lepers he made whole,
He fixed the palsied nerves of weak decay,
He drove out Satan from the tortured soul,
And to the blind gave or restored the day,—
Nay more,—far more unequalled pangs sustained,
Till his lost fallen flock his taintless blood regained.

My feeble feet refused my body's weight,
Nor would my eyes admit the glorious light,

My nerves convulsed shook fearful of their fate,
My mind lay open to the powers of night.
He pitying did a second birth bestow,—
A birth of joy—not like the first of tears and woe.

Ye strengthened feet, forth to his altar move;
Quicken, ye new-strung nerves, the enraptured lyre;
Ye heaven-directed eyes, o'erflow with love;
Glow, glow, my soul, with pure seraphic fire;
Deeds, thoughts, and words, no more his mandates break,
But to his endless glory work, conceive, and speak.

O! penitence, to virtue near allied,
Thou can'st new joys e'en to the blest impart;
The listening angels lay their harps aside
To hear the music of thy contrite heart;
And heaven itself wears a more radiant face,
When charity presents thee to the throne of grace.

Chief of metallic forms is regal gold;
Of elements, the limpid fount that flows;
Give me 'mongst gems the brilliant to behold;
O'er Flora's flock imperial is the rose:
Above all birds the sovereign eagle soars;
And monarch of the field the lordly lion roars.

What can with great leviathan compare,
Who takes his pastime in the mighty main?
What, like the sun, shines through the realms of air,
And gilds and glorifies the ethereal plain—
Yet what are these to man, who bears the sway;
For all was made for him—to serve and to obey.

Thus in high heaven charity is great,
Faith, hope, devotion, hold a lower place;
On her the cherubs and the seraphs wait,
Her, every virtue courts, and every grace;
See! on the right, close by the Almighty's throne,
In him she shines confessed, who came to make her known.

Deep rooted in my heart then let her grow,
That for the past the future may atone;
That I may act what thou hast given to know,
That I may live for thee and thee alone,

And justify those sweetest words from heaven,
'That he shall love thee most whom thou'st most forgiven.'

DAVIES, SAMUEL (1723–1761), born in Delaware, attended "Log College" in Pennsylvania (training school for the New Light Presbyterians) where he was discipled by Samuel Blair, in memory of whom he later composed two elegies. He was ordained as an evangelist in 1747 and sent to organize congregations in Virginia. He applied for a license to conduct services in Williamsburg, thus beginning his efforts for toleration where the Anglican church was established. His first wife died and he remarried, his second wife becoming the "Chara" of many of his poems. Davies continued all his life to promote evangelical Christianity, often preaching in the open when no buildings could accommodate the crowds which gathered. In 1753 he embarked for England with Gilbert Tennant on a fund-raising campaign for the new College of New Jersey (now Princeton). The mission was exceptionally successful and they returned with more than enough money to begin and continue Princeton. With the French and Indian war, Davies became an outspoken advocate of patriotism, and stirred up many young men to enlist in the defense of the colony. He also was involved in teaching the Bible and Catechism to a group of slaves. In 1752, Davies *Miscellaneous Poems* was published. These show the influence of various Calvinist and evangelical writers: Milton, Herbert, Watts, Doddridge, and his friend Edwards. Davies spoke approvingly of Pope's *Messiah*, Young's *Night Thoughts,* and Thomson's *The Seasons.* He said he imitated "the noble Licence of Pindar. . . which is perhaps most natural to me." [Pindaric odes—formal, celebratory poems.] Davies' hymns may be his best poetry. He often composed them in conjunction with a sermon—often on Saturday night. His hymns appeared in Gibbons *Hymns Adapted for Divine Worship* (London 1769) and Rippon's *A Selection of Hymns* (London 1787). Davies *Sermons* were edited and brought out by Thomas Gibbons in England in five volumes in 1766 and two more in 1771. Many subsequent editions were published in England and America up to 1864.

Of Him and thro' Him, and to Him are all Things.
Rom. xi. ult.

Thou only Good! Eternal ALL!
What am I when compar'd with THEE!
A Piece of animated Clay;
An Atom sporting in thy Ray—
The Loss would be but small,
Should I again to Non-Existence fall:
Nay, if thy Glory might but rise,

Cheerful my Being I'd resign,
And fall a willing Sacrifice
To gain a Purpose so divine,
So much more worthy than this little Life of Mine!

Science. An Ode

SCIENCE! bright Beam of Light Divine!
Dawn of immortal Day!
On this thy new-built Temple shine,
And all thy Charms display.

Where wild untutor'd IGNORANCE:
Her savage Revels kept;
And led the rude ferocious Dance,
While gentle REASON Slept;

Where bowling through her native Wood,
With kindred Beasts of Prey,
She rous'd her furious Sons to Blood,
More wild and fierce than they:

Thy Temple, there, expands in Gates
To thee, celestial Guest!
And each of thy young Vot'ries waits
To hail thee to thy Rest.

Hail, SCIENCE! Heaven born Stranger! hail!
Adorn thy humble Shrine:
Deign in this Western World to dwell,
And its wide Wastes refine.

The One Thing Needful Generally Neglected
Luke x. 42. Long Metre

O, Was my Heart but form'd for Woe,
What streams of pitying Tears should flow,
To see the thoughtless Sons of Men
Labour, and toil, and live in vain!

One Thing is needful, one alone;
If this be ours, all is our own:
'Tis needful now, 'twill needful be
In Death, and thro' Eternity.

Without it we are all undone,
Tho' we could call the World our own:
Not all the Joys of Time and Sense
Can countervail the Loss immense.

Yet, (O the Horrors of the Thought!)
The one Thing needful is forgot;
Forgot, while Trifles of an Hour
Our Love, and Hope, and Zeal devour.

Hurry, and Toil, and anxious Care,
The busy Life of Mortals share,
Till Death compels them to bemoan
Their Folly, when their Sands are run.

The Bliss of Heav'n they disregard,
Hell's flaming Terrors rage unfear'd;
Eternity a Trifle seems;
Immense Realities are Dreams.

O Sinners! will you now return?
Or must I still your Madness mourn?
O will you now at length be wise,
And strive to gain the only Prize?

Great GOD! that powerful Grace of thine,
Which rous'd a Soul so dead as mine,
Can rouse these thoughtless Sinners too
The one Thing needful to pursue.

NEWTON, JOHN (1725–1807), at eleven years of age went to sea with his father, a merchant marine commander. In 1742 his father retired and Newton was impressed aboard a navy ship the next year. Although he was made a midshipman, he deserted, only to be captured and degraded. He was exchanged to a slaver off Portugal, and was thereafter involved in the slave trade until 1754. He taught himself Euclid's geometry and enough Latin to read Virgil, Livy, and Erasmus, as well as learning Horace by heart. He also studied the Bible with increased devotion and through Captain Cluny of St. Kitts, came to hold to Calvinist theology. After 1755 he was made surveyor of the tides at Liverpool, where he soon became an enthusiastic disciple of Whitfield. He also met Wesley and formed a lasting friendship with him. His first application for ordination received "the softest refusal imaginable," but in 1764 he was ordained through the influence of the evangelical young Lord Dartmouth. His earliest charge was the curacy of Olney in Buckinghamshire. In 1767, William Cowper came to stay with him and biographers like to debate whether Newton was good or bad for the despondent Cowper. Newton and Cowper together published *Olney Hymns* in 1779. It contained sixty-eight pieces by Cowper and 280 by Newton. Newton moved in 1780 to London, where in 1788 he aided Wilberforce by publishing an account of his experience in the slave trade, "a temperate, restrained, but ghastly recital of the facts" *(National Dictionary of Biography)*. He was apparently an extemporary preacher, and his printed sermons are little valued. His hymns continue among the favorites of our day, with "Amazing Grace" probably the best known hymn of the English-speaking world.

Amazing Grace

Amazing grace—how sweet the sound—
That saved a wretch like me!
I once was lost, but now am found—
Was blind, but now I see.

'Twas grace that taught my heart to fear,
And grace my fears relieved;
How precious did that grace appear
The hour I first believed!

Thro' many dangers, toils and snares,
I have already come;
'Tis grace has brought me safe thus far,
And grace will lead me home.

The Lord has promised good to me!
His word my hope secures;
He will my shield and portion be
As long as life endures.

Yea, when this flesh and heart shall fail,
And mortal life shall cease,
I shall possess within the veil
A life of joy and peace.

When we've been there ten thousand years,
Bright shining as the sun,
We've no less days to sing God's praise
Than when we've first begun.

The Name of Jesus

How sweet the name of Jesus sounds
    In a believer's ear!
It soothes his sorrows, heals his wounds,
    And drives away his fear.

It makes the wounded spirit whole,
    And calms the troubled breast;
'Tis manna to the hungry soul,
    And to the weary rest.

Dear Name! the rock on which I build,
    My shield and hiding-place,
My never-failing treasury filled
    With boundless stores of grace.

By thee my prayers acceptance gain,
    Although with sin defiled;
Satan accuses me in vain,
    And I am owned a child.

Jesus! my Shepherd, Husband, Friend,
    My Prophet, Priest, and King;
My Lord, my Life, my Way, my End,
    Accept the praise I bring.

Weak is the effort of my heart
    And cold my warmest thought:
But, when I see thee as thou art,
    I'll praise thee as I ought.

Till then I would thy love proclaim
    With every fleeting breath;
And may the music of thy name
    Refresh my soul in death.

The Encounter
(In Evil long I took Delight)

In evil long I took delight,
Unawed by shame or fear,
Till a new object struck my sight,
And stopped my wild career:
I saw One hanging on a tree

In agonies and blood,
Who fixed His languid eyes on me,
As near His cross I stood.

Sure never till my latest breath
Can I forget that look:
It seemed to charge me with His death,
Though not a word He spoke:
My conscience felt and owned the guilt,
And plunged me in despair;
I saw my sins His Blood had spilt
And helped to nail Him there.

Alas! I knew not what I did!
But now my tears are vain:
Where shall my trembling soul be hid?
For I the Lord have slain!
A second look He gave, which said,
'I freely all forgive;
This Blood is for thy ransom paid;
I die, that thou mayst live.'

Thus, while His death my sin displays
In all its blackest hue,
Such is the mystery of grace,
It seals my pardon too.
With pleasing grief, and mournful joy,
My spirit now is filled,
That I should such a life destroy,
Yet live by Him I killed!

COWPER, WILLIAM (1731–1800), studied law, entered the Middle Temple, and was called to the bar in 1754. He had lost his mother at an early age, was rebuffed by his uncle when he sought to marry a cousin, and was barely supporting himself as a commissioner of bankrupts in 1759. He struggled against religious doubts and insecurities. Apparently under the pressure of an approaching interview for a clerk's post in the House of Lords, Cowper attempted suicide. He was put in an asylum for eighteen months, after which he stayed with the Unwins, staunch Calvinists, who remained life-long friends and supporters. When Morley Unwin died, Cowper and Mrs. Unwin moved to Olney in Buckinghamshire, where they resided with John Newton, who encouraged Cowper's involvement in evangelism, and hymn-writing. *Olney Hymns* (1779) included hymns by both of them. In 1773 Cowper had a relapse into "madness." After Newton went to London in 1780, Cowper turned more to writing poetry, partly at the encouragement of Mary Unwin. He wrote some moral satires, the famous poem, "John Gilpin's Ride," and *The Task*, which was published with immediate success in 1785. Cowper then began his translation of *Homer* which was published in 1791. Mary Unwin, disabled since 1792, died in 1796, and Cowper sank into a lasting depression out of which he wrote "The Castaway." Cowper feared all his life, especially in his periods of "madness" that he was predestined to damnation. One who saw his face after he died said that with the "calmness and composure" was "mingled, as it were, a holy surprise." Elizabeth Barrett Browning wrote a commemorative poem on Cowper's grave.

There Is A Fountain Filled With Blood

There is a fountain filled with blood,
Drawn from Immanuel's veins;
And sinners plunged beneath that flood,
Lose all their guilty stains.

The dying thief rejoiced to see
That fountain in his day;
And there have I, as vile as he,
Washed all my sins away.

E'er since by faith I saw the stream
Thy flowing wounds supply,
Redeeming love has been my theme,
And shall be till I die.

Dear dying Lamb, thy precious blood
Shall never lose its power,
Till all the ransomed church of God
Be saved, to sin no more.

Sometimes A Light Surprises

Sometimes a light surprises   The Christian while he sings;
It is the Lord, who rises   With healing in his wings:
When comforts are declining,   He grants the soul again
A season of clear shining,   To cheer it after rain.

In holy contemplation   We sweetly then pursue
The theme of God's salvation,   And find it ever new
Set free from present sorrow,   We cheerfully can say,
Let the unknown tomorrow   Bring with it what it may.

It can bring with it nothing   But he will bear us through;
Who gives the lilies clothing   Will clothe his people too:
Beneath the spreading heavens   No creature but is fed;
And he who feeds the ravens   Will give his children bread.

Though vine and fig-tree neither   Their wonted fruit shall bear,
Though all the fields should wither,   Nor flocks nor herds be there;
Yet God the same abiding,   His praise shall tune my voice,
For, while in him confiding,   I cannot but rejoice.

God Moves In A Mysterious Way

God moves in a mysterious way   His wonders to perform;
He plants his footsteps in the sea,   And rides upon the storm.

Deep in unfathomable mines   Of never failing skill
He treasures up his bright designs,   And works his sovereign will.

Ye fearful saints, fresh courage take;   The clouds ye so much dread
Are big with mercy, and shall break   In blessings on your head.

Judge not the Lord by feeble sense,   But trust him for his grace;
Behind a frowning providence   He hides a smiling face.

His purposes will ripen fast,   Unfolding ev'ry hour;
The bud may have a bitter taste,   But sweet will be the flow'r.

Blind unbelief is sure to err,   And scan his work in vain;
God is his own interpreter,   And he will make it plain.

Subjoined To The Yearly Bill Of Mortality
Of The Parish Of All Saints, Northampton, 1792

Thankless for favours from on high,
Man thinks he fades too soon;
Though 'tis his privilege to die,
Would he improve the boon.

But he, not wise enough to scan
His blessed concerns aright,
Would gladly stretch life's little span
To ages, if he might.

To ages in a world of pain,
To ages, where he goes

Galled by affliction's heavy chain,
And hopeless of repose.

Strange fondness of the human heart,
Enamoured of its harm!
Strange world, that costs it so much smart,
And still has power to charm.

Whence has the world her magic power?
Why deem we death a foe?
Recoil from weary life's best hour,
And covet longer woe?

The cause is conscience—conscience oft
Her tale of guilt renews:
Her voice is terrible though soft,
And dread of death ensues.

Then anxious to be longer spared,
Man mourns his fleeting breath:
All evils then seem light, compared
With the approach of death.

'Tis judgment shakes him; there's the fear
That prompts the wish to stay:
He has incurred a long arrear,
And must despair to pay.

Pay!—follow Christ, and all is paid;
His death your peace ensures;
Think on the grave where he was laid,
And calm descend to yours.

Hymn—Jesus, Where'er Thy People Meet

Jesus, where'er thy people meet,
There they behold thy mercy-seat;
Where'er they seek thee, thou art found,
And every place is hallowed ground.

For thou, within no walls confined,
Inhabitest the humble mind;
Such ever bring thee where they come,
And, going, take thee to their home.

Dear shepherd of thy chosen few,
Thy former mercies here renew;
Here to our waiting hearts proclaim
The sweetness of thy saving name.

Here may we prove the power of prayer,
To strengthen faith and sweeten care;
To teach our faint desires to rise,
And bring all heaven before our eyes.

Lord, we are few, but thou art near;
Nor short thine arm, nor deaf thine ear;
O rend the heavens, come quickly down,
And make a thousand hearts thine own!

Retirement

Far from the world, O Lord, I flee,
From strife and tumult far;
From scenes where Satan wages still
His most successful war.

The calm retreat, the silent shade,
With prayer and praise agree;
And seem, by Thy sweet bounty made,
For those who follow Thee.

There if Thy Spirit touch the soul,
And grace her mean abode,
Oh with what peace, and joy, and love,
She communes with her God;

There like the nightingale she pours
Her solitary lays;
Nor asks a witness of her song,
Nor thirsts for human praise.

Author and Guardian of my life,
Sweet source of light Divine,
And all harmonious names in one—
My Saviour! Thou art mine!

What thanks I owe Thee, and what love—
A boundless, endless store—

Shall echo through the realms above,
When time shall be no more.

The Sum Of Life
From "The Garden": "The Task" Book VI

I was a stricken deer, that left the herd
Long since; with many an arrow deep infixed
My panting side was charged, when I withdrew,
To seek a tranquil death in distant shades.
There was I found by one who had himself
Been hurt by the archers. In his side be bore,
And in his hands and feet, the cruel scars
With gentle force soliciting the darts,
He drew them forth, and healed, and bade me live.
Since then, with few associates, in remote
And silent woods I wander, far from those
My former partners of the peopled scene;
With few associates, and not wishing more.
Here much I ruminate, as much I may,
With other views of men and manners now
Than once, and others of a life to come.
I see that all are wanderers, gone astray
Each in his own delusions; they are lost
In chase of fancied happiness, still wooed
And never won. Dream after dream ensues;
And still they dream, that they shall still succeed;
And still are disappoint. Rings the world
With the vain stir, I sum up half mankind,
And add two-thirds of the remaining half,
And find the total of their hopes and fears
Dreams, empty dreams.

To A Young Lady

Sweet stream, that winds through yonder glade,
Apt emblem of a virtuous maid—
Silent and chaste she steals along,
Far from the world's gay busy throng;
With gentle yet prevailing force,
Intent upon her destined course;
Graceful and useful all she does,

Blessing and blest where'er she goes;
Pure-bosom'd as that watery glass,
And Heaven reflected in her face.

The Vicar of Bray (1734)
Anonymous

In good King Charles's golden days,
When Loyalty no harm meant;
A Furious High-Church Man I was,
And so I gain'd Preferment.
Unto my Flock I daily Preach'd,
Kings are by God appointed,
And Damn'd are those who dare resist,
Or touch the Lord's Anointed.
    And this is Law, I will maintain
    Unto my Dying Day, Sir,
    That whatsoever King shall Reign,
    I will be Vicar of Bray, Sir!

When Royal James possest the Crown,
And Popery grew in fashion;
The Penal Law I houted down,
And read the Declaration:
The Church of Rome, I found would fit,
Full well my Constitution,
And I had been a Jesuit,
But for the Revolution.
    And this is Law, I will maintain
    Unto my Dying Day, Sir,
    That whatsoever King shall Reign,
    I will be Vicar of Bray, Sir!

When William our Deliverer came,
To heal the Nation's Grievance,
I turned the Cat in Pan again,
And swore to him Allegiance:
Old Principles I did revoke,
Set Conscience at a distance,
Passive Obedience is a Joke,
A Jest is Non-resistance.
    And this is Law, I will maintain

Unto my Dying Day, Sir,
That whatsoever King shall Reign,
I will be Vicar of Bray, Sir!

When glorious Ann became our Queen,
The Church of England's Glory,
Another face of things was seen,
And I became a Tory:
Occasional Conformists base,
I Damn'd, and Moderation,
And thought the Church in danger was,
From such Prevarication.
    And this is Law, I will maintain
    Unto my Dying Day, Sir,
    That whatsoever King shall Reign,
    I will be Vicar of Bray, Sir!

When George in Pudding time came o'er,
And Moderate Men looked big, Sir,
My Principles I chang'd once more,
And so became a Whig, Sir:
And thus Preferment I procur'd,
From our Faith's Great Defender,
And almost every day abjur'd
The Pope, and the Pretender.
    And this is Law, I will maintain
    Unto my Dying Day, Sir,
    That whatsoever King shall Reign,
    I will be Vicar of Bray, Sir!

The Illustrious House of Hanover,
And Protestant Succession,
To these I lustily will swear,
Whilst they can keep possession:
For in my Faith, and Loyalty,
I never once will faulter,
But George, my Lawful King shall be,
Except the Times should alter.
    And this is Law, I will maintain
    Unto my Dying Day, Sir,
    That whatsoever King shall Reign,
    I will be Vicar of Bray, Sir!

TOPLADY, AUGUSTUS MONTAGUE (1740–1778), was son of an army major who died in battle in 1741. His mother moved to Ireland in 1755, and there Toplady was converted "in an obscure part of Ireland, midst a handful of people met together in a barn, and by the ministry of one who could hardly spell his own name." Although that was a Methodist meeting, he soon became a committed Calvinist, and an outspoken opponent of John Wesley's theological Arminianism. He was ordained in 1764 and became a curate. He had a wide range of friends, men of all denominations and of society in general. He was acquainted with Dr. Johnson. He published *Poems and Hymns on Sacred Subjects* in 1759, but the best-known of his hymns, "Rock of Ages," did not appear until a later edition. He published "The Historic Proof of the Doctrinal Calvinism of the Church of England" in 1774, the best example of his aggressive prose writings. Several of John Wesley's attacks on him, as well as several of his epithets for Wesley were clearly unworthy of those who are supposed to be characterized by love. As Albert Edward Bailey points out, however, "when Toplady published his collection of hymns in 1776, his own "Rock of Ages" and Charles Wesley's "Jesus, lover of my soul," stood, in spite of theology, side by side" (*The Gospel in Hymns*, p. 121). We might amend Bailey's "in spite of theology," to "in unified theology."

Rock Of Ages

Rock of Ages, cleft for me,   Let me hide myself in thee;
Let the water and the blood,   From thy riven side which flowed,
Be of sin the double cure,   Cleanse me from its guilt and pow'r.

Not the labors of my hands   Can fulfill thy law's demands;
Could my zeal no respite know,   Could my tears for ever flow,
All for sin could not atone;   Thou must save, and thou alone.

Nothing in my hands I bring,   Simply to thy cross I cling;
Naked come to thee for dress,   Helpless, look to thee for grace;
Foul, I to the Fountain fly;   Wash me, Saviour or I die.

While I draw this fleeting breath,   When mine eyelids close in death,
When I soar to worlds unknown,   See thee on thy judgment throne,
Rock of Ages, cleft for me,   Let me hide myself in thee.

Hymn

Inspirer and hearer of prayer,
Thou feeder and guardian of thine,
My all to thy covenant care

I sleeping and waking resign;
If thou art my shield and my sun,
The night is no darkness to me,
And fast as my moments roll on,
They bring me but nearer to thee.

Thy minist'ring spirits descend
To watch while thy saints are asleep,
By day and by night they attend,
The heirs of salvation to keep;
Bright seraphs dispatched from the throne,
Repair to the stations assigned,
And angels elect are sent down,
To guard the elect of mankind.

Thy worship no interval knows,
Their fervor is still on the wing:
And while they protect my repose,
They chant to the praise of my King:
I too, at the season ordained,
Their chorus forever shall join,
And love, and adore, without end,
Their faithful Creator, and mine.

Eighteenth Century Hymnody

In the sixteenth and seventeenth centuries lyric poetry began to be a formal art-form where previously it had been primarily words to be sung with music. As did the madrigal, the lyric increasingly became a formal genre of court poetry. Hymn lyrics, however, are a notable exception. Born out of the Protestant Reformation, European hymns influenced English Christian poetry. Singing in English churches had been predominantly Psalm-singing, the form of musical worship prescribed by the Reformed church in Northern Europe, although a few hymns—mostly translations of the older Latin hymns—were sung in England.

The Scottish "kirk" adopted a stricter Psalmody, although it used many of the metrical translations of the "Old Version." James I added a number of his own translations to the service-book, the new version of which, published in 1636, started the "second Scottish Reformation." The question of rival psalm translations was decided by the Long Parliament in 1642. The "New Version" of the Psalms, by Nicholas Brady and Nahum Tate, poet laureate, was sanctioned in 1696, although it was less faithful to the Hebrew than the "Old."

Under James I, George Wither obtained a patent for his *Hymns and Songs of the Church* (1622). Others, including Milton, John Cosin, and Jeremy Taylor published hymns of their own composition. During the Restoration, Samuel Crossman (1664), John Austin (1668), and Richard Baxter (1681) published a number of good hymns. Dryden, Bishops Ken and Patrick, and Joseph Addison published a few hymns at the turn of the century.

Isaac Watts, often called the father of English hymnody, published his *Hymns* in 1707–1709. There were very few hymns in common use up to his time. Watts also published *Psalms* (1709) which were not merely translations, but rather hymns based on Psalms. Watts's was followed by Simon Browne and Phillip Doddridge. In Scotland, Watts' influence showed up in Ralph Erskine's *Gospel Sonnets* (1732).

The Scottish church softened its psalm-singing stand in the late Eighteenth century to include "paraphrases" of scripture. These followed the sense of scriptural passages without the constraints of strict translation. The English Independent hymn-writers (Watts et al.) were followed by the Methodists, and from their ranks Charles Wesley towers. Other notable hymn-writers, who tended toward George Whitfield's "Calvinistic Methodism" were Augustus Toplady, John Newton, and William Cowper.

Christian Pilgrim's Hymn
William Williams, 1745

Guide me, O thou great Redeemer,
Pilgrim through this barren land:
I am weak but thou art mighty;
Hold me with thy powerful hand:
Bread of heaven! Bread of heaven!
Feed me now and evermore!

Open now the crystal fountain
Whence the healing streams do flow;
Let the fiery cloudy pillar
Lead me all my journey through:
Strong Deliverer! Strong Deliverer!
Be thou still my strength and shield.

When I tread the verge of Jordan,
Bid my anxious fears subside;
Death of deaths, and hell's destruction,
Land me safe on Canaan's side:
Songs of praises, songs of praises,
I will ever give to thee.

Come, Thou Almighty King
Anonymous

Come, thou Almighty King,
Help us thy Name to sing,
Help us to praise:
   Father, all glorious,
   O'er all victorious,
   Come, and reign over us,
Ancient of Days.

Come, thou Incarnate Word,
Gird on thy mighty sword,
Our prayer attend:
   Come, and thy people bless,
   And give thy Word success;
   Spirit of Holiness,
On us descend.

Come, Holy Comforter,
Thy sacred witness bear
In this glad hour:
   Thou who almighty art,
   Now rule in every heart,
   And ne'er from us depart,
Spirit of pow'r.

To the great One in Three
Eternal praises be,
Hence evermore.
   His sovereign majesty
   May we in glory see,
   And to eternity
Love and adore.

Come Thou Fount Of Ev'ry Blessing
Robert Robinson

Come, thou Fount of ev'ry blessing,   Tune my heart to sing thy grace;
Streams of mercy never ceasing,   Call for songs of loudest praise.
Teach me some melodious sonnet,   Sung by flaming tongues above;
Praise the mount! I'm fixed upon it,   Mount of God's unchanging love.

Here I raise my Ebenezer;   Hither by thy help I'm come;
And I hope, by thy good pleasure,   Safely to arrive at home.
Jesus sought me when a stranger,   Wand'ring from the fold of God:
He, to rescue me from danger,   Interposed his precious blood.

O to grace how great a debtor   Daily I'm constrained to be;
Let that grace now, like a fetter,   Bind my wandering heart to thee.
Prone to wander, Lord, I feel it,   Prone to leave the God I love;
Here's my heart, O take and seal it,   Seal it for thy courts above.

The God Of Abraham Praise
Thomas Olivers, 1725-99

The God of Abraham praise
Who reigns enthroned above,
Ancient of everlasting days,
And God of love:
To him uplift your voice,
At whose supreme command
From earth we rise, and seek the joys
At his right hand.

Though nature's strength decay,
And earth and hell withstand,
To Canaan's bounds we urge our way
At his command.
The watery deep we pass,
With Jesus in our view;
And through the howling wilderness
Our way pursue.

The goodly land we see,
With peace and plenty blest;
A land of sacred liberty
And endless rest;
There milk and honey flow,
And oil and wine abound,
And trees of life for ever grow,
With mercy crowned.

There dwells the Lord our King,
The Lord our Righteousness,
Triumphant o'er the world and sin,

The Prince of Peace;
On Sion's sacred height
His kingdom he maintains,
And glorious with his saints in light
For ever reigns.

Before the great Three-One
They all exulting stand,
And tell the wonders he hath done
Through all their land:
The listening spheres attend,
And swell the growing fame,
And sing, in songs which never end,
The wondrous name.

The God who reigns on high
The great archangels sing,
And 'Holy, holy, holy,' cry,
'Almighty King!
Who was, and is, the same,
And evermore shall be:
Eternal Father, great "I AM,"
We worship thee.'

The whole triumphant host
Give thanks to God on high;
'Hail! Father, Son, and Holy Ghost,'
They ever cry:
Hail! Abraham's God, and mine!
(I join the heavenly lays)
All might and majesty are thine,
And endless praise.

Hail Thou Once Despised Jesus

Hail, thou once despised Jesus,   Hail, thou Galilean King!
Thou didst suffer to release us: Thou didst free salvation bring.
Hail, thou agonizing Saviour,   Bearer of our sin and shame!
By thy merits we find favor;   Life is given through thy Name.

Paschal Lamb, by God appointed,   All our sins were on thee laid;
By almighty Love anointed,   Thou hast full atonement made:
All thy people are forgiven   Through the virtue of thy blood;
Opened is the gate of heaven,   Peace is made 'twixt man and God.

Jesus, hail! enthroned in glory,   There for ever to abide;
All the heav'nly hosts adore thee,   Seated at they Father's side:
There for sinners thou art pleading;   There thou dost our place prepare;
Ever for us interceding,   Till in glory we appear.

Worship, honor, pow'r, and blessing   Thou art worthy to receive:
Loudest praises without ceasing,   Meet it is for us to give.
Help, ye bright angelic spirits,   Bring your sweetest, noblest lays;
Help to sing our Saviour's merits,   Help to chant Immanuel's praise.

How Firm A Foundation
"K" in Rippon's *Selections*

How firm a foundation, ye saints of the Lord,
Is laid for your faith in his excellent Word!
What more can he say than to you he hath said,
You who unto Jesus for refuge have fled?

"Fear not, I am with thee, O be not dismayed;
I, I am thy God, and will still give thee aid;
I'll strengthen thee, help thee, and cause thee to stand,
Upheld by my righteous, omnipotent hand.

"When through the deep waters I call thee to go,
The rivers of woe shall not thee overflow;
For I will be with thee thy troubles to bless,
And sanctify to thee thy deepest distress.

"When through fiery trials thy pathway shall lie,
My grace, all-sufficient, shall be thy supply;
The flame shall not hurt thee; I only design
Thy dross to consume, and thy gold to refine.

"E'en down to old age all my people shall prove
My sovereign, eternal, unchangeable love;
And when hoary hairs shall their temples adorn,
Like lambs they shall still in my bosom be borne.

"The soul that on Jesus hath leaned for repose,
I will not, I will not desert to his foes;
That soul, though all hell should endeavor to shake,
I'll never, no, never, no, never forsake."

While Shepherd Watched Their Flocks By Night
Nahum Tate

While shepherds watched their flocks by night,
All seated on the ground,
The angel of the Lord came down,
And glory shown around, and glory shown around.

"Fear not," said he—for mighty dread
Had seized their troubled mind—
"Glad tidings of great joy I bring
To you and all mankind, to you and all mankind.

"To you, in David's town this day,
Is born of David's line,
The Saviour, who is Christ, the Lord,
And this shall be a sign: and this shall be a sign:

"The heav'nly Babe you there shall find
To human view displayed,
All meanly wrapped in swathing bands,
And in a manger laid, and in a manger laid."

Thus spake the seraph, and forthwith
Appeared a shining throng
Of angels praising God, who thus
Addressed their joyful song: addressed their joyful song:

"All glory be to God on high,
And to the earth be peace:
Good will henceforth, from heav'n to men,
Begin and never cease! begin and never cease!"

Chapter Six

POETRY OF THE ROMANTIC AGE

1776—American Revolution   1837—Victoria's coronation

The poetry of the romantics was born out of reaction against that of their predecessors—particularly against neoclassical poetry. It might be argued that the romantics were the first "modern" school of poetry, in that they self-consciously defined themselves in opposition to "tradition."

"Romantic" is difficult term. The word originally referred to the vernacular of France; then was extended to refer to all European languages descending from Latin. The term "romance" (French "roman," Middle English "romaunt") was an adventurous tale told in the vernacular. It came to mean a tale of chivalry or extravagant adventure, and sometimes a story that was patently false. (The "roman" is generally recognized as the predecessor of the "novel.") Many of these connotations cling to the word today, although Hollywood re-focused it around the "love story." The term "romantic" was not applied to the era or its poetry until the late Victorian period—about the same time it was applied to a school of music "characterized by the subordination of form to theme, and by imagination and passion" (*Oxford Universal Dictionary*). "Romantic" is also used of a school of painting in which grand landscapes are idealized under dramatic atmospheres.

Like most "schools" and "periods," the English romantic school or period does not lend itself to precise delineation. It is safe to say there were poets tending toward its distinctives as early as the mid-eighteenth century. "Nature poems" on subjects from the natural world were popular much earlier. Edward Young ("Night Thoughts") and James Thomson ("Winter") are often designated romantic harbingers. Thomas Gray's "Elegy Written in A Country Churchyard," like Young's "Night Thoughts," was in the genre of eighteenth century solitary meditations that prefigured the romantic school. William Cowper's "Task" is sometimes seen as the first poem in the romantic era.

The romantic period, however, was not merely the time during which poems having certain distinctives were written. We have chosen to designate the American Revolution as the starting point because it seems an appropriate opening for a period of social ferment and revolution in government, in thought, and in poetry. The ills of the Industrial Revolution were getting "iller." Social scientists, like Malthus and Bentham were giving dire prognoses and prescribing strong medicine for a world that the Deist's Clockmaker God seemed to have abandoned. Strange, homemade sects and cults were being founded.

The Restoration and eighteenth century had been considerably influenced or bolstered by Deism, the philosophy that says a mechanic "God" created a mechanistic universe in which each small part has a part to perform and the natural (inner as well as outer) resources to perform it. The romantic era, in contrast, was bent on tossing off the restraints—those of human arbiters and in many cases those of the Designer as well as. The romantics tended to be attracted to philosophies wilder and more disorderly than Deism. Thomas Paine, the famous pamphleteer of the American Revolution widely proclaimed atheism as the truth leading to liberation. Percy Bysshe Shelley was expelled from Oxford for a writing a pamphlet, *The Necessity of Atheism*, and like Paine, soon launched himself into issues of political liberation. Byron, also was revolutionary in his inclinations, becoming noted as a licentious man. (Byron, however, in distinction from most of the other romantic poets, retained a strong prejudice for aristocracy over against the democracy of the "common man" favored by most of the others.) John Keats died young after a life very moderate in comparison, but he, too, exhibited unrestrained passions for existential truth and beauty. De Quincey and Coleridge were opium addicts much of their lives.

Blake was partially or fully "mad" much of his life. In fact Cowper (who suffered numerous bouts of depression) once said to Blake, "Oh, that I were insane always. Cannot you make me truly insane? You retain health and yet are as insane as any of us. . . . Madness is a refuge from unbelief, from Bacon, Newton, Locke. We are citizens of eternity." This is a particularly poignant remark coming from Cowper who wrote such beautiful hymns, and addressed to Blake who wrote the wonderful devotional poem, "The Lamb." It is even more significant in indicating some of what the romantics were fleeing, varied as their paths of flight seem to have been. One might argue that whereas the Restoration/Enlightenment poets were fleeing the immediate past (Christian creeds with their internecine wars), the romantics were in rebellion against the present (the Deist view of "order" and the evils of industrial society).

Several "doctrines" of the eighteenth century against which the romantics reacted were: 1) the rejection of subjective and emotional poetry in favor of "witty" and "sentimental" but universal verse; 2) a rejection of "homely" language and subjects in favor of classical ones; 3) a rejection of metaphysical themes in favor of manners and morals, 4) and the mistrust of "enthusiasm" in contrast to an all-but-worship of reason. One might reverse each of these and come up with a list of romantic tenets.

The poets of this era were reacting to the contradiction between staid rationalism and the ugliness and suffering of industrial society. A number of Christians, like William Wilberforce and Lord Ashley (later Earl of Shaftesbury) responded with life-long, determined efforts at social reform through political and charitable means. Wilberforce was the great reformer who brought about the abolition of the slave trade in 1807. Shaftesbury gave his entire life both to personal involvement with the industrial poor and to political efforts toward regulating the new institutions of lunatic asylums, child labor, long factory hours, unsafe working conditions, and toward promoting public education. Few of the romantic poets were Christians, however. Most were attracted to radical and utopian philosophies and creeds, although several, after being disenchanted turned to the Christian faith.

There were not many well-known or great Christian poets during the eighteenth century. Hymn-writing, although sometimes neoclassical in style, tended in the more popular hymns toward expressions of faith and emotion and fairly plain (though doctrinally profound) language. The wilder romantics were clearly not Christians, but some critics refer to the more moderate as "Christian romantics." There is an obscurity to the romantics, however, which makes them very "modern." While the eighteenth century was so "reasonable" and "scientific" that Swift could satirize it with "An Argument against Abolishing Christianity," as though such an abolition was imminent, the romantics were not so obvious nor susceptible to satire. Indeed, academic sages are still hotly debating what Blake believed or what he was doing with his poetry. While Blake gave a hundred cults and sects grounds for claiming him, Wordsworth was reticent to an opposite extreme. Shelley claimed for the poet the offices of prophet, legislator, and demi-god, but the poetry of the romantics seems to belie him. Much of it emits much heat with little light. Wordsworth in a famous phrase from his Preface to *The Lyrical Ballads* (second edition, 1800) speaks of poetry as "emotion recollected in tranquillity."

There is much more to romantic poetry than emotions, however. Wordsworth's "feeling intellect" is central to T.S. Eliot's concern in his essay "On the Metaphysical Poets." Eliot sees both the Restoration (neoclassical) poets and the romantics as losing ground during the change in poetry after Donne and the metaphysical poets; however: "In the seventeenth century a dissociation of the sensibility set in from which we have never recovered. . ."

The romantics, without formulating it in the same terms, reacted as though they agreed with Eliot's assessment as applied to their immediate predecessors. They were consciously trying to recover some integration of heart and mind, but emphasizing the importance of the heart.

The romantics wished to achieve a kind of flight in their poetry, while Dryden and Pope would have been horrified by the idea. But the romantics were not trying to escape reason, nor would they have agreed with the modern school of aesthetics that says "a poem should not mean but be." The poem was supposed to teach, whatever else it did. Wordsworth said, "Every great poet is a teacher; I wish either to be considered as a teacher or as nothing." He states the purpose of poetry in another place, "To console the afflicted; to add sunshine to daylight by making the happy happier; to teach the young and the gracious of every age to see, to think, and feel. . ." Cowper had written to Lady Austen something similar about the poet's teaching office:

> I, who scribble rhyme
> To catch the triflers of the time,
> And tell them truths divine and clear
> Which, couched in prose they will not hear.

While the American Revolution started off with lots of glorious idealism and was popularly seen to have concluded with victory for "liberty," the French Revolution was much more significant for the romantics. Almost all of them were strongly allied with the cause of "democracy" in France, and their youthful idealism was so inflamed that some went to France to aid in the cause. The political situation seemed to them a "type" of the constricted and unnatural order of the world in general. They had all the zeal of young and naive Marxists (or perhaps of Puritans of a hundred years earlier). The French Revolution, however, did not go as well as the American. Indeed, it became a bloodbath and a stage upon which incredible tyrannies were played out. All of the romantic poets who lived long enough were bitterly disillusioned by it. Indeed, most of them (even those who did not live long) experienced severe disillusionments of one kind or another. It is perhaps not too harsh to say they set themselves up for disappointment, although some grew immeasurably through it.

The romantics, in a manner similar to the transcendentalists of the next century, were looking for a spiritual unity, underlying truth, that could unify a world falling apart. At the same time, the philosophers of their day such as Kant (to whom Coleridge, at least, was attracted) were saying that spiritual reality could not be experienced—that no one could cross the gap between the noumenal (spiritual) and phenomenal (seen or sensed) worlds.

Many of the romantics looked to the "natural world" and to "natural man," the simple places and the simple souls who might hold the keys to what was intrinsically good and true in the world—and in man. Robert Burns was seen (and apparently portrayed himself) as this sort of "natural genius," a peasant-stock poet and seer. The romantics were optimistic and exhilarated at first in the hope the world was turning over a new leaf. Later, especially after the French Revolution went sour, many were deeply embittered, but some passed through their bitterness and came out of it humbler and wiser.

An evidence that the romantic poets were not just cranks, but representative of their times is the reversal in the popularity of the genres from the previous period. During the Restoration and eighteenth century, prose gained considerable ascendancy over poetry, but during the romantic era, the reverse became the case. Although Robert Southey, who became poet laureate, was not the best among them, he and those who were better became popular poets in their day. Even those who died young and bitter, like Byron, enjoyed considerable contemporary popularity in contrast to many great poets before and after them. romantic novels were popular, too. These included the "historical novels" of Sir Walter Scott, the social novels of Jane Austen, and "Gothic" novels.

In one sense most of the romantics "risked all," and they are respectable as a group for the whole-heartedness of their effort. On the other hand, most of them were incredibly immature, many selfish, even cruel. Some persevered and gained enough humility to approach the Truth they sought.

Many of the poets included here, including several "greats," made clear professions of Christian faith, later if not earlier in their lives. Some included here may not have been Christians. My selections have been made on the basis of the poetry more than biographical information. Because of the ambiguity that characterizes the themes of much romantic poetry, I may have made mistakes. Augustine said that until Christ returns there will be those in the church who are not God's people and those outside the church who are. That principle applies to this anthology.

A Brief Chronology of the Romantic Age

1776	American Revolution
1786	Robert Burns' Publishes *Poems, Chiefly in the Scottish Dialect*
1783	William Blake publishes *Poetical Sketches*
1789	French Revolution begins
1791-92	Thomas Paine published *Rights of Man*
1793-94	Robespierre's Reign of Terror in France
1794	William Blake publishes *Songs of Innocence and of Experience*
1798	Wordsworth and Coleridge publish *Lyrical Ballads*
1800	Wordsworth's "Romantic manifesto," The Preface to the *Lyrical Ballads* (2nd edition) published
1804	Napoleon crowned Emperor
1807	William Wilberforce secures the Abolition of Slavery in Britain
1811-20	George, the Prince of Wales serves as Regent for George III who was declared insane (The Regency)
1815	Napoleon defeated at Waterloo—followed by economic depression in England
1820	George IV accedes to throne
1828	Lord Ashley and others succeed in getting laws passed regulating lunatic asylums
1832	The Reform Bill to clean up government and move toward a more representative government passed Parliament. Sir Walter Scott died
1833	Lord Ashley introduces first efforts toward child labor laws
1837	Victoria's coronation

BARBAULD, ANNA LAETITIA (AIKIN) (1743–1825), was born in Leicestershire, and died at Stoke Newington (now part of London). She, with her brother, John Aiken, published several popular books for children. After the suicide of her husband, Rev. Rochemont Barbauld (1808), she became very active both in literary pursuits and in "radical" causes. She edited the 50 volume British Novelists series, and became known both as a poetess and a writer of essays. She wrote *Poems* (1773), *Hymns in Prose for Children* (1781), *The Female Spectator* (1811), and "Eighteen Hundred and Eleven," a prophetic work predicting England's decline and America's rise.

The Call

Awake, my soul! lift up thine eyes,
See where thy foes against thee rise.
In long array, a numerous host:
Awake, my soul! or thou art lost.

Here giant Danger threatening stands.
Mustering his pale terrific bands:
There pleasure's silken banners spread,
And willing souls are captive led.

See where rebellious passions rage,
And fierce desires and lusts engage:
The meanest foe of all the train
His thousands and ten thousands slain.

Thou tread'st upon enchanted ground,
Perils and snares beset thee round;
Beware of all, guard every part.
But most, the traitor in thy heart.

Come then, my soul, now learn to wield
The weight of thine immortal shield;
Put on the armour from above
Of heavenly truth and heavenly love.

The terror and the charm repel,
And powers of earth, and powers of hell;
The Man of Calvary triumphed here:
Why should His faithful followers fear?

Praise To God

Praise to God, immortal praise,
For the love that crowns our days;
Bounteous source of every joy,
Let thy praise our tongues employ.

For the blessings of the field,
For the stores the gardens yield,
For the vine's exalted juice,
For the generous olive's use.

Flocks that whiten all the plain,
Yellow sheaves of ripened grain;
Clouds that drop their fattening dews
Suns that temperate warmth diffuse.

All that spring, with bounteous hand,
Scatters o'er the smiling land;
All that liberal autumn pours
From her rich o'erflowing stores.

These to thee, my God, we owe,
Source whence all our blessings flow;
And for these my soul shall raise
Grateful vows and solemn praise.

Yet should rising whirlwinds tear
From its stem the ripening ear;
Should the fig-tree's blasted shoot
Drop her green untimely fruit;

Should the vine put forth no more,
Nor the olive yield her store;
Though the sickening flocks should fall,
And the herds desert the stall;

Should thine altered hand restrain
The early and the latter rain,
Blast each opening bud of joy,
And the rising year destroy,—

Yet to thee my soul shall raise
Grateful vows and solemn praise;
And when every blessing 's flown,
Love thee for thyself alone.

DWIGHT, TIMOTHY (1752–1817) was born in Northampton, Massachusetts. His father was a merchant, and his mother, a daughter of Jonathan Edwards. When thirteen years old he entered Yale College. His intense study combined with working as a tutor impaired his health to the point of physical breakdown. In recuperation he devoted himself to hiking and horseback riding, which furnished him with material for a work written later in life, *Travels in New England and New York* (4 volumes, 1821–2). He went on to graduate from Yale in 1769, the first scholar in his class, and began a movement to introduce contemporary English literature into the curriculum. In 1771, Dwight began the " Conquest of Canaan, an epic poem in eleven books." He was licensed to preach in the Congregational church, and entered the army as a chaplain. In 1778 he established an co-educational academy at Northampton that continued for five years. In 1783 he was ordained pastor of a church in Greenfield, Connecticut, where he was noted for his preaching. He is generally recognized as the leader of the Connecticut Wits, a group of intellectual and Christian conservatives centered about Yale and Hartford. The group included John Trumbull, Joel Barlow, Lemuel, Hopkins, David Humphreys, Richard Alsop, Theodore Dwight (Timothy's brother), E. H. Smith, and Mason F. Cogswell. They opposed Deism in theology and favored Federalism in politics, collaborating in *The Anarchiad* (1786-7), *The Echo* (1791-1805, and *The Political Greenhouse* (1799). Dwight's own poetry included "Greenfield Hill" (1794) and "The Triumph of Infidelity." He was elected president of Yale College, in 1795. He wrote a number of political works including *The True Means of Establishing Public Happiness, Two Discourses on the Nature and Danger of Infidel Philosophy* (1798), and *The Duty of Americans, at the Present Crisis* (1798). After his cousin Aaron Burr killed Alexander Hamilton in a duel, he published a sermon on the *Folly, Guilt, and Mischiefs of Dueling* (1805). His sermons at Yale were published in five volumes (*Theology, Explained and Defended,* 1818–19). He also wrote several hymns and other short pieces.

The Smooth Divine

> There smiled the Smooth Divine, unused to wound
> The sinner's heart with hell's alarming sound.
> No terrors on his gentle tongue attend;
> No grating truths the nicest ear offend.
> That strange new birth, that methodistic grace,
> Nor in his heart nor sermons found a place.
> Plato's fine tales he clumsily retold,
> Trite, fireside, moral see-saws, dull as old,—
> His Christ and Bible placed at good remove,
> Guilt hell-deserving, and forgiving love.

'Twas best, he said, mankind should cease to sin:
Good fame required it; so did peace within.
Their honors, well he knew, would ne'er be driven;
But hoped they still would please to go to heaven.
Each week he paid his visitation dues;
Coaxed, jested, laughed; rehearsed the private news;
Smoked with each goody, thought her cheese excelled;
Her pipe he lighted and her baby held.
Or, placed in some great town, with lacquered shoes,
Trim wig, and trimmer gown, and glistening hose,
He bowed, talked politics, learned manners mild,
Most meekly questioned, and most smoothly smiled;
At rich men's jests laughed loud, their stories praised,
Their wives' new patterns gazed, and gazed, and gazed;
Most daintily on pampered turkeys dined,
Nor shrunk with fasting, nor with study pined;
Yet from their churches saw his brethren driven,
Who thundered truth and spoke the voice of heaven.
Chilled trembling guilt in Satan's headlong path,
Charmed the feet back, and roused the ear of death.
"Let fools," he cried, "slave on, while prudent I
Snug in my nest shall live and snug shall die."

The Country Pastor

Ah! knew he but his happiness, of men
Not the least happy he, who, free from broils
And bare ambition, vain and bustling, pomp,
Amid a friendly cure, and competence,
Tastes the pure pleasures of parochial life.
What though no crowd of clients, at his gate,
To falsehood and injustice bribe his tongue,
And flatter into guilt?—what though no bright
And gilded prospects lure ambition on
To legislative pride, or chair of state?
What though no golden dreams entice his mind
To burrow, with the mole, in dirt and mire?
What though no splendid villa, Edened round
With gardens of enchantment, walks of state,
And all the grandeur of superfluous wealth,
Invite the passenger to stay his steed,
And ask the liveried footboy, "Who dwells here?"

What though no swarms, around his sumptuous board,
Of soothing flatterers, humming in the shine
Of opulence, and honey from its flowers
Devouring, till their time arrives to sting,
Inflate his mind; his virtues round the year
Repeating, and his faults, with microscope
Inverted, lessen, till they steal from sight?—
Yet from the dire temptations these present
His state is free; temptations, few can stem;
Temptations, by whose sweeping torrent hurled
Down the dire steep of guilt, unceasing fall
Sad victims, thousands of the brightest minds
That time's dark reign adorn; minds, to whose grasp
Heaven seems most freely offered; to man's eye,
Most hopeful candidates for angels' joys.

    His lot, that wealth, and power, and pride forbids,
Forbids him to become the tool of fraud,
Injustice, misery, ruin: saves his soul
From all the needless labors, griefs, and cares,
That avarice and ambition agonize;
From those cold nerves of wealth, that, palsied, feel
No anguish but its own; and ceaseless lead
To thousand meannesses, as gain allures.

    Though oft compelled to meet the gross attack
Of shameless ridicule and towering pride,
Sufficient good is his; good, real, pure,
With guilt unmingled. Rarely forced from home,
Around his board his wife and children smile;
Communion sweetest, nature here can give,
Each fond endearment, office of delight,
With love and duty blending. Such the joy
My bosom oft has known. His, too, the task
To rear the infant plants that bud around;
To ope their little minds to truth's pure light;
To take them by the hand, and lead them on
In that straight, narrow road where virtue walks;
To guard them from a vain, deceiving world,
And point their course to realms of promised life.
His, too, the esteem of those who weekly hear
His words of truth divine; unnumbered acts
Of real love attesting to his eye
Their filial tenderness. Where'er he walks,

The friendly welcome and inviting smile
Wait on his steps, and breathe a kindred joy.
  Oft too in friendliest association joined,
He greets his brethren, with a flowing heart,
Flowing with virtue; all rejoiced to meet,
And all reluctant parting; every aim,
Benevolent, aiding with purpose kind;
While, seasoned with unblemished cheerfulness,
Far distant from the tainted mirth of vice,
Their hearts disclose each contemplation sweet
Of things divine; and blend in friendship pure,
Friendship sublimed by piety and love.
  All virtue's friends are his: the good, the just,
The pious, to his house their visits pay,
And converse high hold of the true, the fair,
The wonderful, the moral, the divine:
Of saints and prophets, patterns bright of truth,
Lent to a world of sin, to teach mankind
How virtue in that world can live and shine;
Of learning's varied realms; of Nature's works;
And that blessed book which gilds man's darksome
With light from heaven; of blessed Messiah's throne
And kingdom; prophecies divine fulfilled,
And prophecies more glorious yet to come
In renovated days; of that bright world,
And all the happy trains which that bright world
Inhabit, whither virtue's sons are gone:
While God the whole inspires, adorns, exalts;
The source, the end, the substance, and the soul.
  His too the task, the blessed, the useful task,
To invigor order, justice, law, and rule;
Peace to extend, and bid contention cease;
To teach the words of life; to lead mankind
Back from the wild of guilt and brink of wo
To virtue's house and family; faith, hope,
And joy to inspire; to warm the soul
With love to God and man; to cheer the sad,
To fix the doubting, rouse the languid heart;
The wandering to restore; to spread with down
The thorny bed of death; console the poor,
Departing mind, and aid its lingering wing.
  To him her choicest pages Truth expands,

Unceasing, where the soul-entrancing scenes
Poetic fiction boasts are real all:
Where beauty, novelty, and grandeur wear
Superior charms, and moral worlds unfold
Sublimities transporting and divine.

　　Not all the scenes Philosophy can boast,
Though them with nobler truths he ceaseless blends,
Compare with these. They, as they found the mind,
Still leave it; more informed, but not more wise:
These wiser, nobler, better, make the man.

　　Thus every happy mean of solid good
His life, his studies, and profession yield.
With motives hourly new, each rolling day
Allures, through wisdom's path and truth's fair field,
His feet to yonder skies. Before him heaven
Shines bright, the scope sublime of all his prayers,
The meed of every sorrow, pain, and toil.

Chamouni At Sunrise *
Translated from Frederike Brün

From the deep shadow of the still fir-groves
Trembling I look to thee, eternal height!
Thou dazzling summit, from whose top my soul
Floats, with dimmed vision, to the infinite!

Who sank in earth's firm lap the pillars deep
Which hold through ages thy vast pile in place?
Who reared on high, in the clear ether's vault,
Lofty and strong, thy ever-radiant face!

Who poured you forth, ye mountain torrents wild,
Down thundering from eternal winter's breast?
And who commanded, with almighty voice,
"Here let the stiffening billows find their rest"?

Who points to yonder morning-star his path,
Borders with wreaths of flowers the eternal frost?
To whom, in awful music, cries the stream,
O wild Arveiron! in fierce tumult tossed?

Jehovah! God! bursts from the crashing ice;
The avalanche thunders down the steeps the call:

Jehovah! rustle soft the bright tree-tops,
Whisper the silver brooks that murmuring fall.

*(See also S. T. Coleridge's "Hymn Before Sunrise in the Vale of Chamouni.")

WHEATLEY, PHILLIS (1753–1784), born in Africa, was brought to America at the age of seven in a boatload of slave girls. The ship unloaded its "cargo" in Boston, where she was sold to a tailor, John Wheatley, who educated her with his family. Mrs. Wheatley soon recognized Phillis's abilities, and made studying her chief duty—she learned Latin and Greek as well as English. She began to write poetry in her teens. When she was eighteen she travelled to London and there published *Poems on Various Subjects, Religious and Moral* (1773). Back in the United States, after her master amd mistress died, she was apparently freed by the heirs. She married another freed slave, John Peters. She died at the age of thirty-one. *Memoirs and Poems of Phillis Wheatley* was published in 1834. A volume of her letters was published in 1864. *A Life and Works of Phillis Wheatley* was published in 1916, including biography, letters, and her known poems. Her poetry covers a range of traditional English genres, and uses imagery from classical, Christian, and contemporary sources. It serves a double purpose in this anthology—illustrating both the birth of African-American writing in English and a style of poetry that flourished in colonial America during the period before the Revolution.

On Being Brought From Africa to America

Twas mercy brought me from my Pagan land,
Taught my benighted soul to understand
That there's a God, that there's a Saviour too.
Once I redemption neither sought nor knew.
Some view our sable race with scornful eye;
"Their colour is a diabolic dye."
Remember, Christians, Negroes, black as Cain,*
May be refined, and join the angelic train.

*Note: That an educated slave would believe that Cain was black—and apparently that the mark of Cain was dark skin—shows the degree to which a false theology in support of racial slavery was in place in America before the Revolution—not only in the South, but in "enlightened" Boston.

On the Death of the Rev. Mr. George Whitefield, 1770

Hail, happy saint, on thine immortal throne,
Possest of glory, life and bliss unknown;
We hear no more the music of thy tongue,
Thy wonted auditories cease to throng.
Thy sermons in unequaled accents flow'd,
And ev'ry bosom with devotion glow'd;
Thou didst in strains of eloquence refin'd
Inflame the heart and captivate the mind.
Unhappy we the setting sun deplore,
So glorious once, but ah! it shines no more.

Behold the prophet in his tow'ring flight!
He leaves the earth for heav'n's unmeasured height,
And worlds unknown receive him from our sight.
There Whitefield wings with rapid course his way,
And sails to Zion through vast seas of day.
Thy pray'rs, great saint, and thine incessant cries
Have pierc'd the bosom of thy native skies.
Thou, moon, hast seen and all the stars of light,
How he has wrestled with his God by night.
He pray'd that grace in ev'ry heart might dwell.
He long'd to see America excel:
He charg'd its youth that ev'ry grace divine
Should with full lustre in their conduct shine:
That Saviour, which his soul did first receive,
The greatest gift that ev'n a God can give,
He freely offer'd to the num'rous throng,
That on his lips with list'ning pleasure hung.

"Take him, ye wretched, for your only good,
"Take him, ye starving sinners, for your food.
"Ye thrifty, come to this life-giving stream,
"Ye preachers, take him for your joyful theme;
"Take him, my dear Americans," he said,
"Be your complaints on his kind bosom laid;
"Take him, ye Africans, he longs for you.
"Impartial Saviour is his title due;
"Washed in the fountain of redeeming blood,
"You shall be sons and kings. and Priests to God."

Great Countess,* we Americans revere
Thy name, and mingle in thy grief sincere;
New England deeply feels, the Orphans mourn,
Their more than father will no more return.
But, though arrested by the hand of death,
Whitefield no more exerts his lab'ring breath,
Yet let us view him in th' eternal skies.
Let ev'ry heart to this bright vision rise
While the tomb safe retains its sacred trust,
Till life divine re-animates his dust.

*The Countess of Huntingdon, to whom Mr. Whitefield was chaplain.

On the Death of a Young Gentleman

Who taught thee conflict with the pow'rs of night,
To vanquish Satan in the fields of fight?
Who strung thy feeble arms with might unknown,
How great thy conquest, and how bright thy crown!
War with each princedom, throne and pow'r is o'er,
The scene is ended to return no more.
O, could my muse thy seat on high behold,
How decked with laurel, how enrich'd with gold!
O could she bear what praise thine harp employs,
How sweet thine anthems, how divine thy joys!
What heav'nly grandeur should exalt her strain!
What holy raptures in her numbers reign!
To soothe the troubles of the mind to peace,
To still the tumult of life's tossing seas,
To ease the anguish of the parent heart.
What shall my sympathizing verse impart?
Where is the balm to heal so deep a wound?
Where shall a sovereign remedy be found?
Look, gracious Spirit, from thine heav'nly bow'r,
And thy full joys into their bosoms pour;
The raging tempest of their grief control,
And spread the dawn of glory through the soul,
To eye the path the saint departed trod,
And trace him to the bosom of his God.

To the Rev. Dr. Thomas Amory,
on Reading His Sermons on Daily Devotion,
in Which that Duty is Recommended and Assisted

To cultivate in ev'ry noble mind
Habitual grace, and sentiments refin'd,
Thus while you strive to mend the human heart,
Thus while the heav'nly precepts you impart,
O may each bosom catch the sacred fire,
And youthful minds to Virtue's throne aspire!
When God's eternal ways you set in sight
And virtue shines in all her native light,
In vain would Vice her works in night conceal.
For Wisdom's eye pervades the sable veil.

Artists may paint the sun's effulgent rays,
But Amory's pen the brighter God displays;
While his great works in Amory's pages shine.
And while he proves his essence all divine,
The Atheist sure no more can boast aloud
Of chance, or nature, and exclude the God;
As if the clay without the potter's aid
Should rise in various forms, and shapes self-made,
Or worlds above with orb o'er orb profound
Self-mov'd could run the everlasting round.
It cannot be—unerring Wisdom guides
With eye propitious, and o'er all presides.
Still prosper, Amory! still may'st thou receive
The warmest blessings that a muse can give,
And when this transitory fate is o'er,
When kingdoms fall, and fleeting Fame's no more,
May Amory triumph in immortal fame,
A nobler title, and superior name!

Excerpt from **Thoughts on the Works of Providence**

As reason's pow'rs by day our God disclose,
So we may trace him in the night's repose:
Say what is sleep? and dreams how passing strange!
When action ceases, and ideas range
Licentious and unbounded o'er the plains,
Where Fancy's queen in giddy triumph reigns,
Hear in soft strains the dreaming lover sigh

To a kind fair, or rave in jealousy;
On pleasure now, and now on vengeance bent,
The lab'ring passions struggle for a vent.
What pow'r, O man! thy reason then restores,
So long suspended in nocturnal hours?
What secret hand returns the mental train.
And gives improv'd thine active pow'rs again?
From thee, O man, what gratitude should rise
And, when from balmy sleep thou op'st thine eyes,
Let thy first thoughts be praises to the skies.
How merciful our God who thus imparts
O'erflowing tides of joy to human hearts,
When wants and woes might be our righteous lot,
Our God forgetting, by our God forgot!

    Among the mental pow'rs a question rose,
"What most the image of th' Eternal shows?"
When thus to Reason (so let Fancy rove)
Her great companion spoke immortal Love:

    "Say, mighty pow'r, how long shall strife prevail.
"And with its murmurs load the whispering gale?
"Refer the cause to Recollection's shrine,
"Who loud proclaims my origin divine,
"The cause whence heav'n and earth began to be,
"And is not man immortaliz'd by me?
"Reason, let this most causeless strife subside."

    Thus Love pronounced. and Reason thus repli'd:
    "Thy birth, celestial queen! 'tis mine to own,
"In thee resplendent is the Godhead shown;
"Thy words persuade, my soul enraptured feels
"Resistless beauty which thy smile reveals."
Ardent she spoke, and, kindling at her charms.
She clasp'd the blooming goddess in her arms.

    Infinite Love where'er we turn our eyes
Appears: this ev'ry creature's wants supplies;
This most is heard in Nature's constant voice,
This makes the morn, and this the eve rejoice;
This bids the fost'ring rains and dews descend
To nourish all, to serve one gen'ral end.
The good of man: yet man ungrateful pays
But little homage, and but little praise.
To him, whose works array'd with mercy shine,
What songs should rise, how constant, how divine!

CRABBE, GEORGE (1754-1832), apprenticed to a doctor when fourteen, became a village surgeon. He fell in love with a Sarah Elmy, who inspired a number of poems, but since his practice profited little and she would not marry him pennyless, he went to London in 1780. There he tried to gain recognition for his writing. Although Crabbe was a complete stranger to him, Burke responded to a desperate letter, supported him and helped him publish *The Library* in 1781. At Burke's advice and through his influence, Crabbe became a priest in his home-town (1782), and later chaplain to the Duke of Rutland. He published *The Village* in 1783, which Johnson praised and corrected in a minor way before it was published. The same year he married Sarah Elmy. In 1785 he published *Newspaper*, after which there were twenty-two years in which he published nothing. He had a system of periodic "incremations," in which he burned his accumulated manuscripts. Among the works thus destroyed were an *Essay on Botany* (a college official at Cambridge had protested against publishing an English book on such a subject), and three novels. Not only did Crabbe have health problems, but five out of seven of his children died. Towards the end of his life he apparently became addicted to opium. He was an "old-fashioned" clergyman, friend to the poor, and a preacher of homespun morality, but he cared little for "theological speculations" and thought little of "enthusiasts," heartily opposing "Wesleyans, evangelicals and other troublesome innovators." (*Dictionary of National Biography*) *The Parish Register* was finished in 1806 after eight years work. *Tales of Verse* was published in 1812. By 1817, when Crabbe visited London, he was famous. In 1819 he published *Tales of the Hall.* The "realism" of Crabbe's poetry, a harbinger of the romantic movement, preceded Cowper's and Wordsworth's. His work has been praised by Sir Walter Scott, William Wordsworth, Edward Fitzgerald, and John Henry Newman.

Resurrection

The wintry winds have ceased to blow,
And trembling leaves appear;
And fairest flowers succeed the snow,
And hail the infant year.

So, when the world and all its woes
Are vanish'd far away,
Fair scenes and wonderful repose
Shall bless the new-born day,—

When, from the confines of the grave,
The body too shall rise;
No more precarious passion's slave,
Nor error's sacrifice.

'Tis but a sleep—and Sion's king
Will call the many dead:
'Tis but a sleep—and then we sing,
O'er dreams of sorrow fled.

Yes!—wintry winds have ceased to blow,
And trembling leaves appear,
And Nature has her types to show
Throughout the varying year.

ADAMS, JOHN QUINCY (1767–1848) was born in Braintree, Massachusetts, son of John Adams, the second president of the United States. He served as a senator from Massachusetts and in several ministerial posts. As Secretary of State (1817-25) under James Monroe he was largely responsible for enunciating the Monroe Doctrine, stipulating US interest in preventing all foreign invasions of the Western Hemisphere. He became the sixth president of the United States in 1825, and, although his administration was unspectacular, he went on to serve effectively as a Representative from Massachusetts from 1831 to 1848 in which office he actively opposed slavery. He has been cited as one of the most learned men of his time and something of a poet. Among his poems are "Oberon, translated from the German of Wieland" and "Dermot McMorrogh, or the Conquest of Ireland." His *Poems of Religion and Society*, a collection of hymns and other short pieces, with notices of his life and character, was published after his death. He died in the capitol, at Washington.

To A Bereaved Mother

Sure, to the mansions of the blest
When infant innocence ascends,
Some angel brighter than the rest
The spotless spirit's flight attends.
On wings of ecstasy they rise,
Beyond where worlds material roll,
Till some fair sister of the skies
Receives the unpolluted soul.

That inextinguishable beam,
With dust united at our birth,
Sheds a more dim, discolored gleam
The more it lingers upon earth.
Closed in this dark abode of clay,

The stream of glory faintly burns:—
Not unobserved, the lucid ray
To its own native fount returns.

But when the Lord of mortal breath
Decrees his bounty to resume,
And points the silent shaft of death
Which speeds an infant to the tomb—
No passion fierce, nor low desire,
Has quenched the radiance of the flame;
Back to its God the living fire
Reverts, unclouded as it came.

Fond mourner! be that solace thine!
Let hope her healing charm impart,
And soothe, with melodies divine,
The anguish of a mother's heart.
O, think! the darlings of thy love,
Divested of this earthly clod,
Amid unnumbered saints above,
Bask in the bosom of their God.

Of their short pilgrimage on earth
Still tender images remain:
Still, still they bless thee for their birth,
Still filial gratitude retain.
Each anxious care, each rending sigh,
That wrung for them the parent's breast,
Dwells on remembrance in the sky,
Amid the raptures of the blest.

O'er thee, with looks of love, they bend
For thee the Lord of life implore;
And oft, from sainted bliss descend,
Thy wounded quiet to restore.
Oft, in the stillness of the night
They smooth the pillow of thy bed;
Oft, till the morn's returning light,
Still watchful hover o'er thy head.

Hark! in such strains as saints employ,
They whisper to thy bosom peace;
Calm the perturbed heart to joy,
And bid the streaming sorrow cease.

Then dry, henceforth, the bitter tear;
Their part and thine inverted see:—
Thou wert their guardian angel here,
They guardian angels now to thee.

Lord Of All Worlds

Lord of all worlds, let thanks and praise
To thee forever fill my soul;
With blessings thou hast crowned my days,
My heart, my head, my hand control:
O, let no vain presumptions rise,
No impious murmur in my heart,
To crave the boon thy will denies,
Or shrink from ill thy hands impart.

Thy child am I, and not an hour,
Revolving in the orbs above,
But brings some token of thy power,
But brings some token of thy love;
And shall this bosom dare repine,
In darkness dare deny the dawn,
Or spurn the treasures of the mine,
Because one diamond is withdrawn?

The fool denies, the fool alone,
Thy being, Lord, and boundless might;
Denies the firmament, thy throne,
Denies the sun's meridian light;
Denies the fashion of his frame,
The voice he hears, the breath he draws:
O idiot atheist! to proclaim
Effects unnumbered without cause!

Matter and mind, mysterious one,
Are man's for threescore years and, ten;
Where, ere the thread of life was spun?
Where, when reduced to dust again?
All-seeing God, the doubt suppress;
The doubt then only canst relieve
My soul thy Saviour-Son shall bless,
Fly to thy gospel, and believe.

Why Should I Fear In Evil Days

Why should I fear in evil days
With snares encompassed all around?
What trust can transient treasures raise
For them in riches who abound?
His brother who from death can save?
What wealth can ransom him from God?
What mine of gold defraud the grave?
What hoards but vanish at his nod?

To live forever is their dream;
Their houses by their name they call;
While, borne by time's relentless stream,
Around them wise and foolish fall;
Their riches others must divide;
They plant, but others reap the fruit:
In honor man cannot abide,
To death devoted, like the brute.

This is their folly, this their way;
And yet in this their sons delight;
Like sheep, of death the destined prey,
The future scorn of the upright;
The grave their beauty shall consume,
Their dwellings never see them more;
But God shall raise me from the tomb,
And life for endless time restore.

What though thy foe in wealth increase,
And fame and glory crown his head?
Fear not, for all at death shall cease,
Nor fame, nor glory, crown the dead:
While prospering all around thee smiled,
Yet to the grave shalt thou descend;
The senseless pride of fortune's child
Shall share the brute creation's end.

KELLY, THOMAS (1769–1854), son of an Irish judge was born in County Queens and educated at Trinity College, Dublin. He originally planned to become a lawyer, but his evangelical faith led him to be ordained in 1792. He preached in Dublin where his strong emphasis on justification by faith put him at odds with the Anglican Archbishop, who barred him from all the pulpits. He continued to preach, however, in independent churches, a number of which he eventually established himself. He was a popular preacher, especially among the poor to whom he was both a physical and spiritual support, especially during the famine of 1847. A poor Dubliner is quoted as saying to his wife, "Hold up, Bridget! Bedad, there's always Mr. Kelly to pull us out of the bog after we've sunk for the last time." He wrote nearly eight hundred hymns, several of which are still found in our hymnals. His *Hymns on Various Passages of Scripture* was first issued in 1804.

The Head That Once Was Crowned With Thorns

The head that once was crowned with thorns
Is crowned with glory now:
A royal diadem adorns
The mighty victor's brow.

The highest place that heaven affords
Is his, is his by right,
The King of kings and Lord of lords,
And heaven's eternal Light;

The joy of all who dwell above,
The joy of all below,
To whom he manifests his love,
And grants his name to know.

To them the Cross, with all its shame,
With all its grace, is given.
Their name an everlasting name,
Their joy the joy of heaven.

They suffer with their Lord below,
They reign with him above,
Their profit and their joy to know
The mystery of his love.

The cross he bore is life and health,
Though shame and death to him;
His people's hope, his people's wealth,
Their everlasting theme.

The Second Advent

Look, ye saints! The sight is glorious:
See the Man of Sorrows now;
From the fight returned victorious,
Every knee to him shall bow
Crown Him! Crown Him! Crown Him! Crown Him!
Crowns become the Victor's brow.

Crown the Saviour! Angels crown Him!
Rich the trophies Jesus brings;
In the seat of power enthrone Him,
While the vault of heaven rings:
Crown Him! Crown Him! Crown Him! Crown Him!
Crown the Saviour King of kings.

Sinners in derision crowned Him,
Mocking thus the Saviour's claim;
Saints and angels crowd around Him,
Own His title, praise His name:
Crown Him! Crown Him! Crown Him! Crown Him!
Spread abroad the Victor's fame.

Hark, those bursts of acclamation!
Hark, those loud triumphant chords!
Jesus takes the highest station;
O what joy the sight affords!
Crown Him! Crown Him! Crown Him! Crown Him!
King of kings, and Lord of lords!

We Sing Praise Of Him Who Died.

We sing praise of him who died.
Of him who died upon the cross,
The sinner's hope let men deride,
For this we count the world but loss.

Inscribed upon the cross we see
In shining letters, 'God is Love'.
He bears our sins upon the tree;
He brings us mercy from above.

The cross! it takes our guilt away;
It holds the fainting spirit up;

It cheers with hope the gloomy day,
And sweetens every bitter cup.

It makes the coward spirit brave,
And nerves the feeble arm for fight;
It takes its terror from the grave,
And gilds the bed of death with light;

The balm of life, the cure of woe,
The measure and the pledge of love,
The sinners' refuge here below,
The angels' theme in heaven above.

WORDSWORTH, WILLIAM (1770–1850), generally recognized as the foremost romantic poet, was educated at Cambridge and travelled in Europe where he fell in love with the Revolution—and a French girl, who had a daughter by him. After going back to England, he intended to return to France, but was prevented by the outbreak of war between the two countries. He had been politically sympathetic with the French Revolution and was deeply disillusioned by the British opposition to the Republic. He turned for a time to the philosophy of William Godwin (the poet Shelley's father-in-law, who, rejecting God, held that man could solve his problems by the exercise of reason). He received a legacy in 1795 that allowed him to settle down near Coleridge, who became the biggest influence in his literary life. With Coleridge, Wordsworth published *Lyrical Ballads* in 1798, and with the second edition (1800–01), the Preface, which was the manifesto of the romantic movement. He went to Germany for a year, after which he settled in the Lake District with his sister Dorothy. In 1802, after making a settlement with the French woman who bore his child, he married Mary Hutchinson. He gradually turned against revolutionary politics largely because of the excesses of the French Republic and Napoleon's dictatorship. He became poet laureate in 1843, succeeding Southey. Although he wrote in positive terms about elements of Roman Catholic tradition, he opposed various liberal reforms including Catholic emancipation. Wordsworth's brother and his nephew (both named Christopher) became Anglican clergymen. Wordsworth, like Coleridge, seems to have become increasingly orthodox on philosophical and spiritual issues later in life. However, we have few expressions of his beliefs apart from his poetry.

For Inspiration
From the Italian of Michelangelo Buonarroti

The prayers I make will then be sweet indeed,
If Thou the spirit give by which I pray;

My unassisted heart is barren clay,
Which of its native self can nothing feed;

Of good and pious works Thou art the seed
Which quickens where Thou say'st it may;
Unless Thou show us then Thine own true way,
No man can find it! Father, Thou must lead!

Do Thou, then, breathe those thoughts into my mind
By which such virtue may in me be bred
That in Thy holy footsteps I may tread;
The fetters of my tongue do Thou unbind,
That I may have the power to sing of Thee
And sound Thy praises everlastingly.

Hymn—Blest Are The Moments, Doubly Blest

Blest are the moments, doubly blest,
That, drawn from this one hour of rest,
Are with a ready heart bestowed
Upon the service of our God!

Each field is then a hallowed spot,
An altar is in each man's cot,
A church in every grove that spreads
Its living roof above our heads.

Look up to heaven! the industrious sun
Already half his race hath run;
He cannot halt or go astray.
But our immortal spirits may.

Lord, since his rising in the east,
If we have faltered or transgressed,
Guide, from thy love's abundant source,
What yet remains of this day's course;

Help with thy grace, through life's short day,
Our upward and our downward way;
And glorify for us the west,
When we shall sink to final rest.

Ninth Evening Voluntary
Composed upon an evening of extraordinary splendour and beauty

I.

Had this effulgence disappeared
With flying haste, I might have sent
Among the speechless clouds a look
Of blank astonishment;
But 'tis endued with power to stay,
And sanctify one closing day,
That frail Mortality may see—
What is?—ah no, but what can be!
Time was when field and watery cove
With modulated echoes rang,
While choirs of fervent angels sang
Their vespers in the grove;
Or, crowning, star-like, each some sovereign height,
Warbled, for heaven above and earth below,
Strains suitable to both.—Such holy rite,
Methinks, if audibly repeated now
From hill or valley could not move
Sublimer transport, purer love,
Than doth this silent spectacle—the gleam—
The shadow—and the peace supreme!

II.

No sound is uttered,—but a deep
And solemn harmony pervades
The hollow vale from steep to steep,
And penetrates the glades.
Far distant images draw nigh,
Called forth by wondrous potency
Of beamy radiance, that imbues
Whate'er it strikes with gem-like hues.
In vision exquisitely clear,
Herds range along the mountain side,
And glistening antlers are descried,
And gilded flocks appear.
Thine is the tranquil hour, purpureal Eve!
But long as godlike wish or hope divine
Informs my spirit, ne'er can I believe
That this magnificence is wholly thine!
From worlds nor quickened by the sun

A portion of the gift is won;
An intermingling of heaven's pomp is spread
On ground which British shepherds tread!

III.

And if there be whom broken ties
Afflict, or injuries assail,
Yon hazy ridges to their eyes
Present a glorious scale
Climbing suffused with sunny air,
To stop—no record hath told where;
And tempting Fancy to ascend,
And with immortal spirits blend!
—Wings at my shoulders seem to play!
But rooted here, I stand and gaze
On those bright steps that heavenward raise
Their practicable way.
Come forth, ye drooping old men, look abroad,
And see to what fair countries ye are bound!
And if some traveller, weary of his road,
Hath slept since noontide on the grassy ground,
Ye genii, to his covert speed,
And wake him with such gentle heed
As may attune his soul to meet the dower
Bestowed on this transcendent hour.

IV.

Such hues from their celestial urn
Were wont to stream before mine eye
Where'er it wandered in the morn
Of blissful infancy.
This glimpse of glory, why renewed?
Nay, rather speak with gratitude;
For, if a vestige of those gleams
Survived, 'twas only in my dreams.
Dread Power! whom peace and calmness serve
No less than nature's threatening voice,
If aught unworthy be my choice,
From THEE if I would swerve;
Oh, let thy grace remind me of the light
Full early lost, and fruitlessly deplored;
Which, at this moment, on my waking sight

Appears to shine, by miracle restored:
My soul, though yet confined to earth,
Rejoices in a second birth!
—'Tis past; the visionary splendour fades
And night approaches with her shades.

London, 1802
(Immediately following a return from France)

O Friend! I know not which way I must look
For comfort, being, as I am, opprest
To think that now our life is only drest
For show-mean handiwork of craftsman, cook,
Or groom!—We must run glittering like a brook
In the open sunshine, or we are unblest;
The wealthiest man among us is the best.
No grandeur now in nature or in book
Delights us. Rapine, avarice, expense,
This is idolatry; and these we adore—
Plain living and high thinking are no more.
The homely beauty of the good old cause
Is gone; our peace, our fearful innocence,
And pure religion breathing household laws.

Written In Early Spring

I heard a thousand blended notes
While in a grove I sate reclined,
In that sweet mood when pleasant thoughts
Bring sad thoughts to the mind.

To her fair works did Nature link
The human soul that through me ran;
And much it grieved my heart to think
What man has made of man.

Through primrose tufts, in that sweet bower,
The periwinkle trail'd its wreaths;
And 'tis my faith that every flower
Enjoys the air it breathes.

The birds around me hopp'd and play'd,
Their thoughts I cannot measure,

But the least motion which they made
It seem'd a thrill of pleasure.

The budding twigs spread out their fan
To catch the breezy air;
And I must think, do all I can,
That there was pleasure there.

If this belief from Heaven be sent,
If such be Nature's holy plan,
Have I not reason to lament
What man has made of man?

After-Thought
(Sonnet XV in Memorials of a Tour of the Continent)

O Life! without thy chequered scene
Of right and wrong, of weal and woe,
Success and failure, could a ground
For magnanimity be found;
For faith, 'mid ruined hopes, serene?
Or whence could virtue flow?

Pain entered through a ghastly breach—
Nor while sin lasts must effort cease;
Heaven upon earth 's an empty boast;
But, for the bowers of Eden lost,
Mercy has placed within our reach
A portion of God's peace.

The World Is Too Much With Us; Late and Soon

The world is too much with us: late and soon,
Getting and spending, we lay waste our powers:
Little we see in Nature that is ours;
We have given our hearts away, a sordid boon!
This sea that bares her bosom to the moon;
The winds that will be howling at all hours,
And are up-gathered now like sleeping flowers;
For this, for everything we are out of tune;
It moves us not.—Great God! I'd rather be
A Pagan suckled in a creed outworn;
So might I, standing on this pleasant lea,

Have glimpses that would make me less forlorn;
Have sight of Proteus rising from the sea,
Or hear old Triton blow his wreathed horn.

Excerpt from **Ode, Intimations of Immortality**

The thought of our past years in me doth breed
Perpetual benediction: not indeed
For that which is most worthy to be blest,
Delight and liberty, the simple creed
Of childhood, whether busy or at rest,
With new-fledged hope still fluttering in his breast:—
Not for these I raise
The song of thanks and praise;
But for those obstinate questionings
Of sense and outward things,
Fallings from us, vanishings;
Blank misgivings of a creature
Moving about in worlds not realized,
High instincts, before which our mortal nature
Did tremble like a guilty thing surprised:
But for those first affections,
Those shadowy recollections,
Which, be they what they may,
Are yet the fountain-light of all our day,
Are yet a master-light of all our seeing;
Uphold us, cherish, and have power to make
Our noisy years seem moments in the being
Of the eternal Silence: truths that wake,
To perish never;
Which neither listlessness, nor mad endeavour,
Nor man nor boy,
Nor all that is at enmity with joy,
Can utterly abolish or destroy!
Hence, in a season of calm weather,
Though inland far we be,
Our souls have sight of that immortal sea
Which brought us hither:
Can in a moment travel thither—
And see the children sport upon the shore,
And hear the mighty waters rolling evermore.

Then sing, ye birds, sing, sing a joyous song!
And let the young lambs bound
As to the tabor's sound!
We, in thought, will join your throng,
Ye that pipe and ye that play,
Ye that through your hearts to-day
Feel the gladness of the May!
What though the radiance which was once so bright
Be now for ever taken from my sight,
Though nothing can bring back the hour
Of splendour in the grass, of glory in the flower;
We will grieve not, rather find
Strength in what remains behind;
In the primal sympathy,
Which having been must ever be;
In the soothing thoughts that spring
Out of human suffering;
In the faith that looks through death;
In years that bring the philosophic mind.
And, O ye Fountains, Meadows, Hills, and Groves,
Forbode not any severing of our loves!
Yet in my heart of hearts I feel your might;
I only have relinquish'd one delight
To live beneath your more habitual sway:
I love the brooks which down their channels fret
Even more than when I tripp'd lightly as they;
The innocent brightness of a new-born day
Is lovely yet;
The clouds that gather round the setting sun
Do take a sober colouring from an eye
That hath kept watch o'er man's mortality;
Another race hath been, and other palms are won.
Thanks to the human heart by which we live,
Thanks to its tenderness, its joys and fears,
To me the meanest flower that blows can give
Thoughts that do often lie too deep for tears.

Hymn For The Boatmen,
As They Approach The Rapids Under The Castle Of Heidelberg

Jesu! bless our slender Boat,
By the current swept along;

Loud its threatenings—let them not
Drown the music of a song
Breathed thy mercy to implore,
Where these troubled waters roar!

Saviour, for our warning, seen
Bleeding on that precious Rood;
If, while through the meadows green
Gently wound the peaceful flood,
We forgot Thee, do not Thou
Disregard thy Suppliants now!

Hither, like yon ancient Tower
Watching o'er the River's bed,
Fling the shadow of thy power,
Else we sleep among the dead;
Thou who trod'st the billowy sea,
Shield us in our jeopardy!

Guide our Bark among the waves;
Through the rocks our passage smooth;
Where the whirlpool frets and raves
Let thy love its anger soothe:
All our hope is placed in Thee;
Miserere Domine!

The Point At Issue
Sonnet XXX of Part One, Ecclesiastical Sonnets

For what contend the wise?—for nothing less
Than that the Soul, freed from the bonds of Sense,
And to her God restored by evidence
Of things not seen, drawn forth from their recess,
Root there, and not in forms, her holiness;—
For Faith, which to the Patriarchs did dispense
Sure guidance, ere a ceremonial fence
Was needful round men thirsting to transgress;—
For Faith, more perfect still, with which the Lord
Of all, himself a Spirit, in the youth
Of Christian aspiration, deigned to fill
The temples of their hearts who, with his word
Informed, were resolute to do his will,
And worship him in spirit and in truth.

Funeral Service
Sonnet XXI from Ecclesiastical Sonnets, Part Three

From the Baptismal hour, thro' weal and woe,
The Church extends her care to thought and deed;
Nor quits the Body when the Soul is freed,
The mortal weight cast off to be laid low.
Blest Rite for him who hears in faith,
"I know That my Redeemer liveth,"—hears each word
That follows—striking on some kindred chord
Deep in the thankful heart;—yet tears will flow.
Man is as grass that springeth up at morn,
Grows green, and is cut down and withereth
Ere nightfall—truth that well may claim a sigh,
Its natural echo; but hope comes reborn
At Jesu's bidding. We rejoice, "O Death,
Where is thy Sting?—O Grave, where is thy Victory?"

Obligations Of Civil To Religious Liberty
Sonnet X from Ecclesiastical Sonnets, Part Three

Ungrateful Country, if thou e'er forget
The sons who for thy civil rights have bled!
How, like a Roman, Sidney bowed his head,
And Russel's milder blood the scaffold wet;
But these had fallen for profitless regret
Had not thy holy Church her champions bred,
And claims from other worlds inspirited
The star of Liberty to rise. Nor yet
(Grave this within thy heart!) if spiritual things
Be lost, through apathy, or scorn, or fear,
Shalt thou thy humbler franchises support,
However hardly won or justly dear:
What came from heaven to heaven by nature clings,
And, if dissevered thence, its course is short.

My Heart Leaps Up

My heart leaps up when I behold
A rainbow in the sky:
So was it when my life began,
So is it now I am a man,
So be it when I shall grow old

Or let me die!
The child is father of the man:
And I could wish my days to be
Bound each to each by natural piety.

A Gravestone Upon The Floor
In The Cloisters Of Worcester Cathedral

"MISERRIMUS," and neither name nor date,
Prayer, text, or symbol, graven upon the stone;
Nought but that word assigned to the unknown,
That solitary word—to separate
From all, and cast a cloud around the fate
Of him who lies beneath. Most wretched one,
Who chose his epitaph?—Himself alone
Could thus have dared the grave to agitate,
And claim, among the dead, this awful crown;
Nor doubt that He marked also for his own
Close to these cloistral steps a burial-place,
That every foot might fall with heavier tread,
Trampling upon his vileness. Stranger, pass
Softly!—To save the contrite, Jesus bled.

At Florence—From Michael Angelo
Sonnet XXII from Memorials of a Tour of Italy

Eternal Lord! eased of a cumbrous load,
And loosened from the world, I turn to Thee;
Shun, like a shattered bark, the storm, and flee
To thy protection for a safe abode.
The crown of thorns, hands pierced upon the tree,
The meek, benign, and lacerated face,
To a sincere repentance promise grace,
To the sad soul give hope of pardon free.
With justice mark not Thou, O Light divine,
My fault, nor hear it with thy sacred ear;
Neither put forth that way thy arm severe;
Wash with thy blood my sins; thereto incline
More readily the more my years require
Help, and forgiveness speedy and entire.

See the Condemned Alone Within His Cell
Sonnet XII from The Punishment of Death Series

See the Condemned alone within his cell
And prostrate at some moment when remorse
Stings to the quick, and, with resistless force,
Assaults the pride she strove in vain to quell.
Then mark him, him who could so long rebel,
The crime confessed, a kneeling Penitent
Before the Altar, where the Sacrament
Softens his heart, till from his eyes outwell
Tears of salvation. Welcome death! while Heaven
Does in this change exceedingly rejoice;
While yet the solemn heed the State hath given
Helps him to meet the last Tribunal's voice
In faith, which fresh offences, were he cast
On old temptations, might for ever blast.

MONTGOMERY, JAMES (1771–1854), son of a Moravian minister, first a
shop assistant, then a journalist, wrote twenty-two books of verse. He worked
for thirty-three years on a Sheffield paper, for thirty-one of them as editor. He
was twice imprisoned for things he printed. He delivered lectures on poetry at
Sheffield and the Royal Institute in London, and promoted Foreign Missions
and the Bible Society in many parts of the country. He received a royal pension
in 1833. His poetical works include *Greenland and Other Poems* (1819), *The
Christian Psalmist* (1825), *The Christian Poet* (1825), and *The Poet's Portfolio* (1835).
He also published *Original Hymns for Public, Private, and Social Devotion* (1853), for
many of which he is counted one of the better nineteenth century hymn-writers.

Prayer

Prayer is the soul's sincere desire,
Utter'd, or unexpress'd;
The motion of a hidden fire
That trembles in the breast.

Prayer is the burden of a sigh,
The falling of a tear,
The upward glancing of the eye,
When none but God is near.

Prayer is the simplest form of speech
That infant lips can try;

Prayer the sublimest strains that reach
The Majesty on high.

Prayer is the contrite sinners voice
Returning from his ways,
While angels in their songs rejoice,
And cry, Behold, he prays!

Prayer is the Christian's vital breath,
The Christian's native air;
His watchword at the gates of death;
He enters heaven with prayer.

The saints, in prayer, appear as one
In word, and deed, and mind;
While with the Father and the Son
Sweet fellowship they find.

Nor prayer is made by man alone:
The Holy Spirit pleads;
And Jesus, on the eternal throne
For mourners intercedes.

O Thou, by whom we come to God!
The Life, the Truth, the Way!
The path of prayer Thyself hast trod;
Lord, teach us how to pray!

Good Tidings Of Great Joy To All People

Angels from the realms of glory,
Wing your flight o'er all the earth;
Ye who sang creation's story
Now proclaim Messiah's birth;
Come and worship,
Worship Christ, the new-born King.

Shepherds, in the fields abiding,
Watching o'er your flocks by night,
God with man is now residing,
Yonder shines the infant-light;
Come and worship;
Worship Christ, the new-born King.

Sages, leave your contemplations,
Brighter visions beam afar;
Seek the great Desire of Nations;
Ye have seen His natal-star;
Come and worship;
Worship Christ, the new-born King.

Saints, before the altar bending,
Watching long in hope and fear,
Suddenly, the Lord descending,
In His temple shall appear,
Come and worship;
Worship Christ, the new-born King.

Sinners, wrung with true repentance,
Doomed, for guilt, to endless pains,
Justice now revokes the sentence,
Mercy calls you—break your chains;
Come and worship;
Worship Christ, the new-born King.

Come to Calvary's Holy Mountain

Come to Calvary's holy mountain,
Sinners ruined by the fall;
Here's a pure and healing fountain
Flows to you, to me, to all,
In a full, perpetual tide,
Opened when our Saviour died.

Come in poverty and meanness,
Come defiled, without, within;
From infections and uncleanness,
From the leprosy of sin,
Wash your robes, and make them white:
Ye shall walk with God in light.

Come, in sorrow and contrition,
Wounded, impotent, and blind;
Here the guilty, free remission,
Here the troubled, peace may find;
Health this fountain will restore,
He that drinks shall thirst no more.

He that drinks shall live forever;
'Tis a soul-renewing flood:
God is faithful, God will never
Break his covenant in blood;
Signed when our Redeemer died,
Sealed when He was glorified.

The Stranger And His Friend

A Poor wayfaring man of grief
Hath often crossed me on my way,
Who sued so humbly for relief,
That I could never answer, "Nay."
I had not power to ask his name,
Whither He went, or whence He came;
Yet there was something in his eye
That won my love,—I knew not why.

Once, when my scanty meal was spread,
He entered;—not a word He spake;
Just perishing for want of bread,
I gave Him all; He blessed it, brake,
And ate;—but gave me part again:
Mine was an angel's portion then,
For while I fed with eager haste,
That crust was manna to my taste.

I spied Him, where a fountain burst
Clear from the rock; his strength was gone:
The heedless water mocked his thirst:
He heard it, saw it hurrying on:
I ran to raise the sufferer up;
Thrice from the stream He drained my cup,
Dipped, and returned it running o'er;
I drank, and never thirsted more.

'Twas night; the floods were out,—it blew
A winter hurricane aloof;
I heard his voice abroad, and flew
To bid Him welcome to my roof;
I warmed, I clothed, I cheered my guest;
Laid Him on my own couch to rest;
Then made the earth my bed, and seemed
In Eden's garden while I dreamed.

Stripped, wounded, beaten nigh to death,
I found Him by the highway side;
I roused his pulse, brought back his breath,
Revived his spirit, and supplied
Wine, oil, refreshment; He was healed;
I had myself a wound concealed,
But from that hour forgot the smart,
And Peace bound up my broken heart.

In prison I saw Him next, condemned
To meet a traitor's doom at morn;
The tide of lying tongues I stemmed,
And honored Him midst shame and scorn:
 My friendship's utmost zeal to try,
He asked if I for Him would die;
The flesh was weak, my blood run chill,
But the free spirit cried, "I will."

Then in a moment to my view,
The stranger darted from disguise,
The tokens in his hands I knew,
My Saviour stood before mine eyes:
He spake; and my poor name He named,
"Of Me thou hast not been ashamed,
These deeds shall thy memorial be;
Fear not, thou didst them unto Me."

On The Loss Of Friends

Friend after friend departs;
Who hath not lost a friend?
There is no union here of hearts,
That finds not here an end!
Were this frail world our final rest,
Living, or dying, none were blest.

Beyond the flight of time,—
Beyond the reign of death,—
There surely is some blessed clime,
Where life is not a breath:
Nor life's affections transient fire,
Whose sparks fly upward and expire.

There is a world above,
Where parting is unknown,
A long eternity of love,
Formed for the good alone;
And faith beholds the dying here
Translated to that glorious sphere.

Thus star by star declines,
Till all are passed away;
As morning high and higher shines
To pure and perfect day:
Nor sink those stars in empty night,
But hide themselves in heaven's own light.

WORDSWORTH, DOROTHY (1771–1855), sister of William Wordsworth, is noted by one biographer as "the most distinguished of English writers who never wrote a line for the general public." (de Selincourt, *Life*, 1933). She spent her childhood as something of an orphan, separated from her three brothers, but settled with William in 1895 and spent the rest of her life with him, through the time he married and on to his death. Her journals are a great source of information about William and about S. T. Coleridge, to whom she was a close friend. William seems to have made use of her journals in some of his poetry. Very little of her poetry is extant. The poem included here is actually published in William's *Works*, with the notation indicating it is hers.

Loving And Liking

Irregular Verses Addressed To A Child (By My Sister)
Written at Rydal Mount. It arose, I believe, out of a casual expression
of one of Mr Swinburne's children.—William Wordsworth's note

There's more in words than I can teach:
Yet listen, Child!—I would not preach;
But only give some plain directions
To guide your speech and your affections
Say not you *love* a roasted fowl,
But you may love a screaming owl.
And, if you can, the unwieldy toad
That crawls from his secure abode
Within the mossy garden wall
When evening dews begin to fall.
Oh mark the beauty of his eye:
What wonders in that circle lie!

So clear, so bright, our fathers said
He wears a jewel in his head!
And when, upon some showery day,
Into a path or public way
A frog leaps out from bordering grass,
Startling the timid as they pass,
Do you observe him, and endeavour
To take the intruder into favour;
Learning from him to find a reason
For a light heart in a dull season.
And you may love him in the pool,
That is for him a happy school,
In which he swims as taught by nature,
Fit pattern for a human creature,
Glancing amid the water bright,
And sending upward sparkling light.
Nor blush if o'er your heart be stealing
A love for things that have no feeling:
The spring's first rose by you espied,
May fill your breast with joyful pride;
And you may love the strawberry-flower,
And love the strawberry in its bower;
But when the fruit, so often praised
For beauty, to your lip is raised,
Say not you *love* the delicate treat,
But *like* it, enjoy it, and thankfully eat.
Long may you love your pensioner mouse,
Though one of a tribe that torment the house:
Nor dislike for her cruel sport the cat,
Deadly foe both of mouse and rat;
Remember she follows the law of her kind,
And Instinct is neither wayward nor blind.
Then think of her beautiful gliding form,
Her tread that would scarcely crush a worm,
And her soothing song by the winter fire,
Soft as the dying throb of the lyre.
I would not circumscribe your love:
It may soar with the eagle and brood with the dove,
May pierce the earth with the patient mole,
Or track the hedgehog to his hole.
Loving and liking are the solace of life,
Rock the cradle of joy, smooth the deathbed of strife.

You love your father and your mother,
Your grown-up and your baby brother;
You love your sister, and your friends,
And countless blessings which God sends:
And while these right affections play,
You live each moment of your day;
They lead you on to full content,
And liking's fresh and innocent,
That store the mind, the memory feed,
And prompt to many a gentle deed:
But *likings* come, and pass away;
'T is *love* that remains till our latest day:
Our heavenward guide is holy love,
And will be our bliss with saints above.

COLERIDGE, SAMUEL TAYLOR (1772–1834), son of a vicar and school-master, went to Cambridge, which he left (under financial pressure) to enlist as a dragoon under a false name. After returning to Cambridge where the students were stirred by the French Revolution, Coleridge concluded with Robert Southey that small societies of right-minded people could provide an alternative to violent revolution. They outlined plans to establish a "pantisocracy" of 12 men and 12 women on the Susquehanna river in Pennsylvania. Partly at Southey's urging he married in 1795, and soon family economics began to take his attention. Coleridge continued to write—mostly politically oriented poems and essays. In 1797 he and William Wordsworth turned from politics to develop an informal poetry of the imagination. Thus his contributions to *Lyrical Ballads* in 1798. Under the influence of opium he wrote the famous "Kubla Khan," which has been seen as an expression of his view of the two sides of human "genius." "The Rime of the Ancient Mariner" and "Christobel" also express this view of the human spirit in ideas parallel to the New England Transcendentalists. (Emerson was to visit Coleridge later in London.) The latter poem emphasizes the two-sided nature of the life principle (a dualism similar to William Blake's). In 1798 he almost became a Unitarian minister, but the Wedgwood brothers offered him an annuity in order to let him pursue his intellectual concerns. He went to Germany with the Wordsworths where he attended lectures on physiology and biblical criticism at Gottingen. Returning to England he seems to have "fallen in love" with Sara Hutchinson, Wordsworth's future sister-in-law. Meanwhile his opium addiction was increasing and his health failing. In 1804, his health bad, he accepted a post as secretary to the governor of Malta. After returning to England, he separated from his wife and family, who ended up under the care of Southey. He set to work on a periodical oriented toward political and human principles, with Sara Hutchinson as his amanuensis. The strain of their relationship was too much for her, however, and she left for Wales at Wordsworth's encouragement. Coleridge then settled in London, where he went through a dark period of heavy opium use and self-pity. He began to profit from a growing interest in the arts, however, and in 1811-12 gave a series of popular lectures. His psychological approach to Shakespeare's characters was new and exciting to his hearers. His opium habit was dominating his life until, at the home of friends, he read a commentary on I Peter by the 17th century archbishop Robert Leighton. He seems to have undergone a Christian conversion, with a marked shift in outlook thereafter. In 1822, under urging to help those troubled by the scepticism of the age, he began his "Thursday evening classes," which over the years were attended by many young men. Among other distinguished visitors, James Fenimore Cooper called on him in London. Coleridge wrote mostly prose works in his later years, including works on church and state and a major work, never completed, discussing the idea that the *logos* of God was the ultimate key to knowledge of the universe. He influenced not only Wordsworth, but Keats, Byron, and Shelley. Victorian Christians had a variety of responses to him. Some were sceptical of a Christian faith based on a set of symbols. Newman criticised his speculations saying they took "a liberty which no Christian can tolerate," and led to "conclusions that were often heathen rather than Christian." However he seems to have had many "followers:"

> In the latter part of his life, and for the generation which followed, Coleridge was ranked by many young English churchmen of liberal views as the greatest religious thinker of their time. . . .As Carlyle has told in his *Life of Sterling*, the poet's distinction, in the eyes of his audience, lay in his having recovered and preserved his Christian faith after having passed through periods of rationalism and Unitarianism, and faced the full results of German criticism and philosophy. His opinions, however, were at all periods mutable and it would be difficult to state them in any form that would hold good for the whole even of his later writings. (*Encyclopaedia Britannica* 1936 Edition)

In any case, most of his famous poetry is early and gives few clues to what he later believed.

Epitaph on Himself

Stop, Christian passer-by!—Stop, child of God,
And read with gentle breast. Beneath this sod
A poet lies, or that which once seem'd he.
O, lift one thought in prayer for S. T. C.;
That he who many a year with toll of breath
Found death in life, may here find life in death!

Mercy for praise—to be forgiven for fame
He ask'd, and hoped, through Christ. Do thou the same!

Hymn
Before sunrise, in the Vale of Chamouni

Hast thou a charm to stay the morning star
In his steep course—so long he seems to pause
On thy bald awful head, O sovran Blanc?
The Arve and Arveiron at thy base
Rave ceaselessly; but thou, most awful Form!
Risest from forth thy silent sea of pines,
How silently! Around thee and above
Deep is the air and dark, substantial, black,
An ebon mass: methinks thou piercest it
As with a wedge! But when I look again,
It is thine own calm home, thy crystal shrine,
Thy habitation from eternity!
O dread and silent Mount! I gazed upon thee
Till thou, still present to the bodily sense,
Didst vanish from my thought: entranced in prayer
I worshipped the Invisible alone.

Yet, like some sweet beguiling melody,
So sweet, we know not we are listening to it,
Thou, the meanwhile, wast blending with my thought,
Yea, with my life and life's own secret joy;
Till the dilating soul, enwrapt, transfused,
Into the mighty vision passing—there
As in her natural form, swelled vast to Heaven!

Awake, my soul! Not only passive praise
Thou owest! Not alone these swelling tears,
Mute thanks and secret ecstasy! Awake,
Voice of sweet song! Awake, my heart, awake!
Green vales and icy cliffs, all join my hymn.

Thou first and chief, sole sovran of the Vale!
O struggling with the darkness all the night,
And visited all night by troops of stars,
Or when they climb the sky or when they sink!
Companion of the morning-star at dawn,
Thyself earth's rosy star, and of the dawn,
Co-herald! wake, O wake, and utter praise!

Who sank thy sunless pillars deep in earth?
Who filled thy countenance with rosy light?
Who made thee parent of perpetual streams?

And you, ye five wild torrents fiercely glad!
Who called you forth from night and utter death,
From dark and icy caverns called you forth,
Down those precipitous, black, jagged rocks,
For ever shattered, and the same for ever?
Who gave you your invulnerable life,
Your strength, your speed, your fury, and your joy,
Unceasing thunder, and eternal foam?
And who commanded—and the silence came—
Here let the billows stiffen, and have rest?

Ye ice-falls! ye that from the mountain's brow
Adown enormous ravines slope amain—
Torrents, methinks, that heard a mighty voice,
And stopped at once amid their maddest plunge!—
Motionless torrents! silent cataracts!
Who made you glorious as the gates of heaven
Beneath the keen full moon? Who bade the sun
Clothe you with rainbows? Who, with living flowers
Of loveliest blue, spread garlands at your feet?—
God! let the torrents, like a shout of nations,
Answer! and let the ice-plains echo, God!
God! sing, ye meadow-streams, with gladsome voice!
Ye pine-groves, with your soft and soul-like sounds!
And they too have a voice, yon piles of snow,
And in their perilous fall shall thunder, God!

Ye living flowers that skirt the eternal frost!
Ye wild goats sporting round the eagle's nest!
Ye eagles, playmates of the mountain-storm!
Ye lightnings, the dread arrows of the clouds!
Ye signs and wonders of the element!
Utter forth God, and fill the hills with praise.

Thou too, hoar Mount! with thy sky-pointing peaks,
Oft from whose feet the avalanche, unheard,
Shoots downward, glittering through the pure serene
Into the depth of clouds that veil thy breast,
Thou too again, stupendous Mountain! thou
That, as I raise my head, awhile bowed low

In adoration—upward from thy base
Slow-travelling with dim eyes suffused with tears
Solemnly seemest, like a vapoury cloud,
To rise before me! rise, O ever rise;
Rise like a cloud of incense from the earth!
Thou kingly spirit throned among the hills!
Thou dread ambassador from earth to heaven!
Great hierarch! tell thou the silent sky,
And tell the stars, and tell yon rising sun,
Earth, with her thousand voices, praises God.

On An Infant
Which died before baptism

"*Be* rather than *be called* a child of God,"
Death whispered. With assenting nod,
Its head upon its mother's breast
The baby bowed without demur—
Of the kingdom of the blest
Possessor, not inheritor.

MANT, Bishop RICHARD (1776–1848) educated at Winchester and Oxford, won the Chancellor's purse for an English essay at Oxford. He entered the Anglican priesthood and became Chaplain to the Archbishop of Canterbury (1813). After serving as a rector, he became a bishop to the Irish sees, first of Killaloe and then of Down and Connor. He wrote a History of the church in Ireland and on *The Happiness of the Blessed Dead* (1847). He also published sermons, which were popular in his day, as well as poetry. His books of poetry included *The Country Curate* (1804); *Poems in Three Parts* (1806); *The Slave* (1807); *The Holy Days of the Church* . . . (two volumes: 1828, 1831); and *Ancient Hymns from the Roman Breviary* . . . [with] *Original Hymns* (1837). He is chiefly known for his Latin translations.

True Knowledge

What is true knowledge?—Is it with keen eye
Of lucre's sons to thread the mazy way?
Is it of civic rights, and royal sway,
And wealth political, the depths to try?
Is it to delve the earth, or soar the sky;
To marshal nature's tribes in just array;
To mix, and analyze, and mete, and weigh

Her elements, and all her powers descry?
These things, who will may know them, if to know
Breed not vain-glory: but o'er all to scan
God, in his works and word shown forth below;
Creation's wonders; and Redemption's plan;
Whence came we; what to do; and whither go:
This is true knowledge, and "the whole of man."

The House Of God

It is the Sabbath bell, which calls to prayer,
Even to the House of God, the hallowed dome,
Where He who claims it bids his people come
To bow before his throne, and serve Him there
With prayers, and thanks, and praises. Some there are
Who hold it meet to linger now at home,
And some o'er fields and the wide hills to roam,
And worship in the temple of the air!
For me, not heedless of the lone address,
Nor slack to greet my Maker on the height,
By wood, or living stream; yet not the less
Seek I his presence in each social rite
Of his own temple: that He deigns to bless,
There still He dwells, and there is his delight.

The Church Bells

What varying sounds from yon gray pinnacles
Sweep o'er the ear, and claim the heart's reply!
Now the blithe peal of home festivity,
Natal or nuptial, in full concert swells:
Now the brisk chime, or voice of altered bells,
Speaks the due hour of social worship nigh:
And now the last stage of mortality
The deep dull toll with lingering warning tells.
How much of human life those sounds comprise;
Birth, wedded love, God's service, and the tomb!
Heard not in vain, if thence kind feelings rise,
Such as befit our being, free from gloom
Monastic,—prayer that communes with the skies,
And musings mindful of the final doom.

Social Worship

There is a joy, which angels well may prize:
To see, and hear, and aid God's worship, when
Unnumbered tongues, a host of Christian men,
Youths, matrons, maidens, join. Their sounds arise,
"Like many waters;" now glad symphonies
Of thanks and glory to our God; and then,
Seal of the social prayer, the loud Amen,
Faith's common pledge, contrition's mingled cries.
Thus, when the Church of Christ was hale and young,
She called on God, one spirit and one voice;
Thus from corruption cleansed, with health new strung,
Her sons she nurtured. Oh! be theirs, by choice,
What duty bids, to worship, heart and tongue;
At once to pray, at once in God rejoice!

MOORE, THOMAS (1779–1852), educated at Trinity College, Dublin, read law at the Middle Temple and was for a while an official in Bermuda. A friend of Byron and Shelley, and an advocate of Irish nationalism, his major poetic work, *Irish Melodies,* was very popular. It contained such familiar lyrics as "the Last Rose of Summer" and "Believe Me if All Those Endearing Young Charms." He published *Sacred Songs* in 1816, which includes a number of hymns. His best known major poem, "Lalla Rookh," was published in 1817 and earned the highest price ever paid by a publisher for a poem up to that time. He wrote many satirical works portraying regency politics and manners, as well. He is also famous, together with the publisher John Murray, for burning Byron's memoirs, no doubt in order to protect Byron's memory. He later published *The Letters and Journals of Lord Byron.*

The Comforter

Oh! thou who dry'st the mourner's tear,
   How dark this world would be,
If, when deceived and wounded here,
   We could not fly to thee!

The friends who in our sunshine live,
   When winter comes are flown;
And he who has but tears to give,
   Must weep those tears alone;

But thou wilt heal that broken heart,
Which, like the plants that throw
Their fragrance from the wounded part,
Breathes sweetness out of woe.

When joy no longer soothes or cheers,
And even the hope that threw
A moment's sparkle o'er our tears,
Is dimm'd and varnish'd too;

Oh who would bear life's stormy doom,
Did not thy wing of love
Come brightly wafting through the gloom,
One peace-branch from above.

Then sorrow, touch'd by thee, grows bright
With more than rapture's ray;
As darkness shows us worlds of light
We never saw by day.

This World Is All A Fleeting Show

This world is all a fleeting show,
For man's illusion given;
The smiles of joy, the tears of woe,
Deceitful shine, deceitful flow,—
There's nothing true but Heaven!

And false the light on glory's plume,
As fading hues of even;
And love, and hope, and beauty's bloom
Are blossoms gathered for the tomb,—
There's nothing bright but Heaven!

Poor wanderers of a stormy day,
From wave to wave we're driven,
And fancy's flash and reason's ray
Serve but to light the troubled way,—
There's nothing calm but Heaven!

A Prayer

O Thou who dry'st the mourner's tears!
How dark this world would be,

If, when deceived and wounded here,
We could not fly to Thee.
The friends, who in our sunshine live,
When winter comes are flown;
And he, who has but tears to give,
Must weep those tears alone.
But Thou wilt heal that broken heart,
Which, like the plants that throw
Their fragrance from the wounded part,
Breathes sweetness out of woe.

When joy no longer soothes or cheers,
And e'en the hope that threw
A moment's sparkle o'er our tears,
Is dimmed and vanished too!
Oh! who could bear life's stormy doom,
Did not Thy wing of love
Come brightly wafting through the gloom
Our peace-branch from above?
Then sorrow, touched by Thee, grows bright
With more than rapture's ray;
As darkness shows us worlds of light
We never saw by day.

CROLY, GEORGE (1780–1860), who received a LL.D. from Dublin University in 1831, was ordained and laboured in Ireland until 1840, when he went to London and dedicated himself fully to writing. He is best known for his three volume romantic novel, *Salathiel* (1829), about the legendary Wandering Jew. He also wrote for a number of literary journals, including *Blackwoods Magazine*. In 1851 he published *Scenes from Scripture and Other Poems*, and in 1854, *Psalm and Hymns for Public Worship*.

A Dirge

Earth to earth, and dust to dust!
Here the evil and the just,
Here the youthful and the old,
Here the fearful and the bold,
Here the matron and the maid,
In one silent bed are laid;
Here the vassal and the king
Side by side lie withering;

Here the sword and sceptre rust:
"Earth to earth, and dust to dust!"

Age on age shall roll along,
O'er this pale and mighty throng;
Those that wept them, those that weep,
All shall with these sleepers sleep;
Brothers, sisters of the worm,
Summer's sun, or winter's storm,
Song of peace, or battle's roar,
Ne'er shall break their slumbers more;
Death shall keep his silent trust:
"Earth to earth, and dust to dust!"

But a day is coming fast,
Earth, thy mightiest and thy last;
It shall come in fear and wonder,
Heralded by trump and thunder;
It shall come in strife and spoil;
It shall come in blood and toil;
It shall come in empire's groans,
Burning temples, trampled thrones;
Then, ambition, rule thy lust:
"Earth to earth, and dust to dust!"

Then shall come the judgment sign;—
In the east, the King shall shine,
Flashing from heaven's golden gate,
Thousands, thousands round his state,
Spirits with the crown and plume.
Tremble, then, thou sullen tomb;
Heaven shall open on our sight,
Earth be turned to living light,
Kingdoms of the ransomed just:
"Earth to earth, and dust to dust!"

Then thy Mount, Jerusalem,
Shall be gorgeous as a gem;
Then, shall in the desert rise
Fruits of more than Paradise;
Earth by angel feet be trod,
One great garden of her God;—
Till are dried the martyrs' tears,

Through a thousand glorious years.
Now in hope of him we trust:
"Earth to earth, and dust to dust!"

A Supplication

Spirit of God! descend upon my heart;
Wean it from earth, though all its pulses move;
Stoop to my weakness, mighty as thou art,
And make me love thee, as I ought to love.

I ask no dream, no prophet ecstasies,
No sudden rending of the veil of clay;
No angel visitant, no opening skies;—
But take the dimness of the soul away.

Hast thou not bid us love thee, God and King?
All, all thine own—soul, heart, and strength, and mind;
I see thy cross—there teach my heart to cling:
O! let me seek thee,—and O! let me find!

Teach me to feel, that thou art always nigh;
Teach me the struggles of the soul to bear,
To check the rising doubt, the rebel sigh;
Teach me the patience of unanswered prayer.

I know thee glorious! might and mercy all,
All that commands thy creatures' boundless praise;
Yet shall my soul from that high vision fall,
Too cold to worship, and too weak to gaze?

Teach me to love thee, as thine angels love,
One holy passion filling all my frame;
The baptism of the heaven-descended dove,
My heart an altar, and thy love its flame.

ELLIOT, EBENEZER (1781–1849), "the corn-law rhymer," was a Yorkshire ironmonger with border raiders as ancestors and a politically radical, Calvinist father. After a bout of smallpox that left him sickly he began to read extensively and developed a love for the natural world that he says "caused him to desert both alehouse and chapel" and led him to study botany on his own. He had numerous poems and short stories published in periodicals some of which brought him the commendation of Southey. He took over his father's trade and became involved in the movement to repudiate the corn law. In 1831 he produced *Corn-law Rhymes*. Many of his poems artistically portray the life of the rural poor. A famous description of himself goes, "My feelings have been hammered until they have become *cold-short* [brittle] and are apt to snap and fly off in sarcasms."

The Three Marys At Castle Howard, In 1812 And 1837

The lifeless son—the mother's agony,
O'erstrained till agony refused to feel—
That sinner too I then dry-eyed could see;
For I was hardened in my selfish weal,
And strength and joy had strung my soul with steel.
I knew not then what man may live to be,
A thing of life, that feels he lives in vain—
A taper, to be quenched in misery!
Forgive me, then, Caracci! if I seek
To look on this, thy tale of tears, again;
For now the swift is slow, the strong is weak.
Mother of Christ! how merciful is pain!
But if I longer view thy tear-stained cheek,
Heart-broken Magdalen! my heart will break.

Plaint

Dark, deep, and cold the current flows
Unto the sea where no wind blows,
Seeking the land which no one knows.

O'er its sad gloom still comes and goes
The mingled wail of friends and foes,
Borne to the land which no one knows.

Why shrieks for help yon wretch, who goes
With millions, from a world of woes,
Unto the land which no one knows?

Though myriads go with him who goes
Alone he goes where no wind blows,
Unto the land which no one knows.

For all must go where no wind blows,
And none can go for him who goes;
None, none return whence no one knows.

Yet why should he who shrieking goes
With millions, from a world of woes,
Reunion seek with it or those?

Alone with God, where no wind blows,
And Death, his shadow—doom'd, he goes:
That God is there the shadow shows.

O shoreless Deep, where no wind blows!
And thou, O Land which no one knows!
That God is All, His shadow shows.

Song

Child, is thy father dead
Father is gone!
Why did they tax his bread?
God's will be done!
Mother has sold her bed:
Better to die than wed!
Where shall she lay her head?
Home we have none!

Father clammed thrice a week—
God's will be done!
Long for work did he seek,
Work he found none.
Tears on his hollow cheek
Told what no tongue could speak:
Why did his master break?
God's will be done!

Doctor said air was best—
Food we had none;
Father, with panting breast,
Groaned to be gone:
Now he is with the blest—
Mother says death is best!
We have no place of rest—
Yes, we have one!

clammed - fasted

HEBER, REGINALD (1783–1826) attended Oxford College, where he wrote, "Palestine" a prize-winning poem, published in 1807. Sir Walter Scott, with whom he was breakfasting before the poem was submitted suggested several of the well-known lines that Heber inserted impromptu. In 1807 he was ordained; in 1815 he became an Oxford lecturer; and in 1822, preacher at Lincoln's Inn. He became bishop of Calcutta late that year. He established Bishop's College in Calcutta, and was known for his indefatigable involvement throughout his diocese, which encompassed a third of India. He ordained the first native Indian to join the Anglican clergy. In 1811 he published some hymns in *The Christian Observer*. In 1812 he published *Poems and Translations*. Heber died suddenly while ministering in Trichinopoly. In 1841, after his death, his *Poetical Works* were published. All of his well-known hymns were written before he became Bishop of Calcutta. Julian's *Dictionary of Hymnology* refers to "the lyric spirit of Scott and Byron" passing "into our hymns in Heber's verse."

Brightest And Best Of The Sons Of The Morning

Brightest and best of the sons of the morning,
Dawn on our darkness, and lend us thine aid;
Star of the East, the horizon adorning,
Guide where our infant Redeemer is laid.

Cold on his cradle the dewdrops are shining;
Low lies his head with the beasts of the stall;
Angels adore him in slumber reclining,
Maker and Monarch, and Lord over all.

Say, shall we yield him, in costly devotion,
Odours of Edom, and off'rings divine,
Gems of the mountain and pearls of the ocean,
Myrrh from the forest or gold from the mine?

Vainly we offer each ample oblation,
Vainly with gifts would his favor secure;
Richer by far is the heart's adoration;
Dearer to God are the prayers of the poor.

Brightest and best of the sons of the morning,
Dawn on our darkness, and lend us thine aid;
Star of the East, the horizon adorning,
Guide where our infant Redeemer is laid.

Holy, Holy, Holy

Holy, Holy, Holy, Lord God Almighty!
Early in the morning our song shall rise to thee;
Holy, Holy, Holy! Merciful and mighty!
God in three Persons, blessed Trinity!

Holy, Holy, Holy! All the saints adore thee,
Casting down their golden crowns around the glassy sea;
Cherubim and seraphim falling down before thee,
Who wert, and art, and evermore shalt be.

Holy, Holy, Holy! Though the darkness hide thee,
Though the eye of sinful man thy glory may not see,
Only thou art holy; there is none beside thee
Perfect in power, in love, and purity.

Holy, Holy, Holy! Lord God Almighty!
All thy works shall praise thy Name, in earth and sky and sea;
Holy, Holy, Holy! Merciful and Mighty!
God in three Persons, blessed Trinity!

From Greenland's Icy Mountains

From Greenland's icy mountains,　From India's coral strand,
Where Afric's sunny fountains　Roll down their golden sand,
From many an ancient river,　From many a palmy plain,
They call us to deliver　Their land from error's chain.

What though the spicy breezes　Blow soft o'er Ceylon's Isle;
Though ev'ry prospect pleases,　And only man is vile:
In vain with lavish kindness　The gifts of God are strown;
The heathen in his blindness　Bows down to wood and stone.

Can we, whose souls are lighted　With wisdom from on high,
Can we to men benighted　The lamp of life deny?
Salvation! O salvation!　The joyful sound proclaim,
Till each remotest nation　Has learned Messiah's Name.

Waft, waft, ye winds, his story,　And you, ye waters, roll,
Till like a sea of glory　It spreads from pole to pole;
Till o'er our ransomed nature　The Lamb for sinners slain,
Redeemer, King, Creator,　In bliss returns to reign.

DE VERE, Sir AUBREY (1788-1846), of Curragh Chase, County Limerick, is an Irish poet of note. Sir Aubrey wrote *Julian the Apostate* (1822), *The Duke of Mercia, The Song of Faith* (1842), and *Mary Tudor* (1847-posthumously published), among other works. (He is perhaps less well-known than his son, Aubrey Thomas De Vere, who was a friend of Cardinal Newman, Wordsworth, Tennyson, and Carlyle, becoming a Roman Catholic when he was thirty-seven.)

The Right Use of Prayer

Therefore, when thou wouldst pray, or dost thine alms,
Blow not a trump before thee. Hypocrites
Do thus vaingloriously: the common streets
Boast of their largess, echoing their psalms.
On such the laud of men like unctuous balms
Falls with sweet savour. Impious Counterfeits!
Prating of Heaven, for earth their bosom beats:
Grasping at weeds they lose immortal palms.
God needs not iteration nor vain cries;
That Man communion with his God might share
Below, Christ gave the ordinance of prayer.
Vague ambages and witless ecstasies
Avail not. Ere a voice to prayer be given
The heart should rise on wings of love to Heaven.

Sonnet

Ye praise the humble: of the meek ye say,
"Happy they live among their lowly bowers;
The mountains, and the mountain-storms are ours."
Thus, self-deceivers, filled with pride always
Reluctant homage to the good ye pay,
Mingled with scorn like poison sucked from flowers—
Revere the humble; godlike are their powers:
No mendicants for praise of men are they.
The child who prays in faith "Thy will be done"
Is blended with that Will Supreme which moves
A wilderness of worlds by Thought untrod;
He shares the starry sceptre, and the throne:
The man who as himself his neighbour loves
Looks down on all things with the eyes of God!

Reality

Love thy God and love Him only:
And thy breast will ne'er be lonely.
In that one great Spirit meet
All things mighty, grave and sweet.
Vainly strives the soul to mingle
With a being of our kind:
Vainly heart with our hearts are twined.
For the deepest still is single.
An impalpable resistance
Holds like nature's still at distance.
Mortal! Love that Holy One!
Or dwell for aye alone.

Sorrow

Count each affliction, whether light or grave,
God's messenger sent down to thee; do thou
With courtesy receive him; rise and bow;
And, ere his shadow pass thy threshold, crave
Permission first his heavenly feet to lave;
Then lay before him all thou hast; allow
No cloud of passion to usurp thy brow,
Or mar thy hospitality; no wave
Of mortal tumult to obliterate
Thy soul's marmoreal calmness. Grief should be
Like joy, majestic, equable, sedate,
Confirming cleansing, raising, making free;
Strong to consume small troubles; to commend
Great thoughts, grave thoughts, thoughts lasting to the end.

MILMAN, HENRY HART (1791–1868), son of a court physician become a baronet, was a prize-winning poet and scholar at Oxford. He wrote a play, *Fazio,* which was publicly produced. His books, *Samor* (1817), *The Fall of Jerusalem* (1820), *Belshazzar, The Martyr of Antioch* (1822), and *Anne Boleyn,* were all well received. In 1821 he was appointed poetry professor at Oxford. John Keble succeeded him ten years later. He contributed a number of hymns to the collected *Hymns* of his friend Reginald Heber. In 1827 his focus turned to theology as illustrated by his *Bampton Lectures.* He wrote *A History of the Jews* in 1829, which sparked considerable controversy. In the words of Dean Stanley, "it was the first decisive inroad of German theology into England, the first palpable indication that the Bible could be studied like another book, that the characters and events of the sacred history could be treated at once critically and reverently." (Julian's *Dictionary of Hymnology*) He published an edition of Gibbon's *Decline and Fall of the Roman Empire* in 1839 and a *History of Christianity* in 1840. Among his many literary friends were Arthur Hallam and Macauley. Among his minor works were a *Life of Keats* and a *Life of Horace*.

The Holy Field

Beneath our feet and o'er our head
Is equal warning given;
Beneath us lie the countless dead,
Above us is the Heaven!

Their names are graven on the stone,
Their bones are in the clay;
And ere another day is done,
Ourselves may be as they.

Death rides on every passing breeze,
He lurks in every flower;
Each season has its own disease,
Its peril every hour.

Our eyes have seen the rosy light
Of youth's soft cheek decay,
And Fate descend in sudden night
On manhood's middle day.

Our eyes have seen the steps of age
Halt feebly towards the tomb;
And yet shall earth our hearts engage,
And dreams of days to come?

Turn, mortal, turn! thy danger know;
Where'er thy foot can tread
The earth rings hollow from below,
And warns thee of her dead!

Turn, Christian, turn! thy soul apply
To truths divinely given;
The bones that underneath thee lie
Shall live for Hell or Heaven!

Where The Wicked Cease From Troubling, And The Weary Are At Rest

Brother, thou art gone before us: and thy saintly soul is flown
Where tears are wiped from every eye, and sorrow is unknown:
From the burden of the flesh, and from care and fear releas'd,
Where the wicked cease from troubling, and the weary are at rest.

The toilsome way thou'st travelled o'er, and borne the heavy load;
But Christ hath taught thy languid feet to reach His blest abode:
Thou'rt sleeping now, like Lazarus upon his father's breast,
Where the wicked cease from troubling, and the weary are at rest.

Sin can never taint thee now, not doubt thy faith assail,
Nor thy meek trust in Jesus Christ and the Holy Spirit fail:
And there thou'rt sure to meet the good, whom on earth thou lovedst best,
Where the wicked cease from troubling, and the weary are at rest.

Earth to earth, and dust to dust, the solemn priest hath said:
So we lay the turf above thee now, and we seal thy narrow bed:
But thy spirit, brother, soars away among the faithful blest,
Where the wicked cease from troubling, and the weary are at rest.

And when the Lord shall summon us, whom thou hast left behind.
May we, untainted by the world, as sure a welcome find!
May each, like thee, depart in peace, to be a glorious guest,
Where the wicked cease from troubling, and the weary are at rest!

Hymn

When our heads are bowed with woe,
When our bitter tears o'erflow;
When we mourn the lost, the dear,
Gracious Son of Mary, hear!

Thou out throbbing flesh hast worn,
Thou our mortal griefs hast borne,
Thou hast shed the human tear:
Gracious Son of Mary, hear!

When the sullen death-bell tolls
For our own departed souls,
When our final doom is near,
Gracious Son of Mary, hear!

Thou hast bowed the dying head
Thou the blood of life hast shed;
Thou hast filled a mortal bier:
Gracious Son of Mary, hear!

When the heart is sad within
With the thought of all its sin;
When the spirit shrinks with fear,
Gracious Son of Mary, hear!

Thou the shame, the grief, hast known,
Though the sins were not thine own;
Thou hast deigned their load to bear;
Gracious Son of Mary, hear!

Hymn From 'The Martyr Of Antioch'

For thou didst die for me, O Son of God!
By thee the throbbing flesh of man was worn;
Thy naked feet the thorns of sorrow trod,
And tempests beat thy houseless head forlorn.
Thou, that wert wont to stand
Alone, on God's right hand,
Before the ages were, the Eternal, eldest born.

Thy birthright in the word was pain and grief,
Thy love's return in gratitude and hate;
The limbs thou healedst brought thee no relief,
The eyes thou openedst calmly viewed thy fate:
Thou, that wert wont to dwell
In peace, tongue cannot tell
Nor heart conceive the bliss of thy celestial state.

They dragged thee to the Roman's solemn hall,
Where the proud judge in purple splendour sate;
Thou stoodst a meek and patient criminal,
Thy doom of death from human lips to wait;
Whose throne shall be the world
In final ruin hurled,
With all mankind to hear their everlasting fate.

Thou wert alone in that fierce multitude
When 'Crucify him!' yelled the general shout;
No hand to guard thee 'mid those insults rude,

Nor lip to bless in all that frantic rout;
Whose lightest whispered word
The Seraphim had heard,
And adamantine arms from all the heaven broke out.

They bound thy temples with the twisted thorn,
Thy bruised feet went languid on with pain;
Thy blood, from all thy flesh with scourges torn,
Deepened thy robe of mockery's crimson grain;
Whose native vesture bright
Was the unapproached light,
The sandal of whose foot the rapid hurricane.

They smote thy cheek with many a ruthless palm,
With the cold spear thy shuddering side they pierced;
The draught of bitterest gall was all the balm
They gave, to enhance thy unslaked, burning thirst:
Thou at whose words of peace
Did pain and anguish cease,
And the long-buried dead their bonds of slumber burst.

Low bowed thy head convulsed and drooped in death,
Thy voice sent forth a sad and wailing cry;
Slow struggled from thy breast the parting breath,
And every limb was wrung with agony:
That head, whose veilless blaze
Filled angels with amaze,
When at that voice sprang forth the rolling suns on high.

And thou wert laid within the narrow tomb,
Thy clay-cold limbs with shrouding grave-clothes bound;
The sealed stone confirmed thy mortal doom,
Lone watchmen walked thy desert burial-ground,
Whom heaven could not contain,
Not the immeasurable plain
Of vast infinity inclose or circle round.

For us, for us, thou didst endure the pain,
And thy meek spirit bowed itself to shame,
To wash our souls from sin's infecting stain,
To avert the Father's wrathful vengeance flame.
Thou that could'st nothing win
By saving worlds from sin,
Nor aught of glory add to thy all-glorious name.

The Crucifixion

Bound upon the accursed tree,
Faint and bleeding, who is He?
By the flesh with scourges torn,
By the crown of twisted thorn,
By the side so deeply pierced,
By the baffled, burning thirst,
By the drooping, death-dew's brow,
Son of Man! 'tis Thou! 'tis Thou!

Bound upon the accursed tree,
Dread and awful, who is He?
By the sun at noonday pale,
Shiv'ring rock, and rending veil,
Eden promised ere He died
To the felon at His side,
Lord! our suppliant knees we bow,
Son of God! 'tis Thou! 'tis Thou!

Bound upon the accursed tree,
Sad and dying, who is He?
By the last and bitter cry,
Ghost giv'n up in agony,
By the lifeless body laid
In the chamber of the dead,
Crucified! we know Thee now,
Son of Man! 'tis Thou! 'tis Thou!

Bound upon the accursed tree,
Dread and awful, who is He?
By the spoil'd and empty grave,
By the souls He died to save,
By the conquest He hath won,
By the saints before His throne,
By the rainbow round His brow,
Son of God! 'tis Thou! 'tis Thou!

O Help Us, Lord!

O help us, Lord! Each hour of need
Thy heavenly succour give;
Help us in thought and word and deed
Each hour on earth we live.

O help us when our spirits bleed,
With contrite anguish sore,
And when our hearts are cold and dead,
O help us, Lord, the more.

O help us through the prayer of faith
More firmly to believe;
For still the more the servant hath,
The more shall he receive.

O help us, Jesus, from on high,
We know no help but thee,
O help us so to live and die
As thine, in heaven to be.

KEBLE, JOHN (1792–1866), son of a Gloucestershire vicar who educated his sons at home, was a prize-winning Oxford scholar, elected as a Fellow of Oriel at nineteen years old. He was ordained in 1816 and, on the death of his mother in 1823, returned home where he became a rural curate. In 1827 he published *The Christian Year*. In 1830 he published an edition of *Hooker's Works*. In 1831 he was elected to the poetry professorship of Oxford. There in 1835 he preached his famous Assize Sermon on "Natural Apostasy," said by Dr. Newman to have started the Oxford Movement. Soon after that he began to issue the *Tracts for the Times*. In 1835 his father died, and he again returned home where he married and became the Vicar of Hursley, devoting himself to the life of a parish priest thereafter. In 1864 his health deteriorated and in 1866 he passed away followed within six weeks by his wife. Many of his most popular hymns are truncations of longer poems, but most of his poems are true hymns according to Dr. Johnson's definition, to wit "song(s) of adoration to some superior being." Keble's praises, however, are a bit more specific than that.

All Saints' Day

Why blow'st thou not, thou wintry wind,
Now every leaf is brown and sere,
And idly droops, to thee resigned,
The fading chaplet of the year?
Yet wears the pure aerial sky
Her summer veil, half drawn on high,
Of silvery haze, and dark and still
The shadows sleep on every slanting hill.

How quiet shews the woodland scene!
Each flower and tree, its duty done,
Reposing in decay serene,
Like weary men when age is won,
Such calm old age as conscience pure
And self-commanding hearts ensure,
Waiting their summons to the sky,
Content to live, but not afraid to die.

Sure if our eyes were purged to trace
God's unseen armies hovering round,
We should behold by angels' grace
The four strong winds of Heaven fast bound,
Their downward sweep a moment stayed
On ocean cove and forest glade,
Till the last flower of autumn shed
Her funeral odours on her dying bed.

So in Thine awful armoury, Lord,
The lightnings of the judgment-day
Pause yet awhile, in mercy stored,
Till willing heart swear quite away
Their earthly stains; and spotless shine
On every brow in light divine
The Cross by angel hands impressed,
The seal of glory won and pledge of promised rest.

Little they dream, those haughty souls
Whom empires own with bended knee,
What lowly fate their own controls,
Together linked by Heaven's decree;—
As bloodhounds hush their baying wild
To wanton with some fearless child,
So Famine waits, and War with greedy eyes,
Till some repenting heart be ready for the skies.

Think ye the spires that glow so bright
In front of yonder setting sun,
Stand by their own unshaken might?
No—where th'upholding grace is won,
We dare not ask, nor Heaven would tell,
But sure from many a hidden dell,
From many a rural nook unthought of there,
Rises for that proud world the saints' prevailing prayer.

Oh Champions blest, in Jesus' name,
Short be your strife, your triumph full,
Till every heart have caught your flame,
And, lightened of the world's misrule,
Ye soar those elder saints to meet,
Gathered long since at Jesus' feet,
No world of passions to destroy,
Your prayers and struggles o'er, your task all praise and joy.

[Lyra Innocentium] From 'The Waterfall'

Go where the waters fall,
Sheer from the mountain's height—

Mark how a thousand streams in one,—
One in a thousand on they fare,
    Now flashing to the sun,
    Now still as beast in lair.
Now round the rock, now mounting o'er,
In lawless dance they win their way,
    Still seeming more and more
    To swell as we survey,

They rush and roar, they whirl and leap,
Not wilder drives the wintry storm.
    Yet a strong law they keep,
    Strange powers their course inform.

Even so the mighty skyborn stream
Its living waters from above,
    All marred and broken seem,
    No union and no love.

Yet in dim caves they softly blend
In dreams of mortals unespied:
    One is their awful end,
    One their unfailing Guide.

Sun Of My Soul

Sun of my soul, thou Saviour dear,
It is not night if thou be near;
O may no earthborn cloud arise
To hide thee from thy servant's eyes.

When the soft dews of kindly sleep
My weary eyelids gently steep,
Be my last thought, how sweet to rest
For ever on my Saviour's breast.

Abide with me from morn till eve,
For without thee I cannot live;
Abide with me when night is nigh,
For without thee I dare not die.

If some poor wandering child of thine
Have spurned today the voice Divine,
Now, Lord, the gracious work begin;
Let him no more lie down in sin.

Watch by the sick; enrich the poor
With blessings from thy boundless store;
Be every mourner's sleep tonight,
Like infant's slumbers, pure and light.
Come near and bless us when we wake,
Ere through the world our way we take,
Till in the ocean of thy love
We lose ourselves in heav'n above.

United States from Lyra Apostolica

Tyre of the farther West! be thou too warned,
Whose eagle wings thine own green world overspread
Touching two Oceans: wherefore hast thou scorned
Thy fathers' God, O proud and full of bread?
Why lies the Cross unhonoured on thy ground
While in mid air thy stars and arrows flaunt?
That sheaf of darts, will it not fall unbound,
Except, disrobed of thy vain earthly vaunt,
Thou bring it to be blessed where Saints and Angels haunt?

The holy seed, by Heaven's peculiar grace,
Is rooted here and there in thy dark woods;
But many a rank weed round it grows apace,
And Mammon builds beside thy mighty floods,
O'ertopping Nature, braving Nature's God;
O while thou yet hast room, fair fruitful land,
Ere war and want have stained thy virgin sod,
Mark thee a place on high, a glorious stand,

Whence Truth her sign may make o'er forest, lake, and strand.
Eastward, this hour, perchance thou turn'st thine ear,
Listening if haply with the surging sea,
Blend sounds of Ruin from a land once dear
To thee and Heaven. O trying hour for thee!
Tyre mocked when Salem fell; where now is Tyre?
Heaven was against her. Nations thick as waves,
Burst o'er her walls, to Ocean doomed and fire:
And now the tideless water idly laves
Her towers, and lone sands heap her crowned merchants' graves.

Flowers Of The Field
Consider the lilies of the field, how they grow.—St. Matthew vi. 28.

Sweet nurslings of the vernal skies,
Bath'd in soft airs, and fed with dew,
What more than magic in you lies,
To fill the heart's fond view?
In childhood's sports, companions gay,
In sorrow, on life's downward way,
How soothing! in our last decay
Memorials prompt and true.

Relics ye are of Eden's bowers,
As pure, as fragrant, and as fair,
As when ye crown'd the sunshine hours
Of happy wanderers there.
Fall'n all beside—the world of life,
How is it stain'd with fear and strife!
In Reason's world what storms are rife,
What passions range and glare!

But cheerful and unchanged the while
Your first and perfect form ye show,
The same that won Eve's matron smile
In the world's opening glow.
The stars of heaven a course are taught
Too high above our human thought;
Ye may be found if ye are sought,
And as we gaze, we know.

Ye dwell beside our paths and homes,
Our paths of sin, our homes of sorrow,

And guilty man, where'er he roams,
Your innocent mirth may borrow.
The birds of air before us fleet,
They cannot brook our shame to meet—
But we may taste your solace sweet
And come again to-morrow.

Ye fearless in your nests abide—
Nor may we scorn, too proudly wise
Your silent lessons, undescried
By all but lowly eyes:
For ye could draw th' admiring gaze
Of Him who worlds and hearts surveys:
Your order wild, your fragrant maze,
He taught us how to prize.

Ye felt your Maker's smile that hour,
As when He paus'd and own'd you good;
His blessing on earth's primal bower,
Ye felt it all renew'd.
What care ye now, if winter's storm
Sweep ruthless o'er each silken form?
Christ's blessing at your heart is warm,
Ye fear no vexing mood.

Alas! of thousand bosoms kind,
That daily court you and caress,
How few the happy secret find
Of your calm loveliness!
"Live for to-day! to-morrow's light
To-morrow's cares shall bring to sight;
Go sleep like closing flowers at night,
And heaven thy morn shall bless."

Address To Poets

Ye whose hearts are beating high
With the pulse of poesy,
Heirs of more than royal race,
Framed, by Heaven's peculiar grace,
God's own work to do on earth,
(If the word be not too bold,)
Giving virtue a new birth,
And a life that ne'er grow old—

Sovereign masters of all hearts!
Know ye who hath set your parts?
He, who gave you breath to sing,
By whose strength ye sweep the string,
He hath chosen you to lead
His hosannas here below;—
Mount, and claim your glorious meed;
Linger not with sin and wo.

But if ye should hold your peace,
Deem not that the song would cease—
Angels round His glory-throne,
Stars, His guiding hand that own,
Flowers, that grow beneath our feet,
Stones, in earth's dark womb that rest,
High and low in choir shall meet,
Ere His name shall be unblest.

Lord, by every minstrel tongue
Be thy praise so duly sung,
That thine angels' harps may ne'er
Fail to find fit echoing here!
We the while, of meaner birth,
Who in that divinest spell
Dare not hope to join on earth,
Give us grace to listen well.

But should thankless silence seal
Lips that might half-heaven reveal—
Should bards in idol-hymns profane
The sacred soul-enthralling strain,
(As in this bad world below
Noblest things find vilest using,)
Then, thy power and mercy show,
In vile things noble breath infusing.

Then waken into sound divine
The very pavement of thy shrine,
Till we, like heaven's star-sprinkled floor,
Faintly give back what we adore.
Childlike though the voices be,
And untunable the parts,
Thou wilt own the minstrelsy,
If it flow from childlike hearts.

LYTE, HENRY FRANCIS (1793–1847), prize-winner in poetry at Trinity College, Dublin, gave up his intentions of becoming a doctor and became a curate in 1815. Poor health forced him to resign the position, and after a trip to Europe, he married Anne Maxwell in Cornwall. Lyte later held curacies in Hampshire and Devonshire, frequently taking trips abroad for his health. His hymns continue to be among the best known. His poems include *Tales in Verse* (1826), and *Poems Chiefly Religious* (1833). Other poems are included in his *Spirit of the Psalms* (1834), a metrical version of the Psalter. *Miscellaneous Poems,* a collection of verse from his *Remains . . .* was published in 1850. *Poems Chiefly Religious* was re-published in 1868. Lyte wrote the biographical preface to Vaughan's *Sacred Poems,* published in 1847.

Abide With Me

Abide with me: fast falls the eventide;
The darkness deepens; Lord with me abide:
When other helpers fall, and comforts flee,
Help of the helpless, O abide with me.

Swift to its close ebbs out life's little day;
Earth's joys grow dim, its glories pass away;
Change and decay in all around I see;
O thou who changest not, abide with me.

I need thy presence every passing hour;
What but thy grace can foil the tempter's pow'r?
Who like thyself my guide and stay can be?
Through cloud and sunshine, O abide with me.

I fear no foe, with thee at hand to bless:
Ills have no weight, and tears no bitterness.
Where is death's sting? where, grave, thy victory?
I triumph still, if thou abide with me.

Hold thou the cross before my closing eyes;
Shine through the gloom, and point me to the skies:
Heav'n's morning breaks, and earth's vain shadows flee:
In life, in death, O Lord, abide with me.

Praise My Soul The King Of Heaven

Praise, my soul, the King of heaven,
To his feet thy tribute bring;
Ransomed, healed, restored, forgiven,

Who, like me, his praise should sing?
Praise him, praise him, praise him, praise him,
Praise the everlasting King.

Praise him for his grace and favor
To our fathers in distress;
Praise him, still the same for ever,
Slow to chide, and swift to bless;
Praise him, praise him, praise him, praise him,
Glorious in his faithfulness.

Fatherlike, he tends and spares us;
Well our feeble frame he knows;
In his hands he gently bears us,
Rescues us from all our foes;
Praise him, praise him, praise him, praise him,
Widely as his mercy goes.

Angels, help us to adore him;
Ye behold him face to face;
Sun and moon, bow down before him,
Dwellers all in time and space,
Praise him, praise him, praise him, praise him,
Praise with us the God of grace.

COLERIDGE, HARTLEY (1796–1849), eldest son of Samuel Taylor Coleridge, lost his scholarship at Oxford for intemperance. He also failed as a schoolmaster. He spent his boyhood and his later years in the Lake District. In 1833 his *Poems, Songs and Sonnets* was published. The sonnets were particularly well received. He published, in that same year, *Biographia Borealis* (republished in 1836 as *Worthies of Yorkshire and Lancashire*). He contributed to various literary magazines. His *Essays and Marginalia* were published by his brother Derwent in 1851.

Multum Dilexit
"She Loved Much"

She sat and wept beside his feet; The weight
Of sin oppressed her heart; for all the blame,
And the poor malice of the worldly shame,
To her was past, extinct, and out of date:

Only the sin remained,—the leprous state;
She would be melted by the heat of love,

By fires far fiercer than are blown to prove
And purge the silver ore adulterate.

She sat and wept, and with her untressed hair
Still wiped the feet she was so blest to touch:
And He wiped off the soiling of despair
From her sweet soul, because she loved so much.

I am a sinner, full of doubts and fears,—
Make me a humble thing of love and tears!

KNOWLES, HERBERT (1798–1817), lost both his parents when he was quite young and would have become a merchant's clerk, except that some benevolent clergymen and friends raised the money to send him to school. He entered grammar school in Yorkshire, in his own words, "totally ignorant of classical and mathematical literature." He hoped to obtain a scholarship to Cambridge, but his relatives could or would not supplement the project, so in October, 1816, he applied to Southey for help, sending him at the same time "The Three Tabernacles." Southey promised to help him and obtained financial help from other men, as well. Knowles was elected a Cambridge "sizar" (a scholarship student) in January, 1917, but he was seriously sick by then and died in February. Some of his verses were printed in periodicals over the next decade. "Three Tabernacles," better known as "Stanzas in Richmond Churchyard" remains the one poem for which he was noted.

Lines Written In The Church Yard
Of Richmond, Yorkshire

Lord, it is good for us to be here: If thou wilt, let us make here three tabernacles; one for thee, and one for Moses, and one for Elias.—Matt. xvii. 4

Methinks it is good to be here,
If thou wilt, let us build—but for whom?
Nor Elias nor Moses appear;
but the shadows of eve that encompass with gloom
The abode of the dead and the place of the tomb.

Shall we build to Ambition? Ah no!
Affrighted, he shrinketh away;
For see, they would pin him below
In a small narrow cave, and, begirt with cold clay,
To the meanest of reptiles a peer and a prey.

To Beauty? Ah no! she forgets
The charms which she wielded before;

Nor knows the foul worm that he frets
The skin which but yesterday fools could adore,
For the smoothness it held or the tint which it wore.

Shall we build to the purple of Pride,
The trappings which dizen the proud,
Alas! they are all laid aside,
And here's neither dress nor adornments allowed,
But the long winding-sheet and the fringe of the shroud.

To Riches? Alas! 'tis in vain;
Who hid, in their turns have been hid;
The treasures are squandered again;
And here in the grave are all metals forbid
But the tinsel that shines on the dark coffin-lid.

To the pleasures which Mirth can afford,
The revel, the laugh, and the jeer?
Ah! here is a plentiful board!
But the guests are all mute as their pitiful cheer,
And none but the worm is a reveller here.

Shall we build to Affection and Love?
Ah no! they have withered and died,
Or fled with the spirit above.
Friends, brothers, and sisters are laid side by side,
Yet none have saluted and none have replied.

Unto Sorrow?—the dead cannot grieve;
Nor a sob, not a sigh meet mine ear,
Which Compassion itself could relieve.
Ah, sweetly they slumber, nor love, hope, or fear;
Peace! peace is the watchword, the only one here.

Unto Death, to whom monarchs must bow?
Ah no! for his empire is known.
And here there are trophies enow!
Beneath the cold dead, and around the dark stone,
Are the signs of a sceptre that none may disown.

The first tabernacle to Hope we will build,
And look for the sleepers around us to rise!
The second to Faith, which insures it fulfilled;
And the third to the Lamb of the great sacrifice,
Who bequeathed us them both when He rose to the skies.

NEWMAN, Cardinal JOHN HENRY (1801–1890), educated at Oxford College, became one of the leaders in the Oxford Movement, a revival of high church ideals and practices. He was ordained in the Church of England 1824, and became vicar of St. Mary's, Oxford in 1827. He published several books which contributed to the movement, including *Parochial and Plain Sermons* (1834-42), *Lectures on the Prophetical Office of the Church* (1837), and *Universal Sermons* (1843). In 1843, having come to doubt the catholicity of the Church of England, he resigned as vicar, and in 1845 he joined the Roman Catholic Church. He served as first rector of Catholic University, Dublin and published *The Idea of a University* in 1852. He published *Apologia pro Vita Sua* in 1864 in reply to Charles Kingsley's attacks on the Roman Catholic clergy. He disagreed on many matters with another Roman Catholic writer, Henry Manning, especially the enunciation of papal infallibility. (He opposed the enunciation but not the doctrine itself.) In 1879 he was made a cardinal by Pope Leo XIII.

Angel

My work is done,
My task is o'er,
And so I come,
Taking it home;
For the crown is won.
Alleluia,
For evermore.

My Father gave
In charge to me
This child of earth
E'en from its birth,
To serve and save,
Alleluia,
And saved is he.

This child of clay
To me was given,
To rear and train
By sorrow and pain
In the narrow way,
Alleluia,
From earth to heaven.

The Elements: A Tragic Chorus

Man is permitted much
To scan and learn
In Nature's frame:
Till he well-nigh can tame
Brute mischiefs and can touch
Invisible things, and turn
All warring ills to purposes of good.
Thus, as a god below,
He can control,
And harmonize, what seems amiss to flow
As severed from the whole
And dimly understood.

But o'er the elements
One Hand alone,
One Hand has sway
What influence day by day
In straiter belt prevents
The impious Ocean, thrown
Alternate o'er the ever-sounding shore?
Or who has eye to trace
How the Plague came?
Forerun the doublings of the Tempest's race?
Or the Air's weight and flame
On a set scale explore?

Thus God has willed
That man, when fully skilled
Still gropes in twilight dim;
Encompassed all his hours
By fearfullest powers
Inflexible to him.
That so he may discern
His feebleness.
And e'en for earth's success
To Him in wisdom turn,
Who holds for us the Keys of either home,
Earth and the world to come.

Melchizedek

*Without father, without mother, without descent; having neither
beginning of days, nor end of life.*

Thrice bless'd are they, who feel their loneliness;
To whom nor voice of friends nor pleasant scene
Brings that on which the sadden'd heart can lean;
Yea, the rich earth, garb'd in her daintiest dress
Of light and joy, doth but the more oppress,
Claiming responsive smiles and rapture high;
Till, sick at heart, beyond the veil they fly,
Seeking His Presence, who alone can bless.
Such, in strange days, the weapons of Heaven's grace;
When, passing o'er the high-born Hebrew line,
He forms the vessel of His vast design;
Fatherless, homeless, reft of age and place,
Sever'd from earth, and careless of its wreck,
Born through long woe His rare Melchizedek.

The Pillar of the Cloud (Lead, Kindly Light)

Lead, Kindly Light, amid the encircling gloom,
    Lead Thou me on!
The night is dark, and I am far from home—
    Lead Thou me on!
Keep Thou my, feet: I do not ask to see
The distant scene,—one step enough for me.

I was not ever thus, nor pray'd that Thou
    Shouldst lead me on.
I loved to choose and see my path; but now
    Lead Thou me on!
I loved the garish day, and, spite of fears,
Pride ruled my will: remember not past years.

So long Thy power hath blest me, sure it still
    Will lead me on,
O'er moor and fen, o'er crag and torrent, till
    The night is gone;
And with the morn those angel faces smile
Which I have loved long since, and lost awhile.

Taormini

Say, hast thou track'd a traveller's round,
Nor visions met thee there,
Thou couldst but marvel to have found
This blighted world so fair?

And feel an awe within thee rise,
That sinful man should see
Glories far worthier Seraph's eyes
Than to be shared by thee?

Store them in heart! thou shalt not faint
'Mid coming pains and fears,
As the third heaven once nerved a Saint
For fourteen trial-years.

The Path Of The Just

When I look back upon my former race,
Seasons I see, at which the Inward Ray
More brightly burn'd, or guided some new way;
Truth, in its wealthier scene and nobler space
Given for my eye to range, and feet to trace.
And next I mark, 'twas trial did convey,
Or grief, or pain, or strange eventful day,
To my tormented soul such larger grace.

So now, whene'er, in journeying on, I feel
The shadow of the Providential Hand,
Deep breathless stirrings shoot across my breast,
Searching to know what He will now reveal,
What sin uncloak, what stricter rule command,
And girding me to work His full behest.

Desolation

O say not thou art left of God,
Because His tokens in the sky
Thou canst not read: this earth He trod
To teach thee He was ever nigh.

He sees, beneath the fig-tree green,
Nathaniel con His sacred lore;

Shouldst thou thy chamber seek, unseen
He enters through the unopened door.

And when thou liest, by slumber bound,
Outwearied in the Christian fight,
In glory, girt with saints around,
He stands above thee through the night.

When friends to Emmaus bend their course,
He joins, although He holds their eyes:
Or, shouldst thou feel some fever's force,
He takes thy hand, He bids thee rise.

Or on a voyage, when calms prevail,
And prison thee upon the sea,
He walks the waves, He wings the sail,
The shore is gained, and thou art free.

MANGAN, JAMES CLARENCE (1803–1849), son of a Dublin grocer, learned Latin, Spanish, French, and Italian from an erudite cleric before his father's failure in business forced him to get a job with a scrivener, and then with a lawyer, in order to help support his family. He began to drink heavily, and though employed in the library of Trinity College and in the Irish ordnance survey offices, he never was very successful. He contributed verse to various Dublin magazines from 1822. He mastered German in order to read German philosophy, and sent translations to magazines, not only of German but of Turkish, Persian, Arabic, and Coptic, languages he did not know! He knew enough about the cultures to get away with it, though. He also made adaptations of Irish verse, although he did not know Irish, depending on prose translations by friends. He wrote for various magazines, but his drinking became an increasingly serious problem, until it put him in the hospital in 1848. He met with an accident on his recovery and was again hospitalized. In 1849 he died in the cholera epidemic that swept through Dublin that year. His poetry, including many ballads as well as translations, was much reprinted after his death.

S. Patrick's Hymn before Tara (From The Irish)

Christ, as a light,
Illumine and guide me!
Christ, as a shield, overshadow and cover me!
Christ be under me! Christ be over me!
Christ be beside me

On left hand and right!
Christ be before me, behind me, about me!
Christ this day be within and without me!

Christ, the lowly and meek,
Christ, the All-powerful, be
In the heart of each to whom I speak,
In the mouth of each who speaks to me!
In all who draw near me,
Or see me or hear me!

At Tara to-day, in this awful hour,
I call on the Holy Trinity!
Glory to Him who reigneth in power,
The God of the Elements, Father, and Son,
And Paraclete Spirit, which Three are the One,
The ever-existing Divinity!

Salvation dwells with the Lord,
With Christ, the Omnipotent Word.
From generation to generation
Grant us, O Lord, Thy grace and salvation!

HAWKER, ROBERT STEPHEN (1803–1875), became a vicar on the north
Cornish coast, where he pursued his antiquarian and literary interests, as well.
He is said to be the type for the character Canon Tremaine in Mortimer Collin's
Sweet and Twenty, with a distinctive and unforgettable personality. His poetry
includes *The Quest of the Sangraal: Chant the First* (1864) and *Cornish Ballads* (1869).
His *Poetical Works* (1879) and his *Prose Works* (1893) were edited by J.G. Godwin
and his complete poems were published in 1904 as *Cornish Ballads and other Poems*.
His formal reception into the Roman church just before his death sparked an
acrid newspaper controversy.

The Silent Tower of Bottreaux

Tintadgel bells ring o'er the tide,
The boy leans on his vessel's side;
He hears that sound, and dreams of home
Soothe the wild orphan of the foam.
  'Come to thy God in time!'
  Thus saith their pealing chime:
  'Youth, manhood, old age past,
  Come to thy God at last.'

But why are Bottreaux' echoes still?
Her Tower stands proudly on the hill;
Yet the strange chough that home hath found,
The lamb lies sleeping on the ground.
  'Come to thy God in time!'
  Should be her answering chime:
  'Come to thy God at last!'
  Should echo on the blast.

The ship rode down with courses free,
The daughter of a distant sea:
Her sheet was loose, her anchor stored,
The merry Bottreaux bells on board.
  'Come to thy God in time!'
  Rung out Tintadgel chime:
  'Youth, manhood, old age past,
  Come to thy God at last!'

The pilot heard his native bells
Hang on the breeze in fitful swells;
'Thank God!' with reverent brow he cried,
'We'll make the shore with evening's tide.'
  'Come to thy God in time!'
  It was his marriage chime:
  'Youth, manhood, old age past,'
  His bell must ring at last.

Thank God, thou whining knave! on land,
But thank, at sea, the steersman's hand'—
The captain's voice above the gale—
'Thank the good ship and ready sail.'
  'Come to thy God in time!'
  Sad grew the boding chime:
  'Come to thy God at last!'
  Boomed heavy on the blast.

Uprose the sea! as if it heard
The mighty Master's signal-word:
What thrills the captain's whitening lip?
The death-groans of his sinking ship.
  'Come to thy God in time!'
  Swung deep the funeral chime:
  'Grace, mercy, kindness past,
  Come to thy God at last!'

Long did the rescued pilot tell—
When grey hairs o'er his forehead fell,
While those around would hear and weep—
That fearful judgment of the deep.
　　'Come to thy God in time!'
　　He read his native chime:
　　'Youth, manhood, old age past,'
　　His bell rang out at last.

Still when the storm of Bottreaux' waves
Is wakening in his weedy caves:
Those bells, that sullen surges hide,
Peal their deep notes beneath the tide:
　　'Come to thy God in time!'
　　Thus saith the ocean chime:
　　'Storm, billow, whirlwind past,
　　Come to thy God at last!'

BROWNING, ELIZABETH BARRETT (1806–1861), wife of Robert Browning, was an invalid due to a childhood spinal injury. Robert's courtship of her, their eventual elopement and happy marriage in Italy are among the most famous of literary romances. She was delicate in constitution and that delicacy seems to be reflected in her poetry. Her best known work, *Sonnets from the Portugese,* a series of love sonnets addressed to her husband, was published in 1850. She also published a translation of Aeschylus' *Prometheus Bound* (1833), five other volumes of poetry, and a long narrative poem, *Aurora Leigh* (1856), among other works. Her faith is sometimes characterized as profound but unorthodox. Certainly this sonnet sounds the note of faith.

Comfort

Speak low to me, my Saviour, low and sweet
From out the hallelujahs, sweet and low,
Lest I should fear and fall, and miss Thee so,
Who art not missed by any that entreat.
Speak to me as to Mary at Thy feet!
And if no precious gums my hands bestow,
Let my tears drop like amber, while I go
In reach of Thy divinest voice complete
In humanest affection—thus, in sooth,
To lose the sense of losing. As a child,

Whose song-bird seeks the wood for evermore,
Is sung to in its stead by mother's mouth,
Till, sinking on her breast, love-reconciled,
He sleeps the faster that he wept before.

Bereavement

When some Beloveds, 'neath whose eyelids lay
The sweet lights of my childhood, one by one
Did leave me dark before the natural sun,
And I astonied fell, and could not pray,
A thought within me to myself did say,
" Is God less God that thou art left undone?
Rise, worship, bless Him! in this sackcloth spun,
As in that purple! "—But I answer, Nay!
What child his filial heart in words can loose,
If he behold his tender father raise
The hand that chastens sorely? Can he choose
But sob in silence with an upward gaze?
And my great Father, thinking fit to bruise,
Discerns in speechless tears both prayer and praise.

Sleep

"He giveth his beloved sleep."-Psalm cxxvi. 2.

Of all the thoughts of God that are
Borne inward unto souls afar,
Among the Psalmist's music deep,
Now tell me if that any is,
For gift or grace, surpassing this,—
"He giveth his beloved sleep"?

What would we give to our beloved?
The hero's heart, to be unmoved,—
The poet's star-tuned harp, to sweep,—
The patriot's voice, to teach and rouse,—
The monarch's crown, to light the brows?
"He giveth his beloved sleep."

What do we give to our beloved?
A little faith, all undisproved,—
A little dust to overweep,

And bitter memories, to make
The whole earth blasted for our sake,
"He giveth his beloved sleep."

"Sleep soft, beloved!" we sometimes say,
But have no tune to charm away
Sad dreams that through the eyelids creep
But never doleful dream again
Shall break the happy slumber when
"He giveth his beloved sleep."

O earth, so full of dreary noise!
O men, with wailing in your voice!
O delved gold the wailers heap!
O strife, O curse, that o'er it fall!
God strikes a silence through you all,
And "giveth his beloved sleep."

His dews drop mutely on the hill,
His cloud above it saileth still,
Though on its slope men sow and reap;
More softly than the dew is shed,
Or cloud is floated overhead,
"He giveth his beloved sleep."

For me, my heart, that erst did go
Most like a tired child at a show,
That sees through tears the mummers leap,
Would now its wearied vision close,
Would childlike on his love repose
Who "giveth his beloved sleep."

Substitution

When some beloved voice that was to you
Both sound and sweetness, faileth suddenly,
And silence against which you dare not cry,
Aches round you like a strong disease and new—
What hope? What help? What music will undo
That silence to your sense? Not friendship's sigh,
Not reason's subtle count; not melody
Of viols, nor of pipes that Faunus blew;
Not songs of poets, nor of nightingales,

Whose hearts leap upward through the cypress trees
To the clear moon; nor yet the spheric laws
Self-chanted, nor the angels' sweet 'All-hails,'
Met in the smile of God: Nay, none of these,
Speak Thou, availing Christ!—and fill this pause.

Convinced by Sorrow

"There is no God" the foolish saith,
But none, "There is no sorrow."
And nature oft the cry of faith,
In bitter need will borrow:
Eyes which the preacher could not school,
By wayside graves are raised,
And lips say "God be pitiful,"
Who ne'er said, "God be praised."
Be pitiful, O God!

The Meaning Of The Look

I think that look of Christ might seem to say—
"Thou Peter! art thou then a common stone
Which I at last must break my heart upon,
For all God's charge to his high angels may
Guard my foot better? Did I yesterday
Wash thy feet, my beloved, that they should run
Quick to deny me 'neath the morning sun?
And do thy kisses, like the rest, betray?
The cock crows coldly.—Go, and manifest
A late contrition, but no bootless fear!
For when thy final need is dreariest,
Thou shalt not be denied, as I am here;
My voice to God and angels shall attest,
Because I know this man, let him be clear."

WORDWORTH, CHRISTOPHER (1807–1885), was the second of three Christopher Wordsworths. (The other two were his father, an Anglican clergyman and the youngest brother of William, the romantic poet; and Christopher's second son, who became prebendary of Lincoln cathedral.) He was educated at Winchester and Cambridge and was canon, then archdeacon at Westminster before becoming bishop of Lincoln in 1868. He wrote on various classical and theological subjects, as well as authoring *The Memoirs of William Wordsworth* (1851). He also wrote a number of studies of the Bible and church history.

See The Conqueror Mounts In Triumph

See the Conqueror mounts in triumph,
See him come in royal state,
Like a laurelled king returning
To his joyful palace gate;
Hark! the choirs of angel voices
Joyful alleluyas sing,
And the portals wide are opened
To receive their heavenly King.

Who is this that comes in glory,
With the trump of jubilee?
Over battles, over armies,
He has gained the victory;
He who on the cross did suffer,
He who from the grave arose,
He has vanquished sin and Satan,
He by death has spoiled his foes.

Thou hast raised our human nature
To the height on God's right hand;
There we sit in heavenly places,
There with thee in glory stand;
Jesus reigns, adored by angels;
Man with God is on the throne;
Mighty Lord, in thine ascension
We by faith behold our own.

Glory, be to God the Father;
Glory be to God the Son,
Dying, risen, ascending for us,
Who the heavenly realm has won;
Glory to the Holy Spirit;
To one God in persons three;
Glory both in earth and heaven,
Glory, endless glory be.

Hark The Sound Of Holy Voices

Hark the sound of holy voices,
Chanting at the crystal sea,
Alleluya, alleluya,
Alleluya, Lord, to thee!
Multitude, which none can number,
Like the stars in glory stands,
Clothed in white apparel, holding
Palms of victory in their hands.

Patriarch, and holy prophet,
Who prepared the way of Christ,
King, apostle, saint, confessor,
Martyr, and evangelist,
Saintly maiden, godly matron,
Widows who have watched to prayer,
Joined in holy concert, singing
To the Lord of all, are there.

Marching with thy cross their banner,
They have triumphed following
Thee, the captain of salvation,
Thee, their saviour and their king;
Gladly, Lord, with thee they suffered;
Gladly, Lord, with thee they died,
And by death to life immortal
They were born, and glorified.

Now they reign in heavenly glory,
Now they walk in golden light,
Now they drink, as from a river,
Holy bliss and infinite;
Love and peace they taste for ever,
And all truth and knowledge see
In the beatific vision
Of the blessed Trinity.

God of God, the one-begotten
Light of light, Emmanuel,
In whose body joined together
All the saints for ever dwell;
Pour upon us of thy fullness,

That we may for evermore
God the Father, God the Spirit,
One with thee on high, adore.

O Day of Rest and Gladness

O day of rest and gladness,
O day of joy and light,
O balm of care and sadness,
Most beautiful, most bright!
On Thee the high and lowly,
Through ages joined in tune,
Sing, "Holy, holy, holy!"
To the great God triune.

Thou art a port protected
From storms that round us rise;
A garden intersected
With streams of paradise;
Thou art a colling fountain
In life's dry dreary sand;
From thee, like Pisgah's mountain,
We view our promised land.

Today on weary nations
The heavenly manna falls;
To holy convocations
The silver trumpet calls;
Where gospel light is glowing
With pure and radiant beams,
And living water flowing
With soul-refreshing streams.

A day of sweet reflection
Thou art,—a day of love,
A day of resurrection
From earth to things above.
New graces ever gaining
From this our day of rest,
We reach the rest remaining
To spirits of the blest.

BROWN, NATHAN (1807–1886), born in New Hampshire, became both a poet and a missionary. He graduated from Williams College, became a teacher and then editor of the *Vermont Telegraph*. After receiving a call to mission work, he attended the Theological Institution at Newton, Massachusetts, and in 1832 sailed with his wife and child for Burma. He completed the translation of the New Testament in 1848. Physically and mentally exhausted, he returned to the United States in 1855. Out of disagreement with the Missionary Union policy, he did not return to mission work until 1873, when he was sent to Japan. In 1879 he completed the first full translation of the New Testament into Japanese. He died in Yokohama. In addition to writing poetry, Brown translated many favorite English hymns into Burmese and Japanese.

My Soul is Not at Rest

My soul is not at rest. There comes a strange
And secret whisper to my spirit, like
A dream of night, that tells me I am on
Enchanted ground. Why live I here? The vows
Of God are on me, and I may not stop
To play with shadows or pluck earthly flowers,
Till I my work have done, and rendered up
Account. The voice of my departed Lord:
"Go, teach all nations," from the eastern world
Comes on the night air, and awakes my ear.

And I will go. I may no longer doubt
To give up friends, and home, and idol hopes,
And every tender tie that binds my heart
To thee, my country! Why should I regard
Earth's little store of borrowed sweets? I sure
Have had enough of bitter in my cup
To show that never was it his design,
Who placed me here, that I should live in ease,
Or drink at pleasure's fountain. Henceforth, then,
It matters not if storm or sunshine be
My earthly lot, bitter or sweet my cup;
I only pray, God fit me for the work;
God make me holy, and my spirit nerve
For the stern hour of strife. Let me but know
There is an Arm unseen that holds me up,
An Eye that kindly watches all my path,
Till I my weary pilgrimage have done;
Let me but know I have a Friend that waits

To welcome me to glory, and I joy
To tread the dark and death-fraught wilderness.

And when I come to stretch me for the last,
In unattended agony beneath
The cocoa's shade, or lift my dying eyes
From Afric's burning sand, it will be sweet
That I have toiled for other worlds than this.
I know I shall feel happier than to die
On softer bed. And if I should reach heaven—
If one that hath so deeply, darkly sinned—
If one whom ruin and revolt have held
With such a fearful grasp—if one for whom
Satan hath struggled as he hath for me—
Should ever reach that blessed shore, O how
This heart will glow with gratitude and love!
And through the ages of eternal years,
Thus saved, my spirit never shall repent
That toil and suffering once were mine below.

TRENCH, RICHARD CHEVENIX (1807–1886), went to Cambridge, where he was friends with Alfred Tennyson and Arthur Hallam. He went through a period of depression after 1829, in which he found relief through writing poetry. He spent some time in Spain and returned to England where he become a clergyman in 1832. He held several positions and began to read patristic and theological works out of which study came *Notes and Parables* in 1840. He became a close friend of Samuel Wilberforce, who did much to make Trench a public figure. In 1845 Wilberforce got him appointed professor of divinity, later professor of the exegesis of the New Testament at King's College. He was appointed dean of Westminster in 1856 and began the work of bringing the abbey into touch with the people of London, work that continued under his successor, Stanley. As Archbishop of Dublin, he became a central figure in opposing the disestablishment of the Irish church and afterwards in maintaining the bishop's office as independent rather than subordinate to the clergy and laity. He also led the conservatives in the efforts at prayer book revision from 1871 to 1877. He kept the Irish church united during the agitation following disestablishment. He was injured in 1875, never fully recovering, and resigned his office in 1884. He published many books of poetry during his life, including many notable sonnets. His exegetical works on the parables and miracles also distinguished him. He was on the committee for the revised version of the Bible. As a philologist he popularized scientific study of language and first suggested guidelines for the writing of the *Oxford English Dictionary*.

God our Refuge

If there had anywhere appeared in space
Another place of refuge where to flee,
Our hearts had taken refuge in that place,
And not with Thee.
For we against creation's bars had beat
Like prisoned eagles, through great worlds had sought
Though but a foot of ground to plant our feet,
Where Thou wert not.

And only when we found in earth and air,
In heaven or hell, that such might nowhere be—
That we could not flee from Thee anywhere,
We fled to Thee.

What is Man?

What, many times I musing ask'd, is Man,
    If grief and care
Keep far from him? he knows not what he can,
    What cannot bear.

He, till the fire hath proved him, doth remain
    The main part dross:
To lack the loving discipline of pain
    Were endless loss.

Yet when my Lord did ask me on what side
    I were content,
The grief, whereby I must be purified,
    To me were sent,

As each imagined anguish did appear,
    As each withering bliss,
Before my soul, I cried, 'Oh! spare me here:
    Oh no, not this!'—

Like one that having need of, deep within,
    The surgeon's knife.
Would hardly bear that it should graze the skin.
    Though for his life:—

Till He at last, Who best doth understand
    Both what we need,

And what can bear, did take my case in hand,
   Nor crying heed.

Lord, Many Times I Am Aweary Quite

Lord, many times I am aweary quite
Of mine own self, my sin, my vanity;
Yet be not Thou, or I am lost outright,
Weary of me!

And hate against myself I often bear,
And enter with myself in fierce debate:
Take Thou my part against myself, nor share
In that just hate.

Best friends might loathe us, if what things perverse,
We know of our own selves, they also knew;
Lord, Holy One! if Thou who knowest worse,
Should loathe us, too!

WHITTIER, JOHN GREENLEAF (1807–1892), a Quaker, was born in Massachusetts, where he began his writing career with Robert Burns as his chief model. He worked as journalist on the papers of William Garrison in Boston, and published his *Legend of New England in Prose and Verse* in 1829. He became actively involved in the abolition movement, through which he was elected to the Massachusetts legislature in 1835. He became editor of the *Pennsylvania Freeman* and wrote verse published in *Poems Written During the Progress of the Abolition Question* (1838). Other books of his early poetry included *Lays of My Home and Other Poems* (1943), then *Voices of Freedom* (1846). He edited the *National Era* newspaper, in which his poems (1847–1860) were published. In 1849 he published his only long work of fiction, *Leaves from Margaret Smith's Journal in the Province of Massachusetts Bay*. His first collected *Poems* was published that same year. He put out two more prose collections, *Old Portraits and Modern Sketches* (1850) and *Literary Recreations and Miscellanies* (1854). Whittier's *Songs of Labor* (1850) carried on the passionate, but literary plea against slavery. He continued to further his "other reputation" as a poet of the countryside with *The Chapel of the Hermits* (1853), *The Panorama and Other Poems* (1856), and *Home Ballads, Poems, and Lyrics* (1860). *Panorama* included "Barefoot Boy" and *Home Ballads* included "Skipper Ireson's Ride," two of Whittier's more popular poems. During the Civil War, he published *In War Time and Other Poems* (1864), including "Barbara Frietchie," and following the war he turned back to the countryside with *Snow-Bound* (1866) and *Tent on the Beach* (1867), a series of verse narratives. His later poetry, published in *Among the Hills* (1869), *Miriam and Other Poems* (1871), *Hazel-Blossoms*

(1875), *The Vision of Echard* (1878), *St. Gregory's Guest* (1886), and *At Sundown* (1890) focuses on rural and historical settings.

From "Andrew Rykman's Prayer"

Pardon, Lord, the lips that dare
Shape in words a mortal's prayer!
. . .
Not as one who seeks his home
With a step assured I come;
Still behind the tread I hear
Of my life-companion, Fear;
Still a shadow deep and vast
From my westering feet is cast,
Wavering, doubtful, undefined,
Never shapen nor outlined:
From myself the fear has grown,
And the shadow is my own.
Yet, O Lord, through all a sense
Of Thy tender providence
Stays my falling heart on Thee,
And confirms the feeble knee;
And, at times, my worn feet press
Spaces of cool quietness,
Lilied whiteness shone upon;
Hours there be of inmost calm,
Broken but by grateful psalm,
When I love Thee more than fear Thee,
And Thy blessed Christ seems near me,
With forgiving look, as when
He beheld the Magdalen.
Well I know that all things move
To the spheral rhythm of love,—
That to Thee, O Lord of all!

Dear Lord and Father of Mankind
From *The Brewing of Soma*

Dear Lord and Father of mankind,
Forgive our foolish ways!
Reclothe us in our rightful mind,

In purer lives Thy service find,
In deeper reverence, praise.

In simple trust like theirs who heard
Beside the Syrian sea
The gracious calling of the Lord,
Let us, like them, without a word,
Rise up and follow Thee.

Drop Thy still dews of quietness,
Till all our strivings cease;
Take from our souls the strain and stress,
And let our ordered lives confess
The beauty of Thy peace.

Breathe through the heats of our desire
Thy coolness and Thy balm;
Let sense be dumb, let flesh retire;
Speak through the earthquake, wind, and fire,
O still, small voice of calm!

Vesta

O Christ of God! whose life and death
Our own have reconciled,
Most quietly, most tenderly
Take home Thy star-named child!

Thy grace is in her patient eyes,
Thy words are on her tongue;
The very silence round her seems
As if the angels sung.

Her smile is as a listening child's
Who hears its mother call;
The lilies of Thy perfect peace
About her pillow fall.

She leans from out our clinging arms
To rest herself in Thine;
Alone to Thee, dear Lord, can we
Our well-beloved resign.

Oh, less for her than for ourselves
We bow our heads and pray;

Her setting star, like Bethlehem's,
To Thee shall point the way!

Hymns of the Romantic Period

As the poetry of the romantic period (or romantic revival as it is sometimes called) was partly in reaction to the rationalism of the Restoration period, so romantic hymns swung toward a more personal and even "enthusiastic" expression of faith in Christ. The models admired by their authors were the hymns lyrics of the eighteenth century's "Great Awakening" rather than those of the Restoration.

However, since time and God's plan for human history are linear, there is never any going back. Romantic hymns have their own distinctives. They tend toward a self-consciousness the Great Awakening had in much smaller measure. They are "existential" in a more modern sense, having more to do with the human side—even of divine encounters. And despite the language of "enthusiasm," there seems to be generally less fervor and sometimes less confidence than one hears in the great eighteenth century hymns.

All Hail The Power Of Jesus' Name
E . Perronet (1780)

All hail the power of Jesus' name
Let angels prostrate fall;
Bring forth the royal diadem
To crown him Lord of all.

Crown him, ye martyrs of your God,
Who from his altar call;
Praise him whose way of pain ye trod,
And crown him Lord of all.

Ye prophets who our freedom won,
Ye searchers, great and small
By whom the work of truth is done,
Now crown him Lord of all.

Sinners, whose love can ne'er forget
The wormwood and the gall,
Go spread your trophies at his feet,
And crown him Lord of all.

Bless him, each poor oppressed race
That Christ did upward call;
His hand in each achievement trace,
And crown him Lord of all.

Let every tribe and every tongue
To him their hearts enthral:
Lift high the universal song,
And crown him Lord of all.

Just As I Am
Charlotte Elliott, 1836

Just as I am without one plea
But that thy blood was shed for me,
And that thou bidd'st me come to thee,
O Lamb of God I come.

Just as I am and waiting not
To rid my soul of one dark blot,
To thee, whose blood can cleanse each spot,
O Lamb of God I come.

Just as I am, though tossed about
With many a conflict, many a doubt,
Fightings and fears within, without,
O Lamb of God, I come.

Just as I am, poor, wretched, blind;
Sight, riches, healing of the mind,
Yea, all I need, in thee to find,
O Lamb of God, I come.

Just as I am! thou wilt receive,
Wilt welcome, pardon, cleanse, relieve;
Because thy promise I believe,
O Lamb of God, I come.

Just as I am! thy love unknown
Has broken ev'ry barrier down;
Now, to be thine, yea, thine alone,
O Lamb of God, I come.

O Worship The King
Sir Robert Grant, 1833

O worship the King all glorious above,
O gratefully sing his pow'r and his love;
Our Shield and Defender, the Ancient of Days,
Pavilioned in splendor, and girded with praise.

O tell of his might, O sing of his grace,
Whose robe is the light, whose canopy space.
His chariots of wrath the deep thunderclouds form,
And dark is his path on the wings of the storm.

The earth with its store of wonders untold,
Almighty, thy pow'r hath founded of old;
Hath stablished it fast by a changeless decree,
And round it hath cast, like a mantle, the sea.

Thy bountiful care what tongue can recite?
It breathes in the air; it shines in the light;
It streams from the hills; it descends to the plain;
And sweetly distils in the dew and the rain.

Frail children of dust, and feeble as frail,
In thee do we trust, nor find thee to fail;
Thy mercies how tender, how firm to the end,
Our Maker, Defender, Redeemer, and Friend!

O measureless Might! Ineffable Love!
While angels delight to hymn thee above,
The humbler creation, though feeble their lays,
With true adoration shall lisp to thy praise.

Lord With Glowing Heart I'd Praise Thee
Francis Scott Key 1817

Lord with glowing heart I'd praise thee
For the bliss thy love bestows,
For the pardoning grace that saves me,
And the peace that from it flows:

Help, O God, my weak endeavor;
This dull soul to rapture raise:
Thou must light the flame, or never
Can my love be warmed to praise.

Praise, my soul the God who sought thee,
Wretched wand'rer far astray;
Found thee lost, and kindly brought thee
From the paths of death away:

Praise, with love's devoutest feeling,
Him who saw thy guilt-born fear,
And, the light of hope revealing,
Bade the bloodstained cross appear.

Praise thy Saviour God that drew thee
To that cross, new life to give,
Held a blood-sealed pardon to thee,
Bade thee look to him and live:

Praise the grace whose threats alarmed thee,
Roused thee from thy fatal ease,
Praise the grace whose promise warm'd thee,
Praise the grace that whispered peace.

Lord, this bosom's ardent feeling
Vainly would my lips express:
Low before thy footstool kneeling,
Deign thy suppliant's pray'r to bless:

Let thy love, my soul's chief treasure,
Love's pure flame within me raise;
And, since words can never measure,
Let my life show forth thy praise.

Chapter Seven

POETRY OF THE EARLY VICTORIAN PERIOD

1837—Victoria crowned Queen   1861—American Civil War

Our distinguishing of the Victorian period into two sections, Early and Late, is as arbitrary as our other literary divisions. The designation of the whole Victorian period is likewise arbitrary, except in strict application to the reign of that British sovereign. We may nevertheless say certain factors shifted society and poetry significantly from the time of Victoria's ascent to the throne to the end of the First World War: 1) a shift in the "equilibrium" between "religion" and "science," the former dominating still in the Early Victorian, the latter in the Late Victorian; 2) a shift from an optimism about human society (particularly American and British) to a predominant pessimism; 3) a shift from trying to maximize the potential for good in human society to an effort to minimize the evil; and 4) the particular shift in the church and among Christian poets from viewing the church and society as more or less integrated to wrestling with new definitions of them as separate and opposed.

During the Victorian period, the great tension between Christian thought and "enlightenment" secular thought reached an uneasy equilibrium, that continues uneasily among us today. Most particularly in the normalizing of the idea of a secular world, modernism is merely an extension of Victorian thought. In the early Victorian period, Christianity still dominated culture, but it may be argued that dominance ended in the second half.

In other terms, we might say T.S. Eliot's "dissociation of the sensibilities from the intellect" was completed or finally accepted as normal during the Victorian age. One evidence for this is the growing general perspective that affirmed a separation between beliefs and morals: what one affirmed in theory and what one did in practice. The disparity went in both directionsas it does today: some believed better than they acted; others acted better than they believed. Many accounts claim the Victorian age was a period of unprecedented "religious" activity. That religious activity was not all motivated by Christian faith, however. On the other hand, sometimes literary proponents of high standards in human ethics, such as George Eliot (Mary Ann Evans), lived in a manner less exemplary (as she did).

From the standpoint of his attitudes toward Christianity, we might characterize the Victorian poet as belonging to one of four "schools": 1) turning, 2) yearning, 3) returning, or 4) spurning. The "turning" poet was moving away from a Christian worldview. The "yearning" poet had a sort of nostalgia toward Christian faith, but was unsure whether it was still possible to reaffirm the central doctrines of the faith. He was to varying degrees a "searcher" after spiritual truth. The "returning" poet "came back" to Christian faith, having found the alternatives false. The "spurning" poet aggressively rejected Christianity and/or affirmed alternative world views—either the pagan mystical or materialistic "scientism." There is much overlap and combination of these categories in individual poets—especially when viewed over the course of their lifetimes. Nevertheless the tension between Christian faith and the alternatives was practically universal as a major factor in Victorian poetry.

It is perhaps due largely to this tension that the novel came to be the dominant literary genre. The novel allows for great latitude of philosophical and religious "worldview." A novel's "goodness" or "badness" depends on an undefined sense of internal consistency that may vary considerably from the reader's view of what is "good" or "bad" in any moral, philosophical, or religious sense. (In a similar way, the modern movie is allowed tremendous latitude—many contemporary Christians go to see movies they know are "bad" morally, excusing the "badness" and judging on a much lower plain of technical and stylistic "goodness.")

The Victorian age was the period of England's greatest expansion and consolidation as a world power. During this time the center of world culture may be said to have moved from Paris to London. London, itself grew from 2 million to 6.5 million people during Victoria's reign. The development of the steam engine, railways, printing presses, and farm machinery, along with the tremendous growth in factory mechanization contributed to this urbanization of the nation. British merchant fleets carried England's manufactured goods to all the world's ports. This growth and expansion as an urban, industrial, and colonial power brought an overwhelming sense of success, power, and optimism to certain sectors of the society.

Christian poetry of the Early Victorian period, while including a wide range of forms and styles, is most clearly seen in two sorts—the hymn lyric of the "Returning" and the indecisive poem of the "Yearning" poet. Particular in the latter, it is difficult to ascertain purely from the poem itself what the poet believed. In many cases it seems as useless to say he believed none of the basic doctrines of the Christian faith as to say he affirmed all. As always the ultimate determinations on those scores must be made by the Ultimate Critic.

For our purposes, however, we have included here a great deal of poetry that is far less explicitly Christ-centered than we have seen in previous periods. At the same time, we have labored to avoid presenting as Christian those other strains of religious philosophy that multiplied during the Victorian era.

An example of a Victorian poet who maintained a higher degree of "association" (as per T.S. Eliot, again) in the Victorian age, is Christina Rossetti. Such poets as Robert and Mrs. Browning, and Alfred Tennyson, despite lofty wrestlings and poetic dexterity, offer us a "doctrinal" content that is relatively meager, although their works contain "existential" truth, often powerfully presented. We have included the best hymn writers here, but as the Victorian Period went on, there were an increasing number of hymn-writers whose work was embarrassingly void of theological content or poetic beauty.

The "passion" of the romantics and the "wit" of the neoclassical poets, defined in some measure in opposition to each other, both flow into Victorian poetry, along with all of the stylistic paraphernalia of the previous ages. Victorian poets employed the many forms that were already part of the tradition. They did not define their "poetic" primarily in opposition to what had gone before, much less do they seem to have tried to "shake free" from traditional style. Victorian poets often use the traditional elements of poetry to their fullest. They also treated homely and "everyday" subjects with affection.

Victorian poetry was very conscious of the idiom of common speech, which the romantics had advocated in theory, and such as Burns in practice. But for Victorians it was ordinary speech, not the Scottish or country speech that was their basic material. With truth much more in question than in any other age, honesty of expression was felt to be tremendously important. This comes down to us in one of the few poetic shibboleths nearly universal to contemporary criticism—poetic language should never be "false," that is unnatural, artificial, archaic, clichéd, stock, etcetera. To put it paradoxically they held that poetry should not sound too much like poetry. Some attribute this to the effect of journalism, the burgeoning influence of innumerable newspapers, magazines, and journals that continues so much with us today. (C. S. Lewis wrote that one who would write well should avoid reading magazines and newspapers altogether.)

On the other hand, Victorian poetry was poetry—defined over against all other genres, and certainly over against journalism, so while the diction, the words themselves could not be too "poetic," the language and rhythms, and the word order is poetic. (This latter—word order—is one of the distinctions remaining to Victorian, in contrast to modern poetry. Twentieth century poetry is almost as uncomfortable with inversions, etcetera, as with archaic words.) A further variation on this comes most distinctly in Hopkins's watershed poetry—the use of ordinary words (and some unusual ones, too) in very unordinary ways. Victorian poets were doing this in milder ways before Hopkins. Twentieth century poets have tried to take it farther.

The very legitimate concerns over social responsibility that went with the evils of colonial and industrial expansion were reflected in much of Early Victorian literature and some of the poetry. Dickens's novels, for example, nearly all have the disparity between the affluent and the very poor as a backdrop. Sustained efforts toward eliminating such social ills as the slave trade, slave-holding, unregulated factory labor (especially among children and women), and various severe conditions of urban poverty occupied many godly men like Wilberforce and Shaftesbury. Many hymns, both evangelical and liberal, include expressions of the need to affirm the "brotherhood of man" in compassion toward those who suffer, especially from the oppression of their fellow men.

But when all is said, Christian poetry of the Early Victorian period shares the great and simple tenets of the faith—the centricity of Christ and his work, the fellowship of the saints, and the promises of God. There continues the tradition that began with the Anglo-Saxons of crying out in poetry to God for grace applied to the particular trials of the believer and the church. There also continues an evangelical call to the unbeliever—to consider his lost state, Christ's sacrifice on his behalf, and the salvation that is offered him in the gospel.

A Brief Chronology of the Early Victorian Period

1832	First Reform Bill passes
1833	Thomas Carlyle publishes *Sartor Resartus*—his "baptism" into secular "faith"
1837	Victoria ascends to throne
	Charles Dickens publishes *Pickwick Papers*
	Sunday Observance Bill passed by Parliament
1838	Workingman's organization, "The Chartists" draw up "People's Charter"
	Charles Dickens publishes *Oliver Twist*
1830s–40s	Oxford Movement, to strengthen "high church" party in Church of England, led by John Henry Newman
1840s	"Hungry 40's"—great deprivation among England's poor
1845	John Henry Newman becomes a Roman Catholic
	Serious crop failures in England, potato blight in Ireland
1846	Robert Browning marries Elizabeth Barrett, elopes to Italy
	Corn Laws repealed
	Dante Gabriel Rossetti writes "Blessed Damozel"
1847	Karl Marx publishes *Communist Manifesto*
	Charlotte Brontë publishes *Jane Eyre;* Emily Brontë publishes *Wuthering Heights*
1848	Thackeray publishes *Vanity Fair;* Anne Brontë publishes *Tenant of Wildfell Hall*
1850	Alfred Tennyson becomes poet laureate. Publishes *In Memoriam*
1851	Great Exhibition in London
1853	Matthew Arnold's *Poems* published
1854–56	Crimean War against Russia

1857	Arnold elected Professor of Poetry at Oxford
1859	Charles Darwin's *Origin of the Species* published
	Charless Dickens publishes *Tale of Two Cities*
	Tennyson, *Idylls of the King* (first four books)
	Edward Fitzgerald, "Rubaiyat of Omar Khayam"
1861	American Civil War begins

TENNYSON, FREDERICK (1807–1898), son of a Surrey vicar, and older brother of the more famous Alfred, contributed to a collection, *Poems of Two Brothers* (1827) including poetry by Alfred and Charles. He also published *Days and Hours* (1854), *Isles of Greece* (1890), and *Daphne and Other Poems* (1891).

The Holy Tide

The days are sad, it is the Holy tide:
The Winter morn is short, the Night is long;
So let the lifeless Hours be glorified
With deathless thoughts and echo'd in sweet song:
And through the sunset of this purple cup
They will resume the roses of their prime,
And the old Dead will hear us and wake up,
Pass with dim smiles and make our hearts sublime!
The days are sad, it is the Holy tide:
Be dusky mistletoes and hollies strown,
Sharp as the spear that pierced His sacred side,
Red as the drops upon His thorny crown;
No haggard Passion and no lawless Mirth
Fright off the solemn Muse,—tell sweet old tales,
Sing songs as we sit brooding o'er the hearth,
Till the lamp flickers, and the memory fails.

Iona

I landed on Iona's holy isle,
And wandered through its ancient ruins bare,
And felt the great Columba's self was there.
Thirteen long centuries seemed "a little while"
Before the unchanging sea and sky, whose smile
He knew. He trod these paths; he breathed this air;
These waves once rolled responsive to his prayer,
Whose murmuring ripples now my ear beguile.
Nor to the Saint alone closer I stand,

Nearer the Lord I seem, upon this shore;
The solid rock of this historic strand
Helps me to bridge Time's waste of waters o'er,
And grasp His feet, and feel His loving hand
In whom all saints are one for evermore!

An Incident

At the Lord's Table waiting, robed and stoled,
Till all had knelt around, I saw a sign!
In the full chalice sudden splendours shine,
Azure and crimson, emerald and gold.
I stooped to see the wonder, when, behold!
Within the cup a Countenance divine
Looked upward at me through the trembling wine,
Suffused with tenderest love and grief untold.

The comfort of that sacramental token
From Memory's page Time never can erase;
The glass of that rich window may be broken,
But not the mirrored image of His grace,
Through which my dying Lord to me has spoken,
At His own Holy Table, face to face!

PALMER, RAY (1808–1887), born in Rhode Island, worked as a dry-goods clerk in Boston after receiving a home elementary education from his father, a judge. He became a member of Park Street church under pastor Sereno E. Dwight, who helped him gain admission to Phillips Academy in Andover. Palmer graduated from Yale College in 1830. He taught at girls' schools in New York and New Haven, while studying theology, and entered the Congregational ministry in 1835. He pastored churches in Bath, Maine, and Albany, New York, · becoming secretary of the Congregational Union in New York City from 1866-1878. He wrote many hymns, his published volumes including *Hymns and Sacred Pieces* (1865), *Hymns of My Holy Hours* (1868), and *Voices of Hope and Gladness* (1880). He was one of the first American hymn-writers to translate Latin hymns into English.

Hymn—Jesus These Eyes Have Never Seen

Jesus these eyes have never seen
That radiant form of thine;

The veil of sense hangs dark between
Thy blessed face and mine.

I see thee not, I hear thee not,
Yet art thou oft with me;
And earth hath ne'er so dear a spot
As where I meet with thee.

Yet, though I have not seen, and still
Must rest in faith alone,
I love thee, dearest Lord, and will,
Unseen, but not unknown.
When death these mortal eyes shall seal
And still this throbbing heart,
The rending veil shall thee reveal
All glorious as thou art.

My Faith Looks Up To Thee

My faith looks up to thee,
Thou Lamb of Calvary,
Saviour divine!
Now hear me while I pray,
Take all my guilt away,
O let me from this day
Be wholly thine.

May thy rich grace impart
Strength to my fainting heart,
My zeal inspire;
As thou hast died for me,
O may my love to thee
Pure, warm, and changeless be,
A living fire.

While life's dark maze I tread,
And griefs around me spread,
Be thou my guide;
Bid darkness turn to day,
Wipe sorrow's tears away,
Nor let me ever stray
From thee aside.

When ends life's transient dream,
When death's cold sullen stream
Shall o'er me roll,
Blest Saviour, then in love
Fear and distrust remove;
O bear me safe above,
A ransomed soul.

Jesus, Thou Joy Of Loving Hearts
From a Latin hymn attributed to Bernard of Clairvaux, circa 1150

Jesus, thou Joy of loving hearts,
Thou Font of life, thou Light of men,
From the best bliss that earth imparts
We turned unfilled to thee again.

Thy truth unchanged hath ever stood;
Thou savest those that on thee call;
To them that seek thee thou art good,
To them that find thee All in all.

We taste thee, O thou living Bread,
And long to feast upon thee still;
We drink of thee, the Fountainhead,
And thirst our souls from thee to fill.

Our restless spirits yearn for thee,
Where e'er our changeful lot is cast;
Glad when thy gracious smile we see,
Blest when our faith can hold thee fast.

O Jesus, ever with us stay,
Make all our moments calm and bright;
Chase the dark night of sin away,
Shed o'er the world thy holy light.

BONAR, HORATIUS (1808–1889), educated at the University of Edinburgh, was ordained in 1837 in the Church of Scotland. He ministered in Kelso, leaving the Established Church in the "Disruption" of May, 1843, but remaining in Kelso as a minister in the Free Church of Scotland. He received a D.D. from Aberdeen in 1853, and went to the Chalmers Memorial Church in Edinburgh in 1866. In 1883 he was Moderator of the General Assembly of the

Free Church of Scotland. Hymns from his three series of *Hymns of Faith and Hope* (1857–66) were and are widely used in English-speaking churches.

Precedence

'Tis first the true and then the beautiful,
Not first the beautiful and then the true;
First the wild moor, with rock and reed and pool,
Then the gay garden, rich in scent and hue.

'Tis first the good and then the beautiful,—
Not first the beautiful and then the good;
First the rough seed, sown in the rougher soil,
Then the flower-blossom, or the branching wood.

Not first the glad and then the sorrowful,—
But first the sorrowful, and then the glad;
Tears for a day,—for earth of tears is full,
Then we forget that we were ever sad.

Not first the bright, and after that the dark,—
But first the dark, and after that the bright;
First the thick cloud, and then the rainbows arc,
First the dark grave, then resurrection-light.

'Tis first the night,—stern night of storm and war,—
Long night of heavy clouds and veiled skies;
Then the far sparkle of the Morning-star,
That bids the saints awake and dawn arise.

'Thy Way, Not Mine'

Thy way, not mine, O Lord,
However dark it be!
Lead me by Thine own hand,
Choose out the path for me.

Smooth let it be or rough,
It will be still the best;
Winding or straight, it leads
Right onward to Thy rest.

I dare not choose my lot;
I would not, if I might;

Choose Thou for me, my GOD;
So shall I walk aright.

The kingdom that I seek
Is Thine; so let the way
That leads to it be Thine;
Else I must surely stray.

Take Thou my cup, and it
With joy or sorrow fill,
As best to Thee may seem;
Choose Thou my good and ill;
Choose Thou for me my friends,
My sickness or my health;
Choose Thou my cares for me,
My poverty or wealth.

Not mine, not mine the choice,
In things or great or small;
Be Thou my guide, my strength,
My wisdom, and my all!

Not What My Hands Have Done

Not what my hands have done
Can save my guilty soul;
Not what my toiling flesh has borne
Can make my spirit whole.
Not what I feel or do
Can give me peace with God;
Not all my prayers and sighs and tears
Can bear the awful load.

Thy work alone, O Christ,
Can ease this weight of sin;
Thy blood alone, O Lamb of God,
Can give me peace within.
Thy love to me, O God,
Not mine, O Lord, to thee,
Can rid me of this dark unrest,
And set my spirit free.

Thy grace alone, O God,
To me can pardon speak;

Thy pow'r alone, O Son of God,
Can this sore bondage break.
No other work save thine,
No other blood will do;
No strength, save that which is divine,
Can bear me safely through.

I bless the Christ of God;
I rest on love divine;
And with unfalt'ring lip and heart,
I call this Savior mine.
His cross dispels each doubt;
I bury in his tomb
Each thought of unbelief and fear,
Each ling'ring shade of gloom.

I praise the God of grace;
I trust his truth and might;
He calls me his, I call him mine,
My God, my joy, my light.
'Tis he who saveth me,
And freely pardon gives;
I love because he loveth me,
I live because he lives.

Here, O My Lord, I See Thee Face To Face

Here, O my Lord, I see thee face to face;
Here would I touch and handle things unseen,
Here grasp with firmer hand th'eternal grace,
And all my weariness upon thee lean.

Here would I feed upon the bread of God,
Here drink with thee the royal wine of heaven;
Here would I lay aside each earthly load,
Here taste afresh the calm of sin forgiven.

This is the hour of banquet and of song;
This is the heav'nly table spread for me:
Here let me feast, and, feasting, still prolong
The brief, bright hour of fellowship with thee.

I have no help but thine, nor do I need
Another arm save thine to lean upon:

It is enough, my Lord, enough indeed;
My strength is in thy might, thy might alone.

Mine is the sin, but thine the righteousness;
Mine is the guilt, but thine the cleansing blood;
Here is my robe, my refuge, and my peace,
Thy blood, thy righteousness, O Lord my God.

Fill Thou My Life

Fill thou my life, O Lord my God,
   In every part with praise,
That my whole being may proclaim
   Thy being and thy ways.

Not for the lip of praise alone,
   Nor e'en the praising heart,
I ask, but for a life made up
   Of praise in every part.

Praise in the common words I speak,
   Life's common words and tones,
In intercourse at hearth or board
   With my beloved ones.

Fill every part of me with praise:
   Let all my being speak
Of thee and of thy love, O Lord,
   Poor though I be and weak.

So shall no part of day or night
   From sacredness be free;
But all my life, in every step,
   Be fellowship with thee.

From My Old Letters, Conclusion of Book IV

The evening brings all home. For that we wait,
Which is it once our evening and our morn,
The end of evil and the dawn of good.
October sheds the leaf and April brings it;
So one flower fadeth and another springs;
Earth renovates itself. When we are gone,

Our homes will not be vacant; and the crowds
Will swell our cities as when we were there.
Earth liveth on and on amid this change,
Or with us or without us to the end.
That end, ah, would that it were come! All things
Press forward to it, and cry out, Delay not;
For hope deferred has sickened the sad heart,
And men are asking, Shall it ever come?
Shake down your leaves, O many-tinted trees
Of dying autumn; let the forest gale
Of the unsparing north search through and through
Your desolate boughs, and heap the earth with sackcloth.
Another winter soon will lie behind us,—
One winter less to come ere the long spring
Shall o'er us shed its beauty and its balm!
Fling down your stars, O skies! O waiting earth!
Heave with thy final earthquake; and, O sea!
Let loose thy last stern tempest for the day
Of nature's shock, above us and beneath;
Speed on Creation's travail-throes, from which
There comes at last the perfect and the fair.

Hymn—O Love Of God, How Strong And True

O Love of God, how strong and true,
Eternal, and yet ever new,
Uncomprehended and unbought,
Beyond all knowledge and all thought!

O heavenly love, how precious still,
In days of weariness and ill,
In nights of pain and helplessness,
To heal, to comfort, and to bless!

O wide-embracing, wondrous love
We read thee in the sky above;
We read thee in the earth below,
In seas that swell and streams that flow.

We read thee in the flowers, the trees,
The freshness of the fragrant breeze,
The songs of birds upon the wing,
The joy of summer and of spring.

We read thee best in him who came
And bore for us the cross of shame,
Sent by the Father from on high,
Our life to live, our death to die.

O love of God, our shield and stay
Through all the perils of our way;
Eternal love, in thee we rest,
For ever safe, for ever blest.

TENNYSON, Lord ALFRED (1809–1892), who wrote poetry modeled on Milton, Scott, and Pope as a young boy, graduated from Cambridge in 1827. After winning a prize for his poem "Timbuctoo" in 1829, he published *Poems*, "Morte d'Arthur" and in 1850, *Memoriam* in honor of his friend, Arthur Hallam, who had died in 1833. Queen Victoria admired that work and he became poet laureate in 1850. His famous poem "Charge of the Light Brigade" was published in a volume of that name in 1855, *Idylls of the King* in 1859, and *Enoch Arden* in 1864. He published many other books of poetry, including ballads, as in *Ballads and Other Poems* (1880) and drama, such as *Becket* (1884). "Crossing the Bar" appeared in *Demeter and Other Poems* (1889). His reputation as a great poet declined in the late Victorian era, but it has risen again since.

From Idylls of the King

Pray for my soul. More things are wrought by prayer
Than this world dreams of. Wherefore let thy voice
Rise like a fountain for me night and day.
For what are men better than sheep or goats
That nourish a blind life within the brain,
If, knowing God, they lift not hands of prayer
Both for themselves and those who call them friends?
For so the whole round earth is every way
Bound by gold chains about the feet of God.

Late, Late, So Late!

Late, late, so late! and dark the night and chill!
Late, late, so late! but we can enter still.
Too late, too late! ye cannot enter now.

No light had we: for that we do repent;
And learning this, the bridegroom will relent.
Too late, too late! ye cannot enter now.

No light: so late! and dark and chill the night!
O let us in, that we may find the light!
Too late, too late: ye cannot enter now.

Have we not heard the Bridegroom is so sweet!
O let us in, tho' late, to kiss His feet!
No, no, too late! ye cannot enter now.

Forgiving

O Man, forgive thy mortal foe,
Nor ever strike him blow for blow;
For all the souls on earth that live
To be forgiven must forgive.
Forgive him seventy times and seven:
For all the blessed souls in Heaven
Are both forgivers and forgiven!

St. Agnes' Eve

Deep on the convent-roof the snows
Are sparkling to the moon:
My breath to heaven like vapour goes:
May my soul follow soon!
The shadows of the convent-towers
Slant down the snowy sward,
Still creeping with the creeping hours
That lead me to my Lord·
Make Thou my spirit pure and clear
As are the frosty skies,
Or this first snowdrop of the year
That in my bosom lies.

As these white robes are soil'd and dark,
To yonder shining ground;
As this pale taper's earthly spark,
To yonder argent round;
So shows my soul before the Lamb,
My spirit before Thee;
So in mine earthly house I am,
To that I hope to be.
Break up the heavens, O Lord! and far,

Thro' all yon starlight keen,
Draw me, thy bride, a glittering star,
In raiment white and clean.

He lifts me to the golden doors;
The flashes come and go;
All heaven bursts her starry floors,
And strows her lights below,
And deepens on and up! the gates
Roll back, and far within
For me the Heavenly Bridegroom waits,
To make me pure of sin.
The sabbaths of Eternity,
One sabbath deep and wide—
A light upon the shining sea—
The Bridegroom with his bride!

'Strong Son of God'
from In Memoriam, A.H.H. Obit MDCCCXXXIII

Strong Son of God, immortal Love,
    Whom we, that have not seen thy face,
    By faith, and faith alone, embrace,
Believing where we cannot prove;

Thine are these orbs of light and shade;
    Thou madest Life in man and brute;
    Thou madest Death; and lo, thy foot
Is on the skull which thou hast made.

Thou wilt not leave us in the dust:
    Thou madest man, he knows not why,
    He thinks he was not made to die;
And thou hast made him: thou art just.

Thou seemest human and divine,
    The highest, holiest manhood, thou:
    Our wills are ours, we know not how;
Our wills are ours, to make them thine.

Our little systems have their day;
    They have their day and cease to be:
    They are but broken lights of thee,
And thou, O Lord, art more than they.

We have but faith: we cannot know;
    For knowledge is of things we see;
    And yet we trust it comes from thee,
A beam in darkness: let it grow.

Let knowledge grow from more to more,
    But more of reverence in us dwell;
    That mind and soul, according well,
May make one music as before,

But vaster. We are fools and slight;
    We mock thee when we do not fear:
    But help thy foolish ones to bear;
Help thy vain worlds to bear thy light.

Forgive what seemed my sin in me;
    What seemed my worth since I began;
    For merit lives from man to man,
And not from man, O Lord, to thee.

Forgive my grief for one removed,
    Thy creature, whom I found so fair.
    I trust he lives in thee, and there
I find him worthier to be loved.

Forgive these wild and wandering cries,
    Confusions of a wasted youth;
    Forgive them where they fail in truth,
And in thy wisdom make me wise.

Section LV from **In Memoriam**

The wish, that of the living whole
    No life may fail beyond the grave;
    Derives it not from what we have
The likest God within the soul?

Are God and Nature then at strife,
    That Nature lends such evil dreams,
    So careful of the type she seems,
So careless of the single life;

That I, considering everywhere
    Her secret meaning in her deeds,
    And finding that of fifty seeds
She often brings but one to bear;

I falter where I firmly trod,
   And falling with my weight of cares
   Upon the great world's altar-stairs
That slope thro' darkness up to God;

I stretch lame hands of faith, and grope,
   And gather dust and chaff, and call
   To what I feel is Lord of all,
And faintly trust the larger hope.

Section CXXIV from **In Memoriam**

That which we dare invoke to bless;
   Our dearest faith; our ghastliest doubt;
   He, They, One, All; within, without;
The Power in darkness Whom we guess.

I found Him not in world or sun,
   Or eagle's wings, or insect's eye;
   Nor through the questions men may try,
The petty cobwebs we have spun.

If e'er when faith had fallen asleep,
   I heard a voice 'Believe no more'
   And heard an ever-breaking shore
That tumbled in the godless deep;

A warmth within the breast would melt
   And freezing reason's colder part,
   And like a man in wrath the heart
Stood up and answered 'I have felt.'

The Ancient Sage

Thou canst not prove that thou art body alone,
Nor canst thou prove that thou art spirit alone,
Nor canst thou prove that thou art both in one,
Thou canst not prove thou art immortal, no,
Nor yet that thou art mortal—nay, my son,
Thou canst not prove that I, who speak with thee,
Am not thyself in converse with thyself,
For nothing worthy proving can be proven,
Nor yet disproven. Wherefore thou be wise,

Cleave ever to the sunnier side of doubt,
And cling to Faith beyond the forms of Faith!
She reels not in the storm of warring words,
She brightens at the clash of 'Yes' and 'No,'
She sees the best that glimmers through the worst,
She feels the sun is hid but for a night,

Crossing the Bar

Sunset and evening star,
    And one clear call for me!
And may there be no moaning of the bar,
    When I put out to sea,

But such a tide as moving seems asleep,
    Too full for sound and foam,
When that which drew from out the boundless deep
    Turns again home.

Twilight and evening bell,
    And after that the dark
And may there be no sadness of farewell,
    When I embark;

For tho' from out our bourne of Time and Place
    The flood may bear me far,
I hope to see my Pilot face to face
    When I have crost the bar.

BROWNING, ROBERT (1812–89), was brought up in London and educated largely by means of his father's 6,000 book library. He was much influenced by the poetry of Shelley, Byron, and Keats on one hand, and on the other, by his mother's strong nonconformist faith. He destroyed all but two in his first collection of poems, written at age 12. In 1828 he was enrolled for a time in London University. His first published poem (anonymous) appeared in 1833. In 1835 his blank verse narrative poem "Paracelsus" brought him wide recognition and important friends, including Carlyle, Dickens, and Tennyson. Two others, J. Forster, and William Macready influenced him to write a play. His first, *Stafford* (1837) was followed by *Sordello* (1840), which did poorly. In fact he had very little success in his dramatic writing until he published a collection of plays and short poems, *Bells and Pomegranates,* in 1841. In 1845 he began exchanging letters with Elizabeth Barrett, having admired her *Poems* (1844). After their growing relationship attracted the disapproval of her father, they married and eloped to Italy in 1846. Robert published *Christmas-Eve and Easter Day,* in 1850. "Christmas Day" is a kind of spiritual fantasy in which the author is taken in a vision or dream to many different kinds of churches and Christmas celebrations during which he wrestles with which is the true worship or philosophy. George MacDonald, (in a chapter of *A Dish of Orts*), assesses the poem as a vivid picture of affirmation of faith in the midst of doubt. Elizabeth died in 1861, after which Robert returned to England. He published *Men and Women* and *Dramatis Personae* (1864), followed by his greatest success, *The Ring and the Book* (1868–9). He had a wide circle of literary acquaintances in London, was honored by Oxford, and received an honorary fellowship from Balliol College. In 1881 the Browning Society was formed. He published nearly twenty more books before his death, but his poetry is his greatest work. Browning's remains are buried in Westminster Abbey.

Excerpt From **"Pauline"**

O God, where do they tend—these struggling aims?
What would I have? What is this 'sleep' which seems
To bound all? Can there be a 'waking' point
Of crowning life? The soul would never rule;
It would be first in all things, it would have
Its utmost pleasure filled,—but, that complete,
Commanding for commanding sickens it.
The last point I can trace is, rest beneath
Some better essence than itself—in weakness;
This is 'myself'—not what I think should be,
And what is that I hunger for but God?
My God, my God, let me for once look on thee
As though naught else existed, we alone!
And as creation crumbles, my soul's spark
Expands till I can say, 'Even from myself
I need thee, and I feel thee, and I love thee;
I do not plead my rapture in thy works
For love of thee, nor that I feel as one
Who cannot die: but there is that in me
Which turns to thee, which loves, or which should love.'

Why have I girt myself with this hell-dress?
Why have I laboured to put out my life?
Is it not in my nature to adore,
And e'en for all my reason do I not
Feel him, and thank him, and pray to him—now?

Can I forgo the trust that he loves me?
Do I not feel a love which only ONE . . .
O thou pale form, so dimly seen, deep-eyed!
I have denied thee calmly—do I not
Pant when I read of thy consummate power,
And burn to see thy calm pure truths out-flash
The brightest gleams of earth's philosophy?
Do I not shake to hear aught question thee?
If I am erring save me, madden me,
Take from me powers and pleasures,—let me die
Ages, so I see thee! I am knit round
As with a charm, by sin and lust and pride,
Yet though my wandering dreams have seen all shapes
Of strange delight, oft have I stood by thee—
Have I been keeping lonely watch with thee
In the damp night by weeping Olivet,
Or leaning on thy bosom, proudly less,
Or dying with thee on the lonely cross,
Or witnessing thine outburst from the tomb!

Eternity Affirms the Hour

All we have willed or hoped or dreamed of good shall exist;
Not its semblance, but itself; no beauty, nor good, nor power
Whose voice has gone forth, but each survives for the melodist
When eternity affirms the conception of an hour.
The high that proved too high, the heroic for earth too hard,
The passion that left the ground to lose itself in the sky,
Are music sent up to God by the lover and the bard;
Enough that he heard it once: we shall hear it by and by.

Hymn (I Intend to Get to God)

There's heaven above, and night by night
I look right through its gorgeous roof;
No suns and moons though e'er so bright
Avail to stop me; splendour-proof,
I keep the brood of stars aloof.

For I intend to get to God,
For 'tis to God I speed so fast,
For in God's breast, my own abode,

Those shoals of dazzling glory passed,
I lay my spirit down at last.

I lie where I have always lain,
God smiles as he has always smiled;
Ere suns and moons could wax and wane,
Ere stars were thundergirt, or piled
The heavens, God thought on me his child.

God, whom I praise: how could I praise,
If such as I might understand,
Make out and reckon on his ways,
And bargain for his love, and stand,
Paying a price, at his right hand!

VERY, JONES (1813–1880), descendant of New England colonists and sea captains, delivered the English Oration at Harvard College upon his graduation in 1836. He attended Harvard Divinity School for two years, but withdrew after experiencing a time of deep fervor. Soon thereafter he was committed to an asylum in Somerville for a month, apparently against his will. Ralph Waldo Emerson, the transcendentalist, before whom Very had preached, helped Very gain release, pronouncing him "profoundly sane." Although Emerson did not concur with Very's faith, he made the selection and pushed through the publication of Very's *Essays and Poems* in 1839. Very was licensed as a Unitarian preacher in 1843. He lived until his death with two sisters in the family home at Salem, but preached at various churches around Boston. He was a "Quietist," dedicated to waiting upon the Lord as the means by which the Christian is led into obedience. Much of his poetry has a definite prophetic ring—aimed not only at declaring the necessity of the new birth, which he experienced in 1838, but also at decrying the ills of church and society around him. Very was so forthright in his calls to repentance and faith that he alienated many of his associates. He confronted not only Emerson, but Harvard professors as well as many who knew him in Salem. He read widely and was influenced both by the Puritans and the romantics. His sermons are often parallel to later poems.

The Hand and Foot

The hand and foot that stir not, they shall find
Sooner than all the rightful place to go:
Now in their motion free as roving wind,
Though first no snail so limited and slow;
I mark them full of labor all the day,
Each active motion made in perfect rest;

They cannot from their path mistaken stray,
Though 'tis not theirs, yet in it they are blest;
The bird has not their hidden track found out,
The cunning fox though full of art he be;
It is the way unseen, the certain route,
Where ever bound, yet thou art ever free;
The path of Him, whose perfect law of love
Bids spheres and atoms in just order move.

He Was Acquainted with Grief

I cannot tell the sorrows that I feel
By the night's darkness, by the prison's gloom;
There is no sight that can the death reveal
The spirit suffers in a living tomb;
There is no sound of grief that mourners raise,
No moaning of the wind, or dirge-like sea,
Nor hymns, though prophet tones inspire the lays,
That can the spirit's grief awake in thee.
Thou too must suffer as it suffers here
The death in Christ to know the Father's love;
Then in the strains that angels love to hear
Thou too shalt hear the Spirit's song above,
And learn in grief what these can never tell,
A note too deep for earthly voice to swell.

I Was Sick and in Prison

Thou hast not left the rough-barked tree to grow
Without a mate upon the river's bank;
Nor dost Thou on one flower the rain bestow,
But many a cup the glittering drops has drank;
The bird must sing to one who sings again,
Else would her note less welcome be to hear;
Nor hast Thou bid Thy word descend in vain,
But soon some answering voice shall reach my ear;
Then shall the brotherhood of peace begin,
And the new song be raised that never dies,
That shall the soul from death and darkness win,
And burst the prison where the captive lies;
And one by one new-born shall join the strain,
Till earth restores her sons to heaven again.

The New Birth

'Tis a new life;—thoughts move not as they did
With slow uncertain steps across my mind,
In thronging haste fast pressing on they bid
The portals open to the viewless wind
That comes not save when in the dust is laid
The crown of pride that gilds each mortal brow,
And from before man's vision melting fade
The heavens and earth;—their walls are falling now.—
Fast crowding on, each thought asks utterance strong;
Storm-lifted waves swift rushing to the shore,
On from the sea they send their shouts along,
Back through the cave-worn rocks their thunders roar;
And I a child of God by Christ made free
Start from death's slumbers to Eternity.

The Dead

I see them, crowd on crowd they walk the earth
Dry, leafless trees no autumn wind laid bare;
And in their nakedness find cause for mirth,
And all unclad would winter's rudeness dare;
No sap doth through their clattering branches flow,
Whence springing leaves and blossoms bright appear;
Their hearts the living God have ceased to know,
Who gives the springtime to th'expectant year;
They mimic life, as if from him to steal
His glow of health to paint the livid cheek;
They borrow words for thoughts they cannot feel,
That with a seeming heart their tongue may speak;
And in their show of life more dead they live
Than those that to the earth with many tears they give.

The Poor

I walk the streets and though not meanly drest,
Yet none so poor as can with me compare;
For none though weary call me in to rest,
And though I hunger none their substance share;
I ask not for my stay the broken reed,
That fails when most I want a friendly arm;

I cannot on the loaves and fishes feed,
That want the blessing that they may not harm;
I only ask the living word to hear,
From tongues that now but speak to utter death;
I thirst for one cool cup of water clear,
But drink the riled stream of lying breath;
And wander on though in my Father's land,
Yet hear no welcome voice, and see no beckoning hand.

The Harvest

They love me not, who at my table eat;
They live not on the bread that Thou hast given;
The word Thou giv'st is not their daily meat,
The bread of life that cometh down from heaven;
They drink but from their lips the waters dry,
There is no well that gushes up within;
And for the meat that perishes they cry,
When Thou hast vexed their souls because of sin;
Oh send Thy laborers! every hill and field
With the ungathered crop is whitened o'er;
To those who reap it shall rich harvests yield,
In full eared grain all ripened for Thy store;
No danger can they fear who reap with Thee,
Though thick with storms the autumn sky may be.

The Laborers

The workmen shall not always work; who builds,
His house shall finish with the last-raised stone;
The last small measure full the vessel fills;
The last step taken and thy journey's done;
But where is he, who but one hour ago,
Lifted with toiling arm the burden nigh?
And he whose vessel to the brim did flow,
Or he who laid his staff and sandals by?
I see them still at work another way,
From those that late thou sawest thus employed;
And heard them each unto the other say,
As to new tasks they bent them overjoyed,
"The sun is rising, haste! that he may see,
When setting every hand from labor free."

The Settler

When thou art done thy toil, anew art born;
With hands that never touched the spade or plough,
Nor in the furrows strewed the yellow corn,
Or plucked the ripened fruit from off the bough:
Then shall thou work begin;—thy plough and spade
Shall break at early morn the virgin soil;
The swelling hill and thickly wooded glade
With changing aspect own the daily toil;
Thy house shall strike the eye, where none are near,
For thou hast traveled far, where few have trod;
And those who journey hence will taste thy cheer,
And bless thee as a favored one of God;
For He it was Who in this pathless wild,
Upon thy good intent so richly smiled.

The Sower

To want is there to be where I am not,
Abundance waits for me where'er I tread;
The cares of life in me are all forgot,
I have enough and e'en to spare of bread;
Come, taste, and hunger shall be laid at rest;
And thirst once quenched shall never thirst again;
Thou shalt of all I have be long possest,
And long thy life my body shall sustain;
There are who food will give thee, but 'tis theirs;
And hunger rages but the more 'tis fed;
'Twas made from out the grains of scattered tares,
That through my field by wicked hands were spread;
But thou shalt have the wheat that's sown by me,
And in thy bosom's field new harvests ever see.

Beauty

I gazed upon thy face,—and beating life
Once stilled its sleepless pulses in my breast,
And every thought whose being was a strife
Each in its silent chamber sank to rest;
I was not, save it were a thought of thee,
The world was but a spot where thou hadst trod,

From every star thy glance seemed fixed on me,
Almost I loved thee better than my God.
And still I gaze,—but 'tis a holier thought
Than that in which my spirit lived before,
Each star a purer ray of love has caught,
Earth wears a lovelier robe than then it wore,
And every lamp that burns around thy shrine
Is fed with fire whose fountain is Divine.

Faith

There is no faith; the mountain stands within
Still unrebuked, its summit reaches heaven;
And every action adds its load of sin,
For every action wants the little leaven;
There is no prayer; it is but empty sound,
That stirs with frequent breath the yielding air,
With every pulse they are more strongly bound,
Who make the blood of goats the voice of prayer.
Oh heal them, heal them, Father, with thy word,—
Their sins cry out to thee from every side;
From son and sire, from slave and master heard,
Their voices fill the desert country wide;
And bid thee hasten to relieve and save,
By him who rose triumphant o'er the grave.

FABER, FREDERICK WILLIAM (1814–1863) was raised a strict Calvinist in the Anglican church, and after attending Oxford, was ordained and began work as a rector. He had become acquainted with John Henry Newman at Oxford, and began to incline toward the beliefs and rituals of Rome that had attracted Newman. Faber then followed Newman into the Roman church in 1845. He and eight others formed a community in Birmingham and later joined Newman at the founding of his Oratory (literally place of prayer). Newman sent Faber to found a London Oratory in 1849. Having grown up with the inspiration of the hymns of Newton, Cowper and the Wesleys, Faber felt the need for English Catholics to have hymns of their own. He wrote one hundred and fifty during his lifetime, many of which have found their way into Protestant hymnbooks, albeit stripped of their Roman distinctives. Among the best known of these are "Faith of our fathers, living still." (The original version has a stanza referring to Mary's prayers as a means by which England shall be won back to the Roman church.)

My God, How Wonderful Thou Art

My God, how wonderful Thou art,
Thy majesty how bright,
How beautiful Thy mercy-seat,
In depths of burning light!

How dread are Thine eternal years,
O everlasting Lord;
By prostrate spirits day and night
Incessantly adored!

How wonderful, how beautiful,
The sight of Thee must be,
Thine endless wisdom, boundless power,
And awful purity!

O how I fear Thee, living God,
With deepest, tenderest fears,
And worship Thee with trembling hope,
And penitential tears!

Yet I may love Thee too, O Lord,
Almighty as Thou art,
For Thou hast stooped to ask of me
The love of my poor heart.

The Shadow of the Rock

The Shadow of the Rock!
Stay, Pilgrim! stay!
Night treads upon the heels of day;
There is no other resting-place this way.
The Rock is near.
The well is clear.
Rest in the Shadow of the Rock.

The Shadow of the Rock!
The desert wide
Lies round thee like a trackless tide,
In waves of sand forlornly multiplied.
The sun is gone.
Thou art alone.
Rest in the Shadow of the Rock.

The Shadow of the Rock!
All come alone,
All, ever since the sun hath shone,
Who travelled by this road have come alone.
Be of good cheer,
A home is here.
Rest in the Shadow of the Rock.

The Shadow of the Rock!
Night veils the land:
How the palms whisper as they stand!
How the well tinkles faintly through the sand!
Cool water take
Thy thirst to slake,
Rest in the Shadow of the Rock.

The Shadow of the Rock!
Abide! Abide!
This Rock moves ever at thy side,
Pausing to welcome thee at eventide.
Ages are laid
Beneath its shade.
Rest in the Shadow of the Rock.

The Shadow of the Rock!
Always at hand,
Unseen it cools the noon-tide land,
And quells the fire that flickers in the sand.
It comes in sight
Only at night.
Rest in the Shadow of the Rock.

The Shadow of the Rock!
Mid skies storm-riven
It gathers shadows out of heaven,
And holds them o'er us all night cool and even.
Through the charmed air
Dew falls not there.
Rest in the Shadow of the Rock.

The Shadow of the Rock!
To angel's eyes
This Rock its shadow multiplies,
And at this hour in countless places lies.

One Rock, one Shade,
O'er thousands laid.
Rest in the Shadow of the Rock.

The Shadow of the Rock!
To weary feet,
That have been diligent and fleet,
The sleep is deeper and the shade more sweet.
O weary! rest,
Thou art sore pressed.
Rest in the Shadow of the Rock.

The Shadow of the Rock!
Thy bed is made;
Crowds of tired souls like thine are laid
This night beneath the self-same placid shade.
They who rest here
Wake with heaven near.
Rest in the Shadow of the Rock.

The Shadow of the Rock!
Pilgrim! sleep sound;
In night's swift hours with silent bound
The Rock will put thee over leagues of ground,
Gaining more way
By night than day.
Rest in the Shadow of the Rock.

The Shadow of the Rock!
One day of pain
Thou scarce wilt hope the Rock to gain,
Yet there wilt sleep thy last sleep on the plain;
And only wake
In heaven's day-break.
Rest in the Shadow of the Rock.

The Eternity Of God

O Lord! my heart is sick,
Sick of this everlasting change;
And life runs tediously quick
Through its unresting race and varied range:
Change finds no likeness to itself in Thee,
And wakes no echo in Thy mute eternity.

Dear Lord! my heart is sick
Of this perpetual lapsing time,
So slow in grief, in joy so quick,
Yet ever casting shadows so sublime:
Time of all creatures is least like to Thee,
And yet it is our share of Thine eternity.

Oh change and time are storms,
For lives so thin and frail as ours;
For change the work of grace deforms
With love that soils, and help that overpowers;
And time is strong, and, like some chafing sea,
It seems to fret the shores of Thine eternity.

Weak, weak, for ever weak!
We cannot hold what we possess;
Youth cannot find, age will not seek,—
Oh weakness is the heart's worst weariness:
But weakest hearts can lift their thoughts to Thee;
It makes us strong to think of Thine eternity.

Thou hadst no youth, great God!
An Unbeginning End Thou art;
Thy glory in itself abode,
And still abides in its own tranquil heart:
No age can heap its outward years on Thee:
Dear God! Thou art Thyself Thine own eternity!

Without an end or bound
Thy life lies all outspread in light;
Our lives feel Thy life all around,
Making our weakness strong, our darkness bright;
Yet is it neither wilderness nor sea,
But the calm gladness of a full eternity.

Oh Thou art very great
To set Thyself so far above!
But we partake of Thine estate,
Established in Thy strength and in Thy love:
That love hath made eternal room for me
In the sweet vastness of its own eternity.

Oh Thou art very meek
To overshade Thy creatures thus!

Thy grandeur is the shade we seek;
To be eternal is Thy use to us:
Ah, Blessed God! what joy it is to me
To lose all thought of self in Thine eternity.

Self-wearied, Lord! I come;
For I have lived my life too fast:
Now that years bring me nearer home
Grace must be slowly used to make it last;
When my heart beats too quick I think of Thee,
And of the leisure of Thy long eternity.

Farewell vain joys of earth!
Farewell, all love that is not His!
Dear God! be Thou my only mirth,
Thy majesty my single timid bliss!
Oh in the bosom of eternity
Thou dost not weary of Thyself, nor we of Thee!

DE VERE, AUBREY THOMAS (1814–1902), son of Aubrey De Vere, was born and raised in Ireland. He went to Trinity College in Dublin, where he was more interested in philosophy and theology than his other studies. In 1838 he visited Oxford where he met Newman. In 1841 he met William Wordsworth and in 1843 was invited to visit Wordworth at Rydal. During subsequent visits, he became friends with Miss Fenwick, Wordsworth's neighbor and Sara Coleridge, the poet's daughter. In 1845, in London, he saw much of Tennyson and met Carlyle, later getting to know Robert Browning, as well. His first book of poetry was *Waldenses and other Poems* (1842), followed by *The Search after Prosperine and Other Poems* (1843). The Irish famine, during which he was active in practical relief, brought forth a poem, "A Year of Sorrow," and a prose work, *English Misrule and Irish Misdeeds* (1846). During the years of turbulence in Ireland he always held the same intense loyalty for Ireland, but an opposition to violent means of defending her. In 1848, he turned toward the Roman church. He went to Rome in 1851 and was received into that church in Avignon. In 1854 Cardinal Newman, his close friend, appointed him a professor in the new Dublin Catholic University, a position he held until 1858, although he did not actually teach there. He wrote *May Carols* (1857), hymns to Mary and the saints, at the suggestion of Pope Pius IX. He exchanged visits with Tennyson during the ensuing years and published *Inisfail, a Lyrical Chronicle of Ireland* (1862) and *The Legends of St. Patrick* (1872). He also wrote two poetic dramas, *Alexander the Great* (1874) and *St. Thomas of Canterbury* (1876), and in 1876 *Recollections* was published. He was the author of many prose works as well. Sara Coleridge said of him he had more entirely a poet's nature than her own father or any other poet she had known.

Implicit Faith

Of all great Nature's tones that sweep
Earth's resonant bosom, far or near,
Low-breathed or loudest, shrill or deep,
How few are grasped by mortal ear.

Ten octaves close our scale of sound:
Its myriad grades, distinct or twined,
Transcend our hearing's petty bound,
To us as colours to the blind.

In Sound's unmeasured empire thus
The heights, the depths alike we miss;
Ah, but in measured sound to us
A compensating spell there is!

In holy music's golden speech
Remotest notes to notes respond:
Each octave is a world; yet each
Vibrates to worlds its own beyond.

Our narrow pale the vast resumes;
Our sea-shell whispers of the sea:
Echoes are ours of angel-plumes
That winnow far infinity!

—Clasp thou of Truth the central core!
Hold fast that centre's central sense!
An atom there shall fill thee more
Than realms on Truth's circumference.

That cradled Saviour, mute and small,
Was God—is God while worlds endure!
Who holds Truth truly holds it all
In essence, or in miniature.

Know what thou know'st! He knoweth much
Who knows not many things: and he
Knows most whose knowledge hath a touch
Of God's divine simplicity.

NEALE, JOHN MASON (1818–1866), son of two "very pronounced Evangelicals," excelled as a scholar at Cambridge, where his inability at mathematics was the only factor keeping him from very highest honors. "At Cambridge he identified himself with the Church movement, which was spreading there in a quieter, but no less real, way than in the sister University." (Julian's *Dictionary of Hymnology*). He married Sarah Webster, daughter of an evangelical clergyman in 1842, and would have entered into the ministry the next year, but for lung disease that forced him to travel to Madeira, where he stayed until 1844. After 1846 he spent his life as Warden of Sackville College, East Grinstead, where despite church and local opposition, he founded the sisterhood of St. Margaret's, out of which arose an orphanage, a middle school for girls, and a house for the reformation of fallen women. He wrote many hymns, ballads, and poetry. He is particularly noted for his translations of early and medieval Latin hymns and eastern (Greek) hymns. Many of his translations continue to be favorite hymns today.

Good Christian Men Rejoice
Translated from Medieval Latin

Good Christian men, rejoice,
With heart, and soul and voice;
Give ye heed to what we say:
Jesus Christ is born today;
Earth and heav'n before him bow,
And he is in the manger now.
Christ is born today!
Christ is born today!

Good Christian men rejoice,
With heart and soul and voice;
Now ye hear of endless bliss:
Jesus Christ was born for this!
He hath op'ed the heav'nly door,
And man is blessed forevermore.
Christ is born today!
Christ is born today!

Good Christian men, rejoice,
With heart, and soul, and voice;
Now ye need not fear the grave:
Jesus Christ was born to save!
Calls you one and calls you all
To gain his everlasting hall.

Christ is born today!
Christ is born today!

Good King Wenceslas

Good King Wenceslas looked out,
On the Feast of Stephen,
When the snow lay round about,
Deep, and crisp, and even:
Brightly shone the moon that night,
Though the frost was cruel,
When a poor man came in sight,
Gathering winter fuel.

"Hither, page, and stand by me,
If thou know'st it, telling,
Yonder peasant, who is he?
Where and what his dwelling?"
"Sire, he lives a good league hence,
Underneath the mountain;
Right against the forest fence,
By Saint Agnes' fountain."

"Bring me flesh, and bring me wine,
Bring me pine logs hither;
Thou and I will see him dine,
When we bear them thither."
Page and monarch forth they went,
Forth they went together;
Through the rude wind's wild lament,
And the bitter weather.

"Sire, the night is darker now,
And the wind blows stronger;
Fails my heart, I know not how,
I can go no longer."
"Mark my footsteps, good my page.
Tread thou in them boldly;
Thou shalt find the winter's rage
Freeze thy blood less coldly."

In his master's steps he trod,
Where the snow lay dinted;

Heat was in the very sod
Which the Saint had printed.
Therefore, Christian men, be sure,
Wealth or rank possessing,
Ye who now will bless the poor,
Shall yourselves find blessing.

The Guide from St. Stephen The Sabaite

Art thou weary, art thou languid,
Art thou sore distrest?
'Come to me,' saith One, ' and coming
Be at rest!'

Hath he marks to lead me to him,
If he be my guide?
'In his feet and hands are wound-prints,
And his side.'

Hath he diadem as monarch
That his brow adorns?
'Yea, a crown, in very surety,
But of thorns!'

If I find him, if I follow,
What his guerdon here?
'Many a sorrow, many a labour,
Many a tear.'

If I still hold closely to him,
What hath he at last?
'Sorrow vanquished, labour ended,
Jordan past!'

If I ask him to receive me,
Will he say me nay?
'Not till earth, and not till heaven
Pass away!'

Finding, following, keeping, struggling,
Is he sure to bless?
'Angels, martyrs, prophets, virgins,
Answer, Yes!'

ALEXANDER, CECIL FRANCES (NEE: CECIL HUMPHREYS) (1818–1895) was born in Ireland, daughter of a royal marine major. She began to write poetry at age nine (chiefly on tragic subjects), and developed a friendship with Lady Harriet Howard, together with whom she came under the influence of the Oxford movement. They turned to writing tracts, Lady Harriet providing the prose and Miss Humphreys the poetry. In 1846 Miss Humphreys published *Verses for Holy Seasons* (London, 8 volumes). *Hymns for Little Children*, with a preface by John Keble, followed in 1848. By 1869 sixty- nine editions had been published. It contained such universal hymns as "All things bright and beautiful" (the first lines of which were used by James Herriot as titles for his veterinary memoirs), and "Jesus calls us o'er the tumult." In 1850 she married William Alexander, himself a poet, then a rector in Tyrone. In 1867 he became bishop of Raphoe and Derry. Mrs. Alexander died at the palace in Londonderry in 1895, leaving two sons and two daughters. Tennyson said he would be proud to be the author of her ballad, "The Legend of Stumpies's Brae."

The Breastplate of St. Patrick (From the Irish)

I bind unto myself to-day
The strong Name of the Trinity,
By invocation of the same,
The Three in One and One in Three.

I bind this day to me for ever,
By pow'r of faith, Christ's incarnation;
His baptism in Jordan river;
His death on Cross for my salvation;
His bursting from the spiced tomb,
His riding up the heavenly way;
His coming at the day of doom;
I bind unto myself to-day.

I bind unto myself the power
Of the great love of Cherubim;
The sweet 'Well done' in judgment hour,
The service of the Seraphim,
Confessors' faith, Apostles' word,
The patriarchs' prayers, the Prophets' scrolls,
All good deeds done unto the Lord,
And purity of virgin souls.

I bind unto myself to-day
The virtues of the star-lit heaven,
The glorious sun's life-giving ray,
The whiteness of the moon at even,
The flashing of the lightning free,
The whirling wind's tempestuous shocks,
The stable earth, the deep salt sea
Around the old eternal rocks.

I bind unto myself to-day
The pow'r of God to hold, and lead,
His eye to watch, His might to stay,
His ear to hearken to my need;
The wisdom of my God to teach,
His hand to guide, His shield to ward;
The Word of God to give me speech,
His heavenly host to be my guard:

Against the demon snares of sin,
The vice that gives temptation force,
The natural lusts that war within,
The hostile men that mar my course;
Or few or many, far or nigh,
In every place, and in all hours,
Against their fierce hostility,
I bind to me these holy powers:

Against all Satan's spells and wiles,
Against false words of heresy,
Against the knowledge that defiles,
Against the heart's idolatry,
Against the wizard's evil craft,
Against the death-wound and the burning,
The choking wave, the poisoned shaft,
Protect me, Christ, till Thy returning.

Christ be with me, Christ within me,
Christ behind me, Christ before me,
Christ beside me, Christ to win me,
Christ to comfort and restore me,
Christ beneath me, Christ above me,
Christ in quiet, Christ in danger,

Christ in hearts of all that love me,
Christ in mouth of friend and stranger.

I bind unto myself the Name,
The strong Name of the Trinity;
By invocation of the same,
The Three in One, and One in Three.
Of Whom all nature hath creation;
Eternal Father, Spirit, Word:
Praise to the Lord of my salvation,
Salvation is of Christ the Lord.

All Things Bright And Beautiful

All things bright and beautiful,
All creatures great and small,
All things wise and wonderful,
The Lord God made them all.

Each little flower that opens,
Each little bird that sings,
He made their glowing colours,
He made their tiny wings:

The rich man in his castle,
The poor man at his gate,
God made them, high or lowly,
And ordered their estate.

The purple-headed Mountain,
The river running by,
The sunset and the morning,
That brightens up the sky:

The cold wind in the winter,
The pleasant summer sun,
The ripe fruits in the garden,
He made them every one:

He gave us eyes to see them,
And lips that we might tell
How great is God Almighty,
Who has made all things well.

Hymn—The Eternal Gates Lift Up Their Heads

The eternal gates lift up their heads,
The doors are opened wide,
The King of Glory is gone up
Unto his Father's side.

And ever on our earthly path
A gleam of glory lies,
A light still bright behind the cloud
That veils thee from our eyes.

Lift up our hearts, lift up our minds,
And let thy grace be given,
That, while we linger yet below,
Our treasure be in heaven;

That, where thou art at God's right hand
Our hope, our love may be:
Dwell in us now, that we may dwell
For evermore in thee.

Jesus calls us! O'er the tumult

Jesus calls us! O'er the tumult
Of our life's wild restless sea
Day by day his sweet voice soundeth,
Saying, ' Christian, follow me':

As of old Saint Andrew heard it
By the Galilean lake,
Turned from home, and toil, and kindred,
Leaving all for his dear sake.

Jesus calls us from the worship
Of the vain world's golden stores
From each idol that would keep us,
Saying, 'Christian, love me more.'

In our joys and in our sorrows,
Days of toil and hours of ease,
Still he calls, in cares and pleasures,
'Christian, love me more than these.'

Jesus calls us! By thy mercies,
Saviour, may we hear thy call,
Give our hearts to thy obedience,
Serve and love thee best of all.

Reason and Faith

Through paths of pleasant thought I ran,
False Science sang enchanted airs;
She told of nature and of man,
And of the God-like gifts he bears.
But when I sat down by the way,
And thought out life and thought out sin,
The burning truths that round me lay,
And all the weak proud self within;

Still in my single soul there wrought
The sense of sin, the curse of doom,
Till slowly broke upon my thought
An Eastern olive garden's gloom.
Hung on Thy cross 'twixt earth and heaven
I saw Thee, Son of man Divine;
To Thee the bitter pain was given,
But all the heavy guilt was mine.

I know the serpent touched my heart,
I saw his trail on hand and brow;
No sinless thought, no perfect part,
But sullied breast and broken vow.
But then I felt my need of Thee,
And pride's illusions passed away;
And oh! that Thou hast died for me,
Is more than all the world can say.

The wounded fawn in yonder glade,
Beside the doe seeks rest from harm;
The babe that scorned its mother's aid,
Flies to her at the least alarm.
And thus I feel my need of Thee,
When sin and pride would tempt me most;
And oh! that Thou hast died for me,
Is more than all the skeptic's boast.

Touched with a Feeling of Our Infirmities

When, wounded sore, the stricken soul
Lies bleeding and unbound,
One only hand, a pierced hand
Can salve the sinner's wound.

When sorrow swells the laden breast
And tears of anguish flow,
Only one heart, a broken heart,
Can feel the sinner's woe.

When penitence has wept in vain
Over some foul dark spot,
One only stream, a stream of blood,
Can wash away the blot.

'Tis Jesus' blood that washes white,
His hand that brings relief,
His heart that's touched with all our joys,
And feeleth for our grief.

Lift up thy bleeding hand, O Lord,
Unseal that cleansing tide;
We have no shelter from our sin
But in thy wounded side.

BRONTË, ANNE (1820–1849), daughter of Rev. Patrick Brontë, and third of the famous literary sisters (after Charlotte and Emily), was the sixth of six children. Her father, a peculiar character and an Evangelical, attended Cambridge, and became an Anglican priest. Her mother died within a year of her birth, and her two oldest sisters died five years later. She was educated at home, chiefly by her mother's sister. She and her sister Emily concocted an imaginary land called "Gondol" in which they set tales, characters, and pictures. The four surviving siblings made up many pseudonymns and nicknames for themselves and each other. When Anne was sixteen she had a bout of serious illness, during which a Moravian bishop visited her and led her to a fuller understanding of the grace of God through Christ. Her only brother Branwell became an addict to alcohol and opium, and as such, frequently troubled the household. Anne became a governess to the Ingham family (1839) and to the Robinson family (1841-45). In 1845, largely under Charlotte's oversight, poems by the three sisters were published as *Poems by Currer, Ellis, and Acton Bell.* Anne published a novel, *Agnes Grey,* in 1847 and another, *Tenant of Wildfell Hall* (1848). Her Christian faith, though unorthodox in some points, comes through clearly in the second novel, in which a young woman struggles with severe moral dilemmas as the wife of a prodigal husband. [Anne's novel is in considerable contrast to Emily's *Wuthering Heights.*] Branwell died in 1848. Emily died in December of the same year. (Anne refers to her death in the fifth stanza of "Last Lines" below.) Five months later, at twenty-nine, Anne departed this world, comforting her sister in her last words, "Take courage, Charlotte; take courage." Earlier that day she said to someone trying to make her comfortable, "It is not you who can give me ease, but soon all will be well through the merits of our Redeemer."

A Prayer

My God (oh, let me call Thee mine,
Weak, wretched sinner though I be),
My trembling soul would fain be Thine;
My feeble faith still clings to Thee.

Not only for the past I grieve,
The future fills me with dismay;
Unless Thou hasten to relieve,
Thy suppliant is a castaway.

I cannot say my faith is strong,
I dare not hope my love is great;
But strength and love to Thee belong:
Oh, do not leave me desolate!

I know I owe my all to Thee;
Oh, take the heart I cannot give;
Do Thou my Strength, my Saviour be,
And make me to Thy glory live!

The Doubter's Prayer

Eternal Power, of earth and air!
    Unseen, yet seen in all around;
Remote, but dwelling everywhere;
    Though silent heard in every sound;

If e'er thine ear in Mercy lent,
    When wretched mortals cried to Thee,
And if indeed, Thy Son was sent,
    To save lost sinners such as me:

Then hear me now, while kneeling here,
   I lift to thee my heart and eye,
And all my soul ascends in prayer,
   Oh, give me—Give me Faith! I cry.

Without some glimmering in my heart
   I could not raise this fervent prayer;
But, oh! a stronger light impart,
   And in Thy mercy fix it there.

While Faith is with me, I am blest;
   It turns my darkest night to day;
But while I clasp it to my breast,
   I often feel it slide away.

Then, cold and dark, my spirit sinks,
   To see my light of life depart;
And every friend of Hell, methinks,
   Enjoys the anguish of my heart.

What shall I do if all my love,
   My hopes, my toil, are cast away,
And if there be no God above,
   To hear and bless me while I pray?

If this be vain delusion all,
   If death be an eternal sleep
And none can hear my secret call,
   Or see the silent tears I weep!

O help me God! for Thou alone
   Canst my distracted soul relieve;
Forsake it not, it is Thine own,
   Though weak, yet longing to believe.

Oh, drive these cruel doubts away;
   And make me know that Thou art God!
A faith, that shines by night and day,
   Will lighten every earthly load.

If I believe that Jesus died,
   And waking, rose to reign above;
Then surely Sorrow, Sin, and Pride
   Must yield to Peace, and Hope, and Love;

And all the blessèd words he said
  Will strength and holy joy impart:
A shield of safety o'er my head,
  A spring of comfort in my heart.

The Penitent

I mourn with thee, and yet rejoice
That thou shouldst sorrow so;
With angels choirs I join my voice
To bless the sinner's woe.

Though friends and kindred turn away,
And laugh thy grief to scorn;
I hear the great Redeemer say,
"Blessed are ye that mourn."

Hold on thy course, nor deem it strange
That earthly cords are riven:
Man may lament the wondrous change,
But "there is joy in heaven!"

Last Lines
("These lines written, the desk was closed, the pen laid aside
  —for ever."—note by Charlotte Bronte)

I hoped that with the brave and strong
My portioned task might lie;
To toil amid the busy throng
With purpose pure and high;

But God has fixed another part,
And He has fixed it well:
I said so with my breaking heart
When first this trouble fell.

These weary hours will not be lost,
These days of misery,
These nights of darkness, tempest-tost,
Can I but turn to Thee;

With secret labor to sustain
In patience every blow,
To gather fortitude from pain,
And holiness from woe.

If Thou shouldst bring me back to life,
More humble I should be,
More wise, more strengthened for the strife,
More apt to lean on Thee.

Should death be standing at the gate,
Thus should I keep my vow:
But, Lord! whatever be my fate,
Oh, let me serve Thee now.

HOLLAND, J. G. (JOSIAH GILBERT) (1819–1881) from Massachusetts, published his early writings under the *nom de plume* Timothy Titcomb. His novels include: *The Bay-Path* (1857), *Miss Gilbert's Career* (1860), *Arthur Bonnicastle* (1873), *Sevenoaks* (1875), and *Minturn* (1877). Twentieth century critics sometimes characterize his works as "sentimental didacticism," but his books were very popular in his lifetime. His books of poetry include *Bittersweet* (1858) and *Kathrina, Her Life and Mine in a Poem* (1867). In 1870 he was co-founder and the first editor of *Scribner's Monthly* magazine. He was one of the literary figures aquainted with Emily Dickinson.

Wanted

God give us men! A time like this demands
Strong minds, great hearts, true faith, and ready hands;
Men whom the lust of office does not kill;
Men whom the spoils of office cannot buy;
Men who possess opinions and a will;
Men who have honor,—men who will not lie;
Men who can stand before a demagogue,
And damn his treacherous flatteries without winking!
Tall men, sun-crowned, who live above the fog
In public duty, and in private thinking:
For while the rabble, with their thumb-worn creeds,
Their large professions and their little deeds,—
Mingle in selfish strife, lo! Freedom weeps,
Wrong rules the land, and waiting justice sleeps.

There's A Song In The Air!

There's a song in the air!
There's a star in the sky!
There's a mother's deep prayer
And a baby's low cry!
And the star rains its fire while the beautiful sing,
For the manger of Bethlehem cradles a King!

There's a tumult of joy
O'er the wonderful birth,
For the Virgin's sweet boy
Is the Lord of the earth.
Ay! the star rains its fire while the beautiful sing,
For the manger of Bethlehem cradles a King!

In the light of that star
Lie the ages impearled;
And that song from afar
Has swept over the world.
Every hearth is aflame, and the beautiful sing
In the homes of the nations that Jesus is King!

We rejoice in the light,
And we echo the song
That comes down thro' the night
From the heavenly throng.
Ay! we shout to the lovely evangel they bring,
And we greet in His cradle our Saviour and King!

CLOUGH, ARTHUR HUGH (1819–1861) was born in England, and spent five years of childhood in South Carolina. He went to Rugby where he was a favorite pupil of Dr. Thomas Arnold, the headmaster, becoming almost a member of the Arnold family (Matthew Arnold was three years younger than he). He went to Oxford where the Oxford movement both engaged and unsettled his spiritual interests. He became a Fellow of Oriel College in 1841, but resigned after six years out of conscientious inability to subscribe to the Thirty-nine Articles of the Church of England. He published *The Bothie of Tober-na-Vuolich* (1848), and *Ambarvalia* (1849). He was for three years head of University Hall, London, but resigned to accept the invitation of Ralph Waldo Emerson to lecture, teach, and write in America. After a unsuccessful year, he returned to London where he became an Examiner for the Education Office. He married a year later, and published *Amours de Voyage* (1858), first in the *Atlantic Monthly* magazine. After seven years his health failed, and in 1860 he went to Florence hoping to regain his strength. He died late in 1861 and was buried in the Protestant cemetery there. (Elizabeth Barrett Browning's remains had been laid to rest a few months earlier.) Clough's *Dipsychus* and *Mari Magno* were published after his death. His *Poems,* appeared in 1862, with a Memoir by F. T. Palgrave. Clough's poetry is in one sense sceptical and agnostic. There is however, little of the false contentment of the Transcendentalist, or the emotional "prophecy" of the universalist romantic in his work. (Neither Emerson of the former school or Shelley of the latter "school," though resembling Clough in many points, are included in this collection.)

Revival

So I went wrong,
Grievously wrong, but folly crushed itself,
And vanity o'ertoppling fell, and time
And healthy discipline and some neglect,
Labour and solitary hours revived
Somewhat, at least, of that original frame.
Oh, well do I remember then the days
When on some grassy slope (what time the sun
Was sinking, and the solemn eve came down
With its blue vapour upon field and wood to
And elm-embosomed spire) once more again
I fed on sweet emotion, and my heart
With love o'erflowed, or hushed itself in fear
Unearthly, yea celestial. Once again
My heart was hot within me, and, meseemed,
I too had in my body breath to wind
The magic horn of song; I too possessed
Up-welling in my being's depths a fount
Of the true poet-nectar whence to fill
The golden urns of verse.

In a Lecture-Room

Away, haunt thou not me,
Thou vain Philosophy!
Little hast thou bestead,
Save to perplex the head,
And leave the spirit dead.
Unto thy broken cisterns wherefore go,

While from the secret treasure-depths below,
Fed by the skyey shower,
And clouds that sink and rest on hill-tops high,
Wisdom at once, and Power,
Are welling, bubbling forth, unseen, incessantly?
Why labour at the dull mechanic oar,
When the fresh breeze is blowing,
And the strong current flowing,
Right onward to the Eternal Shore?

The Questioning Spirit

The human spirits saw I on a day,
Sitting and looking each a different way;
And hardly tasking, subtly questioning,
Another spirit went around the ring
To each and each: and as he ceased his say,
Each after each, I heard them singly sing,
Some querulously high, some softly, sadly low.
We know not—what avails to know?
We know not—wherefore need we know?
This answer gave they still unto his suing,
We know not, let us do as we are doing.
Dost thou not know that these things only seem?—
I know not, let me dream my dream.
Are dust and ashes fit to make a treasure?
I know not, let me take my pleasure.
What shall avail the knowledge thou hast sought?—
I know not, let me think my thought.
What is the end of strife?—
I know not, let me live my life.
How many days or e'er thou mean'st to move?—
I know not, let me love my love.
Were not things old once new?
I know not, let me do as others do.
And when the rest were over past,
I know not, I will do my duty, said the last.

Thy duty do? rejoined the voice,
Ah, do it, do it, and rejoice;
But shalt thou then, when all is done,
Enjoy a love, embrace a beauty

Like these, that may be seen and won
In life, whose course will there be run;
Or wilt thou be where there is none?
I know not, I will do my duty.

And taking up the word around, above, below,
Some querulously high, some softly, sadly low,
We know not, sang they all, nor ever need we know;
We know not, sang they, what avails to know?
Whereat the questioning spirit, some short space,
Though unabashed, stood quiet in his place.
But as the echoing chorus died away
And to their dreams the rest returned apace,
By the one spirit I saw him kneeling low,
And in a silvery whisper heard him say:
Truly, thou know'st not, and thou need'st not know;

Hope only, hope thou, and believe alway;
I also know not, and I need not know,
Only with questionings pass I to and fro,
Perplexing these that sleep, and in their folly
Imbreeding doubt and sceptic melancholy;
Till that, their dreams deserting, they with me
Come all to this true ignorance and thee.

There Is No God From *Dipsychus*

"There is no God," the wicked saith,
"And truly it's a blessing,
For what He might have done with us
It's better only guessing."

"There is no God," a youngster thinks,
"Or really, if there may be,
He surely didn't mean a man
Always to be a baby."

"There is no God, or if there is,"
The tradesman thinks, "'twere funny
If He should take it ill in me
To make a little money."

"Whether there be," the rich man says,
"It matters very little,

For I and mine, thank somebody,
Are not in want of victual."

Some others, also, to themselves,
Who scarce so much as doubt it,
Think there is none, when they are well,
And do not think about it.

But country folks who live beneath
The shadow of the steeple;
The parson and the parson's wife,
And mostly married people;

Youths green and happy in first love,
So thankful for illusion;
And men caught out in what the world
Calls guilt, in first confusion;

And almost every one when age,
Disease, or sorrows strike him,
Inclines to think there is a God,
Or something very like Him.

Say Not The Struggle Nought Availeth

Say not the struggle nought availeth,
The labour and the wounds are vain,
The enemy faints not, nor faileth,
And as things have been they remain.

If hopes were dupes, fears may be liars;
It may be, in yon smoke concealed,
Your comrades chase e'en now the fliers,
And, but for you, possess the field.

For while the tired waves, vainly breaking,
Seem here no painful inch to gain,
Far back, through creeks and inlets making,
Comes silent, flooding in, the main.

And not by eastern windows only,
When daylight comes, comes in the light,
In front, the sun climbs slow, how slowly,
But westward, look, the land is bright.

Through A Glass Darkly

What we, when face to face we see
The Father of our souls, shall be,
John tells us, doth not yet appear;
Ah! did he tell what we are here!

A mind for thoughts to pass into,
A heart for loves to travel through,
Five senses to detect things near,
Is this the whole that we are here?

Rules baffle instincts—instincts rules,
Wise men are bad—and good are fools,
Facts evil—wishes vain appear,
We cannot go, why are we here?

O may we for assurance' sake,
Some arbitrary judgment take,
And wilfully pronounce it clear,
For this or that 'tis we are here?

　Or is it right, and will it do,
To pace the sad confusion through,
And say:—It doth not yet appear,
What we shall be, what we are here?

Ah yet, when all is thought and said,
The heart still overrules the head;
Still what we hope we must believe,
And what is given us receive;

Must still believe, for still we hope
That in a world of larger scope,
What here is faithfully begun
Will be completed, not undone.

My child, we still must think, when we
That ampler life together see,
Some true result will yet appear
Of what we are, together, here.

The Latest Decalogue

Thou shalt have one God only; who
Would be at the expense of two?

No graven images may be
Worship'd except the currency:

Swear not at all; for, for thy curse
Thine enemy is none the worse:

At church on Sunday to attend
Will serve to keep the world thy friend:

Honour thy parents; that is, all
From whom advancement may befall;

Thou shalt not kill; but needst not strive
Officiously to keep alive;

Do not adultery commit;
Advantage rarely comes of it:
Thou shalt not steal; an empty feat,
Where 'tis so lucrative to cheat:

Bear not false witness; let the lie
Have time on its own wings to fly:

Thou shalt not covet, but tradition
Approves all forms of competition.

With Whom Is No Variableness, Neither Shadow of Turning

It fortifies my soul to know
That though I perish, truth is so;
That, howso'er I stray and range.
Whate'er I do, Thou dost not change.
I steadier step when I recall
That, if I slip, Thou dost not fall.

GREENWELL, DOROTHY "DORA" (1821–1848), was born at Greenwell Ford, Durham, and is noted as a hymn-writer. She published *Poems* in 1848, *The Patience of Hope* in 1861 (prose), *A Present Heaven*, and *Songs of Salvation* in 1874, among other works.

The Man with Three Friends

To one full sound and silently
That slept, there came a heavy cry,

'Awake, arise! for thou hast slain
A man.' 'Yea, have I to mine own pain,'

He answer'd; 'but of ill intent
And malice am I, that naught forecast,
As is the babe innocent.
From sudden anger our strife grew:
I hated not, in times past,
Him whom unwittingly I slew.'

'If it be thus indeed, thy case
Is hard,' they said; ' for thou must die,
Unless with the Judge thou canst find grace.
Hast thou, in thine extremity,
Friends soothfast for thee to plead?'

Then said he, ' I have friends three:
One whom in word and will and deed
From my youth I have served, and loved before
Mine own soul, and for him striven;
To him was all I got given;
And the longer I lived, I have loved him more.

'And another have I, whom (sooth to tell)
I love as I love my own heart well;
And the third I cannot now call
To mind that ever loved at all
He hath been of me, or in aught served;
And yet, may be, he hath well deserved
That I should love him with the rest.

'Now will I first to the one loved best.'
Said the first, ' And art thou so sore bestead?
See, I have gain'd of cloth good store,
So will I give thee three ells and more
(If more thou needest) when thou art dead,
To wrap thee. Now hie thee away from my door:
I have friends many, and little room.'
And the next made answer, weeping sore,
'We will go with thee to the place of doom:
There must we leave thee evermore.'

'Alack!' said the man, 'and well-a-day!'
But the third only answered, ' Yea ';
And while the man spake, all to start soon,

Knelt down and buckled on his shoon,
And said, 'By thee in the Judgement Hall
I will stand and hear what the Judge decree;
And if it be death, I will die with thee,
Or for thee, as it may befall.'

[The three friends are, in order: The World, Wife and Children, Christ.]

PATMORE, COVENTRY (KERSEY DIGHTON) (1823–1896), one of
the few Victorians who seems to have appreciated the metaphysical poets, was
himself a poet, novelist, and essayist. He worked in the library of the British
Museum, London, for nineteen years. He published a series of books of narra-
tive verse telling the story of two marriages, beginning with *The Angel in the House*,
continuing with *The Betrothal*, *The Espousals*, *The Victories of Love*, and *Faithful for Ever*.
Interspersed among these were lyrical "preludes." A last selection was aban-
doned on the death of his wife, Emily, in 1862. He became a Roman Catholic
in 1864 and married again. Together he and his wife, Marianne, translated St.
Bernard on the *Love of God* (1881). *The Unknown Eros and Other Odes* with mysti-
cal poems on divine and married love was published in 1877. *Amelia* (1878) is
his last book of poetry. In later years he wrote essays on literature and philos-
ophy, which were collected in *Principle in Art* (1889), and *Religio Poetae* (1893).
Gerard Manley Hopkins thought highly of Patmore's *English Metrical Law* (1857)
a basic study of meter in English.

Fool And Wise

Endow the fool with sun and moon,
Being his, he holds them mean and low,
But to the wise a little boon
Is great, because the giver's so.

Rods And Kisses

All blessings ask a blessed mood;
The garnish here is more than meat;
Happy who takes sweet gratitude;
Next best, though bitter, is regret.

'Tis well if on the tempest's gloom
You see the covenant of God;
But far, far happier he on whom
The kiss works better than the rod.

Vesica Piscis

In strenuous hope I wrought,
And hope seemed still betray'd;
Lastly I said,
' I have labour'd through the Night, nor yet
Have taken aught;
But at Thy word I will again cast forth the net! '
And, lo, I caught
(Oh, quite unlike and quite beyond my thought,)
Not the quick, shining harvest of the Sea,
For food, my wish,
But Thee!
Then, hiding even in me,
As hid was Simon's coin within the fish,
Thou sigh'd'st, with joy, ' Be dumb,
Or speak but of forgotten things to far-off times to come.'

The Married Lover
From "Angel in the House"

Why, having won her, do I woo?
Because her spirit's vestal grace
Provokes me always to pursue,
But, spirit-like, eludes embrace;
Because her womanhood is such
That, as on court-days subjects kiss
The Queen's hand, yet so near a touch
Affirms no mean familiarness;
Nay, rather marks more fair the height
Which can with safety so neglect
To dread, as lower ladies might,
That grace could meet with disrespect;
Thus she with happy favor feeds
Allegiance from a love so high
That thence no false conceit proceeds
Of difference bridged, or state put by;
Because, although in act and word
As lowly as a wife can be,
Her manners, when they call me lord,
Remind me 'tis by courtesy;
Not with her least consent of will,
Which would my proud affection hurt,

But by the noble style that still
Imputes an unattained desert;
Because her gay and lofty brows,
When all is won which hope can ask,
Reflect a light of hopeless snows
That bright in virgin ether bask;
Because, though free of the outer court
I am, this Temple keeps its shrine
Sacred to Heaven; because, in short,
She's not and never can be mine.

CARY, PHOEBE (1824–1871) was born near Cincinnati, Ohio, the sixth of nine children. She lived nearly her whole life with her older sister Alice. Both of them began writing poetry in their teens and were being published in various magazines by the late 1840's. In 1850 a volume of their poetry, *Poems of Alice and Phoebe Cary*, was published in Philadelphia, and the two poetesses travelled to New York and Boston. They soon settled in New York where they were befriended by Horace Greeley. At first they lived a frugal life supported by their writing, but they quickly made a wide circle of acquaintances and friends in New York's cosmopolitan society, as their literary efforts flourished. Besides editing many of Alice's books, Phoebe published her own *Poems and Parodies* (1854), *Poems of Faith, Hope, and Love* (1868), and *Hymns for All Christians* (1869). Alice died in 1870, a year before Phoebe. Alice's religious poetry tends toward universalism, while Phoebe's expresses a clear faith and understanding of the gospel.

Nearer Home

One sweetly solemn thought
Comes to me o'er and o'er;
I am nearer home to-day
Than I ever have been before;

Nearer my Father's house,
Where the many mansions be;
Nearer the great white throne,
Nearer the, crystal sea;

Nearer the bound of life,
Where we lay our burdens down;
Nearer leaving the cross,
Nearer gaining the crown!

But lying darkly between,
Winding down through the night,
Is the silent, unknown stream,
That leads at last to the light.

Closer and closer my steps
Come to the dread abysm:
Closer Death to my lips
Presses the awful chrism.

Oh, if my mortal feet
Have almost gained the brink;
If it be I am nearer home
Even to-day than I think;

Father, perfect my trust;
Let my spirit feel in death,
That her feet are firmly set
On the rock of a living faith!

Hymn

How dare I in thy courts appear,
Or raise to thee my voice!
I only serve thee, Lord, with fear,
With trembling I rejoice.

I have not all forgot thy word.
Nor wholly gone astray;
I follow thee, but oh, my Lord,
So faint, so far away!

That thou wilt pardon and receive
Of sinners even the chief,
Lord, I believe,—Lord, I believe;
Help thou mine unbelief!

Human And Divine

Vile, and deformed by sin I stand,
A creature earthy of the earth;
Yet fashioned by God's perfect hand,
And in his likeness at my birth.

Here in a wretched land I roam,
As one who had no home but this;
Yet am invited to become
Partaker in a world of bliss.

A tenement of misery,
Of clay is this to which I cling:
A royal palace waits for me,
Built by the pleasure of my King!

My heavenly birthright I forsake,—
An outcast, and unreconciled;
The manner of his love doth make
My Father own me as his child.

Shortened by reason of man's wrong,
My evil days I here bemoan;
Yet know my life must last as long
As his, who struck it from his own.

Turned wholly am I from the way,—
Lost, and eternally undone;
I am of those, though gone astray,
The Father seeketh through the Son.

I wander in a maze of fear,
Hid in impenetrable night,
Afar from God—and yet so near,
He keeps me always in his sight.

I am as dross, and less than dross,
Worthless as worthlessness can be;
I am so precious that the cross
Darkened the universe for me!

I am unfit, even from the dust,
Master! to kiss thy garment's hem:
I am so dear, that thou, though just,
Wilt not despise me nor condemn.

Accounted am I as the least
Of creatures valueless and mean;
Yet heaven's own joy shall be increased
If e'er repentance wash me clean.

Naked, ashamed, I hide my face,
All seamed by guilt's defacing scars;
I may be clothed with righteousness
Above the brightness of the stars.

Lord, I do fear that I shall go
Where death and darkness wait for me;
Lord, I believe, and therefore know
I have eternal life in thee!

Prodigals

Again, in the Book of Books, to-day
I read of that Prodigal, far away
In the centuries agone,
Who took the portion that to him fell,
And went from friends and home to dwell
In a distant land alone.

And when his riotous living was done,
And his course of foolish pleasure run,
And a fearful famine rose,
He fain would have fed with the very swine,
And no man gave him bread nor wine,
For his friends were changed to foes.

And I thought, when at last his state he knew
What a little thing he had to do,
To win again his place:
Only the madness of sin to learn,
To come to himself, repent, and turn,
And seek his father's face.

Then I thought however vile we are,
Not one of us hath strayed so far
From the things that are good and pure,
But if to gain his home he tried,
He would find the portal open wide,
And find his welcome sure.

My fellow-sinners, though you dwell
 In haunts where the feet take hold on hell,
Where the downward way is plain;

Think, who is waiting for you at home,
Repent, and come to yourself, and come
To your Father's house again!

Say, out of the depths of humility,
"I have lost the claim of a child on thee,
I would serve thee with the least!"
And He will a royal robe prepare,
He will call you son, and call you heir;
And seat you at the feast.

Yea, fellow-sinner, rise to-day,
And run till He meets you on the way,
Till you hear the glad words said,
"Let joy through all the heavens resound,
For this, my son, who was lost is found,
And he lives who once was dead. "

Unbelief

Faithless, perverse, and blind,
We sit in our house of fear,
When the winter of sorrow comes to our souls,
And the days of our life are drear.

For when in darkness and clouds
The way of God is concealed,
We doubt the words of his promises,
And the glory to be revealed.

We do but trust in part;
We grope in the dark alone;
Lord, when shall we see thee as thou art,
And know as we are known?

When shall we live to thee
And die to thee, resigned,
Nor fear to hide what we would keep,
And lose what we would find?

For we doubt our Father's care,
We cover our faces and cry,
If a little cloud, like the hand of a man,
Darkens the face of our sky.

We judge of his perfect day
By our life's poor glimmering spark;
And measure eternity's circle
By the segment of an arc.

We say, they have taken our Lord,
And we know not where He lies,
When the light of his resurrection morn
Is breaking out of the skies.

And we stumble at last when we come
On the brink of the grave to stand;
As if the souls that are born of his love
Could slip their Father's hand?

PALGRAVE, FRANCIS TURNER, (1824–1897) was son of the English
historian, Sir Francis Palgrave, a converted Jew, who changed his name from
Cohen to his mother's maiden name at the time of his conversion. The father
was a legal scholar, specializing in legal pedigrees, and writing a number of pop-
ular historical studies, as well. The son was educated at Charterhouse School,
and became a fellow of Exeter College in 1846. He was for a time Gladstone's
secretary, then worked in the government Education Office, after which
(1850–55) he was vice principal of Kneller Hall, a teachers' college. He became
a friend of Alfred Tennyson, spending several summers with him in Europe. In
1885, after resigning from the Education Office, Palgrave followed his friend
John Campbell Shairp into the professorship of poetry at Oxford. His book *The
Passionate Pilgrim* (1858) gives an account of his life, especially his spiritual jour-
ney. He served as editor of *The Golden Treasure of English Lyrics* (1861, 1896), an
excellent anthology. He also edited selections of hymns (1867), of Shakespeare
(1865), of lyrics (1871), of stories for children (1868), and of the poems of
Herrick (1877) and Tennyson (1885). Other of his works include *Visions of
England* (1881), and *Amenophis* (1892)

God's City

O Thou not made with hands,
Not throned above the skies,
Nor walled with shining walls,
Nor framed with stones of price,
More bright than gold or gem,
God's own Jerusalem!

Where'er the gentle heart
Finds courage from above;
Where'er the heart forsook
Warms with the breath of love;
Where faith bids fear depart,
City of God, thou art.

Thou art where'er the proud
In humbleness melts down;
Where self itself yields up;
Where martyrs win their crown;
Where faithful souls possess
Themselves in perfect peace;

Where in life's common ways
With cheerful feet we go;
Where in his steps we tread,
Who trod the way of woe;
Where he is in the heart,
City of God, thou art.

Not throned above the skies,
Nor golden-walled afar,
But where Christ's two or three
In his name gathered are,
Be in the midst of them,
God's own Jerusalem!

MACDONALD, GEORGE (1824–1905), born at Huntley, Aberdeenshire, and educated at King's College, Aberdeen, became a Congregationalist minister in Arundel, Sussex, for three years, and thereafter preached for a short time to a company at Manchester and Bolton. Giving up the ministry, he became a Lecturer at King's College, London, and eventually entered fully into writing. He is chiefly noted for his fiction, which includes short stories, long "fantasies," (notably *Phantastes* and *Lilith*), children's books (notably the two Curdie books and *At the Back of The North Wind*), and many novels, including *David Elginbrod, Robert Falconer, Alec Forbes of Howglen, What's Mine Is Mine, Sir Gibbie,* and *Annals of a Quiet Neighborhood.* The novels fell out of fashion in the twentieth century, but a tremendous revival of severely abridged versions has been underway recently and has led to the republication of all MacDonald's original works. MacDonald's poetic works include *Within and Without* (1855), *The Disciple and Other Poems* (1860), *The Diary of An Old Soul* (1867), and *A Threefold Cord* (1883). He also published a volume of translations from German entitled *Exotics* and is the author of several hymns. MacDonald was acquainted with a wide range of contemporaries, including Lewis Carroll and Samuel Clemens. It is difficult not to see the many parallels between his works (published first) and Clemens famous *Tom Sawyer* and *Huckleberry Finn*. Next to his enduring works, his influence on C.S. Lewis has brought him note among twentieth century Christians. Lewis discusses him in his autobiographical book, *Surprised by Joy*, and makes him a heavenly guide in *The Great Divorce*.

Sonnet

This infant world has taken long to make,
Nor hast Thou done with it, but mak'st it yet,
And wilt be working on when death has set
A new mound in some churchyard for my sake.
On flow the centuries without a break;
Uprise the mountains, ages without let;
The lichens suck; the hard rock's breast they fret;
Years more than past the young earth yet will take.
But in the dumbness of the rolling time
No veil of silence shall encompass me—
Thou wilt not once forget and let me be;
Rather Thou wouldst some old chaotic prime
Invade, and, moved by tenderness sublime,
Unfold a world that I, thy child, might see.

That Holy Thing

They all were looking for a king
To slay their foes and lift them high:
Thou cam'st, a little baby thing
That made a woman cry.

O Son of Man, to right my lot
Naught but Thy presence can avail;
Yet on the road Thy wheels are not,
Nor on the sea Thy sail!

My how or when Thou wilt not heed,
But come down thine own secret stair,
That Thou mayst answer all my need—
Yea, every bygone prayer.

Mammon Marriage

The croak of a raven hoar!
A dog's howl, kennel-tied!
Loud shuts the carriage-door:
The two are away on their ghastly ride
To Death's salt shore!

Where are the love and the grace?
The bridegroom is thirsty and cold!
The bride's skull sharpens her face!
But the coachman is driving, jubilant, bold,
The devil's pace.

The horses shiver'd and shook
Waiting gaunt and haggard
With sorry and evil look;
But swift as a drunken wind they stagger'd
'Longst Lethe brook.

Long since, they ran no more;
Heavily pulling they died
On the sand of the hopeless shore
Where never swell'd or sank a tide,
And the salt burns sore.

Flat their skeletons lie,
White shadows on shining sand;
The crusted reins go high
To the crumbling coachman's bony hand
On his knees awry.

Side by side, jarring no more,
Day and night side by side,
Each by a doorless door,
Motionless sit the bridegroom and bride
On the Dead-Sea-shore.

Dorcas

If I might guess, then guess I would
That, mid the gather'd folk,
This gentle Dorcas one day stood,
And heard when Jesus spoke.

She saw the woven seamless coat—
Half envious, for his sake:
'Oh, happy hands,' she said, 'that wrought
The honoured thing to make!'

Her eyes with longing tears grow dim:
She never can come nigh
To work one service poor for him
For whom she glad would die!

O Thou Of Little Faith!

Sad-hearted, be at peace: the snowdrop lies
Buried in sepulchre of ghastly snow;
But spring is floating up the southern skies,
And darkling the pale snowdrop waits below.

Let me persuade: in dull December's day
We scarce believe there is a month of June;
But up the stairs of April and of May
The hot sun climbeth to the summer's noon.

Yet hear me: I love God, and half I rest.
O better! God loves thee, so all rest thou.
He is our summer, our dim-visioned Best;—
And in his heart thy prayer is resting now.

The Sheep And The Goat

The thousand streets of London gray
Repel all country sights;
But bar not winds upon their way,
Nor quench the scent of new-mown hay
In depth of summer nights.

And here and there an open spot,
Still bare to light and dark,
With grass receives the wanderer hot;
There trees are growing, houses not—
They call the place a park.

Soft creatures, with ungentle guides,
God's sheep from hill and plain,
Flow thitherward in fitful tides,

There weary lie on woolly sides,
Or crop the grass amain.

And from dark alley, yard, and den,
In ragged skirts and coats,
Troop hither tiny sons of men,
Wild things, untaught of word or pen—
The little human goats.

In Regent's Park one cloudless day,
An overdriven sheep,
Arrived from long and dusty way,
Throbbing with thirst and hotness lay,
A panting woollen heap.

But help is nearer than we know
For ills of every name:
Ragged enough to scare the crow,
But with a heart to pity woe,
A quick-eyed urchin came.

Little he knew of field or fold,
Yet knew what ailed; his cap
Was ready cup for water cold;
Though rumpled, stained, and very old,
Its rents were small—good-hap!

Shaping the rim and crown he went,
Till crown from rim was deep.
The water gushed from pore and rent;
Before he came one half was spent—
The other saved the sheep.

O little goat, born, bred in ill,
Unwashed, half-fed, unshorn!
Thou to the sheep from breezy hill
Wast bishop, pastor, what you will,
In London dry and lorn.

And let priests say the thing they please,
My hope, though very dim,
Thinks he will say who always sees,
In doing it to one of these
Thou didst it unto him.

What Christ Said

I said, "Let me walk in the fields."
He said, "No; walk in the town."
I said, "There are no flowers there."
He said, "No flowers, but a crown."

I said, "But the skies are black,
There is nothing but noise and din;"
And he wept as he sent me back;
"There is more," he said, "there is sin."

I said, "But the air is thick,
And fogs are veiling the sun."
He answered, "Yet souls are sick,
And souls in the dark undone."

I said, "I shall miss the light,
And friends will miss me, they say."
He answered, "Choose tonight
If I am to miss you, or they."

I pleaded for time to be given.
He said, "Is it hard to decide?
It will not seem hard in Heaven
To have followed the steps of your Guide."

I cast one look at the fields,
Then set my face to the town;
He said, "My child, do you yield?
Will you leave the flowers for the crown?"

Then into his hand went mine;
And into my heart came he;
And I walk in a light divine,
The path I had feared to see.

Rest (I)

When round the earth the Father's hands
Have gently drawn the dark;
Sent off the sun to fresher lands,
And curtained in the lark;
'Tis sweet, all tired with glowing day,
To fade with fading light,

And lie once more, the old weary way,
Upfolded in the night.

If mothers o'er our slumbers bend,
And unripe kisses reap,
In soothing dreams with sleep they blend,
Till even in dreams we sleep.
And if we wake while night is dumb,
'Tis sweet to turn and say,
It is an hour ere dawning come,
And I will sleep till day.

There is a dearer, warmer bed,
Where one all day may lie,
Earth's bosom pillowing the head,
And let the world go by.
Hast thou not wisdom to enwrap
My waywardness about,
In doubting safety on the lap
Of Love that knows no doubt?

Lo! Lord, I sit in thy wide space,
My child upon my knee;
She looketh up unto my face,
And I look up to thee.

Father's Hymn for the Mother to Sing

My child is lying on my knees;
The signs of heaven she reads:
My face is all the heaven she sees,
Is all the heaven she needs.

And she is well, yea, bathed in bliss,
If heaven is in my face—
Behind it, all is tenderness,
And truthfulness and grace.

I mean her well so earnestly,
Unchanged in changing mood;
My life would go without a sigh
To bring her something good.

I also am a child, and I
Am ignorant and weak;
I gaze upon the starry sky,
And then I must not speak;

For all behind the starry sky,
Behind the world so broad,
Behind men's hearts and souls doth lie
The Infinite of God.

If true to her, though troubled sore,
I cannot choose but be;
Thou, who art peace for evermore,
Art very true to me.

If I am low and sinful, bring
More love where need is rife;
Thou knowest what an awful thing
It is to be a life.

Sonnets Suggested by St. Augustine

I

What love I when I love Thee, O my God?
Not corporal beauty, nor the limb of snow,
Nor of loved light the white and pleasant flow,
Nor manna showers, nor streams that flow abroad,
Nor flowers of Heaven, nor small stars of the sod:
Not these, my God, I love, who love Thee so;
Yet love I something better than I know:—
A certain light on a more golden road;
A sweetness, not of honey or the hive;
A beauty, not of summer or the spring;
A scent, a music, and a blossoming
Eternal, timeless, placeless, without gyve,
Fair, fadeless, undiminish'd, ever dim,—
This, this is what I love in loving Him.

II

This, this is what I love, and what is this?
I ask'd the beautiful earth, who said—'not I.'
I ask'd the depths, and the immaculate sky
And all the spaces said—'not He but His.'

And so, like one who scales a precipice,
Height after height, I scaled the flaming ball
Of the great universe, yea, pass'd o'er all
The world of thought, which so much higher is.
Then I exclaimed, 'To whom is mute all murmur
Of phantasy, of nature, and of art,
He, than articulate language bears a firmer
And grander meaning in his own deep heart.
No sound from cloud or angel.' Oh, to win
That voiceless voice—'My servant, enter in'!

A Prayer

When I look back upon my life nigh spent,
Nigh spent, although the stream as yet flows on,
I more of follies than of sins repent,
Less for offence than Love's shortcomings moan.
With self, O Father, leave me not alone—
Leave not with the beguiler the beguiled;
Besmirched and ragged, Lord, take back thine own:
A fool I bring thee to be made a child.

The Birthday Crown

If aught of simple song have power to touch
Your silent being, O ye country flowers,
   Twisted by tender hands
   Into a royal brede,

O hawthorn, tear thou not the soft white brow
Of the small queen upon her rustic throne;
   But breathe thy finest scent
   Of almond round about.

And thou, laburnum, and what other hue
Tinct deeper gives variety of gold,
   Inwoven lily, and vetch
   Bedropp'd with summer's blood,

I charge you wither not this long June day!
O, wither not until the sunset come,
   Until the sunset's shaft
   Slope through the chestnut tree;

Until she sit, high-gloried round about
With the great light above her mimic court—
   Her threads of sunny hair
   Girt sunnily by you!

What other crown that queen may wear one day,
What drops may touch her forehead not of balm,
   What thorns, what cruel thorns,
   I will not guess to-day.

Only, before she is discrown'd of you,
Ye dying flowers, and thou, O dying light,
   My prayer shall rise—'O Christ!
   Give her the unfading crown.

'The crown of blossoms worn by happy bride,
The thorny crown o'er pale and dying lips,
   I dare not choose for her—
   Give her the unfading crown!'

Rest (II)

Who dwelleth in that secret place,
   Where tumult enters not,
Is never cold with terror base,
   Never with anger hot:
For if an evil host should dare
   His very heart invest,
God is his deeper heart, and there
   He enters in to rest.

When mighty sea-winds madly blow.
   And tear the scattered waves,
Peaceful as summer woods, below
   Lie darkling ocean caves:
The wind of words may toss my heart,
   But what is that to me!
'Tis but a surface storm—Thou art
   My deep, still, resting sea.

A Christmas Carol

Babe Jesus lay in Mary's lap;
The sun shone on His hair;

And this is how she saw, mayhap,
The crown already there.

For she sang: "Sleep on, my little King,
Bad Herod dares not come;
Before Thee sleeping, holy thing,
The wild winds would be dumb.

"I kiss Thy hands, I kiss Thy feet,
My child so long desired;
Thy hands shall never be soiled, my sweet,
Thy feet shall never be tired.

For Thou art the King of Men, my son;
Thy crown I see it plain;
And men shall worship Thee, every one,
And cry, Glory! Amen!"

Babe Jesus opened his eyes so wide!
At Mary looked her Lord.
And Mary stinted her song and sighed.
Babe Jesus said never a word.

Lost And Found

I missed him when the sun began to bend;
I found him not when I had lost his rim;
With many tears I went in search of him,
Climbing high mountains which did still ascend,
And gave me echoes when I called my friend;
Through cities vast and charnel-houses grim,
And high cathedrals where the light was dim,
Through books and arts and works without an end,
But found him not—the friend whom I had lost.
And yet I found him—as I found the lark,
A sound in fields I heard but could not mark;
I found him nearest when I missed him most;
I found him in my heart, a life in frost,
A light I knew not till my soul was dark.

PROCTOR, ADELAIDE ANNE (1825–1864), best known as the writer of "The Lost Chord," was the daughter of Bryan Waller Proctor, "Barry Cornwall," mid-Victorian playwright and poet. She showed early abilities in music and poetry, further enhanced by acquaintance through her father with

such men as Charles Lamb, Leigh Hunt, and Charles Dickens. She submitted
poetry to Dickens's magazine under the pseudonym Miss Berwick, fearing that
his friendship with her would influence his editorial decisions. He accepted the
work, only discovering her identity years later. A collection of her poetry, with
introduction by Dickens, was published in 1858. In 1851 Adelaide Proctor
became a Roman Catholic. She wrote a number of hymns that may be found in
contemporary hymnals.

A Lost Chord

Seated one day at the Organ,
I was weary and ill at ease,
And my fingers wandered idly
Over the noisy keys.

I do not know what I was playing,
Or what I was dreaming then;
But I struck one chord of music,
Like the sound of a great Amen.

It flooded the crimson twilight,
Like the close of an Angel's Psalm,
And it lay on my fevered spirit
With a touch of infinite calm.

It quieted pain and sorrow,
Like love overcoming strife;
It seemed the harmonious echo
From our discordant life.

It linked all perplexed meanings
Into one perfect peace,
And trembled away into silence
As if it were loth to cease.

I have sought, but I seek it vainly,
That one lost chord divine,
Which came from the soul of the Organ,
And entered into mine.

It may be that Death's bright angel
Will speak in that chord again,
It may be that only in Heaven
I shall hear that grand Amen.

A Legend

I

The Monk was preaching: strong his earnest word;
From the abundance of his heart he spoke,
And the flame spread,—in every soul that heard
Sorrow and love and good resolve awoke:—
The poor lay brother, ignorant and old,
Thanked God that he had heard such words of gold.

II

'Still let the glory, Lord, be thine alone,'—
So prayed the Monk, his heart absorbed in praise:
Thine be the glory: if my hands have sown
The harvest ripened in Thy mercy's rays,
It was Thy blessing, Lord, that made my word
Bring light and love to every soul that heard.

III

'O Lord, I thank Thee that my feeble strength
Has been so blest; that sinful hearts and cold
Were melted at my pleading,—knew at length
How sweet Thy service and how safe Thy fold:
While souls that loved Thee saw before them rise
Still holier heights of loving sacrifice.'

IV

So prayed the Monk: when suddenly be heard
An Angel speaking thus: 'Know, O my Son,
The words had all been vain, but hearts were stirred,
And saints were edified, and Sinners won,
By his, the poor lay Brother's humble aid
Who sat upon the pulpit stair and prayed.'

Give Me Thy Heart

With echoing steps the worshippers
Departed one by one;
The organ's pealing voice was stilled,
The vesper hymn was done;

The shadows fell from roof and arch,
Dim was the incensed air,
One lamp alone with trembling ray,
Told of the Presence there!

In the dark church she knelt alone;
Her tears were falling fast;
'Help, Lord,' she cried, 'the shades of death
Upon my soul are cast!

Have I not shunned the path of sin
And chosen the better part?'
What voice came through the sacred air?
'My child, give me thy heart!

'For I have loved thee with a love
No mortal heart can show;
A love so deep, My Saints in Heaven
Its depths can never know:

When pierced and wounded on the Cross,
Man's sin and doom were Mine,
I loved thee with undying love;
Immortal and divine.'

In awe she listened, and the shade
Passed from her soul away;
In low and trembling voice she cried,
'Lord, help me to obey!'

The Divine Presence

All but unutterable Name!
Adorable, yet awful sound!
Thee can the sinful nations frame
Save with their foreheads on the ground?

Soul-searching and all-cleansing Fire;
To see Thy countenance were to die:
Yet how beyond the bound retire
Of Thy serene immensity?

Thou mov'st beside us, if the spot
We change—a noteless, wandering tribe;
The orbits of our life and thought
In Thee their little arcs describe.

In their dead calm, at cool of day,
We hear Thy voice, and turn, and flee:

Thy love outstrips us on our way!
From Thee, O God, we fly—to Thee.

Sorrow

Count each affliction, whether light or grave,
God's messenger sent down to thee; do thou
With courtesy receive him; rise and bow;
And, ere his shadow pass thy threshold, crave
Permission first his heavenly feet to lave;
Then lay before him all thou hast; allow
No cloud of passion to usurp thy brow,
Or mar thy hospitality; no wave
Of mortal tumult to obliterate
Thy soul's marmoreal calmness. Grief should be
Like joy, majestic, equable, sedate;
Confirming, cleansing, raising, making free;
Strong to consume small troubles; to commend
Great thoughts, grave thoughts, thoughts lasting to the end.

Per Pacem Ad Lucem

I do not ask, O Lord, that life may be
    A pleasant road;
I do not ask that thou would'st take from me
    Aught of its load;

I do not ask that flowers should always spring
    Beneath my feet;
I know too well the poison and the sting
    Of things too sweet.

For one thing only, Lord, dear Lord, I plead
    Lead me aright—
Though strength should falter, and though heart should bleed—
    Through peace to light.

I do not ask, O Lord, that thou should'st shed
    Full radiance here;
Give but a ray of peace, that I may tread
    Without a fear.

I do not ask thy cross to understand,
    My way to see—

Better in darkness just to feel thy hand,
   And follow thee.

Joy is like restless day; but peace divine
Like quiet night: Lead me,
O Lord—till perfect day shall shine
   Through peace to light.

Thankfulness

My God, I thank thee who hast made
   The earth so bright;
So full of splendour and of joy,
   Beauty and light;
So many glorious things are here,
   Noble and right!

I thank thee, too, that thou hast made
   Joy to abound;
So many gentle thoughts and deeds
   Circling us round,
That on the darkest spot of earth
   Some love is found.

I thank thee more that all our joy
   Is touched with pain;
That shadows fall on brightest hours;
   That thorns remain;
So that earth's bliss may be our guide,
   And not our chain.

For thou who knowest, Lord, how soon
   Our weak heart clings,
Hast given us joys, tender and true,
   Yet all with wings,
So that we see, gleaming on high,
   Diviner things!

I thank thee, Lord, that thou hast kept
   The best in store;
We have enough, yet not too much
   To long for more:
A yearning for a deeper peace,
   Not known before.

I thank thee, Lord, that here our souls,
　　Though amply blest
Can never find, although they seek,
　　A perfect rest—
Nor ever shall, until they lean
　　On Jesus' breast.

Judge Not

Judge not; the workings of his brain
And of his heart thou canst not see;
What looks to thy dim eyes a stain,
In God's pure light may only be
A scar, brought from some well-won field,
Where thou wouldst only faint and yield.

The look, the air, that frets thy sight
May be a token that below
The soul has closed in deadly fight
With some infernal fiery foe,
Whose glance would scorch thy smiling grace,
And cast thee shuddering on thy face!

The fall thou darest to despise,—
May be the angel's slackened hand
Has suffered it, that he may rise
And take a firmer, surer stand;
Or, trusting less to earthly things,
May henceforth learn to use his wings.

And judge none lost; but wait and see,
With hopeful pity, not disdain;
The depth of the abyss may be
The measure of the height of pain
And love and glory that may raise
This soul to God in after days!

Unexpressed

Dwells within the soul of every Artist
More than all his effort can express;
And he knows the best remains unuttered
Sighing at what we call his success.

Vainly he may strive; he dare not tell us
All the sacred mysteries of the skies;
Vainly he may strive, the deepest beauty
Cannot be unveiled to mortal eyes.

And the more devoutly that he listens,
And the holier message that is sent,
Still the more his soul must struggle vainly,
Bowed beneath a noble discontent.

No great Thinker ever lived and taught you
All the wonder that his soul received;
No true Painter ever set on canvas
All the glorious vision he conceived.

No Musician ever held your spirit
Charmed and bound in his melodious chains,
But be sure he heard, and strove to render,
Feeble echoes of celestial strains.

No real Poet ever wove in numbers
All his dream; but the diviner part,
Hidden from all the world, spake to him only
In the voiceless silence of his heart.

So with Love: for Love and Art united
Are twin mysteries; different, yet the same:
Poor indeed would be the love of any
Who could find its full and perfect name.

Love may strive, but vain is the endeavor
All its boundless riches to unfold;
Still its tenderest, truest secret lingers
Ever in its deepest depths untold.

Things of Time have voices: speak and perish.
Art and Love speak; but their words must be
Like sighings of illimitable forests,
And waves of an unfathomable sea.

The Dark Side

Thou hast done well, perhaps,
To lift the bright disguise,
And lay the bitter truth

Before our shrinking eyes;
When evil crawls below
What seems so pure and fair,
Thine eyes are keen and true
To find the serpent there:
And yet—I turn away;
Thy task is not divine,—
The evil angels look
On earth with eyes like thine.

Thou hast done well, perhaps,
To show how closely wound
Dark threads of sin and self
With our best deeds are found,
How great and noble hearts,
Striving for lofty aims,
Have still some earthly chord
A meaner spirit claims;
And yet—although thy task
Is well and fairly done—
Methinks for such as thou
There is a holier one.

Shadows there are, who dwell
Among us, yet apart,
Deaf to the claim of God,
Or kindly human heart;
Voices of earth and heaven
Call, but they turn away,
And Love, through such black night
Can see no hope of day;
And yet—our eyes are dim,
And thine are keener far:
Then gaze till thou canst see
The glimmer of some star.

The black stream flows along
Whose waters we despise,—
Show us reflected there
Some fragment of the skies;
'Neath tangled thorns and briers,
(The task is fit for thee,)
Seek for the hidden flowers,

We are too blind to see;
Then will I thy great gift
A crown and blessing call;
Angels look thus on men,
And God sees good in all!

The Pilgrims

The way is long and dreary,
The path is bleak and bare;
Our feet are worn and weary,
But we will not despair.

More heavy was Thy burden,
More desolate Thy way,
O Lamb of God who takest
The sin of the world away,
Have mercy on us.

The snows lie thick around us
In the dark and gloomy night;
And the tempest wails above us,
And the stars have hid their light;
But blacker was the darkness
Round Calvary's Cross that day;
O Lamb of God who takest
The sin of the world away,
Have mercy on us.

Our hearts are faint with sorrow,
Heavy and hard to bear;
For we dread the bitter morrow,
But we will not despair:
Thou knowest all our anguish,
And Thou wilt bid it cease,—
O Lamb of God who takest
The sin of the world away,
Give us Thy Peace!

Words

Words are lighter than the cloud-foam
Of the restless ocean spray;

Vainer than the trembling shadow
That the next hour steals away.
By the fall of summer rain-drops
Is the air as deeply stirred;
And the rose-leaf that we tread on
Will outlive a word.

Yet, on the dull silence breaking
With a lightning flash, a Word,
Bearing endless desolation
On its blighting wings, I heard:
Earth can forge no keener weapon,
Dealing surer death and pain,
And the cruel echo answered
Through long years again.

I have known one word hang starlike
O'er a dreary waste of years,
And it only shone the brighter
Looked at through a mist of tears;
While a weary wanderer gathered
Hope and heart on Life's dark way,
By its faithful promise, shining
Clearer day by day.

I have known a spirit calmer
Than the calmest lake, and clear
As the heavens that gazed upon it,
With no wave of hope or fear;
But a storm had swept across it,
And its deepest depths were stirred,
(Never, never more to slumber,)
Only by a word.

I have known a word more gentle
Than the breath of summer air;
In a listening heart it nestled,
And it lived forever there.
Not the beating of its prison
Stirred it ever, night or day;
Only with the heart's last throbbing
Could it fade away.

Words are mighty, words are living:
Serpents with their venomous stings,
Or bright angels, crowding round us,
With heaven's light upon their wings:
Every word has its own spirit,
True or false, that never dies;
Every word man's lips have uttered
Echoes in God's skies.

BLACKMORE, RICHARD DODDRIDGE (1825–1900), educated at Oxford, tried both teaching and the law, but gave both up upon receiving an inheritance. He is author of the well-known *Lorna Doone: A Romance of Exmoor* (1869), and of more than ten other novels, including *Craddock Nowell* (1866), *Clara Vaughan* (1864), and *Christowell* (1882). He published five books of poetry, as well, including *Poems by Melanter* (1853) and *Fringilla* (1895). He also translated *Hero and Leander* by Musaeus, Virgil's *Georgics* and the *Idylls* of Theocritus. His books are particularly noted for their secondary characters and descriptions of the west country of England.

Dominus Illuminatio Mea

In the hour of death, after this life's whim,
When the heart beats low, and the eyes grow dim,
And pain has exhausted every limb—
The lover of the Lord shall trust in Him.

When the will has forgotten the lifelong aim,
And the mind can only disgrace its fame,
And a man is uncertain of his own name—
The power of the Lord shall fill this frame.

When the last sigh is heaved, and the last tear shed,
And the coffin is waiting beside the bed,
And the widow and child forsake the dead—
The angel of the Lord shall lift this head.

For even the purest delight may pall,
And power must fail, and the pride must fall,
And the love of the dearest friends grow small—
But the glory of the Lord is all in all.

For the Holy Family by Michelangelo In the National Gallery

In this picture the Virgin Mother is seen withholding from
the Child Saviour the prophetic writings in which his sufferings
are foretold. Angelic figures beside them examine a scroll.

Turn not to the prophet's page, O Son! He knew
All that Thou hast to suffer, and hath writ.
Not yet Thine hour of knowledge. Infinite
The sorrows that Thy manhood's lot must rue
And dire acquaintance of Thy grief. That clue
The spirits of Thy mournful ministerings
Seek through yon scroll in silence. For these things
The angels have desired to look into.
Still before Eden waves the fiery sword,—
Her Tree of Life unransomed: whose sad Tree
Of Knowledge yet to growth of Calvary
Must yield its Tempter,—Hell the earliest dead
Of Earth resign,—and yet, O Son and Lord,
The Seed o' the woman bruise the serpent's head.

Lost Days

The lost days of my life until to-day,
What were they, could I see them on the street
Lie as they fell? Would they be ears of wheat
Sown once for food but trodden into clay?
Or golden coins squandered and still to pay?
Or drops of blood dabbling the guilty feet?
Or such spilt water as in dreams must cheat
The undying throat of Hell, athirst alway?

I do not see them here; but after death
God knows I know the faces I shall see,
Each one a murdered self, with low last breath.
"I am thyself,—what hast thou done to me?"
"And I—and I—thyself," (lo! each one saith,)
"And thou thyself to all eternity!"

World's Worth

'Tis of the Father Hilary.
He strove, but could not pray; so took

The steep coiled stair, where his feet shook
A sad blind echo. Ever up
He toiled. 'Twas a sick sway of air
That autumn noon within the stair,
As dizzy as a turning cup.
His brain benumbed him, void and thin;
He shut his eyes and felt it spin;
The obscure deafness hemmed him in.
He said: "O world, what world for me?"

He leaned unto the balcony
Where the chime keeps the night and day;
It hurt his brain, be could not pray.
He had his face upon the stone:
Deep 'twixt the narrow shafts, his eye
Passed all the roofs to the stark sky,
Swept with no wing, with wind alone.
Close to his feet the sky did shake
With wind in pools that the rains make;
The ripple set his ayes to ache.
He said: "O world, what world for me?"

He stood within the mystery
Girding God's blessed Eucharist:
The organ and the chaunt had ceas'd
The last words paused against his ear
Said from the altar: drawn round him
The gathering rest was dumb and dim.
And now the sacring-ball rang clear
And ceased; and all was awe—the breath
Of God in man that warranteth
The inmost utmost things of faith.
He said: "O God, my world in Thee!"

The Heart Of The Night

From child to youth; from youth to arduous man;
From lethargy to fever of the heart;
From faithful life to dream-dowered days apart;
From trust to doubt; from doubt to brink of ban;—
Thus much of change in one swift cycle ran
Till now. Alas, the soul!—how soon must she

Accept her primal immortality—
The flesh resume its dust whence it began?

O Lord of work and peace! O Lord of life!
O Lord, the awful Lord of will! though late,
Even yet renew this soul with duteous breath:
That when the peace is garnered in from strife,
The work retrieved, the will regenerate,
This soul may see thy face, O Lord of death!

ROSSETTI, DANTE GABRIEL (GABRIEL CHARLES DANTE)

(1828–1882), brother of Christina and leading personality of the Pre-Raphaelite Brotherhood, is chiefly noted as a painter, although he wrote and translated poetry, as well. His best known poem is "The Blessed Damozel." His collection of poetry, *Poems* (1870), was buried in the coffin of his wife and painting model, Elizabeth Siddall. (The poems were recovered a few years later.) His *Ballads and Sonnets* was published in 1881. He was involved in the "arts and crafts movement" that the Pre-Raphaelite Brotherhood began as an effort to reaffirm the value of hand-craftsmanship over against factory production. Holman Hunt and J. E. Millais were the other "founders." Their short-lived magazine, *The Germ*, declared their purpose, to "enforce and encourage an entire adherence to the simplicity of nature." The name of their group may be understood by another statement of purpose as painters: "to paint things as they probably did look and happen, not as, by rules of art developed under Raphael, they might be supposed gracefully, deliciously, or sublimely to have happened." Rossetti's work has a characteristic note of melancholy his sister's poetry sometimes shares. However, her faith seems more to overcome it and her poetry sounds a stronger call of hope.

Saint Luke the Painter
For a Drawing

Give Honour unto Luke Evangelist:
For he it was (the aged legends say)
Who first taught Art to fold her hands and pray.
Scarcely at once she dared to rend the mist
Of devious symbols; but soon having wist
How sky-breadth and field-silence and this day
Are symbols also in some deeper way,
She looked through these to God and was God's priest.
And if, past noon, her toil began to irk,
And she sought talismans, and turned in vain

To soulless self-reflections of man's skill,—
Yet now, in this the twilight, she might still
Kneel in the latter grass to pray again,
Ere the night cometh and she may not work.

CLEPHANE, ELIZABETH (1830–1869), daughter of a Scottish sheriff, is chiefly noted as a hymn-writer. Her hymns appeared in the *Family Treasury*, under the general title, *Breathings on the Border*. The editor, Rev W. Arnot, introduced them, "These lines express the experiences, the hopes, and the longings of a young Christian lately released. Written on the very edge of this life, with the better land fully in the view of faith, they seem to us footsteps printed on the sands of time, where these sands touch the ocean of Eternity. These footprints of one whom the Good Shepherd led through the wilderness into rest, may, with God's blessing, contribute to comfort and direct succeeding pilgrims." (*Dictionary of Hymnology*)

Beneath The Cross Of Jesus

Beneath the cross of Jesus
I fain would take my stand,
The shadow of a mighty Rock
Within a weary land;
A home within the wilderness,
A rest upon the way,
From the burning of the noontide heat,
And the burden of the day.

Upon the cross of Jesus
Mine eye at times can see
The very dying form of One
Who suffered there for me:
And from my stricken heart with tears
Two wonders I confess,
The wonders of redeeming love
And my own worthlessness.

I take, O cross, thy shadow,
For my abiding place:
I ask no other sunshine than
The sunshine of his face;
Content to let the world go by,
To know no gain or loss;

My sinful self my only shame,
My glory, all the cross.

Ninety And Nine

There were ninety and nine that safely lay
In the shelter of the fold,
But one was out on the hills away,
Far off from the gates of gold—
　　Away on the mountains wild and bare,
　　Away from the tender Shepherd's care,
　　Away from the tender Shepherd's care.

"Lord, thou hast here thy ninety and nine;
Are they not enough for thee?"
But the Shepherd made answer:
"This of mine has wandered away from me,
　　And although the road be rough and steep,
　　I go to the desert to find my sheep,
　　I go to the desert to find my sheep."

But none of the ransomed ever knew
How deep were the waters crossed;
Nor how dark was the night that the Lord passed thro'
Ere he found his sheep that was lost.
　　Out in the desert he heard its cry—
　　Sick and helpless and ready to die,
　　Sick and helpless and ready to die.

"Lord, whence are those blooddrops all the way
That mark out the mountain's track?"
"They were shed for one who had gone astray
Ere the Shepherd could bring him back."
　　Lord whence are thy hands so rent and torn?"
　　"They're pierced tonight by many a thorn;
　　They're pierced tonight by many a thorn."

But all thro' the mountains, thunder-riv'n,
And up from the rocky steep,
There arose a glad cry to the gate of heav'n,
"Rejoice! I have found my sheep!"
　　And the angels echoed around the throne,
　　"Rejoice, for the Lord brings back his own!
　　Rejoice, for the Lord brings back his own!"

DICKINSON, EMILY (1830–1886) daughter of a lawyer, lived in Amherst, Massachusetts, where she attended Mount Holyoke Female Seminary for a year. She was a reclusive and private person. Despite writing nearly 1800 poems, she published nothing in her own lifetime. Her poetry is "romantic," that is derived from observations and meditations on phenomena of "nature," but it is also metaphysical, making use of unusual and extended metaphors. Her poems are very "spare," condensing a great deal of meaning into a few words and lines, which characteristic makes reading them feel like working at riddles. Some of her poems refer to a sweetheart who is far away—this "lover" of the poems is apparently based on Charles Wadsworth of Philadelphia, whom she only met through letters in which she sought spiritual guidance. He moved to San Francisco in 1862, and her poems of absent love date from this time. Dickinson sent poems to various others, including the editor, Samuel Bowles, the essayist, Thomas Ffigginson, Dr. J. G. Holland, and her friend, the writer, Helen Hunt Jackson. Her faith, though isolated and often crankily expressed, is evident throughout her poetry. After she died her poems were published as *Poems* (1890); *Poems: Second Series* (1891); *Poems: Third Series* (1896); *The Single Hound* (1914); *Further Poems* (1929); *Unpublished Poems* (1936); and *Bolts of Melody* (1945). *Letters of Emily Dickinson* was published in 1894. In some of the editions, her poems were heavily edited. A careful collection of all her verse became available in 1955 in a three volume variorum text, *The Complete Poems of Emily Dickinson* (editor, Thomas H. Johnson). A one volume version was published in 1960. Dickinson is now recognized as a major American poet.

Then I Am Ready to Go (No. 279)

Tie the Strings to my Life, My Lord,
Then, I am ready to go!
Just a look at the Horses—
Rapid! That will do!

Put me in on the firmest side—
So I shall never fall—
For we must ride to the Judgment—
And it's partly, down Hill—

But never I mind the steepest—
And never I mind the Sea—
Held fast in Everlasting Race—
By my own Choice, and Thee—

Goodbye to the Life I used to live—
And the World I used to know—

And kiss the Hills, for me, just once—
Then—I am ready to go!

I Should Have Been Too Glad (No. 313)

I should have been too glad, I see
Too lifted—for the scant degree
Of Life's penurious Round—
My little Circuit would have shamed
This new Circumference—have blamed—
The homelier time behind.

I should have been too saved—I see—
Too rescued—Fear too dim to me
That I could spell the Prayer
I knew so perfect—yesterday—
That Scalding One—Sabachthani—
Recited fluent—here—

Earth would have been too much—I see—
And Heaven—not enough for me—
I should have had the Joy
Without the Fear—to justify—
The Palm—without the Calvary—
So Savior—Crucify—

Defeat—whets Victory—they say—
The Reefs—in old Gethsemane—
Endear the Coast—beyond!
'Tis Beggars—Banquets—can define—
'Tis Parching—vitalizes Wine—
"Faith" bleats—to understand!

The Lily (No. 392)

Through the Dark Sod—as Education—
The Lily passes sure—
Feels her white foot—no trepidation—
Her faith—no fear—

Afterward—in the Meadow—
Swinging her Beryl Bell—
The Mold-life—all forgotten—now—
In Ecstasy—and Dell—

I Choose Just A Crown (No. 508)

I'm ceded—I've stopped being Theirs—
The name They dropped upon my face
With water, in the country church
Is finished using, now,
And They can put it with my Dolls,
My childhood, and the string of spools,
I've finished threading—too—

Baptized, before, without the choice,
But this time, consciously, of Grace—
Unto supremest name—
Called to my Full—The Crescent dropped—
Existence's whole Arc, filled up,
With one small Diadem.

My second Rank—too small the first—
Crowned—Crowing—on my Father's breast—
A half unconscious Queen—
But this time—Adequate—Erect,
With Will to choose, or to reject,
And I choose, just a Crown—

That I Did Always Love (No. 549)

That I did always love
I bring thee Proof
That till I loved
I never lived—Enough—

That I shall love alway—
I argue thee
That love is life—
And life hath Immortality—

This—dost thou doubt—Sweet—
Then have I
Nothing to show
But Calvary—

The Morning After Death (No. 1078)

The Bustle in a House
The Morning after Death

Is solemnest of industries
Enacted upon Earth—

The Sweeping up the Heart
And putting Love away
We shall not want to use again
Until Eternity.

Of Paul and Silas (No. 1166)

Of Paul and Silas it is said
They were in Prison laid
But when they went to take them out
They were not there instead.

Security the same insures
To our assaulted Minds—
The staple must be optional
That an Immortal binds.

Unexpected Friends (No. 1180)

"Remember me" implored the Thief!
Oh Hospitality!
My Guest "Today in Paradise"
I give thee guaranty.

That Courtesy will fair remain
When the Delight is Dust
With which we cite this mightiest case
Of compensated Trust.

Of all we are allowed to hope
But Affidavit stands
That this was due where most we fear
Be unexpected Friends.

The Broad-minded Preacher (No. 1207)

He preached upon "Breadth" till it argued him narrow—
The Broad are too broad to define
And of "Truth" until it proclaimed him a Liar—
The Truth never flaunted a Sign—

Simplicity fled from his counterfeit presence
As Gold the Pyrites would shun—
What confusion would cover the innocent Jesus
To meet so enabled a Man!

A Marrowless Assembly (No. 1274)

The Bone that has no Marrow,
What Ultimate for that?
It is not fit for Table.
For Beggar or for Cat.

A Bone has obligations—
A Being has the same—
A Marrowless Assembly
Is culpabler than shame.

But how shall finished Creatures
A function fresh obtain?
Old Nicodemus' Phantom
Confronting us again !

How Brittle Are the Piers (No. 1433)

How brittle are the Piers
On which our Faith doth tread—
No Bridge below doth totter so—
Yet none hath such a Crowd.

It is as old as God—
Indeed—'twas built by him—
He sent his Son to test the Plank,
And he pronounced it firm.

The Road to Bethlehem (No. 1487)

The Savior must have been
A docile Gentleman—
To come so far so cold a Day
For little Fellowmen—

The Road to Bethlehem
Since He and I were Boys

Was leveled, but for that 'twould be
A rugged billion Miles—

Partings (No. 1732)

My life closed twice before its close—
It yet remains to see
If Immortality unveil
A third event to me.

So huge, so hopeless to conceive
As these that twice befell.
Parting is all we know of heaven,
And all we need of hell.

KINGSLEY, HENRY (1830–1876), son of a Northamptonshire rector and brother of Charles Kingsley (*The Water Babies*), was a novelist and journalist. He left Oxford without taking a degree, prospected for gold in Australia, and served for a time as a trooper in the Sydney Mounted Police. He wrote *Geoffrey Hamlyn* (1859), *Ravenshoe* (1862), *The Hillyars and the Burtons* (1865), *Mademoiselle Mathilde* (1868) among other novels, as well as essays, short stories and children's tales. The popularity of his novels diminished and he worked as a journalist, editing the Edinburgh *Daily Review*. He is described as an "impulsive, convivial, but insecure man." (*Oxford Companion to English Literature*)

Magdalene

Magdalene at Michael's gate
    Tirled at the pin;
On Joseph's thorn sang the blackbird,
    'Let her in! Let her in!'

'Hast thou seen the wounds?' said Michael
    'Know'st thou thy sin?'
'It is evening, evening,' sang the blackbird,
    'Let her in! Let her in!'

'Yes, I have seen the wounds,
    And I know my sin.'
'She knows it well, well, well,' sung the blackbird,
    'Let her in! Let her in!'

'Thou bringest no offerings,' said Michael.
   'Nought save sin.'
And the blackbird sang, 'She is sorry, sorry, sorry,
   Let her in! Let her in!'

When he had sung himself to sleep,
   And night did begin,
One came and open'd Michael's gate,
   And Magdalen went in.

ROSSETTI, CHRISTINA GEORGINA (1830–1894), daughter of a Neopolitan refugee, and sister of Dante Gabriel (painter and poet), is widely known for her children's verses and her Christian poetry. She was educated at home, was a model for many PreRaphaelite painters, and published a variety of works. Her poetry books include *Goblin Market* (1862), *The Prince's Progress* (1864), *Sing-Song, A Nursery Rhyme Book* (1872), *A Pageant and Other Poems* (1881), *Time Flies* (1885), and *New Poems* (1896). She also published *Anno Domini* (1874), a book of prayers for every day of the year and *Letter and Spirit of the Decalogue* (1883). She spent her last years, after an illness in 1874, in seclusion as an invalid. Her poetry is lyrical and profound. "Her sonnets are amongst the finest in the English language." *(Dictionary of English Hymnody)* "She is known for her ballads and her mystical religious lyrics, marked by symbolism, vividness of detail, and intensity of feeling." *(The Reader's Encyclopedia)*

Who Has Seen The Wind?

Who has seen the wind?
   Neither I nor you:
But when the leaves hang trembling
   The wind is passing thro'.

Who has seen the wind?
   Neither you nor I:
But when the trees bow down their heads
   The wind is passing by.

An Emerald Is As Green As Grass

An emerald is as green as grass;
   A ruby red as blood;
A sapphire shines as blue as heaven;
   A flint lies in the mud.

A diamond is a brilliant stone,
    To catch the world's desire;
An opal holds a fiery spark;
    But a flint holds fire.

Up-Hill

Does the road wind up-hill all the way?
    Yes, to the very end.
Will the day's journey take the whole long day?
    From morn to night, my friend.

But is there for the night a resting-place?
    A roof for when the slow dark hours begin.
May not the darkness hide it from my face?
    You cannot miss that inn.

Shall I meet other wayfarers at night?
    Those who have gone before.
Then must I knock, or call when just in sight?
    They will not keep you standing at that door.

Shall I find comfort, travel-sore and weak?
    Of labour you shall find the sum.
Will there be beds for me and all who seek?
    Yea, beds for all who come.

Last Prayer

Before the beginning Thou hast foreknown the end,
Before the birthday the death-bed was seen of Thee:
Cleanse what I cannot cleanse, mend what I cannot mend,
O Lord All-Merciful, be merciful to me.

While the end is drawing near I know not mine end;
Birth I recall not, my death I cannot foresee:
O God, arise to defend, arise to befriend,
O Lord All-Merciful, be merciful to me.

From "Christ Our All in All"

Thy lovely saints do bring Thee love,
Incense and joy and gold;

Fair star with star, fair dove with dove,
Beloved by Thee of old.
I, Master, neither star nor dove,
Have brought Thee sins and tears;
Yet I too bring a little love
Amid my flaws and fears.
A trembling love that faints and fails
Yet still is love of Thee,
A wondering love that hopes and hails
Thy boundless Love of me;
Love kindling faith and pure desire,
Love following on to bliss,
A spark, O Jesus, from Thy fire,
A drop from Thine abyss.

The Three Enemies

THE FLESH: 'Sweet, thou art pale.'
                    'More pale to see,
                    Christ hung upon the cruel tree
                    And bore His Father's wrath for me.'

                    'Sweet, thou art sad.'
                    'Beneath a rod
                    More heavy, Christ for my sake trod
                    The winepress of the wrath of God.'

                    'Sweet, thou art weary.'
                    'Not so Christ;
                    Whose mighty love of me sufficed
                    For Strength, Salvation, Eucharist.'

                    'Sweet, thou art footsore.'
                    'If I bleed,
                    His feet have bled; yea in my need
                    His Heart once bled for mine indeed.'

THE WORLD: 'Sweet, thou art young.'
                    'So He was young
                    Who for my sake in silence hung
                    Upon the Cross with Passion wrung.'

                    'Look, thou art fair.'
                    'He was more fair

Than men, Who deigned for me to wear
A visage marred beyond compare.'

'And thou hast riches.'
'Daily bread:
All else is His: Who, living, dead,
For me lacked where to lay His Head.'

'And life is sweet.'
'It was not so
To Him, Whose Cup did overflow
With mine unutterable woe.'

THE DEVIL: 'Thou drinkest deep.'
'When Christ would sup
He drained the dregs from out my cup:
So how should I be lifted up?'

'Thou shalt win Glory.'
'In the skies,
Lord Jesus, cover up mine eyes
Lest they should look on vanities.'

'Thou shalt have Knowledge.'
'Helpless dust!
In thee, O Lord, I put my trust:
Answer Thou for me, Wise and Just.'

'And Might.'—
'Get thee behind me, Lord,
Who has redeemed and not abhorred
My soul, oh keep it by Thy Word.'

Consider The Lilies Of The Field

Solomon most glorious in array
Put not on his glories without care:—
Clothe us as Thy lilies of a day,
As the lilies Thou accountest fair,
Lilies of Thy making,
Of Thy love partaking,
Filling with free fragrance earth and air:
Thou Who gatherest lilies, gather us and wear.

To Set Forth Thee

Lord, grant us calm, if calm can set forth Thee;
Or tempest, if a tempest set Thee forth;
Wind from the east or west or south or north,
Or congelation of a silent sea,
With stillness of each tremulous aspen tree.

Still let fruit fall, or hang upon the tree;
Still let the east and west, the south and north,
Curb in their winds, or plough a thundering sea;
Still let the earth abide to set Thee forth,
Or vanish like a smoke to set forth Thee.

Heaviness May Endure For A Night, But Joy Cometh In The Morning,

No thing is great on this side of the grave,
Nor any thing of any stable worth:
Whatso is born from earth returns to earth:
No thing we grasp proves half the thing we crave:
The tidal wave shrinks to the ebbing wave:
Laughter is folly, madness lurks in mirth:
Mankind sets off a-dying from the birth:
Life is a losing game, with what to save?
Thus I sat mourning like a mournful owl,
And like a doleful dragon made ado,
Companion of all monsters of the dark:
When lo the light cast off its nightly cowl,
And up to heaven flashed a carolling lark,
And all creation sang its hymn anew.

While all creation sang its hymn anew
What could I do but sing a stave in tune?
Spectral on high hung pale the vanishing moon
Where a last gleam of stars hung paling too.
Lark's lay—a cockcrow—with a scattered few
Soft early chirpings—with a tender croon
Of doves—a hundred thousand calls, and soon
A hundred thousand answers sweet and true.
These set me singing too at unawares:
One note for all delights and charities,
One note for hope reviving with the light,

One note for every lovely thing that is;
Till while I sang my heart shook off its cares
And revelled in the land of no more night.

If Only

If I might only love my God and die!
But now He bids me love Him and live on,
Now when the bloom of all my life is gone,
The pleasant half of life has quite gone by.
My tree of hope is lopped that spread so high;
And I forget how summer glowed and shone,
While autumn grips me with its fingers wan,
And frets me with its fitful windy sigh.
When autumn passes then must winter numb,
And winter may not pass a weary while,
But when it passes spring shall flower again:
And in that spring who weepeth now shall smile,
Yea, they shall wax who now are on the wane,
Yea, they shall sing for love when Christ shall come.

Who Shall Deliver Me?

God strengthen me to bear myself;
That heaviest weight of all to bear,
Inalienable weight of care.

All others are outside myself;
I lock my door and bar them out,
The turmoil, tedium, gad-about.

I lock my door upon myself,
And bar them out; but who shall wall
Self from myself, most loathed of all?

If I could once lay down myself,
And start self-purged upon the race
That all must run! Death runs apace.

If I could set aside myself,
And start with lightened heart upon
The road by all men overgone!

God harden me against myself,
This coward with pathetic voice
Who craves for ease, and rest, and joys:

Myself, arch-traitor to myself;
My hollowest friend, my deadliest foe,
My clog whatever road I go.

Yet One there is can curb myself,
Can roll the strangling load from me,
Break off the yoke and set me free.

After Communion

Why should I call Thee Lord, who art my God?
Why should I call Thee Friend, who art my Love?
Or King, Who art my very Spouse above?
Or call Thy Sceptre on my heart Thy rod?
Lo now Thy banner over me is love,
All heaven flies open to me at Thy nod:
For Thou hast lit Thy flame in me a clod,
Made me a nest for dwelling of Thy Dove.
What wilt Thou call me in our home above,
Who now hast called me friend? how will it be
When Thou for good wine settest forth the best?
Now Thou dost bid me come and sup with Thee,
Now Thou dost make me lean upon Thy breast:
How will it be with me in time of love?

None Other Lamb

None other Lamb, none other Name,
None other Hope in heav'n or earth or sea,
None other Hiding-place from guilt and shame,
None beside thee!

My faith burns low, my hope burns low;
Only my heart's desire cries out in me
By the deep thunder of its want and woe,
Cries out to thee.

Lord, thou art Life, though I be dead;
Love's fire thou art, however cold I be:

Nor heav'n have I, nor place to lay my head,
Nor home, but thee.

In The Bleak Midwinter

In the bleak midwinter
Frosty wind made moan;
Earth stood hard as iron,
Water like a stone;
Snow had fallen, snow on snow,
Snow on snow,
In the bleak midwinter,
Long ago.

Our God, heaven cannot hold him
Nor earth sustain;
Heaven and earth shall flee away
When he comes to reign:
In the bleak mid-winter
A stable-place sufficed
The Lord God almighty,
Jesus Christ.

Enough for him, whom cherub
Worship night and day,
A breastful of milk,
And a manger full of hay;
Enough for him, whom angels
Fall down before,
The ox and ass and camel
Which adore.

Angels and archangels
May have gathered there,
Cherubim and seraphim
Thronged the air:
But only his mother
In her maiden bliss
Worshipped the Beloved
With a kiss.

What can I give him,
Poor as I am?
If I were a shepherd

I would bring a lamb;
If I were a wise man
I would do my part;
Yet what I can I give him—
Give my heart.

What Are These That Glow From Afar

What are these that glow from afar,
These that lean over the golden bar,
Strong as the lion, pure as the dove,
With open arms, and hearts of love?
They the blessed ones gone before,
They the blessed for evermore,
Out of great tribulation they went
Home to their home of heaven content.

What are these that fly as a cloud,
With flashing heads and faces bowed,
In their mouths a victorious psalm,
In their hands a robe and a palm?
Welcoming angels these that shine,
Your own angel, and yours, and mine;
Who have hedged us, both day and night,
On the left hand and on the right.

Light above light, and bliss beyond bliss,
Whom words cannot utter, lo, who is this?
As a king with many crowns he stands,
And our names are graven upon his hands;
As a priest, with God-uplifted eyes,
He offers for us his sacrifice;
As the Lamb of God, for sinners slain,
That we too may live, he lives again.

God the Father give us grace
To walk in the light of Jesus' face;
God the Son give us a part
In the hiding-place of Jesus' heart;
God the Spirit so hold us up
That we may drink of Jesus' cup;
God almighty, God three in One,
God almighty, God alone.

Service And Strength

Service and strength, God's angels and archangels;
His seraphs fires, and lamps his cherubim:
Glory to God from highest and from lowest,
Glory to God in everlasting hymn
From all his creatures.

Princes that serve and Powers that work his pleasure.
Heights that soar toward him, depths that sink toward him;
Flames fire out-flaming, chill beside his essence;
Insight all-probing, save where scant and dim
Toward its Creator.

Sacred and free, exultant in God's pleasure,
His will their solace, thus they wait on him;
And shout their shout of ecstasy eternal,
And trim their splendours that they burn not dim
Toward their Creator.

Wherefore with angels, wherefore with archangels,
With lofty cherubs, loftier seraphim,
We laud and magnify our God almighty,
And veil our faces rendering love to him
With all his creatures.

BROWN, THOMAS EDWARD (1830–1897), after attending King William's College, Isle of Man, went to Oxford, where he received academic honors in classics and law and history. He was ordained in 1855, after which he served as an educator for many years. He published a number of verse narratives, many of them set in his native Isle of Man, beginning with "Betsy Lee" in a periodical (1873), and that with three others in a book, *Fo'c'sle Yarns*, in 1881. *The Doctor and other Poems* (1887) was followed by *The Manx Witch and Other Poems* (1889), and *Old John* (1893). He had a life-long friendship with many of the old Manx "salts," and one of his objects was to record the old ways of life and speech on the Isle of Man, before they disappeared. A collected edition of his poems was published in 1900. Both George Eliot and Robert Browning appreciated the *Yarns*. In addition to his job as educator, Brown was a curate from 1884 to 1893. In 1893 he returned to his old home and in 1897 died of a stroke while addressing the students of Clifton College.

Pain

The man that hath great griefs I pity not;
'Tis something to be great
In any wise, and hint the larger state,
Though but in shadow of a shade, God wot!

Moreover, while we wait the possible,
This man has touched the fact,
And probed till he has felt the core, where, packed
In pulpy folds, resides the ironic ill.

And while we others sip the obvious sweet—
Lip-licking after-taste
Of glutinous rind, lo! this man hath made haste,
And pressed the sting that holds the central seat.

For thus it is God stings us into life,
Provoking actual souls
From bodily systems, giving us the poles
That are His own, not merely balanced strife.

Nay, the great passions are His veriest thought,
Which whoso can absorb,
Nor, querulous halting, violate their orb,
In him the mind of God is fullest wrought.

Thrice happy such an one! Far other he
Who dallies on the edge
Of the great vortex, clinging to a sedge
Of patent good, a timorous Manichee;

Who takes the impact of a long-breathed force,
And fritters it away
In eddies of disgust, that else might stay
His nerveless heart, and fix it to the course.

For there is threefold oneness with the One;
And he is one, who keeps
The homely laws of life; who, if he sleeps,
Or wakes, in his true flesh God's will is done.

And he is one, who takes the deathless forms,
Who schools himself to think
With the All-thinking, holding fast the link,
God-riveted, that bridges casual storms.

But tenfold one is he, who feels all pains
Not partial, knowing them
As ripples parted from the gold-beaked stem,
Wherewith God's galley onward ever strains.

To him the sorrows are the tension-thrills
Of that serene endeavour
Which yields to God for ever and for ever
The joy that is more ancient than the hills.

Land, Ho!

Know 'tis but a loom of land,
Yet is it land, and so I will rejoice,
I know I cannot hear His voice
Upon the shore, nor see Him stand;
Yet is it land, ho! land.

The land! the land! the lovely land!
Far off, dost say? Far off—ah, blessed home!
Farewell! farewell! thou salt sea-foam!
Ah, keel upon the silver sand—
Land, ho! land.

You cannot see the land, my land,
You cannot see, and yet the land is there—
My land, my land, through murky air—
I did not say 'twas close at hand—
But—land, ho! land.

Dost hear the bells of my sweet land,
Dost hear the kine, dost hear the merry birds?
No voice, 'tis true, no spoken words,
No tongue that thou may'st understand—
Yet is it land, ho! land.

It's clad in purple mist, my land,
In regal robe it is apparelled,
A crown is set upon its head,
And on its breast a golden band
Land, ho! land.

Dost wonder that I long for land?
My land is not a land as others are—
Upon its crest there beams a star,

And lilies grow upon the strand
Land, ho! land.

Give me the helm! there is the land!
Ha! lusty mariners, she takes the breeze!
And what my spirit sees it sees—
Leap, bark, as leaps the thunderbrand—
Land, ho! land.

Indwelling

If thou could'st empty all thy self of self
Like to a shell dishabited,
Than might He find thee on the ocean shelf
And say—"This is not dead,"
And fill thee with Himself instead;
But thou art all replete with very thou
And hast such shrewd activity,
That when He comes He says: "This is enow
Unto itself; 'twere better let it be,
It is so small and full, there is no room for Me."

Disguises

High stretched upon the swinging yard,
I gather in the sheet;
But it is hard
And stiff, and one cries haste.
Then He that is most dear in my regard
Of all the crew gives aidance meet;
But from His hands, and from His feet,
A glory spreads wherewith the night is starred:

Moreover of a cup most bitter-sweet
With fragrance as of nard,
And myrrh, and cassia spiced,
He proffers me to taste.
Then I to Him:—'Art Thou the Christ?'
He saith—'Thou say'st.'

Like to an ox
That staggers 'neath the mortal blow,
She grinds upon the rocks:—

Then straight and low
Leaps forth the levelled line, and in our quarter locks
The cradle's rigged; with swerving of the blast
We go,
Our Captain last—
Demands
'Who fired that shot?' Each silent stands—
Ah, sweet perplexity!
This too was He.

I have an arbour wherein came a toad
Most hideous to see—
Immediate, seizing staff or goad,
I smote it cruelly.
Then all the place with subtle radiance glowed—
I looked, and it was He!

THOMSON, JAMES (1834–1882), born in Scotland, the son of a seaman, attended the Royal Caledonian Asylum school in London. He became an army schoolmaster, in which capacity he served at various posts in England and Ireland. His poetry was published in various journals under the *nom de plume*, "B.V.," which he took from two favorite writers, Shelley ("Bysshe") and the German Hardenberg (Novalis—"Vanolis"). His propensity to alcoholism lost him his post in 1862. He came back to London in 1868 and lodged with the "freethinker," Charles Bradlaugh, editor of the *National Reformer*. Thomson supported himself writing poetry, essays, translations, and stories. His long poem, "Weddah," an Arabian love story, led to his acquaintance with W.M. Rossetti. In 1872 Thomson went as an employee of an English gold-mining company to Colorado. In 1873 he was a war reporter in Spain, after which he wrote his best-known poem, "The City of the Dreadful Night." His first book of poetry, *City of Dreadful Night and Other Poems*, was published in 1880, followed immediately by a second volume. His alcoholism led to his death. His *Satires and Profanities* (1884) was published after his death. The "dark" tone or mood of his poetry—often pessimistic unto despair—affected the poetry of his age and since.

Songs in the Desert

Songs in the Desert! songs of husky breath
And undivine Despair;
Songs that are Dirges, but for life, not Death,
Songs that infect the air;

Have sweetened bitterly my food and wine,
The heart corroded and the Dead Sea brine.

So potent is the Word, the Lord of Life,
And so tenacious Art,
Whose instinct urges to perpetual strife
With Death, Love's counterpart;
The magic of their music, might, and light
Can keep one living in his own despite.

The Doom of a City (last part)

"Thy Church has long been becoming the Fossil of a Faith;
The Form of dry bones thou hast, but where are the blood and breath?
Dry bones, that seem a whole, with dead sinews binding the parts,
Inert save when bejuggled to ghastly galvanic starts:
Though thou swearest to thy people, 'The King is but sick, not dead'—
Gaining the time while you choose you another in His stead;
Though thy scribes and thy placemen all; most of whom know the fact,
Vouchsafe in His name to write, pretend to His will to act:
Where are the signs of His life?—While living He never ceased
To thrill with the breath of His being thy realm from the West to the East;
While He lived He fought with sin, with fleshly lust and pride;
While He lived His poor and mean were wealthy and dignified;
While He lived His reign was freedom, faith, chastity, peace, and love;
And the symbol borne on His banner was not the raven but dove;
While He lived there yawned a Hell with a Devil for His foes,
And a God-ruled Heaven of triumph before His followers rose;
While He lived the noblest of men were wholly devoted to Him,
The saints, the bards, the heroes, in soul and mind and limb,—
Who now without a Leader, mournful in silence wait,
Girding each one himself to his lonely fight with Fate.

"But thou, O Queen, art false: a liar, if He is dead
And becoming a mammoth fossil whose aeon is wholly sped;
A traitor if still He lives and shall for ever reign,
For thou spurnest the laws most sacred of all He doth ordain.
Should Christ come now from Heaven, to reap the harvest sown
When He buried Himself in earth, watered with blood of His own,
How many Christians indeed could He gather with strictest care
From the two hundred myriads who claim in Him a share?
He agonised to save thee and thy children all;
And He saveth scarcely enough to delay thy deadly fall.

"For fall thou wilt, thou must—so proud as thy state is now,
Thou and thy sisters all, scarce better or worse than thou,
If ye do not all repent, and cleanse each one her heart
From the foulness circling with its blood to poison every part.
Woe to thy pampered rich in their arrogant selfishness;
Woe to thy brutelike poor who feel but their bread-distress;
Woe to thy people who dare not live without hope of wealth,
Who look but to fruits of the earth for their life and saving health;
Woe to thy rulers who rule for the good of themselves alone,
Fathers who give their children crying for bread a stone;
Woe to thy mighty men whose strength is unused or sold;
Thy sages who shut their eyes when Truth is stern to behold;
Woe to thy prophets who smile Peace, Peace, when it is a sword;
Thy poets who sing their own lusts instead of hymns of the Lord;
Thy preachers who preach the life of what they feel to be death;
Thy sophists who sail wild seas without the compass of faith;
Thy traders trading in lies and in human bodies and souls;
Thy good men cursing those better who strive on to loftier goals:—
The final Doom evolveth, burdened with woe on woe,
Sure as the justice of God while yet by His patience slow;
For the earth is pervaded wholly, through densest stone and clod,
With the burning fire of the law of the Truth of the Living God;
Consuming the falsehood, the evil, the pride, the lust, the shame,
With ever-burning, unrelenting, irresistable flame;
Until all save the purest spirit, eternal, of truth and love,
Be altogether consumed away beneath as well as above.'

BARING-GOULD, SABINE (1834–1924),educated in Germany, France, and at Cambridge, became a curate in a coal-mining village of Yorkshire "neglected even by the Dissenters." He began his ministry from a small office in a Post Office building, which became a night school as well as a chapel. He wrote his famous hymn "Onward Christian Soldiers" in 1865, as a processional for school children walking to a neighboring village for a school festival. Arthur Sullivan later wrote the tune for it. One night he rescued a mill-girl from a flooding river and from this event blossomed a romance. He married Grace Taylor in 1868. Theirs was a long and happy marriage. In 1872 he inherited his family's estate. He became lord of the manor, justice of the peace, and appointed himself rector of the parish, in which capacities he completed his life. Baring-Gould was a prolific writer. His works include, *Iceland* (1861), *The Book of Werewolves* (1865), *Post-Medieval Preachers* (1865), *Curious Myths of The Middle Ages* (1866-68), *The Origin and Development of Religious Belief* (1869–1870), *Lives of the Saints* in fifteen volumes (1872–1877), *Some Modern Difficulties* (1740), *Mehelah*

(1880), and *John Herring* (1883). He published eighty-five books, and Bailey *(The Gospel in Hymns)* says the literary catalogue of the British museum lists more titles by him than by any other author of his time. His literary secret: ". . . simply that I stick to a task when I begin it."

Onward Christian Soldiers

Onward, Christian soldiers,   Marching as to war,
With the cross of Jesus   Going on before.
Christ, the royal Master,   Leads against the Foe:
Forward into battle   See his banners go!

  Onward, Christian soldiers,   Marching as to war,
  With the cross of Jesus   Going on before.

Like a mighty army   Moves the Church of God;
Brothers we are treading   Where the saints have trod.
We are not divided,   All one body we,
One in hope and doctrine,   One in charity.

Crowns and thrones may perish,   Kingdoms rise and wane,
But the Church of Jesus   Constant will remain.
Gates of hell can never   'Gainst the Church prevail;
We have Christ's own promise,   And that cannot fail.

Onward, then, ye faithful,   Join our happy throng,
Blend with ours your voices   In the triumph-song:
Glory, laud, and honor   Unto Christ, the King;
This thro' countless ages   Men and angels sing.

Now The Day Is Over

Now the day is over, Night is drawing nigh,
Shadows of the evening Steal across the sky.

Jesus, give the weary Calm and sweet repose;
With thy tend'rest blessing May our eyelids close.

Grant to little children Visions bright of thee;
Guard the sailors, tossing On the deep blue sea.

Comfort ev'ry suff'rer Watching late in pain;
Those who plan some evil From their sin restrain.

Through the long night-watches May thine angels spread
Their white wings above me, Watching round my bed.

Glory to the Father, Glory to the Son,
And to thee, blest Spirit, Whilst all ages run.

BROOKS, PHILLIPS (1835–1893) was baptized in a Unitarian church, although his ancestors on either side were Puritans and Congregationalists. His parents were repelled by elements of Unitarian theology, however, and turned to the Episcopal church. After being raised in that church, he went to Harvard, where Lowell, Holmes, Agassiz, and Longfellow were among his professors. He entered the Episcopal Theological Seminary in Virginia. As an Episcopal priest, his first churches were in Philadelphia, and in 1869 was called to Trinity Church in Boston, where he gradually gained a high reputation. He was generally recognized as a peace-maker and reconciler, preaching the gospel, but without undue controversy. While loyal to his own communion, he claimed the Episcopal Church had something important to learn from the Puritans. He was elected bishop of Massachusetts in 1891. He preached in Westminster Abbey six months before his death. Beside publishing sermons and lectures, he authored books on various moral and doctrinal matters and a collection of travel letters. His carol, "O, Little Town of Bethlehem," is the work for which he is most widely known.

Our Burden Bearer

The little sharp vexations
And the briars that cut the feet,
Why not take all to the Helper
Who has never failed us yet?
Tell Him about the heartache,
And tell Him the longings too,
Tell Him the baffled purpose
When we scarce know what to do.
Then, leaving all our weakness
With the One divinely strong
Forget that we bore the burden
And carry away the song.

O Little Town Of Bethlehem

O little town of Bethlehem,
    How still we see thee lie;

Above thy deep and dreamless sleep
   The silent stars go by:
Yet in thy dark streets shineth
   The everlasting Light;
The hopes and fears of all the years
   Are met in thee tonight.

For Christ is born of Mary;
   And gathered all above,
While mortals sleep, the angels keep
   Their watch of wondering love.
O morning stars, together
   Proclaim the holy birth;
And praises sing to God the King,
   And peace to men on earth.

How silently, how silently
   The wondrous gift is giv'n!
So God imparts to human hearts
   The blessings of his heaven.
No ear may hear his coming,
   But in this world of sin,
Where meek souls will receive him still,
   The dear Christ enters in.

Where children, pure and happy,
   Pray to the Blessed Child;
Where misery cries out to thee,
   Son of Mother mild;
Where charity stands watching,
   And faith holds wide the door,
The dark night wakes, the glory breaks,
   And Christmas comes once more.

O holy Child of Bethlehem,
   Descend to us, we pray;
Cast out our sin, and enter in,
   Be born in us today.
We hear the Christmas angels
   The great glad tidings tell;
O come to us, abide with us,
   Our Lord Emmanuel.

HAVERGAL, FRANCES RIDLEY (1836–1879), daughter of a country cleric, was born and buried at Astley, a small town on the banks of the Severn River near the Malvern Hills in Worcestershire. She was the youngest of six children. Her father, who ministered in the place of her birth for more than twenty years, was also a musician, poet, and hymn-writer. When she was ten years old her father received an appointment as a canon of the cathedral in the City of Worcester. There, in her teens, she entered into "missionary work," teaching Sunday School to younger children of the city. She went to boarding school in England, where she later said she "began to have faith and conscious hope in Christ." She also went on to boarding school in Germany. She found her student life in Germany "bracing" in that she met more hostility than she had previously encountered and had to be careful that her life brought credit to her professed faith. She went on to study, French, German, Italian, Latin, Greek, and Hebrew. In addition she learned enough Welsh in Wales to be able to participate intelligently in Sunday services. She was an intensive student of the Bible and an accomplished pianist and vocalist. After she returned to England, she helped edit a hymnal, *Songs of Grace and Glory,* and after her father's death finished a collection of his hymns, *Havergals Psalmody,* to which she also contributed some lyrics. She once said, "I prefer to sing Scripture words, because he did not promise that our words should not return to him void." Nevertheless her own collections of hymns include *The Thoughts of God,* and *Loyal Responses, Kept for the Master's Use, Morning Bells,* and *Little Pillows.* In later life, she was actively involved in many mission efforts oriented often toward the poor. She died of respiratory illness. She once said, "I have such a craving for the music of heaven."

The One Reality

Fog wreaths of doubt in blinding eddies drifted,
Whirlwinds of fancy, countergusts of thought,
Shadowless shadows where warm lives were sought,
Numb feet, that feel not their own tread, uplifted
On clouds of formless wonder, lightning-rifted!
What marvel that the whole world's life should seem,
To helpless intellect, a Brahma-dream,
From which the real and restful is out-sifted?
Through the dim storm a white peace-bearing Dove
Gleams, and the mist rolls back, the shadows flee,
The dream is past. A clear calm sky above,
Firm rock beneath; a royal-scrolled tree,
And One, thorn-diademed, the King of Love,
The Son of God who gave Himself for me.

Trusting Jesus

I am trusting Thee, Lord Jesus,   Trusting only Thee;
Trusting Thee for full salvation,   Great and free.

I am trusting Thee for pardon;   At Thy feet bow,
For Thy grace and tender mercy,   Trusting now.

I am trusting Thee for cleansing   In the crimson flood;
Trusting Thee to make me holy   By Thy blood.

I am trusting Thee to guide me;   Thou alone shalt lead!
Every day and hour supplying   All my need.

I am trusting Thee for power;   Thine can never fail!
Words which Thou Thyself shalt give me,   Must prevail.

I am trusting Thee, Lord Jesus: Never let me fall!
I am trusting Thee forever,   And for all.

On The Lord's Side

Who is on the Lord's side?   Who will serve the King?
Who will be His helpers,   Other lives to bring?
Who will leave the world's side?   Who will face the foe?
Who is on the Lord's side?   Who for Him will go?

By Thy call of mercy,   By Thy grace divine,
We are on the Lord's side;   Saviour, we are Thine.

Not for weight of glory,   Not for crown and palm,
Enter we the army,   Raise the warrior-psalm;
But for Love that claimeth   Lives for whom He died:
He whom Jesus nameth   Must be on His side.

By Thy love constraining,   By Thy grace divine,
We are on the Lord's side;   Savior, we are Thine.

Jesus, Thou hast bought us,   Not with gold or gem,
But with Thine own Life-blood,   For Thy diadem.
With Thy blessing filling   Each who comes to Thee,
Thou hast made us willing   Thou hast made us free.

By Thy grand redemption,   By Thy grace divine,
We are on the Lord's side;   Saviour, we are Thine.

Fierce may be the conflict　Strong may be the foe,
But the King's own army　None can overthrow.
Round His standard ranging,　Victory is secure,
For His truth unchanging　Makes the triumph sure.

Joyfully enlisting　By Thy grace divine,
We are on the Lord's side;　Saviour, we are Thine.

Chosen to be soldiers　In an alien land;
"Chosen, called, and faithful,"　For our Captain's band;
In the service royal　Let us not grow cold;
Let us be right loyal,　Noble, true, and bold.

Master, Thou wilt keep us,　By Thy grace divine,
Always on the Lord's side,　Saviour, always Thine.

True-Hearted, Whole-Hearted

True-hearted, whole-hearted, faithful and loyal,
King of our lives, by Thy grace we will be!
Under Thy standard, exalted and royal,
Strong in Thy strength, we will battle for Thee!

True-hearted, wholehearted! Fullest allegiance
Yielding henceforth to our glorious King;
Valiant endeavour and loving obedience
Freely and joyously now would we bring.

True-hearted! Saviour, Thou knowest our story;
Weak are the hearts that we lay at Thy feet,
Sinful and treacherous! yet, for Thy glory,
Heal them and cleanse them from sin and deceit.

Whole-hearted! Saviour, beloved and glorious,
Take Thy great power, and reign Thou alone
Over our wills and affections victorious,
Freely surrendered, and wholly Thine own.

Half-hearted, false-hearted! Heed we the warning!
Only the whole can be perfectly true;
Bring the whole offering, all timid thought scorning,
True-hearted only if whole-hearted too.

Half-hearted! Saviour, shall aught be withholden,
Giving Thee part who hast given us all?

Blessings outpouring, and promises golden
Pledging with never reserve or recall.

Half-hearted! Master, shall any who knows Thee
Grudge Thee their lives, who hast laid down Thine own?
Nay; we would offer the hearts that we owe Thee,—
Live for Thy love and Thy glory alone.

Sisters, dear sisters, the call is resounding,
Will ye not echo the silver refrain,
Mighty and sweet, and in gladness abounding,—
"True-hearted, wholehearted! " ringing again?

Jesus is with us, His rest is before us,
Brightly His standard is waving above.
Brothers, dear brothers, in gathering chorus,
Peal out the watchword of courage and love!

Peal out the watchword, and silence it never,
Song of our spirits, rejoicing and free!
"True-hearted, whole-hearted, now and forever,
King of our lives, by Thy grace we will be!"

Under The Surface

I.

On the surface, foam and roar,
Restless heave and passionate dash,
Shingle rattle along the shore,
Gathering boom and thundering crash.

Under the surface, soft green light,
A hush of peace and an endless calm,
Winds and waves, from a choral height,
Falling sweet as a far-off psalm.

On the surface, swell and swirl,
Tossing weed and drifting waif,
Broken spars that the mad waves whirl,
Where wreck-watching rocks they chafe.

Under the surface, loveliest forms,
Feathery fronds with crimson curl,
Treasures too deep for raid of storms,
Delicate coral and hidden pearl.

II.

On the surface, lilies white,
A painted skiff with a singing crew,
Sky-reflections soft and bright,
Tremulous crimson, gold, and blue.

Under the surface, life in death,
Slimy tangle and oozy moans,
Creeping things with watery breath,
Blackening roots and whitening bones.

On the surface, a shining reach,
A crystal couch for moonbeams rest,
Starry ripples along the beach,
Sunset songs from the breezy west.

Under the surface, glooms and fears,
Treacherous currents swift and strong,
Deafening rush in the drowning ears,—
Have ye rightly read my song?

Consecration Hymn (Take My Life)

Take my life and let it be
Consecrated, Lord, to Thee.

Take my moments and my days;
Let them flow in ceaseless praise.

Take my hands, and let them move
At the impulse of Thy love.

Take my feet and let them be
Swift and "beautiful" for Thee.

Take my voice, and let me sing
Always, only, for my King.

Take my lips, and let them be
Filled with messages from Thee.

Take my silver and my gold;
Not a mite would I withhold.

Take my intellect, and use
Every power as Thou shalt choose.

Take my will, and make it Thine;
It shall be no longer mine.

Take my heart, it is Thine own;
It shall be Thy royal throne.

Take my love; my Lord, I pour
At Thy feet its treasure-store.

Take myself, and I will be
Ever, only, ALL for Thee.

Perfect Peace (Like A River Glorious)

Like a river glorious   Is God's perfect peace
Over all victorious   In its bright increase.
Perfect yet it floweth   Fuller every day;
Perfect yet it groweth   Deeper all the way.

> Stayed upon Jehovah,
> Hearts are fully blest,
> Finding as He promised,
> Perfect peace and rest.

Hidden in the hollow   Of His blessed hand,
Never foe can follow,   Never traitor stand.
Not a surge of worry,   Not a shade of care,
Not a blast of hurry   Touch the spirit there.

Every joy or sorrow   Falleth from above,
Traced upon our dial   By the Sun of Love.
We may trust Him solely   All for us to do;
They who trust Him wholly   Find Him wholly true.

Conclusion to The Thoughts of God

They say there is a hollow, safe and still,
A point of coolness and repose
Within the center of a flame, where life might dwell
Unharmed and unconsumed, as in a luminous shell,
Which the bright walls of fire enclose
In breachless splendor, barrier that no foes
     Could pass at will.

There is a point of rest
At the great center of the cyclone's force,
A silence at its secret source;—
A little child might, slumber undistressed,
Without the ruffle of one fairy curl,
In that strange central calm amid the mighty whirl.

So, in the center of these thoughts of God,
Cyclones of power, consuming glory-fire,—
　　As we fall o'erawed
Upon our faces, and are lifted higher
By His great gentleness, and carried nigher

Than unredeemed angels, till we stand
Even in the hollow of His hand,
Nay, more! we lean upon His breast—
There, there we find a point of perfect rest
And glorious safety. There we see
His thoughts to usward, thoughts of peace
That stoop in tenderest love; that still increase
With increase of our need; that never change,
That never fail, or falter, or forget.
　　O pity infinite!
　　O royal mercy free!
O gentle climax of the depth and height
Of God's most precious thoughts, most wonderful,
　　most strange!
"For I am poor and needy, yet
The Lord Himself, Jehovah, thinketh upon me!"

Vessels of Mercy Prepared Unto Glory
(Rom. ix. 23.)

Vessels of mercy, prepared unto glory!
This is your calling and this is your joy!
This, for the new year unfolding before ye,
Tells out the terms of your blessed employ.

Vessels, it may be, all empty and broken
Marred in the Hand of inscrutable skill;
(Love can accept the mysterious token!)
Marred but to make them more beautiful still.
Jer xviii. 4.

Vessels, it may be, not costly or golden;
Vessels, it may be, of quantity small,
Yet by the Nail in the Sure Place upholden,
Never to shiver and never to fall.

Isa. xxii 23,24.

Vessels to honor, made sacred and holy,
Meet for the use of the Master we love,
Ready for service, all simple and lowly,
Ready, one day, for the temple above.

2 Tim. ii. 21.

Afterwards

Light after darkness, gain after loss,
Strength after weakness, crown after cross;
Sweet after bitter, hope after fears,
Home after wandering, praise after tears.

Sheaves after sowing, sun after rain,
Sight after mystery, peace after pain;
Joy after sorrow, calm after blast,
Rest after weariness, sweet at last.

Near after distant, gleam after gloom,
Love after loneliness, life after tomb;
After long agony, rapture of bliss—
Right was the pathway leading to this.

BLISS, PHILIP (1838–1876), of a Pennsylvania Methodist family, joined a Baptist church at the age of twelve. He moved to Chicago where, with George F. Root, he conducted musical institutes and conventions. He became a member of a congregational church. The first of his books of songs and hymns was *The Charm*, published in 1871. Ira D. Sankey was associated with him in preparing his last book, *Gospel Hymns and Sacred Songs* (1875). He and his wife were aboard a train going from Pennsylvania to Chicago, when a trestle collapsed beneath it. Bliss escaped but was burned while trying to rescue his wife.

Last Hymn

I know not what awaits me,
God kindly veils mine eyes;
And o'er each step of my onward way

He makes new scenes to rise;
And every joy he sends me comes
A sweet and glad surprise.

One step I see before me.
'Tis all I need to see,
The light of heaven more brightly shines
When earth's illusions flee;
And sweetly thro' the silence comes
His loving "Follow me."

O blissful lack of wisdom,
'Tis blessed not to know;
He holds me with his own right hand,
And will not let me go,
And lulls my troubled soul to rest
In him who loves me so.

Soon I go, not knowing,
I would not if I might;
I'd rather walk in the dark with God
Than go alone in the light;
I'd rather walk by faith with him
Than go alone by sight.

MATHESON, GEORGE (1842–1906) was born and educated in Glasgow, Scotland. He became blind while a boy, but persevered and entered the Scottish Presbyterian ministry (Kirk of Scotland) in 1868. He ministered in Innellan (Firth of Clyde) and Edinburgh. He published various theological and popular works, including *Aids of the Study of German Theology* (1874); *Natural Elements of Revealed Theology* (1881), *The Psalmist and the Scientist* (1887), *Sidelights from Patmos* (1897), *The Sceptre Without a Sword* (1901), and several books on *Representative Men of the Bible* and *Representative Women of the Bible*.

Make Me A Captive

Make me a captive, Lord,
   And then I shall be free;
Force me to render up my sword,
   And I shall conqueror be.
I sink in life's alarms
   When by myself I stand;
Imprison me within thine arms,
   And strong shall be my hand.

My heart is weak and poor
    Until it master find:
It has no spring of action sure,
    It varies with the wind:
It cannot freely move
    Till thou hast wrought its chain;
Enslave it with thy matchless love,
    And deathless it shall reign.

My power is faint and low
    Till I have learned to serve:
It wants the needed fire to glow,
    It wants the breeze to nerve;
It cannot drive the world
    Until itself be driven;
Its flag can only be unfurled
    When Thou shalt breathe from heaven.

My will is not my own
    Till thou hast made it thine;
If it would reach a monarch's throne
    It must its crown resign;
It only stands unbent
    Amid the clashing strife,
When on thy bosom it has leant
    And found in thee its life.

O Love That Wilt Not Let Me Go

O Love that wilt not let me go,
I rest my weary soul in thee;
I give thee back the life I owe,
That in thine ocean depths its flow
May richer, fuller be.

O Light that flowest all my way,
I yield my flickering torch to thee;
My heart restores its borrowed ray,
That in thy sunshine's blaze its day
May brighter, fairer be.

O Joy that seekest me through pain,
I cannot close my heart to thee;
I trace the rainbow through the rain,

And feel the promise is not vain
That morn shall tearless be.

O Cross that liftest up my head,
I dare not ask to fly from thee;
I lay in dust life's glory dead,
And from the ground there blossoms red
Life that shall endless be.

MYERS, FREDERICK WILLIAM HENRY (1843–1901), went to
Cambridge where he won a number of literary prizes and scholarships. After
graduation he toured Europe, Canada, and the United States, (where he suc-
cessfully completed a dangerous swim across the river below Niagara Falls). He
spent a few years as classical lecturer at Cambridge, then became a school
inspector for most the rest of his life. He published a number of books of poet-
ry until his interest in "psychical research" took up most of his leisure time.
Among his books of poetry are *St. Paul* (1867), a collection (1870), and *The
Renewal of Youth* (1882). His prose works include a monograph on Wordsworth
(1881), and essays on other writers (Virgil, Rossetti, Victor Hugo, and Trench).
The last twenty years of his life were largely given to research into mesmerism,
clairvoyance, and other such phenomena. *The Dictionary of National Biography* men-
tions this interest in connection with his poem "The Implicit Promise of
Immortality" and "another reason strongly drawing him to such studies. . . a
deep modification of his early religious beliefs." Displacing the "intensely per-
sonal emotion" that underlay (as he records) the early poems of "St. Paul" and
"John the Baptist" was a "disillusionment caused by wider knowledge;" and for
fresh light, it would seem, he began to look to "the scientific study of imper-
fectly explored phenomena." This apparently led him to affirm that telepathy
legitimately occurred, especially under circumstances of crisis, as when someone
was facing death. His health failed in 1900 and he went abroad hoping to
restore it, but died in Rome in 1901. He is representative of others of his time
(and since) in whom "scientific" superstition seems to have choked the seed of
Christian faith.

Surrender to Christ

See, when a fireship in mid ocean blazes
Lone on the battlefields a swimmer stands,
Looks for a help, and findeth none, and raises
High for a moment melancholy hands;

Then the sad ship, to her own funeral flaring,
Holds him no longer in her arms, for he

Simple and strong and desolate and daring
Leaps to the great embraces of the sea.

So when around me for my soul's affrighting,
Madly red-litten of the woe within,
Faces of men and deeds of their delighting
Stare in a lurid cruelty of sin,

Thus as I weary me and long and languish,
Nowise availing from that pain to part,—
Desperate tides of the whole world's anguish
Forced through the channels of a single heart,—

Then let me feel how infinite around me
Floats the eternal peace that is to be,
Rush from the demons, for my King has found me,
Leap from the universe and plunge in Thee!

Hymn—Hark What A Sound

Hark what a sound, and too divine for hearing,
Stirs on the earth and trembles in the air!
Is it the thunder of the Lord's appearing?
Is it the music of his people's prayer?

Surely he cometh, and a thousand voices
Shout to the saints, and to the deaf are dumb;
Surely he cometh, and the earth rejoices,
Glad in his coming who hath sworn, 'I come.'

This hath he done and shall we not adore him?
This shall he do and can we still despair?
Come, let us quickly fling ourselves before him,
Cast at his feet the burden of our care.

Yea, through life, death, through sorrow and through sinning
He shall suffice me, for he hath sufficed:
Christ is the end, for Christ was the beginning,
Christ the beginning, for the end is Christ.

Spirituals

"Spiritual" is a general term used to refer to a hymn or song that appears to be
oral in its origins, rather than literary—one that uses language from the every-

day speech of those who sing it. It might also be said that "spirituals" (from the Bible phrase "hymns and spiritual songs") use more "homely" tunes, often borrowed from folk songs.

"White spirituals" originated among the congregations of England and New England in the eighteenth century. Many of their melodies are traceable to English, Irish, Welsh and Scots folk tunes. Other tunes were composed in imitation of folk tunes and appeared in collections such as *The Cluster of Spiritual Songs* (Jesse Mercer, 1823), *The Virginia Harmony* (James P. Carrell, 1831), *Southern Harmony* (William Walker, 1835–54), and *The Sacred Harp* (B.F. King, 1844).

The last-named was a collection based on a tradition of the Appalachian Mountains, in turn based on British and Gaelic singing. The original titles of the pieces did not refer to the texts, but to places, either where they were written or in some sort of commemoration.

"Negro Spirituals" are a result of the melding of African and white spiritual traditions. Samuel Davies (see biographical paragraph in Restoration and Eighteenth Century section) formed Negro congregations in Virginia as early as 1755. Isaac Watts's hymns were the chief form of singing among them. The form of hymn that became most popular among black congregations, however, was the verse-refrain, leader-response type. These were transformed and often much improved in the black churches. Other black spirituals owed nothing to white tradition, however. Many originated with early Christian converts among slaves in the southern United States. They arose as songs of praise, songs of suffering, and work-songs, probably composed and modified, not by one author, but by many. Their origins, like those of other forms of folk song, are impossible to determine in most cases. The earliest records of most were probably not written down until many years after they were composed and sung.

Negro spirituals have elements of African music in them, as well as Christian themes. The African elements most commonly cited are the rhythm, the interval, and the verse forms. Most of them have texts directly from the Bible or applying biblical themes to the life of the slave and the lot of mankind.

Recent interpretations of the spirituals have tended to see them as allegorical, and as expressions of the slaves' desire to escape, hidden under a guise of Christian imagery. Judging by the words, themselves, and the beautiful and powerful tunes that have accompanied them, this interpretation is oversimplified. No one can doubt that there is a longing to escape behind such songs as "Deep River" and "Nobody Knows the Trouble I've Seen," but the Christian hope expressed in both is unequivocal.

Early published collections include *Slave Songs of the United States* (1867), *Jubilee Songs* (1872), and *Cabin and Plantation Songs* (1874). Negro spirituals were first publicized before the American public in 1871 by the Fisk Jubilee singers. Since then they have been published, recorded, and adapted by a multitude of writers, singers, and composers.

Because the two spiritual traditions, white and black were parallel and since they converged in the revivals of the mid-nineteenth century, it is now sometimes difficult to distinguish which tunes and words came from which tradition. It is generally agreed that many more recent genres of American music owe a great deal to the spiritual tradition.

Were You There
Anonymous

Were you there when they crucified my Lord?
Were you there when they crucified my Lord?
Oh-oh-oh Sometimes it causes me to tremble, tremble, tremble.
Were you there when they crucified my Lord?

Were you there when they nailed him to the tree?
Were you there when they nailed him to the tree?
Oh-oh-oh Sometimes it causes me to tremble, tremble, tremble.
Were you there when they nailed him to the tree?

Were you there when they pierced him in the side?
Were you there when they pierced him in the side?
Oh-oh-oh sometimes, it causes me to tremble, tremble, tremble.
Were you there, when they pierced him in the side?

Were you there, when the sun refused to shine?
Were you there, when the sun refused to shine?
Oh-oh-oh sometimes, it causes me to tremble, tremble, tremble.
Were you there, when the sun refused to shine?

Were you there when they laid him in the tomb?
Were you there when they laid him in the tomb?
Oh-oh-oh sometimes it causes me to tremble, tremble, tremble.
Were you there when they laid him in the tomb?

Were you there when he rose up from the dead?
Were you there when he rose up from the dead?
Oh-oh-oh sometimes it causes me to tremble, tremble, tremble.
Were you there when he rose from the dead?

Nobody Knows the Trouble I've Seen
Anonymous

Oh, Nobody knows the trouble I've seen,
Nobody knows but Jesus.

Nobody knows the trouble I've seen, oh
Nobody knows but him.

Sometimes I'm up, sometimes I'm down,
Oh——yes——Lord,
Sometimes I'm almost to the ground,
Oh——yes——Lord.

Oh, Nobody knows the trouble I've seen,
Nobody knows but Jesus.
Nobody knows the trouble I've seen, oh
Nobody knows but him.

Sometimes I'm up, sometimes, I'm down
Oh——yes——Lord,
But all the time I'm heavenly bound,
Oh——yes——Lord.

Oh, Nobody knows the trouble I've seen,
Nobody knows but Jesus.
Nobody knows the trouble I've seen, oh
Nobody knows but him.

If you get there before I do,
Oh——yes——Lord,
Tell all my friends I'm a-coming there, too,
Oh——yes——Lord.

Oh, Nobody knows the trouble I've seen,
Nobody knows but Jesus.
Nobody knows the trouble I've seen,
Nobody knows, but nobody knows,
But nobody knows but him.

Deep Spring
Anonymous

As on the cross, the Saviour hung,
And wept, and bled, and died,
He pour'd salvation on a wretch
That languished at his side.

His crimes, with inward grief and shame,
The penitent confessed,

And turned his dying eyes to Christ,
And thus his pray'r address'd:

"Jesus, thou Son and heir of heaven!
Thou spotless lamb of God!
I see thee bathed in sweat and tears,
And welt'ring in thy blood.

"Yet quickly from these scenes of woe,
In triumph thou shalt rise,
Burst through the gloomy shades of death,
And shine above the skies."

Wondrous Love
Anonymous

What wondrous love is this! Oh, my soul! Oh, my soul!
What wondrous love is this! Oh, my soul!
    What wondrous love is this,
    That caused the Lord of bliss
To bear the dreadful curse for my soul, for my soul,
To bear the dreadful curse for my soul.

When I was sinking down, sinking down, sinking down,
When I was sinking down, sinking down,
    When I was sinking down
    Beneath God's righteous frown,
Christ laid aside His crown for my soul, for my soul,
Christ laid aside His crown for my soul.

And when from death I'm free, I'll sing on, I'll sing on,
And when from death I'm free, I'll sing on,
    And when from death I'm free,
    I'll sing and joyful be,
And through eternity I'll sing on, I'll sing on,
And through eternity I'll sing on.

The Angel Of Death
Anonymous

There's a man going 'round taking names,
There's a man going 'round taking names,
He took my mother's name and he filled my heart with pain,
There's a man going 'round taking names.

There's a man going 'round taking names,
There's a man going 'round taking names,
He took my father's name and he filled my heart with pain,
There's a man going 'round taking names.
There's a man going 'round taking names,
There's a man going 'round taking names,
He took my sister's name and he filled by heart with pain,
There's a man going 'round taking names.

There's a man going 'round taking names,
There's a man going 'round taking names,
He took my brother's name and he filled my heart with pain,
There's a man going 'round taking names.

There's a man going 'round taking names,
There's a man going 'round taking names,
He took my sweetheart's name and he filled my heart with pain,
There's a man going 'round taking names.

A Poor Wayfaring Stranger
Anonymous

I am a poor wayfaring stranger
While traveling through this world of woe,
Yet there's no sickness, toil or danger
In that bright world to which I go.

I'm going there to see my father,
I'm going there no more to roam,
I'm only going over Jordan,
I'm only going home.

I know dark clouds will gather around me,
I know my way is rough and steep,
Yet beauteous fields lie just before me,
Where God's redeemed their vigils keep.

I'm going there to see my mother,
She said she'd meet me when I come,
I'm only going over Jordan,
I'm only going over home.

I'll soon be freed from every trial,
My body asleep in the old churchyard,

I'll drop the cross of self-denial,
And enter on my great reward.

I'm going there to see my classmates,
Who have gone before me, one by one,
I'm only going over Jordan,
I'm only going over home.

I want to wear a crown of glory
When I get home to that good land,
I want to shout salvation's glory
In concert with that blood-washed band.

I'm going there to see my Savior,
To sing his praise forevermore,
I'm only going over Jordan.
I'm only going over home.

The Cherry-Tree Carol
(Medieval origins)

When Joseph was an old man,
An old man was he,
He married Virgin Mary,
The Queen of Galilee.

As Joseph and Mary
Were walking one day:
"Here are apples, here are cherries
Enough to behold."

Then Mary spoke to Joseph
So meek and so mild:
"Joseph, gather me some cherries,
For I am with child."

Then Joseph flew in anger,
In anger flew he:
"Let the father of the baby
Gather cherries for thee."

Then Jesus spoke a few words,
A few words spoke he:
"Let my mother have some cherries;
Bow low down, cherry-tree."

The cherry-tree bowed low down,
Bowed low down to the ground,
And Mary gathered cherries
While Joseph stood around.

Then Joseph took Mary
All on his right knee:
"O, what have I done?
Lord have mercy on me!"

Then Joseph took Mary all,
All on his left knee:
"O, tell me, little baby,
When thy birthday will be."

"On the sixth day of January
My birthday will be,
When the stars in the elements
Shall tremble with glee."

Deep-River
Anonymous

Deep river, my home is over Jordan,
Deep river, Lord, I want to cross over into camp ground.

O, don't you want to go to that gospel feast,
That promised land, where all is peace?

Deep river, my home is over Jordan,
Deep river, Lord, I want to cross over into camp ground.

Stars Begin To Fall
Anonymous

I Tink I hear my brudder say,
Call de nation great and small;
I lookee on de God's right hand
When de stars begin to fall.

Oh, what a mournin', sister,
Oh, what a mournin', brudder,
Oh, what a mournin',
When de stars begin to fall!

Give Me Jesus
Anonymous

Oh, when I come to die,
Oh, when I come to die,
Oh, when I come to die,
Give me Jesus.
In that mornin' when I rise,
That mornin' when I rise,
In that mornin' when I rise,
Give me Jesus.

Give me Jesus, give me Jesus,
You may have all this world, give me Jesus,
Oh, give me Jesus, give me Jesus,
You may have all this world, give me Jesus.

Dark midnight was my cry,
Dark midnight was my cry,
Dark midnight was my cry,
Give me Jesus.

I heard a mourner say,
I heard a mourner say,
I heard a mourner say,
Give me Jesus.

Swing Low, Sweet Chariot
Anonymous

I looked over Jordan, and what did I see?
Comin' fo' to carry me home?
A band of angels comin' after me.
Comin' fo' to carry me home.

Swing low, sweet chariot,
Comin' fo' to carry me home;
Swing low, sweet chariot,
Comin' fo' to carry me home.

If you get there before I do,
Comin' fo' to carry me home.
Tell all my friends I'm comin' too.
Comin' fo' to carry me home.

The brightest day that ever I saw
Comin' fo' to carry me home.
When Jesus washed my sins away.
Comin' fo' to carry me home.

Swing low, sweet chariot,
Comin' fo' to carry me home;
Swing low, sweet chariot,
Comin' fo' to carry me home.

Chapter Eight

POETRY OF THE LATE VICTORIAN PERIOD

1861—Beginning of American Civil War   1918—End of First World War

While we are officially marking the end of this period of literature with the publication of Gerard Manley Hopkins's poetry, nothing nearly so neat happened in fact. It is still difficult for us to speak with much objectivity about the Late Victorian age, since a great deal that was central to its tensions and habits is still with us—much of it unconscious and unexamined. Similarly, our literature, especially perhaps our Christian literature, has made few great departures from that of the Late Victorian period. John Drinkwater in his *Victorian Poetry* (1924) says "the spirit of an age is hardly ever definable to the age itself," and to the degree we are still closely linked to the Victorian Age, we indeed have difficulty defining it.

Where there had been many non-Christian poets in the romantic age, they at least defined themselves in contrast to Christianity. In the Victorian Age, scientific rationalism and non-Christian poetry not only defined themselves against Christianity, but quite self-consciously increasingly believed they were supplanting it. In the view of such, Kant's "noumenal" and "phenomenal" were divided up between poetry and science, and Christianity excluded from either sphere.

"Science" continued to rise in influence and to claim more and more dominance over "religion." George MacDonald writes in the midst of this period (1868):

There are some indications of that strong reaction of the present century towards ancient forms of church life. This reaction seems to me a further consequence of that admiration of power of which I have spoken. [MacDonald saw British society and literature as increasingly elevating and desiring power over against truth and beauty.] For, finding the progress of discovery in the laws of nature constantly bring[s] an assurance most satisfactory to the intellect, men began to demand a similar assurance in other matters; and whatever department of human thought could not be subjected to experiment or did not admit of logical proof began to be regarded with suspicion. The highest realms of human thought—where indeed only grand conviction, and that the result not of research, but of obedience to the voice within, can be had—came to be by such regarded as regions where, no scientific assurance being procurable, it was only to his loss that a man should go wandering: the whole affair was unworthy of him. And if there be no guide of humanity but the intellect, and nothing worthy of its regard but what that intellect can isolate and describe in the forms peculiar to its operations,—that is, if a man has relations to nothing beyond his definition, is not a creature of the immeasurable,—then these men are right. (*England's Antiphon*, p.314)

Specifically three "watershed" prose works proclaiming a materialistic worldview were published in the Late Victorian Period. The first of these was Darwin's *Origin of the Species*, followed by other works by Darwin, Thomas Huxley, and Herbert Spenser, all dedicated to establishing and reinforcing an evolutionary view over against biblical creation. The second was Marx and Engles *Das Kapital*, the political principles of which influenced its own age less than the 20th century, but which was nonetheless a leading example of a materialistic worldview applied to history, economics, and social relations. A third (relatively late) major contribution to the materialistic worldview of the period was Sigmund Freud's series of books and monographs. The first of these translated into English was *On the Psychical Mechanism of Hysterical Phenomena* (translated 1909). Freud, "The Father of Modern Psychology," put forth the theories attributing behavior primarily to organic and environmental factors. All three of these works and many related to them denied any ultimate truth to Christianity or spiritual reality. The "spurning" school of poets (see introduction to Early Victorian Period) found in them further "proof" with which to aggressively deny the doctrines of eternal soul and sin in man, the Creatorhood of God, and the saving grace of Christ.

Various social and intellectual leaders seem to have agreed that religion might be ultimately illusionary, but maintained nonetheless that it was socially "necessary" for the maintenance of order in human society. The alternative to faith, of course, was logically an acknowledgment that the universe had no real order, that chaos was the ultimate reality, and human affairs therefore suspended between the logical necessity of either artificial order or of natural anarchy. Religion at best, in such a view, is one of the artificial forces by which the artificial order may be maintained.

Even the conservative or orthodox church (much of which came to call itself fundamentalist or primitive or evangelical) was influenced by this pervasive outlook, albeit in a defensive posture against it. The common themes that might be summarized as a withdrawal from the intellectual arena on the one hand, and the "gambling of all" in purely rational apologetics (leading nearly always to a heretical universalism or Deism) on the other, are abundantly evident in evangelical Christian literature in the first instance, and liberal Christian literature in the second. Anglican and Catholic literature contain both strains—defensive orthodoxy or concessionary "liberal" theology.

The continuing moral and social problems resulting from urban, colonial, and industrial expansion seen in the light of the new secular theories gave increasing impetus to "social Darwinism," the theory that mankind, too, was subject to "survival of the fittest." The idea that some races were superior to other races, that the poor somehow deserved to be poor, that mankind must regulate his own evolution—by controlling reproduction, etcetera—had been stated or implied in the work of Thomas Malthus, *On the Principle of Population* (1798). Darwin derived his ideas about "natural selection" first from this work. After Darwin's major works were published and based on them, Sir Francis Galton wrote "Inquiries into Human Faculty and its Development"(1883), which politely proposed most of the main points of "social Darwinism" or social engineering that have been instituted among us today. [From this time until the World War II, it was considered "chic" among intellectuals to defend and affirm "eugenics," the "science" of limiting and controlling human repro- duction and thus, evolution. After World War II, due to the strong association of the "science of eugenics" with the Nazis, who pursued the theory to its log- ical conclusions, the language of British and American proponents was changed, and the "eugenics" agenda went underground. Nevertheless "eugenics" remains an important doctrine of opponents of the biblical world view in both coun- tries today.]

England had outlawed the slave trade in the Early Victorian Period. It might be argued that the failure of the United States to succeed in doing so short of a Civil War was partly due to a racism re-entrenched through the theories of "social Darwinism." The atmosphere these materialist speculations produced in British and later American society was anarchic to say the least. If men are only animals, then what is poetry?

Using the four "schools" of Victorian poetry suggested in the introduction to the previous section, 1) Turning, 2) Yearning, 3) Returning, or 4) Spurning, we might say the "Turning" and "Spurning" poets found themselves more pop- ular in the Late than the Early Victorian period. "Yearning" poets, like Arthur Clough and "Returning" poets, like the Meynells, Francis Thompson, and Gerard Manley Hopkins, continue to speak, if in increasingly isolated voices.

Victorian poets saw themselves trying to do a much smaller job much more carefully than previous poets in previous periods. Late Victorian (and some Early Victorian) poetry is "mood" poetry to a far greater degree than anything previous. Words often seem to have been chosen for their lack of particular association, so that in aggregate they may contribute to a larger "mood." (For example Poe, technically earlier than this period, is a noted practitioner of this. He deliberately uses condensed alliteration and stark imagery in much of his poetry toward the reinforcement of mood.)

Victorian poets, including nearly all the "greats," were concerned, if not with "truth" at least with "right living" (morals or ethics), and perhaps most desperately so those poets who were most insecure regarding "truth." Many of the "Turning" and "Spurning" schools viewed the poet as the only true prophet (much as Shelley had). This view was espoused by such as Matthew Arnold, whose view of "good" poetry had to do with a number of indistinct principles. Nevertheless he seems to make poetry the effective substitute for religion. Arnold and others of the time, like the "pagan" romantics, viewed poetry as the source of what "truth" was available to man—that the poet was the seer or even maker of truth with a small "t." The logic of this view would lead to the idea that "the poem should not mean but be," the modernist description, a sub-heading of the greater modern view of all human creativity, "Art for Art's sake."

The terms "puritan" and "puritanical" as they are used among us would be much more accurately rendered "Victorian." The Victorian age was very much a period of preoccupation with doing right—outward morality—along with a dark sense that something in and among people was very destructive. Many Victorians went to church as much to "do right" as out of any desire to "believe" or "know" right. If a kind of desperation regarding truth trembled beneath the human landscape of Victorian England and America, then one of its manifestations was the desire to solidify and reinforce rules of behavior at all levels.

Among the Late Victorians, many Catholic poets stand out as sustained voices. Many "fundamentalists" or "evangelicals," on the other hand, retreated to the writing of or barely evangelistic or else revivalist hymns. The theological depth and poetic excellence of hymns tended to decrease as the Victorian Age wound down and the Twentieth Century began. There was an increasing turn toward "sentimental" and individualistic lyrics.

Despite all these distinctions, Christian poetry continued alive and well to the end of the Victorian Period. Christian poetry more than English poetry in general or in any one of its periods, is its own nation and period. What may be different in the Victorian period is the scope of the nominally Christian and non-Christian "schools" of poetry, and their conscious intention to supplant orthodox Christianity. What may also be different, when seen in contrast to what went before, is the degree to which the church and Christian poetry took up a defensive posture.

A Brief Chronology of the Late Victorian Period

1861	American Civil War begins
	Elizabeth Browning dies
	Dickens, *Great Expectations*
1862	Christina Rossetti publishes *Goblin Market and Other Poems*

1863	Emancipation Proclamation in United States
1864	American Civil War over
	Newman publishes *Apologia Pro Vita Sua*
1865	Lewis Carroll, *Alice in Wonderland*
	President Abraham Lincoln assassinated
1867	Second Reform Bill passed
	Marx and Engles, *Das Capital*
1868	Wilkie Collins, *The Moonstone*
1870–71	Franco-Prussian War
1871	Darwin's *Descent of Man* published
1872	George Eliot (Mary Ann Evans), *Middlemarch*
1892	Tennyson dies
1901	Death of Victoria
1909	First English translation of Freud's work published
1914	World War I begins
1918	World War I ends
	Hopkins's poetry published by Bridges

HOPKINS, GERARD MANLEY (1844–1889), an English poet, teacher and clergy-man, was educated at Oxford and after winning two prizes for poetry, became a Roman Catholic in 1865. He was sponsored by John Henry Newman in his studies for the Jesuit priesthood and was ordained in 1874. Hopkins, talented in music and painting as well as writing, wrote no poetry for seven years, until, in response to the wish of his Rector, he wrote the famous "Wreck of the Deutschland"(1875) to commemorate the loss of a group of nuns aboard that ship. His poetry was not published in his lifetime, but in 1918, his friend, Robert Bridges, who had received them in letters, published them and they became very influential overnight. Hopkins's poetry is characterized by "sprung rhythm," and dense metaphor and wordplay that some critics attribute to traditional Welsh poetic technique. (Similar techniques in the poetry of another "Welsh poet," Dylan Thomas, might lend credence to this idea, although Thomas was much influenced by Hopkins.) He became professor of Greek at Dublin University in 1884. Hopkins work is generally recognized as foundational to "modern" poetry, rather than being characteristic of Victorian poetry. W. H. Auden and C. Day Lewis, among other British and American poets were much influenced by his poetry. His letters, notebooks, and papers were published from 1835 to 1938.

8

He hath abolished the old drouth,
And rivers run where all was dry,

The field is sopp'd with merciful dew.
He hath put a new song in my mouth,
The words are old, the purport new,
And taught my lips to quote this word
That I shall live, I shall not die,
But I shall when the shocks are stored
See the salvation of the Lord.

16

Myself unholy, from myself unholy
To the sweet living of my friends I look—
Eye-greeting doves bright-counter to the rook,
Fresh brooks to salt sand-teasing waters shoaly:—
And they are purer, but alas! not solely
The unquestion'd readings of a blotless book.
And so my trust, confused, struck, and shook
Yields to the sultry siege of melancholy.
He has a sin of mine, he its near brother;
Knowing them well I can but see the fall.
This fault in one I found, that in another:
And so, though each have one while I have all,
No better serves me now, save best; no other
Save Christ: to Christ I look, on Christ I call.

19

Let me be to Thee as the circling bird,
Or bat with tender and air-crisping wings
That shapes in half-light his departing rings,
From both of whom a changeless note is heard.
I have found my music in a common word,
Trying each pleasurable throat that sings
And every praised sequence of sweet strings,
And know infallibly which I preferred.
The authentic cadence was discovered late
Which ends those only strains that I approve,
And other science all gone out of date
And minor sweetness scarce made mention of:
I have found the dominant of my range and state—
Love, O my God, to call Thee Love and Love.

God's Grandeur

The world is charged with the grandeur of God.
It will flame out, like shining from shook foil;
It gathers to a greatness, like the ooze of oil
Crushed. Why do men then now not reck his rod?

Generations have trod, have trod, have trod;
And all is seared with trade; bleared, smeared with toil;
And wears man's smudge and shares man's smell: the soil
Is bare now, nor can foot feel, being shod.

And for all this, nature is never spent;
There lives the dearest freshness deep down things;
And though the last lights off the black West went,
Oh, morning, at the brown brink eastward, springs—
Because the Holy Ghost over the bent
World broods with warm breast and with ah! bright wings.

The Windhover: To Christ our Lord

I caught this morning morning's minion, king-
    dom of daylight's dauphin, dapple-dawn-drawn Falcon, in
        his riding
  Of the rolling level underneath him steady air, and striding
High there, how he rung upon the rein of a wimpling wing
In his ecstasy! then off, off forth on swing,
    As a skate's heel sweeps smooth on a bow-bend: the hurl and
      gliding
    Rebuffed the big wind. My heart in hiding
Stirred for a bird,—the achieve of, the mastery of the thing!

Brute beauty and valour and act, oh, air, pride, plume, here
    Buckle! AND the fire that breaks from thee then, a billion
Times told lovelier, more dangerous, O my chevalier!

    No wonder of it: sheer plod makes plough down sillion
Shine, and blue-bleak embers, ah my dear,
    Fall, gall themselves, and gash gold-vermilion.

Hurrahing in Harvest

Summer ends now; now, barbarous in beauty, the stooks rise
Around; up above, what wind-walks! what lovely behaviour

Of silk-sack clouds! has wilder, wilful-wavier
Meal-drift moulded ever and melted across skies?

I walk, I lift up, I lift up heart, eyes,
Down all that glory in the heavens to glean our Saviour;
And, eyes, heart, what looks, what lips yet gave you a
Rapturous love's greeting of realer, of rounder replies?

And the azurous hung hills are his world-wielding shoulder
Majestic—as a stallion stalwart, very-violet-sweet!—
These things, these things were here and but the beholder
Wanting; which two when they once meet,
The heart rears wings bold and bolder
And hurls for him, O half hurls earth for him off under his feet.

Pied Beauty

Glory be to God for dappled things—
    For skies of couple-colour as a brinded cow;
        For rose-moles all in stipple upon trout that swim;
Fresh-firecoal chestnut-falls; finches' wings;
    Landscape plotted and pieced—fold, fallow, and plough;
        And all trades, their gear and tackle and trim.
All things counter, original, spare, strange;
    Whatever is fickle, freckled (who knows how?)
        With swift, slow; sweet, sour; adazzle, dim;
He fathers-forth whose beauty is past change:
        Praise him.

The Lantern Out of Doors

    Sometimes a lantern moves along the night,
    That interests our eyes. And who goes there?
    I think; where from and bound, I wonder, where,
    With, all down darkness wide, his wading light?

    Men go by me whom either beauty bright
    In mould or mind or what not else makes rare:
    They rain against our much-thick and marsh air
    Rich beams, till death or distance buys them quite.

    Death or distance soon consumes them: wind
    What most I may eye after, be in at the end
    I cannot, and out of sight is out of mind.

Christ minds: Christ's interest, what to avow or amend
There, eyes them, heart wants, care haunts, foot follows kind,
Their ransom, their rescue, and first, fast, last friend.

Inversnaid

This darksome burn, horseback brown,
His rollrock highroad roaring down,
In coop and in comb the fleece of his foam
Flutes and low to the lake falls home.

A windpuff-bonnet of fawn-froth
Turns and twindles over the broth
Of a pool so pitchblack, fell-frowning,
It rounds and rounds Despair to drowning.

Degged with dew, dappled with dew
Are the groins of the braes that the brook treads through,
Wiry heathpacks, flitches of fern,
And the beadbonny ash that sits over the burn.

What would the world be, once bereft
Of wet and of wildness? Let them be left,
O let them be left, wildness and wet;
Long live the weeds and the wilderness yet.

74

*Justus quidem tu es, Domine, si disputem tecum; verumtamen
justa loquar ad te: Quare via impiorum prosperatur? &c.*

Thou art indeed just, Lord, if I contend
With thee; but, sir, so what I plead is just.
Why do sinners' ways prosper? and why must
Disappointment all I endeavour end?

Wert thou my enemy, O thou my friend,
How wouldst thou worse, I wonder, than thou dost
Defeat, thwart me? Oh, the sots and thralls of lust
Do in spare hours more thrive than I that spend,

Sir, life upon thy cause. See, banks and brakes
Now, leaved how thick! laced they are again
With fretty chervil, look, and fresh wind shakes

Them; birds build—but not I build; no, but strain,
Time's eunuch, and not breed one work that wakes.
Mine, O thou lord of life, send my roots rain.

The Debt

Thee, God, I come from, to Thee go,
All day long I like fountain flow
From Thy hand out, swayed about
Mote-like in Thy mighty glow.

What I know of Thee I bless,
As acknowledging Thy stress;
On my being, and as seeing
Something of Thy holiness.

Once I turned from Thee and hid,
Bound on what Thou hadst forbid;
Sow the wind I would; I sinned:
I repent of what I did.

Bad I am, but yet Thy child.
Father, be Thou reconciled.
Spare Thou me, since I see
With Thy might that Thou art mild.

I have life left with me still
And Thy purpose to fulfil;
Yes, a debt to pay Thee yet:
Help me, Sir, and so I will.

The Habit Of Perfection

Elected Silence, sing to me
And beat upon my whorled ear,
Pipe me to pastures still, and be
The music that I care to hear.

Shape nothing, lips; be lovely-dumb:
It is the shut, the curfew sent
From there where all surrenders come
Which only makes you eloquent.

Be shelled, eyes, with double dark
And find the uncreated light;
This ruck and reel which you remark
Coils, keeps and teases simple sight.

Palate, the hutch of tasty lust,
Desire not to be rinsed with wine:
The can must be so sweet, the crust
So fresh that come in fasts divine!

Nostrils, your careless breath that spend
Upon the stir and keep of pride,
What relish shall the censers send
Along the sanctuary side!

BRIDGES, ROBERT SEYMOUR (1844–1930), had as his first major Christian influences friends at Eton, particularly his young relative, Digby Mackworth Dolben, whose dream was to establish an Anglican "Brotherhood." Attending Oxford, Bridges met Gerard Manley Hopkins, but Bridges's "religious sympathies" faded and he became more interested in philosophy and natural science. His first book of poems was published in 1873 and was praised by Andrew Lang. But Bridges published nothing more in his own name for ten years. Anonymously, he produced *The Growth of Love; A poem in Twenty-four Sonnets* in 1876. He received his medical degree (1874) and practiced at St. Bartholomew's, the Hospital for Sick Children, and the Great Northern Hospital. In 1879 and 1880 he published two more collections of *Poems, by the Author of the Growth of Love,* which were well but not widely received. In 1884 he married Monica Waterhouse. Residing at Yattendon until 1904, he and a lifelong friend produced *The Yattendon Hymnal,* which influenced the reform of hymns and the revival of sixteenth and seventeenth century music. Bridges also wrote eight dramas and a long narrative poem, *Eros and Psyche* (1885). His essays "On the elements of Milton's Blank Verse in *Paradise Lost*" (1887) and "On the Prosody of *Paradise Regained* and *Samson Agonistes*" (1889) were the first discussions of the beginning of the modern development in English verse in which natural phrase accent was to reassert itself. Bridges had discussed this in earlier years with Hopkins and later with W. J. Stone, who published *Classical Metres in English Verse* (1899), which Bridges republished with his own criticism in *Milton's Prosody* (1901). In 1913 he was appointed Poet Laureate. Bridges edited Hopkins's poems for publication in 1918. Those poems became a major influence on twentieth century poetry thereafter. At eighty-five he published his magnum opus, *The Testament of Beauty.*

Noel. Christmas Eve, 1913

Pax hominibus bonae voluntatis

A Frosty Christmas Eve
   when the stars were shining
Fared I forth alone
   where westward falls the hill,
And from many a village
   in the water'd valley
Distant music reach'd me
   peals of bells aringing:
The constellated sounds
   ran sprinkling on earth's floor
As the dark vault above
   with stars was spangled o'er.
Then sped my thought to keep
   that first Christmas of all
When the shepherds watching
   by their folds ere the dawn
Heard music in the fields
   and marveling could not tell
Whether it were angels
   or the bright stars singing.
Now blessed be the tow'rs
   that crown England so fair
That stand up strong in prayer
   unto God for our souls:
Blessed be their founders
   (said I) an' our country folk
Who are ringing for Christ
   in the belfries to-night
With arms lifted to clutch
   the rattling ropes that race
Into the dark above
   and the mad romping din.
But to me heard afar
   it was starry music
Angels' song, comforting
   as the comfort of Christ
When he spake tenderly
   to his sorrowful flock:
The old words came to me
   by the riches of time

Mellow'd and transfigured
    as I stood on the hill
Heark'ning in the aspect
    of th' eternal silence.

Thee Will I Love, My God And King

Thee will I love, my God and King
Thee will I sing,
My strength and tower:
For evermore thee will I trust,
O God most just
Of truth and power;
Who all things hast
In order placed,
Yea, for thy pleasure hast created;
And on thy throne
Unseen, unknown,
Reignest alone
In glory seated.

Set in my heart thy love I find;
My wandering mind
To thee thou leadest:
My trembling hope, my strong desire
With heavenly fire
Thou kindly feedest.
Lo, all things fair
Thy path prepare.
Thy beauty to my spirit calleth,
Thine to remain
In joy or pain,
And count it gain
Whate'er befalleth.

O more and more thy love extends;
My life befriends
With heavenly pleasure;
That I may win thy paradise,
Thy pearl of price,
Thy countless treasure;
Since but in thee
I can go free

From earthly care and vain oppression,
This prayer I make
For Jesus sake
That thou me take
In thy possession.

HICKEY, EMILY HENRIETTA (1845–1924), was the second daughter of an Irish clergyman. She was educated in private school and at University College. She took correspondence classes from Cambridge University and received a First Class Honors certificate therefrom. In 1881, she was co-founder with Frederick Furnivall of the Browning Society. She published many books of poetry beginning in 1881 with *A Sculptor and Other Poems*, and including *Poems* (1896), *Later Poems* (1913), and *Devotional Poems* (1922). Her poetical works include *Litanies of the Most Holy Rosary* (1910) and *Prayers from the Divine Liturgy* (1910). She wrote various prose works and translations from Old English as well as short stories and papers that were contributed to English and American magazines.

Song

Beloved, it is morn!
A redder berry on the thorn,
A deeper yellow on the corn,
For this good day new-born:
Pray, Sweet, for me
That I may be
Faithful to God and thee.

Beloved, it is day!
And lovers work, as children play,
With heart and brain untired alway:
Dear love, look up and pray.
Pray, Sweet, for me
That I may be
Faithful to God and thee.

Beloved, it is night!
Thy heart and mine are full of light,
Thy spirit shineth clear and white,—
God keep thee in his sight!
Pray, Sweet, for me
That I may be
Faithful to God and thee.

MEYNELL, ALICE (1847–1922), who became a Roman Catholic in 1868, was an active literary figure with her husband Wilfrid at the center of a sort of coterie, including many of the writers of her time. Francis Thompson is one of the best-known among those the Meynells befriended and encouraged. Alice, herself, published her first book of verse, *Preludes*, with the encouragement of Alfred Tennyson and Coventry Patmore, in 1875. She married Wilfrid in 1877 and they had eight children. She wrote essays that were published in *Merry England* (1883-95), a monthly magazine her husband founded. Other books of her poetry included: *Poems* (1893), *Later Poems* (1901), *Father of Women* (1918), and *Last Poems* (1923). Her books of essays include *The Rhythm of Life* (1893), *The Color of Life* (1896), *The Children* (1896), *The Spirit of Peace* (1898), *Ceres Runaway* (1910), and *The Second Person Singular* (1921). Her verse was popular enough to earn her mention as a possible successor to Tennyson as poet laureate.

Unto Us A Son Is Given

Given, not lent,
And not withdrawn—once sent,
This Infant of mankind, this One,
Is still the little welcome Son.

New every year,
New born and newly dear,
He comes with tidings and a song,
The ages long, the ages long;

Even as the cold
Keen winter grows not old,
As childhood is so fresh, foreseen,
And spring in the familiar green—

Sudden as sweet
Come the expected feet.
All joy is young, and new all art,
And He, too, Whom we have by heart.

Via, Et Veritas, Et Vita

'You never attained to Him?' 'If to attain
Be to abide, then that may be.'
'Endless the way, followed with how much pain!'
    'The way was He.'

Messina, 1908

Lord, Thou hast crushed Thy tender ones, o'erthrown
        Thy strong, Thy fair; Thy man thou hast unmanned,
Thy elaborate works unwrought, Thy deeds undone,
        Thy lovely sentient human plan unplanned;
Destroyer, we have cowered beneath Thine own
        Immediate, unintelligible hand.

Lord, Thou hast hastened to retrieve, to heal,
        To feed, to bind, to clothe, to quench the brand,
To prop the ruin, to bless, and to anneal;
        Hast sped Thy ships by sea, Thy trains by land,
Shed pity and tears:—our shattered fingers feel
        Thy mediate and intelligible hand.

The Crucifixion

        Oh, man's capacity
For spiritual sorrow, corporal pain!
Who has explored the deepmost of that sea,
With heavy links of a far-fathoming chain?

        That melancholy lead,
Let down in guilty and in innocent hold,
Yea into childish hands delivered,
Leaves the sequestered floor unreached, untold.

        One only has explored
The deepmost; but He did not die of it.
Not yet, not yet He died. Man's human Lord
Touched the extreme; it is not infinite.

        But over the abyss
Of God's capacity for woe He stayed
One hesitating hour; what gulf was this?
Forsaken He went down, and was afraid.

Easter Night

All night had shout of men and cry
Of woeful women filled His way;
Until that noon of sombre sky
On Friday, clamour and display

Smote Him; no solitude had He.
No silence, since Gethsemane.

Public was Death; but Power, but Might,
But Life again, but Victory,
Were hushed within the dead of night,
The shutter'd dark, the secrecy.
And all alone, alone, alone,
He rose again behind the stone.

To Conscripts

Compel them to come in—St. Luke's Gospel

You 'made a virtue of necessity'
By divine sanction; you, the loth, the grey,
The random, gentle, unconvinced; O be
The crowned!—you may, you may.

You, the compelled, be feasted! You, the caught,
Be freemen of the gates that word unlocks!
Accept your victory from that unsought,
That heavenly paradox.

To A Daisy

Slight as thou art, thou art enough to hide
Like all created things, secrets from me,
And stand a barrier to eternity,
And I, how can I praise thee well and wide

From where I dwell—upon the hither side?
Thou little veil for so great mystery,
When shall I penetrate all things and thee,
And then look back? For this I must abide,

Till thou shalt grow and fold and be unfurled
Literally between me and the world.
Then shall I drink from in beneath a spring,

And from a poet's side shall read his book.
O daisy mine, what will it be to look
From God's side even of such a simple thing?

THOMSON, EDWARD WILLIAM (1849–1924), son of a Canadian banker and man of letters, was born near Toronto and attended public schools and Trinity College Grammar School. Zealous for the popular causes represented by the North in the Civil War, he enlisted in the 3rd and 5th Pennsylvania Volunteer cavalry regiments during the last year of the Civil War. After the war he served in the Queen's Own Rifles in Toronto during the Fenian Raid of 1866. Thomson was a civil engineer until 1878. He moved to Boston and became a political writer, author, and journalist. He wrote short stories and poems. His poetry appeared in periodicals and in *When Lincoln Died, The Many-Mansioned House and Other Poems.*

Aspiration

My friend conceived the soul hereafter dwells
In any heaven the inmost heart desires,
The heart, which craves delight, at pain rebels,
And balks, or obeys the soul till life expires.

He deem'd that all the eternal Force contrives
Is wrought to revigorate its own control,
And that its alchemy some strength derives
From every tested and unflagging soul.

He deem'd a spirit which avails to guide
A human heart, gives proof of energy
To be received in That which never bides,
But ever toils for what can never be—

A perfect All—toward which the Eternal strives
To urge for ever every atom's range,
The Ideal, which never unto Form arrives,
Because new concept emanates from change.

He deem'd the inmost heart is what aligns
Man's aspiration, noble or impure,
And that immortal Tolerance assigns
Each soul what Aspiration would secure.

And if it choose what highest souls would rue—
Some endless round of mortal joys inane—
Such fate befits what souls could not subdue
The heart's poor shrinking from the chrism of pain.

•　　•　　•　　•　　•

My friend reviewed, nigh death, how staunch the soul
Had waged in him a conflict, never done,
To rule the dual self that fought control,
Spirit and flesh inextricably one.

His passionless judgement ponder'd well the past,
Patient, relentless, ere he spoke sincere,—
'Through all the strife my soul prevail'd at last,
It rules my inmost heart's desire here;

'My Will craves not some paradise of zest
Where mortal joys eternally renew,
Nor blank nirvana, nor elysian rest,
Nor palaced pomp to bombast fancy true;

'It yearns no whit to swell some choiring strain
In endless amplitudes of useless praise;
It dares to aspire to share the immortal pain
Of toil in moulding Form from phase to phase.

'To me, of old, such fate some terror bore,
But now great gladness in my spirit glows,
While death clings round me friendlier than before
To loose the soul that mounts beyond repose.'

•   •   •   •

Yet, at the end, from seeming death he stirr'd
As one whose sleep is broke by sudden shine,
And whisper'd Christ, as if the soul had heard
Tidings of some exceeding sweet design.

VAN DYKE, HENRY (1852–1933) born in Germantown, Pennsylvania, became a Presbyterian minister and later a professor at Princeton. He became most famous as a preacher while serving the Brick Church in New York City. Van Dyke wrote a number of books popular in his time, including outdoor adventures, moral tales (from sermons), short stories, travel sketches, literary criticism, and poetry. His essays on outdoor life included *Little Rivers* (1895) and *Fisherman's Luck* (1899). His moral tales included *The Story of the Other Wiseman* (1896) and *The First Christmas Tree* (1897). He published three collections of short stories: *The Ruling Passion* (1901), *The Blue Flower* (1902), and *The Unknown Quantity* (1912). He was called as a professor of English literature at Princeton (1908–09). From 1913–17 he served as minister to the Netherlands, and resigned in order to be free to raise public sentiment against pre-World War I Germany. He served as a navy chaplain during the war. Van Dyke's best known lyric is his "Hymn of Joy," written to Beethoven's Ninth Symphony.

Victoria

Be of good cheer, I have overcome the world.—John 16:33

Thy victory is in the heart,
Thy kingdom is within;
When outward pride and pomp depart,
Thy glory doth begin.

Thine army, ever in the field,
Is led by love and light;
Thy followers fall but never yield,
Triumphant in the right.

O King most meek and wonderful,
Grant us among Thy host,
To follow Thee, to fight for Thee,
Knights of the Holy Ghost.

Work

Let me but do my work from day to day
In field or forest, at the desk or loom,
In roaring market-place or tranquil room;
Let me but find it in my heart to say,
When vagrant wishes beckon me astray,
"This is my work; my blessing, not my doom;
Of all who live, I am the one by whom
This work can best be done in the right way."

Then shall I see it not too great, nor small,
To suit my spirit and to prove my powers;
Then shall I cheerful greet the labouring hours,
And cheerful turn, when the long shadows fall
At eventide, to play and love and rest,
Because I know for me my work is best.

The Gospel Of Labor

Yet often I think the king of that country,
comes out from His tireless host,
And walks in this world of the weary
as if He loved it the most;
For here in the dusty confusion,

with eyes that are heavy and dim,
He meets again the laboring men
who are looking and longing for Him.

He cancels the curse of Eden,
and brings them a blessing instead:
Blessed are they that labor,
for Jesus partakes of their bread,
He puts His hand to their burdens,
He enters their homes at night:
Who does his best shall have as his guest
the Master of life and light.

And courage will come with His presence,
and patience return at His touch,
And manifold sins be forgiven
to those who love Him much;
And the cries of envy and anger
will change to the songs of cheer,
For the toiling age will forget its rage
when the Prince of Peace draws near.

This is the gospel of labor,
ring it, ye bells of the kirk!
The Lord of Love comes down from above
to live with the men who work.
This is the rose that He planted,
here in the thorn-cursed soil:
Heaven is blessed with perfect rest,
but the blessing of earth is toil.

Foundations

Those things which cannot be shaken.—Hebrews 12:28

Now again the world is shaken,
Tempests break on sea and shore;
Earth with ruin overtaken,
Trembles while the storm-winds roar.
He abideth who confideth,
God is God forevermore.

Thrones are falling, heathen raging,
Peoples dreaming as of yore

Vain imaginations, waging
Man with man, unmeaning war.
He abideth who confideth,
Christ is King forevermore.

Human wisdom in confusion,
Casts away the forms it wore;
Ancient error, new illusion,
Lose the phantom fruit they bore.
He abideth who confideth,
Truth is truth forevermore.

Right eternal, Love immortal,
Built the House where we adore;
Mercy is its golden portal,
Virtue its unshaken floor.
He abideth who confideth,
God is God forevermore.

OXENHAM, JOHN (1852–1941) first wrote war poetry during the South African War—one of these poems, "Hymn for the Men at the Front," became popular throughout the English-speaking world during World War I. He predicted something like the League of Nations in a poem written in 1898, "Policeman X." He published his first book of poems, *Bees in Amber*, before World War I, during which he lost a son. His war poetry continued to be Christ-centered, despite the loss of his son on the front, while increasing the note of pathos that was to characterize subsequent "modern" war poetry, especially during World War II. *All's Well* was his second book of poetry. As of the 1930s, his books of poetry had sold more than a million copies.

Fair Raiment

O that my prayers could raiment you in splendour,—
Heaven's mystic grace soft-spun to golden haze,
Gemmed with the radiant jewels of the tender
God-given memories of good, glad days!

O that my love could clothe you with the glory
Of its own vision of your loveliness,
Fined and refined with touch absolutory,
Wove and inwove with eucharistic grace!

O that my joy could clothe you with the wonder
Of its own joyfulness in that you are!

What though our paths lie as the poles asunder,
I can thank God and worship from afar.

O that my hope could clothe you in its glowing
All-radiant faith in that which yet shall be,
When, with a gladness beyond mortal knowing,
Love claims its crown of immortality.

My Treasure

Treasure I sought
Over land and sea,
And dearly I bought
Prosperity.
But nought that I gained,
On land or sea,
Brought ever a lasting good to me.

Pleasure I sought
Over sea and land,
And snatched at life
With eager hand.
But nought that I found,
On land or sea,
Brought ever a lasting joy to me.

For treasure of earth
Is fleeting gain,
And Pleasure is but
A mask for pain.
Life asketh more,
And ever stands,
With outstretched hands by an opening door.

And then at last
My wanderings o'er,
All that I sought,
And God's good more,
Lay waiting for me
At my own door,—
Yea, more than I sought was at my door.

He let me scour
The world, to show

His Love and Power
Must all bestow.
All mine own strivings
Had brought me nought;
He gave me more than all I had sought.

So Little And So Much

In that I have so greatly failed Thee, Lord,
Have grace!
And in Thy outer courts deny me not
A place!

So little of fair work for Thee have I
To show;
So much of what I might have done, I did
Not do.

Yet Thou hast seen in me at times the will
For good,
Although so oft I did not do all that
I would.

Thou knowest me through and through, and yet Thou canst
Forgive.
Only in hope of Thy redeeming grace
I live.

Vimy Ridge

Tread softly here! Go reverently and slow!
Yea, let your soul go down upon its knees,
And with bowed head, and heart abased, strive hard
To grasp the future gain in this sore loss!
For not one foot of this dank sod but drank
Its surfeit of the blood of gallant men,
Who, for their faith, their hope,—for Life and Liberty,
Here made the sacrifice,—here gave their lives,
And gave right willingly—for you and me.
From this vast altar pile the souls of men
Sped up to God in countless multitudes;
On this grim cratered ridge they gave their all,
And, giving, won

The Peace of Heaven and Immortality.
Our hearts go out to them in boundless gratitude;
If ours—then God's; for His vast charity
All sees, all knows, all comprehends—save bounds.
He has repaid their sacrifice;—and we—?
God help us if we fail to pay our debt
In fullest full and all unstintingly!

The Pruner

God is a zealous pruner,
For He knows—
Who, falsely tender, spares the knife
But spoils the rose.

Watchman! What Of The Night?

Watchman! What of the night?
No light we see,—
Our souls are bruised and sickened with the sight
Of this foul crime against humanity.
The Ways are dark—
    "I See The Morning Light!"

—The Ways are dark;
Faith folds her wings; and Hope, in piteous plight,
Has dimmed her radiant lamp to feeblest spark.
Love bleeding lies—
    "I See The Morning Light!"

—Love bleeding lies,
Struck down by this grim fury of despight,
Which once again her Master crucifies.
He dies again—
    "I See The Morning Light!"

—He dies again,
By evil slain! Who died for man's respite
By man's insensate rage again is slain.
O woful sight!—
    "I See, The Morning Light!

—Beyond the war-clouds and the reddened ways,
I see the Promise of the Coming Days!

I see His Sun arise, new-charged with grace
Earth's tears to dry and all her woes efface
Christ lives! Christ loves! Christ rules!
No more shall Might,
Though leagued with all the Forces of the Night,
Ride over Right. No more shall Wrong
The world's gross agonies prolong.
Who waits His Time shall surely see
The triumph of His Constancy;—
When, without let, or bar, or stay,
The coming of His Perfect Day
Shall sweep the Powers of Night away;—
And Faith, replumed for nobler flight,
And Hope, aglow with radiance bright,
And Love, in loveliness bedight,
   Shall Greet The Morning Light!"

Profit And Loss

Profit?—Loss?
Who shall declare this good—that ill?—
When good and ill so intertwine
But to fulfil the vast design
Of an Omniscient Will?—
When seeming gain but turns to loss,—
When earthly treasure proves but dross,—
And what seemed loss but turns again
To high, eternal gain?

Wisest the man who does his best,
And leaves the rest
To Him Who counts not deeds alone,
But sees the root, the flower, the fruit,
And calls them one.

Hammer And Anvil

Hammer, Hammer,
Strike your fill!
Anvil, anvil,
Lie there still!

When you're the hammer,
Strike your fill!
When you're the anvil,
Lie there still!

Dies Ire-Dies Pacis [1915]

"Only through Me!" . . . The clear, high call comes pealing,
Above the thunders of the battle-plain;——
"Only through Me can Life's red wounds find healing;
Only through Me shall Earth have peace again.

Only through Me! . . . Love's Might, all might transcending,
Alone can draw the poison-fangs of Hate.
Yours the beginning!—Mine at nobler ending,——
Peace upon Earth, and Man regenerate!

Only through Me can come the great awaking;
Wrong cannot right the wrongs that Wrong hath done;
Only through Me, all other gods forsaking,
Can ye attain the heights that must be won.

Only through Me shall Victory be sounded;
Only through Me can Right wield righteous sword;
Only, through Me shall Peace be surely founded;
Only through Me! Then bid Me to the Board!"

Can we not rise to such great height of glory?
Shall this vast sorrow spend itself in vain?
Shall future ages tell the woeful story,——
Christ by His own was crucified again?

Hymn—In Christ There Is No East Or West

In Christ there is no East or West,
In him no South or North,
But one great fellowship of love
Throughout the whole wide earth.

In him shall true hearts everywhere
Their high communion find,
His service is the golden cord
Close-binding all mankind.

Join hands, then, brothers of the faith,
Whate'er your race may be!
Who serves my Father as a son
Is surely kin to me.

In Christ now meet both East and West,
In him meet South and North,
All Christly souls are one in Him
Throughout the whole wide earth.

MAY PROBYN

'Is It Nothing To You'

We were playing on the green together,
My sweetheart and I—
O! so heedless in the gay June weather
When the word went forth that we must die.
O! so merrily the balls of amber
And of ivory toss'd we to the sky,
While the word went forth in the King's chamber
That we both must die.

O! so idly straying thro' the pleasaunce
Pluck'd we here and there
Fruit and bud, while in the royal presence
The King's son was casting from his hair
Glory of the wreathen gold that crown'd it,
And, ungirdling all his garments fair,
Flinging by the jewell'd clasp that bound it,
With his feet made bare.

Down the myrtled stairway of the palace,
Ashes on his head,
Came he, thro' the rose and citron alleys,
In rough sark of sackcloth habited,
And in the hempen halter—O! we jested
Lightly, and we laugh'd as he was led
To the torture, while the bloom we breasted
Where the grapes grew red.

O! so sweet the birds, when he was dying,
Piped to her and me—

Is no room this glad June day for sighing—
He is dead, and she and I go free!
When the sun shall set on all our pleasure
We will mourn him—What, so you decree
We are heartless? Nay, but in what measure
Do you more than we?

CHAPMAN, J. WILBUR (1859–1918) was educated at Lake Forest University (Illinois) and Lane Theological Seminary before he was ordained to the Presbyterian ministry. He served for nearly twenty years as a pastor in Philadelphia, Albany, and New York City, before becoming an evangelist. In that capacity he travelled throughout the world for ten years, assisted by Charles M. Alexander as his musical director. Chapman then became the first director of the Winona Lake Bible and Chautauqua Conference (Indiana). He was involved in starting the conferences at Montreat, North Carolina, and Stony Brook, Long Island. In 1917, Chapman was elected moderator of the Presbyterian General Assembly. He published eight books, and wrote a number of hymns, including the well known ones included here.

One Day!

One day when heaven was filled with his praises,
One day when sin was as black as could be,
Jesus came forth to be born of a virgin—
Dwelt amongst men, my example is he!

Living he loved me; dying, he saved me;
Buried he carried my sins far away;
Rising, he justified freely, for ever:
One day he's coming—O, glorious day!

One day they led him up Calvary's mountain,
One day they nailed him to die on a tree;
Suffering anguish, despised and rejected:
Bearing our sins, my Redeemer is he!

One day they left him alone in the garden,
One day he rested, from suffering free;
Angels came down o'er his tomb keeping vigil;
Hope of the hopeless, my Saviour is he!

One day the grave could conceal him no longer,
One day the stone rolled away from the door;

Then he arose, over death he had conquered;
Now is ascended, my Lord evermore!

One day the trumpet will sound for his coming,
One day the skies with his glories will shine;
Wonderful day, my beloved ones bringing;
Glorious Saviour, this Jesus is mine!

Jesus What A Friend For Sinners

Jesus! What a Friend for sinners!
Jesus! Lover of my soul;
Friends may fail me, foes assail me,
He, my Saviour, makes me whole.

Hallelujah! what a Saviour!
Hallelujah! what a Friend!
Saving, helping, keeping, loving.
He is with me to the end.

Jesus! what a strength in weakness!
Let me hide myself in him;
Tempted, tried, and sometimes failing,
He, my strength, my victory wins.

Jesus! what a help in sorrow!
While the billows over me roll,
Even when my heart is breaking,
He, my comfort, helps my soul.

Jesus! what a guide and keeper!
While the tempest still is high,
Storms about me, night overtakes me,
He, my pilot, hears my cry.

Jesus! I do now receive him,
More than all in him I find,
He hath granted me forgiveness,
I am his, and he is mine.

REESE, LIZETTE WOODWORTH (1856–1935) lyric poet from
Baltimore, was a high school teacher for much of her life. Her earliest book of
poetry was *A Branch of May* (1887). She also published *A Handful of Lavender*
(1891), *A Quiet Road* (1896) and *A Wayside Lute* (1909). The latter includes her

most widely known poem, the sonnet "Tears." She went on to publish *Spicewood* (1920), *Wild Cherry* (1923), *Little Henrietta* (1927), *White April* (1930), *Pastures* (1933), and *The Old House in the Country* (1936). *Selected Poems* was published in 1926, followed by two autobiographical narratives, *A Victorian Village* (1929) and *The York Road* (1931). Her poetry, though personal, marks a movement away from Victorian sentiment toward a more romantic treatment of natural subjects.

At Cockcrow

The stars are gone out spark by spark;
A cock crows; up the cloudy lane,
A cart toils creaking through the dark:
Lord, in Thy sight all roads are plain,
Or run they up or down,
Sheep-tracks, highways to town,
Or even that little one,
Beneath the hedge, where seldom falls the sun.

If it were light, I would go west;
I would go east across the land;
But it is dark; I needs must rest
Till morn breaks forth on every hand:
Lord, choose for me,
The road that runs to Thee.

Prayer of an Unbeliever

Draw closer to me, God, than were I one,
With the hedged comfort of a creed about,
With not a shadow's shadow of a doubt
That You are father, and each man a son.
Because I halt means not the will to roam,
But through the stubble a surer track to find:
Confused of foot, the ear, the eye less kind,
One fears to miss the steps which lead to home.
Who gives not to a wayfarer at the end
A roof? To beggar a sustaining cup?
Else waits the crumbling ditch from dew to dew.
Even this to me, if by that way I mend,
By such a bitter hand be lifted up,
To stumble to that lodging which is You.

THOMPSON, FRANCIS (1859–1907), educated at Ushaw College, a Roman Catholic seminary, studied medicine at Manchester, but never received a degree. He tried to earn a living in London as a cobbler, errand-boy, and matchseller, eventually becoming addicted to opium, sick and starving to the point of attempting suicide in 1888. He wrote some poetry during this period, and a few poems were accepted by Wilfrid Meynell for publication in *Merry England*. Wilfrid and Alice befriended him and persuaded him to enter a hospital, on discharge from which he took up residence with the Meynells. His poems were good enough to be admired by Robert Browning, and in 1893, the Meynells helped Thompson arrange for the publication of *Poems*, which contained the famous "Hound of Heaven." Thompson once wrote, "To be the poet of the return to nature is something, but I would rather be the poet of the return to God." Other of his volumes include *Sister Songs* (1895), *New Poems* (1897), and several prose works, including *Health and Holiness* (1905), *Life of St. Ignatius Loyola* (1909), and *Essays on Shelley* (1909). His poetry shows an influence (as does Alice Meynell's) of the metaphysical poets. He died of tuberculosis.

The Hound Of Heaven

> I fled Him, down the nights and down the days;
> I fled Him, down the arches of the years;
> I fled Him, down the labyrinthine ways
> Of my own mind and in the mist of tears
> I hid from Him, and under running laughter.

>   Up vistaed hopes I sped;
>   And shot, precipitated,
> Adown Titanic glooms of chasmed fears,
> From those strong Feet that followed, followed after.
>   But with unhurrying chase,
>   And unperturbed pace,
> Deliberate speed, majestic instancy,
>   They beat—and a Voice beat
>   More instant than the Feet—
> 'All things betray thee, who betrayest Me.'

>   I pleaded, outlaw-wise,
> By many a hearted casement, curtained red,
> Trellised with intertwining charities;
> (For, though I knew His love Who followed,
>   Yet was I sore adread
> Lest, having Him, I must have naught beside.)
> But, if one little casement parted wide,

The gust of His approach would clash it to:
Fear wist not to evade, as Love wist to pursue.
Across the margent of the world I fled,
And troubled the gold gateways of the stars,
Smiting for shelter on their clanged bars;
  Fretted to dulcet jars
And silvern chatter the pale ports o' the moon.
I said to Dawn: Be sudden—to Eve: Be soon;
With thy young skiey blossoms heap me over
  From this tremendous Lover—
Float thy vague veil about me, lest He see!
I tempted all His servitors, but to find
My own betrayal in their constancy,
In faith to Him their fickleness to me,
Their traitorous trueness, and their loyal deceit.
To all swift things for swiftness did I sue;
Clung to the whistling mane of every wind.
But whether they swept, smoothly fleet,
The long savannahs of the blue;
  Or whether, Thunder-driven,
They clanged his chariot 'thwart a heaven,
Plashy with flying lightnings round the spurn o' their feet:—
Fear wist not to evade as Love wist to pursue.
  Still with unhurrying chase,
  And unperturbed pace,
Deliberate speed, majestic instancy,
  Came on the following Feet,
  And a Voice above their beat—
'Naught shelters thee, who wilt not shelter Me.'

I sought no more that after which I strayed
  In face or man or maid;
But still within the little children's eyes
  Seems something, something that replies,
They at least are for me, surely for me!
I turned me to them very wistfully;
But just as their young eyes grew sudden fair
  With dawning answers there,
Their angel plucked them from me by the hair.
'Come then, ye other children, Nature's-share
With me' (said I) 'your delicate fellowship;
  Let me greet you lip to lip,
  Let me twine with you caresses,

Wantoning
With our Lady-Mother's vagrant tresses,
Banqueting
With her in her wind-walled palace,
Underneath her azured dais,
Quaffing, as your taintless way is,
From a chalice
Lucent-weeping, out of the dayspring.'
So it was done:
I in their delicate fellowship was one—
Drew the bolt of Nature's secrecies.
I knew all the swift importings
On the wilful face of skies;
I knew how the clouds arise
Spumed of the wild sea-snortings;
All that's born or dies
Rose and drooped with; made them shapers
Of mine own moods, or wailful or divine;
With them joyed and was bereaven.
I was heavy with the even,
When she lit her glimmering tapers
Round the day's dead sanctities,
I laughed in the morning's eyes.
I triumphed and I saddened with all weather,
Heaven and I wept together,
And its sweet tears were salt with mortal mine:
Against the red throb of its sunset-heart
I laid my own to beat,
And share commingling heat;
But not by that, by that, was eased my human smart.
In vain my tears were wet on Heaven's grey cheek.
For ah! we know not what each other says,
These things and I; in sound I speak
Their sound is but their stir, they speak by silences.
Nature, poor stepdame, cannot slake my drouth;
Let her, if she would owe me,
Drop yon blue bosom-veil of sky, and show me
The breasts o' her tenderness:
Never did any milk of hers once bless
My thirsting mouth.
Nigh and nigh draws the chase,
With unperturbed pace,

Deliberate speed, majestic instancy;
    And past those noised Feet
    A voice comes yet more fleet—
'Lo! naught contents thee, who content'st not Me.'

Naked I wait Thy love's uplifted stroke!
My harness piece by piece Thou hast hewn from me,
    And smitten me to my knee;
    I am defenceless utterly.
    I slept, methinks, and woke,
And, slowly gazing, find me stripped in sleep.
In the rash lustihead of my young powers,
    I shook the pillaring hours
And pulled my life upon me; grimed with smears,
I stand amid the dust o' the mounded years—
My mangled youth lies dead beneath the heap.
My days have crackled and gone up in smoke,
Have puffed and burst as sun-starts on a stream,
    Yea, faileth now even dream
The dreamer, and the lute the lutanist;
Even the linked fantasies, in whose blossomy twist
I swung the earth a trinket at my wrist,
Are yielding; cords of all too weak account
For earth with heavy griefs so overplussed.
    Ah! is Thy love indeed
A weed, albeit an amaranthine weed,
Suffering no flowers except its own to mount?
    Ah! must—
    Designer infinite!—
Ah! must Thou char the wood ere Thou canst limn with it?
My freshness spent its wavering shower i' the dust;
And now my heart is as a broken fount,
Wherein tear-drippings stagnate, spilt down ever
    From the dank thoughts that shiver
Upon the sighful branches of my mind.
    Such is; what is to be?
The pulp so bitter, how shall taste the rind?
I dimly guess what Time in mists confounds;
Yet ever and anon a trumpet sounds
From the hid battlements of Eternity;
Those shaken mists a space unsettle, then
Round the half-glimpsed turrets slowly wash again.
    But not ere him who summoneth

I first have seen, enwound
With glooming robes purpureal, cypress-crowned;
His name I know, and what his trumpet saith.
Whether man's heart or life it be which yields
  Thee harvest, must Thy harvest-fields
  Be dunged with rotten death?

  Now of that long pursuit
  Comes on at hand the bruit;
  That Voice is round me like a bursting sea:
  'And is thy earth so marred,
  Shattered in shard on shard?
  Lo, all things fly thee, for thou fliest Me!

  Strange, piteous, futile thing!
Wherefore should any set thee love apart?
Seeing none but I makes much of naught' (He said),
'And human love needs human meriting:
  How hast thou merited—
Of all man's clotted clay the dingiest clot?
  Alack, thou knowest not
How little worthy of any love thou art!
Whom wilt thou find to love ignoble thee,
  Save Me, save only Me?
All which I took from thee I did but take,
  Not for thy harms,
But just that thou might'st seek it in My arms.
  All which thy child's mistake
Fancies as lost, I have stored for thee at home:
  Rise, clasp My hand, and come!'

Halts by me that footfall:
Is my gloom, after all,
Shade of His hand, outstretched caressingly?

'Ah, fondest, blindest, weakest,
I am He Whom thou seekest!
Thou dravest love from thee, who dravest Me.'

Love's Varlets

Love, he is nearer (though the moralist
Of rule and line cry shame on me), more near
To thee and to the heart of thee, be't wist,

Who sins against thee even for the dear
Lack that he hath of thee; than who, chill-wrapt
In thy light-thought-on customed livery,
Keeps all thy laws with formal service apt,
Save that great law to tremble and to be
Shook to his heart-strings if there do but pass
The rumour of thy pinions. Such one is
Thy varlet, guerdoned with the daily mass
That feed on thy remainder-meats of bliss.
More hath he of thy bosom, whose slips of grace
Fell through despair of thy close-gracious face.

Heaven And Hell

'Tis said there were no thought of hell,
Save hell were taught; that there should be
A Heaven for all's self-credible.
Not so the thing appears to me.
'Tis Heaven that lies beyond our sights,
And hell too possible that proves;
For all can feel the God that smites,
But ah, how few the God that loves!

To A Snowflake

What heart could have thought you?—
Past our devisal
(O filigree petal!)
Fashioned so purely,
Fragilely, surely,
From what Paradisal
Imagineless metal,
Too costly for cost?
Who hammered you, wrought you,
From argentine vapour?—
God was my shaper.
Passing surmisal,
He hammered, He wrought me,
From curled silver vapour,
To lust of His mind:—
Thou could'st not have thought me!
So purely, so palely,

Tinily, surely,
Mightily, frailly,
Insculped and embossed,
With His hammer of wind,
And His graver of frost.'

The Kingdom Of God ('In no Strange Land')

O World invisible, we view thee,
O world intangible, we touch thee,
O world unknowable, we know thee,
Inapprehensible, we clutch thee!

Does the fish soar to find the ocean,
The eagle plunge to find the air—
That we ask of the stars in motion
If they have rumour of thee there?

Not where the wheeling systems darken,
And our benumbed conceiving soars!
The drift of pinions, would we hearken,
Beats at our own clay-shuttered doors.

The angels keep their ancient places;—
Turn but a stone, and start a wing!
'Tis ye, 'tis your estranged faces,
That miss the many-splendoured thing.

But (when so sad thou canst not sadder)
Cry;—and upon thy so sore loss
Shall shine the traffic of Jacob's ladder
Pitched betwixt Heaven and Charing Cross.

Yea, in the night, my Soul, my daughter,
Cry,—clinging Heaven by the hems;
And lo, Christ walking on the water
Not of Gennesareth, but Thames!

BEECHING, HENRY CHARLES (1859–1919), while at Oxford, contributed poetry to an undergraduate magazine, *Waifs and Strays*, and, together with J.W. Mackail and J.B.B. Nichols, put out two volumes of poetry, *Mensae Secundae*, and *Love in Idleness*. With the same collaborators he published *Love's Looking Glass* in 1891. In 1882 Beeching was ordained a deacon and became a curate in Liverpool. In 1885 he accepted a "living" in Berkshire that he held for

fifteen years. There he devoted much of his time to literary work, particularly
the study of English poets. In 1890 he married Mary Plow, a niece of Robert
Bridges. In 1895 he published *Love In a Garden and Other Poems.* In 1900 Beeching
became chaplain of Lincoln's Inn and professor of pastoral theology at King's
College, London. He preached at Oxford, Cambridge, and also in Dublin. He
produced several volumes of sermons and lectures in London, including *Religio
Laici, The Bible Doctrine of Atonement,* and a work on Shakespeare. In 1911 he was
appointed dean of Norwich.

Knowledge after Death

Siccine separat amara mors?
Is death so bitter? Can it shut us fast
Off from ourselves, that future from this past,
When time compels us through those narrow doors?
Must we supplanted by ourselves in the course,
Changelings, become as they who know at last
A river's secret, never having cast
One guess, or known one doubt, about its source?

Is it so bitter? Does not knowledge here
Forget her gradual growth, and how each day
Seals up the sum of each world-conscious soul?
So tho' our ghosts forget us, waste no tear;
We, being ourselves, would gladly be as they,
And we, being they, are still ourselves made whole.

Prayers

God who created me
Nimble and light of limb,
In three elements free,
To run, to ride, to swim:
Not when the sense is dim,
But now from the heart of joy,
I would remember Him:
Take the thanks of a boy.

Jesu, King and Lord,
Whose are my foes to fight,
Gird me with thy sword
Swift and sharp and bright.
Thee would I serve if I might;

And conquer if I can,
From day-dawn till night,
Take the strength of a man.

Spirit of Love and Truth,
Breathing in grosser clay,
The light and flame of youth,
Delight of men in the fray,
Wisdom in strength's decay;
From pain, strife, wrong to be free,
This best gift I pray,
Take my spirit to Thee.

HULL, ELEANOR (1860–1935), after Celtic studies at the University of Dublin, joined the staff of the *Literary World* and contributed scholarly material to various encyclopedias and periodicals. In 1899 she founded the Irish Texts Society together with F. York Powell. She belonged to various other societies connected with Irish folklore. She published a number of books on early Irish mythology and literature, including *The Cuchulain Saga in Irish Literature* (1898), *Pagan Ireland, and Early Christian Ireland* (1904), and *The Poem Book of the Gael* (1912). She wrote an extensive history of the Irish people and was editor of the *Lives of the Celtic Saints* series.

The Soul's Desire
From the Irish

It were my soul's desire
To see the face of God;
It were my soul's desire
To rest in His abode.

It were my soul's desire
To study zealously;
This, too, my soul's desire,
A clear rule set for me.

It were my soul's desire
A spirit free from gloom;
It were my soul's desire
New life beyond the Doom.

It were my soul's desire
To shun the chills of hell;

It were my soul's desire
Within His house to dwell.

It were my soul's desire
To imitate my King,
It were my soul's desire
His ceaseless praise to sing.

It were my soul's desire,
When heaven's gate is won,
To find my soul's desire
Clear shining like the sun.

Grant, Lord, my soul's desire,
Deep waves of cleansing sighs;
Grant, Lord, my soul's desire
From earthly cares to rise.

This still my soul's desire—
Whatever life afford—
To gain my soul's desire
And see Thy face, O Lord.

GUINEY, LOUISE IMOGEN (1861–1920), born in New England and educated at the Convent of the Sacred Heart in Providence, Rhode Island, became a respected poet and editor, especially in England where she resided after 1901 until her death. Her father was severely wounded in the Civil War Battle of the Wilderness. He died of his wounds in 1877 and apparently furnished her with the recurring imagery of the "knight" in her poetry. She published *Songs at the Start* (1884), *Goose-quill Papers* (1885), *The White Sail* (1887), and *A Roadside Harp* (1893). She was appointed postmistress in Auburndale, Massachusetts, where residents resented the "Irish-Catholic" at the stamp window and boycotted the office. Despite re-appointment by President McKinley in 1897, she resigned. She published *A Little English Gallery* (1894), *Nine Sonnets Written at Oxford* (1895), *Patrins* (1897), and *England and Yesterday* (1898). After her move to England, she began to research neglected authors. She contributed to the revival of Henry Vaughan's works and the preservation of William Hazlitt's fame. She worked with the Jesuit, Geoffrey Bliss, on *Recusant Poets, 1535–1735: A Catholic Anthology from St. Thomas More to Pope,* but it was not published in her lifetime. The first volume was published in 1938. She also wrote a number of biographies and published the works of various poets. Her own best works she published in *Happy Ending* (1909).

The Kings

A man said unto his Angel:
'My spirits are fallen low,
And I cannot carry this battle:
O brother! Where might I go?

'The terrible Kings are on me
With spears that are deadly bright;
Against me so from the cradle
Do fate and my fathers fight.'

Then said to the man his Angel:
'Thou wavering witless soul
Back to the ranks! What matter
To win or to lose the whole,

'As judged by the little judges
Who hearken not well, nor see?
Not thus, by the outer issue,
The Wise shall interpret thee.

'Thy will is the sovereign measure
And only event of things:
The puniest heart defying,
Were stronger than all these Kings.

'Though out of the past they gather,
Mind's Doubt, and Bodily Pain,
And pallid Thirst of the Spirit
That is kin to the other twain,

'And Grief, in a cloud of banners,
And ringletted Vain Desires,
And Vice, with spoils upon him
Of thee and thy beaten sires,—

'While Kings of Eternal evil
Yet darken the hills about,
Thy part is with broken sabre
To rise on the last redoubt;

'To fear not sensible failure,
Nor covet the game at all,
But fighting, fighting, fighting,
Die, driven against the wall.'

The House of Christmas

There fared a mother driven forth
Out of an inn to roam;
In the place where she was homeless
All men are at home.
The crazy stable close at hand,
With shaking timber and shifting sand,
Grew a stronger thing to abide and stand
Than the square stones of Rome.

For men are homesick in their homes,
And strangers under the sun,
And they lay their heads in a foreign land
Whenever the day is done.
Here we have battle and blazing eyes,
And chance and honour and high surprise,
But our homes are under miraculous skies
Where the yule tale was begun.

A Child in a foul stable,
Where the beasts feed and foam,
Only where He was homeless
Are you and I at home;
We have hands that fashion and heads that know,
But our hearts we lost—how long ago!—
In a place no chart nor ship can show
Under the sky's dome.

This world is wild as an old wives' tale,
And strange the plain things are.
The earth is enough and the air is enough
For our wonder and our war;
But our rest is as far as the fire-drake swings
And our peace is put in impossible things
Where clashed and thundered unthinkable wings
Round an incredible star.

To an open house in the evening
Home shall men come,
To an older place than Eden
And a taller town than Rome.
To the end of the way of the wandering star,
To the things that cannot be and that are,

To the place where God was homeless
And all men are at home.

Note: The last stanza of this poem is wrongly attributed to G.K. Chesterton as "Home
At Last" in The World's Great Religious Poetry (1923) 1945.

Deo Optimo Maximo

All else for use, One only for desire;
Thanksgiving for the good, but thirst for Thee:
Up from the best, whereof no man need tire,
Impel Thou me.

Delight is menace if Thou brood not by,
Power is a quicksand, Fame a gathering jeer.
Oft as the morn (though none of earth deny
These three are dear),

Wash me of them, that I may be renewed,
And wander free amid my freeborn joys:
Oh, close my hand upon Beatitude!
Not on her toys.

COLERIDGE, MARY ELIZABETH (1861–1907), great grand-niece of
Samuel Taylor Coleridge, was educated at home where she showed literary abil-
ity as a child, writing poetry and mystical romances. When she was twenty she
began to write for periodicals. In 1893 she published her first novel, *The Seven
Sleepers of Ephesus*, a fantasy novel that was praised by Robert Louis Stevenson.
Her first book of poetry, *Fancy's Following*, was published in 1896 through the
influence of Robert Bridges. In 1897 she published a historical romance, *The
King With Two Faces*, which was an immediate success. She published a book of
essays, *Non Sequitur*, in 1900. In addition to her literary production, she taught
working-women in her home and taught English literature at the Working
Women's College. Just before her sudden death from illness, she finished a short
Life of Holman Hunt, the painter. It was published after her death, as well as *Poems,
New and Old*, and *Gathered Leaves*, a volume of unpublished stories and essays.

I Saw a Stable

I saw a stable, low and very bare,
     A little child in a manger.
The oxen knew Him, had Him in their care,
     To men He was a stranger.

The safety of the world was lying there,
　　And the world's danger.

A Huguenot

O a gallant set were they,
As they charged on us that day,
A thousand riding like one!
Their trumpets crying,
And their white plumes flying,
And their sabres flashing in the sun.

O, a sorry lot were we,
As we stood beside the sea,
Each man for himself as he stood!
We were scatter'd and lonely—
A little force only
Of the good men fighting for the good.

But I never loved more
On sea or on shore
The ringing of my own true blade.
Like lightning it quiver'd,
And the hard helms shiver'd,
As I sang, ' None maketh me afraid!'

Lord of the Winds

Lord of the winds, I cry to Thee,
　　I that am dust,
And blown about by every gust
　　I fly to Thee.

Lord of the waters, unto Thee I call.
I that am weed upon the waters borne,
　　And by the waters torn,
Tossed by the waters, at Thy feet I fall.

From *Death*

Bid me remember, O my gracious Lord,
The flattering words of love are merely breath!
O not in roses wreathe the shining sword,

Bid me remember, O my gracious Lord,
The bitter taste of death!

Wrap not in clouds of dread for me that hour
When I must leave behind this house of clay,
When the grass withers and the shrunken flower!
Bid me, O Lord, in that most dreadful hour,
Not fall, but fly away!

HINKSON, KATHERINE TYNAN (1861–1931), better known by her maiden name, spent her early years in rural County Dublin, Ireland. She attended convent school until an attack of measles endangered her eyesight. She became an Irish nationalist like her father, but was more interested in literature than politics. Her father published her first book, *Louise de la Valliere* in 1885. She made the acquaintances of Wilfrid and Alice Meynell, William and Christina Rossetti, William Butler Yeats and his family, and George Russell (AE) through it. She then began the writing career that was to provide her living—through the production of more than a hundred novels. She published several collections of poetry as well. In 1883 she married Henry Albert Hinkson, a scholar of Trinity College, Dublin, a lawyer and a novelist. After her marriage she lived in England until 1916. Her two sons were officers in the British army during World War I and her daughter Pamela is known as a novelist. George Russell described her as "happy in religion, friendship, children," and "instantly kindling to beauty."

Of An Orchard

Good is an Orchard, the Saint saith,
To meditate on life and death,
With a cool well, a hive of bees,
A hermit's grot below the trees.

Good is an Orchard: very good,
Though one should wear no monkish hood;
Right good when Spring awakes her flute,
And good in yellowing time of fruit:

Very good in the grass to lie
And see the network 'gainst the sky,
A living lace of blue and green
And boughs that let the gold between.

The bees are types of souls that dwell
With honey in a quiet cell;

The ripe fruit figures goldenly
The soul's perfection in God's eye.

Prayer and praise in a country home,
Honey and fruit: a man might come
Fed on such meats to walk abroad
And in his Orchard talk with God.

Lux in Tenebris

At night what things will stalk abroad,
What veiled shapes and eyes of dread!
With phantoms in a lonely road
And visions of the dead.

The kindly room when day is here,
At night takes ghostly terrors on;
And every shadow hath its fear,
And every wind its moan.

Lord Jesus, Day-Star of the world,
Rise Thou, and bid this dark depart,
And all the east, a rose uncurled,
Grow golden at the heart!

Lord, in the watches of the night,
Keep Thou my soul! a trembling thing
As any moth that in daylight
Will spread a rainbow wing.

Sheep and Lambs

All in the April morning,
    April airs were abroad;
The sheep with their little lambs
    Pass'd me by on the road.

The sheep with their little lambs
    Pass'd me by on the road;
All in an April evening
    I thought on the Lamb of God.

The lambs were weary, and crying
    With a weak human cry,

I thought on the Lamb of God
   Going meekly to die.

Up in the blue, blue mountains
   Dewy pastures are sweet:
Rest for the little bodies,
   Rest for the little feet.

But for the Lamb of God
   Up on the hill-top green,
Only a cross of shame
   Two stark crosses between.

All in the April evening,
   April airs were abroad;
I saw the sheep with their lambs,
   And thought on the Lamb of God.

A Prayer

Now wilt me take for Jesus' sake,
   Nor cast me out at all;
I shall not fear the foe awake,
   Saved by thy City wall;
But in the night without affright
   Shall hear him steal without,
Who may not scale thy wall of might,
   Thy bastion, nor redoubt.

Full well I know that to the foe
   Wilt yield me not for aye,
Unless mine own hand should undo
   The gates that are my stay—
My folly and pride should open wide
   Thy doors and set me free
'Mid tigers striped and panthers pied
   Far from thy liberty.

Unless by debt myself I set
   Outside thy loving ken,
And yield myself by weight of debt
   Unto my fellow-men;
Deal with my guilt Thou as Thou wilt,
   And ' Hold!' I shall not cry,

So I be thine in storm and shine,
Thine only till I die.

I Would Choose To Be A Doorkeeper In The House Of The Lord

I would choose to be a doorkeeper
In the House of the Lord,
Rather than lords and ladies
In satin on the sward.
To draw the bolts for the white souls
Would be my rich reward:
And I the happy doorkeeper
To the House of the Lord.

Of all troop in not one comes out
From the House of the Lord,
Those who have won from sin and death,
From age and grief abhorred.
There is more room within its courts
Than palaces afford;
So great it is and spacious
In the House of the Lord.

They come with shining faces
To the House of the Lord;
The broken hearts and weary
That life has racked and scored:
They come hurrying and singing
To sit down at his board,
They are young and they are joyful
In the House of the Lord.

There are lilies and daisies
In the House of the Lord.
The lover finds his lover
With a long, long regard.
The mothers find their children,
Strayed from their watch and ward.
O the meetings and the greetings
In the House of the Lord!

I would be a humble doorkeeper
In the House of the Lord,
Where the courts are white and shining

In the light of the Word.
When the saved souls come trooping
For the gates to be unbarred,
O blessed is the doorkeeper
In the House of the Lord!

SCOTT, FREDERICK GEORGE (1861–1944), son of a Montreal profes-
sor of anatomy, attended high school in Canada and Kings College in London.
He entered the clergy in 1884 as a deacon, became a priest in 1886, and
returned to Canada, where he served in various offices of the church in Quebec.
He published *Soul's Quest, and Other Poems* in 1888, and six more books of poet-
ry before World War I. He served as a chaplain in the war, being six times
wounded. His *In the Battle Silences, and Other Poems written at the Front* was published
in 1916. After the war he served again in the Church of Canada, becoming
Canon of Quebec Cathedral in 1906 and Archdeacon of Quebec from 1925
to 1933. He published various short stories and pamphlets as well as five more
books of poetry: *In Sun and Shade: A Book of Poems* (1926); *New Poems* (1929);
Selected Poems (1933); *Collected Poems* (1934); and *Poems* (1936).

The Sting of Death

'Is Sin, then, fair?'
Nay, love, come now,
Put back the hair
From his sunny brow;
See, here, blood-red
Across his head
A brand is set,
The word—'Regret'.

'Is Sin so fleet
That while he stays,
Our hands and feet
May go his ways?'
Nay, love, his breath
Clings round like death,
He slakes desire
With liquid fire.

'Is Sin Death's sting?'
Ay, sure he is,
His golden wing

Darkens man's bliss;
And when Death comes,
Sin sits and hums
A chaunt of fears
Into man's ears.

'How slayeth Sin?'
First, God is hid,
And the heart within
By its own self chid;
Then the maddened brain
Is scourged by pain
To sin as before
And more and more,
For evermore.

MACKAY, JESSIE (1864–1938), of Highland descent, was born in New Zealand and attended Normal Training College. She became a journalist, contributing poetry, articles and literary pieces to papers in New Zealand, Australia, and Britain. She was published in *Time and Tide* (London) among other periodicals. Her interests included feminism, prohibition, and international matters. Her books of poetry include *Verse, Land of the Morning* (1909), *Poems* (1910), *Bride of the Rivers* (1926), and *Vigil* (1935).

In Galilee

Herod the King came sounding through
Capernaum gate with a revelling crew;
Beyond his garden of sycophants,
He saw but a thousand crawling ants.

Judas the Mammonite masked his heart
With a crooked smile in Capernaum mart,
And up the street as he went his way,
He saw but a thousand masks of clay.

John the Dreamer walked up and down
The streets of old Capernaum town;
And naught he saw with his raptured eye
But a thousand phantoms hurrying by.

Soft as snow to Capernaum drew
Jesus the Christ, and no man knew.

He saw as in a painted scroll
The ant, the mask, and the phantom soul.

But in and over and back of them all,
He saw, by old Capernaum wall,
The angel of each to whom was given
To stand before their God in Heaven.

JOHNSON, LIONEL PIGOT (1867–1902), of a high church Anglican family, went to Oxford where he was influenced by the "aestheticism" of Walter Pater. He became a poet, classicist, critic, and journalist, beginning with a carefully written weekly review. In 1891 he became a Roman Catholic, and although he never fulfilled his schoolboy aspiration to become a priest, he regarded writers as a "third order of the priesthood." He published *The Fools of Shakespeare* (1887), *The Art of Thomas Hardy* (1894), *Poems* (1895), and *Ireland* (1891). Two critical works were published after his death, *Post Liminium* (1912) and *Reviews and Critical Papers* (1921). He is said to have strained his "abnormally nervous" constitution to the breaking point by solitary bouts of heavy drinking. Johnson was among the members of the Rhymers Club, founded in 1891 by William Butler Yeats, and nominally dedicated to "art for art's sake." Other members included Earnest Dowson and Arthur Symons. Johnson was the most traditional, consciously resisting much of the decadence and the philistinism of the Victorian era. He distinguished between style and technique, "Style, the perfection of workmanship, we cannot do without that; but still less can we endure the dexterous and polished imitation of that."

Cadgwith

My windows open to the autumn night,
In vain I watched for sleep to visit me:
How should sleep dull mine ears, and dim my sight,
Who saw the stars, and listened to the sea?

Ah, how the City of our God is fair!
If, without sea, and starless though it be,
For joy of the majestic beauty there,
Men shall not miss the stars, nor mourn the sea.

My Own Fate

Each in his Proper gloom;
Each in his dark, just place.

The builders of their doom
Hide, each his awful face.

Not less than saints, are they
Heirs of Eternity:
Perfect, their dreadful way;
A deathless company.

Lost! lost! fallen and lost!
With fierce wrath ever fresh:
Each suffers in the ghost
The sorrows of the flesh.

O miracle of sin!
That makes itself an home,
So utter black within,
Thither Light cannot come!

O mighty house of hate!
Stablished and guarded so,
Love cannot pass the gate,
Even to dull its woe!

Now, Christ compassionate!
Now, bruise me with thy rod:
Lest I be mine own fate,
And kill the Love of God.

The Precept Of Silence

I know you: solitary griefs,
Desolate passions, aching hours!
I know you: tremulous beliefs,
Agonized hopes, and ashen flowers!

The winds are sometimes sad to me;
The starry spaces, full of fear:
Mine is the sorrow on the sea,
And mine the sigh of places drear.

Some players upon plaintive strings
Publish their wistfulness abroad:
I have not spoken of these things,
Save to one man, and unto God.

A Burden Of Easter Vigil

Awhile meet Doubt and Faith;
For either sigheth and saith,
    That He is dead
To-day: the linen cloths cover His head,
That hath, at last, whereon to rest; a rocky bed.

Come! for the pangs are done,
That overcast the sun,
    So bright to-day!
And moved the Roman soldier: come away!
Hath sorrow more to weep? Hath pity more to say?

Why wilt thou linger yet?
Think on dark Olivet;
    On Calvary stem:
Think, from the happy birth at Bethlehem,
To this last woe and passion at Jerusalem!

This only can be said:
He loved us all; is dead;
    May rise again.
But if He rise not? Over the far main,
The sun of glory falls indeed: the stars are plain.

CARMICHAEL, AMY WILSON (1867–1951), was the adopted daughter of Robert Wilson, chairman of the Keswick Convention. She worked as a missionary in Japan until, after a breakdown in her health, she moved to South India, where she worked with the Church of England Zenana Missionary Society. She wrote *Things As They Are* (1903), a realistic and moving account of mission life, which influenced many young people toward involvement in foreign missions. She started the Dohnavur Fellowship, a ministry aimed at redeeming children devoted to pagan temple service (which often involved prostitution). The Fellowship became independent of the Zenana Missionary Society in 1926. After a fall in 1931, she was crippled by arthritis, but she continued to be a primary force at the center of the Fellowship. She wrote many devotional and inspirational books and poems.

Yet Listen Now

Yet listen now,
Oh, listen with the wondering olive trees,

And the white moon that looked between the leaves,
And gentle earth that shuddered as she felt
Great drops of blood. All torturing questions find
Answer beneath those old grey olive trees.
There, only there, we can take heart to hope
For all lost lambs—Aye, even for ravening wolves.
Oh, there are things done in the world today
Would root up faith, but for Gethsemane.
For Calvary interprets human life,
No path of pain but there we meet our Lord;
And all the strain, the terror and the strife
Die down like waves before His peaceful word,
And nowhere but beside the awful Cross,
And where the olives grow along the hill,
Can we accept the unexplained, the loss,
The crushing agony,—and hold us still.

Do We Not Hear Thy Footfall?

Do we not hear Thy footfall, O Beloved,
Among the stars on many a moonless night?
Do we not catch the whisper of Thy coming
On winds of dawn, and often in the light
Of noontide and of sunset almost see Thee?
Look up through shining air
And long to see Thee, O Beloved, long to see Thee,
And wonder that Thou art not standing there?

And we shall hear Thy footfall, O Beloved,
And starry ways will open, and the night
Will call her candles from their distant stations,
And winds shall sing Thee, noon, and mingled light
Of rose-red evening thrill with lovely welcome;
And we, caught up in air,
Shall see Thee, O Beloved, we shall see Thee,
In hush of adoration see Thee there.

BARLOW, JANE (c.1870–1917), of County Dublin, Ireland, although edu-
cated at home, eventually received an honorary D. Litt. from the University of
Dublin. She published continuously from 1892 through 1913, commencing
with *Irish Idylls* and ending with *Doings and Dealings*. Between these her published
works included *Kerrigan's Quality* (1893), *The End of Elfintown* (1894), *The Battle of*

the *Frogs and Mice* (1894), *Creel of Irish Stories* (1897), *Irish Neighbour* (1907), *Irish Ways* (1909), *Mac's Adventures and Flaws* (1911), and *Doings and Dealings* (1913). She enjoyed music as well as writing.

Christmas Rede

Full clear and bright this Christmas night range fields of Heaven
    fire-sown;
But beam from star fled ne'er so far as mine Heart's Light hath flown
Since kindest eyes beneath yon skies fell dark and left me lone.

Ah, Mary blest! on kingly quest wise men had miss'd their way,
But evermore they saw before a star of soothfast ray,
And follow'd, till its lamp stood still where He who lit it lay.

Such light to friend their search had end, now mine doth but begin,
Yet, mother sweet, may wand'ring feet anigh thy Mansion win,
Above that roof no star for proof need shine to guide them in.

If kindest eyes in olden wise smile soft to bid me learn
That Love, the flower of Earth's dim hour, hath found a bower eterne
Shall burn rose-red while stars be sped; tho' stars dropt dead would
    burn.

BELLOC, HILAIRE (1870–1953), French-born son of an early suffragette, worked as a journalist, served in the French artillery, and graduated from Oxford in 1894. He married a Californian in 1896, and became a British citizen in 1902, serving in Parliament from 1906 to 1910. His writing career began with the publication of *Verses and Sonnets* (1895) and *The Bad Child's Book of Beasts* (1896). He published another book of light children's verse, *Cautionary Tales*, in 1907. He also published historical works, notably *Danton* (1899) and *Robespierre* (1901); satirical works, such as *Lambkin's Remains* (1900) and *Mr. Burden* (1904); an account of a pilgrimage, *The Path To Rome* (1902); some adult light verse, *The Modern Traveller* (1898); *Heroic Poem in Praise of Wine* (1932), and a few satirical novels, which were illustrated by G.K. Chesterton, with whom he shared a life-long friendship. He also published several long historical works, *Europe and Faith* (1920), *History of England* (four volumes from 1925 to 1931), and a series of biographies from *James II* (1928) to *Wolsey* (1930). He carried on scholarly controversies with H.G. Wells over the latter's *Outline of History* and with the Protestant historian G.C. Coulton.

Love And Honour

Love wooing Honour, Honour's love did win
And had his pleasure all a summer's day.
Not understanding how the dooms begin,
Love wooing Honour, wooed her life away.
Then wandered he a full five years' unrest
Until, one night, this Honour that had died
Came as he slept, in youth grown glorified
And smiling like the Saints whom God has blest.

But when he saw her on the clear night shine
Serene with more than mortal light upon her,
The boy that careless was of things divine,
Small Love, turned penitent to worship Honour.
So Love can conquer Honour: when that's past
Dead Honour risen outdoes Love at last.

The Prophet Lost In The Hills At Evening

Strong God which made the topmost stars
To circulate and keep their course,
Remember me; whom all the bars
Of sense and dreadful fate enforce.

Above me in your heights and tall,
Impassable the summits freeze,
Below the haunted waters call
Impassable beyond the trees.

I hunger and I have no bread.
My gourd is empty of the wine.
Surely the footsteps of the dead
Are shuffling softly close to mine!

It darkens. I have lost the ford.
There is a change on all things made.
The rocks have evil faces, Lord,
And I am awfully afraid.

Remember me. The Voids of Hell
Expand enormous all around.
Strong friend of souls, Emmanuel,
Redeem me from accursed ground.

The long descent of wasted days,
To these at last have led me down;
Remember that I filled with praise
The meaningless and doubtful ways
That lead to an eternal town.

I challenged and I kept the Faith,
The bleeding path alone I trod;
It darkens. Stand about my wraith,
And Harbour me, almighty God.

Her Faith

Because my faltering feet may fail to dare
The first descendant of the steps of Hell
Give me the Word in time that triumphs there.
I too must pass into the misty hollow
Where all our living laughter stops: and hark!
The tiny stuffless voices of the dark
Have called me, called me, till I needs must follow:
Give me the Word and I'll attempt it well.

Say it's the little winking of an eye
Which in that issue is uncurtained quite;
A little sleep that helps a moment by
Between the thin dawn and the large daylight.
Ah! tell me more than yet was hoped of men;
Swear that's true now, and I'll believe it then.

Almighty God, Whose Justice Like a Sun

Almighty God, whose justice like a sun
Shall coruscate along the floors of Heaven,
Raising what's low, perfecting what's undone,
Breaking the proud and making odd things even.
The poor of Jesus Christ along the street
In your rain sodden, in your snows unshod,
They have nor hearth, nor sword, nor human meat,
Nor even the bread of men: Almighty God.

The poor of Jesus Christ whom no man hears
Have waited on your vengeance much too long.
Wipe out not tears but blood: our eyes bleed tears.

Come smite our damned sophistries so strong
That thy rude hammer battering this rude wrong
Ring down the abyss of twice ten thousand years.

JOHNSON, JAMES WELDON (1871–1938), born in Florida and educat-
ed at Atlanta and Columbia Universities, was principal of the Colored High
School in Jacksonville before being admitted to the Florida bar in 1897. In
1901 he moved to New York where he wrote for vaudeville and light opera with
his brother, J. Rosamond Johnson. He served seven years as US Consul in
Venezuela, became secretary of the NAACP, and was professor of Creative
Literature at Fisk University. He published *Fifty Years and Other Poems* (1918), and
Gods Trombones (1927), as well as a novel, *The Autobiography of an Ex-Colored Man*
(1912), a prose account, *Black Manhattan* (1930), and his own autobiography,
Along This Way (1933). He also put together two collections of *American Negro
Spirituals* (1925, 1926) and edited the *Book of American Negro Poetry*.

Envoy

If homely virtues draw from me a tune
In jingling rhyme—or in ambitious rune;
Or if the smoldering future should inspire
My hand to try the seer's prophetic lyre;
Or if injustice, brutishness, and wrong
Stir me to make a weapon of my song;

O God, give beauty, truth, strength to my words—
Oh, may they fall like sweetly cadenced chords,
Or burn like beacon fires from out the dark,
Or speed like arrows, swift and sure to the mark.

The Creation

And God stepped out on space,
And He looked around and said,
"I'm lonely
I'll make me a world."

And far as the eye of God could see
Darkness covered everything,
Blacker than a hundred midnights
Down in a cypress swamp.

Then God smiled,
And the light broke,
And the darkness rolled up on one side,
And the light stood shining on the other,
And God said, "That's good!"

Then God reached out and took the light in His hands,
And God rolled the light around in His hands,
Until He made the sun;
And He set that sun a-blazing in the heavens.
And the light that was left from making the sun
God gathered up in a shining ball
And flung against the darkness,
Spangling the night with the moon and stars.
Then down between
The darkness and the light
He hurled the world;
And God said, "That's good!"

Then God himself stepped down—
And the sun was on His right hand,
And the moon was on His left;
The stars were clustered about His head,
And the earth was under His feet.
And God walked, and where He trod
His footsteps hollowed the valleys out
And bulged the mountains up.

Then He stopped and looked and saw
That the earth was hot and barren.
So God stepped over to the edge of the world
And He spat out the seven seas;
He batted His eyes, and the lightnings flashed;
He clapped His hands, and the thunders rolled;
And the waters above the earth came down,
The cooling waters came down.

Then the green grass sprouted,
And the little red flowers blossomed,
The pine-tree pointed his finger to the sky,
And the oak spread out his arms;
The lakes cuddled down in the hollows of the ground,
And the rivers ran down to the sea;
And God smiled again,

And the rainbow appeared,
And curled itself around His shoulder.

Then God raised His arm and He waved His hand
Over the sea and over the land,
And He said, "Bring forth! Bring forth!"
And quicker than God could drop His hand,
Fishes and fowls
And beasts and birds
Swam the rivers and the seas,
Roamed the forests and the woods,
And split the air with their wings,
And God said, "That's good!"

Then God walked around
And God looked around
On all that He had made.
He looked at His sun,
And He looked at His moon,
And He looked at His little stars;
He looked on His world
With all its living things,
And God said, "I'm lonely still."

Then God sat down
On the side of a hill where He could think;
By a deep, wide river He sat down;
With His head in His hands,
God thought and thought,
Till He thought, "I'll make me a man!"

Up from the bed of the river
God scooped the clay;
And by the bank of the river
He kneeled Him down;
And there the great God Almighty,
Who lit the sun and fixed it in the sky,
Who flung the stars to the most far corner of the night,
Who rounded the earth in the middle of His hand—
This Great God,
Like a mammy bending over her baby,
Kneeled down in the dust
Toiling over a lump of clay
Till He shaped it in His own image;

Then into it He blew the breath of life,
And man became a living soul.
Amen. Amen.

Go Down, Death

Weep not, weep not,
She is not dead;
She's resting in the bosom of Jesus.
Heart-broken husband—weep no more;
Grief-stricken son—weep no more;
Left-lonesome daughter—weep no more;
She's only just gone home.

Day before yesterday morning,
God was looking down from his great, high heaven,
Looking down on all his children,
And his eye fell on Sister Caroline,
Tossing on her bed of pain.
And God's big heart was touched with pity,
With the everlasting pity.

And God sat back on his throne,
And he commanded that tall, bright angel
    standing at his right hand:
Call me Death!
And that tall, bright angel cried in a voice
That broke like a clap of thunder:
Call Death!—Call Death!
And the echo sounded down the streets of heaven
Till it reached away back to that shadowy place,
Where Death waits with his pale, white horses.

And Death heard the summons,
And he leaped on his fastest horse,
Pale as a sheet in the moonlight.
Up to the golden street Death galloped,
And the hoofs of his horse struck fire from the gold,
But they didn't make no sound.
Up Death rode to the Great White Throne,
And waited for God's command.

And God said: Go down, Death, go down,
Go down to Savannah, Georgia,

Down in Yamacraw,
And find Sister Caroline.
She's borne the burden and the heat of the day,
She's labored long in the vineyard,
And she's tired—
She's weary—
Go down, Death, and bring her to me.

And Death didn't say a word,
But he loosed the reins of his pale, white horse,
And he clamped the spurs to his bloodless sides,
And out and down he rode,
Through heaven's pearly gates,
Past suns and moons and stars;
On Death rode,
Leaving the lightning's flash behind;
Straight on down he came.

While we were watchin—round her bed,
She turned her eyes and looked away,
She saw what we couldn't see;
She saw Old Death. She saw Old Death,
Coming like a falling star.
But Death didn't frighten Sister Caroline;
He looked to her like a welcome friend.
And she whispered to us: I'm going home,
And she smiled and closed her eyes.

And Death took her up like a baby,
And she lay in his icy arms,
But she didn't feel no chill.
And Death began to ride again—
Up beyond the evening star,
Out beyond the morning star,
Into the glittering light of glory,
On to the Great White Throne.
And there he laid Sister Caroline
On the loving breast of Jesus.

And Jesus took his own hand and wiped away her tears,
And he smoothed the furrows from her face,
And the angels sang a little song,
And Jesus rocked her in his arms,

And kept a-saying: Take your rest,
Take your rest, take your rest.

Weep not—weep not,
She is not dead;
She's resting in the bosom of Jesus.

DUNBAR, PAUL LAURENCE (1872–1906) born in Dayton, Ohio, published his first book of poetry, *Oak and Ivy*, in 1893. He extracted poems from that work and his second one, *Majors and Minors* (1895) for *Lyrics of Lowly Life* (1896), which began to establish his reputation. As a black poet, he wrestled with the peculiar pressures of writing primarily for white readers. His range is very wide, from classical genre pieces to poems in European dialects to poems in African-American dialect. The latter were popular, but, as a defined genre (as in the works of Joel Chandler Harris, Mark Twain, and the spiritual tradition being popularized by the Fisk Jubilee Singers) tended toward the light and humorous, and did not allow the poet the depth of expression of which he and poetry were capable. On the other hand, the real struggles of his life and friends seemed remote from the literary world where he was attempting to "make it." There is, therefore an artificiality about much of his work, but, as often, an open-hearted honesty. Sometimes they overlap in the same work. In addition to four novels, his other works include *Lyrics of the Hearthside* (1899), *Lyrics of Love and Laughter* (1903), and *Lyrics of Sunshine and Shadow*. His *Complete Poems* were published in 1913.

A Prayer

O Lord, the hard-won miles
Have worn my stumbling feet:
Oh, soothe me with thy smiles,
And make my life complete.

The thorns were thick and keen
Where'er I trembling trod;
The way was long between
My wounded feet and God.

Where healing waters flow
Do thou my footsteps lead.
My heart is aching so;
Thy gracious balm I need.

Hymn

When storms arise
And dark'ning skies
About me threatening lower,
To thee, O Lord, I raise mine eyes,
To thee my tortured spirit flies
For solace in that hour.

The mighty arm
Will let no harm
Come near me nor befall me;
Thy voice shall quiet my alarm,
When life's great battle waxeth warm—
No foeman shall appall me.

Upon thy breast
Secure I rest,
From sorrow and vexation;
No more by sinful cares oppressed,
But in thy presence ever blest,
O God of my salvation.

We Wear The Mask

We wear the mask that grins and lies,
It hides our checks and shades our eyes,
This debt we pay to human guile;
With torn and bleeding hearts we smile,
And mouth with myriad subtleties.

Why should the world be overwise,
In counting all our tears and sighs?
Nay, let them only see us, while
   We wear the mask.

We smile, but, O great Christ, our cries
To thee from tortured souls arise.
We sing, but oh the clay is vile
Beneath our feet, and long the mile;
But let the world dream otherwise,
   We wear the mask!

A Hymn After Reading "Lead, Kindly Light"

Lead gently, Lord, and slow,
For oh, my steps are weak,
And ever as I go,
Some soothing sentence speak;

That I may turn my face
Through doubt's obscurity
Toward thine abiding-place,
E'en tho' I cannot see.

For lo, the way is dark;
Through mist and cloud I grope,
Save for that fitful spark,
The little flame of hope.

Lead gently, Lord, and slow,
For fear that I may fall;
I know not where to go
Unless I hear thy call.

My fainting soul doth yearn
For thy green hills afar;
So let thy mercy burn—
My greater, guiding star!

Theology

There is a heaven, for ever, day by day,
The upward longing of my soul doth tell me so.
There is a hell, I'm quite as sure; for pray,
If there were not, where would my neighbours go?

Resignation

Long had I grieved at what I deemed abuse;
But now I am as grain within the mill.
If so be thou must crush me for thy use,
Grind on, O potent God, and do thy will!

Distinction

"I am but clay," the sinner plead,
Who fed each vain desire.
"Not only clay," another said,
"But worse, for thou art mire."

A Spiritual

De 'cession's stahted on de gospel way,
De Capting is a-drawin' nigh:
Bettah stop a-foolin' an' a-try to pray;
Lif' up yo' haid w'en de King go by!

Oh, sinnah mou'nin' in de dusty road,
Hyeah's de minute fu' to dry yo' eye:
Dey's a moughty One a-comin' fu' to baih yo' load;
Lif' up yo' haid w'en de King go by!

Oh, widder weepin' by yo' husban's grave,
Hit's bettah fu' to sing den sigh:
Hyeah come de Mastah wid de powah to save;
Lif' up yo' haid w'en de King go by!

Oh, orphans a-weepin' lak de widder do,
An' I wish you'd tell me why:
De Mastah is a mammy an' a pappy too;
Lif' up yo' haid w'en de King go by!

Oh, Moses sot de sarpint in de wildalness
W'en de chillun had commenced to die:
Some 'efused to look, but hit cuohed de res';
Lif' up yo' haid w'en de King go by!

Bow down, bow 'way down,
    Bow down,
But lif' up yo' haid w'en de King go by!

Slow Through The Dark

Slow moves the pageant of a climbing race;
Their footsteps drag far, far below the height,
And, unprevailing by their utmost might,
Seem faltering downward from each hard won place.

No strange, swift-sprung exception we; we trace
A devious way thro' dim, uncertain light,—
Our hope, through the long vistaed years, a sight
Of that our Captain's soul sees face to face.
Who, faithless, faltering that the road is steep,
Now raiseth up his drear insistent cry?
Who stoppeth here to spend a while in sleep
Or curseth that the storm obscures the sky?
Heed not the darkness round you, dull and deep;
The clouds grow thickest when the summit's nigh.

The Place Where The Rainbow Ends

There's a fabulous story
Full of splendor and glory,
That Arabian legends transcends;
Of the wealth without measure,
The coffers of treasure,
At the place where the rainbow ends.

Oh, many have sought it,
And all would have bought it,
With the blood we so recklessly spend;
But none has uncovered,
The gold, nor discovered
The spot at the rainbow's end.

They have sought it in battle,
And e'en where the rattle
Of dice with man's blasphemy blends;
But howe'er persuasive,
It still proves evasive,
This place where the rainbow ends.

I own for my pleasure,
I yearn not for treasure,
Though gold has a power it lends;
And I have a notion,
To find without motion,
The place where the rainbow ends.

The pot may hold pottage,
The place be a cottage,

That a humble contentment defends,
Only joy fills its coffer,
But spite of the scoffer,
There's the place where the rainbow ends.

Where care shall be quiet,
And love shall run riot,
And I shall find wealth in my friends;
Then truce to the story,
Of riches and glory;
There's the place where the rainbow ends.

When All Is Done

When all is done, and my last word is said,
And ye who loved me murmur, "He is dead,"
Let no one weep for fear that I should know,
And sorrow too that ye should sorrow so.

When all is done and in the oozing clay,
Ye lay this cast-off hull of mine away,
Pray not for me, for, after long despair,
The quiet of the grave will be a prayer.

For I have suffered loss and grievous pain,
The hurts of hatred and the world's disdain,
And wounds so deep that love, well-tried and pure,
Had not the pow'r to ease them or to cure.

When all is done, say not my day is o'er,
And that thro' night I seek a dimmer shore:
Say rather that my morn has just begun—
I greet the dawn and not a setting sun,
    When all is done.

CHESTERTON, G.K. (GILBERT KEITH) (1874–1936), writer and social critic, became a journalist and reviewer after graduating from University College in London. In 1900 he published a book of poetry, *The Wild Knight*, after which he published three books of social criticism taken from his journalistic works, *The Defendant* (1901), *Twelve Types* (1902), and *Heretics* (1905). He and Hillaire Belloc went through parallel political shifts from liberal to radical to "Distributionist," favoring more equitable land ownership as essential to a healthy nation, from which position he wrote *What's Wrong With The World* (1910).

He is perhaps best known for his fiction, notably the Father Brown mysteries (1911, 1914, 1926, 1927, and 1935), but his first major work of fiction was *The Napoleon of Notting Hill* (1904), which was followed by short stories, *The Club of Queer Trades* (1905) and *The Man Who Was Thursday* (1908). He also was noted as a literary critic, publishing books on Robert Browning, Charles Dickens, George Bernard Shaw, the Victorian Age, William Blake, William Cobbett, and Robert Louis Stevenson. He maintained friendships with H. G. Wells, George Bernard Shaw, and Max Beerbohm, as well as Belloc, among others. He wrote *Orthodoxy* in 1909, and after converting from the Anglican to the Roman Catholic church in 1922, *The Catholic Church and Conversion* (1926), *St. Francis of Assisi* (1923), *The Everlasting Man* (1925) and *St. Thomas Aquinas* (1933). He was a master of the ballad, paradoxical repartee, humorous-serious essay, and didactic prose.

The World State

Oh, how I love Humanity,
With love so pure and pringlish,
And how I hate the horrid French,
Who never will be English!

The International Idea,
The largest and the clearest,
Is welding all the nations now,
Except the one that's nearest.

This compromise has long been known,
This scheme of partial pardons,
In ethical societies
And small suburban gardens—

The villas and the chapels where
I learned with little labour
The way to love my fellow-man
And hate my next-door neighbour.

The Sword Of Surprise

Sunder me from my bones, O sword of God,
Till they stand stark and strange as do the trees;
That I whose heart goes up with the soaring woods
May marvel as much at these.

Sunder me from my blood that in the dark
I hear that red ancestral river run,
Like branching buried floods that find the sea
But never see the sun.

Give me miraculous eyes to see my eyes,
Those rolling mirrors made alive in me,
Terrible crystal more incredible
Than all the things they see.

Sunder me from my soul, that I may see
The sins like streaming wounds, the life's brave beat;
Till I shall save myself, as I would save
A stranger in the street.

Fantasia

The happy men that lose their heads
They find their heads in heaven
As cherub heads with cherub wings,
And cherub haloes even:
Out of the infinite evening lands
Along the sunset sea,
Leaving the purple fields behind,
The cherub wings beat down the wind
Back to the groping body and blind
As the bird back to the tree.

Whether the plumes be passion-red
For him that truly dies
By headsman's blade or battle-axe,
Or blue like butterflies,
For him that lost it in a lane
In April's fits and starts,
His folly is forgiven then:
But higher, and far beyond our ken,
Is the healing of the unhappy men,
The men that lost their hearts.

Is there not pardon for the brave
And broad release above,
Who lost their heads for liberty
Or lost their hearts for love?
Or is the wise man wise indeed

Whom larger thoughts keep whole?
Who sees life equal like a chart,
Made strong to play the saner part,
And keep his head and keep his heart,
And only lose his soul.

The Convert

After one moment when I bowed my head
And the whole world turned over and came upright,
And I came out where the old road shone white,
I walked the ways and heard what all men said,
Forests of tongues, like autumn leaves unshed,
Being not unlovable but strange and light;
Old riddles and new creeds, not in despite
But softly, as men smile about the dead.

The sages have a hundred maps to give
That trace their crawling cosmos like a tree,
They rattle reason out through many a sieve
That stores the sand and lets the gold go free:
And all these things are less than dust to me
Because my name is Lazarus and I live.

Ultimate

The vision of a haloed host
That weep around an empty throne;
And, aureoles dark and angels dead,
Man with his own life stands alone.

'I am,' he says his bankrupt creed;
'I am,' and is again a clod:
The sparrow starts, the grasses stir,
For he has said the name of God.

The Holy Of Holies

'Elder father, though thine eyes
Shine with hoary mysteries,
Canst thou tell me what in the heart
Of a cowslip blossom lies?'

'Smaller than all lives that be,
Secret as the deepest sea,
Stands a little house of seeds,
Like an elfin's granary. '

'Speller of the stones and weeds,
Skilled in Nature's crafts and creeds,
Tell me what is in the heart
Of the smallest of the seeds.'

'God Almighty, and with Him
Cherubim and Seraphim,
Filling all eternity—
Adonai Elohim.'

PICKTHALL, MARJORIE LOWRY CHRISTIE (1883–1922), daughter of an Anglican priest, was born in London and came to Canada when she was six. She was educated in Toronto, and worked as a librarian at Trinity College of the University of Toronto. In 1914 she published *Drift of Pinions,* which brought her several awards and wide recognition as a lyric poet. Her poems and stories were printed in many Canadian and American periodicals.

Resurgam

I shall say, Lord, 'Is it music, is it morning,
Song that is fresh as sunrise, light that sings?'
When on some hill there breaks the immortal warning
Of half forgotten springs.

I shall say, Lord, 'I have loved you, not another,
Heard in all quiet your footsteps on my road,
Felt your strong shoulder near me, O my brother,
Lightening the load.'

I shall say, Lord, 'I remembered, working, sleeping,
One face I looked for, one denied and dear.
Now that you come my eyes are blind with weeping,
But you will kiss them clear.'

I shall say, Lord, 'Touch my lips, and so unseal them;
I have learned silence since I lived and died.'
I shall say, Lord, 'Lift my hands, and so reveal them,
Full, satisfied.'

I shall say, Lord, 'We will laugh again to-morrow,
Now we'll be still a little, friend with friend.
Death was the gate and the long way was sorrow.
Love is the end.'

Quiet

Come not the earliest petal here, but only
Wind, cloud, and star,
Lovely and far,
Make it less lonely.

Few are the feet that seek her here, but sleeping
Thoughts sweet as flowers
Linger for hours,
Things winged, yet weeping.

Here in the immortal empire of the grasses,
Time, like one wrong
Note in a song,
With their bloom, passes.

JERROLD, SYDNEY E. (Madame Marie Christopher)

Earthly Joy

The shining cup of earthly joy
    I took with praise to Thee,
And held it dear because it was
    Thy loving cup to me.

The jewelled cup of earthly joy
    I kissed for love of Thee,
Because within its limpid depths
    Thine image I could see.

I drank the cup of earthly joy
    With many a thought of Thee,
And drinking it, I seemed to taste
    Perfect felicity.

But now the cup of earthly joy
    No longer flows for me,

Lest I should satisfy my soul
    With something less than Thee.

Non Te Rapiet Quisquam De Manua Mea

No airy stretch of sky to rest my eyes on,
Bright sea or dappled land,
My homeliest home, my fairest far horizon
The hollow of His hand.

Inviolable toughness of my hiding,
Almighty to withstand;
The chosen sanctuary of my abiding,
The stronghold of His hand.

Whence neither charm can hire nor power can move me
The spirit's Holy Land,
Fairer than flowers below or stars above me—
The heaven of His hand.

Hope

Chosen to walk in Heavenly places
Within His light and shade,
If strait and bare Thy earthly spaces,
    Be not afraid.

Called by Thy name in Easter's garden,
Steeped in His sun Who rose,
Be not dismayed for roads that harden
    Or doors that close.

Drawn, lifted, sealed by Love unchanging,
His wonders to declare,
Mid noise and throng, fear no estranging,
    He keeps thee there.

Fashioned to gaze where Truth is shining,
To live where Peace lies dear,
Frame not thy steps to labyrinths twining
    In darkness here.

Long must the voyage be that leads thee
At last to such an End.

Welcome, each wind and wave that speeds thee
        To such a Friend.

"A little while," He saith, " and sorrow
Shall hide in mist the shore,
But I will see you on the morrow
        For evermore."

The Beggar Maid

Dreaming, waking, the beggar maid
        Held her through the city's din,
The pitiless glare and the pitiful shade
        Whose strands are woven of beauty and sin.
But the pools by the wayside shone like flame
        Where Love's likeness burned for a breath and sped,
And a Voice through the multitudes called her name,
        And "I know some day He will come," she said.

He came at last and He set her free
        From the tangled meshes of beauty and sin,
He clad her in gold and embroidery,
        Fair without and shining within.
Loved and lowly she stood at His side,
        With gold of His crowning upon her head.
"I have called, thou art Mine, My chosen Bride,
        In thee I will set My Throne," He said.

Lost in light is the beggar's array,
        Thro' the mists of glory the city unseen,
But shadow and echo make mocking play
        That a beggar maid should be crowned a queen.
And she marvels much that the thing should be,
        "Am I waking or dreaming here where I stand?"—
" What matter? My dreams come true," saith He,
        "And no one shall snatch thee out of My Hand."

John In Prison

I hardly saw His Face.
I knew Him not till Heaven had given sign.
He passed, yet never did His eyes meet mine
For one short perfect space.

Yet mine it was to call
"Behold the Lamb of God "—and they who heard
Went from my side, sought Him, and at a word
Followed Him, leaving all.

I scarcely heard His voice—
Not me He called to Him from Jordan's side—
Yet to the Bridegroom have I led the Bride,
And I, His friend, rejoice.

And now—'"What things you see
Relate to John," He saith—" The prophecies
Are all fulfilled, and blessed be he who is
Not scandalised in Me."

Not blessed who baptised,
Watched, prayed and thundered to prepare His way,
Bore witness to the Light—but blessed they
Who are not scandalised.

Lord, be it ever so—
Before Thy Face to show the way of peace
I go, a passing voice that must decrease
Whilst Thou, the Lord, must grow.

The ways of peace are mine—
Though sharp and shining be the sword's way home
The Spirit and the Bride shall whisper "Come":
Then shall my eyes meet Thine.

Christopher

Was this Thy Passover—
The rage of wind and flood, night and despair,
And Thou the Burden past my strength to bear
    That made me Christopher?

No form nor loveliness
A weight unseen that bowed my shoulders down,
Only Thy strangling arms around me thrown
    To feel for all caress.

Thus art Thou come and gone.
The cold grey light shows all things as before,

No heavenly gleam, no print upon the shore
   Where I am left alone.

So will it ever be:
The wild, dark night, the sullen clouded day.
Are these Thy tokens, and is this the way
   Thou comest unto me?

But 'twixt the day and night
There comes a moment when drowsed hope is stirred,
And worn-out faith is quickened at Thy word,
   And smouldering love burns bright.

Carrying, not carried here;
But I shall know it was Thy arms upbore
When, standing on the radiant morning shore,
   Thou callest, Christopher.

Late Victorian Hymns

The nineteenth century continued a strong period of hymn-writing. It is strik-ing the degree to which Protestant poetry seems to have retreated to this one lit-erary bastion. Roman Catholic poets continued to produce general poetry dur-ing the Victorian age, but with very few exceptions, hymns are the sole genre in which Protestants continued to write and publish in any volume.

Alfred, Lord Tennyson had this to say about hymn-writing:

> A good hymn is the most difficult thing in the world to write. In a good hymn you have to be commonplace and poetical. The moment you cease to be commonplace and put in any expression at all out of the common, it ceases to be a hymn. Of all hymns I like Heber's "Holy, Holy, Holy" better than most, it is in a fine metre, too. What will people come to in a hundred years? do you think they will give up all religious forms and go and sit in silence in the Churches lis-tening to organs? (from *Alfred Lord Tennyson: A Memoir by His Son*, quot-ed in *Victorian and Later Poets*)

In America two sorts of hymns came to dominate after the Civil War: "lib-eral" hymns, as suitable for universalist as Christian churches, and "Moody-Sankey" hymns, associated with "fundamentalist" revival. L. F. Benson (*The English Hymn*) describes the latter:

> They carried the more emotional and less cultivated element of reli-gious people off its feet, and furnished for a time the familiar songs

of vast numbers hitherto unacquainted with hymns and unused to public worship. The new melodies penetrated even the music halls and were whistled by the man on the street. . . Easy, catchy, sentimental, swaying with a soft or a martial rhythm and culminating in a taking refrain; calling for no musical knowledge to understand and no skill to render them; inevitably popular, with the unfailing appeal of clear melody. (Bailey, *The Gospel in Hymns*)

It was not just the melodies that were effective, however. While many of the lyrics were inferior, some of them were good poetry of a simple sort.

Hymn-writing continued an important genre of Christian poetry up to the mid-twentieth century. While hymns continue to be an important part of our church music, contemporary Christian musical lyrics are being composed along two other lines: those that have followed popular musical styles and others (going full circle, we might say), chiefly scripture songs composed for contemporary worship.

Adeste Fideles
Anonymous, 1751, Translated by Frederick Oakeley, 1841

O come, all ye faithful,
Joyful and triumphant;
O come ye, O come ye to Bethlehem;
Come and behold Him
Born, the King of Angels;
O come, let us adore Him,
O come, let us adore Him,
O come, let us adore Him, Christ the Lord.

God of God,
Light of Light,
Lo! He abhors not the Virgin's womb;
Very God,
Begotten, not created;
O come, let us adore Him,
O come, let us adore Him,
O come, let us adore Him, Christ the Lord.

Sing, choirs of angels;
Sing in exultation,
Sing, all ye citizens of Heav'n above:
Glory to God
All glory in the highest;

O come, let us adore Him,
O come, let us adore Him,
O come, let us adore Him, Christ the Lord.

Yea, Lord, we greet Thee,
Born this happy morning;
Jesus, to Thee be glory given;
Word of the Father,
Now in flesh appearing;
O come, let us adore Him,
O come, let us adore Him,
O come, let us adore Him, Christ the Lord.

And Didst Thou Love The Race That Loved Not Thee?
Jean Ingelow, 1820–1897

And didst thou love the race that loved not thee?
And didst thou take to heaven a human brow?
Dost plead with man's voice by the marvellous sea?
Art thou his kinsman now?

O God, O kinsman loved, but not enough,
O Man, with eyes majestic after death,
Whose feet have toiled along our pathways rough,
Whose lips drawn human breath:

By that one likeness which is ours and thine,
By that one nature which doth hold us kin,
By that high heaven where, sinless, thou dost shine
To draw us sinners in;

By thy last silence in the judgment hall,
By long foreknowledge of the deadly tree,
By darkness, by the wormwood and the gall
I pray thee visit me.

Come, lest this heart should, cold and cast away,
Die ere the guest adored she entertain:
Lest eyes which never saw thine earthly day
Should miss thy heavenly reign.

The Church's One Foundation
Samuel J. Stone, 1839-1900

The Church's one foundation
Is Jesus Christ, her Lord;
She is his new creation
By water and the word:
From heaven he came and sought her
To be his holy bride,
With his own blood he bought her,
And for her life he died.

Elect from every nation,
Yet one o'er all the earth,
Her charter of salvation
One Lord, one faith, one birth;
One holy name she blesses,
Partakes one holy food,
And to one hope she presses
With every grace endued.

Though with a scornful wonder
Men see her sore opprest,
By schisms rent asunder,
By heresies distrest,
Yet saints their watch are keeping,
Their cry goes up, 'How long?'
And soon the night of weeping
Shall be the morn of song.

'Mid toil, and tribulation,
And tumult of her war,
She waits the consummation
Of peace for evermore;
Till with the vision glorious
Her longing eyes are blest,
And the great Church victorious
Shall be the Church at rest.

Yet she on earth hath union
With God the three in One,
And mystic sweet communion
With those whose rest is won:
O happy ones and holy!

Lord, give us grace that we,
Like them the meek and lowly,
On high may dwell with thee.

Harvest Home (Come, Ye Thankful People, Come)
Henry Alford, 1844, 1867

Come, ye thankful people, come,   Raise the song of harvest-home:
All is safely gathered in,   Ere the winter storms begin;
God, Our Maker, doth provide   For our wants to be supplied:
Come to God's own temple, come,   Raise the song of harvest-home.

All the world is God's own field,   Fruit unto his praise to yield;
Wheat and tares together sown,   Unto joy or sorrow grown:
First the blade, and then the ear,   Then the full corn shall appear:
Lord of harvest, grant that we   Wholesome grain and pure may be.

For the Lord our God shall come,   And shall take his harvest home;
From his field shall in that day   All offences purge away;
Give his angels charge at last   In the fire the tares to cast,
But the fruitful ears to store   In the garner evermore.

Even so, Lord, quickly come   To thy final harvest-home;
Gather thou thy people in,   Free from sorrow, free from sin;
There for ever purified,   In thy presence to abide:
Come, with all thine angels, come,   Raise the glorious harvest-home.

Day Is Dying In The West
Mary A. Lathbury, 1877

Day Is dying in the west;   Heav'n is touching earth with rest;
Wait and worship while the night   Sets her evening lamps alight
Through all the sky.

> Holy, Holy, Holy, Lord God of hosts!
> Heav'n and earth are full of thee!
> Heav'n and earth are praising thee,
> O Lord Most High.

While the deep'ning shadows fall,   Light of light, on whom we call
Through the glory and the grace   Of the stars that veil thy face,
Our hearts ascend.

And when fading from our sight   Pass the stars, the day, the night,
Lord of Glory, on our eyes   Let eternal morning rise,
And shadows end.

Funeral Hymn
William Walsham Howe, 1864

For all the saints who from their labors rest,
Who thee by faith before the world confessed,
Thy Name, O Jesus, be forever blessed.
    Alleluia.

Thou wast their rock, their fortress and their might:
Thou, Lord, their Captain in the well-fought fight;
Thou in the darkness drear, the one true Light.
    Alleluia.

O may thy soldiers, faithful, true and bold,
Fight as the saints who nobly fought of old,
And win, with them, the victor's crown of gold.
    Alleluia.

O blest communion, fellowship divine!
We feebly struggle; they in glory shine;
Yet all are one in Thee, for all are thine.
    Alleluia.

And when the strife is fierce, the warfare long,
Steals on the ear the distant triumph song,
And hearts are brave again, and arms are strong,
    Alleluia.

The golden evening brightens in the west;
Soon, to faithful warriors cometh rest;
Sweet is the calm of paradise the blest.
    Alleluia.

But lo! there breaks a yet more glorious day;
The saints triumphant rise in bright array;
The King of glory passes on His way.
    Alleluia.

From earth's wide bounds, from ocean's farthest coast,
Through gates of pearl streams in the countless host,

Singing to the Father, Son and Holy Ghost,
 Alleluia, Amen.

Father I Know That All My Life
Anna L. Waring, 1850

Father, I know that all my life Is portioned out for me;
The changes that are sure to come, I do not fear to see:
I ask thee for a present mind, Intent on pleasing thee.

I would not have the restless will That hurries to and fro,
Seeking for some great thing to do, Or secret thing to know;
I would be treated as a child, And guided where I go.

I ask thee for the daily strength, To none that ask denied,
A mind to blend with outward life, While keeping at thy side,
Content to fill a little space, If thou be glorified.

In service which thy will appoints There are no bonds for me;
My secret heart is taught the truth That makes thy children free;
A life of self-renouncing love Is one of liberty.

For The Beauty Of The Earth
F.S. Pierpoint, 1835-1917

For the beauty of the earth,
For the beauty of the skies,
For the love which from our birth
Over and around us lies:

 Father, unto thee we raise
 This our sacrifice of praise.

For the beauty of each hour
Of the day and of the night,
Hill and vale, and tree and flower.
Sun and moon and stars of light:

For the joy of ear and eye.
For they heart and brain's delight,
For the mystic harmony
Linking sense to sound and sight:

For the joy of human love,
Brother, sister, parent, child,
Friends on earth, and friends above,
For all gentle thoughts and mild:

For each perfect gift of thine
To our race so freely given,
Graces human and divine,
Flowers of earth and buds of heaven:

Father, unto thee we raise
This our sacrifice of praise.

God Rest Ye Merry, Gentlemen
Traditional carol

God rest ye merry, gentlemen,   Let nothing you dismay,
Remember Christ our Saviour   Was born on Christmas day,
To save us all from Satan's pow'r   When we were gone astray;

O tidings of comfort and joy, comfort and joy,
O tidings of comfort and joy.

From God our heav'n-ly Father,   A blessed angel came;
And unto certain shepherds   Brought tidings of the same:
How that in Bethlehem was born   The Son of God by name.

O tidings of comfort and joy, comfort and joy,
O tidings of comfort and joy.

'Fear not then,' said the angel, ' Let nothing you affright,
This day is born a Saviour Of a pure virgin bright,
To free all those who trust in him From Satan's pow'r and might.'

O tidings of comfort and joy, comfort and joy,
O tidings of comfort and joy.

The shepherds at those tidings Rejoiced much in mind,
And left their flocks a feeding, In tempest, storm and wind:
And went to Bethlehem straightway, The Son of God to find.

O tidings of comfort and joy, comfort and joy,
O tidings of comfort and joy.

Great Is Thy Faithfulness
Thomas O. Chisholm, 1923

"Great is thy faithfulness," O God my Father,
There is no shadow of turning with thee;
Thou changest not, thy compassions, they fail not;
As thou hast been thou for ever wilt be.

"Great is thy faithfulness! Great is thy faithfulness!"
Morning by morning new mercies I see:
All I have needed thy hand hath provided—
"Great is thy faithfulness," Lord unto me!

Summer and winter, and springtime and harvest,
Sun, moon and stars in their courses above,
Join with all nature in manifold witness
To thy great faithfulness, mercy and love.

Pardon for sin and a peace that endureth,
Thine own dear presence to cheer and to guide;
Strength for today and bright hope for tomorrow,
Blessings all mine, with ten thousand beside!

Have Thine Own Way, Lord!
Adelaide A. Pollard, 1902

Have thine own way, Lord! Have thine own way!
Thou art the Potter; I am the clay.
Mold me and make me after thy will,
While I am waiting, yielded and still.

Have thine own way, Lord! Have thine own way!
Search me and try me, Master, today!
Whiter than snow, Lord, wash me just now,
As in thy presence humbly I bow.

Have thine own way, Lord! Have thine own way!
Wounded and weary, help me I pray!
Power—all power—surely is thine!
Touch me and heal me, Saviour divine!

Have thine own way, Lord! Have thine own way!
Hold o'er my being absolute sway!
Fill with thy Spirit till all shall see
Christ only, always, living in me!

He Leadeth Me
Joseph H. Gilmore, 1862

He leadeth me: O blessed thought!
O words with heav'n-ly comfort fraught!
What-e'er I do, wher-e'er I be,
Still 'tis God's hand that leadeth me.

    He leadeth me, he leadeth me;
      By his own hand he leadeth me.

Sometimes 'mid scenes of deepest gloom,
Sometimes where Eden's bowers bloom,
By waters calm, o'er troubled sea,
Still 'tis his hand that leadeth me.

Lord, I would clasp thy hand in mine,
Nor ever murmur nor repine;
Content, whatever lot I see,
Since 'tis my God that leadeth me.

And when my task on earth is done,
When, by thy grace, the vict'ry's won,
E'en death's cold wave I will not flee,
Since God through Jordan leadeth me.

I Love To Tell The Story
Katherine Hankey, 1866

I love to tell the story   Of unseen things above,
Of Jesus and his glory,   Of Jesus and his love.
I love to tell the story,   Because I know 'tis true;
It satisfies my longings   As nothing else can do.

    I love to tell the story,
    'Twill be my theme in glory
    To tell the old, old story
    Of Jesus and his love.

I love to tell the story;   More wonderful it seems
Than all the golden fancies   Of all our golden dreams.
I love to tell the story,   It did so much for me;
And that is just the reason   I tell it now to thee.

I love to tell the story;   'Tis pleasant to repeat
What seems, each time   I tell it, More wonderfully sweet.

I love to tell the story,   For some have never heard
The message of salvation   From God's own holy Word.

I love to tell the story;   For those who know it best
Seem hungering and thirsting   To hear it, like the rest.
And when in scenes of glory,   I sing the new, new song,
'Twill be the old, old story,   That I have loved so long.

Immortal, Invisible
Walter Chalmers Smith, 1824-1908

Immortal, invisible, God only wise,
In light inaccessible hid from our eyes,
Most blessed, most glorious, the Ancient of Days,
Almighty, victorious, Thy great Name we praise.

Unresting, unhasting, and silent as light,
Nor wanting, nor wasting, Thou rulest in might;
Thy justice like mountains high soaring above
Thy clouds which are fountains of goodness and love.

Great Father of Glory, pure Father of Light,
Thine angels adore thee, all veiling their sight;
All praise we would render; O help us to see
'Tis only the splendor of light hideth thee!

In Emmanuel's Land
Anne R. Cousin, 1857, based on Samuel Rutherford, 1600–1661

The sands of time are sinking,   The dawn of heaven breaks,
The summer morn I've sighed for,   The fair sweet morn awakes;
Dark, dark hath been the midnight,   But day-spring is at hand,
And glory, glory dwelleth   In Emmanuel's land.

The King there in his beauty   Without a veil is seen;
It were a well-spent journey   Though sev'n deaths lay between:
The Lamb with his fair army   Doth on Mount Zion stand,
And glory, glory dwelleth   In Emmanuel's land.

O Christ, he is the fountain,   The deep sweet well of love!
The streams on earth I've tasted   More deep I'll drink above:
There to an ocean fulness   His mercy doth expand,
And glory, glory dwelleth   In Emmanuel's land.

The bride eyes not her garment,   But her dear bridegroom's face;
I will not gaze at glory,   But on my King of grace;
Not at the crown he gifteth,   But on his pierced hand:
The Lamb is all the glory   Of Emmanuel's land.

In The Cross Of Christ I Glory
John Bowring, 1825

In the cross of Christ I glory,
Towering o'er the wrecks of time;
All the light of sacred story
Gathers round its head sublime.

When the woes of life o'ertake me,
Hopes deceive and fears annoy,
Never shall the cross forsake me:
Lo, it glows with peace and joy.

When the sun of bliss is beaming
Light and love upon my way,
From the cross the radiance streaming
Adds more luster to the day.

Bane and blessing, pain and pleasure,
By thy cross are sanctified;
Peace there is that knows no measure,
Joys that through all time abide.

In the cross of Christ I glory,
Towering o'er the wrecks of time;
All the light of sacred story
Gathers round its head sublime.

It Came Upon The Midnight Clear
Edmund Sears, 1850

It came upon the midnight clear,
That glorious song of old,
From angels bending near the earth
To touch their harps of gold:
"Peace on the earth, good will to men,
From heav'ns all-gracious King:"
The world in solemn stillness lay,
To hear the angels sing.

Still through the cloven skies they come,
With peaceful wings unfurled,
And still their heav'nly music floats
O'er all the weary world:
Above its sad and lowly plains
They bend on hov'ring wing,
And ever o'er its Babel-sounds
The blessed angels sing.

And ye, beneath life's crushing load,
Whose forms are bending low,
Who toil along the climbing way
With painful steps and slow,
Look now! for glad and golden hours
Come swiftly on the wing:
O rest beside the weary road,
And hear the angels sing.

For lo, the days are hast'ning on,
By prophet bards foretold,
When with the ever-circling years
Comes round the age of gold;
When peace shall over all the earth
Its ancient splendors fling,
And the whole world give back the song
Which now the angels sing.

It Is Well With My Soul
Horatio G. Spafford, 1828-1888

When peace, like a river, attendeth my way,
When sorrows like sea-billows roll;
What-ever my lot, thou hast taught me to say,
It is well, it is well with my soul.

>   It is well—with my soul
>   It is well, it is well, with my soul.

Though Satan should buffet, though trials should come,
Let this blest assurance control,
That Christ has regarded my helpless estate,
And has shed his own blood for my soul.

My sin—O the bliss of this glorious thought!
My sin, not in part, but the whole,
Is nailed to the cross and I bear it no more;
Praise the Lord, praise the Lord, O my soul!

O Lord, haste the day when the faith shall be sight,
The clouds be rolled back as a scroll,
The trump shall resound and the Lord shall descend;
"Even so"—it is well with my soul.

Jesus I Am Resting, Resting
Jean Sophia Pigott, 1876

Jesus I am resting, resting   In the joy of what thou art;
I am finding out the greatness   Of thy loving heart.
Thou hast bid me gaze upon thee,   As thy beauty fills my soul,
For by thy transforming power,   Thou hast made me whole.

Jesus I am resting, resting   In the joy of what thou art;
I am finding out the greatness   Of thy loving heart.

O how great thy lovingkindness,   Vaster, broader than the sea!
O how marvelous thy goodness   Lavished all on me!
Yes, I rest in thee, Beloved,   Know what wealth of grace is thine,
Know thy certainty of promise   And have made it mine.

Simply trusting thee, Lord Jesus,   I behold thee as thou art,
And thy love, so pure, so changeless,   Satisfies my heart;
Satisfies its deepest longings,   Meets, supplies its ev'ry need,
Compasseth me round with blessings: Thine is love indeed.

Ever lift thy face upon me   As I work and wait for thee;
Resting 'neath thy smile, Lord Jesus,   Earth's dark shadows flee.
Brightness of my Father's glory,   Sunshine of my Father's face,
Keep me ever trusting, resting,   Fill me with thy grace.

Judge Eternal, Throned In Splendours
Henry Scott Holland, 1847–1918

Judge eternal, throned in splendours
Lord of lords and King of kings,
With thy living fire of judgment
Purge this realm of bitter things:

Solace all its wide dominion
With the healing of thy wings.

Still the weary folk are pining
For the hour that brings release,
And the city's crowded clangour
Cries aloud for sin to cease,
And the homesteads and the woodlands
Plead in silence for their peace.

Crown, O God, thine own endeavour;
Cleave our darkness with thy sword;
Feed the faint and hungry heathen
With the richness of thy word;
Cleanse the body of this empire
Through the glory of the Lord.

Let All The Multitudes Of Light
F. B. MacNutt, 1873-1949

Let all the multitudes of light,
    Their songs in concert raising,
With earth's triumphal hymns unite.
    The risen Saviour praising.
Ye heavens, his festival proclaim!
    Our King returneth whence he came,
With victory amazing.

For us he bore the bitter tree,
    To death's dark realm descending;
Our foe he slew, and set us free,
    Man's ancient bondage ending.
No more the tyrant's chains oppress;
    O conquering Love! thy name we bless,
With thee to heaven ascending.

Jesus, to thee be endless praise,
    For this thy great salvation;
O holy Father! thine always
    Be thanks and adoration;
Spirit of life and light, to thee
    Eternal praise and glory be;
One God of all creation!

Lord, Who Hast Made Me Free
G. W. Briggs, 1875–1959

Lord, who hast made me free,
Whose hand upholdeth me,
In wondrous love hath found me,
In willing bonds hath bound me;
Nor life nor death for ever
Me from thy love can sever.

O love, how deep, how high,
On cross of shame to die!
Such love can never fail me,
Thy grace shall still avail me;
In life thou wilt uphold me,
In death thine arms enfold me.

My strength is not my own:
I trust in thee alone,
And welcome each to-morrow,
Let it bring joy or sorrow;
For thou art still beside me,
Thy hand will alway guide me.

Lord of my life and guide.
In thee let me abide
Thy way more clearly knowing,
To fuller stature growing,
Till I at last before thee
With eyes unveiled adore thee.

Nearer, My God, To Thee
Sarah Flower Adams, 1841

Nearer, my God, to Thee,
Nearer to Thee!
E'en though it be a cross
That raiseth me;
Still all my song shall be,
Nearer, my God, to Thee,
Nearer to Thee

Though like the wanderer,
The sun gone down,

Darkness be over me,
My rest a stone;
Yet in my dreams I'd be
Nearer, my God, to Thee,
Nearer to Thee!

There let my way appear
Steps unto heaven;
All that Thou sendest me
In mercy given;
Angels to beckon me
Nearer, my God, to Thee,
Nearer to Thee!

Then, with my waking thoughts
Bright with Thy praise,
Out of my stony griefs,
Altars I'll raise;
So by my woes to be
Nearer, my God, to Thee,
Nearer to Thee!

Or, if on joyful wing,
Cleaving the sky,
Sun, moon, and stars forgot,
Upward I fly,
Still all my song shall be
Nearer, my God, to Thee,
Nearer to Thee!

O Come To My Heart, Lord Jesus
Emily E. S. Elliott, 1864

Thou dost reign on high   With a kingly crown,
Yet thou camest to earth for me,
And in Bethlehem's home   Was there found no room
For thy holy nativity:
    O, come to my heart, Lord Jesus,
    There is room in my heart for thee.

Heaven's arches rang   When the angels, sang,
Proclaiming thy royal degree;
But of lowly birth   Didst thou come to earth,
And In great humility:

The foxes found rest, And the birds their nest,
In the shade of the forest tree;
But thy couch was the sod, O thou Son of God,
In the deserts of Galilee:

Thou camest, O Lord, With the living word
That should set thy people free;
But with mocking scorn, And with crown of thorn,
They bore thee to Calvary:

When heav'ns arches shall ring, And her choirs shall sing,
At thy coming to victory,
Let thy voice call me home, Saying "Yet there is room,
There is room at my side for thee."
   And my heart shall rejoice, Lord Jesus,
      When thou comest and callest for me.

O The Deep, Deep Love Of Jesus
Samuel Trevor Francis, 1834-1925

O the deep, deep love of Jesus!
Vast, unmeasured, boundless, free;
Rolling as a mighty ocean
In its fullness over me.
Underneath me, all around me,
Is the current of thy love;
Leading onward, leading homeward,
To thy glorious rest above.

O the deep, deep love of Jesus!
Spread his praise from shore to shore;
How he loveth, ever loveth,
Changeth never, never-more;
How he watches o'er his loved ones,
Died to call them all his own;
How for them he intercedeth,
Watcheth o'er them from the throne.

O, the deep, deep love of Jesus!
Love of ev'ry love the best:
'Tis an ocean vast of blessing,
'Tis a haven sweet of rest.
O the deep, deep love of Jesus!

'Tis a heav'n of heav'ns to me;
And it lifts me up to glory,
 For it lifts me up to thee.

Stand Up, Stand Up For Jesus!
G. Duffield, 1818-88

Stand up, stand up for Jesus!
Ye soldiers of the cross,
Lift high his royal banner;
It must not suffer loss.
From victory unto victory
His army he shall lead,
Till every foe is vanquished,
And Christ is Lord indeed.

Stand up, stand up for Jesus!
The solemn watchword hear:
If while ye sleep he suffers,
Away with shame and fear;
Where'er ye meet with evil,
Within you or without,
Charge for the God of freedom,
And put the foe to rout.

Stand up, stand up for Jesus!
The trumpet call obey:
Forth to the mighty conflict
In this his glorious day.
Ye that are men now serve him
Against unnumbered foes;
Let courage rise with danger,
And strength to strength oppose.

Stand up, stand up for Jesus!
Stand in his strength alone;
The arm of flesh will fail you,
Ye dare not trust your own.
Put on the Gospel armour,
Each piece put on with prayer;
Where duty calls or danger,
Be never wanting there!

Stand up, stand up for Jesus!
The strife will not be long;
This day the noise of battle,
The next the victor's song.
To him that overcometh
A crown of life shall be;
He with the King of Glory,
Shall reign eternally.

This Is My Father's World
Maltbie D. Babcock, 1901

This is my Father's world,   And to my listening ears,
All nature sings, and round me rings   The music of the spheres.
This is my Father's world: I rest me in the thought
Of rocks and trees, of skies and seas;   His hands the wonders wrought.

This is my Father's world,   The birds their carols raise,
The morning light, the lily white,   Declare their Maker's praise.
This is my Father's world: He shines in all that's fair;
In the rustling grass I hear him pass,   He speaks to me everywhere.

This is my Father's world,   O let me ne'er forget
That though the wrong seems oft so strong,   God is the Ruler yet.
This is my Father's world: The battle is not done;
Jesus who died shall be satisfied,   And earth and heav'n be one.

To God Be The Glory
Fanny J. Crosby, 1875

To God be the glory, great things he hath done!
So loved he the world that he gave us his Son,
Who yielded his life an atonement for sin,
And opened the life-gate that we may go in.

Praise the Lord, praise the Lord, Let the earth hear his voice!
Praise the Lord, praise the Lord, Let the people rejoice!
O come to the Father, thro' Jesus the Son
And give him the glory,—great things he hath done!

O perfect redemption, the purchase of blood!
To every believer the promise of God;
The vilest offender who truly believes,
That moment from Jesus forgiveness receives.

Great things he hath taught us, great things he hath done,
And great our rejoicing through Jesus the Son;
But purer, and higher, and greater will be
Our wonder, our transport, when Jesus we see.

Up From The Grave He Arose
Robert Lowry, 1874

Low in the grave he lay—Jesus, my Saviour,
Waiting the coming day—Jesus, my Lord.

Up from the grave he arose!
With a mighty triumph o'er his foes!
He arose a victor from the dark domain,
And he lives for ever with his saints to reign.
He arose! He arose!
Hallelujah! Christ arose.

Vainly they watch his bed—Jesus, my Saviour;
Vainly they seal the dead—Jesus, my Lord.

Death cannot keep his prey—Jesus, my Saviour;
He tore the bars away—Jesus, my Lord.

We Have Not Known Thee As We Ought
Thomas Benson Pollock, 1889

We have not known thee as we ought,
Nor learned thy wisdom, grace, and pow'r;
The things of earth have filled our thought,
And trifles of the passing hour.
Lord, give us light thy truth to see,
And make us wise in knowing thee.

We have not feared thee as we ought,
Nor bowed beneath thine awful eye,
Nor guarded deed, and word, and thought,
Remembering that God was nigh.
Lord, give us faith to know thee near,
And grant the grace of holy fear.

We have not loved thee as we ought,
Nor cared that we are loved by thee;
Thy presence we have coldly sought,

And feebly longed thy face to see.
Lord, give a pure and loving heart
To feel and own the love thou art.

We have not served thee as we ought;
Alas! the duties left undone,
The work with little fervor wrought,
The battles lost, or scarcely won!
Lord, give the zeal, and give the might,
For thee to toil, for thee to fight.

When shall we know thee as we ought,
And fear, and love, and serve aright!
When shall we, out of trial brought,
Be perfect in the land of light!
Lord, may we day by day prepare
To see thy face, and serve thee there.

What A Friend We Have In Jesus
Joseph Scriven, 1855

What a friend we have in Jesus,   All our sins and griefs to bear!
What a privilege to carry   Ev'rything to God in prayer!
O what peace we often forfeit,   O what needless pain we bear,
All because we do not carry   Ev'rything to God in prayer.

Have we trials and temptations?   Is there trouble anywhere?
We should never be discouraged: Take it to the Lord in prayer!
Can we find a friend so faithful,   Who will all our sorrows share?
Jesus knows our every weakness—   Take it to the Lord in prayer!

Are we weak and heavy laden,   Cumbered with a load of care?
Precious Saviour, still our Refuge—   Take it to the Lord in prayer!
Do thy friends despise, forsake thee?   Take it to the Lord in prayer!
In his arms he'll take and shield thee,   Thou wilt find a solace there.

Wonderful Grace Of Jesus
Haldor Lillenas, 1885-?

Wonderful grace of Jesus, Greater than all my sin;
How shall my tongue describe it, Where shall its praise begin?
Taking away my burden, Setting my spirit free;
For the wonderful grace of Jesus reaches me.

Wonderful the matchless grace of Jesus,
Deeper than the mighty rolling sea;
Higher than the mountain, sparkling like a fountain,
All sufficient grace for even me,
Broader than the scope of my transgressions,
Greater far than all my sin and shame,
O magnify the precious name of Jesus,
Praise his Name!

Wonderful grace of Jesus, Reaching a mighty host,
By it I have been pardoned, Saved to the uttermost,
Chains have been torn asunder, Giving me liberty;
For the wonderful grace of Jesus reaches me.

Wonderful grace of Jesus, Reaching the most defiled,
By its transforming power, Making him God's dear child,
Purchasing peace and heaven, For all eternity;
And the wonderful grace of Jesus reaches me.

Chapter Nine

TWENTIETH CENTURY POETRY

1918 - Hopkins's poetry published   1965 - T.S. Eliot dies

One popular view of recent literature and art has it that the twentieth century is divorced from all that went before. In this scenario, World War I inflicted a fatal wound in western culture and World War II administered the *coup de grâce*. Western culture died, and "modern" art and poetry built atop the decaying wreckage. (Some might modify the picture and say modern art and poetry are the decaying wreckage, while the most critical cite them as agents of the wreck and decay.)

Poetry and art are important to a culture, but contrary to the view of poet as ultimate prophet (a vision that has carried over to the twentieth century), spiritual and philosophical values are fundamental to and not products of literary ones.

> T.S. Eliot quotes Jacques Maritain, "By showing us where moral truth and genuine supernatural are situate, religion saves poetry from the absurdity of believing itself destined to transform ethics and life: saves it from overweening arrogance." (*The Use of Poetry and the Use of Criticism*). Furthermore it is an arrogance which paralyzes the poet, for when he has failed as God, he feels that he has failed as poet. (Roseann Miller Trott, *The Isolation of the Imagination in Samuel Johnson and Samuel Taylor Coleridge*, unpub'd paper, Wellesley College, 1971).

The fragmented state of twentieth century art and literature is not the cause, but a result of a "decayed" or "wrecked" culture. The philosophical legacy of the Victorian era (see intro to Victorian section) although itself held together by an often artificial bond of moral affirmation, was a retreat of Christianity on the one hand and the ascendancy of pragmatism on the other hand. If the Victorian era was a period of moral affirmation, the twentieth century has been the opposite. If the Victorian era was a period of reaffirming formal ideals, the twentieth century has been the opposite. If the Victorian era was a time where Christians found their cultural foundations cracking, in the twentieth century full demolition took place.

While nothing has happened in the twentieth century that does not have its roots in earlier periods, most of what has happened in this century has reaffirmed the worst expectations of Christians and many of the aspirations of those "moderns" who believe truth is relative, unknowable, or non-existent.

In the twentieth century, the church completed the Victorian withdrawal to those two strongholds of retreat: the hilltop fortress of the high church—and the underground bunker of the evangelical. Those non-Christian thinkers and poets who longed for a glimpse of enduring truth were left outside to wander among the detritus of what was once Christian culture. For Christian poetry to emerge from such a scenario involves one of three journeys: 1) out of the high bastions, 2) out of the deep caves (never dropping the torch of faith, which is a constant temptation in such a journey), or 3) back along the tortured ways and into the strongholds where the faith has been maintained. In other words, the Christian poet in order to be anything but a provincial voice needs to venture out of safety into the hostile post-Christian culture. The unbelieving twentieth century poet who is hungry for Truth, on the other hand, has had to search out the old and moss-grown paths that lead to Christ.

Poetry, despite the chaotic state of twentieth century "culture" has continued. Literature, although often the harbinger of change among the arts, is in other ways the most conservative of them. Literature has to do with words and words with sense. While words can be (and are) deliberately stripped of sense in much modern poetry, the poet cannot "pull off" what the modern painter or sculptor can. A painting that excludes all elements of meaning (what some call the "referential" aspects of art) may be sold for a grand sum of money and the artist both support himself and draw a great deal of attention to himself, his "philosophy," and his work. For this to happen, the artist needs only a convinced buyer, although usually he has a critic-patron to help do the convincing. A writer, however, must sell his work to a publisher, who is seldom a self-conscious philanthropist, and who, therefore, must sell the book, in turn, to the general reading public. Selling something to one or two wealthy patrons is one thing, but selling something to the public is another. Economic considerations, therefore have kept literature a relatively conservative art. Poetry can afford to be the most "radical" form of literature since poetry is not usually the sole means by which the poet supports himself. Like the modern painter the poet may "create" in the manner he pleases—and has done so, but where economics does not hold the modern poet back, words and sense do.

Hopkins reminded the twentieth century that words could be used for purposes other than strict denotation, but poets have always known this. Poets have always stretched the language, coining words, sharpening them, limbering up syntax, and creating or reducing the structures of formal English. Hopkins may have stretched the bounds of precedent, using some words and phrases purely for their connotations. Certainly his commitment to exact correspondence between poetic images and particular reality was significantly less than that of most poets gone before. Moderns were impressed by this. They were also much taken with a new edition of John Donne's poems, which became available to the twentieth century reader within a few years of the publication of Hopkins's works. What Donne did with startling use of metaphor, Hopkins did with words. As Donne's conjunction of unlikes had offended the more conservative, so did Hopkins'. But neither had subversive motives—neither wished to weaken or deny the sense of language or of reality—rather they wished to refresh poetry with a new and legitimate use of imagery and word with which to depict reality.

Modern critics and poets, however, regarding Truth and Meaning as illusions, began to imitate or extend Hopkins's linguistic liberties to proclaim their new gospel. Modern poetry, like modern art became a race to see who could push his "experiments" farthest toward complete unmeaning, toward a point of none but an existential significance. "Art for art's sake," originally the motto of those who wished to replace a poetry of sentiment and groundless moralism with a poetry of well-crafted form became "a poem should not mean but be" (Archibald MacLeish, *Ars Poetica*, 1926). This was not a sort of sadistic movement to destroy the language or poetry (although some instances make one wonder) but, at least in part, a reaction against the opposite tendency in Victorian times—the tendency toward brave and noble-sounding assertions of things the poet scarcely believed.

> Against all (preceding) accounts of the function of art stands another, which belongs distinctively to the 20th century—the theory of art as form, or formalism. The impact of formalism can best be seen by noting what it was reacting against: art as representative, art as expression, art as a vehicle of truth and knowledge or moral betterment or social improvement.
>
> Formalists do not deny that art is capable of doing these things, but they believe that the true purpose of art is subverted by its being made to do these things. "Art for art's sake, not art for life's sake" is the watchword of formalism. Art is to be enjoyed, to be savoured, for the perception of the intricate arrangements of lines and colours, of musical tones, of words and combinations of these. (*Encyclopedia Britannica*, 10th ed.)

The new emphasis, however, was more and more an abandonment of respect for language as the vehicle for communicating things of significance—as the messenger of meaning.

As twentieth century poetry became self-consciously experimental, poets became less concerned to say anything of universal import, rather they tried to see what poetry could be made into or what, within fashionable limitations, it still could be made to do. This is not to say the modern poet is not serious. Often he writes as though he believed what Oscar Wilde said:

It is through Art, and through Art only, that we can realize our per-
fection; through Art and Art only that we can shield ourselves from
the sordid perils of actual existence. (*The Critic as Artist*, 1891)

If it is possible to summarize twentieth century poetry, then, it is by saying
that twentieth century poetry has been heavily influenced by "formalism," the
idea that the poem's chief significance exists in and of itself, not in relation to
"outer reality"—the poem's form is what matters, far more than its meaning.

Twentieth century poetry is divided into various camps and schools focused
about particular aspects of poetic form. Three "schools" may be distinguished
in post-WWI English poetry. The first school looked back to Walt Whitman,
Gerard Manley Hopkins and the French Symbolists. It's chief poets were Ezra
Pound and T.S. Eliot. In Eliot's early works, the influence of the Symbolists and
the metaphysical poets of the 17th century is clear. . .

in the juxtaposition of not immediately associated images. His
[Eliot's] *Wasteland* (1922) equaled Joyce's *Ulysses* in the revolutionary
effect it had upon young writers of the time. (*New Catholic Encyclopedia*,
1981)

Eliot seems to have been the single most significant twentieth century poet.
By the 1930s, however, some poets, were revolting against what was "bourgeois"
in him.

The second school, which was Marxist in its ideals and therefore wildly
romantic in its vision, included many young poets who had not been involved
in World War I, and who felt the revolution in Russia embodied mankind's
hope, including W. H. Auden, Julian Bell, Cecil Day Lewis, William Empson,
Stephen Spender, and Richard Eberhart. Christopher Isherwood and Louis
MacNeice also became associated with these poets. This "Pylon School" knew
of the Russian situation mainly through journalism and literature. They adopt-
ed the factory machine and the railroad locomotive as their primary symbols.
They tended to swing more to the left as the decade went on, and when the
Spanish Civil War began, many of them (eg., George Orwell) got involved on
behalf of the Marxists. (A few others got involved on the side of Franco, eg.,
Roy Campbell). The horrors of modern warfare combined with the various
intrigues and massacres of that war disillusioned many. When the Soviet Union
carried out its purge trials in 1937 and then signed a non-aggression pact with
Hitler in 1939, disillusionment was complete for almost all. Some, like Auden,
gained the beginnings of a Christian vision out of their romantic betrayal.
(This movement was in many ways like that of the romantics when they became
disillusioned with the French Revolution.)

The third school, the "neo-romantics," arose, partly in reaction to the
Auden or "Pylon School" group. The best known among these is Dylan

Thomas, but it included others like Vernon Watkins and David Gascoyne. They reacted against the impersonalism of the Pylon School, producing poetry that was personal, surreal, and concerned with eschatology or the end of things. Sometimes known as "The Apocalyptics" these poets were also romantic, but on an individual and human level rather than in terms of social values. They looked to Henry Miller and Nicolai Berdyaev as comrades in prose and philosophy. Dylan Thomas brought together personal experience, especially of his native Wales, with Freudian and Biblical imagery in poetry that is dense and subtle, with many-faceted imagery. Correlations are often seen between his and Hopkins's poetry. After Eliot, Thomas was the dominant poetic figure until his death in the 1950s.

In America, Poetry continued to show the worst faults of the Victorian period into the 20th century. Stephen Crane published two volumes of poetry in 1895 and 1899 that signalled a change. He and Edwin Arlington Robinson may be said to be the first American moderns, with Whitman and Emily Dickinson as fore-runners. Robert Frost became the dominant American voice beginning with *North of Boston* in 1914, but although he was modern in his scepticism, he was conservative in style. Frost maintained an illusion of "meaning" and poetic "moral" without any commitment to Truth. Ezra Pound and his disciple, Hilda Doolittle (H.D.), and eventually Amy Lowell made up the "Imagist" school. Pound went on to other experiments. Experiment became the key to American poetry. William Carlos Williams and Marianne Moore experimented as Frost had with dialect-sounding rhythms and words, and with syllabic verse. T.S. Eliot (self-exiled like Pound) while over-shadowing English poetry affected American poetry as well.

Eliot was converted to Christ. His poem "Four Quartets" may be said to commemorate that conversion and is a manifesto of modern poetry as well as of Christian faith. Few other modern Americans expressed anything of their faiths, until the sixties and seventies. Among the exceptions are minor poets who tended to be more declarative than poetic and a few good poets whose works include explicit statements of faith that tend to be subtle.

Other Americans, like Carl Sandburg, Vachel Lindsay, Edgar Lee Masters, and Stephen Vincent Benet looked for subject and styles in the people, places, and language of their fellow Americans, experimenting in the same sense Frost did, using traditional forms and subjects, but avoiding thematic commitments, except in fragmentary and incidental forms.

Some "modern poets," then, concentrate on images—producing distinct and particular metaphors to be strung together by association rather than in relation to a central theme. Some concentrate on the difficult task of constructing poems in which no word positively carries its denotation, or no sentence says anything strictly referring to perceived reality. Eliot and Thomas, for example, while both wrote poems with strong themes, often lead the reader up poetic paths where their footprints become indistinct. The reader who follows carefully may avoid getting lost, but he must take short cuts of his own across parts of the poem's landscape. Other moderns write poems chiefly intending to parody various aspects of traditional poetry—without capitals, without punctuation, without verbs, without any semblance of traditional form. Some write with a certain nostalgia for poems that "meant," but no longer try to convey a theme, rather hint at a single emotion or a particular facet of ennui—poetry of "mood," rather than meaning. Most twentieth century poetry is quite autobiographical and introspective. More than the romantics, modern poets are interested in reporting inner landscapes as much as outer. The romantics still believed experience was universal and communicable. Fewer moderns do.

Christian poets of the twentieth century fall into two general categories: those who followed Hopkins into a modern poetry that retained meaning, and those who continued to model their work on traditional models, with little reference to the modern movement. Of those who followed Hopkins into a modern style, another division may be made—between those who developed their poetic style along with their faith and those who developed their poetic style as secular moderns and came to Christian faith afterward. A great number of poets fall into the last category, including T.S. Eliot and W. H. Auden. Some twentieth century poets, like C. S. Lewis, through a literary education, tended toward the traditional before they came to faith, and some Christians, like Charles Williams, after failing in more traditional styles, found their true metier in modern poetic techniques.

Eliots's, Lewis's, and to some degree Auden's spiritual progresses may be traced in their poetry. Like the Metaphysical poets of the seventeenth century, twentieth century Christian poets reveal much of themselves.

The present state of Christian poetry is the next step, as it were, in a very long and continuous tradition. Despite the "modern" claim that the tradition is dead, the modern movement itself is part of something very much alive. While most contemporary Christian poets still follow in the train of Hopkins and Eliot, there is room for the spiral to continue, for old approaches to poetry to be revived and modified and for new approaches to be subjected to the old. God's glory remains the object of Christian poetry, an ever ancient and continually fresh sacrifice of praise.

A Brief Chronology of the First Half of the Twentieth Century

1911	John Masefield's *Everlasting Mercy* published
1917	T.S. Eliot's *Prufrock and Other Observations* published
	Russian Revolution begins
1918	World War I ends

Hopkins's poetry published by Bridges (Hopkins d. 1889)
1922   Eliot's *Wasteland* published
1930   Masefield succeeds Robert Bridges as poet laureate
           Eliot's *Ash Wednesday* published
1934   Elizabeth Scott Stam executed by Chinese Communists
1935–1943 Eliot's *Four Quartets* published
1939   World War II begins
1942   C. S. Lewis's *Screwtape Letters* published
           Pearl Harbor attacked, United States enters World War II
1945   World War II ends
1946   W. H. Auden emigrates to the United States
           Dylan Thomas' *Deaths and Entrances* published
1948   Eliot receives Nobel Prize for Literature
1950   Beginning of Korean Conflict
1952   John Donne's *Divine Poems* (re-)published
1953   Dylan Thomas dies
1954   C. S. Lewis becomes Professor of Medieval and Renaissance Literature at Cambridge
1963   President Kennedy assassinated, C. S. Lewis dies
1965   T.S. Eliot dies

MASEFIELD, JOHN (1878–1967), educated at King's School, Warwick, went as apprentice aboard a sailing ship that went around Cape Horn. He lived in the United States for several years after that, working in a factory, after which he returned to England and worked as a journalist. In 1902 he published his best-known verse in *Salt-Water Ballads,* which includes "Sea Fever" and "Cargoes," frequently found in school anthologies. His long narrative poem, *The Everlasting Mercy,* published in 1911, was written in strikingly colloquial English and is the story of a brawler's conversion. He published two poetic dramas, *The Tragedy of Nan* (1909) and *The Tragedy of Pompey The Great* (1910). Masefield's other long narrative poems, including *Dauber* (1913) and *Reynard the Fox* (1919), do not seem to reach the standard set by *The Everlasting Mercy.* He wrote several novels of adventure, *Sard Harker* (1924), *Odtaa* (1926), and *Basilissa* (1940). In 1930 he succeeded Robert Bridges as the fifteenth poet laureate of England. His two autobiographical works are *In the Mill* (1941) and *So Long To Learn* (1952). His writing is both sentimental and vigorous, elements that lend a measure of balance to the whole. Sadly his latter works are void of the faith that seemed so vigorous in *The Everlasting Mercy.* His unbelief is extreme in his last sonnet, which says "There is no God, but we who breathe the air,/Are God ourselves and touch God everywhere."

Excerpts from The Everlasting Mercy

From '41 to '51
I was my folk's contrary son;
I bit my father's hand right through
And broke my mother's heart in two.
I sometimes go without my dinner
Now that I know the times I've gi'n her.

From '51 to '61
I cut my teeth and took to fun.
I learned what not to be afraid of
And what stuff women's lips are made of;
I learned with what a rosy feeling
Good ale makes floors seem like the ceiling,
And how the moon gives shiny light
To lads as roll home singing by't.

From '61 to '67
I lived in disbelief of Heaven.
I drunk, I fought, I poached, I whored,
I did despite unto the Lord.
I cursed, 'would make a man look pale,
And nineteen times I went to gaol.

    •   •   •   •

I opened the window wide and leaned
Out of the pigstye of that fiend
And felt a cool wind go like grace
About the sleeping market-place.
The clock struck three, and sweetly, slowly,
The bells, chimed Holy, Holy, Holy;
And in a second's pause there fell
The cold note of the chapel bell,
And then a cock crew, flapping wings
And summat made me think of things.
How long those ticking clocks had gone
From church and chapel, on and on,
Ticking the time out, ticking slow
To men and girls who'd come and go,
And how they ticked in belfry dark
When half the town was bishop's park,
And how they'd rung a chime full tilt
The night after the church was built,

And how that night was Lamberts' Feast,
The night I'd fought and been a beast.
And how a change had come. And then
I thought, "you tick the different men."

What with fight and what with drinking
And being alone there thinking
My mind began to carp and tetter,
"If this life's all, the beasts are better."
And then I thought, "I wish I'd seen
The many towns this town has been;
I wish I knew if they'd a-got
A kind of summat we've a-not,
If them as built the church so fair
Were half the chaps folk say they were;
For they'd the skill to draw their plan,
And skill's a joy to any man;
And they'd the strength, not skill alone,
To build it beautiful in stone;
And strength and skill together thus
O, they were happier men than us.

But if they were, they had to die
The same as every one and I.
And no one lives again, but dies,
And all the bright goes out of eyes,
And all the skill goes out of hands,
And all the wise brain understands,
And all the beauty, all the power
Is cut down like a withered flower.
In all the show from birth to rest
I give the poor dumb cattle best."

I wondered, then, why life should be,
And what would be the end of me
When youth and health and strength were gone
And cold old age came creeping on?
A keeper's gun? The Union ward?
Or that new quod at Hereford?
And looking round I felt disgust
At all the nights of drink and lust,
And all the looks of all the swine
Who'd said that they were friends of mine;

And yet I knew, when morning came,
The morning would be just the same,
For I'd have drinks and Jane would meet me
And drunken Silas Jones would greet me,
And I'd risk quod and the keeper's gun
Till all the silly game was done.
"For parson chaps are mad, supposin'
A chap can change the road he's chosen."

    •   •   •   •

O Christ who holds the open gate,
O Christ who drives the furrow straight,
O Christ, the plough, O Christ, the laughter,
Of holy white birds flying after,
Lo, all my heart's field red and torn,
And Thou wilt bring young green corn,
The young green corn divinely springing,
The young green corn forever singing;
And when the field is fresh and fair
Thy blessed feet shall glitter there,
And we will walk the weeded field,
And tell the golden harvest's yield,
The corn that makes the holy bread
By which the soul of man is fed,
The holy bread, the food unpriced,
Thy everlasting mercy, Christ.

    •   •   •   •

How swift the summer goes,
Forget-me-not, pink, rose.
The young grass when I started
And now the hay is carted,
And now my song is ended,
And all the summer spended;
The blackbird's second brood
Routs beech leaves in the wood;
The pink and rose have speeded,
Forget-me-not has seeded.
Only the winds that blew,
The rain that makes things new,
The earth that hides things old,
And blessings manifold.

O lovely lily clean,
O lily springing green,

O lily bursting white,
Dear lily of delight,
Spring in my heart agen
That I may flower to men.

NOYES, ALFRED (1880–1959) was educated for a time at Oxford University. After leaving university, he went to sea and began his writing career with *The Loom of Years* (1902), followed steadily all his life by other volumes of poetry. He apparently supported himself successfully with his verse, which was published in at least thirteen volumes, including *Poems* (1904), *Drake, an English Epic* (2 volumes 1906-08), *Tales of the Mermaid Tavern* (1913), and *The Torchbearers* (a trilogy on the progress of science, 1922–30). His best known poem is "The Highwayman." He also wrote criticism, *Some Aspects Of Modern Poetry* (1924), and *The Opalescent Parrot* (1929), some short stories, a novel, and a controversial biography of Voltaire. After his second marriage, he became a Roman Catholic (1925), which he describes in *The Unknown God*. His poetry is traditional and mildly sentimental. *The Edge of the Abyss* is a call for a return to Christian philosophy.

Resurrection

When all the altar lights were dead,
And mockery choked the world's desire;
When every faith on earth had fled,
A spirit rose on wings of fire.

He rose and sang. I never heard
A song of such ecstatic breath;
And, though I caught no throbbing word,
I knew that he had conquered death.

He sang no comfortable things;
But as a shaft had pierced him through;
And dark stain between his wings
Grew darker as the glory grew.

He sang the agonies of loss;
Of farewells, and love's last kiss.
He sang in heaven as on a cross,
A spirit crucified with bliss.

Over these ruined shrines he rose,
These crumbling graves where all men grope!

Racked by the universal throes,
And singing the eternal hope.

The Double Fortress

Time, wouldst thou hurt us? Never shall we grow old.
Break as thou wilt these bodies of blind clay,
Thou canst not touch us here, in our stronghold,
Where two, made one, laugh all thy powers away.

Though ramparts crumble and rusty gates grow thin,
And our brave fortress divine to a hollow shell,
Thou shalt hear heavenly laughter, far within,
Where, young as Love, two hidden lovers dwell.

We shall go clambering our twisted stairs
To watch the moon through rifts in our grey towers.
Thou shalt hear whispers, kisses, and sweet prayers
Creeping through all our creviced walls like flowers.

Wouldst wreck us, Time? When thy dull leaguer brings
The last wall down, look heavenward. We have wings

The Anvil

Stand like a beaten anvil, when thy dream
Is laid upon thee, golden from the fire.
Flinch not, though heavily through that furnace-gleam
The black forge-hammers fall on thy desire.

Demoniac giants round thee seem to loom.
'Tis but the world-smiths heaving to and fro.
Stand like a beaten anvil. Take the doom
Their ponderous weapons deal thee, blow on blow.

Needful to truth as dew-fall to the flower
Is this wild wrath and this implacable scorn.
For every pang, new beauty, and new power,
Burning blood-red shall on thy heart be born.
Stand like a beaten anvil. Let earth's wrong
Beat on that iron and ring back in song.

Night Journey

Thou who never canst err, for Thyself art the Way,
Thou whose infinite kingdom is flooded with day;
Thou whose eyes behold all, for Thyself art the Light,
Look down on us gently who journey by night.

By the pity revealed in Thy loneliest hour
Forsaken, self-bound and self emptied of power,
Thou who even in death hadst all heaven in sight,
Look down on us gently who journey by night.

On the road to Emmaus they thought Thou wast dead,
Yet they saw Thee and knew in the breaking of bread.
Though the day was far spent, in Thy face there was light.
Look down on us gently who journey by night.

KELLER, HELEN ADAMS (1880–1968) was born in Alabama and at the age of two became both deaf and blind as a result of a severe illness. When she was seven, Anne Sullivan (Mrs. John A. Macy) of the Perkins Institute of the Blind became her tutor and taught her sign language and braille. In 1890 she learned to speak through the teaching of Sarah Fuller of the Horace Mann school. Keller went to preparatory school in Boston and entered Radcliffe College (1900) from which she graduated with honors in 1904. She served thereafter on the Massachusetts Commission for the Blind and many other platforms in behalf of people with disabilities. Her autobiography, *Story of My Life*, was published in 1903. She also wrote *Optimism* (1903), *The World I Live In* (1908), *Song of the Stone Wall* (1910), *Out of the Dark* (1913), and *Midstream—My Later Life* (1929). Helen Keller spoke to men blinded in both world wars. She spoke with presidents Roosevelt and Eisenhower, with Mark Twain, Enrico Caruso, Jascha Heifetz, and Carl Sandburg. Up into her seventies she travelled around the world speaking and encouraging others.

In The Garden Of The Lord

The word of God came unto me,
Sitting alone among the multitudes;
And my blind eyes were touched with light.
And there was laid upon my lips a flame of fire.

I laugh and shout for life is good,
Though my feet are set in silent ways.

In merry mood I leave the crowd
To walk in my garden. Ever as I walk
I gather fruits and flowers in my hands.
And with joyful heart I bless the sun
That kindles all the place with radiant life.
I run with playful winds that blow the scent

Of rose and jessamine in eddying whirls.
At last I come where tall lilies grow,
Lifting their faces like white saints to God.
While the lilies pray, I kneel upon the ground;
I have strayed into the holy temple of the Lord.

ROPE, HENRY E. G. (EDWARD GEORGE) (1880–1978) was born in Shrewsbury, England, attended Shrewsbury School, Oxford (Christ Church), and Beda College, Rome. He worked as an editorial assistant on the *Oxford English Dictionary* and lectured in English at the University of Breslau, Germany, before being ordained a priest in the Roman Catholic Church (1915). He served as a curate and chaplain for many years before becoming archivist of the Venerable English College in Rome. His prose works include *Flee to the Fields* (1934); *Fisher and More* (1935); and *The Schola Saxonum, the Hospital and the English College in Rome* (1951). His books of poetry include: *Religionis Ancilla* (1916), *Soul's Belfry* (1919); *The City of the Grail* (1923); *The Hills of Home* (1925); and *Dream Holiday* (1964).

The Wasted Years

The wasted years, the wasted years,
No purpose firm, no contrite tears
Can ever bring to me again
The wasted years, the squandered grain.

The wasted years, the wasted years,
The source of looming, frowning fears,
Pursue me, threatening to bear
My foolish soul unto despair.

The wasted days, the wasted days,
A storm of dust along the ways,
Vain, devastating, venom-fraught,
The busy pursuance of naught;

The wasted hours, the wasted hours,
Of sinful thoughts and squander'd powers
The wasted moments millionfold,
The wasted dower of grace untold;

The certain death, the nearing doom
The crucifix dispels the gloom,
From wanhope and mistrust doth keep
The prodigal, the hundredth sheep.

The City of the Grail

Where lies the city of the Holy Grail,
And who will guide me thither?
For spent with sorrow, oft at point to fail
The heart doth sink, the holy purpose wither.

Where shall I find the city, by what token
Know her for Heaven's chosen,
Way-weary oftentimes and nigh heart-broken,
Beset with robber fiends that lure and cozen?

The city high-uplifted o'er the plain,
Dawn-girdled, starry-crown'd,
Whose bells sink down upon the world like rain—
In this sad fleeting world may she be found?

ANGEL: The city of the Grail abides in Heaven,
With sorrow unacquainted,
Yet many a foreglimpse on this earth is given,
This earth so many-troubled, many-sainted.

The city of the Grail is God's own palace,
And needs not sun or moon,
But manifold amid earth's recreant malice
Reflections of her mirror'd light are strewn.

Dear child, how oft beside me hast thou stept
To these most holy places,
And oftentimes the heart within thee leapt
Born on the wave of high accepted graces.

How many a belfried eyrie saw we lifted
Rock-pillar'd in the sky,

Forth-gazing like a watchtower o'er the rifted
Brave mountain-heart of elder Italy,

And Norman river-valleys husht at even,
And Kerry's haunted shore—
To win thee forward were these shadows
Until the light shall dawn for evermore.

O'DONNELL, CHARLES L. (1884–1934) was born in Indiana and studied at Notre Dame, Holy Cross, Harvard, and Catholic University. He was ordained a priest in the Roman Catholic Church (1910) and, after teaching English there for eighteen years, was made president of Notre Dame (1928). His prose writing included *Newman's Gentleman* (1916). His books of poetry are *The Dead Musician and Other Poems* (1916), *Cloister and Other Poems* (1922), and *A Rime of the Rood and Other Poems* (1928). He edited *Notre Dame Verse* (1917).

Resolution

Love, You have struck me straight, my Lord!
Past innocence, past guilt,
I carry in my soul the sword
You buried to the hilt.

And though to eyes in terrible pain
Heaven and earth may reel,
For fear You may not strike again
I will not draw the steel.

Security

Outwit me, Lord, if ever hence
This unremembering brain
Should urge these most inconstant feet
To quit Thy side again.

Be not too sure of me though death
Still find me at Thy side,—
Let Pain, Thy soldier, break my legs
Before I shall have died.

And when at length this heart is stopped,
Leave not a final chance,
But send some kind centurion,
An expert with the lance.

Process

The seed, Lord, falls on stony ground
Which sun and rain can never bless—
Until the soil is broken found—
With harvest fruitfulness.

Plow then the rock, and plow again,
That so some blade of good may start,
After the searching share of pain
Has cut a furrow through my heart.

WYLIE, ELINOR (HOYT) (1885–1928), an American poet, noted also for her novels, anonymously published her first book of poetry, *Incidental Numbers* (1912). Thereafter, she published under her own name and won a prize for her *Nets to Catch the Wind* (1921). (The title was taken from the seventeenth century poem "The Devil's Law Case" by John Webster.) Having married Philip Hichborn in 1905, she left him and eloped with Horace Wylie in 1910, marrying Wylie after Hichborn's death in 1915. They were divorced in 1921 and in 1925 she married the poet William Rose Benet. Her other books of poetry include *Black Armour* (1923), *Trivial Breath* (1928), and *Angels and Earthly Creatures* (sonnets, 1929). Apparently influenced by Elizabethan and metaphysical poetry, her poems are noted for sharp but subtle imagery and thematic irony. Her novels include *Jennifer Lorn* (1923), *The Venetian Glass Nephew* (1925), *The Orphan Angel* (*Mortal Image*, England) (1926), and *Mr. Hodge and Mr. Hazard* (1928). Benet edited *Collected Poems of Elinor Wylie* (1932) and *Last Poems of Elinor Wylie* were published in 1942–43.

King Honour's Eldest Son

His father's steel, piercing the wholesome fruit
Of his mother's flesh, wrought acidly to mar
Its own Damascus, staining worse than war
A purity intense and absolute;
While her clean stock put forth a poisoned shoot,
In likeness of a twisted scimitar,
Sleek as a lovelock, ugly as a scar,
Wrong as the firstborn of a mandrake root.

There was a waning moon upon his brow,
A fallen star upon his pointed chin;
He mingled Ariel with Caliban,
But such a blossom upon such a bough

Convinced his poor progenitors of sin
In having made a something more than man.

A Crowded Trolley Car

The rain's cold grains are silver-gray
Sharp as golden sands,
A bell is clanging, people sway
Hanging by their hands.

Supple hands, or gnarled and stiff,
Snatch and catch and grope;
That face is yellow-pale, as if
The fellow swung from rope.

Dull like pebbles, sharp like knives,
Glances strike and glare,
Fingers tangle, Bluebeard's wives
Dangle by the hair.

Orchard of the strangest fruits
Hanging from the skies;
Brothers, yet insensate brutes
Who fear each other's eyes.

One man stands as free men stand,
As if his soul might be
Brave, unbroken; see his hand
Nailed to an oaken tree.

Twelfth Night

It has always been King Herod that I feared;
King Herod and his kinsmen, ever since. . . .
I do not like the colour of your beard;
I think that you are wicked, and a prince.

I keep no stable . . . how your horses stamp!. . .
If you are wise men, you will leave me soon;
I have been frightened by a thievish tramp
Who counted bloody silver in the moon.

You get no lodging underneath these roofs,
No, though you pay in frankincense and myrrh;

Your harness jangles with your horses' hooves;
Be quiet; you will wake him if you stir.

This is no church for Zoroastrians,
Nor resting-place for governors from Rome;
Oh, I have knowledge of your secret plans;
Your faces are familiar; go home.

And you, young captain of the lion stare,
Subdue your arrogance to this advice;
You should forbid your soldiery to swear,
To spit at felons, and to play at dice.

You have perceived, above the chimney ledge,
Hanging inverted by Saint David's harp
His sword from heaven, with the double edge
Which, for your service, is no longer sharp.

He sleeps, like some ingenuous shepherd boy
Or carpenter's apprentice, but his slim
And wounded hands shall never more destroy
Another giant; do not waken him.

The counterpane conceals the deeper wound
Which lately I have washed with vinegar;
Now let this iron bar be importuned;
I say you shall not speak to him of war.

Doomsday

The end of everything approaches;
I hear it coming
Loud as the wheels of painted coaches
On turnpikes drumming;
Loud as the pomp of plumy hearses,
Or pennoned charges;
Loud as when every oar reverses
Venetian barges;
Loud as the caves of covered bridges
Fulfilled with rumble
Of hooves; and loud as cloudy ridges
When glaciers tumble;
Like creeping thunder this continues
Diffused and distant,

Loud in our ears and in our sinews,
Insane, insistent;
Loud as a lion scorning carrion
Further and further;
Loud as the ultimate loud clarion
Or the first murther.

ELIOT, T.S. (THOMAS STEARNES) (1888–1965), perhaps the best known modern poet writing in English, was born and raised in St. Louis, Missouri, but was also, by temperament, education, and ancestry, a New Englander. He studied at Harvard, then went to England where he worked as a teacher, bank clerk, editor and critic. He studied at Oxford and the Sorbonne. Eliot published *Prufrock and Other Observations* in 1917 and *Poems* in 1919. *The Waste Land* (1922) brought him wide recognition. He was editor of a critical review, *The Criterion,* and became a director of the publishing house Faber and Faber. In 1927 he converted to the Anglican faith and became a British citizen. *Ash Wednesday* (1930) and *Four Quartets* (1935-1943) are his other major poetical works. He published a great deal of critical writing, including *The Sacred Wood* (1920) and *To Criticize the Critic* (1965). His book, *On Poetry and Poets* (1957) and his essays on John Donne and on tradition are well known expositions of his philosophy of poetry. He wrote a number of plays, including *Murder in the Cathedral* (1935), *Family Reunion* (1939), and *The Cocktail Party* (1950). In 1948 he was awarded the Nobel Prize in Literature. Although he was a "modern" in that his allusions and metaphors are complex and not always clearly referential, he did much to promote classical standards (poetry as an intellectual experience as well as an experience of the sensibilities) and helped revive interest in six-teenth and seventeenth century poetry. Two of his philosophical works, *The Idea of a Christian Society* and *Notes towards the Definition of Culture,* were published in one volume, *Christianity and Culture,* in 1968.

Canto IV From Little Gidding

The dove descending breaks the air
With flame of incandescent terror
Of which the tongues declare
The one discharge from sin and error.
The only hope, or else despair
Lies in the choice of pyre or pyre—
To be redeemed from fire by fire.

Who then devised the torment? Love.
Love is the unfamiliar Name

Behind the hands that wove
The intolerable shirt of flame
Which human power cannot remove,
We only live, only suspire
Consumed by either fire or fire.

Canto I From **Ash-Wednesday**

Because I do not hope to turn again
Because I do not hope
Because I do not hope to turn
Desiring this man's gift and that man's scope
I no longer strive to strive towards such things
(Why should the aged eagle stretch its wings?)
Why should I mourn
The vanished power of the usual reign?

Because I do not hope to know again
The infirm glory of the positive hour
Because I do not think
Because I know I shall not know
The one veritable transitory power
Because I cannot drink
There, where trees flower, and springs flow, for there is
    nothing again

Because I know that time is always time
And place is always and only place
And what is actual is actual only for one time
And only for one place
I rejoice that things are as they are and
I renounce the blessed face
And renounce the voice
Because I cannot hope to turn again
Consequently I rejoice, having to construct something
Upon which to rejoice

And pray to God to have mercy upon us
And I pray that I may forget
These matters that with myself I too much discuss
Too much explain
Because I do not hope to turn again
Let these words answer

For what is done, not to be done again
May the judgement not be too heavy upon us

Because these wings are no longer wings to fly
But merely vans to beat the air
The air which is now thoroughly small and dry
Smaller and dryer than the will
Teach us to care and not to care
Teach us to sit still.

Pray for us sinners now and at the hour of our death
Pray for us now and at the hour of our death.

Section VI of Choruses from "The Rock"

It is hard for those who have never known persecution,
And who have never known a Christian,
To believe these tales of Christian persecution.
It is hard for those who live near a Bank
To doubt the security of their money.
It is hard for those who live near a Police Station
To believe in the triumph of violence.
Do you think that the Faith has conquered the World
And that lions no longer need keepers?
Do you need to be told that whatever has been, can still be?
Do you need to be told that even such modest attainments
As you can boast in the way of polite society
Will hardly survive the Faith to which they owe their
                    significance?
Men! polish your teeth on rising and retiring;
Women! polish your fingernails:
You polish the tooth of the dog and the talon of the cat.
Why should men love the Church? Why should they love her laws?
She tells them of Life and Death, and of all that they would forget.
She is tender where they would be hard, and hard where they like to
        be soft.
She tells them of Evil and Sin, and other unpleasant facts.
They constantly try to escape
From the darkness outside and within
By dreaming of systems so perfect that no one will need to be good.
But the man that is will shadow
The man that pretends to be.
And the Son of Man was not crucified once for all,

The blood of the martyrs not shed once for all,
The lives of the Saints not given once for all:
But the Son of Man is crucified always
And there shall be Martyrs and Saints.
And if blood of Martyrs is to flow on the steps
We must first build the steps;
And if the Temple is to be cast down
We must first build the Temple.

Excerpt from Section X of Choruses from **"The Rock"**

O Light Invisible, we praise Thee!
Too bright for mortal vision.
O Greater Light, we praise Thee for the less;
The eastern light our spires touch at morning,
The light that slants upon our western doors at evening,
The twilight over stagnant pools at batflight,
Moon light and star light, owl and moth light,
Glow-worm glowlight on a grassblade.
O Light Invisible, we worship Thee!

We thank Thee for the lights that we have kindled,
The light of altar and of sanctuary;
Small lights of those who meditate at midnight
And lights directed through the coloured panes of windows
And light reflected from the polished stone,
The gilded carven wood, the coloured fresco.
Our gaze is submarine, our eyes look upward
And see the light that fractures through unquiet water.
We see the light but see not whence it comes.
O Light Invisible, we glorify Thee!

The Hippopotamus

Similiter et omnes reveantur Diaconos, ut mandatum Jesu Christi; et Episcopum, ut Jesum Christum, existentem filium Patris; Presbyteros autem, ut concilium Dei et conjunctionem Apostolorum. sine his Ecclesia non vocatur; de quibus suadeo vos sic habeo.
S. Ignatii Ad Trallianos

And when this epistle is read among you, cause that it be read also in the church of the Laodiceans.

The broad-backed hippopotamus
Rests on his belly in the mud;

Although he seems so firm to us
He is merely flesh and blood.

Flesh and blood is weak and frail,
Susceptible to nervous shocks;
While the True Church can never fail
For it is based upon a rock.

The hippo's feeble steps may err
In compassing material ends,
While the True Church need never stir
To gather in its dividends.

The 'potamus can never reach
The mango on the mango-tree;
But fruits of pomegranate and peach
Refresh the Church from over the sea.

At mating time the hippo's voice
Betrays inflexions hoarse and odd,
But every week we hear rejoice
The Church, at being one with God.

The hippopotamus's day
Is passed in sleep; at night he hunts;
God works in a mysterious way—
The Church can sleep and feed at once.

I saw the 'potamus take wing
Ascending from the damp savannas,
And quiring angels round him sing
The praise of God, in loud hosannas.

Blood of the Lamb shall wash him clean
And him shall heavenly arms enfold,
Among the saints he shall be seen
Performing on a harp of gold.

He shall be washed as white as snow,
By all the martyr'd virgins kist,
While the True Church remains below
Wrapt in the old miasmal mist.

There Shall Always Be The Church

There shall always be the Church and the World
And the Heart of Man
Shivering and fluttering between them, choosing and chosen,
Valiant, ignoble, dark and full of light
Swinging between Hell Gate and Heaven Gate.
And the Gates of Hell shall not prevail.

LINDSAY, RUTH TEMPLE

The Hunters

'The Devil, as a roaring lion, goeth about seeking whom he may devour.'

The Lion, he prowleth far and near,
Nor swerves for pain or rue;
He heedeth nought of sloth nor fear,
He prowleth—prowleth through
The silent glade and the weary street,
In the empty dark and the full noon heat;
And a little Lamb with aching Feet—
He prowleth too.

The Lion croucheth alert, apart—
With patience doth he woo;
He waiteth long by the shuttered heart,
And the Lamb—He waiteth too.
Up the lurid passes of dreams that kill,
Through the twisting maze of the great Untrue,
The Lion followeth the fainting will—
And the Lamb—He followeth too.

From the thickets dim of the hidden way
Where the debts of Hell accrue,
The Lion leapeth upon his prey:
But the Lamb—He leapeth too.
Ah! loose the leash of the sins that damn,
Mark Devil and God as goals,
In the panting love of a famished Lamb,
Gone mad with the need of souls.

The Lion, he strayeth near and far;
What heights hath he left untrod?

He crawleth nigh to the purest star,
On the trail of the saints of God.
And throughout the darkness of things unclean,
In the depths where the sin-ghouls brood,
There prowleth ever with yearning mien—
A Lamb as white as Blood!

SHOVE, FREDEGOND (1889–1949) was the daughter of the historian F. W. Maitland, Fellow of Trinity College, Cambridge, and Professor of English Law, whose widow married Charles Darwin's son Francis. Fredegond thus became step-sister to Bernard Darwin and Frances Cornford. She married Gerald Shove, a Cambridge classical scholar, and spent most of her life in or near the University. Her collected works were published as *Poems* in 1956.

The New Ghost

'And he casting away his garment rose and came Jesus.'

And he cast it down, down, on the green grass,
Over the young crocuses, where the dew was—
He cast the garment of his flesh that was full of death,
And like sword his spirit showed out of the cold sheath.

He went a pace or two, he went to meet his Lord,
And, as I said, his spirit looked like a clean sword,
And seeing him the naked trees began shivering,
And all the birds cried out aloud as it were late spring.

And the Lord came on, He came down, and saw
That a soul was waiting there for Him, one without flaw,
And they embraced in the churchyard where the robins play,
And the daffodils hang their heads, as they burn away.

The Lord held his head fast, and you could see
He kissed the unsheathed ghost that was gone free—
As a hot sun, on a March day, kisses the cold ground;
And the spirit answered, for he knew well that his peace was found.

The spirit trembled, and sprang up at the Lord's word—
As on a wild, April day, springs up a small bird—
So the ghost's feet lifting him up, he kissed the Lord's cheek
And for the greatness of their love neither of them could speak.

But the Lord went then, to show him the way,
Over the young crocuses, under the green may
That was not quite in flower yet—to a far-distant land;
And the ghost followed, like a naked cloud holding the sun's hand.

The Farmer

I see a farmer walking by himself
In the ploughed field, returning like the day
To his dark nest. The plovers circle round
In the gray sky; the blackbird calls; the thrush
Still sings-but all the rest have gone to sleep.
I see the farmer coming up the field,
Where the new corn is sown, but not yet sprung;
He seems to be the only man alive
And thinking through the twilight of this world.
I know that there is war behind those hills,
And I surmise, but cannot see the dead,
And cannot see the living in their midst—
So awfully and madly knit with death.
I cannot feel, but know that there is war,
And has been now for three eternal years,
Behind the subtle cinctures of those hills.
I see the farmer coming up the field,
And as I look, imagination lifts
The sullen veil of alternating cloud,
And I am stunned by what I see behind
His solemn and uncompromising form:
Wide hosts of men who once could walk like him
In freedom, quite alone with night and day,
Uncounted shapes of living flesh and bone,
Worn-dull, quenched dry, gone blind and sick, with war;
And they are him and he is one with them;
They see him as he travels up the field.
O God, how lonely freedom seems today!
O single farmer walking through the world,
They bless the seed in you that earth shall reap,
When they, their countless lives, and all their thoughts,
Lie scattered by the storm: when peace shall come
With stillness, and long shivers, after death.

LEWIS, C. S. (CLIVE STAPLES) (1898–1963), student at Campbell College, Belfast, World War I ambulance driver, and graduate of Oxford University, where he was a Fellow for thirty years, became Professor of Medieval and Renaissance English at Cambridge in 1954. Like his friend, J. R. R. Tolkien, he was a scholar, but he is best known for popular works such as *Screwtape Letters,* published in 1942. Lewis had previously published *Out of the Silent Planet* (1938), and subsequently *Perelandra* (1943) and *That Hideous Strength* (1945), which comprise a science fiction trilogy. His fictional tale of a bus-trip from hell to heaven, *The Great Divorce,* is another popular work. *Till We Have Faces,* which he once cited as the best of his fictional works, was published in 1956. His critical works include *Allegory of Love* (1936) and *Preface to Paradise Lost* (1942). His popular Christian apologetical books include *Mere Christianity* and *The Four Loves.* Lewis also wrote a popular philological book, *Studies in Words* (1960). Most widely read of all his works are the "Narnia Books," seven books for children (of all ages), which are set in the mysterious land of Narnia. Lewis has probably had more literary and apologetic effect than any other twentieth century Christian, with the possible exception of Solzhenitsyn. His writings continue to be popular among a wide range of readers. He wrote with a light-heartedness that lends credence to his fierce logic and firm faith. His poems may be found in *Poems: C. S. Lewis* (1964) and *C. S. Lewis: Narrative Poems* (1969).

On A Theme From Nicolas Of Cusa
(De Docta Ignorantia, III. ix.)

When soul and body feed, one sees
Their differing physiologies.
Firmness of apple, fluted shape
Of celery, or tight-skinned grape
I grind and mangle when I eat,
Then in dark, salt, internal heat,
Annihilate their natures by
The very act that makes them I.

But when the soul partakes of good
Or truth, which are her savoury food,
By some far subtler chemistry
It is not they that change, but she,
Who feels them enter with the state
Of conquerors her opened gate,
Or, mirror-like, digests their ray
By turning luminous as they.

Reason

Set on the soul's acropolis the reason stands
A virgin, arm'd, commercing with celestial light,
And he who sins against her has defiled his own
Virginity: no cleansing makes his garment white;
So clear is reason. But how dark, imagining,
Warm, dark, obscure and infinite, daughter of Night:
Dark is her brow, the beauty of her eyes with sleep
Is loaded and her pains are long, and her delight.
Tempt not Athene. Wound not in her fertile pains
Demeter, nor rebel against her mother-right.
Oh who will reconcile in me both maid and mother,
Who make in me a concord of the depth and height?
Who make imagination's dim exploring touch
Ever report the same as intellectual sight?
Then could I truly say, and not deceive,
Then wholly say, that I B E L I E V E.

Prayer

Master, they say that when I seem
    To be in speech with you,
Since you make no replies, it's all a dream
    —One talker aping two.

They are half right, but not as they
    Imagine; rather, I
Seek in myself the things I meant to say,
    And lo! the wells are dry.

Then, seeing me empty, you forsake
    The Listener's role, and through
My dead lips breathe and into utterance wake
    The thoughts I never knew.

And thus you neither need reply
    Nor can; thus, while we seem
Two talking, thou art One forever, and I
    No dreamer, but thy dream.

Stephen To Lazarus

But was I the first martyr, who
Gave up no more than life, while you,
Already free among the dead,
Your rags stripped off, your fetters shed,
Surrendered what all other men
Irrevocably keep, and when
Your battered ship at anchor lay
Seemingly safe in the dark bay
No ripple stirs, obediently
Put out a second time to sea
Well knowing that your death (in vain
Died once) must all be died again?

The Apologist's Evening Prayer

From all my lame defeats and oh! much more
From all the victories that I seemed to score;
From cleverness shot forth on Thy behalf
At which, while angels weep, the audience laugh;
From all my proofs of Thy divinity,
Thou who wouldst give no sign, deliver me.

Thoughts are but coins. Let me not trust, instead
Of Thee, their thin-worn image of Thy head.
From all my thoughts, even from my thoughts of Thee,
O thou fair Silence, fall, and set me free.
Lord of the narrow gate and the needle's eye,
Take from me all my trumpery lest I die.

After Prayers, Lie Cold

Arise my body, my small body, we have striven
Enough, and He is merciful; we are forgiven.
Arise small body, puppet-like and pale, and go,
White as the bedclothes into bed, and cold as snow,
Undress with small, cold fingers and put out the light,
And be alone, hush'd mortal, in the sacred night,
—A meadow whipt flat with the rain, a cup
Emptied and clean, a garment washed and folded up,
Faded in colour, thinned almost to raggedness
By dirt and by the washing of that dirtiness.

Be not too quickly warm again. Lie cold; consent
To weariness' and pardon's watery element.
Drink up the bitter water, breathe the chilly death;
Soon enough comes the riot of our blood and breath.

CLEVELAND, PHILIP JEROME (1903–), was born in Beverly, Massachusetts, and studied at the Boston Museum of Fine Arts, Berkshire Christian College, and New England School of Theology. He became a Congregational minister, serving as chaplain at Babson College, then as a pastor in Nova Scotia, Connecticut, and Pennsylvania. He became pastor of First Congregational Church in New Bedford, Massachusetts, in 1961. His diverse ministry included service as a jail chaplain, a newspaper editor, a radio pianist, and a Sears and Roebuck Santa Claus. Among his prose works are *Her Master: A Religious Romance* (1928), *Beauty's Pilgrim, a Portrait of Jesus* (1937), and a novel, *End of Dreams* (1943). His devotional works also include *Three Churches and a Model T* (1960), *It's Bright in My Valley* (1962), and *Have a Wonderful Time!* (1966). Cleveland's poetry was published in various anthologies including *Masterpieces of Religious Verse* (1948), *A Treasury of Religious Verse* (1962), and *American Lyric Poems* (1964).

I Yield Thee Praise

For thoughts that curve like winging birds
Out of the summer dusk each time
I drink the splendor of the sky
And touch the wood-winds swinging by—
I yield Thee praise.

For waves that lift from autumn seas
To spill strange music on the land,
The broken nocturne of a lark
Flung out upon the lonely dark—
I yield Thee praise.

For rain that piles gray torrents down
Black mountain-gullies to the plain,
For singing fields and crimson flare
At daybreak, and the sea-sweet air—
I yield Thee praise.

For gentle mists that wander in
To hide the tired world outside

That in our hearts old lips may smile
Their blessing through lifes afterwhile—
I yield Thee praise.

For hopes that fight like stubborn grass
Up through the clinging snows of fear
To find the rich earth richer still
With kindliness and honest will—
I yield Thee praise.

By Night

The tapers in the great God's hall
Burn ageless, beautiful and white,
But only with the fall of dusk
Disclose to earth their faithful light.

Earth keeps her lamps of beauty, too,
Fairer than stars in fields above;
Dark hours of grief and pain reveal
The undreamed constancy of love.

There Is A Love

There is a love that tumbles like a stream,
Frothing and foaming down a budded way;
There is a love like ocean depths that move
Hidden, eternal—winter as in May.

There is a love that stumbles through its lines
Trying to say what love can never say;
There is another—patient, tender, strong
Serving and blessing till the close of day.

MASON, R. A. K. (RONALD ALLISON KELLS) (1905–1971), born and educated in Auckland, began writing as a boy and completed most of his major poems by the age of 25. After taking a classics degree, he published *The Beggar* in 1924, which brought him some notice. His *No New Thing, Poems 1924-1929*, published in 1934, focuses on a Christ figure, who is primarily a suffering servant and a persecuted laborer. By the 1930s Mason was largely involved in political and trade-union activities. He wrote little during this time, but some of his dramatic works were published in 1941 in *The Dark Will Lighten*. *Collected Poems* was published in 1962.

On The Swag

His body doubled
under the pack
that sprawls untidily
on his old back
the cold wet deadbeat
plods up the track

The cook peers out:
'oh curse that old lag
here again
with his clumsy swag
made of a dirty old
turnip-bag'

'Bring him in cook
from the grey level sleet
put silk on his body
slippers on his feet,
give him fire
and bread and meat

Let the fruit be plucked
and the cake be iced,
the bed be snug
and the wine be spiced
in the old cove's nightcap:
for this is Christ.'

Judas Iscariot

Judas Iscariot
sat in the upper
room with the others
at the last supper

And sitting there smiled
up at his master
whom he knew the morrow
would roll in disaster

At Christ's look he guffawed—
for then as thereafter

Judas was greatly
given to laughter

Indeed they always said
that he was the veriest
prince of good fellows
and the whitest and merriest

All the days of his life
he lived gay as a cricket
and would sing like the thrush
that sings in the thicket.

STAM, ELISABETH ALDEN SCOTT (1906–1934), daughter of a Presbyterian minister, at six months of age went to China where her parents were sent as missionaries. She attended school in Tung Chow, near Peking, and finished her last year in high school, while on furlough, in Springfield, Massachusetts. She attended Wilson College in Chambersburg, Pennsylvania, and then Moody Bible Institute in Chicago. There she met John Stam, whom she married five years later (1933) after going back to China as a missionary herself. She had a daughter, Helen, born in 1934. Three months later Stam was put to death, along with her husband, by Chinese Communist soldiers in Anhwei Province. In the looted wreckage of her home, a number of her poems were found on paper scraps wrapped around chinaware that had been thus preserved by a faithful cook.

"Stand Still, And See"
Exodus 14:13.

"I'm Standing, Lord.
There is a mist that blinds my sight.
Steep jagged rocks, front, left, and right.
Lower, dim, gigantic, in the night.
    Where is the way?

"I'm Standing, Lord.
The black rock hems me in behind.
Above my head a moaning wind
Chills and oppresses heart and mind.
    I am afraid!

"I'm Standing, Lord.
The rock is hard beneath my feet.

I nearly slipped, Lord, on the sleet.
So weary, Lord, and where a seat?
    Still must I stand?"

He answered me, and on His face
A look ineffable of grace,
Of perfect, understanding love,
Which all my murmuring did remove.

    "I'm Standing, Lord.
Since Thou hast spoken, Lord, I see
Thou hast beset; these rocks are Thee;
And, since Thy love encloses me,
    I stand and sing!"

Two Names

I

When Lucifer was lowliest in Heaven,
There was a Spirit with no name at all
Nor any work to do, before the Fall.
But God had said to her there should be given
Two names more beautiful than Morn or Even,
For time and for eternity. They call
Her Pain because on earth she wears a pall—
A horrid cloak of piercing colors seven—
More feared by men than the black robe of Death;
And Pain appears, at the first, gasping breath;
Wrapping her cloak of many and many a fold
Round man; nor can be bought with tears or gold.
To men on earth her face she may not show;
She is too beautiful for earth below.

II

Pain is her name; her face she may not show,
But covers up her eyes serene and bold;
Eyes of a child, which fairyland will hold;
Eyes of a sage, which all experience know;
Eyes of a mother, clear and gray, as flow
Down a clean mountain rock, snow-cold
And fresh and pure, snow-waters. I am told
Her mouth is sweeter than one sees below.
So close she lived to God when up above,

And to the Son of God when He was Man,
She has led multitudes to God, who well,
Had quite forgotten God, as vigor can,
She has the place of Lucifer who fell—
Her name, through all the ages, shall be Love.

Ring Sonnet

Dearest, when thou desirest to buy a ring,—
Sweetheart, in this obey me without fail;
Give me no diamond which is for sale—
It is too glittering, too cold a thing.
Buy me no platinum; I cannot sing
Of such a metal, precious, but too pale!
And bandits' robbing soon would end the tale.
Thy love is more than ransom for a king.
It is enough that I should have thy heart
And when thou tak'st me, Lover, for thy bride,
Give me a ring of gold, not thick nor wide,
Pure gold like thee, God's finest work of art.
I also thought; into the Heavens new,
Where streets are gold, I might take thy ring, too.

BETJEMAN, Sir JOHN (1906–1984), had T.S. Eliot as one of his teachers before he went to Oxford. He published *Mount Zion* (verse) and *Ghastly Good Taste* (architecture) in 1933. He published four more volumes of poetry gathered in *Collected Poems* (1958). His love for British small towns and older architecture show up in much of his poetry. He published a sort of verse biography, *Summoned By Bells*, in 1960. In 1972 he succeeded C. Day Lewis as poet laureate of England.

Undenominational

Undenominational
    But still the church of God
He stood in his conventicle
    And ruled it with a rod.

Undenominational
    The walls around him rose,
The lamps within their brackets shook
    To hear the hymns he chose.

"Glory" "Gopsal" "Russell Place"
　"Wrestling Jacob" "Rock"
"Saffron Walden" "Safe at Home"
　"Dorking" "Plymouth Dock"

I slipped about the chalky lane
　That runs without the park,
I saw the lone conventicle
　A beacon in the dark.

Revival ran along the hedge
　And made my spirit whole
When steam was on the window panes
　And glory in my soul.

St. Saviour's, Aberdeen Park,
Highbury, London, N.

With oh such peculiar branching and overreaching of wire
Trolley-bus standards pick their threads from the London sky
Diminishing up the perspective, Highbury-bound retire
Threads and buses and standards with plane trees volleying by
And, more peculiar still, that ever-increasing spire
Bulges over the housetops, polychromatic and high.

Stop the trolley-bus, stop! And here, where the roads unite
Of weariest worn-out London—no cigarettes, no beer,
No repairs undertaken, nothing in stock—alight;
For over the waste of willow-herb, look at her, sailing clear,
A great Victorian church, tall, unbroken and bright
In a sun that's setting in Willesden and saturating us here.
These were the streets my parents knew when they loved and won—
The brougham that crunched the gravel, the laurel-girt paths that wind,
Geranium-beds for the lawn, Venetian blinds for the sun,
A separate tradesman's entrance, straw in the mews behind,
Just in the four-mile radius where hackney carriages run,
Solid Italianate houses for the solid commercial mind.

These were the streets they knew; and I, by descent, belong
To these tall neglected houses divided into flats.
Only the church remains, where carriages used to throng
And my mother stepped out in flounces and my father stepped out
　in spats

To shadowy stained-glass matins or gas-lit evensong
And back in a country quiet with doffing of chimney hats.

Great red church of my parents, cruciform crossing they knew—
Over these same encaustics they and their parents trod
Bound through a red-brick transept for a once familiar pew
Where the organ set them singing and the sermon let them nod
And up this coloured brickwork the same long shadows grew
As these in the stencilled chancel where I kneel in the presence of
    God.
Wonder beyond Time's wonders, that Bread so white and small
Veiled in golden curtains, too mighty for men to see,
Is the Power that sends the shadows up this polychrome wall,
Is God who created the present, the chain-smoking millions and me;
Beyond the throb of the engines is the throbbing heart of all—
Christ, at this Highbury altar, I offer myself to Thee.

Blame The Vicar

When things go wrong it's rather tame
To find we are ourselves to blame,
It gets the trouble over quicker
To go and blame things on the Vicar.

The Vicar, after all, is paid
To keep us bright and undismayed.
The Vicar is more virtuous too
Than lay folks such as me and you.
He never swears, he never drinks,
He never should say what he thinks.
His collar is the wrong way round,
And that is why he's simply bound
To be the sort of person who
Has nothing very much to do
But take the blame for what goes wrong
And sing in tune at Evensong.

For what's a Vicar really for
Except to cheer us up? What's more,
He shouldn't ever, ever tell
If there is such a place as Hell,
For if there is it's certain he
Will go to it as well as we.

The Vicar should be all pretence
And never, never give offence.
To preach on Sunday is his task
And lend his mower when we ask
And organize our village fetes
And sing at Christmas with the waits
And in his car to give us lifts
And when we quarrel, heal the rifts.

To keep his family alive
He should industriously strive
In that enormous house he gets,
And he should always pay his debts,
For he has quite six pounds a week,
And when we're rude he should be meek
And always turn the other cheek.
He should be neat and nicely dressed
With polished shoes and trousers pressed,
For we look up to him as higher
Than anyone, except the Squire.

Dear People, who have read so far,
I know how really kind you are,
I hope that you are always seeing
Your Vicar as a human being,
Making allowances when he
Does things with which you don't agree.
But there are lots of people who
Are not so kind to him as you.
So in conclusion you shall hear
About a parish somewhat near,
Perhaps your own or maybe not,
And of the Vicars that it got.

One parson came and people said,
Alas! Our former Vicar's dead!
And this new man is far more 'Low'
Than dear old Reverend so-and-so,
And far too earnest in his preaching,
We do not really like his teaching,
He seems to think we're simply fools
Who've never been to Sunday Schools."
That Vicar left, and by and by

A new one came, "He's much too 'High'‚"
The people said, "too like a saint,
His incense makes our Mavis faint."
So now he's left and they're alone
Without a Vicar of their own.
The living's been amalgamated
With one next door they've always hated.

Dear readers, from this rhyme take warning,
And if you heard the bell this morning
Your Vicar went to pray for you,
A task the Prayer Book bids him do.
"Highness" or "Lowness" do not matter,
You are the Church and must not scatter,
Cling to the Sacraments and pray
And God be with you every day.

AUDEN, W. H. (WYSTAN HUGH) (1907–1973), graduate of Oxford, became well-known as a political radical in the 1930s. He wrote a number of verse dramas with Christopher Isherwood during that time, including *The Dog Beneath the Skin* (1935), *The Ascent of F6* (1936), and *On the Frontier* (1938). He travelled extensively in Europe, China, and elsewhere. In 1937 he collaborated with Louis MacNeice on *Letters from Iceland*. He edited the *Oxford Book of Light Verse* in 1938, and in 1939, Auden came to the United States, where he became an American citizen in 1946. His books of poetry include *Poems* (1930), *The Orators* (1932), *The Dance of Death* (1933), *Look Stranger* (1936), *The Double Man* (1941), *For the Time Being* (1944), *The Age of Anxiety* (1947), *Nones* (1951), *The Shield of Achilles* (1955), *Homage to Clio* (1960), and *About the House* (1965). An authorized collection of his poems was published after his death. He won the Pulitzer prize for poetry for *The Age of Anxiety*. He revived interest in opera libretti as a writing genre, as well as writing translations, editing anthologies, and publishing essays on various topics. The dedication to his collected poems reads:

For Christopher Isherwood And Chester Kallman

Although you be, as I am, one of those
Who feel a Christian ought to write in prose,
For poetry is magic: born in sin, you
May read it to exorcise the Gentile in you.

Part II of **Memorial For The City**
(in Memoriam Charles Williams, d. April 1945)

Alone in a room Pope Gregory whispered his name
While the Emperor shone on a centreless world
From wherever he happened to be; the New City rose
Upon their opposition, the yes and no
Of a rival allegiance; the sword, the local lord
Were not all: there was home and Rome;
Fear of the stranger was lost on the way to the shrine.

The facts, the acts of the City bore a double meaning:
Limbs became hymns; embraces expressed in jest
A more permanent tie; infidel faces replaced
The family foe in the choleric's nightmare;
The children of water parodied in their postures
The infinite patience of heaven;
Those born under Saturn felt the gloom of the day of doom.

Scribes and innkeepers prospered; suspicious tribes combined
To rescue Jerusalem from a dull god,
And disciplined logicians fought to recover thought
From the eccentricities of the private brain
For the Sane City; framed in her windows, orchards, ports,
Wild beasts, deep rivers and dry rocks
Lay nursed on the smile of a merciful Madonna.

In a sandy province Luther denounced as obscene
The machine that so smoothly forgave and saved
If paid; he announced to the Sinful City a grinning gap
No rite could cross; he abased her before the Grace:
Henceforth division was also to be her condition;
Her conclusions were to include doubt,
Her loves were to bear with her fear; insecure, she endured.

Saints tamed, poets acclaimed the raging herod of the will;
The groundlings wept as on a secular stage
The grand and the bad went to ruin in thundering verse;
Sundered by reason and treason the City
Found invisible ground for concord in measured sound,
While wood and stone learned the shameless
Games of man, to flatter, to show off, be pompous, to romp.

Nature was put to the Question in the Prince's name;
She confessed, what he wished to hear, that she had no soul;
Between his scaffold and her coldness the restrained style,
The ironic smile became the worldly and devout,
Civility a city grown rich: in his own snob way
The unarmed gentleman did his job
As a judge to her children, as a father to her forests.

In a national capital Mirabeau and his set
Attacked mystery; the packed galleries roared
And history marched to the drums of a clear idea,
The aim of the Rational City, quick to admire,
Quick to tire: she used up Napoleon and threw him away;
Her pallid affected heroes
Began their hectic quest for the prelapsarian man.

The deserts were dangerous, the waters rough, their clothes
Absurd but, changing their Beatrices often,
Sleeping little, they pushed on, raised the flag of the Word
Upon lawless spots denied or forgotten
By the fear or the pride of the Glittering City;
Guided by hated parental shades,
They invaded and harrowed the hell of her natural self.

Chimeras mauled them, they wasted away with the spleen,
Suicide picked them off; sunk off Cape Consumption,
Lost on the Tosspot Seas, wrecked on the Gibbering Isles
Or trapped in the ice of despair at the Soul's Pole,
They died, unfinished, alone; but now the forbidden,
The hidden, the wild outside were known:
Faithful without faith, they died for the Conscious City.

RIDLER, ANNE BARBARA (NEE: BRADBY) (1912–) daughter of a
Rugby house-master, graduated from Kings College, London. She worked for a
number of years as an editor for Faber and Faber and married Vivian Bradby in
1938. She has two sons and two daughters. Her first book of poetry, *Poems*, was
published in 1939, followed by *A Dream Observed* (1941), *The Nine Bright Shiners*
(1943), *The Golden Bird* (1951), *A Matter of Life and Death* (1959), *Selected Poems*
(New York—1961), and *Some Time After* (1972). Her long introduction to
Charles Williams's *The Images of the City and Other Essays* (1958, 1970) is an excel-
lent biography of Williams. She contributed to *Ten Oxford Poets* (1978) and has
written many plays, including *Cain* (1943), *The Shadow Factory: A Nativity Play*
(1946), and *The Trial of Thomas Cranmer* (1956). She has also written numerous

libretti, verse-plays, translations, critical works, and edited various anthologies. Her *New and Selected Poems* was published in 1988, her *Collected Poems* in 1994.

Making Love, Killing Time

The clock within us, speaking time
By heart-beat seconds and by mental years,
Is garrulous in any gear,
So life at once seems short and endless.
Who is not glad to find the hour later than he thought?
For so he has killed, not time
But the inward timing of the ceaseless rote.
Its beat, which makes him count the cost
Of that creation which, loving, he cannot resist,
Hurries him on to end whatever was begun—
The child, to be grown, the poem, to be done.

But in each other's arms,
Or on the tide of prayer, when we
Encountering souls support each other, like swimmers in a
 blissful sea,
The cost is known as the cause of bliss,
And the gabbling rote is heard as a murmur of peace.
So making love we say, but love makes us
Again to be as in our listening-time,
When hearing our heart-beat we took it for the world's,
And with no wish to escape it, then and there
Loved what we were.

Before Sleep

Now that you lie
In London afar
And may sleep longer
Though lonelier,
For I shall not wake you
With a nightmare—
Heaven plant such peace in us
As if no parting stretched between us.

The world revolves
And is evil;
God's image is

Wormeaten by the devil.
May the good angel
Have no rival
By our beds, and we lie curled
At the sound unmoving centre of the world.

In our good nights
When we were together,
We made, in that stillness
Where we loved each other,
A new being, of both
Yet above either.
So, when I cannot share your sleep,
Into this being, half yours, I creep.

For a Child Expected

Lovers whose lifted hands are candles in winter,
Whose gentle ways like streams in the easy summer,
Lying together
For secret setting of a child, love what they do,
Thinking they make that candle immortal, those streams forever flow,
And yet do better than they know.

So the first flutter of a baby felt in the womb,
Its little signal and promise of riches to come,
Is taken in its father's name;
Its life is the body of his love, like his caress,
First delicate and strange, that daily use
Makes dearer and priceless.

Our child was to be the living sign of our joy,
Restore to each the other's lost infancy;
To a painter's pillaging eye
Poet's coiled hearing, add the heart we might earn
By the help of love; all that our passion would yield
We put to planning our child.

The world flowed in; whatever we liked we took:
For its hair, the gold curls of the November oak
We saw on our walk;
Snowberries that make a Milky Way in the wood
For its tender hands; calm screen of the frozen flood
For our care of its childhood.

But the birth of a child is an uncontrollable glory;
Cat's cradle of hopes will hold no living baby,
Long though it lay quietly.
And when a baby stirs and struggles to be born
It compels humility: what we began
Is now its own.

For as the sun that shines through glass
So Jesus in His Mother was.
Therefore every human creature,
Since it shares a divine nature,
In candle-gold passion or white
Sharp star should show its own way of light.
May no parental dread or dream
Darken our darling's early beam:
May she grow to her right powers
Unperturbed by passion of ours.

Edlesborough

Beyond the Chiltern coast, this church:
A lighthouse in dry seas of standing corn.
Bees hive in the tower; the outer stone
Pared and frittered in sunlight, flakes with the years:
Clunch crumbles, but silence, exaltation endures.

The brass-robed Rector stretched on his tomb endures.
Within, we go upon the dragon and the bat,
Walk above the world, without,
Uplifted among lavender, beech and sycamore,
Shades of the sea-born chalk, indelible and austere.

If we see history from this hill
It is upon its own conditions, here
Each season swirls and eddies the circle of a year
Round the spectator church, and human eyes
Take, on its plinth, a long focus of centuries.

We seem like gods on any hill.
From here all toil resembles rest, and yet
Unlike a god we feel ourselves shut out.
Surely that farm in a carved blue curve of trees,
So still with all its creatures, holds the unattainable peace?

It is Time's camouflage deceives us.
There it extends like space: whatever moves
(A horse to drink, a reaper to stack the sheaves)
Displays the movement in its whole succession,
Not a change of terms, only a changed relation.

Deceit or truth? The dead possess the hill
In battlements of totternhoe or slate;
The view is ours, the range and ache of sight.
Their death, our life, so far apart, unite
If Time serves: in a common space unrolls
This Resurrection field, with sheaves in glory like risen souls.

Cranmer and the Bread of Heaven

> . . . the bread had nothing to do with the Body
> that was what he was dying for—Dom Gregory Dix on Cramner

Dear master, was it really for this you died?
To make the separation clear
That heaven is elsewhere, nowise here?
That the divine bitter yeast is not inside
Our common bread; this body, loved so
In its young crocus light, and the full orb of manhood,
And the paean of sound, all that our senses know
Is not the matter of God?

The 'last enchantments of the Middle Age'
In this case, were a faggot fire
And rubbish pitched beside the pyre;
A couple of burnt doors, from this so-intellectual rage
Remain, and the proposition (if dying made it plain)
Flesh turns to ashes, bread cannot turn to God.
Yet how if the question that cost so much pain
Itself was wrongly made?

A change takes place: to this all can assent;
But question 'what place does it take?
Or none at all?'—there's the mistake,
There we confuse our terms. For this is an event,
Not subject to a physical experiment
As water is split for energy; no gain
In splitting hairs. We know that God can enter
To what He first contained;

We know the kingdom of heaven suffers violence,
But not atomic. Who can weigh
Love in a man's heart? So we still say
'Body and soul' as though they were at variance.
Who can weigh Love? Yet sensibly he burns,
His conflagration is eyes, hands, hearts:
So is he sensed, but in and out of the eternal,
Because the sense departs.

Some Time After

Where are the poems gone, of our first days?
　　Locked on the page
Where we for ever learn our first embrace.
　　Love come of age
Takes words as said, but never takes for granted
　　His holy luck, his pledge
That what is truly loved is truly known.
　　Now in that knowledge
Love unillusioned is not love disenchanted.

Modern Love

In *Almost Cinderella*, the author said, 'he had wanted to recreate for adults
the impact the story had upon children . . . Prince Charming . . . begins to
strangle Cinderella in a very stylised way as the clock strikes. It is part of
the mockery of the cliche of love at first sight.'
The London Times, 7 December 1966

That strong god whose touch made Dante tremble,
Who made the sun rise and the stars fall,
And could make saints of you and me for an hour,
Now that the world is wise has lost his power:
He was only a pantomime uncle after all.

'Love for another is simply the willing of good' *
True for the Middle Ages, a genuine thrill,
But now such childish fancies are outgrown.
This is the truth for modern, adult man:
'Love is simply the perfect wish to kill.'

* Aquinas

EVERSON, WILLIAM (BROTHER ANTONIUS) (1912–) son of a Norwegian composer, was born in California, where he dropped out of college to marry a high-school sweetheart. He was influenced early by the "mythical pantheism" of Robinson Jeffers, and after spending the war as a conscientious objector in Oregon work camps, he was associated with the San Francisco "Beat" movement and Kenneth Rexroth. He converted to the Catholic church in 1949 and became a Dominican monk, Brother Antonius. *The Residual Years: Poems 1934-1948* was published 1948 (revised edition 1968). In 1959 he published *The Crooked Lines of God.* It was followed by *The Hazards of Holiness: Poems 1957-1960* in 1962. He left the Dominicans in 1969, publishing *Man-Fate: The Swansong of Brother Antonius* in 1974. *The Veritable Years 1946-1966* (1978) and *The Masks of Drought* (1980) are subsequent books of poetry. Like Bob Dylan, the troubadour, Everson seems to be in and out of "Christian phases" in his poetry. His latest passions seem to be more "ecological" than theological.

Passion Week

Christ-cut: the cedar
Bleeds where I gashed it.

Lance wound under the narrow rib.

Eve's orifice: the agony of Abel
Enacted out on the Tree.

Blood gushed
From the gash.

The Holy Ghost
Gusted out of the sky
Aghast.
Our Guest.

Bleed cedar.
Little cedar,
Lanced,
Axe-opened,
The ache of sacrifice.

Pour out,
As Christ,
Those pearls of pain,
Bequeathed.

O bleed
Little cedar,

Bleed for the blooded Heart,
For the pang of man . . .

The earth's
Old ache.

Zone Of Death

Wind is not nigh.

No Holy Ghost,
Spirit outspilt,
Burnt this charred day.

What sin did this?
Could I?

Hot light blares.
Stars, outblistered now,
Mark time, extinct.

Night might bring
The seasonal constellations
In its sphere,
But night is nowhere.
Sun. Sand.
The noon-crazy jays
Cackle and gibber,
Jar on the gritted ear.

Dawn sneaked in unsmelt.
No wine, no water here.

Now the lance-riddled man
On yon pronged tree,
Stretched in the death-tread there,
Opens his executing eye
And gibbets me.

L'ENGLE, MADELEINE (Mrs. Hugh Franklin) (1918–), well-known author of many "fantasy" novels for young people, was born in New York City and married in 1946. She attended Smith College, New College, and Columbia University. She has taught in New York since 1960, been on the faculty and/or writer-in-residence at several universities and colleges, and is active in several authors' and church organizations. She published her first book, *The Small Rain* in 1945. She is perhaps best known for her "juvenile" novels, including the series *A Wrinkle In Time* (1962), *A Wind in the Door* (1973), and *A Swiftly Tilting Planet* (1978). Her work covers a wide range, including such powerful novels as *The Love Letter* and *The Summer of the Great-grandmother* (1974). She has won many literary awards including the Newbery medal in 1963. Her husband Hugh, an actor, is most widely known for his television roles. Her book about writing, *Walking On Water* (1981), has encouraged many others. Her books of poetry include *The Risk of Birth* (date?), *Lines Scribbled on an Envelope* (1969) and *The Weather of the Heart* (1978).

The Risk Of Birth

This is no time for a child to be born,
With the earth betrayed by war & hate
And a comet slashing the sky to warn
That time runs out & the sun burns late.

That was no time for a child to be born,
In a land in the crushing grip of Rome;
Honor & truth were trampled to scorn—
Yet here did the Savior make His home.

When is the time for love to be born?
The inn is full on the planet earth,
And by a comet the sky is torn—
Yet Love still takes the risk of birth.

Lines Scribbled On An Envelope
While Riding The 104 Broadway Bus:

There is too much pain
I cannot understand
I cannot pray

I cannot pray for all the little ones with bellies bloated by
        starvation in India;
for all the angry Africans striving to be separate in a world
        struggling for wholeness;
for all the young Chinese men and women taught that
        hatred and killing are good and compassion evil;
or even all the frightened people in my own city looking
        for truth in pot or aid.

Here I am
and the ugly man with beery breath beside me reminds me
    that it is not my prayers that waken your concern, my
    Lord;
my prayers, my intercessions are not to ask for your love
for all your lost and lonely ones,
your sick and sinning souls,
but mine, my love, my acceptance of your love.
Your love for the woman sticking her umbrella and her
    expensive
parcels into my ribs and snarling, "Why don't you watch
where you're going?"
Your love for the long-haired, gum-chewing boy who shoves
    the old lady aside to grab a seat,
Your love for me, too, too tired to look with love,
too tired to look at Love, at you, in every person on the
    bus.
Expand my love, Lord, so I can help to bear the pain,
help your love move my love into the tired prostitute with
    false eyelashes and bunioned feet,
the corrupt policeman with his hand open for graft,
the addict, the derelict, the woman in the mink coat and
    discontented mouth,
the high school girl with heavy books and frightened eyes.

Help me through these scandalous particulars
to understand
your love.

Help me to pray.

LEVERTOV, DENISE (1923–) was born in England, of a Welsh mother and Jewish father. Her mother's ancestors include the mystic Angel Jones, and her father's, the Hasidic "Rav of Northern White Russia," Schneour Zaiman. Her father converted to Christianity and became an Anglican priest. She served as a nurse in wartime London, and published her first book of poetry in 1946. In 1948 she emigrated to the United States where her husband, Michael Goodman, introduced her to a number of important poets, particularly of the "Imagist" and "Black Mountain" schools. She became an American citizen in 1955. Her prose works include *The Poet in the World* (1973) and *Light Up the Cave* (1981). She has taught poetry at various universities. Her poetry, of which she has published fifteen books, is often referred to as having a "sacramental" sense.

Her *Selected Poems* were published in England in 1986. Among her other books
of poetry are *Oblique Prayers* (1984), and *Breathing the Water* (1987).

Perhaps No Poem But All I Can Say And I Cannot Be Silent

As a devout Christian, my father
took delight and pride in being
(like Christ and the Apostles)
a Jew.
  It was
  Hasidic lore, his heritage,
  he drew on to know
  the Holy Spirit as Shekinah.

My Gentile mother, Welsh through and through,
and like my father sustained
by deep faith, cherished
all her long life the words
of Israel Zangwill, who told her,
'You have a Jewish soul.'

I their daughter ('flesh of their flesh,
   bone of their bone')
writing, in this Age of Terror, a libretto
about El Salvador, the suffering,
   the martyrs,

look from my page to watch
the apportioned news—those foul
dollops of History
each day thrusts at us, pushing them
into our gullets—
   and see that,
   in Lebanon
  so-called Jews have permitted
  so-called Christians
  to wreak pogrom ('thunder of devastation')
  on helpless folk (of a tribe
  anciently kin to their own, and now
  concentrated
   in Camps . . .)

My father—my mother—
I have longed for you.

Now I see
         it is well you are dead,
dead and
gone from Time,
gone from this time whose weight
of shame your bones, weary already
from your own days and years of
tragic History,
could surely not have borne.

St. Peter And The Angel

Delivered out of raw continual pain,
smell of darkness, groans of those others
to whom he was chained—

unchained, and led
past the sleepers,
door after door silently opening—
out!
         And along a long street's
majestic emptiness under the moon:

one hand on the angel's shoulder, one
feeling the air before him,
eyes open but fixed . . .

And not till he saw the angel had left him,
alone and free to resume
the ecstatic, dangerous, wearisome roads of
what he had still to do,
not till then did he recognize
this was no dream. More frightening
than arrest, than being chained to his warders:
he could hear his own footsteps suddenly.
Had the angel's feet
made any sound? He could not recall.
No one had missed him, no one was in pursuit.
He himself must be
the key, now, to the next door,
the next terrors of freedom and joy.

Oblique Prayer

Not the profound *dark*
night of the soul

and not the austere desert
to scorch the heart at noon,
grip the mind
in teeth of ice at evening

but gray,
a place
without clear outlines,

the air
heavy and thick

the soft ground clogging
my feet if I walk,
sucking them downwards
if I stand.

Have you been here?
Is it

a part of human-ness

to enter
no man's land?

I can remember
    (is it asking you
    that
    makes me remember?)
even here

the blessed light that caressed the world
before I stumbled into
this place of mere
not-darkness.

SHAW, LUCI (1928–), was born in England, and was brought up in Australia and Canada. She graduated from Wheaton College (near Chicago) in 1953 and married Harold Shaw, founder of Harold Shaw Publishers. Her books of poetry include *Adam Among the Television Trees* (1971), *Listen to The Green* (1971), *The Secret Trees* (1976), *The Sighting* (1981), *Postcard from the Shore* (1985), and *Polishing the Petoskey Stone* (1990). She also published *God in the Dark* (1989), dealing with her "journey through grief" and with Madeleine L'Engle *Winter Song* (1996), a collection of Christmas readings. She has been writer in residence at Regent College.

Reluctant prophet

Both were dwellers
in deep places (one
in the dark bowels
of ships and great fish
and wounded pride.
The other
in the silvery belly
of the seas). Both
heard God saying
"Go!"
but the whale
did as he was told.

It is as if infancy
were the whole of incarnation

One time of the year
the new-born child
is everywhere,
planted in madonnas' arms
hay mows, stables,
in palaces or farms,
or quaintly, under snowed gables,
gothic angular or baroque plump,
naked or elaborately swathed,
encircled by Della Robbia wreaths,
garnished with whimsical
partridges and pears,
drummers and drums,
lit by oversize stars,
partnered with lambs,
peace doves, sugar plums,
bells, plastic camels in sets of three
as if these were what we need
for eternity.

But Jesus the Man is not to be seen.
We are too wary, these days,
of beards and sandalled feet.

Yet if we celebrate, let it be
that He
has invaded our lives with purpose,
striding over our picturesque traditions,
our shallow sentiment,
overturning our cash registers,
wielding His peace like a sword,
rescuing us into reality,
demanding much more
than the milk and the softness
and the mother warmth
of the baby in the storefront creche,

(only the Man would ask
all, of each of us)
reaching out
 always, urgently, with strong
effective love
(only the Man would give
His life and live
again for love of us).

Oh come, let us adore Him—
Christ—the Lord.

Onlookers

*"Sickness is a place . . . where there's no company,
where nobody can follow."*—Flannery O'Connor

Behind our shield of health, each
of us must sense another's anguish
second-hand; we are agnostic
in the face of dying. So Joseph
felt, observer of the push
and splash of birth, and even Mary,
mourner, under the cross's arm.

Only their son, and God's,
in bearing all our griefs

felt them first-hand, climbing
himself our rugged hill of pain.
His nerves, enfleshed, carried
the messages of nails, the tomb's
chill. His ever-open wounds
still blazon back to us the penalty
we never bore, and heaven
gleams for us more real,
crossed with that human blood.

AFTERWORD

The most important thing to say in conclusion hardly needs to be said—that there are many, rather myriad, wonderful Christian poets and poems I have failed to include here—and many, many more to come.

My chiefest motive in beginning this collection, and in carrying the effort to this imperfect stage of completion has been the desire, first, to understand my own poor efforts at glorifying Christ in poetry in the midst of a multitude no man can number. And secondly, my motive has been to help other Christian writers of poetry toward a sense of their place in the tradition in which all stand—to help each in composing or performing the everlasting music that each, in T. S. Eliot's words, "modifies," as he or she writes—or "sings" to use a word from the final paragraph of George MacDonald's anthology, *England's Antiphon:*

> But the singers will yet sing on to him that hath ears to hear. When he returns to seek them, the shadowy door will open to his touch, the long-drawn aisles receding will guide his eye to the carven choir, and there they will stand, the sweet singers, content to repeat the ancient psalm and new song to the prayer of the humblest whose heart would join in England's Antiphon.

England's—yes—but also that of the whole English-speaking world, and of course, that only a section of the whole choir that sings and will sing around the throne for all eternity.

BIBLIOGRAPHIES

I. Individual Poets - Books and Collections.

Auden, W. H. *W. H. Auden, Collected Poems.* Ed. Edward Mendelson. New York: Random House, 1976.

Belloc, Hilaire. *H. Belloc: Complete Verse.* Ed. W.N. Roughead. London: Gerald Duckworth, 1970.

Beowulf: And the Fight at Finnsburg. Ed. Fr. Klaeber. Boston: D.C. Heath and Company, 1922 (1968).

Betjeman, John. *Church Poems.* London: John Murray Publisher, 1932 (1981).

Bonar, Horatius. *My Old Letters.* New York: Robert Carter and Bros., 1877.

Bradstreet, Anne. *Works of Anne Bradstreet.* Ed. Jeannine Hensley. Cambridge, Massachusetts: Harvard University Press, 1967.

Bridges, Robert. *Poetical Works of Robert Bridges Excluding The Eight Dramas.* Ed. Humphrey Milford. London: Oxford University Press, 1914. (Oxford Edition)

Brontë , Anne. *Best Poems of the Brontë Sisters.* Ed. Susan Rattiner. Mineola, New York: Dover Publications, 1997. (Dover Thrift Editions)

Caedmon. *Metrical Paraphrase of Parts of the Holy Scriptures in Anglo-Saxon: with an English Translation, Notes, and a Verbal Index.* Benjamin Thorpe. London: Society of Antiquaries in London, 1832.

Cary, Alice and Phoebe. *The Poetical Works of Alice and Phoebe Cary.* Ed. Mary Clemmer. New York: Hurd and Houghton, 1877. (The Riverside Press, Cambridge)

Chaucer, Geoffrey. *The Works of Geoffrey Chaucer.* 2nd Edition: Ed. F. N. Robinson. Boston: Houghton Mifflin Company, 1961 (1933).

Chesterton, G.K. *Collected Poems of G.K. Chesterton.* New York: Dodd, Meade and Co., 1911 (1932, 1961).

Crashaw, Richard. *Poems of Richard Crashaw.* Ed. L.C. Martin. Oxford: Clarendon Press, 1927 (1957).

Davies, Samuel. *Collected Poems of Samuel Davies, 1723-1761.* Ed. Richard Beale Davis. Gainesville, Florida: Scholars Facsimiles & Reprints , 1968.

Donne, John. *John Donne's Poetry: Authoritative Texts and Criticism.* Ed. A. L. Clements. New York: W. W. Norton and Company, 1966.

Donne, John. *John Donne's Poetry: Norton Critical Edition.* Ed. A. L. Clements. New York: W. W. Norton and Company, 1966.

Drummond, William. *William Drummond of Hawthorden: Poems and Prose.* Ed. Robert H. MacDonald. Edinburgh and London: Scottish Academic Press, 1976.

Dunbar, Paul Laurence. *The Complete Poems of Paul Laurence Dunbar.* Ed. Willian Dean Howells. New York: Dodd, Mead & Company, 1960. (1913)

Dunbar, William. *William Dunbar: Poems.* Ed. James Kinsley. Oxford: The Clarendon Press, 1958.

Eliot, T.S. (Thomas Sternes). *T.S. Eliot: The Complete Poems and Plays.* New York: Harcourt and Brace and Company, 1952.

Erskine, Ralph. *Gospel Sonnets or Spiritual Songs: In Six Parts.* Edinburgh: J. Ruthven and Sons, 1812 (orig? 25th ed in 1795 !)

Gower, John. *Selections from John Gower.* Ed. J.A.W. Bennett. Oxford: Clarendon Press, 1968.

Havergal, Frances Ridley. *Kept for the Master's Use.* New York: F. M. Lupton Publishing Company, 1880 (?).

Havergal, Frances Ridley. *Poems by Frances Ridley Havergal with a Sketch of Her Life.* Ed. "W. M. L. J." New York: E. P. Dutton and Company, 1882. (copyright, 1881)

Havergal, Frances Ridley. *The Poetical Works of Frances Ridley Havergal.* London: Nisbet and Company, 1902?.

Herbert, George. *Works of George Herbert.* Ed. T. E. Hutchinson. Oxford: Oxford University Press, 1941 (1959).

Herrick, Robert. *Poetical Works of Robert Herrick.* Ed. L.C. Martin. Oxford: Clarendon Press, 1956.

Hopkins, Gerard Manley. *Poems of Gerard Manley Hopkins.* Ed. W.H. Gardner and N.H. Mackenzie. London: Oxford U. Press, 1918 (Second Edition with appendix of additional poems and a critical introduction by Charles Williams, 1930-1944).

Johnson, James Weldon. *God's Trombones.* New York: Viking Press, 1927 (1969).

Jerrold, Sydney E. (Madame Marie Christopher). *Parvulus and other Poems.* London: Burns, Oats and Washbourne, 1940.

L'Engle, Madeleine (Mrs. Hugh Franklin). *Lines Scribbled on an Envelope.* New York: Doubleday, 1969.

Lewis, C.S. *C.S. Lewis: Poems.* Ed. Walter Hooper. New York: Harcourt, Brace and World, 1964 (1965).

Lydgate, John. *John Lydgate: Poems.* Ed. John Norton-Smith. Oxford: Clarendon Press, 1966.

Masefield, John. *The Everlasting Mercy.* New York: The Macmillan Company, 1915 (1911).

Meynell, Alice. *Poems of Alice Meynell.* Ed. Humphrey Milford. London: Oxford University Press, 1940-41. (Collected Edition - 1913)

Milton, John. *Poems of John Milton.* Ed. James Holly Hanford. New York: The Ronald Knox Press, 1936 (1946).

Noyes, Alfred. *Alfred Noyes: Collected Poems In One Volume.* New York: Clark McCutcheon, 1966. (Second edition)

Oxenham, John. *Selected Poems of John Oxenham.* London: Ernest Benn Limited, 1931 (1924).

Patmore, Coventry. *Selected Poems of Coventry Patmore.* Ed. Derek Patmore. London: Chatto and Windus, 1931.

Proctor, Adelaide A. *The Poems of Adelaide A. Proctor.* New York: Thomas Y Crowell & Company Publishers, undated. (Dedication dated 1858)

Raleigh, Sir Walter. *Sir Walter Raleigh: Selected Prose and Poetry.* Ed. Agnes M.C. Latham. London: The Athlone Press, 1965.

Raleigh, Sir Walter and Wotton, Sir Henry. *The Poems of Sir Walter Raleigh Collected and Authenticated with Those of Sir Henry Wotton and Other Courtley Poems From 1540 to 1650.* Ed. J. Hannah, D.C.L. London: George Bell and Sons, 1910.

Ridler, Anne (Bradby). *Selected Poems By Anne Ridler.* New York: The Macmillan Company, 1961.

Ridler, Anne (Bradby). *Some Time After & Other Poems.* London: Faber and Faber, Ltd., 1972.

Rossetti, Christina. *Selected Poems of Christina Rossetti.* Ed. Marya Zaturenska. London: MacMillan, 1970.

Shaw, Luci. *Polishing the Petoskey Stone.* Wheaton, Ill.: Harold Shaw Publishers, 1990.

Stam, Elisabeth Alden Scott . *The Faith of Betty Scott Stam in Poem and Verse.* Eds. Clara and Charles E. Scott. New York: Fleming H. Revell Company, 1938.

Taylor, Edward. *The Poems of Edward Taylor.* Ed. Donald E. Stanford. New Haven (and London): Yale University Press, 1966 (1960).

Thompson, Francis. *Complete Poetical Works of Francis Thompson.* Wilfrid Meynell. New York: Modern Library, undated (Executor's note, dated 1913).

Thomson, James. *Poems of James Thomson "B.V."* Ed. Gordon Hall Gerould. New York: Henry Holt and Company, 1927.

Vaughan, Henry. *Works of Henry Vaughan.* Ed. L. C. Martin. Oxford: Oxford University Press, 1914 (1963).

Very, Jones. *Essays and Poems Boston:* Charles C. Little and James Brown, 1839. (Reprint Edition In *The Romantic Tradition in American Literature* series. Ed. Harold Bloom. New York: Arno Press, Inc, 1972.)

Very, Jones. *Jones Very: Selected Poems.* Ed. Nathan Lyons. New Brunswick, New Jersey: Rutgers University Press, 1966.

Wheatley, Phillis. *Life and Works of Phillis Wheatley.* Ed. G. Herbert Renfro. Original: 1916. Reprint: Salem, New Hampshire: Ayer Company Publishing, 1984.

Williams, Charles. *The Region of the Summer Stars.* Oxford: Oxford University Press, 1969 (1950). (Original edition: London: Oxford University Press, 1944.)

Wordsworth, William. *The Complete Poetical Works of William Wordsworth.* (Students Cambridge Edition) Boston: Houghton Mifflin Company, 1932 (1904).

Wotton, Sir Henry *see*: Ralegh, Sir Walter and... *The Poems of Sir Watler Raleigh*, etc.
Ed. J. Hannah

II. Anthologies of Poems from Periods, Places, Genres, and Schools of Poetry

American Anthology 1787–1900, An: Selections Illustrating the Editor's Critical Review of American Poetry In the Nineteenth Century. Ed. Edmund Clarence Stedman. New York: Greenwood Press, 1968 (1900).

American Folk Poetry: An Anthology. Ed. Duncan Emrich. Boston: Little, Brown and Company, 1974.

American Puritans: Their Prose and Poetry, The. Ed. Perry Miller. Garden City, New York: Doubleday and Company, Inc., 1956.

Ancient English Christmas Carols: MCCCC to MDCC. Ed. Edith Rickert. London: Chatto & Windus, 1925 (Also New York: Oxford University Press)

Anglo-Saxon Poetry. Ed. and Tr. R. K. Gordon. London: Dent/Everyman's, 1926, 1967.

Anthology of Contemporary Catholic Poetry, An. Ed. Maurice Leahy. London: Cecil Palmer, dedication and acknowledgment dated 1931.

Anthology of New Zealand Verse. Eds. Robert Chapman and Jonathan Bennett. London and Wellington: Oxford University Press, 1956.

Atlantic Book of British and American Poetry, The. Ed. Dame Edith Sitwell. Boston and Toronto: Little Brown and Company (Atlantic Monthly Press), c.1958.

Beautiful Poems On Jesus. Ed. Basil Miller. Beacon Hill Press, c.1948. Books for Libraries Reprint, Freeport, NY, 1968.

Best Loved Religious Poems, The: Gleaned from Many Sources. James Gilchrist Lawson. New York, (London and Edinburgh) Fleming H. Revell Company, 1933.

Book of American Negro Poetry. Ed. James Weldon Johnson. New York: Harcourt, Brace & Co., 1931.

Book of Religious Verse. Ed. Helen Gardner. New York: Oxford University Press, 1972 (Originally *The Faber Book of Religious Verse.* England: Faber and Faber.)

Book of Scottish Verse. Ed. R. L. Mackie. London: Oxford U. Press, (1934), 1960.

British Poetry and Prose: A Book of Readings. Eds. Paul Robt. Lieder, Robt. M. Lovett, Robt. K. Root. Cambridge Mass: (Houghton Mifflin) Riverside Press, 1928.

Burning Bright: An Anthology of Sacred Poetry. Ed. Patricia Hampl. New York: Ballantine Books, 1995.

Christ and the Fine Arts: An Anthology of World-Famous Pictures, Poetry, Hymns and Stories Centering in the Life of Christ. Ed. Cynthia Pearl Maus. New York: Harper and Brothers Publishers, 1959 (1938).

Christian Poetry: A Brief Survey. Ed. Elizabeth Jennings. New York: Hawthorne Books, 1965. (Volume 12 of the *Twentieth Century Encyclopedia of Catholicism.*)

Christian's Treasury of Stories and Songs, Prayers and Poems, and Much More for Young and Old, The. Ed. Lissa Roche. Wheaton, Illinois: Crossway Books, 1995.

Classic Selections From the Best Authors: Adapted to the Study of Vocal Expression. S. S. Curry. Boston: The Expression Company, 1888.

Colonial American Poetry. Kenneth Silverman. New York: Hafner Publishing Company, 1968.

Columbia Anthology of British Poets. Eds. Carl Woodring and James Shapiro. New York: Columbia University Press, 1995.

Contemporary Religious Poetry. Ed. Paul Ramsey. New York / Mahwah, New Jersey: Paulist Press, 1987.

Country of the Risen King, The: An Anthology of Christian Poetry. Compiler, Merle Meeter. Grand Rapids, Baker Book House, 1978.

Devotional Poets of the XVII Century. [Introduction by Sir Henry Newbolt] London and Edinburgh: Thomas Nelson and Sons Ltd. [c.1910 - 1931].

Early English Carols. Ed. Richard Leighton Greene. Oxford: Oxford University Press, 1935 (revised edition 1977).

Early English Christian Poetry. Ed. and Tr. Charles W. Kennedy. New York: Oxford University Press, 1952 (1968).

Early English Poems. Selected and Edited by Henry S. Pancoast and John Duncan Spaeth. New York: Henry Holt & Company, 1911.

Earth Is the Lords: Poems of the Spirit, The. Ed. Helen Plotz. London: Thomas Y. Crowell, Company, 1965.

England's Antiphon. Ed. George MacDonald. London: Macmillan and Company, 1868. (Now back in print, available from Johannesen Publishers, P.O. Box 24, Whitethorn, CA 95589)

English Catholic Poems. Chaucer to Dryden. Ed. Elbridge Colby. Freeport, New York: Books for Libraries Press, Incorporated, reprint 1967. (1936)

English Lyrics before 1500. Ed. Theodore Silverstein. Northwestern / University of York, 1971. (York Medieval Series).

English Madrigals in the Time of Shakespeare. Ed. F. A. Cox. London: J. Dent and Company, 1974.

English Poetry 1170–1892. Ed. John Matthews Manly. London: Ginn and Company, 1907.

English Sacred Lyrics. Ed. Anonymous. London: Kegan, Paul, Trench & Co., 1884.

English Verse 1300–1500. Ed. John Anthony Burrow. New York: Longman Group Limited, 1977.

English Verse in Five Volumes. Ed. W. Peacock. London: Oxford University Press 1928–1931.

Everyman Book of English Verse. Ed. John Wain. London: J. M. Dent & Sons, 1981.

Faber Book of Religious Verse, The. London: Faber and Faber. See: *Book of Religious Verse.* Ed. Helen Gardner. New York: Oxford University Press, 1972.

Faber Book of Twentieth Century Verse: 1900–1950. Ed. John Heath-Stubbs and David Wright. London: Faber and Faber, 1953.

Gems of the British Sacred Poets. Ed. Isaac Williams. Oxford, c.1845.

Golden Book of Catholic Poets, The. Ed. Alfred Noyes. Philadelphia and New York: J. Lippincott Co., 1946.

Golden Treasury, The. Ed. Francis Turner Palgrave. New York: Walter J. Black (Classics Club Edition), 1932 (1861, 1897).

Harper Anthology of Poetry, The. Ed. John Frederick Nims. New York: Harper and Row, 1981.

Harper Book of Christian Poetry. Ed. Anthony S. Mercatante. New York: Harper and Row, 1972.

Home Book of Modern Verse, The. Ed. Burton Egbert Stevenson. New York: Holt, Rinehart and Winston, (1925) 1953.

Home Book of Verse, The (2 volumes). Ed. Burton Egbert Stevenson. New York: Holt, Rinehart and Winston, Inc., 1913.

Inspirational and Devotional Verse: 365 Choice Poems. Bob Jones, Jr. Grand Rapids, Mich.: Zondervan Publishing House, 1946.

Library of Choice Literature and Encyclopedia of Universal Authorship: Selected from the Standard Authors of All Nations and All Time, 2d edition, volumes I - X. Eds. Ainsworth R. Spofford, Charles Gibbon. Philadelphia: Gebbie Publishing Co., 1895..

Major Poets; English and American, The. Coffin, Charles M. New York: Harcourt, Brace and World, 1954 (1969). (2nd edition, revised, Ed. Gerrit Hubbard Roeloff)

Manual of Mystic Verse: Being a Choice of Meditative and Mystic Poems Made and Annotated by Louise Collier Willcox. Ed. Louise Collier Willcox. New York: E. P. Dutton and Company, 1917 (Harper and Brothers, 1910).

Men Who March Away: Poems of the First World War. Ed. I. M. Parsons. London: Chatto & Windus, 1965.

Metaphysical Lyrics and Poems of the Seventeenth Century: Donne to Butler. Ed. Herbert J.C. Grierson. New York: Oxford University Press, 1959 (1921).

Modern American Poetry, Mid-Century Edition. Ed. Louis Untermeyer. New York: Harcourt, Brace and Company, 1950 (1919).

Modern Australian Poets. Ed. H. M. Green. Melbourne: Melbourne University Press, 1946 (1952).

Modern British Poetry: A Critical Anthology. Ed. Louis Untermeyer. New York: Harcourt, Brace and Company, 1920 (1942 - fifth revised edition).

Modern Religious Verse and Prose: An Anthology. Ed. Fred Merrifield. New York: Charles Scribner's Sons, 1925.

New British Poets. Ed. Kenneth Rexroth. New York: New Directions, 1949.

New Oxford Book of Christian Verse, The. Ed. Donald Davie. Oxford: Oxford University Press, 1981.

New Oxford Book of English Verse, The. Ed. Arthur Quiller-Couch. London: Oxford University Press, 1st edition, 1900; new edition 1939.

Norton Anthology of English Literature, Vols I and II . Gen Ed. M. H. Abrams. New York: W.W. Norton and Company, 1962 (1968).

Our Land and Its Literature. Ed. Orton Lowe. New York (and London): Harper and Brothers Publishers, 1936.

Oxford Anthology of English Literature, Volume I. The Middle Ages through the Eighteenth Century. General Eds. Frank Kermode and John Hollander. New York: Oxford University Press, 1973.

Oxford Book of American Verse. Ed. F. O. Matthiessen. New York, Oxford University Press, 1950.

Oxford Book of Canadian Verse: In English and French. Ed. A. J.M. Smith. Toronto, London, New York: Oxford University Press, 1960.

Oxford Book of Christian Verse. Ed. Lord David Cecil. Oxford: Oxford University Press, 1940 (1951).

Oxford Book of Eighteenth Century Verse. Ed. David Nichol Smith. London: Oxford University Press, (1926), 1958.

Oxford Book of English Mystical Verse XIII–XX Centuries. Eds. D.H.S. Nicholson and A.H.E. Lee. Oxford: Clarendon Press 1917 (1962).

Oxford Book of Irish Verse: XVIIth Century–XXth Century. Eds. Donagh MacDonagh and Lennox Robinson. Oxford: Clarendon Press, 1958 (1959).

Oxford Book of Medieval English Verse. Eds. Celia and Kenneth Sisam. Oxford: Clarendon Press, 1970.

Oxford Book of Religious Verse. Ed. Helen Gardiner. New York: Oxford University Press, 1972.

Oxford Book of Seventeenth Century Verse. Eds. H.J.C. Grierson and G. Bullough. Oxford: Clarendon Press, 1934 (1958).

Oxford Book of 20th Century English Verse. Ed. Philip Larkin. London: Oxford University Press, 1973.

Oxford Book of Victorian Verse. Ed. Arthur Quiller-Couch. Oxford: Clarendon Press, 1912 (1955).

Oxford Dictionary of the Christian Church. Ed. F.L. Cross. London: Oxford University Press, 1957.

Pace, Roy Bennett. *English Literature.* Boston: Allyn and Bacon, 1918 (1927).

The Pilgrim's Staff: Poems Divine and Moral. Ed. Fitzroy Carrington. New York: Duffield and Company, 1906.

Poems of Christmas. Ed. Myra Cohn Livingston. New York: Atheneum, 1983.

Poems of Religious Sorrow, Comfort, and Aspiration. New York: Sheldon and Company Publishers, 1863.

Poems of Sunshine and Shadow. Compiled by Ord L. Morrow and John I. Paton. Lincoln, Nebraska: Back to the Bible Publishers, 1962.

Poems To Enjoy: Anthology for Junior High School Grades. Eds. W. P. Percival and J. G. S. Brash. Toronto: Thomas Nelson & Sons (Canada), 1955.

Poems: Wadsworth Handbook and Anthology. Main, C.F. and Seng, Peter J. Belmont California: Wadsworth Publishing Company, 1961 (1965).

Poems Worth Knowing: A Collection of Poems Worthy of Lifelong Remembrance. Compiled by Grace B. Faxon. Dansville, N.Y.: F. A. Owen Publishing Co., undated.

Poetry of the English Renaissance 1509–1660. Eds. J. William Hebel and Hoyt H. Hudson. New York: F. S. Crofts and Co., 1929 (1947).

Poets of the English Language: in Five Volumes. Ed. not indicated (W.H. Auden?). New York: Viking Press, 1950 (1962). [Include extensive "calendars" of British and American poetry for each period near the beginning of each volume]

Prayer Poems: An Anthology for Today. Compiled by O. V. & Helen Armstrong. Nashville: Abingdon Press: copyright 1942, Whitmore and Stone.

Prose and Poetry of England. Eds. Julian L. Maline and Wilfred M. Mallon. New York: L.W. Singer Co., 1949.

Religious Lyrics of the XIVth Century, Second Edition. Ed. Carleton Brown, revised by G.V. Smithers. Oxford: Clarendon Press, 1924 (1957).

Religious Lyrics of the XVth Century. Ed. Carleton Brown. Oxford: Clarendon Press, 1939 (1962).

Renaissance Poetry. Ed. Leonard Dean. Englewood Cliffs, N.J.: Prentice Hall, Inc., 1950 (1964). (Volume III [of seven] in English Masterpieces: An Anthology of Imaginative Literature from Chaucer to T.S. Eliot. Gen. Ed. Maynard Mack.)

Sacred Poets of England and America: for Three Centuries, The. Ed. Rufus W. Griswold. New York: D. Appleton and Company, 1848. (Philadelphia: Geo. S. Appleton, 1848).

Scenes in the Life of our Saviour: By the Poets and Painters. Ed. R. W. Griswold. 1845. [Includes a poem by Nathaniel Hawthorne.]

Selection of Religious Lyrics, A. Ed. Donald Gray. Oxford: Clarendon Press, 1975.

Song Book, The: Words and Tunes from the Best Poets and Musicians. Ed. John Hullah. London (and New York): Macmillan and Company, 1892 (1866).

Songs of Praise. Words Ed. Percy Dearmer and Music Eds. Ralph Vaughan Williams and Martin Shaw. London: Oxford University Press, 1969 (1936).

Spiritual Songs: From English Mss. of Fourteenth to Sixteenth Centuries. Ed. Francis M. M. Comper. London: Society for Promoting Christian Knowledge, 1936. (also New York: The MacMillan Company.)

Thorpe, Benjamin. *Metrical Paraphrase of Parts of the Holy Scriptures In Anglo-Saxon with An English Translation, Notes and A Verbal Index.* London: Society of Antiquaries of London, 1832.

Three Middle English Religious Poems. Ed. R.H. Bowers. Gainesville, Florida: University of Florida Monograph, 1963.

Treasury of Poems for Worship and Devotion, A. Ed. Charles L. Wallis. New York: Harper and Brothers Publishers, 1959.

Treasury of Religious Verse, The. Ed. Donald T. Kauffman. New York: Fleming H. Revell, 1962.

Treasury of Sacred Song: Selected from the Lyrical Poetry of Four Centuries [12th through 16th]. Ed. Francis T. Palgrave. Oxford: Clarendon Press, 1890.

Twelve Centuries of English Poetry and Prose. Eds. Alphonso Gerald Newcomber, Alice E. Andrews, Howard Judson Hall. Chicago, Atlanta, New York: Scott, Foresman and Company, 1928 (1910).

University Carol Book, The: A Collection of Carols from Many Lands, for All Seasons. Ed. Erik Routley. Brighton: H. Freeman and Company (95a St. George's Road), c.1961.

Victorian and Later English Poets. Eds. James Stephens, Edwin L. Beck, and Royall H. Snow. New York, Cincinnati, Chicago, Boston, Atlanta: American Book Company, 1934 (1949).

Women in Praise of the Sacred. Ed. Jane Hirschfield. New York, Harper-Collins, 1994.

World's Great Religious Poetry. Ed. Caroline Miles Hill. New York: MacMillan Company, 1924.

III. Biography, Criticism and History

Bailey, Albert Edward. *The Gospel In Hymns: Backgrounds and Interpretations.* New York: Charles Scribner's Sons, 1950.

Barfield, Owen. *Poetic Diction: A Study In Meaning.* Wesleyan University Press (1928, 1952) 1973. [Foreword by Howard Nemerov]

Bennett, J.A.W. *Poetry of the Passion: Studies In 12 Centuries of English Verse.* Oxford: Clarendon Press, 1982.

Bennett, Joan. *Five Metaphysical Poets: Donne, Herbert, Vaughan, Crashaw, and Marvell.* Cambridge: University Press, 1966.

Biographical Dictionary of Hymn Authors. Ed. Gadsby.

Buckley, Vincent. *Poetry and the Sacred.* London: Chatto and Windus, 1968.

Burrage, Henry S., D. D. *Baptist Hymn Writers and Their Hymns.* Portland, Maine: Brown, Thurston and Company, 1888.

Cambridge Guide to Literature in English, The. Ed. Ian Ousby. London: Cambridge University Press, 1988.

Chilton, Eleanor Carroll and Agar, Herbert. *The Garment of Praise: The Necessity for Poetry.* Garden City, New York: Doubleday, Doran and Company, 1929.

Companion to the Hymnal: A Handbook to the 1964 Methodist Hymnal. Eds Fred D.Gealy, Austin C. Lovelace, and Carlton R. Young. Nashville/New York: Abingdon Press, 1970.

Concise Encyclopedia of English and American Poets and Poetry. Eds. Stephen Spender and Donald Hall. New York: Hawthorn Books, 1963.

Coulson, John. *Religion and Imagination: In and of a Grammar of Assent.* Oxford: Clarendon Press, 1981.

Daiches, David. *God and the Poets: The Gifford lectures,* 1983. Oxford: Clarendon Press, 1984.

Dictionary - Handbook to Hymns for the Living Church. Ed. Donald P. Hustad. Carol Stream, Illinois: Hope Publishing Company, 1978.

Dictionary of Hymnology: Setting Forth the Origin and History of Christian Hymns of All Ages and Nations. Ed. John Julian, D.D. London: John Murray, First ed. 1892, 2nd ed. 1907 (with New Supplement. London and Beccles: William Clowes and Sons, Ltd.), 1925.

Dixon, James Main. *The Spiritual Meaning of In Memoriam.* New York: Abingdon Press, 1920. (Treats a wider range of literary and religious subjects than titles indicates)

Duncan, Joseph E. *The Revival [Renewal?] of Metaphysical Poetry.* New York: Farrar, Straus and Giroux, 1969.

Earth Is the Lords: Poems of The Spirit, The. Ed. Helen PIotz. London: Thomas Y. Crowell Co., 1965.

English Poets: Vol I; Chaucer to Donne. Ed. Thomas Humphry Ward. London and New York: Macmillan and Co., 1900.

English Poets: Vol III; Addison to Blake. Ed. Thomas Humphry Ward. London and New York: Macmillan and Co., 1880 (1902).

English Poets: Vol IV; The Nineteenth Century, Wordsworth to Rossetti. Ed. Thomas Humphry Ward. London and New York: Macmillan and Co., 1890.

Fairchild, Hoxie Neale. *Religious Trends In English Poetry, Vol I: 1700–1740, Protestantism and the Cult of Sentiment.* New York: Columbia University Press, 1939 (1958).

Fairchild, Hoxie Neale. *Religious Trends In English Poetry, Vol II: 1740–1780, Religious Sentimentalism In the Age of Johnson.* New York: Columbia University Press, 1942.

Fairchild, Hoxie Neale. *Religious Trends In English Poetry, Vol III: 1780–1830, Romantic Faith.* New York: Columbia University Press, 1949.

Fairchild, Hoxie Neale. *Religious Trends In English Poetry, Vol IV: 1830–1880; Christianity and Romanticism in the Victorian Era.* New York: Columbia University Press, 1957.

Fraser, Rebecca. *The Brontës: Charlotte Brontë and Her Family.* New York: Fawcett Columbine, 1988.

Halewood, William H. *The Poetry of Grace: Reformation Themes and Structures In English Seventeenth Century Poetry.*

Halleck, Reuben Post. *History of English Literature.* New York, Cincinnati, Chicago: American Book Company, 1900.

Handbook to the Hymnal. Eds. William Chalmers Covert and Calvin Weiss Laufer. Chicago: R.R. Donnelley and Sons Company, 1946 (1935), for Presbyterian Board of Christian Education.

Hymns and Hymn Writers of the Church: An Annotated Edition of the Methodist Hymnal. Eds. Charles S. Nutter and Wilbur F. Tillett. New York: Eaton and Mains, 1911.

Jennings, Elizabeth. *Christian Poetry.* New York: Hawthorn Books Publishers, 1965.

Lewis, C. S. *English Literature in the Sixteenth Century excluding Drama:* Clark Lectures, Trinity College, Cambridge, 1944. *The Oxford History of English Literature* series, Eds. F. P Wilson and Bonamy Dobree. Oxford: Clarendon Press, 1944.

Lives of the English Sacred Poets. Robert Aris Willmot. London: Society for Promoting Christian Knowledge.

Machen, Minnie Gresham. *The Bible in Browning.* New York: Macmillan Company, 1903.

Martz, Louis. *The Poetry of Meditation: A Study in English Religious Literature of the Seventeenth Century.* New Haven: Yale University Press, 1962 (2nd edition).

Metaphysical Poetry: Critical Anthology. Stratford-Upon-Avon Studies, Vol 11. New York: St. Martin's Press, 1970.

Metaphysical Poets: Collected Critical Essays. Ed. Frank Kermode. New York: Fawcett, 1969.

Mims, Edwin. *The Christ of the Poets.* Nashville: Abingdon-Cokesbury Press, 1948.

Morris, David B. *The Religious Sublime: Christian Poets and Critical Tradition In 18th Century England.* University Press of Kentucky, 1972.

Noon, William T., S. J. *Poetry and Prayer.* New Brunswick, NJ: Rutgers University Press, 1967.

Our Hymnody: A Manual of the Methodist Hymnal. Ed. Robert Guy McCutcheon; 2nd Edition, with index of scriptural texts by Fitzgerald Sale Parker. New York/Nashville: Abingdon-Cokesbury Press, 1937.

Oxford Companion to American Literature, The. Ed. James D. Hart. New York: Oxford University Press, 1948 (First Edition, 1941).

Oxford Companion to Twentieth Century Poets. Ed. Ian Hamilton. Oxford: Oxford University Press, 1994.

Paul Laurence Dunbar: Twayne United States Authors Series. By Peter Revell.. Boston: Twayne Publishers, Division of G. K. Hall & Company, 1979.

Poetry of Grace: Reformation Themes and Structures in English Seventeenth Century Poetry, The. Ed. William H. Halewood. New Haven: Yale University Press, (1907), 1970.

Pollock, John. *Shaftesbury: The Poor Man's Earl.* London: Hodder & Stoughton, 1985.

Protestant Poetics and the Seventeenth Century Religious Lyric. Barbara Kiefer Lewalski. Princeton: Princeton University Press, 1979.

Religion and Modern Literature: Essays in Theory and Criticism. Eds. G. B. Tennyson and Edward E. Ericson, Jr. Grand Rapids: William B. Eerdmans Publishing Company, 1975.

Routley, Erik. *The English Carol.*

Strong, Augustus Hopkins. *The Great Poets and Their Theology.* Philadelphia: American Baptist Publishing Society, 1897 (1939).

Summers, Joseph H. *The Heirs of Donne and Jonson.* New York (and London): Oxford University Press, 1970.

Swardson, Harold R. *Poetry and the Fountain of Light.* Columbia: University of Missouri Press, 1962.

The Use of Poetry and the Use of Criticism. T.S. Eliot. Cambridge: Harvard University Press, 1933.

Wordsworth's "Natural Methodism." Ed. Richard E. Brantley. New Haven: Yale University Press, 1975.

Worshiping Church: A Hymnal: Worship Leaders' Edition. Ed. Donald P. Hustad. Carol Stream, Illinois: Hope Publishing Company, 1990, 1991.

ACKNOWLEDGMENTS

W. H. Auden, Part II of "Memorial for the City," from *W. H. Auden: Collected Poems*, Ed. by Edward Meldelson, copyright 1974 by the Estate of W. H. Auden, reprinted by permission of Random House, Inc.

John Betjeman, "Undenominational," "St. Saviour's Aberdeen Park," and "Blame the Vicar," from *Collected Poems*, copyright 1958, by permission of John Murray Publishers, Ltd.

Philip Jerome Cleveland, "I Yield Thee Praise," and "By Night," by courtesy of Phillips Library, Peabody Essex Museum, Salem, Massachusetts.

T.S. Eliot, Canto I from "Ash Wednesday" in *Collected Poems 1909–1962*, copyright 1930 and renewed 1958 by T.S. Eliot, reprinted by permission of Harcourt, Inc.; Section VI of "Choruses from the Rock" in *Collected Poems 1909–1962* by T.S. Eliot, copyright 1936 by Harcourt, Inc., copyright 1964, 1963 by T.S. Eliot, reprinted by permission of the publisher; Canto IV from "Little Gidding" in *Four Quartets*, copyright 1942 by T.S. Eliot and renewed by Esme Valerie Eliot, reprinted by permission of Harcourt, Inc.

William Everson, "Passion Week" and "Zone of Death" from *The Hazards of Holiness*, by Brother Antonius, copyright 1962 by Brother Antonius. Used by permission of Doubleday, a division of Random House, Inc.

Charles WS. Kennedy, translator, "Lines (743–866) from the Ascension of the Redeemer" from *Early English Christian Poetry*, Ed. Charles W. Kennedy, copyright 1963 by Oxford University Press, Inc. Used by permission of Oxford University Press, Inc.

Madeleine L'Engle, "The Risk of Birth" from *The Risk of Birth*, copyright 1974, by Madeleine L'Engle. Used by permission of Harold Shaw Publishers, Wheaton, Illinois; "Lines Scribbled on An Envelope While Riding the 104 Broadway Bus" by Madeleine L'Engle, copyright 1969 by Crosswicks, Ltd. This usage granted by permission.

C. S. Lewis, "On a Theme from Nicolas of Cusa," "Reason," "Prayer," "Stephen to Lazarus," "The Apologist's Evening Prayer," and "After Prayers Lie Cold," from *Poems*, by C. S. Lewis, copyright 1964 by the Executors of Estate of C. S. Lewis Pte. Ltd., reprinted by permission of Harcourt, Inc.

Denise Levertov, "Perhaps No Poem But All I Can Say And I Cannot Be Silent," "St. Peter and the Angel," and "Oblique Prayer" from *Oblique Prayers*, copyright 1984 by Denise Levertov. Reprinted by permission of New Directions Publishing Corp.

R.A.K. Mason, "On the Swag," and "Judas Iscariot" from *Anthology of New Zealand Verse*, copyright 1956, by permission of Hoken Library, University

ALPHABETICAL INDEX OF AUTHORS

ALPHABETICAL INDEX OF POEMS